Language Awareness

FIFTH EDITION

Language
Awareness

EDITORS
Paul Eschholz
Alfred Rosa
Virginia Clark

ST. MARTIN'S PRESS   New York

Senior editor: *Mark Gallaher*
Project editor: *Bruce Glassman*
Production supervisor: *Christine Pearson*
Cover design: *John Jeheber*
Cartoonist: *Jeff Danziger*

For information, write:
St. Martin's Press, Inc.
175 Fifth Avenue
New York, NY 10010

ISBN: 0-312-02081-3

Acknowledgments

I DISCOVERING LANGUAGE

"Coming to an Awareness of Language" from *The Autobiography of Malcolm X* by Malcolm X with the
assistance of Alex Haley. Copyright © 1964 by Alex Haley and Malcolm X. Copyright © 1965 by Alex
Haley and Betty Shabazz. Reprinted by permission of Random House, Inc.

"A Brief History of English" from *Understanding English* by Paul Roberts. Copyright © 1958 by Paul
Roberts. Reprinted by permission of Harper & Row, Publishers, Inc.

"The Power of Words" from *The Word-A-Day Vocabulary Builder* by Bergen Evans. Copyright © 1963
by Bergen Evans. Reprinted by permission of Random House, Inc.

"Contemporary American Graffiti" by Donald V. Mehus. Reprinted by permission of the publisher from
The American Language in the 1970s by Herman A. Estrin and Donald V. Mehus, © 1974, Boyd & Fraser
Publishing Company, pp. 79–84.

"The Sounds of Silence" by Edward T. Hall and Mildred Reed Hall originally appeared in *Playboy*
Magazine: copyright © 1971 by Playboy. Reprinted by permission of Edward T. Hall and Mildred Reed
Hall.

II AMERICAN ENGLISH TODAY

"Language on the Skids" by Edwin Newman reprinted with permission from the November 1979 *Reader's
Digest,* the Naval War College Review, and Edwin Newman. © 1979 by The Reader's Digest Assn., Inc.

Acknowledgments and copyrights are continued at the back of the book on pages 480–482, which constitute an extension of the copyright page.

PREFACE

Since the first edition of *Language Awareness* appeared in 1974, its purpose has been twofold: to foster an appreciation of the richness, flexibility, and vitality of the English language and to encourage and help students to use their language more responsibly and effectively in speech and particularly in writing. Because of these twin purposes, *Language Awareness* has been used in a variety of different courses over the years. Its primary use, however, has been and continues to be in college composition courses. Clearly, many instructors believe as we do that the study of language and the study of writing go hand in hand.

The study of language has many facets; so, while covering a broad spectrum of topics (including the history of English, contemporary debates on the state of American English, the language of prejudice and of euphemism, for example), we have tried to concentrate on those areas in which language use exerts the widest social effects—politics, advertising, media, and gender roles. Opening students' eyes to the power of language—its ability to shape and to manipulate one's understanding, perceptions, and cultural attitudes—is, we believe, one of the worthiest goals a writing class can pursue.

We also provide extensive material to help students improve their abilities as readers and writers. As in the fourth edition, the general introduction to *Language Awareness* provides a discussion of reading and writing that includes guidelines and questions students can use to increase their abilities as thoughtful, analytical readers, as well as explanations of how the various writing strategies can be put to work. At the end of the text we have appended an alternate table of contents that classifies the reading selections in *Language Awareness* according to the rhetorical strategies they exemplify. Also, we have included a detailed glossary that defines rhetorical terms and concepts important to the study of writing.

The readings in *Language Awareness* have been chosen not only for their subject matter but also to provide students of composition with practical illustrations of rhetorical principles and techniques. After each selection, in addition to questions on the content of the essay, we have provided questions that address these rhetorical concerns, adding cross-references to the glossary where useful. The vocabulary list after each selection calls attention to a few words that students will find worth adding to their own active vocabularies. Finally, each reading is followed by two or more writing topics, and each section concludes with topics and instructions for short essays, usually making use of what students have learned from two or more of the readings in the section. In our own teaching we have found such topics helpful in promoting both writing and classroom discussion of language issues.

As always, we have emphasized pieces written in nontechnical language on topics and issues of current interest. Guided by comments and advice from many colleagues across the country who have used the fourth edition, we have retained in this new edition those essays that teachers and students have valued most. But over half of the selections in *Language Awareness* are new to this edition. Among the new essays are Donald V. Mehus' analysis of contemporary American graffiti; Ron Rosenbaum's examination of "hard sell" tactics by advertisers of the eighties; Rachel Jones' poignant argument in favor of standard English; and, Stephen King's provocative look at the "horrors" of children's television programs. In response to the many requests for actual political speeches for analysis, we have added John F. Kennedy's inaugural address and Ronald Reagan's basic 1984 campaign speech. Many instructors asked us to include more on advertising, so we have expanded that section, adding Jeffrey Schrank's analysis of advertising techniques and Jib Fowles' classification of the emotional appeals that advertising makes. Other users asked us to expand the section on sexism and language so we have added five new essays that discuss such topics as gender differences in speech, the question of a possible anti-male bias in English, and the negative reactions to the word *feminism*.

The Part entitled "Media and Language" is also new to this edition. This section has been created in response to reader demand for essays that explore the ways in which language is both used and abused in the media. The essays by Neil Postman, Herbert Gans, and *Consumer Reports* focus on the ways in which language is used to shape the news. Censorship and its effects is the subject of the essays by Nat Hentoff and Stephen King. In the last essay in the section, Robert MacNeil takes an in-depth look at the way language is used in one particular area of sportscasting: football.

All of our aims in *Language Awareness* are serious ones, but a serious book need not be humorless or unnecessarily academic. Paul Roberts' "How to Say Nothing in 500 Words" offers some useful advice about writing, while taking a tongue-in-cheek approach to a composition on football. There's also Edwin Newman's humorous analysis of "advertisin' "; Donald V. Mehus' "Contemporary American Graffiti"; and, Jack Rosenthal's "Gender Benders"—among others. Indeed, we like to think that readers of *Language Awareness* will have as much fun using this edition as we have had in preparing it.

ACKNOWLEDGMENTS

We are grateful to the following colleagues across the country who have sent helpful reactions and suggestions for this fifth edition: Yuxuf Abana, Iowa State University; Larry Andrews, University of Nebraska—Lincoln; Marilyn J. Atlas, Ohio University; Dorothy Behnke, Sterling College; Margaret Benner, Towson State University; Kathleen A. Bieke, Northwest Community College; Ellen M. Bommarito, Michigan Technological University; Charley Boyd, University of Oregon; Mary M. Brown, Marion College; Sue Lane Brown, Wharton County Junior College; Judith Bruce, Nebraska Wesleyan University; Marsha C. Bryant, University of Florida; Anne Burley, Towson State University; Sandra Coats, Wharton County Junior College; Eve Crook, Nassau Community College; G.B. Crump, Central Missouri State University; Antonia Dempster, Genessee Community College; Diana Y. Dreyer, Slippery Rock University; Patricia Bernadt Durfee, Broome Community College; Linda Eickoff, Hope College; Nicholas G. Evans, West Virginia University; Richard Freed, Eastern Kentucky University; Elizabeth Gardner, Elizabethtown College; Alan Goodell, Mt. Hood Community College; Philip B. Graham, Ohio State University; Christine R. Gray, University of Maryland—College Park; J. Leo Harris, Southeastern Missouri University; Sally Widenmann Harrison, University of California—Davis; Edward Heckler, Pan American University; Robert Henderson, Southeastern Oklahoma State University; Vicki L. Hill, Southern Methodist University; John Huntley, University of Iowa; Blanche Jamison, Southeastern Oklahoma State University; B.J. Johnson, Xavier University; Frances S. Johnson, Old Dominion University; Robert Johnson, Loretto Heights College; Stella Kaplan, Pace University; Terrance B. Kearns, University of Central Arkansas; Larry P. Kent, Harper College; George Kerrick, Middle Tennessee State University; Les Keyser, College of Staten Island; Valerie Whiteson Klasewitz, San Jose State University; Daniel M. Larimer, Northampton County Area Community College; Audrey Lattie, Charles S. Mott Community College; Susan Lavin, Florida International University; Judith Longo, Ocean County College; Robert J. Lysiak, Appalachian State University; Adelio F. Maccentelli, Essex Community College; Glenn A. Mayer, SUNY at Oneonta; Kevin McCarthy, University of Florida; Mildred C. Melendez, Sinclair Community College; W. Bede Mitchell, Washtenaw Community College; Sharon M. Morrow, University of Southern Indiana; Denise Murray, San Jose State University; Alma E. Nuggent, Villa Julie College; Candace O'Donnell, Elizabethtown College; Reza Ordoubadian, Middle Tennessee State University; Paul Pavich, Fort Lewis College; Carroll V. Peterson, Fort Lewis College; Doris M. Piatak, Kishwaukee College; Bennett A. Rafoth, Indiana University of Pennsylvania; Ruth S. Ralph, American University;

Karren Rhodes, University of Oregon; Judy Richards, Community College of Philadelphia; Patrick S.J. Ruffin, Drexel University; Diane Scharper, Towson State University; Deborah Shaller, Towson State University; Wayne H. Slater, University of Maryland—College Park; Sally K. Slocum, University of Akron; Frank Edmund Smith, William R. Harper College; Kary D. Smout, Duke University; Louise N. Soldani, Anna Maria College; Mary Jo Stirling, Santa Monica College; Stephanie A. Tingley, Youngstown State University; Becky Tompkins, University of Akron; Rosalie Riegle Troester, Saginaw Valley State University; Cynthia Tuell, University of California—Los Angeles; Shaila Van Sickle, Fort Lewis College; E. Von Furhmann, University of Southern Indiana; Jacquelin Webber, American River College; M.T. Webster, University of Akron; Deanna M. White, University of Texas—San Antonio; Stephen Whittaker, University of Scranton; Joseph Wilson, Anna Maria College.

We would like to express our appreciation to the staff at St. Martin's Press, especially Mark Gallaher, Bruce Glassman, and Steve Morenberg. Special thanks go to Patricia Paquin for her assistance with the apparatus and the instructor's manual. Finally, we are grateful to all our students at the University of Vermont for their enthusiasm for language study and writing and their invaluable responses to materials included in this book. They teach us something new every day.

PAUL ESCHHOLZ
ALFRED ROSA
VIRGINIA CLARK

CONTENTS

Introduction   1

I   DISCOVERING LANGUAGE   7

Malcolm X   **Coming to an Awareness of Language   9**
"I saw that the best thing I could do was get a hold of a dictionary—
to study, to learn some new words."

Helen Keller   **The Day Language Came into My Life   13**
The celebrated deaf and blind writer recalls her discovery of language.

Paul Roberts   **A Brief History of English   17**
"In 1500 English was a minor language spoken by a few people on a
small island. Now it is perhaps the greatest language of the
world. . . ."

Bergen Evans   **The Power of Words   29**
"Words are the tools for the job of saying what you want to say."

Donald V. Mehus   **Contemporary American Graffiti   37**
"Where is the best graffiti found? Who creates it, and why?"

Edward T. Hall and Mildred Reed Hall   **The Sounds of Silence   42**
"Few of us realize how much we depend on our body movement in
our conversation."

WRITING ASSIGNMENTS FOR "DISCOVERING
LANGUAGE"   55

II   AMERICAN ENGLISH TODAY   57

Edwin Newman   **Language on the Skids   59**
A popular television news commentator decries the "high crimes and
misdemeanors" that Americans visit upon the English language.

Harvey Daniels   **Is There Really a Language Crisis?   63**
Another commentator claims that ". . . reports of the death of the English language are greatly exaggerated."

S. I. Hayakawa   **Why English Should Be Our Official
Language   71**
A leading semanticist believes that we must avoid a "country divided
along linguistic and cultural lines."

Alice Roy **The English Only Movement**   75

A college teacher questions the real motives of the English only movement.

Dorothy Z. Seymour **Black Children, Black Speech**   84

"Should children who speak Black English be excused from learning the Standard in school? Should they perhaps be given books in Black English to learn from?"

Rachel L. Jones **What's Wrong with Black English**   93

A student's goal is to see more black people, like herself, "less dependent on a dialect that excludes them from full participation. . . ."

Richard Rodriquez **Caught Between Two Languages**   97

"What I needed to learn in school was that I had the right—and the obligation—to speak the public language of los gringos."

WRITING ASSIGNMENTS FOR "AMERICAN ENGLISH TODAY"   106

III   THE LANGUAGE OF POLITICS AND PROPAGANDA   109

George Orwell **Politics and the English Language**   111

The English language is like the air we breathe. When it becomes polluted, we all suffer.

Newman P. Birk and Genevieve B. Birk **Selection, Slanting, and Charged Language**   125

Two researchers describe some ways in which language can be manipulated to create particular impressions.

Stuart Chase **Gobbledygook**   138

A commentator on the dynamics of our language rambles through the obscurities of bureaucratic jargon.

Donna Woolfolk Cross **Propaganda: How Not to Be Bamboozled**   149

"If we are to continue to be a government 'by the people,' let us become informed about the methods of propaganda, so that we can be the masters, and not the slaves of our destiny."

John F. Kennedy **Inaugural Address**   161

A young president implores his fellow Americans to "Ask not what your country can do for you—ask what you can do for your country."

The New York Times **The Ronald Reagan Basic 1984 Campaign Speech**   167

A synthesis of the public language Reagan used to persuade voters to return him to the White House in 1984.

WRITING ASSIGNMENTS FOR "THE LANGUAGE OF POLITICS AND PROPAGANDA"   173

IV ADVERTISING AND LANGUAGE   177

Jeffrey Schrank **The Language of Advertising Claims   179**
"Students, and many teachers, are notorious believers in their immunity to advertising."

Ron Rosenbaum **The Hard Sell   188**
A New York writer believes that contemporary advertising has succeeded by boldly scaring and humiliating consumers.

Jay Rosen **The Presence of the Word in TV Advertising   199**
A journalism professor claims that "flipping [channels] with the sound off is a good way of investigating television ads."

Edwin Newman **Gettin' Rich by Droppin' the G   204**
A language watchdog observes "an article of faith among advertisers that dropping the *g* on words ending in *ing* is the sure path to riches."

Consumers Union **It's Natural! It's Organic! Or Is It?   207**
A nonprofit consumer group wants us to read labels carefully. Many products don't deliver what they seem to promise.

Jib Fowles **Advertising's Fifteen Basic Appeals   216**
A mass media professor examines the basic emotional appeals that advertising makes to each one of us.

Hugh Rank **Intensify/Downplay   235**
This helpful schema can be used in identifying and analyzing advertising tactics.

WRITING ASSIGNMENTS FOR "ADVERTISING AND LANGUAGE"   242

V PREJUDICE AND STEREOTYPES   245

Gordon Allport **The Language of Prejudice   247**
A leading expert on prejudice discusses some of the ways in which language itself, very often subtly, expresses and even causes prejudice.

S. I. Hayakawa **Words with Built-in Judgments   259**
The power of some words to hurt and victimize is made clear by this leading language expert.

Charles F. Berlitz **The Etymology of the International Insult   264**
A prominent foreign language teacher wonders how people will "ever be able to rise above using insult as a weapon."

William Raspberry **What It Means to Be Black   269**
The noted black newspaper columnist bemoans the "tragically limited definition of blackness."

WRITING ASSIGNMENTS FOR "PREJUDICE AND STEREOTYPES"   273

VI   SEXISM AND LANGUAGE   275

Alleen Pace Nilsen   **Sexism in English**   277

A study of the dictionary provides some surprising linguistic evidence for the view of gender in our society.

Eugene R. August   **Real Men Don't: Anti-Male Bias in English**   289

Could it be that the English language victimizes males as much as it does females?

Jack Rosenthal   **Gender Benders**   303

"Deep within language lurks the powerful force of Hidden Gender."

Casey Miller and Kate Swift   **One Small Step for Genkind**   307

Two pioneers in the study of sexism and language demonstrate the ways in which language discriminates against women.

Cyra McFadden   **In Defense of Gender**   320

A woman speaks out against the "neutering" of the English language.

John Pfeiffer   **Girl Talk-Boy Talk**   325

One investigator takes a hard look at just what characterizes the communication between males and females.

Catharine R. Stimpson   **The "F" Word**   334

For many Americans "Feminism is an X-rated word."

WRITING ASSIGNMENTS FOR "SEXISM AND LANGUAGE"   339

VII   EUPHEMISM AND TABOOS   343

Neil Postman   **Euphemism**   345

A professor of media ecology argues that while some euphemisms are bad, others serve worthwhile social purposes.

S. I. Hayakawa   **Verbal Taboo**   350

"In every language there seem to be certain 'unmentionables'—words of such strong affective connotations that they cannot be used in polite discourse."

Barbara Lawrence   **Four-Letter Words Can Hurt You**   354

"Why should any word be called obscene? Don't they all describe natural human functions?"

Stephen Hilgartner, Richard C. Bell, and Rory O'Connor   **The Language of Nuclear War Strategists**   358

"Nuclear war strategists have developed an esoteric, highly specialized vocabulary. In their ultrarational world, they talk in cool, clinical language about *megatons* and *megadeaths*."

WRITING ASSIGNMENTS FOR "EUPHEMISM AND TABOOS"   367

VIII MEDIA AND LANGUAGE 371

Neil Postman **Now . . . This** 373

Media watcher Postman points out the frightening implications of television news programs that fail to see life as a complex series of interrelated events.

Herbert J. Gans **The Messages Behind the News** 385

A sociologist discovers that the news, far from being impartial, presents a "picture of a nation and society as it ought to be."

Nat Hentoff **When Nice People Burn Books** 398

A columnist shows us how "dumb" supposedly intelligent people can behave once censorship is unleashed.

Stephen King **Now, You Take "Bambi" or "Snow White"**—*That's* **Scary!** 406

Our most popular horror writer answers the question, "Do I believe that all violent or horrifying programming should be banned from network TV?"

Consumer Reports **Advertising in Disguise: How the Hidden Hand of a Corporate Ghostwriter Can Turn a News Report into a Commercial** 412

A report on how some large corporations, using sophisticated techniques, have been able to "insert product plugs in the media under the guise of news."

Robert MacNeil **Pigskin English** 420

A respected news reporter comes to the conclusion that "football commentators do not mangle the language nearly to the extent that I believed."

WRITING ASSIGNMENTS FOR "MEDIA AND LANGUAGE" 425

IX WRITING WELL: USING LANGUAGE RESPONSIBLY 427

Paul Roberts **How to Say Nothing in 500 Words** 429

Some negative advice that may have positive results.

Donald Hall **Writing Honestly** 441

"Good writing is an intricate interweaving of inspiration and discipline."

Linda Flower **Writing for an Audience** 447

"The goal of the writer is to create a momentary common ground between the reader and the writer."

William Zinsser **Simplicity** 451

"If you find that writing is hard, it's because it *is* hard. It's one of the hardest things that people do."

Donald M. Murray   **The Maker's Eye: Revising Your Own Manuscripts   457**

Like most writers, Murray knows that writing is rewriting.

Jacqueline Berke   **The Qualities of Good Writing   462**

"Suffice it to say here that whatever the topic, whatever the occasion, expository writing should be readable, informative, and, wherever possible, engaging."

WRITING ASSIGNMENTS FOR "WRITING WELL: USING LANGUAGE RESPONSIBLY"   467

Rhetorical Table of Contents   468

Glossary of Rhetorical Terms   472

Introduction

Language Awareness is a collection of readings aimed at college writing students and designed to emphasize the crucial role language plays in virtually every aspect of our lives. Most of us think of language as we think of the air we breathe: we cannot survive without it, but we take it for granted nearly all of the time. Seldom are we conscious of language's real power to lead us (or mislead us) or of the effect our own use of language has on others. Even rarer is the recognition that our perceptions of the world are influenced, our very thoughts at least partially shaped, by language, it is also true that liberation begins with our awareness of that fact. To foster such an awareness is one of the goals of this book. We hope, therefore, that as you use this text you will gain a heightened appreciation of the richness, flexibility, and vitality of your language and be moved to explore its possibilities further.

THE STUDY OF LANGUAGE

Language is one of humankind's greatest achievements and one of its most important resources. *Language Awareness* represents the most immediate and interesting fields of language study with a diverse range of thought-provoking essays grouped into nine broad sections. The first section, "Discovering Language," provides an overview of the central issues: the power of words to shape our thinking, the way the English language has evolved, our responsibilities as users of language, and how communication transcends language. Section two, "American English Today," presents some of the arguments that characterize the contemporary debates over usage and literacy, the English Only movement, and bilingual and bidialectal education. In the third section, "The Language of Politics and Propaganda," various writers point out ways that language can be used to manipulate our thinking (or to keep us from thinking at all) as they illustrate the abuses language suffers at the hands of politicians. "Advertising and Language," the fourth section, discusses some of the ways advertisers use language to create a positive image for a product, to imply what they cannot say directly, and to exploit consumer vulnerability.

Section five, "Prejudice and Stereotypes," explores the way words can lock us into particular categories, create powerfully discriminatory impressions, and deeply affect our judgments about others. Section six, "Sexism and Language," concentrates specifically on sterotypical images of women and men implied in our language and suggests some of the difficulties involved in overcoming linguistic prejudice. In "Euphemisms and Taboos," section seven, the readings explore sensitive topics that we tend to cloak in "nice" language and confront some of our culture's "dirty words" to determine how and why these words may seem offensive. The section on "Media and Language," section eight, raises critical questions about the objectivity of network news, the relationship between advertising and the news, and how and why we censor—or fail to censor.

Finally—because our further purpose in this fifth edition of *Language Awareness,* as in earlier editions is to encourage you to write more responsibly and effectively—we have included in our final section, "Writing Well," six essays in which professional writers reflect on their craft, on the way they write. Each writer offers practical advice on the qualities of good writing and the writing process—getting started, drafting, identifying an audience, being truthful to yourself and your audience, revising, and editing. Although this section is at the end of the book, you may find the readings useful as you start your writing course, because together they provide a detailed overview of the composing process. Or, as you work on particular assignments during the school term, you may want to look at one or more of these essays for direction and encouragement about specific aspects of your writing.

The common denominator of all good writing is the writer's conscious concern for language, and this concern is emphasized, in various ways, by every essay in *Language Awareness.* We have chosen them not only because they explore important issues of language and communication, but also because they provide excellent models of how writers give effective expression to their thoughts. Thus, reading and studying the selections throughout the text, by making you more sensitive to how you use language yourself and to how the language of others affects you, can help you become a better reader and, perhaps most important, a better writer. The more aware you are of the many subtleties and complexities of language use, the greater your mastery and control of language will be. This sense of control will, in turn, allow you to read more thoughtfully and critically and to achieve greater competence and confidence in your own writing.

THE IMPORTANCE OF READING WELL

Reading, whatever your reason for doing so, is most rewarding when you do it actively, in a thoughtful spirit, and with an alert and inquiring mind. For writers—and in one way or another we are all writers—there are special reasons to cultivate the habits and skills of careful, attentive reading. By analyzing the ideas and techniques of the writers you read, you can increase your mastery and refine your own personal style as a writer. Furthermore, for everything you write you will be your own first reader and critic. How well you are able to read your own drafts will powerfully affect how well you can revise them; and revising well is crucial to writing well. So, close, critical reading of what others have written is useful and important practice for anyone who wishes to improve his or her writing skills.

Your first important task as a reader sensitive to language is to read every essay assigned from this text at least twice. In your first reading you will be concerned primarily with understanding the points about language a writer is trying to make. In your second reading—and perhaps even a third—you can refine and develop your understanding of the content, working especially at the difficult passages and analyzing more carefully the author's purpose and his or her means of achieving that purpose. You should determine which features of the essay's organization and style seem particularly successful, so you can learn from them and, perhaps, adapt them to your own work. You may also begin to look for the general strategy or strategies a writer uses to develop the essay's ideas. For example, Malcom X uses *narration* to tell the story of his "Coming to an Awareness of Language." In "The Language of Advertising Claims," Jeffrey Shrank uses *classification* to explain the different strategies and techniques advertisers use to manipulate the public. In her essay "Black Children, Black Speech," Dorothy Z. Seymour uses *comparison and contrast* to detail the similarities and differences between Black English and Standard English. And in "Real Men Don't: Anti-Male Bias in English," Eugene R. August uses *argumentation* to convince us that men as well as women are victimized by language. These and the other rhetorical forms—*description, definition, analogy, cause and effect, process analysis,* and *example* (or *illustration*)—are important ways of structuring our thoughts and getting our point across to others. (The Glossary at the end of *Language Awareness,* explains these and other rhetorical terms in detail. In developing your understanding of these rhetorical forms, you may find it helpful to consult the Glossary as well as the alternate table of contents at the beginning, which classifies the essays in the text according to the rhetorical patterns that they demonstrate.)

Expanding your awareness of how writers use language, then, will require you to pay careful attention not only to what an essay says but also to the way it has been put together. To do so most effectively, as you read, keep a pencil in your hand and use it. Make note, first, of your own responses. If you disagree with a fact or a conclusion, object in the margin: "*NO!*" If you feel skeptical, indicate that response: "*Why?*" If you are impressed by an argument or a turn of phrase, compliment the writer:

"*Good!*" Mark words or passages you don't understand at first reading. A question mark in the margin may do the job, or you may want to circle words or phrases in the text. During the second reading you can look up the words and puzzle out the difficult passages. Be sure, as well, to highlight key points. Mark off the essay into its main sections, such as the introduction, body, and conclusion.

Write in whatever marginal notes come naturally to you. These quick, brief responses will help you later when you begin asking and answering for yourself more specific analytical questions. When annotating a text, don't be timid. Mark up your book as much as you like. But don't let annotating become burdensome or meaningless. It should be an aid, not a chore, and a word or phrase is usually as good as a sentence. To avoid annotating or underlining more than necessary, always ask yourself why you believe the sentence or paragraph is important. You may, in fact, want to delay much of your annotating until a second reading, so that your first reading can be fast and free.

Once you've finished reading and annotating an essay, you'll want to make sure that you've gotten everything from it you can. One good way to complete your analysis is to answer some basic questions about the essay's content and form. Here are several such questions that you may find useful:

1. What does the author want to say about language? What is the essay's main idea or thesis?
2. What are the chief supporting ideas, and how do they relate to the main idea?
3. What is the author's general purpose? Is it to *persuade* you to a particular point of view? to *explain* a subject to you? to *entertain* you? to *tell* a story? or to *describe* a language phenomenon? Does the author state his or her purpose directly? If not, how do you know what the author's purpose is?
4. What strategy or rhetorical form—narration, comparison and contrast, definition, argument, etc.—does the author use as the principal form for the essay?
5. Why and how does the author's writing strategy suit both the subject and the purpose?
6. What other strategies or rhetorical forms does the author use? Where and for what reason(s)?
7. How is the essay structured? How does its organization relate to its main idea and to the author's purpose?
8. What is the author's attitude toward the essay's subject—enthusiastically positive, objective, ironic, hostile, etc.?
9. To whom is the essay addressed? What should the audience expect from this particular type of essay—to find out how something works, to discover what something means, to understand why something happened?
10. Does the author supply enough information to support the essay's ideas

and enough details to make its descriptions precise? Is all of the information relevant and, as far as you can tell, accurate?

11. Has the author left out any information that you think might be relevant to
the thesis? Does he or she fail to consider any important views—including
perhaps your own view?

12. Does the author assume anything without supporting the assumption or
even stating it? Are these assumptions acceptable, or would you challenge
them?

13. Overall, how effective is the essay? Has the writer accomplished his or her
purpose?

Each of the essays in *Language Awareness* is followed by questions for
analysis similar to the ones suggested above, but usually more specific. In
addition to content questions on the language issues explored in each
essay, we have provided questions that direct your attention to specific
rhetorical principles and techniques illustrated by the selection. Each essay
is also followed by a list of words that you will find worth adding to your
active vocabulary, including paragraph references to help you see each
word in its original context in the essay. The questions on content and
rhetoric as well as the vocabulary items work best when you try to answer
them as fully as you can, remembering and considering many details from
the selection to support your answers.

LEARNING TO WRITE WELL

As we suggested before, one of our main purposes in encouraging you to
give such thoughtful attention to the essays in *Language Awareness* is to
help increase your own competence and confidence as a writer. By considering how a variety of writers have solved the problem of providing an
opening and closing paragraph for their essays, you can achieve a fuller
understanding of the possibilities available to you as you work on introductions and conclusions in essays of your own. Similarly, the essays you
read in *Language Awareness* will show you how writers develop coherent
paragraphs, how they use transitional words and phases to create clear
connections among the parts of their essays, how they choose words carefully to bring about an appropriate response in their readers. Increasing
your sensitivity to matters like these can have a big impact on your own
writing.

Furthermore, recognizing how and why the writers in *Language
Awareness* have used certain rhetorical strategies will help you put these
powerful patterns of thought and organization into practice for yourself.
You'll see, for example, that a writer who wants to explain the differences
between the language of men and the language of women will naturally

choose the strategy of *comparison and contrast* to provide her essay's structure. On the other hand, if a writer wants to explain *why* such differences exist, you'll see that no amount of comparing will do the job: it will be necessary to use the strategy of analyzing *cause and effect*. If a writer wants to communicate the meaning of a term like "jargon" or "euphemism," the strategy of *definition* suggests itself naturally. Every topic and purpose for writing will suggest one or another writing strategy. As you write, you may often wish to plan your strategy before you start, consciously deciding which one or which combination of strategies best fits what you have to say and what you want to accomplish. When you've completed a rough draft, you need to read what you've written, making sure that your choice of strategy was a good one and that it expresses your content accurately and effectively. The sort of reading *Language Awareness* encourages will help you become more skilled at making the decisions that lead to such improvement in your own writing.

   Language Awareness will also provide you with many possibilities for practicing your writing skills. Each essay in the text is followed by two or more writing assignments based upon the essay's content and/or its rhetorical features. These assignments will give you a chance to use the essay as a model or as a starting point for an essay of your own. At the end of each section of the text, we have provided further topics and instructions for writing that bring together ideas from several different selections, allowing you to synthesize your thoughts about the overall subject of a section. Finally, at the end of the book there is a list of suggested topics for longer papers involving some library research. Each of the many suggestions is designed to help you think more closely about some particular aspect of language as you refine your ability to express your thoughts forcefully and coherently in writing.

PART I

Discovering Language

I know what he said, but who ever takes weather-people literally?

COMING TO AN AWARENESS OF LANGUAGE

Malcolm X

*On February 21, 1965, Malcolm X, the Black Muslim leader,
was shot to death as he addressed an afternoon rally in
Harlem. He was thirty-nine years old. In the course of his
brief life he had risen from the world of thieving, pimping,
and drug pushing to become one of the most articulate and
powerful blacks in America during the early 1960s.*

With the assistance of Alex Haley, later the author of
Roots, *Malcolm X told his story in* The Autobiography of
Malcolm X, *a moving account of his search for fulfillment. In
the following selection taken from the* Autobiography,
*Malcolm X narrates the story of how his frustration at not
being able to express himself in the letters he wrote led to his
discovery of the power of language.*

I've never been one for inaction. Everything I've ever felt strongly about, 1
I've done something about. I guess that's why, unable to do anything else,
I soon began writing to people I had known in the hustling world, such as
Sammy the Pimp, John Hughes, the gambling house owner, the thief
Jumpsteady, and several dope peddlers. I wrote them all about Allah and
Islam and Mr. Elijah Muhammad. I had no idea where most of them lived.
I addressed their letters in care of the Harlem or Roxbury bars and clubs
where I'd known them.

I never got a single reply. The average hustler and criminal was too 2
uneducated to write a letter. I have known many slick sharp-looking hus-
tlers, who would have you think they had an interest in Wall Street;
privately, they would get someone else to read a letter if they received one.
Besides, neither would I have replied to anyone writing me something as
wild as "the white man is the devil."

What certainly went on the Harlem and Roxbury wires was that Detroit 3
Red was going crazy in stir, or else he was trying some hype to shake up
the warden's office.

During the years that I stayed in the Norfolk Prison Colony, never did 4
any official directly say anything to me about those letters, although, of

course, they all passed through the prison censorship. I'm sure, however, they monitored what I wrote to add to the files which every state and federal prison keeps on the conversion of Negro inmates by the teachings of Mr. Elijah Muhammad.

But at that time, I felt that the real reason was that the white man knew   5
that he was the devil.

Later on, I even wrote to the Mayor of Boston, to the Governor of   6
Massachusetts, and to Harry S. Truman. They never answered; they probably never even saw my letters. I handscratched to them how the white
man's society was responsible for the black man's condition in this wilderness of North America.

It was because of my letters that I happened to stumble upon starting to   7
acquire some kind of a homemade education.

I became increasingly frustrated at not being able to express what I   8
wanted to convey in letters that I wrote, especially those to Mr. Elijah
Muhammad. In the street, I had been the most articulate hustler out there—
I had commanded attention when I said something. But now, trying to
write simple English, I not only wasn't articulate, I wasn't even functional.
How would I sound writing in slang, the way I would *say* it, something
such as, "Look, daddy, let me pull your coat about a cat. Elijah
Muhammad—"

Many who today hear me somewhere in person, or on television, or   9
those who read something I've said, will think I went to school far beyond
the eighth grade. This impression is due entirely to my prison studies.

It had really begun back in the Charlestown Prison, when Bimbi first   10
made me feel envy of his stock of knowledge. Bimbi had always taken
charge of any conversation he was in, and I had tried to emulate him. But
every book I picked up had few sentences which didn't contain anywhere
from one to nearly all of the words that might as well have been in
Chinese. When I just skipped those words, of course, I really ended up
with little idea of what the book said. So I had come to the Norfolk Prison
Colony still going through only book-reading motions. Pretty soon, I
would have quit even these motions, unless I had received the motivation
that I did.

I saw that the best thing I could do was get hold of a dictionary—to   11
study, to learn some words. I was lucky enough to reason also that I should
try to improve my penmanship. It was sad. I couldn't even write in a
straight line. It was both ideas together that moved me to request a dictionary along with some tablets and pencils from the Norfolk Prison Colony school.

I spent two days just riffling uncertainly through the dictionary's pages.   12
I'd never realized so many words existed! I didn't know *which* words I
needed to learn. Finally, just to start some kind of action, I began copying.

In my slow, painstaking, ragged handwriting, I copied into my tablet   13
everything printed on that first page, down to the punctuation marks.

I believe it took me a day. Then, aloud, I read back, to myself,   14
everything I'd written on the tablet. Over and over, aloud, to myself, I read
my own handwriting.

I woke up the next morning, thinking about those words—immensely   15
proud to realize that not only had I written so much at one time, but I'd
written words that I never knew were in the world. Moreover, with a little
effort, I also could remember what many of these words meant. I reviewed
the words whose meanings I didn't remember. Funny thing, from the
dictionary's first page right now, that "aardvark" springs to my mind. The
dictionary had a picture of it, a long-tailed, long-eared, burrowing African
mammal, which lives off termites caught by sticking out its tongue as an
anteater does for ants.

I was so fascinated that I went on—I copied the dictionary's next page.   16
And the same experience came when I studied that. With every succeeding
page, I also learned of people and places and events from history. Actually
the dictionary is like a miniature encyclopedia. Finally the dictionary's A
section had filled a whole tablet—and I went on into the B's. That was the
way I started copying what eventually became the entire dictionary. It went
a lot faster after so much practice helped me pick up handwriting speed.
Between what I wrote in my tablet, and writing letters, during the rest of
my time in prison I would guess I wrote a million words.

I suppose it was inevitable that as my word-base broadened, I could for   17
the first time pick up a book and read and now begin to understand what
the book was saying. Anyone who has read a great deal can imagine the
new world that opened. Let me tell you something: from then until I left
that prison, in every free moment I had, if I was not reading in the library,
I was reading on my bunk. You couldn't have gotten me out of books with
a wedge. Between Mr. Muhammad's teachings, my correspondence, my
visitors . . . and my reading of books, months passed without my even
thinking about being imprisoned. In fact, up to then, I never had been so
truly free in my life.

QUESTIONS ON CONTENT

1. What motivated Malcolm X "to acquire some kind of a homemade
education"(7)?

2. What does Malcolm X mean when he says that he was "going through
only book-reading motions"(10)? How did he decide to solve this problem?

3. In paragraph 8 Malcolm X points to the difference between being "ar-

ticulate" and being "functional" in his speaking and writing. What exactly is the distinction that he makes?

4. Why did the word *aardvark* spring to mind when Malcolm X recalled his study of the first page of the dictionary?

5. In what ways is the dictionary like a "miniature encyclopedia"(16)? How are dictionaries and encyclopedias different?

6. What is the nature of the freedom that Malcolm X refers to in the final sentence?

QUESTIONS ON RHETORIC

1. Malcolm X narrates his experiences as a prisoner in the first person. Why is the first person particularly appropriate? (Glossary: *Point of View*)

2. How has Malcolm X organized his essay? (Glossary: *Organization*)

3. The first sentences of paragraphs 1 and 2 are both short declarative sentences. Why are they especially effective as introductory sentences?

4. Could paragraphs 12, 13, and 14 be combined into a single paragraph? What would be gained or lost if they were to be combined?

5. Why is Malcolm X's relatively simple vocabulary in this narrative appropriate? (Glossary: *Diction*)

VOCABULARY

frustrated (8)   functional (8)   inevitable (17)
articulate (8)   emulate (10)

WRITING TOPICS

1. All of us have been in situations in which our ability to use language seemed inadequate—for example, when taking an exam; being interviewed for a job; giving directions; or expressing sympathy, anger, or grief. Write a brief essay in which you recount one such frustrating incident in your life. In preparing to write your narrative, you may find it helpful to ask yourself such questions as: Why is the incident important to me? What details are necessary for me to re-create the incident in an interesting and engaging way? How can my narrative of the incident be most effectively organized? Compare your experiences with those of your classmates.

2. Malcolm X solved the problems of his own illiteracy by carefully studying the dictionary. Would this be a practical solution to the national problem of illiteracy? Are there any alternatives to Malcolm X's approach? What are they?

THE DAY LANGUAGE CAME INTO MY LIFE

Helen Keller

Helen Keller (1880–1968) became blind and deaf at the age of eighteen months as the result of a disease. It wasn't until she was seven years old that her family hired Anne Sullivan to be her teacher. As Keller learned to think and communicate through language, the world opened up to her. Thus, she is in a unique position to remind us of what it is like to pass from the "fog" of prethought into the world where "everything had a name, and each name gave birth to a new thought."

The most important day I remember in all my life is the one on which my teacher, Anne Mansfield Sullivan, came to me. I am filled with wonder when I consider the immeasurable contrast between the two lives which it connects. It was the third of March 1887, three months before I was seven years old.

On the afternoon of that eventful day, I stood on the porch, dumb, expectant. I guessed vaguely from my mother's signs and from the hurrying to and fro in the house that something unusual was about to happen, so I went to the door and waited on the steps. The afternoon sun penetrated the mass of honeysuckle that covered the porch and fell on my upturned face. My fingers lingered almost unconsciously on the familiar leaves and blossoms which had just come forth to greet the sweet southern spring. I did not know what the future held of marvel or surprise for me. Anger and bitterness had preyed upon me continually for weeks and a deep languor had succeeded this passionate struggle.

Have you ever been at sea in a dense fog, when it seemed as if a tangible white darkness shut you in, and the great ship, tense and anxious, groped her way toward the shore with plummet and sounding-line, and you waited with beating heart for something to happen? I was like that ship before my education began, only I was without compass or sounding-line and had no way of knowing how near the harbor was. "Light! give me light!" was the wordless cry of my soul, and the light of love shone on me in that very hour.

13

I felt approaching footsteps. I stretched out my hand as I supposed to   4
my mother. Someone took it, and I was caught up and held close in the
arms of her who had come to reveal all things to me, and, more that all
things else, to love me.

The morning after my teacher came she led me into her room and gave   5
me a doll. The little blind children at the Perkins Institution had sent it and
Laura Bridgman had dressed it; but I did not know this until afterward.
When I had played with it a little while, Miss Sullivan slowly spelled into
my hand the word "d-o-l-l." I was at once interested in this finger play and
tried to imitate it. When I finally succeeded in making the letters correctly
I was flushed with childish pleasure and pride. Running downstairs to my
mother I held up my hand and made the letters for doll. I did not know
that I was spelling a word or even that words existed; I was simply making
my fingers go in monkeylike imitation. In the days that followed I learned
to spell in this uncomprehending way a great many words, among them
pin, hat, cup and a few verbs like *sit, stand* and *walk.* But my teacher had
been with me several weeks before I understood that everything has a
name.

One day, while I was playing with my new doll, Miss Sullivan put my   6
big rag doll into my lap also, spelled "d-o-l-l" and tried to make me understand that "d-o-l-l" applied to both. Earlier in the day we had had a tussle
over the words "m-u-g" and "w-a-t-e-r." Miss Sullivan had tried to impress
it upon me that "m-u-g" is *mug* and that "w-a-t-e-r" is *water,* but I
persisted in confounding the two. In despair she had dropped the subject
for the time, only to renew it at the first opportunity. I became impatient
at her repeated attempts and, seizing the new doll, I dashed it upon the
floor. I was keenly delighted when I felt the fragments of the broken doll
at my feet. Neither sorrow nor regret followed my passionate outburst. I
had not loved the doll. In the still, dark world in which I lived there was
no strong sentiment or tenderness. I felt my teacher sweep the fragments to
one side of the hearth, and I had a sense of satisfaction that the cause of my
discomfort was removed. She brought me my hat, and I knew I was going
out into the warm sunshine. This thought, if a wordless sensation may be
called a thought, made me hop and skip with pleasure.

We walked down the path to the well-house, attracted by the fragrance   7
of the honeysuckle with which it was covered. Some one was drawing
water and my teacher placed my hand under the spout. As the cool stream
gushed over one hand she spelled into the other the word *water,* first
slowly, then rapidly. I stood still, my whole attention fixed upon the
motions of her fingers. Suddenly I felt a misty consciousness as of something forgotten—a thrill of returning thought; and somehow the mystery of
language was revealed to me. I knew then that "w-a-t-e-r" meant the
wonderful cool something that was flowing over my hand. The living word

awakened my soul, gave it light, hope, joy, set it free! There were barriers still, it is true, but barriers that could in time be swept away.

I left the well-house eager to learn. Everything had a name, and each name gave birth to a new thought. As we returned to the house every object which I touched semed to quiver with life. That was because I saw every-thing with the strange, new sight that had come to me. On entering the door I remembered the doll I had broken. I felt my way to the hearth and picked up the pieces. I tried vainly to put them together. Then my eyes filled with tears; for I realized what I had done, and for the first time I felt repentance and sorrow.

I learned a great many new words that day. I do not remember what they all were; but I do know that *mother, father, sister, teacher* were among them—words that were to make the world blossom for me, "like Aaron's rod, with flowers." It would have been difficult to find a happier child than I was as I lay in my crib at the close of that eventful day and lived over the joys it had brought me, and for the first time longed for a new day to come.

QUESTIONS ON CONTENT

1. Keller defines her most important day as the day Anne Sullivan came into her life. Knowing the importance Keller places on language, why do you suppose she chose as her most important day the one on which she understood language for the first time?

2. Until she learned language, Keller could not express her feelings. Nevertheless, she experienced many emotions. What were some of these emotions? What usually precipitated them? When language came to Keller, she experienced a feeling she had never had before. What was that feeling?

3. In paragraphs 7 and 8, Keller explains how "the mystery of language" was revealed to her and how it affected her. In your own words, what was that mystery and what was its significance for Keller?

QUESTIONS ON RHETORIC

1. In her opening sentence, Keller says her meeting with Anne Sullivan was wonderful in that it brought together two lives of such contrast. Read over Keller's story and make a list of Keller's and Sullivan's personality traits. Then, using examples from the text, explain how Keller uses telling details to enhance this contrast.

2. Keller believed that over time words would make her world open up. Identify the parts of speech of her first words. In what way do these parts of speech open up one's world? Does this give you any insight into the nature of writing?

3. Keller uses a narrative (Glossary: *Narrative*) to make her point that language is the key to life and learning. Why do you suppose she chose this method? Could she have made her point as effectively using another writing strategy, cause and effect analysis for example? (Glossary: *Cause and Effect Analysis*)

VOCABULARY

languor (2)   plummet (3)   confounding (6)
tangible (3)

WRITING TOPICS

1. In paragraph 3, Keller uses the metaphor of being lost in a fog to explain her feeling of helplessness and her fustration at not being able to communicate. Perhaps you have had a similar feeling over an inability to communicate with parents or teachers or of not being able to realize some other longed-for goal. In an essay, describe these feelings using a metaphor or some other figure of speech of your own creation.

2. Keller explains that she felt no remorse when she shattered her doll. "In the still, dark world in which I lived there was no strong sentiment or tenderness." However, once she understood that things had names, Keller was able to feel repentance and sorrow. In your own words, try to describe why you think this is true. You may want to discuss this in class or do some research of your own into the ways language alters perception among people who are blind and deaf.

A BRIEF HISTORY OF ENGLISH

Paul Roberts

In the following selection from his book Understanding English, *the late Professor Paul Roberts recounts the major events in the history of England and discusses their relationship to the development of the English language. He shows us how the people who invaded England influenced the language and how, in recent times, the rapid spread of English has resulted in its becoming a major world language.*

HISTORICAL BACKGROUNDS

No understanding of the English language can be very satisfactory without a notion of the history of the language. But we shall have to make do with just a notion. The history of English is long and complicated, and we can only hit the high spots.   1

The history of our language begins a little after A.D. 600. Everything   2
before that is pre-history, which means that we can guess at it but can't prove much. For a thousand years or so before the birth of Christ our linguistic ancestors were savages wandering through the forests of northern Europe. Their language was a part of the Germanic branch of the Indo-European Family.

At the time of the Roman Empire—say, from the beginning of the   3
Christian Era to around A.D. 400—the speakers of what was to become English were scattered along the northern coast of Europe. They spoke a dialect of Low German. More exactly, they spoke several different dialects, since they were several different tribes. The names given to the tribes who got to England are *Angles, Saxons,* and *Jutes.* For convenience, we can refer to them as Anglo-Saxons.

Their first contact with civilization was a rather thin acquaintance with   4
the Roman Empire on whose borders they lived. Probably some of the Anglo-Saxons wandered into the Empire occasionally, and certainly Roman merchants and traders traveled among the tribes. At any rate, this period saw the first of our many borrowings from Latin. Such words as

17

kettle, wine, cheese, butter, cheap, plum, gem, bishop, church were borrowed at this time. They show something of the relationship of the Anglo-Saxons with the Romans. The Anglo-Saxons were learning, getting their first taste of civilization.

They still had a long way to go, however, and their first step was to help smash the civilization they were learning from. In the fourth century the Roman power weakened badly. While the Goths were pounding away at the Romans in the Mediterranean countries, their relatives, the Anglo-Saxons, began to attack Britain.

The Romans had been the ruling power in Britain since A.D. 43. They had subjugated the Celts whom they found living there and had succeeded in setting up a Roman administration. The Roman influence did not extend to the outlying parts of the British Isles. In Scotland, Wales, and Ireland the Celts remained free and wild, and they made periodic forays against the Romans in England. Among other defense measures, the Romans built the famous Roman Wall to ward off the tribes in the north.

Even in England the Roman power was thin. Latin did not become the language of the country as it did in Gaul and Spain. The mass of people continued to speak Celtic, with Latin and the Roman civilization it contained in use as a top dressing.

In the fourth century, troubles multiplied for the Romans in Britain. Not only did the untamed tribes of Scotland and Wales grow more and more restive, but the Anglo-Saxons began to make pirate raids on the eastern coast. Furthermore, there was growing difficulty everywhere in the Empire, and the legions in Britain were siphoned off to fight elsewhere. Finally, in A.D. 410, the last Roman ruler in England, bent on becoming emperor, left the islands and took the last of the legions with him. The Celts were left in possession of Britain but almost defenseless against the impending Anglo-Saxon attack.

Not much is surely known about the arrival of the Anglo-Saxons in England. According to the best early source, the eighth-century historian Bede, the Jutes came in 449 in response to a plea from the Celtic king, Vortigern, who wanted their help against the Picts attacking from the north. The Jutes subdued the Picts but then quarreled and fought with Vortigern, and, with reinforcements from the Continent, settled permanently in Kent. Somewhat later the Angles established themselves in eastern England and the Saxons in the south and west. Bede's account is plausible enough, and these were probably the main lines of the invasion.

We do know, however, that the Angles, Saxons, and Jutes were a long time securing themselves in England. Fighting went on for as long as a hundred years before the Celts in England were all killed, driven into Wales, or reduced to slavery. This is the period of King Arthur, who was not entirely mythological. He was a Romanized Celt, a general, though probably not a king. He had some success against the Anglo-Saxons, but it was only temporary. By 550 or so the Anglo-Saxons were firmly established. English was in England.

OLD ENGLISH

All this is pre-history, so far as the language is concerned. We have no record of the English language until after 600, when the Anglo-Saxons were converted to Christianity and learned the Latin alphabet. The conversion began, to be precise, in the year 597 and was accomplished within thirty or forty years. The conversion was a great advance for the Anglo-Saxons, not only because of the spiritual benefits but because it reestablished contact with what remained of Roman civilization. This civilization didn't amount to much in the year 600, but it was certainly superior to anything in England up to that time.   11

It is customary to divide the history of the English language into three periods: Old English, Middle English, and Modern English. Old English runs from the earliest records—i.e., seventh century—to about 1100; Middle English from 1100 to 1450 or 1500; Modern English from 1500 to the present day. Sometimes Modern English is further divided into Early Modern, 1500–1700, and Late Modern, 1700 to the present.   12

When England came into history, it was divided into several more or less autonomous kingdoms, some of which at times exercised a certain amount of control over the others. In the century after the conversion the most advanced kingdom was Northumbria, the area between the Humber River and the Scottish border. By A.D. 700 the Northumbrians had developed a respectable civilization, the finest in Europe. It is sometimes called the Northumbrian Renaissance, and it was the first of the several renaissances through which Europe struggled upward out of the ruins of the Roman Empire. It was in this period that the best of the Old English literature was written, including the epic poem *Beowulf*.   13

In the eighth century, Northumbrian power declined, and the center of influence moved southward to Mercia, the kingdom of the Midlands. A century later the center shifted again, and Wessex, the country of the West Saxons, became the leading power. The most famous king of the West Saxons was Alfred the Great, who reigned in the second half of the ninth century, dying in 901. He was famous not only as a military man and administrator but also as a champion of learning. He founded and supported schools and translated or caused to be translated many books from Latin into English. At this time also much of the Northumbrian literature of two centuries earlier was copied in West Saxon. Indeed, the great bulk   14 of Old English writing which has come down to us is in the West Saxon dialect of 900 or later.

In the military sphere, Alfred's great accomplishment was his suc-   15
cessful opposition to the Viking invasions. In the ninth and tenth centuries, the Norsemen emerged in their ships from their homelands in Denmark and the Scandinavian peninsula. They traveled far and attacked and plundered at will and almost with impunity. They ravaged Italy and Greece, settled in France, Russia, and Ireland, colonized Iceland and Greenland, and discovered America several centuries before Columbus. Nor did they overlook England.

After many years of hit-and-run raids, the Norsemen landed an army on   16
the east coast of England in the year 866. There was nothing much to oppose them except the Wessex power led by Alfred. The long struggle ended in 877 with a treaty by which a line was drawn roughly from the northwest of England to the southeast. On the eastern side of the line Norse rule was to prevail. This was called the Danelaw. The western side was to be governed by Wessex.

The linguistic result of all this was a considerable injection of Norse   17
into the English language. Norse was at this time not so different from English as Norwegian or Danish is now. Probably speakers of English could understand, more or less, the language of the newcomers who had moved into eastern England. At any rate, there was considerable interchange and word borrowing. Examples of Norse words in the English language are *sky, give, law, egg, outlaw, leg, ugly, scant, sly, crawl, scowl, take, thrust.* There are hundreds more. We have even borrowed some pronouns from Norse—*they, their,* and *them.* These words were borrowed first by the eastern and northern dialects and then in the course of hundreds of years made their way into English generally.

It is supposed also—indeed, it must be true—that the Norsemen influ-   18
enced the sound structure and the grammar of English. But this is hard to demonstrate in detail.

A SPECIMEN OF OLD ENGLISH

We may now have an example of Old English. The favorite illustration is   19
the Lord's Prayer, since it needs no translation. This has come to us in several different versions. Here is one:

Fæder ure,
þu þe eart on heofonum,
si þin nama gehalgod.
Tobecume þin rice.

Gewurþe ðin willa on eorðan swa swa on heofonum.
Urne gedæghwamlican hlaf syle us to dæg.
And forgyf us ure gyltas, swa swa we forgyfað urum gyltendum.
And ne gelæd þu us on costnunge,
ac alys us of yfele. Soþlice.

Some of the differences between this and Modern English are merely 20
differences in orthography. For instance, the sign *æ* is what Old English
writers used for a vowel sound like that in modern *hat* or *and.* The *th*
sounds of modern *thin* or *then* are represented in Old English by *þ* or *ð.* But
of course there are many differences in sound too. *Ure* is the ancestor of
modern *our,* but the first vowel was like that in *too* or *ooze. Hlaf* is modern
loaf; we have dropped the *h* sound and changed the vowel, which in *hlaf*
was pronounced something like the vowel in *father.* Old English had some
sounds which we do not have. The sound represented by *y* does not occur
in Modern English. If you pronounce the vowel in *bit* with your lips
rounded, you may approach it.

In grammar, Old English was much more highly inflected than Modern 21
English is. That is, there were more case endings for nouns, more person
and number endings for verbs, a more complicated pronoun system, various endings for adjectives, and so on. Old English nouns had four cases—
nominative, genitive, dative, accusative. Adjectives had five—all these
and an instrumental case besides. Present-day English has only two cases
for nouns—common case and possessive case. Adjectives now have no
case system at all. On the other hand, we now use a more rigid word order
and more structure words (prepositions, auxiliaries, and the like) to express
relationships than Old English did.

Some of this grammar we can see in the Lord's Prayer. *Heofonum,* for 22
instance, is a dative plural; the nominative singular was *heofon. Urne* is an
accusative singular; the nominative is *ure.* In *urum glytendum* both words
are dative plural. *Forgyfaþ* is the first person plural form of the verb. Word
order is different: "urne gedæghwamlican hlaf syle us" in place of "Give
us our daily bread." And so on.

In vocabulary Old English is quite different from Modern English. 23
Most of the Old English words are what we may call native English: that
is, words which have not been borrowed from other languages but which
have been a part of English ever since English was a part of Indo-European.
Old English did certainly contain borrowed words. We have seen that
many borrowings were coming in from Norse. Rather large numbers had
been borrowed from Latin, too. Some of these were taken while the Anglo-
Saxons were still on the Continent (*cheese, butter, bishop, kettle,* etc.); a
large number came into English after the conversion (*angel, candle, priest,*

martyr, radish, oyster, purple, school, spend, etc.). But the great majority of Old English words were native English.

Now, on the contrary, the majority of words in English are borrowed,   24 taken mostly from Latin and French. Of the words in *The American College Dictionary* only about 14 percent are native. Most of these, to be sure, are common, high-frequency words—*the, of, I, and, because, man, mother, road,* etc.; of the thousand most common words in English, some 62 percent are native English. Even so, the modern vocabulary is very much Latinized and Frenchified. The Old English vocabulary was not.

MIDDLE ENGLISH

Sometime between the years 1000 and 1200 various important changes   25 took place in the structure of English, and Old English became Middle English. The political event which facilitated these changes was the Norman Conquest. The Normans, as the name shows, came originally from Scandinavia. In the early tenth century they established themselves in northern France, adopted the French language, and developed a vigorous kingdom and a very passable civilization. In the year 1066, led by Duke William, they crossed the Channel and made themselves masters of England. For the next several hundred years, England was ruled by kings whose first language was French.

One might wonder why, after the Norman Conquest, French did not   26 become the national language, replacing English entirely. The reason is that the Conquest was not a national migration, as the earlier Anglo-Saxon invasion had been. Great numbers of Normans came to England, but they came as rulers and landlords. French became the language of the court, the language of the nobility, the language of polite society, the language of literature. But it did not replace English as the language of the people. There must always have been hundreds of towns and villages in which French was never heard except when visitors of high station passed through.

But English, though it survived as the national language, was pro-   27 foundly changed after the Norman Conquest. Some of the changes—in sound structure and grammar—would no doubt have taken place whether there had been a Conquest or not. Even before 1066 the case system of English nouns and adjectives was becoming simplified; people came to rely more on word order and prepositions than on inflectional endings to communicate their meanings. The process was speeded up by sound changes which caused many of the endings to sound alike. But no doubt the Conquest facilitated the change. German, which didn't experience a Norman Conquest, is today rather highly inflected compared to its cousin English.

But it is in vocabulary that the effects of the Conquest are most obvi- 28
ous. French ceased, after a hundred years or so, to be the native language
of very many people in England, but it continued—and continues still—to
be a zealously cultivated second language, the mirror of elegance and
civilization. When one spoke English, one introduced not only French
ideas and French things but also their French names. This was not only
easy but socially useful. To pepper one's conversation with French expressions was to show that one was well-bred, elegant, *au courant*. The
last sentence shows that the process is not yet dead. By using *au courant*
instead of, say, *abreast of things,* the writer indicates that he is no dull clod
who knows only English but an elegant person aware of how things are
done in *le haut monde.*

Thus French words came into English, all sorts of them. There were 29
words to do with government: *parliament, majesty, treaty, alliance, tax,
government;* church words: *parson, sermon, baptism, incense, crucifix,
religion;* words for foods: *veal, beef, mutton, bacon, jelly, peach, lemon,
cream, biscuit;* colors: *blue, scarlet, vermilion;* household words: *curtain,
chair, lamp, towel, blanket, parlor;* play words: *dance, chess, music,
leisure, conversation;* literary words: *story, romance, poet, literary;*
learned words: *study, logic, grammar, noun, surgeon, anatomy, stomach;*
just ordinary words of all sorts: *nice, second, very, age, bucket, gentle,
final, fault, flower, cry, count, sure, move, surprise, plain.*

All these and thousands more poured into the English vocabulary be- 30
tween 1100 and 1500 until, at the end of that time, many people must have
had more French words than English at their command. This is not to say
that English became French. English remained English in sound structure
and in grammar, though these also felt the ripples of French influence. The
very heart of the vocabulary, too, remained English. Most of the high-
frequency words—the pronouns, the prepositions, the conjunctions, the
auxiliaries, as well as a great many ordinary nouns and verbs and
adjectives—were not replaced by borrowings.

Middle English, then, was still a Germanic language, but it differed 31
from Old English in many ways. The sound system and the grammar
changed a good deal. Speakers made less use of case systems and other
inflectional devices and relied more on word order and structure words to
express their meanings. This is often said to be a simplification, but it isn't
really. Languages don't become simpler; they merely exchange one kind of
complexity for another. Modern English is not a simple language, as any
foreign speaker who tries to learn it will hasten to tell you.

For us Middle English is simpler than Old English just because it is 32
closer to Modern English. It takes three or four months at least to learn to
read Old English prose and more than that for poetry. But a week of good
study should put one in touch with the Middle English poet Chaucer.

Indeed, you may be able to make some sense of Chaucer straight off, though you would need instruction in pronunciation to make it sound like poetry. Here is a famous passage from the *General Prologue to the Canterbury Tales,* fourteenth century:

> Ther was also a nonne, a Prioresse,
> That of hir smyling was ful symple and coy,
> Hir gretteste oath was but by Seinte Loy,
> And she was cleped° Madame Eglentyne.   named
> Ful wel she song the service dyvyne,
> Entuned in hir nose ful semely.
> And Frenshe she spak ful faire and fetisly,°   elegantly
> After the scole of Stratford-atte-Bowe,
> For Frenshe of Parys was to hir unknowe.

EARLY MODERN ENGLISH

Sometime between 1400 and 1600 English underwent a couple of sound changes which made the language of Shakespeare quite different from that of Chaucer. Incidentally, these changes contributed much to the chaos in which English spelling now finds itself.   33

One change was the elimination of a vowel sound in certain unstressed positions at the end of words. For instance, the words *name, stone, wine, dance* were pronounced as two syllables by Chaucer but as just one by Shakespeare. The *e* in these words became, as we say, "silent." But it wasn't silent for Chaucer; it represented a vowel sound. So also the words *laughed, seemed, stored* would have been pronounced by Chaucer as two-syllable words. The change was an important one because it affected thousands of words and gave a different aspect to the whole language.   34

The other change is what is called the Great Vowel Shift. This was a systematic shifting of half a dozen vowels and diphthongs in stressed syllables. For instance, the word *name* had in Middle English a vowel something like that in the modern word *father; wine* had the vowel of modern *mean; he* was pronounced something like modern *hey; mouse* sounded like *moose; moon* had the vowel of *moan.* Again the shift was thoroughgoing and affected all the words in which these vowel sounds occurred. Since we still keep the Middle English system of spelling these words, the differences between Modern English and Middle English are often more real than apparent.   35

The vowel shift has meant also that we have come to use an entirely different set of symbols for representing vowel sounds than is used by writers of such languages as French, Italian, or Spanish, in which no such vowel shift occurred. If you come across a strange word—say, *bine*—in an   36

English book, you will pronounce it according to the English system, with the vowel of *wine* or *dine*. But if you read *bine* in a French, Italian, or Spanish book, you pronounce it with the vowel of *mean* or *seen*.

These two changes, then, produced the basic differences between   37 Middle English and Modern English. But there were several other developments that had an effect upon the language. One was the invention of printing, an invention introduced into England by William Caxton in the year 1475. Where before books had been rare and costly, they suddenly became cheap and common. More and more people learned to read and write. This was the first of many advances in communication which have worked to unify languages and to arrest the development of dialect differences, though of course printing affects writing principally rather than speech. Among other things it hastened the standardization of spelling.

The period of Early Modern English—that is, the sixteenth and seven-   38 teenth centuries—was also the period of the English Renaissance, when people developed, on the one hand, a keen interest in the past and, on the other, a more daring and imaginative view of the future. New ideas multiplied, and new ideas meant new language. Englishmen had grown accustomed to borrowing words from French as a result of the Norman Conquest; now they borrowed from Latin and Greek. As we have seen, English had been raiding Latin from Old English times and before, but now the floodgates really opened, and thousands of words from the classical languages poured in. *Pedestrian, bonus, anatomy, contradict, climax, dictionary, benefit, multiply, exist, paragraph, initiate, scene, inspire* are random examples. Probably the average educated American today has more words from French in his vocabulary than from native English sources, and more from Latin than from French.

The greatest writer of the Early Modern English period is of course   39 Shakespeare, and the best-known book is the King James Version of the Bible, published in 1611. The Bible (if not Shakespeare) has made many features of Early Modern English perfectly familiar to many people down to the present time, even though we do not use these features in present-day speech and writing. For instance, the old pronouns *thou* and *thee* have dropped out of use now, together with their verb forms, but they are still familiar to us in prayer and in Biblical quotations: "Whither thou goest, I will go." Such forms as *hath* and *doth* have been replaced by *has* and *does;* "Goes he hence tonight?" would now be "Is he going away tonight?"; Shakespeare's "Fie, on't, sirrah" would be "Nuts to that, Mac." Still, all these expressions linger with us because of the power of the works in which they occur.

It is not always realized, however, that considerable sound changes   40 have taken place between Early Modern English and the English of the present day. Shakespearian actors putting on a play speak the words, properly enough, in their modern pronunciation. But it is very doubtful that this pronunciation would be understood at all by Shakespeare. In Shakespeare's time, the word *reason* was pronounced like modern *raisin; face* had the sound of modern *glass;* the *l* in *would, should, palm* was pronounced. In these points and a great many others the English language has moved a long way from what it was in 1600.

RECENT DEVELOPMENTS

The history of English since 1700 is filled with many movements and   41
countermovements, of which we can notice only a couple. One of these is
the vigorous attempt made in the eighteenth century, and the rather half-
hearted attempts made since, to regulate and control the English language.
Many people of the eighteenth century, not understanding very well the
forces which govern language, proposed to polish and prune and restrict
English, which they felt was proliferating too wildly. There was much talk
of an academy which would rule on what people could and could not say
and write. The academy never came into being, but the eighteenth century
did succeed in establishing certain attitudes which, though they haven't
had much effect on the development of the language itself, have certainly
changed the native speaker's feeling about the language.

In part, a product of the wish to fix and establish the language was the   42
development of the dictionary. The first English dictionary was published
in 1603; it was a list of 2,500 words briefly defined. Many others were
published with gradual improvements until Samuel Johnson published his
English Dictionary in 1755. This, steadily revised, dominated the field in
England for nearly a hundred years. Meanwhile in America, Noah Webster
published his dictionary in 1828, and before long dictionary publishing
was a big business in this country. The last century has seen the publication
of one great dictionary: the twelve-volume *Oxford English Dictionary,*
compiled in the course of seventy-five years through the labors of many
scholars. We have also, of course, numerous commercial dictionaries
which are as good as the public wants them to be if not, indeed, rather
better.

Another product of the eighteenth century was the invention of "En-   43
glish grammar." As English came to replace Latin as the language of
scholarship, it was felt that one should also be able to control and dissect
it, parse and analyze it, as one could Latin. What happened in practice was
that the grammatical description that applied to Latin was removed and
superimposed on English. This was silly, because English is an entirely
different kind of language, with its own forms and signals and ways of

producing meaning. Nevertheless, English grammars on the Latin model were worked out and taught in the schools. In many schools they are still being taught. This activity is not often popular with school children, but it is sometimes an interesting and instructive exercise in logic. The principal harm in it is that it has tended to keep people from being interested in English and has obscured the real features of English structure.

But probably the most important force on the development of English in the modern period has been the tremendous expansion of English-speaking peoples. In 1500 English was a minor language, spoken by a few people on a small island. Now it is perhaps the greatest language of the world, spoken natively by over a quarter of a billion people and as a second language by many millions more. When we speak of English now, we must specify whether we mean American English, British English, Australian English, Indian English, or what, since the differences are considerable. The American cannot go to England or the Englishman to America confident that he will always understand and be understood. The Alabaman in Iowa or the Iowan in Alabama shows himself a foreigner every time he speaks. It is only because communication has become fast and easy that English in this period of its expansion has not broken into a dozen mutually unintelligible languages.

QUESTIONS ON CONTENT

1. What are the three major periods in the history of the English language? When did each occur?

2. Roberts is careful to describe the relationship between historical events in England and the development of the English language. In what ways did historical events affect the English language?

3. When the Anglo-Saxons invaded England, their language, with some modifications, became the language of the land. How does Roberts explain the fact that French did not become the language of England after the invasion of William the Conqueror?

4. How would you characterize in social terms the French words that were brought into English by the Norman Conquest? In what areas of life did French have the greatest influence?

5. Explain what changes the English language underwent as a result of the Great Vowel Shift. What is the importance of this linguistic phenomenon for the history of English?

6. Why, according to Roberts, have school children tended not to be interested in the study of the English language?

QUESTIONS ON RHETORIC

1. What is Roberts's thesis in this essay? (Glossary: *Thesis*) Where is it stated?

2. Why is a chronological organization appropriate for this essay? (Glossary: *Organization*)

3. Roberts makes extensive use of examples in his essay. Of what value are these examples for the reader? (Glossary: *Examples*)

4. How does Roberts use comparison and contrast to help him discuss Old English? (Glossary: *Comparison and Contrast*)

5. Roberts uses the pronouns *we, our,* and *us* throughout his essay. What effect does this have on you?

VOCABULARY

forays (6)	impunity (15)	zealously (28)
siphoned (8)	facilitated (25)	linger (39)
conversion (11)		

WRITING TOPICS

1. Using your dictionary, identify the language from which each of the following words was borrowed:

barbecue	hustle
buffalo	marmalade
casino	orangutan
decoy	posse
ditto	raccoon
fruit	veranda

What other examples of borrowed words can you find in your dictionary? Write an essay in which you show with examples that today "the majority of words in English are borrowed" (24).

2. During its relatively brief 1400-year history, the English language has consistently been characterized by change. How is American English still changing today? What effects, if any, have the Vietnam War, the NASA space program, the drug culture, computers and other new technology, the women's movement, and/or recent waves of immigration had on American English?

THE POWER OF WORDS

Bergen Evans

"Words are the tools for the job of saying what you want to say," writes the late Bergen Evans, an authority on the uses and abuses of the English language. With this sentence he introduces the central point of his article and emphasizes a major theme of Language Awareness: *the importance of the word. In this selection, Evans develops his analogy of words as tools and discusses the importance of an effective vocabulary.*

Words are the tools for the job of saying what you want to say. And what you want to say are your thoughts and feelings, your desires and your dislikes, your hopes and your fears, your business and your pleasure—almost everything, indeed, that makes up *you*. Except for our vegetablelike growth and our animallike impulses, almost all that we are is related to our use of words. Man has been defined as a tool-using animal, but his most important tool, the one that distinguishes him from all other animals, is his speech.

As with other tools, the number and variety of the words we know should meet all our needs. Not that any man has ever had a vocabulary exactly fitted to his every need at all times. The greatest writers—those who have shown the rest of us how *in*adequate our own command of words is—have agonized over their verbal shortcomings. But we can approach our needs. The more words we know, the closer we can come to expressing precisely what we want to.

We can, for instance, give clear instructions, and reduce misunderstandings. If we say, "See that he does it," we should make sure that the person spoken to knows what he is to do when he *sees,* that it is clear to him who *he* is and what *it* is and what must be accomplished to *do* it.

Some of history's great disasters have been caused by misunderstood directions. The heroic but futile charge of the Light Brigade at Balaclava in the Crimean War is a striking example. "Someone had blundered," Tennyson wrote. That was true, and the blunder consisted of the confusion over one word, which meant one thing to the person speaking but another to the person spoken to.

The brigade was ordered to charge "the guns." The man who gave the   5
order was on a hilltop and had in mind a small battery which was very plain
to him but was concealed from the soldiers in the valley by a slight rise.
The only guns *they* could see were the main Russian batteries at the far end
of the valley. Therefore they assumed that "the guns" referred to the
batteries *they* saw. The command seemed utter madness, but it was a
command and the leader of the brigade, after filing a protest, carried it out.

Fortunately, most misunderstandings don't have such disastrous con-   6
sequences. But the continual confusion about such general terms as *thing,
deal, it, fix,* and the like, certainly can be frustrating. Taken as a whole, the
exasperation, humiliation, disappointment and quarreling caused by misunderstandings probably produce a thousand times the misery and suffering
that the Light Brigade endured.

So the wise man, who wants peace of mind, and the efficient man, who   7
wants to get on with the the job, will take the trouble to use specific terms
instead of doubtful ones.

Besides clarity, a large vocabulary provides variety. And that is useful;   8
it is the basis for discrimination, since it provides a larger number of tools
to choose from. A hammer won't do when a file is called for. Furthermore
a large and varied vocabulary makes the speaker or writer more interesting.
It allows him to avoid the dullness of repetition and to provoke attention.
The interesting man is much more likely to be persuasive than the dull one.
Dull people bore us. We don't listen to them. We hear them, but with a
secret distaste. Instead of listening to them, we think only about getting
away from them. Therefore a varied vocabulary is very useful for winning
others to our point of view.

Thomas Wolfe reveled in words with more glory and gusto than per-   9
haps any man since Shakespeare or Rabelais. On seeing a shabby little
man lying dead on a subway bench, Wolfe was struck with the thought of
the dull and miserable existence such a man must have had because of the
sterility of his speech. "Poor, dismal, ugly, sterile, shabby little man,"
Wolfe wrote in his essay, "Death the Proud Brother," "with your little
scrabble of harsh oaths, and cries, and stale constricted words, your piti-
ful little designs and feeble purposes. . . . Joy, glory, and magnificence
were here for you upon this earth, but you scrabbled along the pavements
rattling a few stale words like gravel in your throat, and would have none
of them."

When Caliban, the half-human monster in Shakespeare's last play,   10
The Tempest, furiously denies that he owes any gratitude to his master,
the magician Prospero, he demands to know what Prospero has ever done
for him. The magician passes over all the many benefits he has confer-
red on the wretched creature, to stress only one: he has taught him to
speak.

I . . . took pains to make thee speak.
When thou didst not, savage,
Know thine own meaning, but wouldst gabble like
A thing most brutish, I endow'd thy purposes
With words that made them known.

The simple fact is that we all begin as Calibans—and do not know even   11
our own purposes until we endow them with words. We do not, indeed,
know ourselves. The pleasure you will feel as you develop your vocabulary
is not solely the pleasure that comes with increased power; it is also the
greater pleasure that comes with increased knowledge, especially of yourself. You will begin to appreciate expression as an art and to feel not only
the advantage of commanding words but the satisfaction. You will notice
that this or that phrase which someone utters in your hearing or which you
see in the newspapers is very good.

And you will be pleased that it *is* good, just as you are pleased to see   12
a forward pass completed, or a long putt holed, or a dance step gracefully
executed. For words are to the mind what such actions are to the body.

You will see that the rightness of a well-chosen word is not merely a   13
source of pleasure; it may provoke the most serious consequences or
avoid the gravest danger. When, for example, America and Russia confronted each other during the Cuban crisis in 1962, and the world hovered
for a few days on the brink of disaster, the use of the word *quarantine*
instead of *blockade* was extremely important. A *blockade* is an act of
war. No one knew quite what a *quarantine* meant, under the circumstances. But the very use of the word indicated that, while we were determined to protect ourselves, we wanted to avoid war. It was all a part
of giving Russia some possibility of saving face. We wanted her missiles
and planes out of Cuba and were prepared to fight even a nuclear war to
get them out. But we certainly preferred to have them removed peace-
fully. We did not want to back Russia into a corner from which there
could have been no escape except by violence.

Thus the use of *quarantine,* a purposefully vague word, was part of our   14
strategy. Furthermore, it had other advantages over *blockade*. It is commonly associated with a restriction imposed by all civilized nations on
people with certain communicable diseases to prevent them from spreading
their disease throughout the community. It is a public health measure
which, for all the inconvenience that it may impose on the afflicted individual, serves the public welfare. Thus, whereas a blockade would have
been an announcement that we were proceeding aggressively to further our
own interests, regardless of the rights of others, quarantine suggested a
concern for the general welfare. In addition, it suggested that what was
going on in Cuba was a dangerous disease which might spread.

So, as you develop a larger vocabulary you will be increasingly aware   15 of what is going on. You will enjoy what you read more. New pleasures will be opened to you.

You will understand more. Difficult books whose meaning has been   16
uncertain will become readable. The great poets who have enlarged our experience, the philosophers who have shaped our thoughts, the historians who have sought for patterns in the human story, the essayists whose observations have delighted men for centuries—all these and more will be available to you. And in sharing their thoughts your own world will expand. This particular benefit of an increased vocabulary is dramatically apparent in the strides that children make in comprehension as they progress in their use of language. Increased learning increases the child's word stock and the increased word stock makes learning easier. The National Conference on Research in English says "a child's ability to read, to speak, to write, and to think is inevitably conditioned by his vocabulary."

This goes for an adult too. Words cannot be separated from ideas. They   17
interact. The words we use are so associated with our experiences and what the experiences mean to us that they cannot be separated. The idea comes up from our subconscious clothed in words. It can't come any other way.

We don't know how words are stored in our minds, but there does seem   18
to be a sort of filing system. The filing system appears to be controlled by a perverse if not downright wacky filing clerk. Everyone has tried to remember a word and been unable to. Sometimes it is a common word, one that we *know* we know. Yet it won't come when we want it. It can be almost a form of torture trying to recall it, but no amount of fuming or fretting helps. Then suddenly, usually sometime later when it is no longer useful to us, it will come to mind readily. When we are searching for one of these words—often for a person's name—we will come up with other words or names that we know are close to but not exactly the one we want. This is curious in itself. For if we can't remember the word we want, how do we know the other word is very much like it? It's as though the filing clerk had seen the word we actually wanted or was even holding it in his hand but wouldn't give it to us.

Often we know that the unacceptable word has the same sound or   19
begins with the same letter as the word we can't remember. And when we finally recall the word we wanted, we find this is so. It seems as though our mental filing systems were arranged alphabetically and cross-indexed for similarity of internal sound. If we are well-read, we can call up a host of synonyms (words that mean the same thing) for many words, which suggests more crossfiling. Furthermore, words have subtle and complex associations. The speech and writing of some people who have sustained brain injuries or suffered strokes indicate a curious kind of damage. Some injured people seem to lose all proper names, some all adjectives, and many mix up capitals and small letters. This indicates that the interlocking

connections of words in our minds are more complex than we can imagine. The chances are that the most spectacular computer is a simple gadget compared to the human mind.

For our purposes, our ignorance of how this intricate filing system   20 works does not matter. What matters to a person trying to enlarge his vocabulary is the many connections among the words he knows. Once we master a word, it is connected in our mind with scores of other words in what appears to be an infinite number of relationships and shades of meaning. A new word does not drop as a single addition into our word stock. Each new word learned enlarges a whole complex of thinking and is itself enlarged in meaning and significance.

A vocabulary is a tool which one uses in formulating the important   21 questions of life, the questions which must be asked before they can be answered. To a large extent, vocabulary shapes all the decisions we make. Most decisions, of course, are shaped by our emotions, by circumstances, and by the forces which may hold us back or urge us on. These circumstances and forces are largely beyond our control. But our speech is a sort of searchlight that helps us to see these things more clearly and to see ourselves in relation to them. At least it helps us call things by their right names.

To a great extent our speech affects our judgments. We don't always—   22 sometimes we can't—distinguish between words and things. A slogan, for example, especially if it rhymes, or is alliterative (that is, has a number of words that begin with the same sound), or has a strong rhythm, will move us to action. It convinces us that the action is necessary. "Motorists wise Simonize" is far more effective in promoting sales than "Simonize, wise motorists" or "Wise motorists, Simonize" would have been. It's the witchery of rhythm, one of the most subtle and dangerous of unseen forces that move and muddle our minds. Seduced by "Fifty-four forty or fight," our great-grandfathers almost went to war in 1844. And there are historians who trace much of the misery of the modern world to the fascination that Grant's "Unconditional surrender" held for four generations of Americans.

Certainly anyone who develops the valuable habit of examining his   23 own prejudices will find that many of them are, at bottom, verbal. A situation automatically calls forth a single word. The word is bathed in emotion. So whenever the situation is repeated, it produces the same emotional response. There is no effort to be rational, to see what is actually going on. The word triggers the response. But the more words one has at his command, the greater the possibility that he may be his own master. It takes words to free us from words. Removing an emotionally charged word from a phrase and substituting a neutral synonym often gives us an insight that nothing else can.

Speech is the means of relating our separate experiences and emotions,   24
of combining them, reliving them and, as far as we can, understanding
them. If we did not have the words *justice, equal, radiation*—and a thousand others like them—our minds and our whole lives would be much
narrower. Each new word of this kind increases the scope of thought and
adds its bit to humanity. Once we have the word, of course, it seems
natural and it is an effort to imagine being without it.

Consider that remarkable British phrase which Lord Broughton in-   25
vented during the reign of George IV (1820–1830): "His Majesty's opposition." Political parties rose in seventeenth-century England during a
period of limited civil war and they behaved as if parliamentary victories
were military ones. When one party gained power it immediately pro-
ceeded to impeach the leaders of the other party, demanding their very
heads. But after a hundred and fifty years of peace and prosperity, men's
tempers began to cool. A sense of fairness compelled them to grant their
neighbor the right to a different opinion and even to grant that men who
opposed them might still be loyal and honorable. But the atmosphere Lord
Broughton described had to precede the medieval concept of Fortune's
wheel.

Once uttered, the phrase helped to further the idea it described. Men   26
saw that criticism of an administration can be as much a part of good
government as the government itself and that a man was not necessarily a
traitor because he disagreed with the party in power.

Many studies have established the fact that there is a high correlation   27
between vocabulary and intelligence and that the ability to increase one's
vocabulary throughout life is a sure reflection of intellectual progress.

It is hard to stretch a small vocabulary to make it do all the things that   28
intelligent people require of words. It's like trying to plan a series of menus
from the limited resources of a proverty-stricken war-torn country compared to planning such a series in a prosperous, stable country. Words are
one of our chief means of adjusting to all the situations of life. The better
control we have over words, the more successful our adjustment is likely
to be.

QUESTION ON CONTENT

1. Acording to Evans, how can a large vocabulary help you? Explain.

2. What, according to Evans, is the cause for misunderstandings between
people? How can the chances of misunderstanding be reduced?

3. What does Evans believe is the relationship between vocabulary and
intelligence?

4. Explain how a large vocabulary increases one's awareness of what is going on.

5. Many newspapers carry regular "vocabulary building" columns, and the *Reader's Digest* has had for years a section called "It Pays to Increase Your Word Power." What does the continuing popularity of these features suggest about the attitude of many Americans toward language?

6. Evans says, "The words we use are so associated with our experiences and what the experiences mean to us that they cannot be separated" (17). What associations do the following words have for you as a result of your own experiences?

    dinner
    money
    Thanksgiving
    fear
    success

Compare your associations with those of your classmates.

QUESTIONS ON RHETORIC

1. What is Evans's thesis, and where is it stated? (Glossary: *Thesis*)

2. Consider the central analogy of Evans's essay: words as a tool. How effective is the analogy? What other extended analogy does Evans use? (Glossary: *Analogy*)

3. What is the purpose of Evans's reference to Caliban, a character in Shakespeare's *The Tempest?*

4. What technique does Evans use to support his generalization that "the rightness of a well-chosen word is not merely a source of pleasure; it may provoke the most serious consequences or avoid the gravest danger" (13)? (Glossary: *Examples*)

5. How would you describe the author's tone? Would you say that the author's tone is formal, conversational, preachy, chatty, or informal? (Glossary: *Tone*)

VOCABULARY

futile (4)	inevitably (16)	intricate (20)
exasperation (6)	subconscious (17)	muddle (22)
communicable (14)	perverse (18)	correlation (27)

WRITING TOPICS

1. Evans makes the point that words must be defined for communication to be effective. As a writer you will often need to define, and the more

precise your definitions, the more clearly you will communicate. One way of defining a term is to place it in a class of similar items and then to show how it is different from the other items in that class. For example,

Word	Class	Characteristics
a *watch*	is a *mechanical device*	*for telling time and is usually carried or worn*
semantics	is an *area of linguistics*	*concerned with the study of the meaning of words*

Certainly such definitions are not complete, and one could write an entire paragraph, essay, or book to define these terms more fully. This process, however, is useful for getting started in both thinking and writing.

Place each of the following terms in a class, and then write a statement differentiating each term:

paper clip
pamphlet
anxiety
freedom

Now write a brief essay in which you fully define one of the above terms, or one of your own choosing.

2. Evans argues that an improvershed vocabulary certainly limits one's perceptions of and ability to deal with the world. Using examples from your own personal experiences, discuss how your vocabulary has affected you—has it ever made you feel restricted or at a disadvantage, or has it ever given you the feeling that you were in charge, in complete control of the situation? You might wish to consider your work in a particular job or area of academic study.

3. Most of us while we were growing up heard from our parents and teachers that it was important to have a large vocabulary. Is it difficult to acquire a large vocabulary? Why hasn't "vocabulary-building" become a regular part of the public school curriculum, or if it has, what have been the results? What exactly is involved in increasing your vocabulary— memorizing, practice, writing, reading, speaking, all of these?

CONTEMPORARY AMERICAN GRAFFITI

Donald V. Mehus

T-shirts and bumper stickers are everywhere, and they remind us that Americans love to express their opinions publicly. When Donald Mehus wrote this essay in the late 1970s, a different kind of public writing was coming into its own. According to Mehus, American graffiti was flowering into "witty and provocative comments on some of the most vital concerns of our time—war and peace, government and politics, the individual and society."

New York City has long been waging a seemingly losing battle against air pollution and trash-littered streets. In an appeal for public cooperation to help alleviate these conditions, the municipal sanitation department recently put up posters around the city asking: "Did you make New York dirty today?" On one of the posters a long-suffering resident scribbled a plaintive retort: "New York makes *me* dirty *every* day!"

This heartfelt remark is a characteristic example of the American version of graffiti, the ancient art of anonymous, unauthorized wall writing. Graffiti dates back at least as far as the Egypt of the Pharaohs; scholars have long busied themselves collecting and deciphering specimens from the ancient walls of Egypt, Athens, and Pompeii.

During the past few years the United States has witnessed its own flowering of this special form of spontaneous, personal expression. The best examples of contempory American graffiti, whether lightly humorous or bitterly vitriolic, are often witty and provocative comments on some of the most vital concerns of our time—war and peace, government and politics, the individual and society.

Until recently comparatively little serious attention has been given to American graffiti. Lately, however, this often vividly imaginative writing has been accorded a measure of respectful recognition. Such publications as the *New York Times* and *Newsweek* have devoted substantial articles to the subject. Several authors readily admit that they took titles for some of their works directly from graffiti. The playwright Edward Albee first saw the conundrum "Who's Afraid of Virginia Woolf?" on a restroom wall in a bar of New York's Greenwich Village. Robert Saffron found the title for

37

his book "Is the U.S. Ready for Self-Government?" scribbled beneath an assortment of protest slogans on a subway wall.

A number of short book collections, including *Graffiti* and *Great Wall Writings,* both compiled by Robert Reisner, have been published. During recent years, as Reisner points out, the best American graffiti has gradually become more sophisticated, more intellectual and witty. Partly this is because simple obscenities scrawled on walls—a large share of graffiti everywhere, both past and present—have in this permissive age lost much of their shock value. At the same time people have become more alert to the problems, complexities, and absurdities of the age. Reflecting the mood of the troublous times, graffiti has also become more cynical.

According to some observers, American graffiti came of age during the late 1960's, when the widespread protest movement against United States involvement in the Vietnam War and against a range of national ills reached its peak of intensity. Much of the best wall writings suddenly became more pointed and articulate, more socially conscious, much more vitriolic. One bitter comment reported first seen at Harvard University read: "War is good business—invest your sons." Another proclaimed: "Bombing can end the war—bomb the Pentagon." A third cynic caustically urged: "Ban the H-bomb; save the world for conventional warfare."

While much of the best graffiti opposes rather than favors something, a protest slogan may occasionally be amended so as to reverse its original intention. Thus someone once appended to the traditional anti-American sign long familiar throughout the world, "Yankee Go Home," this personal request: "—and take me with you!"

Where is the best graffiti found? Who creates it, and why? Reisner reports that the best graffiti is often seen in large urban areas, particularly at universities and in the restrooms of coffeehouses and smart bars. Graffiti seems to be written predominantly by men; lately, however, women have become increasingly productive. The liveliest writing is often by students, hippies, and young business people. Graffiti is produced for a variety of reasons: to express an opinion, to voice an insult, to share a joke, to assert one's own individuality, to protest social and political conditions.

Some of the wittiest and most learned graffiti, according to Reisner, is on religious subjects. One pithy exchange by several persons ranged through various abstruse areas: contemporary theological debate, the atheistical views of the 19th century German philosopher Nietzsche, the position of Odin as the supreme deity of Scandinavian mythology.

The exchange began with the now-famous two lines: "God is dead. Nietzsche." Immediately following, in another hand, appeared: "Nietzsche is dead. God." A third writer dismissed both assertions: "They are both dead. Odin." Elsewhere an anonymous philosopher-theologian

made a brilliant if somewhat heretical attempt to resolve the dilemma:
"God is not dead. He just doesn't want to get involved."

The public seems to take particular relish in striking back at the inflated   11
claims of omnipresent advertising. Some businessmen, however, actually
welcome anonymous additions to their posters; they hope that graffiti may
suggest—as some has—ideas for future ads. Graffiti writers are quick to
deflate rhetorical questions even on altruistic posters for worthy causes.
When a placard asked: "If the President finds time to help the mentally
retarded, what are you doing that's so important?" some disgruntled citizen wrote underneath: "Working to get them out of Washington."

Predictably, America's racial troubles and the Federal laws against dis-   12
crimination in housing, employment, and education have prompted widespread comment by wall writers. Much of this writing is regrettably virulent
and bitter, the targets fairly clear. But occasionally one is not quite sure how
to interpret certain graffiti, such as this equivocally misanthropic remark
seen in a bar: "We hate all people, regardless of race, creed, or color."

By far the most popular subject of graffiti has doubtless always been   13
the relation between the sexes. Much of this kind of wall writing is of
course merely meaningless obscenities. But some is marked by genuine
wit. One such example enjoins the reader to "Love thy neighbor, but don't
get caught." Another offers a suggestion for alleviating a water shortage:
"Save water; bathe with friends." A third smacks of what has been termed
"pseudograffiti"—a pithy statement that while wittily pregnant, lacks the
apparent spontaneity of true graffiti: "Before Freud, sex was a pleasure;
now it is a necessity."

As amusing and perceptive as graffiti may sometimes be, it has by no   14
means won universal approval. Often graffiti merely defaces, like much of
the huge, psychedelic lettering covering the sides of many New York
subway cars. We have no idea how many people simply look in dismay at
such graffiti and refrain from comment. But not infrequently a dissenter
registers his objection. Wrote one: "I think people who write on walls are
immature and troubled and need psychological help."

Pleas by authorities do not seem to help much to stem the flood. When   15
a sign appeared in a bar requesting: "Do not write on walls," a patron re-
torted: "You want we should type maybe?" But perhaps the ultimate futility
of trying to halt the spread of graffiti was reflected in this injunction written
on a freshly-painted wall: "Stop vandalism—don't scribble on walls."

QUESTIONS ON CONTENT

1. How does Mehus define graffiti?

2. Mehus wrote his essay in the late 1970s, when "graffiti was flower-

ing.'' What does he mean by this? What does the timing of this flowering tell us about the nature of graffiti, its purpose, the emotions that inspire it?

3. According to Mehus, graffiti is lately being taken more seriously in the United States than it had been. How does he know?

4. What changes does Mehus note in the tone of American graffiti? What does the "best graffiti do," according to Mehus?

5. Mehus names four major groups responsible for graffiti. Who are they? What are their favorite topics? Where is the best graffiti found? What motivates people to write graffiti, according to Mehus? Can you think of other reasons?

6. How does Mehus differentiate between graffiti and pseudograffiti? Do you agree with his distinction? Why or why not?

QUESTIONS ON RHETORIC

1. Mehus begins his essay with an example of contemporary American graffiti. How does this example and the other examples used in the essay help Mehus develop his argument? Do you think he is opposed, sympathetic, or objective in his handling of this subject? Explain.

2. Look at the first sentence in each of Mehus's paragraphs. How does each one help to unify the paragraph? (Glossary: *Topic Sentence*)

3. Choosing several examples, show how Mehus moves from the general to the specific to make his argument.

4. Mehus uses words such as *vitriolic, cynical, misanthropic,* and *caustic* to characterize graffiti and the people who create it. What do these words tell you about the type of attitude Mehus perceives as prevailing toward the people who write graffiti? Review the essay. Has Mehus left out any emotions and situations that you think inspire graffiti? Describe them.

VOCABULARY

alleviate (1)	caustically (6)	virulent (12)
plaintive (1)	pithy (9)	misanthropic (12)
vitriolic (3)	abstruse (9)	pregnant (13)
conundrum (4)	altruistic (11)	injunction (15)
cynical (5)		

WRITING TOPICS

1. Check out the graffiti on your college campus. What do the scribbled epithets tell you about the concerns and issues of the other students? Have you ever written any graffiti? If so, what issues motivated you? If not, what do you think of people who use graffiti as a means of communicating their ideas? Write an essay presenting your views on campus graffiti.

2. These days many people want their neighbors to know what they are thinking. However, instead of scribling on walls, they have made lucrative industries out of the manufacturing of bumper stickers and T-shirts that describe a full range of attitudes and complaints. Looking at Mehus's three kinds of graffiti—"true" graffiti, "meaningless obscenities," and pseudo-graffiti—pseudograffiti being that which "lacks the apparent spontaneity of true graffiti"—do you agree with his distinctions and in which category would you place bumper stickers and T-shirts? Give some examples of what you feel are pseudograffiti and real graffiti and, in an essay, discuss the similarities and differences between the two.

THE SOUNDS
OF SILENCE

Edward T. Hall and Mildred Reed Hall

*Until recently, few Americans were aware of the significance
of body language. In this article, Edward and Mildred Hall
discuss the crucial effects that "your posture, gestures, facial
expressions, costume, the way you walk, even your treatment
of time and space and material things" may have. The Halls
use numerous examples as they contrast the body language of
Americans with that of other cultures both to explain what
body language is and to emphasize the importance of
respecting the power and diversity of "the sounds of
silence."*

Bob leaves his apartment at 8:15 A.M. and stops at the corner drugstore   1
for breakfast. Before he can speak, the counterman says, "The usual?"
Bob nods yes. While he savors his Danish, a fat man pushes onto the
adjoining stool and overflows into his space. Bob scowls and the man pulls
himself in as much as he can. Bob has sent two messages without speaking
a syllable.

Henry has an appointment to meet Arthur at 11 o'clock; he arrives at   2
11:30. Their conversation is friendly, but Arthur retains a lingering hostility. Henry has unconsciously communicated that he doesn't think the
appointment is very important or that Arthur is a person who needs to be
treated with respect.

George is talking to Charley's wife at a party. Their conversation is   3
entirely trivial, yet Charley glares at them suspiciously. Their physical
proximity and the movements of their eyes reveal that they are powerfully
attracted to each other.

José Ybarra and Sir Edmund Jones are at the same party and it is   4
important for them to establish a cordial relationship for business reasons.
Each is trying to be warm and friendly, yet they will part with mutual
distrust and their business transaction will probably fall through. José, in
Latin fashion, moved closer and closer to Sir Edmund as they spoke, and
this movement was miscommunicated as pushiness to Sir Edmund, who

kept backing away from this intimacy, and this was miscommunicated to José as coldness. The silent languages of Latin and English cultures are more difficult to learn than their spoken languages.

In each of these cases, we see the subtle power of nonverbal communication. The only language used throughout most of the history of humanity (in evolutionary terms, vocal communication is relatively recent), it is the first form of communication you learn. You use this preverbal language, consciously and unconsciously, every day to tell other people how you feel about yourself and them. This language includes your posture, gestures, facial expressions, costume, the way you walk, even your treatment of time and space and material things. All people communicate on several different levels at the same time but are usually aware of only the verbal dialog and don't realize that they respond to nonverbal messages. But when a person says one thing and really believes something else, the discrepancy between the two can usually be sensed. Nonverbal-communication systems are much less subject to the conscious deception that often occurs in verbal systems. When we find ourselves thinking, ''I don't know what it is about him, but he doesn't seem sincere,'' it's usually this lack of congruity between a person's words and his behavior that makes us anxious and uncomfortable.

Few of us realize how much we all depend on body movement in our conversation or are aware of the hidden rules that govern listening behavior. But we know instantly whether or not the person we're talking to is ''tuned in'' and we're very sensitive to any breach in listening etiquette. In white middle-class American culture, when someone wants to show he is listening to someone else, he looks either at the other person's face or, specifically, at his eyes, shifting his gaze from one eye to the other.

If you observe a person conversing, you'll notice that he indicates he's listening by nodding his head. He also makes little ''Hmm'' noises. If he agrees with what's being said, he may give a vigorous nod. To show pleasure or affirmation, he smiles; if he has some reservations, he looks skeptical by raising an eyebrow or pulling down the corners of his mouth. If a participant wants to terminate the conversation, he may start shifting his body position, stretching his legs, crossing or uncrossing them, bobbing his foot or diverting his gaze from the speaker. The more he fidgets, the more the speaker becomes aware that he has lost his audience. As a last measure, the listener may look at his watch to indicate the imminent end of the conversation.

Talking and listening are so intricately intertwined that a person cannot do one without the other. Even when one is alone and talking to oneself, there is part of the brain that speaks while another part listens. In all conversations, the listener is positively or negatively reinforcing the speaker all the time. He may even guide the conversation without knowing it, by laughing or frowning or dismissing the argument with a wave of his hand.

The language of the eyes—another age-old way of exchanging   9
feelings—is both subtle and complex. Not only do men and women use their eyes differently but there are class, generation, regional, ethnic and national cultural differences. Americans often complain about the way foreigners stare at people or hold a glance too long. Most Americans look away from someone who is using his eyes in an unfamiliar way because it makes them self-conscious. If a man looks at another man's wife in a certain way, he's asking for trouble, as indicated earlier. But he might not be ill mannered or seeking to challenge the husband. He might be a European in this country who hasn't learned our visual mores. Many American women visiting France or Italy are acutely embarrassed because, for the first time in their lives, men really look at them—their eyes, hair, nose, lips, breasts, hips, legs, thighs, knees, ankles, feet, clothes, hairdo, even their walk. These same women, once they have become used to being looked at, often return to the United States and are overcome with the feeling that "No one ever really looks at me anymore."

Analyzing the mass of data on the eyes, it is possible to sort out at least   10
three ways in which the eyes are used to communicate: dominance vs. submission, involvement vs. detachment and positive vs. negative attitude. In addition, there are three levels of consciousness and control, which can be categorized as follows: (1) conscious use of the eyes to communicate, such as the flirting blink and the intimate nose-wrinkling squint; (2) the very extensive category of unconscious but learned behavior governing where the eyes are directed and when (this unwritten set of rules dictates how and under what circumstances the sexes, as well as people of all status categories, look at each other); and (3) the response of the eye itself, which is completely outside both awareness and control—changes in the cast (the sparkle) of the eye and the pupillary reflex.

The eye is unlike any other organ of the body, for it is an extension of   11
the brain. The unconscious pupillary reflex and the cast of the eye have been known by people of Middle Eastern origin for years—although most are unaware of their knowledge. Depending on the context, Arabs and others look either directly at the eyes or deeply *into* the eyes of their interlocutor. We became aware of this in the Middle East several years ago while looking at jewelry. The merchant suddenly started to push a particular bracelet at a customer and said, "You buy this one." What interested us was that the bracelet was not the one that had been consciously selected by the purchaser. But the merchant, watching the pupils of the eyes, knew what the purchaser really wanted to buy. Whether he specifically knew *how* he knew is debatable.

A psychologist at the University of Chicago, Eckhard Hess, was the   12 first to conduct systematic studies of the pupillary reflex. His wife re- marked one evening, while watching him reading in bed, that he must be very interested in the text because his pupils were dilated. Following up on this, Hess slipped some pictures of nudes into a stack of photographs that he gave to his male assistant. Not looking at the photographs but watching his assistant's pupils, Hess was able to tell precisely when the assistant came to the nudes. In further experiments, Hess retouched the eyes in a photograph of a woman. In one print, he made the pupils small, in another, large; nothing else was changed. Subjects who were given the photographs found the woman with the dilated pupils much more attractive. Any man who has had the experience of seeing a woman look at him as her pupils widen with reflex speed knows that she's flashing him a message.

13 The eye-sparkle phenomenon frequently turns up in our interviews of couples in love. It's apparently one of the first reliable clues in the other person that love is genuine. To date, there is no scientific data to explain eye sparkle; no investigation of the pupil, the cornea or even the white sclera of the eye shows how the sparkle originates. Yet we all know it when we see it.

14 One common situation for most people involves the use of the eyes in the street and in public. Although eye behavior follows a definite set of rules, the rules vary according to the place, the needs and feelings of the people, and their ethnic background. For urban whites, once they're within definite recognition distance (16–32 feet for people with average eyesight), there is mutual avoidance of eye contact—unless they want something specific: a pickup, a handout or information of some kind. In the West and in small towns generally, however, people are much more likely to look at and greet one another, even if they're strangers.

15 It's permissible to look at people if they're beyond recognition dis- tance, but once inside this sacred zone, you can only steal a glance at strangers. You *must* greet friends, however; to fail to do so is insulting. Yet, to stare too fixedly even at them is considered rude and hostile. Of course, all of these rules are variable.

16 A great many blacks, for example, greet each other in public even if they don't know each other. To blacks, most eye behavior of whites has the effect of giving the impression that they aren't there, but this is due to white avoidance of eye contact with *anyone* in the street.

17 Another very basic difference between people of different ethnic back- grounds is their sense of territoriality and how they handle space. This is the silent communication, or miscommunication, that caused friction be- tween Mr. Ybarra and Sir Edmund Jones in our earlier example. We know from research that everyone has around himself an invisible bubble of space that contracts and expands depending on several factors: his emo- tional state, the activity he's performing at the time and his cultural back-

ground. This bubble is a kind of mobile territory that he will defend against intrusion. If he is accustomed to close personal distance between himself and others, his bubble will be smaller than that of someone who's accustomed to greater personal distance. People of North European heritage—English, Scandinavian, Swiss and German—tend to avoid contact. Those whose heritage is Italian, French, Spanish, Russian, Latin American or Middle Eastern like close personal contact.

People are very sensitive to any intrusion into their spatial bubble. If someone stands too close to you, your first instinct is to back up. If that's not possible, you lean away and pull yourself in, tensing your muscles. If the intruder doesn't respond to these body signals, you may then try to protect yourself, using a briefcase, umbrella or raincoat. Women—especially when traveling alone—often plant their pocketbook in such a way that no one can get very close to them. As a last resort, you may move to another spot and position yourself behind a desk or a chair that provides screening. Everyone tries to adjust the space around himself in a way that's comfortable for him; most often, he does this unconsciously. 18

Emotions also have a direct effect on the size of a person's territory. When you're angry or under stress, your bubble expands and you require more space. New York psychiatrist Augustus Kinzel found a difference in what he calls Body-Buffer Zones between violent and nonviolent prison inmates. Dr. Kinzel conducted experiments in which each prisoner was placed in the center of a small room and then Dr. Kinzel slowly walked toward him. Nonviolent prisoners allowed him to come quite close, while prisoners with a history of violent behavior couldn't tolerate his proximity and reacted with some vehemence. 19

Apparently people under stress experience other people as looming larger and closer than they actually are. Studies of schizophrenic patients have indicated that they sometimes have a distorted perception of space, and several psychiatrists have reported patients who experience their body boundaries as filling up an entire room. For these patients, anyone who comes into the room is actually inside their body, and such an intrusion may trigger a violent outburst. 20

Unfortunately, there is little detailed information about normal people who live in highly congested urban areas. We do know, of course, that the noise, pollution, dirt, crowding and confusion of our cities induce feelings of stress in most of us, and stress leads to a need for greater space. The man who's packed into a subway, jostled in the street, crowded into an elevator and forced to work all day in a bull pen or in a small office without auditory or visual privacy is going to be very stressed at the end of his day. He needs places that provide relief from constant overstimulation of his nervous system. Stress from overcrowding is cumulative and people can tolerate more crowding early in the day than later; note the increased bad temper 21 during the evening rush hour as compared with the morning melee. Certainly one factor in people's desire to commute by car is the need for privacy and relief from crowding (except, often, from other cars); it may be the only time of the day when nobody can intrude.

In crowded public places, we tense our muscles and hold ourselves stiff, and thereby communicate to others our desire not to intrude on their space and, above all, not to touch them. We also avoid eye contact, and the total effect is that of someone who has "tuned out." Walking along the street, our bubble expands slightly as we move in a stream of strangers, taking care not to bump into them. In the office, at meetings, in restaurants, our bubble keeps changing as it adjusts to the activity at hand.

Most white middle-class Americans use four main distances in their business and social relations: intimate, personal, social and public. Each of these distances has a near and a far phase and is accompanied by changes in the volume of the voice. Intimate distance varies from direct physical contact with another person to a distance of six to eighteen inches and is used for our most private activities—caressing another person or making love. At this distance, you are overwhelmed by sensory inputs from the other person—heat from the body, tactile stimulation from the skin, the fragrance of perfume, even the sound of breathing—all of which literally envelop you. Even at the far phase, you're still within easy touching distance. In general, the use of intimate distance in public between adults is frowned on. It's also much too close for strangers, except under conditions of extreme crowding.

In the second zone—personal distance—the close phase is one and a half to two and a half feet; it's at this distance that wives usually stand from their husbands in public. If another woman moves into this zone, the wife will most likely be disturbed. The far phase—two and a half to four feet—is the distance used to "keep someone at arm's length" and is the most common spacing used by people in conversation.

The third zone—social distance—is employed during business transactions or exchanges with a clerk or repairman. People who work together tend to use close social distance—four to seven feet. This is also the distance for conversations at social gatherings. To stand at this distance from someone who is seated has a dominating effect (e.g., teacher to pupil, boss to secretary). The far phase of the third zone—seven to twelve feet—is where people stand when someone says, "Stand back so I can look at you." This distance lends a formal tone to business or social discourse. In an executive office, the desk serves to keep people at this distance.

The fourth zone—public distance—is used by teachers in classrooms or speakers at public gatherings. At its farthest phase—25 feet and beyond—it is used for important public figures. Violations of this distance can lead to serious complications. During his 1970 U.S. visit, the president of

France, Georges Pompidou, was harassed by pickets in Chicago, who were permitted to get within touching distance. Since pickets in France are kept behind barricades a block or more away, the president was outraged by this insult to his person, and President Nixon was obliged to communicate his concern as well as offer his personal apologies.

It is interesting to note how American pitchmen and panhandlers exploit the unwritten, unspoken conventions of eye and distance. Both take advantage of the fact that once explicit eye contact is established, it is rude to look away, because to do so means to brusquely dismiss the other person and his needs. Once having caught the eye of his mark, the panhandler then locks on, not letting go until he moves through the public zone, the social zone, the personal zone and, finally, into the intimate sphere, where people are most vulnerable.

Touch also is an important part of the constant stream of communication that takes place between people. A light touch, a firm touch, a blow, a caress are all communications. In an effort to break down barriers among people, there's been a recent upsurge in group-encounter activities, in which strangers are encouraged to touch one another. In special situations such as these, the rules for not touching are broken with group approval and people gradually lose some of their inhibitions.

Although most people don't realize it, space is perceived and distances are set not by vision alone but with all the senses. Auditory space is perceived with the ears, thermal space with the skin, kinesthetic space with the muscles of the body and olfactory space with the nose. And, once again, it's one's culture that determines how his senses are programmed— which sensory information ranks highest and lowest. The important thing to remember is that culture is very persistent. In this country, we've noted the existence of culture patterns that determine distance between people in the third and fourth generations of some families, despite their prolonged contact with people of very different cultural heritages.

Whenever there is great cultural distance between two people, there are bound to be problems arising from differences in behavior and expectations. An example is the American couple who consulted a psychiatrist about their marital problems. The husband was from New England and had been brought up by reserved parents who taught him to control his emotions and to respect the need for privacy. His wife was from an Italian family and had been brought up in close contact with all the members of her large family, who were extremely warm, volatile and demonstrative.

When the husband came home after a hard day at the office, dragging his feet and longing for peace and quiet, his wife would rush to him and smother him. Clasping his hands, rubbing his brow, crooning over his weary head, she never left him alone. But when the wife was upset or anxious about the day, the husband's response was to withdraw completely and leave her alone. No comforting, no affectionate embrace, no attention—just solitude. The woman became convinced her husband didn't love her and, in desperation, she consulted a psychiatrist. Their problem wasn't basically psychological but cultural.

Why has man developed all these different ways of communicating messages without words? One reason is that people don't like to spell out certain kinds of messages. We prefer to find other ways of showing our feelings. This is especially true in relationships as sensitive as courtship. Men don't like to be rejected and most women don't want to turn a man down bluntly. Instead, we work out subtle ways of encouraging or discouraging each other that save face and avoid confrontations. 32

How a person handles space in dating others is an obvious and very sensitive indicator of how he or she feels about the other person. On a first date, if a woman sits or stands so close to a man that he is acutely conscious of her physical presence—inside the intimate-distance zone—the man usually construes it to mean that she is encouraging him. However, before the man starts moving in on the woman, he should be sure what message she's really sending; otherwise, he risks bruising his ego. What is close to someone of North European background may be neutral or distant to someone of Italian heritage. Also, women sometimes use space as a way of misleading a man and there are few things that put men off more than women who communicate contradictory messages—such as women who cuddle up and then act insulted when a man takes the next step. 33

How does a woman communicate interest in a man? In addition to such familiar gambits as smiling at him, she may glance shyly at him, blush and then look away. Or she may give him a real come-on look and move in very close when he approaches. She may touch his arm and ask for a light. As she leans forward to light her cigarette, she may brush him lightly, enveloping him in her perfume. She'll probably continue to smile at him and she may use what ethologists call preening gestures—touching the back of her hair, thrusting her breasts forward, tilting her hips as she stands or crossing her legs if she's seated, perhaps even exposing one thigh or putting a hand on her thigh and stroking it. She may also strike her wrists as she converses or show the palm of her hand as a way of gaining his attention. Her skin may be unusually flushed or quite pale, her eyes brighter, the pupils larger. 34

If a man sees a woman whom he wants to attract, he tries to present himself by his posture and stance as someone who is self-assured. He moves briskly and confidently. When he catches the eye of the woman, he may hold her glance a little longer than normal. If he gets an encouraging smile, he'll move in close and engage her in small talk. As they converse, his glance shifts over her face and body. He, too, may make preening gestures—straightening his tie, smoothing his hair or shooting his cuffs. 35

How do people learn body language? The same way they learn spoken   36
language—by observing and imitating people around them as they're growing up. Little girls imitate their mothers or an older female. Little boys
imitate their fathers or a respected uncle or a character on television. In this
way, they learn the gender signals appropriate for their sex. Regional, class
and ethnic patterns of body behavior are also learned in childhood and
persist throughout life.

Such patterns of masculine and feminine body behavior vary widely   37
from one culture to another. In America, for example, women stand with
their thighs together. Many walk with their pelvis tipped slightly forward
and their upper arms close to their body. When they sit, they cross their
legs at the knee or, if they are well past middle age, they may cross their
ankles. American men hold their arms away from their body, often swing-
ing them as they walk. They stand with their legs apart (an extreme example is the cowboy, with legs apart and thumbs tucked into his belt).
When they sit, they put their feet on the floor with legs apart and, in some
parts of the country, they cross their legs by putting one ankle on the other
knee.

Leg behavior indicates sex, status and personality. It also indicates   38
whether or not one is at ease or is showing respect or disrespect for the
other person. Young Latin-American males avoid crossing their legs. In
their world of *machismo,* the preferred position for young males when with
one another (if there is no older dominant male present to whom they must
show respect) is to sit on the base of their spine with their leg muscles
relaxed and their feet wide apart. Their respect position is our military
equivalent; spine straight, heels and ankles together—almost identical to
that displayed by properly brought up young women in New England in the
early part of this century.

American women who sit with their legs spread apart in the presence   39
of males are *not* normally signaling a come-on—they are simply (and often
unconsciously) sitting like men. Middle-class women in the presence of
other women to whom they are very close may on occasion throw themselves down on a soft chair or sofa and let themselves go. This is a signal
that nothing serious will be taken up. Males, on the other hand, lean back
and prop their legs up on the nearest object.

The way we walk, similarly, indicates status, respect, mood and eth-   40
nic or cultural affiliation. The many variants of the female walk are too
well known to go into here, except to say that a man would have to be
blind not to be turned on by the way some women walk—a fact that made
Mae West rich before scientists ever studied these matters. To white
Americans, some French middle-class males walk in a way that is both
humorous and suspect. There is a bounce and looseness to the French
walk, as though the parts of the body were somehow unrelated. Jacques

Tati, the French movie actor, walks this way; so does the great mime, Marcel Marceau.

Blacks and whites in America—with the exception of middle- and upper-middle-class professionals of both groups—move and walk very differently from each other. To the blacks, whites often seem incredibly stiff, almost mechanical in their movements. Black males, on the other hand, have a looseness and coordination that frequently makes whites a little uneasy; it's too different, too integrated, too alive, too male. Norman Mailer has said that squares walk from the shoulders, like bears, but blacks and hippies walk from the hips, like cats. 41

All over the world, people walk not only in their own characteristic way but have walks that communicate the nature of their involvement with whatever it is they're doing. The purposeful walk of North Europeans is an important component of proper behavior on the job. Any male who has been in the military knows how essential it is to walk properly (which makes for a continuing source of tension between blacks and whites in the Service). The quick shuffle of servants in the Far East in the old days was a show of respect. On the island of Truk, when we last visited, the inhabitants even had a name for the respectful walk that one used when in the presence of a chief or when walking past a chief's house. The term was *sufan*, which meant to be humble and respectful. 42

The notion that people communicate volumes by their gestures, facial expressions, posture and walk is not new; actors, dancers, writers and psychiatrists have long been aware of it. Only in recent years, however, have scientists begun to make systematic observations of body motions. Ray L. Birdwhistell of the University of Pennsylvania is one of the pioneers in body-motion research and coined the term *kinesics* to describe this field. He developed an elaborate notation system to record both facial and body movements, using an approach similar to that of the linguist, who studies the basic elements of speech. Birdwhistell and other kinesicists such as Albert Sheflen, Adam Kendon and William Condon take movies of people interacting. They run the film over and over again, often at reduced speed for frame-by-frame analysis, so that they can observe even the slightest body movements not perceptible at normal interaction speeds. These movements are then recorded in notebooks for later analysis. 43

To appreciate the importance of nonverbal-communication systems, consider the unskilled inner-city black looking for a job. His handling of time and space alone is sufficiently different from the white middle-class pattern to create great misunderstandings on both sides. The black is told to appear for a job interview at a certain time. He arrives late. The white interviewer concludes from his tardy arrival that the black is irresponsible and not really interested in the job. What the interviewer doesn't know is that the black time system (often referred to by blacks as C. P. T.—colored 44 people's time) isn't the same as that of whites. In the words of a black student who had been told to make an appointment to see his professor: "Man, you *must* be putting me on. I never had an appointment in my life."

The black job applicant, having arrived late for his interview, may 45
further antagonize the white interviewer by his posture and his eye behavior. Perhaps he slouches and avoids looking at the interviewer; to him, this is playing it cool. To the interviewer, however, he may well look shifty and sound uninterested. The interviewer has failed to notice the actual signs of interest and eagerness in the black's behavior, such as the subtle shift in the quality of the voice—a gentle and tentative excitement—an almost imperceptible change in the cast of the eyes and a relaxing of the jaw muscles.

Moreover, correct reading of black-white behavior is continually com- 46
plicated by the fact that both groups are comprised of individuals—some of whom try to accommodate and some of whom make it a point of pride *not* to accommodate. At present, this means that many Americans, when thrown into contact with one another, are in the precarious position of not knowing which pattern applies. Once identified and analyzed, nonverbal-communication systems can be taught, like a foreign language. Without this training, we respond to nonverbal communications in terms of our own culture; we read everyone's behavior as if it were our own, and thus we often misunderstand it.

Several years ago in New York City, there was a program for sending 47
children from predominantly black and Puerto Rican low-income neighborhoods to summer school in a white upper-class neighborhood on the East Side. One morning, a group of young black and Puerto Rican boys raced down the street, shouting and screaming and overturning garbage cans on their way to school. A doorman from an apartment building nearby chased them and cornered one of them inside a building. The boy drew a knife and attacked the doorman. This tragedy would not have occurred if the doorman had been familiar with the behavior of boys from low-income neighborhoods, where such antics are routine and socially acceptable and where pursuit would be expected to invite a violent response.

The language of behavior is extremely complex. Most of us are lucky 48
to have under control one subcultural system—the one that reflects our sex, class, generation and geographic region within the United States. Because of its complexity, efforts to isolate bits of nonverbal communication and generalize from them are in vain; you don't become an instant expert on people's behavior by watching them at cocktail parties. Body language isn't something that's independent of the person, something that can be donned and doffed like a suit of clothes.

Our research and that of our colleagues has shown that, far from being 49
a superficial form of communication that can be consciously manipulated,

nonverbal-communication systems are interwoven into the fabric of the personality and, as sociologist Erving Goffman has demonstrated, into society itself. They are the warp and woof of daily interactions with others and they influence how one expresses oneself, how one experiences oneself as a man or a woman.

Nonverbal communications signal to members of your own group what kind of person you are, how you feel about others, how you'll fit into and work in a group, whether you're assured or anxious, the degree to which you feel comfortable with the standards of your own culture, as well as deeply significant feelings about the self, including the state of your own psyche. For most of us, it's difficult to accept the reality of another's behavioral system. And, of course, none of us will ever become fully knowledgeable of the importance of every nonverbal signal. But as long as each of us realizes the power of these signals, this society's diversity can be a source of great strength rather than a further—and subtly powerful—source of divison.

50

QUESTIONS ON CONTENT

1. Describe the phenomenon the Halls call "pupillary reflex," and discuss any examples of it that you have noticed.

2. To what extent, according to the Halls, does ethnic background produce differences in nonverbal-communication behavior?

3. What do the Halls mean by the "invisible bubble of space" surrounding each of us? What factors may affect its size at any given time?

4. What are the four distances used by most white middle-class Americans in social and business situations? Describe the varying sensory inputs at each distance (auditory, olfactory, tactile, visual, and so forth).

5. What are "preening gestures"? Give some examples.

6. To illustrate many of the points that the Halls make in their essay, play a game, such as this one, that uses nonverbal communication. Divide players into small groups to act out situations involving body language—a tough cop ticketing a motorist (of either sex); one person trying to give directions to another but not succeeding; a man trying to be friendly with a woman (or vice versa) who really does not wish to be bothered but who also does not wish to be impolite. All the players should discuss each performance not on the basis of the dialogue but on the basis of how well the performers illustrate an awareness of body language. What conclusions can you draw about the relationship between body language and verbal language?

QUESTIONS ON RHETORIC

1. What is the function of the first four paragraphs. (Glossary: *Beginnings*)

2. Would you describe the diction of this essay as formal or informal? Support your conclusions with specific examples from the text. (Glossary: *Diction*)

3. The Halls use comparison and contrast as well as classification in this essay. Identify several examples of each rhetorical technique. (Glossary: *Comparison and Contrast, Division and Classification*)

4. The Halls start several of their paragraphs with questions. What do they achieve by doing so? (Glossary: *Rhetorical Questions*)

VOCABULARY

savors (1)	dilated (12)	inhibitions (28)
proximity (3)	vehemence (19)	volatile (30)
cordial (4)	melee (21)	precarious (46)
congruity (5)		

WRITING TOPICS

1. Using examples from your own experience, discuss the implications of the Halls's statement: "Once identified and analyzed, nonverbal communication systems can be taught, like a foreign language. Without this training, we respond to nonverbal communications in terms of our own culture; we read everyone's behavior as if it were our own, and thus we often misunderstand it."

2. Time is a very important ingredient in nonverbal communication, and Americans apparently place a high value on promptness. How important do you think time is? Are there occasions when it is acceptable or even polite to be late? Are Americans in your experience obsessed with time? Is your sense of time different from that of your parents?

3. How do you handle space? Do you have a strong sense of territoriality, always seeking out the same chair or table in certain situations? When people invade your space bubble, how do you feel? At what distances do you operate most comfortably? In what ways does an awareness of how you handle space help you to deal with it more effectively?

WRITING ASSIGNMENTS FOR "DISCOVERING LANGUAGE"

1. Like Malcom X, we can all tell of an experience that has been unusually significant for us. Think about your own experiences. Identify one incident that has been especially important for you and write an essay about it. In preparing to write, ask yourself such questions as these: Why is the incident important for me? What aspects of the incident might interest someone else? What details will help me re-create the incident in the most engaging way? How can my narrative of the incident be most effectively organized?

2. The writers in this section have at least one thing in common: they all agree that using language is an indispensable aspect of being human. "Everything had a name, and each name gave birth to a new thought," Helen Keller says at the end of her essay. "Except for our vegetablelike growth and our animallike impulses, almost all that we are is related to our use of words," said Bergen Evans in the first paragraph of his essay. But much of modern psychology and many New Age practices encourage us to really "feel" our emotions and "experience" the truth of those feelings. Does this idea conflict with the ideas of thinkers such as Keller, Evans, and the other writers in this section? In your own words, what is the role of language in humanity?

3. It has often been said that language reveals the character of the person using it. Write an essay in which you analyze the character of a particular writer or speaker with whom you are familiar, based on his or her use of language.

4. Paul Roberts argues that "no understanding of the English language can be very satisfactory without a notion of the history of the language." What exactly does Roberts mean by "understanding"? Write an essay in which you substantiate or dispute his claim.

5. No two writers in this section "sound alike." Through choice of words and length and structure of sentences, each creates a "style" uniquely his or her own. Examine some of your own work: term papers and reports, letters to friends and relatives, or essays for college applications. Do you hear a distinct "voice" in your own writing? Do you notice a difference between the way you sound in letters to friends and in college papers? Does your writing tend to be more formal in some kinds of writing than in others? Does your vocabulary differ for different kinds of writing? Write an essay discussing your findings.

PART II

American
English
Today

Jill, fax Farble and ask her what our phone conver-sation just meant.

LANGUAGE ON
THE SKIDS

Edwin Newman

Edwin Newman, besides being a television newsman and commentator, is the author of Strictly Speaking *and* A Civil Tongue—*two very popular books that have established his reputation as an advocate of correct usage and a guardian of American English. In "Language on the Skids," Newman provides numerous examples of redundant, flabby, and self-important language. He believes the English language is being abused and argues for the responsible use of language.*

It is typical of the English spoken on this side of the Atlantic that enough is almost never enough. Cecil Smith, television critic of the Los Angeles *Times,* considered CBS's "Bicentennial Minutes" not merely unique but singularly unique. Sen. Abraham Ribicoff of Connecticut was worried not only about nuclear proliferation but about the spread of nuclear proliferation. And Reggie Jackson, the *New York Times* advised its readers, "stole second successfully," which is better than stealing it unsuccessfully.

All of this is redundancy, to which we have become addicted. A large part of our speech and writing is unnecessary and boring, which makes reading and conversation a chore. We slog through the repetitious, and tarry when we should be moving on. Redundancy triumphs.

One reason for our extravagant use of words is the feeling that an idea is more effective if it is repeated and reinforced. That is why Jimmy Carter once described the international situation as very dormant. (Those were the days!) It is why he said that the place where he would meet Leonid Brezhnev would depend not merely on a mutual decision but on "a mutual decision between us." You can't be too careful when dealing with the Russians.

Another cause is a failure to understand what words mean. The New York *Daily News* would not have said of a motion picture that it "extolled the evils of the advertising business" if it knew what *extolled* meant. The weather forecaster at the CBS station in Washington, D.C., would not have said, "Tomorrow afternoon, the temperature will gradually plummet. . . ." And what could have led the New Bedford, Mass., *Standard Times* to run this headline: "Tie vote kills bottle bill, but not fatally"?

59

There is a third reason for our extravagant use of words—a desire to make what is being done, however simple and routine it may be, sound grand and complicated. Thus, two newspapers in Nevada announce that they intend to put up a building. Do they call it a building? No. It is to be "a community-information center." The Postal Service issues statements about "sortation" of mail. Not sorting. Sortation. The Los Angeles City Teachers' Mathematics Association, at its Annual Recognition Dinner, schedules an associative hour rather than a cocktail hour. What does one do during an associative hour? Get acquainted? Not since computer language has descended on us. One interfaces on a personal basis. By the way, if any well-dressed women are present, it is possible that their dress reflects "Executive Wardrobe Engineering."

Why is such language used? Self-importance, of course, but also because it serves as a fence that keeps others outside and respectful, or leads them to ignore what is going on inside because it is too much trouble to find out. So you may hear about "a horizontal analysis spanning the formal vertical departmental structure" intended to "identify multi-purpose citizen contacts requiring timely responses." Or you may hear of a California school district that closes schools not because there are fewer pupils than expected but because of "accelerated enrollment slippage."

This sort of language is increasingly characteristic of a society where engaged couples are said to be in a commitment situation, and where an economist may refer to work as labor-force participation. In Boston, the Metropolitan District commission did not want to say, "Keep off the ice." It urged that "all persons terminate using any body of water under MDC control for any ice-related recreation." It could have been worse. It could have been ice-related recreation-oriented activity.

There is, of course, a technique involved, but it is easy to grasp. Never say that a tank may spring a leak. Say there may be a "breach of containment." Never say of a product that people won't buy it. Say that it "met consumer resistance." In Knoxville, Tenn., a nurse won a product-naming contest with the suggestion that dust covers for medical equipment be called instead "sterility maintenance covers." That was worth $500 and a lunch at the Hyatt Regency Hotel.

I want to turn now to what I take to be the new pastime. It is "izing." A reporter I know, covering a Presidential visit to Boston, asked the Secret Service where he could park his car. The Secret Service could not help. What should he do, then? "If I were you," the Secret Service man replied, "I would put myself in a chauffeurized situation." The head of the United States Professional Tennis Association proposed "to focalize all major USPTA activities and programs from a single site." Would he be the focalist? Some plastic surgeons, advertising a customized approach, promise "wrinkles youthfulized." This, apparently, leaves the patient with young wrinkles.

Sports broadcasters often have only a shaky grip on grammar and on the connection between words and meaning. During one football game, the announcer told viewers that because of the way some of the boxes in the Superdome were placed, he could not visually see them. This sort of thing is by no means confined to the sports world. For example, we have all heard about alleged victims. They have become confused in some journalistic minds with intended victims, but intended victims are sometimes rendered as would-be victims, who apparently go out in the hope of being robbed.   10

An ironic thing is happening now. As we demand more and more openness from those in public life—unwisely, it seems to me—our language becomes more and more obscure, turgid, ponderous and overblown. The candor expected of public officials about their health, their money, their private lives is offset in public matters by language that conceals more than it tells, and often conceals the fact that there is little or nothing worth telling.   11

We ought to demand that our leaders speak better English, so that we know what they are talking about and, incidentally, so that they do. Some safety does lie in more sensible public attitudes, especially toward the public-relations and advertising techniques now widely used by politicians. It lies also in independent reporting by those of us in the news business, and in greater skepticism on the part of the public, and in an unremitting puncturing of the overblown. In all of this, language is crucial.   12

I have been told that my view is cranky and pedantic, that I want to keep the language from growing, and to impose a standard and rigid English. Far from it. Our language should be specific and concrete, eloquent where possible, playful where possible, and personal so that we don't all sound alike. Instead, high crimes and misdemeanors are visited upon it, and those who commit them do not understand that the crimes are crimes against themselves. The language belongs to all of us. We have no more valuable possession.   13

QUESTIONS ON CONTENT

1. In his opening paragraph Newman gives three examples of our extravagant use of words: "singularly unique," "the spread of nuclear proliferation," and "stole second successfully." Explain what the problem is in each case.

2. Newman believes that for most Americans "enough is almost never enough" (1). What does he see as the causes of our extravagance with words?

3. Why, according to Newman, do people use language that promotes

self-importance? Is such usage ever appropriate or legitimate in your opinion? Explain.

4. What relationship does Newman see between society and the language used?

5. What does Newman believe we can do to correct the situation he describes?

6. In his final paragraph Newman admits that people sometimes find him "cranky and pedantic." What do you think? Are the language abuses that he cites really "high crimes and misdemeanors" against American English? Explain.

QUESTIONS ON RHETORIC

1. What is Newman's thesis in the essay? Where is it stated? (Glossary: *Thesis*)

2. What is the topic sentence in paragraph 4? How is it related to the other sentences in the paragraph? (Glossary: *Topic Sentence*)

3. How would you describe Newman's tone in this essay? (Glossary: *Tone*) Does he ever come across as "cranky and pedantic"?

4. Discuss Newman's use of irony in paragraph 8. (Glossary: *Irony*) What do you suppose was his intent?

5. Without his many examples, how persuasive would Newman's argument be? Did you think that he could have used more examples at any points in the essay? If so, where?

6. What purpose is served by the question that begins paragraph 6? (Glossary: *Rhetorical Question*)

VOCABULARY

unique (1)	extolled (4)	turgid (11)
redundancy (2)	plummet (4)	ponderous (11)

WRITING TOPICS

1. One area of language abuse that Newman discusses is sports. Carefully read the sports section of your local or school newspaper and/or listen to the broadcast of several sports events, collecting examples for an essay on the language abuses of sports broadcasters and writers. Do you agree with Newman's assessment of their language?

2. Write an essay in which you discuss the redundant, highfalutin', and obscure language that you regularly encounter. Where in your experience is such language most common? What effect has this language abuse had on you?

IS THERE REALLY
A LANGUAGE CRISIS?

Harvey Daniels

*For the last ten or fifteen years writers like Edwin Newman
have warned of the widespread corruption of our language
and the demise of Standard English. Such language
critics—or pop grammarians, as Harvey Daniels prefers to
call them—complain that "jargon is rampant; the kids talk
funny; politicians brutalize the language in their endless
attempts to mislead us; bureaucrats pollute the environment
with obfuscation and bluster; the verbal test scores of our
schoolchildren are plunging; substandard dialects are often
accepted or even encouraged in the schools; non-English
speakers are infiltrating our cities; and no one in school or
business can write a simple English sentence correctly." In
the following chapter from his book* Famous Last Words: The
American Language Crisis Reconsidered, *Daniels takes issue
with the "trivial obsessions" of the critics. He believes that
much of their "scolding and fussing about language focuses
on red-penciling the superficial niceties of written and spoken
utterances, rather than on understanding where they come
from and what they might mean."*

The deathwatch over American English has begun again. After all the   1
shocks and assaults of her long life, and after all of her glorious recoveries,
the Mother Tongue now faces the final hour. Around the bedside cluster
the mourners: Edwin Newman, John Simon, Clifton Fadiman, Tony Ran-
dall, and Ann Landers. In darkened ranks behind stand somber professors
of freshman composition, a few school board members, a representative
from the National Assessment of Educational Progress, and the entire
usage panel of the *American Heritage Dictionary*. Like all deaths, this one
evokes in the bereaved the whole range of human feeling: anger, frustration, denial, despair, confusion, and grim humor. It has been a long,
degenerative disease and not pretty to watch.

Is there room for hope? Is it really, uh, terminal? The specialists leave   2
no room for miracles—the prognosis is firm. The obituaries have been
prepared and, in some cases, already published. Services will be announced. Memorials are referred to the Educational Testing Service. *Re-
quiescat in pace* American English.

Yet, curiously, the language clings to life. She even weakly speaks   3
from time to time, in delirium no doubt, for her words are in jargon, cant,
argot, doublespeak, and various substandard dialects. She splits infinitives
and dangles participles, and one of the watchers actually thought he heard
her begin a sentence with *hopefully*. How can one so ill survive? It is
torture to see this. It must end.

But it won't. If this is death in life, it is still the normal condition of   4
American English and of all other human languages. As compelling as the
medical metaphors may be, languages really are not very much like people, healthy or sick, and make poor candidates for personification. The
illnesses, the abuses, the wounds, the sufferings of a language reside in the
minds and hearts of its users, as do its glories, triumphs, and eras of
progress. Our language is an essentially neutral instrument with which we
communicate, more or less, and into which we pour an abundance of
feeling. It is our central cultural asset and our cherished personal friend,
but it is not, in many ways, what we think it is or would like it to be.

But here is another story about death which I believe does tell us   5
something important about the present state of American English. In Chicago, during the Christmas season of 1978, twenty-six Spanish-speaking
people were killed in a series of tragic fires. Many of them perished
because they could not understand the instructions that firemen shouted in
English. When the city promptly instituted a program to teach the firefighters a few emergency phrases in Spanish, a storm of protest arose.
"This is America," proclaimed the head of the Chicago Firefighters Union,
"let them speak English." A local newspaper columnist suggested, with
presumably innocent irony: "Let's stop catering to the still-flickering nationalistic desires to perpetuate the Latin heritage." The city's top-rated
television newscaster used his bylined editorial minute to inveigh against
the Spanish-teaching program in the firehouses.

An exasperated resident wrote to the letters column of the Chicago   6
Tribune: "I object to bilingual everything. It is a pretty low sort of person
who wants to enjoy the benefits of this country while remaining apart from
it, hiding in an ethnic ghetto." Another letter writer huffed: "What does it
take to bring home to these stiff-necked Latinos that when they move to a
foreign country the least they can do is learn the language? I, for one, am
fed up with the ruination of the best country in the world." Still another
correspondent was even more succinct: "If they can't understand two
words—don't jump—they should go back where they came from." And

after my own brief article on the language controversy appeared, an angry firefighter's wife wrote me to explain her husband's awful dilemma in being stationed in the Latino community. "Why should he risk his life for nothing?" she wondered.

What does this story, which concerns speakers of Spanish, tell us about the current state of English? It reminds us that our attitudes about the speech-ways of other people are as much a part of the linguistic environment as nouns, verbs, and adjectives—and that today these attitudes appear unusually harsh and unforgiving. In the Chicago controversy, some otherwise decent people were willing to imply—and some plainly stated—that people who don't talk right can damn well take their chances in a burning building. And while the underlying hostilities that give rise to such sentiments may not begin with language, it is clear that we frequently use language as both a channel and an excuse for expressing some of our deepest prejudices. Admittedly, our unforgiving attitudes about certain kinds of language do not often decide matters of life and death. Judging by the angry reaction to the fire crisis in Chicago, it is a good thing that they don't.

It seems worth noting that this particular outpouring of linguistic intolerance occurred in the midst of a period of more general concern about the fate of the English language. For the last decade we have been increasingly hearing about the sudden and widespread corruption of our native tongue. Standard English is supposedly becoming an endangered species; jargon is rampant; the kids talk funny; politicians brutalize the language in their endless attempts to mislead us; bureaucrats pollute the environment with obfuscation and bluster; the verbal test scores of our schoolchildren are plunging; substandard dialects are often accepted or even encouraged in the schools; non-English speakers are infiltrating our cities; and no one in school or business can write a simple English sentence correctly.

We have been having a "literacy crisis"—a panic about the state of our language in all of its uses, reading and writing and speaking. Predictions of linguistic doom have become a growth industry. *Time* magazine asks: "Can't Anyone Here Speak English?" while *Newsweek* explains "Why Johnny Can't Write." *TV Guide* warns of "The New Illiteracy," *Saturday Review* bemoans "The Plight of the English Language," and even United Airline's *Mainliner Magazine* blusters "Who's Been Messing Around with Our Mother Tongue?" Pop grammarians and language critics appear in every corner of the popular media, relentlessly detailing the latest abuses of language and pillorying individual abusers.

Blue-ribbon commissions are impaneled to study the declining language skills of the young, and routinely prescribe strong doses of "The Basics" as a remedy. Astute educational publishers crank out old-fangled grammar books. English professors offer convoluted explanations of the crisis and its causes, most of which lay the blame on public school English teachers. The *New York Times Magazine* adds Spiro Agnew's former speechwriter to its roster as a weekly commentator "On Language." The president of the United States goes on record as encouraging the "back-to-basics" movement generally and the rebirth of grammar instruction in particular. Scores of books on illiteracy are published, but none outsells *Strictly Speaking*. Edwin Newman, house grammarian of the National Broadcasting Company had posed the question first, and apparently most frighteningly: "Will America be the death of English?" His answer was frightening too: "My mature, considered judgment is that it will."

It was in the midst of this ripening language panic that the Spanish courses were begun in a few Chicago firehouses. The resulting controversy and debate would surely have happened anyway, since the expression of linguistic prejudice is one of humankind's most beloved amusements. But I also believe that the dispute was broadened, extended, and made more explicitly cruel by the prevailing climate of worry about the overall deterioration of American English. 11

The public had repeatedly been informed that the language was in a mess, that it was time to draw the line, time to clean up the tongue, time to toughen our standards, time to quit coddling inadequate speakers. In Chicago, that line was drawn in no uncertain terms. Obviously, the connections between the "language crisis," with its mythical Mother Tongue writhing on her deathbed, and the all-too-real events of that recent Chicago winter are subtle and indirect. 12

Language is changing, yes. People "misuse" language constantly— use it to lie, mislead, and conceal. Few of us write very well. Young people do talk differently from grownups. Our occupations do generate a lot of jargon. We do seem to swear more. I do not personally admire each of these phenomena. But reports of the death of the English language are greatly exaggerated. 13

English is not diseased, it has not been raped and ravaged, it is not in peril. A language cannot, by its very nature, suffer in such ways. In fact, it cannot suffer at all. One of the sternest of the pop grammarians, Richard Mitchell, has said in one of his calmer moments: 14

> There is nothing wrong with English. We do not live in the twilight of a dying language. To say that our English is outmoded or corrupt makes as much sense as to say that multiplication has been outmoded by Texas Instruments and corrupted because we've all forgotten the times tables. You may say as often as you please that six times seven is forty-five, but arithmetic will not suffer.

Mitchell goes on to say that the real problem we face lies not in the language itself but in the ignorance and stupidity of its users. I agree, although my definition of ignorance and stupidity is quite different from his.

At least some of the ignorance from which we suffer is ignorance of the history of language and the findings of linguistic research. History shows us that language panics, some just as fierce as our present one, are as familiar a feature of the human chronicle as wars. In fact, one of the persistent characteristics of past crises has been the inevitable sense that everything was fine until the moment at hand, 1965, or 1789, or 2500 B.C., when suddenly the language (be it American English, British English, or Sumerian) began the final plunge to oblivion. Looking at the history of prior language crises gives us a reassuring perspective for evaluating the current one. 15

But we need more than reassurance—we need facts, or at least the closest thing to them, about the nature of language and how it works. The study of linguistics, which has emerged only during the present century, provides just such crucial information. The fact that the sponsors of the language crisis almost unanimously condemn modern linguistics suggests the irreconcilable difference between the critic's and the linguist's views of language. The linguist's work is not to ridicule poor speakers and praise good ones; not to rank various languages according to their supposed superiority in expressing literary or scientific concepts; not to defend the Mother Tongue from real or imagined assaults. Instead, the linguist tries to understand and explain some of the wonderfully complex mechanisms which allow human beings to communicate with each other. This does not mean that linguists don't have opinions about good and bad language, or even that some of them won't cringe at a dangling *hopefully*. But their main business is not evaluative but explanatory, not prescriptive but descriptive—an orientation which is utterly alien to the work of the contemporary language critics. 16

Even if a review of the history of language and linguistic research does tend to deflate our sense of crisis, this does not mean that the widespread fear of linguistic corruption is meaningless. Far from it. Something is indeed going on, and the wordsmiths of our society have been able to spread their concern about it quite easily to people who do not make their living by teaching, writing, or editing English. . . . 17

All this worry about a decline extends well beyond the speaking and writing of American English. It represents a much wider concern about the direction of our society, our culture, as a whole. We have displaced (to use some jargon) much of our anxiety about current cultural changes into concern for the language which of necessity reflects them. Today, as at certain other moments in the past, talking about language has become a way of talking about ourselves, and about what we mean by knowledge, learning, education, discipline, intelligence, democracy, equality, patriotism, and truth. 18

But there are problems, serious ones. Language itself cannot be asked 19 to carry the weight of such grave issues alone. To the extent that we assign our problems mainly to language, and explain them mostly by reference to aspects of language, we often defeat our own purposes. The critics, in this sense, are actually compounding the problems they profess to solve. First, they are promulgating or reinforcing ideas about language that are just plain wrong. If language is as important as the critics unanimously claim, then we should at least try to tell the truth about it, even if the facts run counter to our favorite prejudices. Second, the ministrations of the critics, with their inaccurate notions about the workings of language, threaten to bring back old—or to inspire new—teaching curricula and techniques that will hinder, rather than enhance, our children's efforts to develop their reading and writing and speaking skills.

Third, the critics, ironically enough, often trivialize the study of lan-   20
guage. Through their steadfast preoccupation with form—with spelling and punctuation and usage and adolescent jargon and bureaucratic bluster and political doublespeak—they deflect us from meaning. Of course we know that form and content are intimately related, as the study of political propaganda reveals. Yet the real study of propaganda involves penetrating beyond the surface features to the message which is being sent, to the messages unsent, and to the purposes of the senders. But much of the current scolding and fussing about language focuses on red-penciling the superficial niceties of written and spoken utterances, rather than on understanding where they come from and what they might mean.

For all their trivial obsessions, the critics do also offer a deeper, more   21
general message. As they advise us to strengthen our democracy by cleaning up the language, they also encourage us to continue using minor differences in language as ways of identifying, classifying, avoiding, or punishing anyone whom we choose to consider our social or intellectual inferior. And this is the gravest problem which the language crisis has given us: it has reinforced and occasionally glorified some of the basest hatreds and flimsiest prejudices in our society. Surely this unfortunate side effect has been mainly inadvertent—but just as surely, it affects us all.

QUESTIONS ON CONTENT

1. What, according to Daniels, is the "normal condition" of American English? Why isn't he concerned about all the so-called abuses cited by language watchdogs and pop grammarians?

2. In paragraphs 5 and 6 Daniels relates the story of the 1978 fires in Chicago. What does this story have to do with the current state of English in the United States? Why does Daniels think that it is more than coincidence that the Chicago incident happened at the same time that there was

growing public awareness of and concern about the decline of the English language?

3. What solutions have been offered for the "literacy crisis"? What is Daniels's attitude toward these solutions?

4. Daniels states that there are several irreconcilable differences between language critics and linguists. What exactly are these differences?

5. Daniels believes that the pop grammarians and language critics are "actually compounding the problems they profess to solve" (19). What reasons does he give for his opinion? Do you find yourself agreeing or disagreeing with Daniels?

6. What does Daniels think is the "gravest problem" that the current language crisis has strapped us with?

QUESTIONS ON RHETORIC

1. How would you characterize Daniels's writing: formal, informal, colloquial? How appropriate is his style to his subject and his argument?

2. How has Daniels organized his essay? You may find it helpful to make an outline of the essay so that you can see how the parts are related.

3. How would you characterize Daniels's tone in this essay? (Glossary: *Tone*) What is his attitude toward pop grammarians? toward the current language crisis? (Glossary: *Attitude*)

4. How does paragraph 13 function in the context of the essay?

5. Why do you think Daniels quotes Richard Mitchell in paragraph 14? Does he make effective use of the quotation? Why, or why not?

6. Why does Daniels find "medical metaphors" used to describe the language crisis generally unsatisfactory?

VOCABULARY

somber (1)	argot (3)	convoluted (10)
bereaved (1)	inveigh (5)	coddling (12)
prognosis (2)	succinct (6)	inadvertent (21)
cant (3)	obfuscation (8)	

WRITING TOPICS

1. After reading what both Newman ("Language on the Skids," p. 59) and Daniels have to say about the language crisis in America, what is your position? Are you more in agreement with watchdog Newman or with linguist Daniels? Explain.

2. While you were in high school you were probably exposed to the "back

to basics'' movement. What exactly did ''back to basics'' mean in your area? How did it affect the curriculum? Did this approach adequately address students' language problems in writing, reading, and speaking?

3. Daniels believes that by insisting upon correctness, pop grammarians ''encourage us to continue using minor differences in language as ways of identifying, classifying, avoiding, or punishing anyone whom we choose to consider our social or intellectual inferior'' (21). Have you ever reacted to anyone negatively or positively on the basis of the English that he or she used, or have you ever been judged on that same basis? Write an essay in which you recount one such incident and discuss how language prejudiced opinion.

WHY ENGLISH SHOULD BE OUR OFFICIAL LANGUAGE

S. I. Hayakawa

S. I. Hayakawa, a former senator from California, is honorary chairman of U.S. English, Washington, D.C. In this essay, Hayakawa argues that the institution of bilingual education in our schools promises to divide the culture in two. In 1981, to prevent this division, Hayakawa introduced to the United States Senate a constitutional amendment decreeing English the official language of America. To date it has not passed into law.

The familiar truism that characterizes the United States as "a nation of immigrants" needs some qualification. We are a nation of immigrants, yes, but not a nation of separate immigrant enclaves. Rather, we are a country composed of various racial, cultural, linguistic, and ethnic groups constantly undergoing integration and assimilation and thereby constantly creating a new culture influenced by—even evolved from—diverse heritages. That is the concept of the melting pot.

But in the past few years, strong resistance to the melting pot idea has arisen—especially among those who claim to speak for our Hispanic-American citizens. Instead of a melting pot, they say, the national ideal should be a salad bowl in which different elements do not melt but mingle, retaining their distinctive character. A key element in the "salad bowl agenda" is the use of so-called bilingual education to encourage the maintenance of, and primary allegiance to, the Spanish language among those of Hispanic heritage.

Unfortunately, a great deal of confusion exists over the term "bilingual education." Bilingualism can mean anything from knowing two languages—a feat we all would heartily applaud—to "binationalism," a course our country must escape. But bilingual education means something quite specific to many who say they speak for Hispanics. For example:

● "The present monolingual, monocultural, Anglocentric public education system must be replaced by a multilingual, multicultural, pluralistic one," according to Robert Cordova, an assistant professor at the University of Northern Colorado, Greeley. "The Hispanic population is becom-

ing larger, and Hispanic culture is becoming stronger. . . . American
society and ideas of old no longer exist.''

• ''Spanish should be included in commercials shown throughout   5
America. Every American child ought to be taught both English and Spanish,'' says Mario Obledo, president of the League of United Latin American Citizens, a group originally founded to help Hispanics learn English.

• ''If the present rate of growth of Spanish speakers continues, it is not   6
unlikely that we will soon have to consider [a law making both English and
Spanish the official U.S. languages] a possibility,'' said Josue Gonzales,
now president of the National Association for Bilingual Education, in
testimony before Congress over a decade ago.

As these quotations illustrate, a very real move is afoot to split the U.S.   7
into a bilingual and bicultural society. This move is being spearheaded not
by rank-and-file Hispanics, but by their political leaders, by certain bilingual education teachers, and by Hispanic lobbying organizations.

Deeply concerned by the specter of a country divided along linguistic   8
and cultural lines, I introduced in the U.S. Senate, in April 1981, a constitutional amendment that would establish English as our official national
language. Others have introduced the same amendment in successive years.

The movement is growing. Six states have passed laws declaring En-   9
glish as their official language. Whenever the question has been submitted
to a popular referendum, it has won by an overwhelming majority. Perhaps
not surprisingly, approximately half the voters of Hispanic background
usually support it.

The national organization leading this movement is U.S. English, on   10
whose board I serve as honorary chairman. Our critics have tried to tar us
with a wide brush as xenophobes and racists, but it is not we who endeavor
to segregate children and society along racial or linguistic lines. (I am a
nonwhite immigrant, three of the six members of our board are immigrants, and all of us know at least one language other than English—hardly
the sort of people likely to embrace xenophobia.)

We are concerned about the future unity of our nation. We are con-   11
vinced Americans must share a common language. And that language must
be English.

We recognize that using a child's native language might help ad-   12
vance his education under some circumstances—but with two provisions.
First, bilingual education must be chosen freely by local school authorities, not imposed by federal or state governments. And second, the bilingual education program must be truly transitional, preparing the
student for transfer into a standard English classroom after one or not
more than two years.

Countless millions of immigrants successfully made the transition from   13
their native tongues to English and became assimilated into the American

mainstream. It is condescending and insulting to single out today's immigrants and suggest they cannot do the same.

QUESTIONS ON CONTENT

1. In his opening paragraph, Hayakawa gives his definition of what has been called the "melting pot" of America. Do you agree with his definition? Explain your answer.

2. In your own words, describe the ideal of the "salad bowl" concept. What is one of its key elements?

3. Who does Hayakawa say is responsible for the move toward bilingualism? Briefly, what are three of the reasons the proponents of bilingualism give for its necessity? Are their arguments convincing?

4. Under certain conditions, Hayakawa says, bilingualism could be used in the schools. What are these conditions?

QUESTIONS ON RHETORIC

1. What is the central idea of Hayakawa's essay? Is it stated or implied?

2. In paragraph 7, Hayakawa charges that "a very real move is afoot to split the U.S. into a bilingual and bicultural society." In paragraph 3, Hayakawa says that binationalism is "a course our country must escape." Toward the end of his essay, Hayakawa defends himself against charges of xenophobia and racism. What kind of evidence does Hayakawa offer in support of each of those three statements? Is some evidence more convincing than others? Cite examples from the text to support your answer.

3. Would you describe Hayakawa's tone as forceful, ironic, or angry? What words in the essay lead you to this conclusion? (Glossary: *Tone*)

4. Reread the opening sentence in each of Hayakawa's paragraphs. How is each of these sentences related to the central idea or thesis of the essay as a whole? Did you find that these sentences work to make his argument more persuasive?

VOCABULARY

truism (1)	pluralistic (4)	referendum (9)
enclaves (1)	specter (8)	xenophobia (10)
ethnic (1)		

WRITING TOPICS

1. Hayakawa is adamant that the United States must remain English speaking; as he states, binationalism is "a course our country must escape." However, he does not give concrete examples of the consequences of

binationalism. Following class discussion or reading on the subject, write an essay in which you explore some of the possible consequences of making both English and Spanish the official languages of our country. You may wish to start with Hayakawa's reference to the segregation of schoolchildren in paragraph 10.

2. Today, in our schools, Spanish-speaking children must learn English. How do you think most English-speaking students would react if they were forced to learn Spanish in school? Have you ever studied a foreign language? Write an essay in which you discuss some of the difficulties in learning a second language.

3. Hayakawa's position can be viewed as a desire to maintain the continuity of American culture. On the other hand, as Hayakawa points out, critics can view it as a form of xenophobia. You may remember that when Israel recently passed a law defining the word *Jew*, with the intention of maintaining the "purity" of Israel's citizenry, many Americans, including many American Jews, accused the Israeli Parliament of xenophobia. Look up the word *xenophobia* in your desk dictionary, then reread Hayakawa's essay. In your opinion can the word rightfully be applied to the issues of national purity in Israel and the English Only movement in the United States? Can it be used in one case but not the other? Write an essay in which you state your own position and defend it with examples from your reading or personal experience.

THE ENGLISH ONLY MOVEMENT

Alice Roy

*Alice Roy, a writing teacher at the California State
University in Los Angeles, challenges the notion of the
melting pot set forth by S. I. Hayakawa in his essay. Roy
offers an alternative look at history and the ways immigrants
have assimilated into our culture. She further charges that
motives and issues having little to do with the preservation of
the English language are at the heart of the move to make
English our official language.*

In 1986, California became the first state in the country to adopt an   1
amendment to the state constitution declaring English the official language.
This was accomplished through a voter initiative sponsored by "U.S.
English," founded by S. I. Hayakawa in 1983. The initiative was Proposition 63, called "English Only," and it passed by a wide margin, 73%
for, 27% against. U.S. English and another group known as "English
First," led by former Virginia legislator Larry Pratt, are working throughout the country to make English the official language. Many people have
adopted "English Only" as the cover label for all such groups and legislative actions; others use "official English" for the purpose.

Membership in official-English groups appears to be increasing. U.S.   2
English nearly doubled its membership from 150,000 in 1983 to 275,000
in 1986. English First has enrolled 200,000 members just since its beginning in 1986. It may be that this growth spurt is over, that is, that all who
are going to join such groups have done so. However, leaders of the two
groups and opponents as well predict increasing membership and activity
in the 1990s and extending into the 21st century (Orenstein 1).

What do official-English acts and amendments do? Most, like Califor-   3
nia's, declare English to be the state's official language. Others say the
state shall not require use of any other language. Some explicitly permit
bilingual education; however, only a few have this feature, and none
except for Arizona are in the West or Southwest. Some require all official
proceedings and publications to be in English. Some, in the form of legislative resolutions, urge passage of federal official-English laws or amendments. A few, among them California's, empower citizens and businesses

of the state to sue to enforce official-English laws. Several declare English to be the basic language in public schools. Such acts and amendments may also forbid state legislatures from passing any law which diminishes or ignores the official status of English (Orenstein 3).

Thirty-one state legislatures have considered or are considering actions 4 to make English the official state or national language. These proposals take varying forms, sometimes as voter initiatives on the ballot, more often as state legislative bills. Twelve have passed: Illinois and Nebraska in the 1920s; Arkansas, Mississippi, North Dakota, California, Georgia, Virginia, Nevada, Indiana, Kentucky, and Tennessee since 1984. (Hawaii's state constitutional amendment, passed in 1978, declares English and Hawaiian to be the state's official languages.) In a few other states bills or initiatives are pending but are not predicted to succeed. In 1981, Hayakawa proposed an amendment to the U.S. Constitution to make English the official language. Similar bills have been introduced every year since then, but none have been voted out of committee (Orenstein 1,2).

In strictly numerical terms, official English has not had much legisla- 5 tive success. And, in practical terms, a survey of official-English states found no changes in education or government policy resulting from official-English legislation (Orenstein 2). However, at another level of activity, a lot is going on. For example, in a small town in California, the mayor vowed that election information and "other things" would only come out in English. In Whittier, California, there are plans for legislation calling for state services to be available only in English, including driver's tests, welfare applications, and state university financial aid forms. Leaders of official-English groups are reviewing laws and regulations to see which ones do not comply with legislation or amendments already passed. Members of official-English groups work to insure that school notices will not be sent home in any language other than English. Furthermore, members of some city councils campaign and are elected to office based on a platform supporting English Only. In an administrative action that was later ruled illegal, three judges in a municipal court imposed an English Only order on Latino employees during their work hours in the courthouse. There are efforts to remove non-English business signs, to stop the translations of city newsletters, and to cut bilingual education funds (Chen and Calderone 8). Indeed, two of the explicitly cited goals in the solicitation letter from English First are to make sure that states can "limit bilingual programs *without having the anti-English coalitions overturn them in the courts*" [emphasis theirs]; and to work for "passage at the Constitutional level, which will end the bilingual ballot" (Pratt 4).

What is the cause of this apparent linguistic chauvinism? The English 6 Only movement appeals to a fairly simple sentiment—that everyone should speak English. Underneath this, however, are anti-immigrant and divisive sentiments that rest on economic fears. The U.S. economy is currently in a period of slow growth, the annual budget deficit is not reducing, and agriculture and some industries are in a depressed state. At such times, competition for limited resources pits segments of the population against each other. Proposals for national legislation reflect or exacerbate people's fears that immigrant workers may take jobs from U.S. citizens, that the state of the economy is to be blamed on foreign imports, and that bilingual education allows non-English-speaking groups to increase their political power. Angry taxpayers blame immigrants for depleting an already tight budget with the use of social services such as education, literacy, health, and jobs programs. Funding of bilingual education and misconceptions about the quality and goals of bilingual education increase fears and distrust (Chen and Calderone 7).

Seeing the sorts of things that English Only groups do *not* have as goals   7
helps to substantiate this economic interpretation. For example, there have been fears in California that the courts might be able to prohibit foreign language advertising. Analysis of an issue of *Business and Community Impact*, a publication of the Chamber of Commerce in a Los Angeles community with a large Asian population, shows a full-page ad for a realty and insurance agency, mostly in English with a few lines in Chinese; a column of English, advertising a bank, paralleled by a column with the same information in Chinese; and a page giving a Chinese-language summary of the sixteen-page magazine. The head of the U.S. English California office says there is no danger of such economic nonsense as interfering with advertising (Orenstein 2). Translation: bilingual is all right if it makes money.

The English Only movement rests on a few myths or misconceptions,   8
some of which we all learned overtly in grade school social studies, some we acquired more implicitly, and some that we as English teachers directly participate in.

The first myth is that earlier immigrant populations all learned English.   9
The solicitation letter for the group English First, signed by Jim Horn, Representative to the Texas Legislature, begins:

> I don't know about your forefathers but when mine came to America, the first thing they did was learn English.
> They wanted to be part of the American dream, and they knew that learning English wasn't just a practical necessity. It was a moral obligation.
> Tragically, many immigrants these days refuse to learn English!

Similarly, Larry Pratt, head of English First, says that it is "something that generations of immigrants have taken for granted: when coming to the U.S. one learns English. In fact, those immigrants were proud to have learned English" (4). But in actual fact it wasn't taken for granted. From the beginning of our history, linguistic difference has been an issue. Benjamin Franklin worried about the Germans—they had little knowledge of English, they had their own German press, and Franklin was afraid they would need translators to tell one half of Congress what the other half was saying (Pinon 4). Three-quarters of a century later, the first California state constitution was written in both English and Spanish.

The myth that all immigrants learned English right away is closely   10
related to the second myth, that of the "melting pot" as a description of ethnic relations in the U.S. The melting pot metaphor encodes the widely held belief that previous immigrant groups arrived, jumped into the common cauldron, and came out homogenized. That kind of assimilation was possible for white Northern Protestant Europeans, for linguistic, cultural, racial, and religious reasons. However, we have inherited a "sanitized romanticism" about our immigration history (Janken 4). Certainly the immigrant experience is a deep-running theme in our country's history. Immigrants came to improve their condition, not so much for themselves as for their children and grandchildren. There was a strong sense that this would take a couple of generations to accomplish. The upward mobility that characterizes this immigrant experience must be seen in a context of persecution—not just the persecution being fled from, but the persecution experienced here as well. Immigrants made up the largest proportion of membership in social protest movements in the U.S. in the first thirty years of the 20th century. Was this because they came from places where they experienced persecution and exploitation? Or was it because they perceived inequity and exploitation here in the midst of the American dream? We have just recently celebrated the Statue of Liberty centennial. In 1882, shortly before the Statue of Liberty was placed in the New York harbor, the Chinese Exclusion Act was passed by Congress. This act was connected to the economic crisis then, for which Chinese were partly blamed. We know that after World War I, immigration restrictions were imposed on eastern and southern Europeans, including Jews who were denied refuge from Nazism. Our "nation of immigrants" legend is largely that of white Europeans. It ignores Blacks, Chicanos, and Native Americans in American history. These groups had no choice of residence: Blacks were brought, Chicanos and Native Americans were displaced—these were not the "huddled masses yearning to breathe free" (Janken 4,5).

The community of Monterey Park in Los Angeles is a modern example   11
of the melting pot myth. It is a suburb of Los Angeles, technically, but quite close to the center of town, well within the metropolitan area. It is now being called the first suburban Chinatown (Arax 1). In the past ten years, a rapid increase in Asian population has occurred—the proportion is now 40% Asian, 37% Latino, 22% Anglo, and 1% Black. Longtime Anglo

and Latino residents remember it before the Asian influx. Some Anglos remember the community before the Chicano influx.

A few years ago, Monterey Park was euphorically designated an all-American city because of its apparent racial harmony. The sixteen-page *Monterey Park Living,* a community activities publication with articles in the Fall 1986 issue of the Monterey Park Golf Course, the Senior Citizens' Center, medical emergency services, and the recreation schedule, has a single page fully in Chinese, summarizing the information contained in the magazine. Now, however, that community is racially polarized. One night in June of 1986, at 1:30 A.M., when most residents who attend such meeting had gone home, the Monterey Park City Council passed a resolution urging control of U.S. borders, denouncing cities that provide sanctuary to refugees, instructing local police to cooperate vigorously with immigration authorities, and endorsing legislation to make English the official language of the United States (Ono and Calderon 6). Clearly the English Only movement is part of a larger reaction—it is not just linguistic.

At the 1986 convention, the National Council of Teachers of English passed a resolution urging rejection of the tenets of official-English groups. NCTE president Nancy McHugh has received many letters attacking her personally or attacking the NCTE stand generally.[1] These letters make frequent reference to the melting pot:

> Dear "Nancy,"
> How could you be elected president of NCTE with the grossly narrow view you hold on English? Now a retired English instructor of 50 years, I am *shocked* to learn of your position. We are ONE nation of the most ethnic people in the world who've become U.S. citizens.

Or, as another letter-writer said:

> I'm horrified at the position of your organization—Glad *I'm* not a member! The *melting pot* is our greatest strength—The immigrant groups which succeed are those who learn the language!

Along with the melting pot myth, this writer raises the issue of the relationship between language and upward mobility. The third myth that the official-English movement rests on is that language exists and can be learned out of social context. Leaders of the movement often reject bilingual education in favor of holding children who speak limited or no English separate from regular schooling until they have learned enough English to cope in English-speaking classes:

> It is clear that an intensive period of instruction, perhaps as much as a year, should be provided so that a student can study English full time during that period. Then the student is ready to study the other courses in the curriculum—in English (Pratt 4).

Research shows, however, that children who study academic content in their early grade school years, using their native language and developing native language literacy, do as well as native speakers in the long run, and better than those students who are held back from beginning their education until they can do so in English. Theory and research in language acquisition tell us that language does not respond to a head-on assault, that rather we learn a language best when we use it to learn or do something else (for example, see Krashen; Swain and Lapkin; and Brumfit and Johnson). Another letter to McHugh echoes the previous writer's belief that knowing English will get the knower a job:

> We . . . strongly object to those who seek to deny recent immigrants the social and economic opportunities that are only available to those knowing English.

Yet it is more likely that once people have jobs they will learn English than it is that people will learn English before they get jobs. In earlier waves of immigration, men who went out to work learned English, though it was described as "broken English," while the women who stayed at home taking care of children and aged parents did not.

The fourth myth on which the official-English movement relies is that language can be controlled and preserved against change. Other letter writers to Nancy McHugh say: 15

> (1) I think it incredible that you could oppose such a movement as the one pushing for the legal protection of the English language. You may want to pay taxes so *some* can use bilingual voting ballots, etc., but I don't. It's your money. U.S. ENGLISH ALL THE WAY!

> (2) In my opinion, I believe there should be a National Academy of English Language Standards to which *ALL* teachers and public speakers should belong.

> (3) As a retired teacher of English, I can't believe the National Council of English Teachers would pass an official resolution opposing the movement for the legal protection of the English language in America! All one has to do is read any newspaper in the country or visit any legislature to discover the deplorable lack of the use of standard English in our country.

But language can be neither controlled nor preserved against change. The French Academy has not succeeded in keeping English words out of French. The Spanish Academy has not succeeded in getting all Spanish-speaking people—even in Spain—to speak Castilian Spanish. And two hundred years of English teachers' exhortations and imprecations to get students to stop saying *lay* for *lie* and to stop using *they* for indefinite singular reference have not succeeded.

What needs to be done? What can we do?   16

One local group in Los Angeles has a tutorial program called Building   17
Rainbows. Its goals are to help students learn about each others' cultures

and to stay in school, to get parents involved in their children's education, and to build parents' leadership in community institutions (Ono and Calderon 7).

A recent *ERIC/CLL* (Clearinghouse on Languages and Linguistics) [18] *News Bulletin* describes programs designed to bring parents of children identified as Limited–English Speaking into tutoring relationships with school classes (Simich-Dudgeon 3).

Our professional organizations provide leadership and information— [19] the NCTE and the Linguistic Society of America have both passed resolutions opposing English Only legislation. We can work for greater funding of programs to help non–English speakers learn English. For example, in the Los Angeles School District, 192,000 adult students study English in adult education programs; 40,000 are on waiting lists (May 16).

Remembering that money talks, we can inform students and the public [20] that we can enrich our resources, industry, tax collection, and consumerism through immigrant populations. At a time when Pacific Rim commercial activity in particular and worldwide exchange in general is increasing, the restriction of use of languages is a particularly parochial aim. We speak for the economic usefulness of a multilingual population.

Most especially, as teachers of English at all levels, we can teach our [21] students to respect and enjoy cultural and linguistic diversity. This means relinquishing a value-laden approach to teaching English that makes the use of a certain kind of English a moral or ethical virtue—where correctness replaces cleanliness right up there next to godliness. We must relinquish as well the purity of the received canon of English literature in order to draw on the richness of minor and minority writing. We as English teachers have inherited an elitist view of English, but we don't have to perpetuate it. Although community action is important, we can do our work in our workplace by refusing to collude in the myths and by learning and teaching how language and society interact.

NOTES

[1] I thank Nancy NcHugh for making copies of some of these letters available to me for this study.

WORKS CITED

Arax, Mark. "Monterey Park: Nation's 1st Suburban Chinatown." *Los Angeles Times.* 6 April 1987, sec I:1 + .

Brumfit, C. J., and K. Johnson, eds. *The Communicative Approach to Language Teaching.* Oxford: Oxford University Press, 1979.

Business and Community Impact. November 1986.

Chen, W., and J. Calderone. "Language Rights and Structural Change." *NDM National Bulletin,* Spring 1987:5–13.

Horn, Jim. "English First" solicitation letter, no date (mailed 1986).

Janken, Kenneth. "The Forgotten 'Immigrant Experience' ." *The New Democrat.* August 1986: 4–5.

Krashen, Stephen D. *Principles and Practice in Second Language Acquisition.* Oxford/New York: Pergamon Press, 1982.

May, Lee. "Alien Law Puts Strain on English Classes." *Los Angeles Times.* 25 February 1987, sec I: 16.

Monterey Park Living. September-November 1986.

Ono, Carol, and Jose Calderon. "No Torch of Liberty in the All-American City." *The New Democrat.* August 1986: 6–7.

Orenstein, Mike, " 'Official English' Battle Widens." *Hispanic Link Weekly Report.* 20 April 1987: 4.

Pinon, Fernando. "The Case for Language Equity." *Hispanic Link Weekly Report.* 20 April 1987: 4.

Pratt, Larry. "The Case for English First." *Hispanic Link Weekly Report.* 20 April 1987: 4.

Simich-Dudgeon, Carmen. "Involving Limited-English-Proficient Parents as Tutors in Their Children's Education." *ERIC/CLL News Bulletin.* March 1987: 3–4, 7.

Swain, Merrill, and Sharon Lapkin. *Evaluating Bilingual Education: A Canadian Case Study.* Clevedon, Avon, England: Multilingual Matters Ltd., n.d.

QUESTIONS ON CONTENT

1. What, for Roy, is the stated motive of the English Only movement? What does she believe to be the real motive? How did she arrive at this conclusion?

2. In paragraph 3, Roy describes the scope of English Only legislation. Over what aspects of everyday life could it have influence?

3. Roy states that several myths about the United States are used to support the English Only movement. Name these myths. What arguments does she use to counter these myths? How does she use the example of Monterey Park to support her position? Is her argument convincing?

4. At the end of her essay, Roy offers several solutions to the language problem. Briefly describe them. Do you think these solutions are realistic? Why or why not?

QUESTIONS ON RHETORIC

1. What is Roy's thesis in this essay? (Glossary: *Thesis*) Where is it best stated?

2. In the first five paragraphs of her essay, Roy describes the goals and efforts of the English Only movement, yet her intention is to argue against

it. Why do you think she chose to use this beginning? (Glossary: *Beginnings*) How else could Roy have started her essay?

3. Roy supports her argument with different types of evidence. (Glossary: *Evidence*) What types of evidence does she use? Do you find her evidence convincing? Explain.

4. How does Roy's position as a writing teacher add authority to her essay?

5. Would you describe the tone of Roy's essay as emotional or would you say it was objective? Use examples of Roy's diction (Glossary: *Diction*) to support your answer.

VOCABULARY

explicitly (4)	assimilation (9)	influx (10)
chauvinism (5)	inequity (9)	euphorically (11)
exacerbate (5)	exploitation (9)	polarized (11)
implicitly (7)		

WRITING TOPICS

1. Roy argues that the English Only movement is a threat to our culture in much the same way that S. I. Hayakawa argues the threat of bilingualism in his essay. Although the two authors are in complete disagreement, what are some of the similar means each uses to convince the reader? In your opinion which of these means are more effective? Why? Using examples from both articles, write an essay to support your conclusions.

2. Hayakawa and some of the other writers in this section present their point of view in fewer words than Roy. In your opinion what are the disadvantages and the advantages of brevity in this kind of writing? What does Roy's essay include that the others do not? Prepare an outline of Roy's and of another essay in this section to help you in your discussion.

3. The English Only movement has inspired many writers to take sides on this issue. One such writer, Edwin M. Yoder, wrote an essay in 1986 for the *Akron Beacon Journal* titled "The Alarmist Proponents of English." In it Yoder disputes Roy's theory that English Only is an attempt to control the present influx of immigrants. However, he also concedes only one virtue on behalf of English Only proponents: that our present culture is drifting away from the standards of civilization contained in such works as the King James Bible, Shakespeare's plays, Bunyan's *Pilgrim's Progress*, and books of common law brought here by early settlers. "Perhaps if we used the language of Shakespeare and the King James Bible as tenderly as our ancestors did, legal measures to assure its primacy would not be needed. Its appeal to new arrivals would be irresistible," Yoder writes. In a short essay, discuss your reaction to this third point of view.

BLACK CHILDREN, BLACK SPEECH

Dorothy Z. Seymour

*In this essay, linguist and long-time elementary-school
reading teacher Dorothy Seymour discusses an important
question facing present-day educators: On the basis of
available evidence, how does one approach the conflict
between the patterns of a nonstandard dialect, which the
child learns either at home or from other children, and the
equivalent patterns of Standard English? The issue, as you
can well imagine, is highly controversial and emotional.
Seymour first analyzes the distinguishing features of Black
English and then considers the impact of Black English on
schools in America, before making her case for a program of
bidialectism. She believes that teachers and parents need to
be informed about nonstandard language in order to
implement such a program in our nation's schools.*

"Cmon, man, les git goin'!" called the boy to his companion. "Dat   1
bell ringin'. It say, 'Git in rat now!' " He dashed into the school yard.

"Aw, f'get you," replied the other. "Whe' Richuh? Whe' da' muv-   2
vuh? He be goin' to schoo'."

"He in de' now, man!" was the answer as they went through the door.   3

In the classroom they made for their desks and opened their books. The   4
name of the story they tried to read was "Come." It went:

Come, Bill, come
Come with me.
Come and see this.
See what is here.

The first boy poked the second. "Wha' da' wor'?"

"Da' wor' *is,* you dope."   5

"*Is?* Ain't no wor' *is.* You jivin' me? Wha' da' wor' mean?"   6

"Ah dunno. Jus' *is.*"   7

To a speaker of Standard English, this exchange is only vaguely com-   8
prehensible. But it's normal speech for thousands of American children. In

addition it demonstrates one of our biggest educational problems: children whose speech style is so different from the writing style of their books that they have difficulty learning to read. These children speak Black English, a dialect characteristic of many inner-city Negroes. Their books are, of course, written in Standard English. To complicate matters, the speech they use is also socially stigmatized. Middle-class whites and Negroes alike scorn it as low-class poor people's talk.

Teachers sometimes make the situation worse with their attitudes toward Black English. Typically, they view the children's speech as "bad English" characterized by "lazy pronunciation," "poor grammar," and "short, jagged words." One result of this attitude is poor mental health on the part of the pupils. A child is quick to grasp the feeling that while school speech is "good," his own speech is "bad," and that by extension he himself is somehow inadequate and without value. Some children react to this feeling by withdrawing; they stop talking entirely. Others develop the attitude of "F'get you, honky." In either case, the psychological results are devastating and lead straight to the dropout route.

It is hard for most teachers and middle-class Negro parents to accept the idea that Black English is not just "sloppy talk" but a dialect with a form and structure of its own. Even some eminent black educators think of it as "bad English grammar" with "slurred consonants" (Professor Nick Aaron Ford of Morgan State College in Baltimore) and "ghettoese" (Dr. Kenneth B. Clark, the prominent educational psychologist).

Parents of Negro school children generally agree. Two researchers of Columbia University report that the adults they worked with in Harlem almost unanimously preferred that their children be taught Standard English in school.

But there is another point of view, one held in common by black militants and some white liberals. They urge that middle-class Negroes stop thinking of the inner-city dialect as something to be ashamed of and repudiated. Black author Claude Brown, for example, pushes this view.

Some modern linguists take a similar stance. They begin with the premise that no dialect is intrinsically "bad" or "good," and that a nonstandard speech style is not defective speech but different speech. More important, they have been able to show that Black English is far from being a careless way of speaking the Standard; instead, it is a rather rigidly-constructed set of speech patterns, with the same sort of specialization in sounds, structure, and vocabulary as any other dialect.

THE SOUNDS OF BLACK ENGLISH

Middle-class listeners who hear black inner-city speakers say "dis" and "tin" for "this" and "thin" assume that the black speakers are just being careless. Not at all; these differences are characteristic aspects of the dialect. The original cause of such substitutions is generally a carryover from one's original language or that of his immigrant parents. The interference from that carryover probably caused the substitution of /d/ for the voiced *th* sound in *this,* and /t/ for the unvoiced *th* sound in *thin.* (Linguists represent language sounds by putting letters within slashes or brackets.) Most speakers of English don't realize that the two *th* sounds of English are lacking in many other languages and are difficult for most foreigners trying to learn English. Germans who study English, for example, are surprised and confused about these sounds because the only Germans who use them are the ones who lisp. These two sounds are almost nonexistent in the West African languages which most black immigrants brought with them to America.

Similar substitutions used in Black English are /f/, a sound similar to 15 the unvoiced *th,* in medial word-position, as in *birfday* for *birthday,* and in final word-position, as in *roof* for *Ruth* as well as /v/ for the voiced *th* in medial position, as in *bruvver* for *brother.* These sound substitutions are also typical of Gullah, the language of black speakers in the Carolina Sea Island. Some of them are also heard in Caribbean Creole.

Another characteristic of the sounds of Black English is the lack of /l/ 16 at the end of words, sometimes replaced by the sound /w/. This makes words like *tool* sound like *too.* If /l/ occurs in the middle of a Standard English word, in Black English it may be omitted entirely: "I can hep you." This difference is probably caused by the instability and sometimes interchangeability of /l/ and /r/ in West African languages.

One difference that is startling to middle-class speakers is the fact that 17 Black English words appear to leave off some consonant sounds at the end of words. Like Italian, Japanese and West African words, they are more likely to end in vowel sounds. Standard English *boot* is pronounced *boo* in Black English. *What* is *wha. Sure* is *sho. Your* is *yo.* This kind of difference can make for confusion in the classroom. Dr. Kenneth Goodman, a psycholinguist, tells of a black child whose white teacher asked him to use *so* in a sentence—not "sew a dress" but "the other *so."* The sentence the child used was "I got a *so* on my leg."

A related feature of Black English is the tendency in many cases not to 18 use sequences of more than one final consonant sound. For example, *just* is pronounced *jus', past* is *pass, mend* sounds like *men* and *hold* like *hole. Six* and *box* are pronounced *sick* and *bock.* Why should this be? Perhaps because West African languages, like Japanese, have almost no clusters of consonants in their speech. The Japanese, when importing a foreign word, handle a similar problem by inserting vowel sounds between every consonant, making *baseball* sound like *besuboru.* West Africans probably made a simpler change, merely cutting a series of two consonant sounds down to one. Speakers of Gullah, one linguist found, have made the same kind of adaptation of Standard English.

Teachers of black children seldom understand the reason for these [19] differences in final sounds. They are apt to think that careless speech is the cause. Actually, black speakers aren't "leaving off" any sounds; how can you leave off something you never had in the first place?

Differences in vowel sounds are also characteristic of the nonstandard [20] language. Dr. Goodman reports that a black child asked his teacher how to spell rat. "R-a-t," she replied. But the boy responded "No ma'am, I don't mean rat mouse, I mean rat now." In Black English, *right* sounds like *rat.* A likely reason is that in West African languages, there are very few vowel sounds of the type heard in the word *right.* This type is common in English. It is called a glided or dipthongized vowel sound. A glided vowel sound is actually a close combination of two vowels; in the word *right* the two parts of the sound "eye" are actually "ah-ee." West African languages have no such long, two-part, changing vowel sounds; their vowels are generally shorter and more stable. This may be why in Black English, *time* sounds like *Tom, oil* like *all,* and *my* like *ma.*

LANGUAGE STRUCTURE

Black English differs from Standard English not only in its sounds but also [21] in its structure. The way the words are put together does not always fit the description in English grammar books. The method of expressing time, or tense, for example, differs in significant ways.

The verb *to be* is an important one in Standard English. It's used as an [22] auxiliary verb to indicate different tenses. But Black English speakers use it quite differently. Sometimes an inner-city Negro says "He coming"; other times he says "He be coming." These two sentences mean different things. To understand why, let's look at the tenses of West African languages; they correspond with those of Black English.

Many West African languages have a tense which is called the habit- [23] ual. This tense is used to express action which is always occurring and it is formed with a verb that is translated as *be.* "He be coming" means something like "He's always coming," "He usually comes," or "He's been coming."

In Standard English there is no regular grammatical construction for [24] such a tense. Black English speakers, in order to form the habitual tense in English, use the word *be* as an auxiliary: *He be doing it. My Momma be working. He be running.* The habitual tense is not the same as the present tense, which is constructed in Black English without any form of the verb *to be: He do it. My Momma working. He running.* (This means the action is occurring right now.)

There are other tense differences between Black English and Standard   25
English. For example, the nonstandard speech does not use changes in grammar to indicate the past tense. A white person will ask, "What did your brother say?" and the black person will answer, "He say he coming." (The verb *say* is not changed to *said.*) "How did you get here?" "I walk." This style of talking about the past is paralleled in the Yoruba, Fante, Hausa, and Ewe languages of West Africa.

Expression of plurality is another difference. The way a black child will   26
talk of "them boy" or "two dog" makes some white listeners think Negroes don't know how to turn a singular word into a plural word. As a matter of fact, it isn't necessary to use an *s* to express plurality. In Chinese and Japanese, singular and plural are not generally distinguished by such inflections; plurality is conveyed in other ways. For example, in Chinese it's correct to say "There are three book on the table." This sentence already has two signals of the plural, *three* and *are;* why require a third? This same logic is the basis of plurals in most West African languages, where nouns are often identical in the plural and the singular. For example, in Ibo, one correctly says *those man,* and in both Ewe and Yoruba one says *they house.* American speakers of Gullah retain this style; it is correct in Gullah to say *five dog.*

Gender is another aspect of language structure where differences can be   27
found. Speakers of Standard English are often confused to find that the nonstandard vernacular often uses just one gender of pronoun, the masculine, and refers to women as well as men as *he* or *him.* "He a nice girl," even "Him a nice girl" are common. This usage probably stems from West African origins, too, as does the use of multiple negatives, such as "Nobody don't know it."

Vocabulary is the third aspect of a person's native speech that could   28
affect his learning of a new language. The strikingly different vocabulary often used in Negro Nonstandard English is probably the most obvious aspect of it to a casual white observer. But its vocabulary differences don't obscure its meaning the way different sounds and different structure often do.

Recently there has been much interest in the African origins of words   29
like *goober* (peanut), *cooter* (turtle), and *tote* (carry), as well as others that are less certainly African, such as *to dig* (possibly from the Wolof *degan,* "to understand"). Such expressions seem colorful rather than low-class to many whites; they become assimilated faster than their black originators do. English professors now use *dig* in their scholarly articles, and current advertising has enthusiastically adopted *rap.*

Is it really possible for old differences in sound, structure, and vocab-   30 ulary to persist from the West African languages of slave days into present-day inner city Black English? Easily. Nothing else really explains such regularity of language habits, most of which persist among black people in various parts of the Western Hemisphere. For a long time scholars believed that certain speech forms used by Negroes were merely leftovers from archaic English preserved in the speech of early English settlers in America and copied by their slaves. But this theory has been greatly weakened, largely as the result of the work of a black linguist, Dr. Lorenzo Dow Turner of the University of Chicago. Dr. Turner studied the speech of Gullah Negroes in the Sea Islands off the Carolina coast and found so many traces of West African languages that he thoroughly discredited the archaic-English theory.

When anyone learns a new language, it's usual to try speaking the new   31
language with the sounds and structure of the old. If a person's first language does not happen to have a particular sound needed in the language he is learning, he will tend to substitute a similar or related sound from his native language and use it to speak the new one. When Frenchman Charles Boyer said "Zees ees my heart," and when Latin American Carmen Miranda sang "Souse American way," they were simply using sounds of their native languages in trying to pronounce sounds of English. West Africans must have done the same thing when they first attempted English words. The tendency to retain the structure of the native language is a strong one, too. That's why a German learning English is likely to put his verb at the end: "May I a glass beer have?" The vocabulary of one's original language may also furnish some holdovers. Jewish immigrants did not stop using the word *bagel* when they came to America; nor did Germans stop saying *sauerkraut*.

Social and geographical isolation reinforces the tendencies to retain old   32
language habits. When one group is considered inferior, the other group avoids it. For many years it was illegal to give any sort of instruction to Negroes, and for slaves to try to speak like their masters would have been unthinkable. Conflict of value systems doubtless retards changes, too. As Frantz Fanon observed in *Black Skin, White Masks,* those who take on white speech habits are suspect in the ghetto, because others believe they are trying to "act white." Dr. Kenneth Johnson, a black linguist, put it this way: "As long as disadvantaged black children live in segregated communities and most of their relationships are confined to those within their own subculture, they will not replace their functional nonstandard dialect with the nonfunctional standard dialect."

Linguists have made it clear that language systems that are different are   33
not necessarily deficient. A judgment of deficiency can be made only in comparison with another language system. Let's turn the tables on Standard English for a moment and look at it from the West African point of

view. From this angle, Standard English: (1) is lacking in certain language sounds, (2) has a couple of unnecessary language sounds for which others may serve as good substitutes, (3) doubles and drawls some of its vowel sounds in sequences that are unusual and difficult to imitate, (4) lacks a method of forming an important tense, (5) requires an unnecessary number of ways to indicate tense, plurality and gender, and (6) doesn't mark negatives sufficiently for the result to be a good strong negative statement.

Now whose language is deficient?   34

How would the adoption of this point of view help us? Say we accepted   35
the evidence that Black English is not just a sloppy Standard but an organized language style which probably has developed many of its features on the basis of its West African heritage. What would we gain?

The psychological climate of the classroom might improve if teachers   36
understood why many black students speak as they do. But we still have not reached a solution of the main problem. Does the discovery that Black English has pattern and structure mean that it should not be tampered with? Should children who speak Black English be excused from learning the Standard in school? Should they perhaps be given books in Black English to learn from?

Any such accommodation would surely result in a hardening of the new   37
separatism being urged by some black militants. It would probably be applauded by such people as Roy Innis, Director of C.O.R.E., who is currently recommending dual autonomous education systems for white and black. And it might facilitate learning to read, since some experiments have indicated that materials written in Black English syntax aid problem readers from the inner city.

But determined resistance to the introduction of such printed materials   38
into schools can be expected. To those who view inner-city speech as bad English, the appearance in print of sentences like "My mama, he work" can be as shocking and repellent as a four-letter word. Middle-class Negro parents would probably mobilize against the move. Any stratagem that does not take into account such practicalities of the matter is probably doomed to failure. And besides, where would such a permissive policy on language get these children in the larger society, and in the long run? If they want to enter an integrated America they must be able to deal with it on its own terms. Even Professor Toni Cade of Rutgers, who doesn't want "ghetto accents" tampered with, advocates mastery of Standard English because, as she puts it, "if you want to get ahead in this country, you must master the language of the ruling class." This has always been true, wherever there has been a minority group.

The problem then appears to be one of giving these children the ability   39
to speak (and read) Standard English without denigrating the vernacular and those who use it, or even affecting the ability to use it. The only way

to do this is to officially espouse bidialectism. The result would be the ability to use either dialect equally well—as Dr. Martin Luther King did—depending on the time, place, and circumstances. Pupils would have to learn enough about Standard English to use it when necessary, and teachers would have to learn enough about the inner-city dialect to understand and accept it for what it is—not just a "careless" version of Standard English but a different form of English that's appropriate in certain times and places.

Can we accomplish this? If we can't, the result will be continued 40 alienation of a large section of the population, continued dropout trouble with consequent loss of earning power and economic contribution to the nation, but most of all, loss of faith in America as a place where a minority people can at times continue to use those habits that remind them of their link with each other and with their past.

QUESTIONS ON CONTENT

1. How does Seymour define Black English?

2. What characteristics of Black English establish it as a distinct dialect rather than as improper usage of Standard English? How does Seymour account for the differences between Black English and Standard English?

3. Why does Seymour believe that Black children need facility with Standard English as well?

4. What distinction does Seymour make between a person's language being "different" and its being "defective"? In what ways is this distinction important to her argument?

5. In what ways, according to Seymour, is Standard English "deficient" when looked at from the West African point of view?

6. Why does Seymour advocate a program of bidialectism? What does she believe such a program will require of teachers, parents, and students?

QUESTIONS ON RHETORIC

1. What is Seymour's purpose in this essay? Does she seem to be more interested in explaining the issues to her readers or in persuading them to her point of view? (Glossary: *Purpose*) Do you think that she accomplishes her purpose? Why, or why not?

2. In what ways do the first seven paragraphs form an appropriate introduction for Seymour's essay? (Glossary: *Beginnings*)

3. Seymour presents her argument inductively; that is, she first introduces the problem, then examines and analyzes the evidence, and finally draws

a conclusion based on her considered analysis. Is this organization effective given the nature of her topic? Could she have, for example, introduced her solution early in the essay? Why, or why not?

4. Seymour frequently cites authorities to strengthen her argument. What exactly is gained with each of these citations?

5. Seymour's essay includes a great deal of technical linguistic information about the sounds, structure, and vocabulary of Black English. Did you have any difficulties understanding her descriptions and explanations? Has Seymour done anything to accommodate readers without a linguistics background? If so, what? (Glossary: *Technical Language*)

6. How would you characterize Seymour's tone in this essay? (Glossary: *Tone*) Did you find it appropriate for her argument? Why, or why not?

7. Do you think paragraph 34 could be joined to paragraph 33? Why do you suppose Seymour chooses to make a separate, one-sentence paragraph?

8. In paragraphs 34–36 Seymour presents a series of questions. How do these questions function in the context of the essay? (Glossary: *Rhetorical Questions*)

VOCABULARY

stigmatized (8)	intrinsically (13)	stratagem (38)
devastating (9)	assimilated (29)	denigrating (39)
eminent (10)	autonomous (37)	vernacular (39)
repudiated (12)		

WRITING TOPICS

1. According to Seymour, linguists believe that when children become ashamed of their language, they become ashamed of themselves. Write an essay in which you first discuss how your attitude toward other people is affected by the way they speak. Second, discuss the nature of the relationship between one's use of language and one's feelings of self-worth. Be sure to describe any specific experiences that have made these relationships clear for you.

2. How important do you believe it is for individuals to understand the characteristics of nonstandard dialects like Black English? Write an essay in which you evaluate the possible advantages for individuals and for American society as a whole.

3. Many critics of bidialectism argue that while materials written in Black English syntax may facilitate learning for many inner-city children, they also make these children dependent on a dialect that excludes them from full participation in the American way of life. Where do you stand on the issue of bidialectism? Cite reasons to support your position.

WHAT'S WRONG WITH BLACK ENGLISH

Rachel L. Jones

*Rachel L. Jones was a sophomore at Southern Illinois
University when she published the following essay in*
Newsweek *in December 1982. Jones argues against a belief
she perceives in some of her fellow black students and black
authorities that "talking white" is a betrayal of her racial
heritage.*

W illiam Labov, a noted linguist, once said about the use of black   1
English, "It is the goal of most black Americans to acquire full control of
the standard language without giving up their own culture." He also suggested that there are certain advantages to having two ways to express
one's feelings. I wonder if the good doctor might also consider the goals
of those black Americans who have full control of standard English but
who are every now and then troubled by that colorful, grammar-to-the-
winds patois that is black English. Case in point—me.

I'm a 21-year-old black born to a family that would probably be con-   2
sidered lower-middle class—which in my mind is a polite way of describing a condition only slightly better than poverty. Let's just say we rarely if
ever did the winter-vacation thing in the Caribbean. I've often had to
defend my humble beginnings to a most unlikely group of people for an
even less likely reason. Because of the way I talk, some of my black peers
look at me sideways and ask, "Why do you talk like you're white?"

The first time it happened to me I was nine years old. Cornered in the   3
school bathroom by the class bully and her sidekick, I was offered the
opportunity to swallow a few of my teeth unless I satisfactorily explained
why I always got good grades, why I talked "proper" or "white." I had
no ready answer for her, save the fact that my mother had from the time I
was old enough to talk stressed the importance of reading and learning, or
that L. Frank Baum and Ray Bradbury were my closest companions. I read
all my older brothers' and sisters' literature textbooks more faithfully than
they did, and even lightweights like the Bobbsey Twins and Trixie Belden
were allowed into my bookish inner circle. I don't remember exactly what
I told those girls, but I somehow talked my way out of a beating.

I was reminded once again of my "white pipes" problem while apart- 4
ment hunting in Evanston, Ill., last winter. I doggedly made out lists of
available places and called all around. I would immediately be invited
over—and immediately be turned down. The thinly concealed looks of
shock when the front door opened clued me in, along with the flustered
instances of "just getting off the phone with the girl who was ahead of you
and she wants the rooms." When I finally found a place to live, my
roommate stirred up old memories when she remarked a few months later,
"You know, I was surprised when I first saw you. You sounded white over
the phone." Tell me another one, sister.

I should've asked her a question I've wanted an answer to for years: 5
how does one "talk white"? The silly side of me pictures a rabid white
foam spewing forth when I speak. I don't use Valley Girl jargon, so that's
not what's meant in my case. Actually, I've pretty much deduced what
people mean when they say that to me, and the implications are really
frightening.

It means that I'm articulate and well versed. It means that I can talk as 6
freely about John Steinbeck as I can about Rick James. It means that
"ain't" and "he be" are not staples of my vocabulary and are only used
around family and friends. (It is almost Jekyll and Hyde-ish the way I can
slip out of academic abstractions into a long, lean, double-negative-filled
dialogue, but I've come to terms with that aspect of my personality.) As a
child, I found it hard to believe that's what people meant by "talking
proper"; that would've meant that good grades and standard English were
equated with white skin, and that went against everything I'd ever been
taught. Running into the same type of mentality as an adult has confirmed
the depressing reality that for many blacks, standard English is not only
unfamiliar, it is socially unacceptable.

James Baldwin once defended black English by saying it had added 7
"vitality to the language," and even went so far as to label it a language
in its own right, saying, "Language [i.e., black English] is a political
instrument" and a "vivid and crucial key to identity." But did Malcolm X
urge blacks to take power in this country "any way y'll can"? Did Martin
Luther King Jr. say to blacks, "I has been to the mountaintop, and I done
seed the Promised Land"? Toni Morrison, Alice Walker and James Baldwin did not achieve their eloquence, grace and stature by using only black
English in their writing. Andrew Young, Tom Bradley and Barbara Jordan
did not acquire political power by saying, "Y'all crazy if you ain't gon
vote for me." They all have full command of standard English, and I don't
think that knowledge takes away from their blackness or commitment to
black people.

I know from experience that it's important for black people, stripped of 8
culture and heritage, to have something they can point to and say, "This

is ours, *we* can comprehend it, *we* alone can speak it with a soulful flourish.'' I'd be lying if I said that the rhythms of my people caught up in ''some serious rap'' don't sound natural and right to me sometimes. But how heartwarming is it for those same brothers when they hit the pavement searching for employment? Studies have proven that the use of ethnic dialects decreases power in the marketplace. ''I be'' is acceptable on the corner, but not with the boss.

Am I letting capitalistic, European-oriented thinking fog the issue? Am   9 I selling out blacks to an ideal of assimilating, being as much like white as possible? I have not formed a personal political ideology, but I do know this: it hurts me to hear black children use black English, knowing that they will be at yet another disadvantage in an educational system already full of stumbling blocks. It hurts me to sit in lecture halls and hear fellow black students complain that the professor ''be tripping dem out using big words dey can't understand.'' And what hurts most is to be stripped of my own blackness simply because I know my way around the English language.

I would have to disagree with Labov in one respect. My goal is not so   10 much to acquire full control of both standard and black English, but to one day see more black people less dependent on a dialect that excludes them from full participation in the world we live in. I don't think I talk white, I think I talk right.

QUESTIONS ON CONTENT

1. When did Jones first realize that she ''talked white''?

2. After years of reflection, Jones figured out what people meant by the expression ''talk white.'' What ''frightening implications'' did these words hold for her? What is the ''depressing reality'' they confirmed?

3. Jones insists that talking white does not detract from her blackness. What kind of arguments does she use to persuade her readers? Which of her arguments do you find most convincing?

4. What is black English? Where does Jones define the term?

5. Jones names five major concerns she has for blacks who refuse to learn standard English. What are they and where are they stated? Can you think of any other concerns?

QUESTIONS ON RHETORIC

1. Jones begins her essay with a quote from a noted linguist. How does his point of view set the tone for Jones's essay? What is that tone? Give examples of Jones' diction to support your answer (Glossary: *Diction*).

2. Jones relies on a liberal use of examples to illustrate her main point.

Choose several passages that show the variety of ways in which Jones uses examples and discuss how these examples help persuade her readers.

3. Jones says talking white means being "articulate and well versed." Is Jones herself articulate and well versed? Give examples of Jones's diction and presentation to support your answer.

4. Jones concludes with a reference to the quote she used in the beginning of her essay. What purpose does this reiteration serve? Is it effective? Explain your answer.

VOCABULARY

linguist (1)	deduced (5)	staples (6)
patois (1)	articulate (6)	dialect (10)
doggedly (4)		

WRITING TOPICS

1. On many college campuses across the country, students are demanding inclusion of a black studies program in the curriculum. How are black issues being dealt with on your campus? What are some of the arguments students make for including black history in the school curriculum? What are some of the arguments against it? Are there plans to include black history in your school's curriculum? How do you feel about it? In light of what you have read in this section, write an essay exploring the issue.

2. Rachel Jones was just a sophomore in college when she wrote this essay, yet her writing and the expression of her ideas show remarkable sophistication and care. Reread Jones's essay with an eye to what her writing style says about her personality; then write an essay showing how Jones might argue that these qualities should be taken for granted in any definition of blackness.

CAUGHT BETWEEN TWO LANGUAGES

Richard Rodriguez

Speaking and writing English well are difficult enough for those brought up in the language; for those who were not, they can be complicated and even wounding experiences. Like millions of Americans, Richard Rodriguez learned English as a second language. He was born in 1944 in San Francisco, but his parents were from Mexico, and Spanish was the language spoken at home. As a child Rodriguez had a painful struggle to master what he calls his "public" language. In the following essay from Hunger of Memory, *Rodriguez relates the hardships and confusion of growing up in a world divided by two languages in order to argue forcefully against bilingual education in America.*

I remember to start with that day in Sacramento—a California now   1
nearly thirty years past—when I first entered a classroom, able to understand some fifty stray English words.

The third of four children, I had been preceded to a neighborhood   2
Roman Catholic school by an older brother and sister. But neither of them had revealed very much about their classroom experiences. Each afternoon they returned, as they left in the morning, always together, speaking in Spanish as they climbed the five steps of the porch. And their mysterious books, wrapped in shopping-bag paper, remained on the table next to the door, closed firmly behind them.

An accident of geography sent me to a school where all my classmates   3
were white, many the children of doctors and lawyers and business executives. All my classmates certainly must have been uneasy on that first day of school—as most children are uneasy—to find themselves apart from their families in the first institution of their lives. But I was astonished.

The nun said, in a friendly but oddly impersonal voice, "Boys and   4
girls, this is Richard Rodriguez." (I heard her sound out: *Rich-heard Road-ree-guess.*) It was the first time I had heard anyone name me in English. "Richard," the nun repeated more slowly, writing my name down in her black leather book. Quickly I turned to see my mother's face dissolve in a watery blur behind the pebbled glass door.

Many years later there is something called bilingual education—a   5
scheme proposed in the late 1960s by Hispanic-American social activists,
later endorsed by congressional vote. It is a program that seeks to permit
non-English-speaking children, many from lower-class homes, to use their
family language as the language of school. (Such is the goal its supporters
announce.) I hear them and am forced to say no: It is not possible for a
child—any child—ever to use his family's language in school. Not to
understand this is to misunderstand the public uses of schooling and to
trivialize the nature of intimate life—a family's "language."

Memory teaches me what I know of these matters; the boy reminds the   6
adult. I was a bilingual child, a certain kind—socially disadvantaged—the
son of working-class parents, both Mexican immigrants.

In the early years of my boyhood, my parents coped very well in   7
America. My father had steady work. My mother managed at home. They
were nobody's victims. Optimism and ambition led them to a house (our
home) many blocks from the Mexican south side of town. We lived among
gringos and only a block from the biggest, whitest houses. It never occurred to my parents that they couldn't live wherever they chose. Nor was
the Sacramento of the fifties bent on teaching them a contrary lesson. My
mother and father were more annoyed than intimidated by those two or
three neighbors who tried initially to make us unwelcome. ("Keep your
brats away from my sidewalk!") But despite all they achieved, perhaps
because they had so much to achieve, any deep feeling of ease, the confidence of "belonging" in public was withheld from them both. They
regarded the people at work, the faces in crowds, as very distant from us.
They were the others, *los gringos*. That term was interchangeable in their
speech with another, even more telling, *los americanos*.

I grew up in a house where the only regular guests were my relations.   8
For one day, enormous families of relatives would visit and there would be
so many people that the noise and the bodies would spill out to the back-
yard and front porch. Then, for weeks, no one came by. (It was usually a
salesman who rang the doorbell.) Our house stood apart. A gaudy yellow
in a row of white bungalows. We were the people with the noisy dog. The
people who raised pigeons and chickens. We were the foreigners on the
block. A few neighbors smiled and waved. We waved back. But no one in
the family knew the names of the old couple who lived next door; until I
was seven years old, I did not know the names of the kids who lived across
the street.

In public, my father and mother spoke a hesitant, accented, not always   9
grammatical English. And they would have to strain—their bodies tense—
to catch the sense of what was rapidly said by *los gringos*. At home they
spoke Spanish. The language of their Mexican past sounded in counterpoint to the English of public society. The words would come quickly,

with ease. Conveyed through those sounds was the pleasing, soothing, consoling reminder of being at home.

During those years when I was first conscious of hearing, my mother and father addressed me only in Spanish; in Spanish I learned to reply. By contrast, English (inglés), rarely heard in the house, was the language I came to associate with *gringos*. I learned my first words of English overhearing my parents speak to strangers. At five years of age, I knew just enough English for my mother to trust me on errands to stores one block away. No more.

I was a listening child, careful to hear the very different sounds of Spanish and English. Wide-eyed with hearing, I'd listen to sounds more than words. First, there were English (*gringo*) sounds. So many words were still unknown that when the butcher or the lady at the drugstore said something to me, exotic polysyllabic sounds would bloom in the midst of their sentences. Often, the speech of people in public seemed to me very loud, booming with confidence. The man behind the counter would literally ask, "What can I do for you!" But by being so firm and so clear, the sound of his voice said that he was a *gringo;* he belonged in public society.

I would also hear then the high nasal notes of middle-class American speech. The air stirred with sound. Sometimes, even now, when I have been traveling abroad for several weeks, I will hear what I heard as a boy. In hotel lobbies or airports, in Turkey or Brazil, some Americans will pass, and suddenly I will hear it again—the high sound of American voices. For a few seconds I will hear it with pleasure, for it is now the sound of *my* society—a reminder of home. But inevitably—already on the flight headed for home—the sound fades with repetition. I will be unable to hear it anymore.

When I was a boy, things were different. The accent of *los gringos* was never pleasing nor was it hard to hear. Crowds at Safeway or at bus stops would be noisy with sound. And I would be forced to edge away from the chirping chatter above me.

I was unable to hear my own sounds, but I knew very well that I spoke English poorly. My words could not stretch far enough to form complete thoughts. And the words I did speak I didn't know well enough to make into distinct sounds. (Listeners would usually lower their heads, better to hear what I was trying to say.) But it was one thing for *me* to speak English with difficulty. It was more troubling for me to hear my parents speak in public; their high-whining vowels and guttural consonants; their sentences that got stuck with "eh" and "ah" sounds; the confused syntax; the hesitant rhythm of sounds so different from the way *gringos* spoke. I'd notice, moreover, that my parents' voices were softer than those of *gringos* we'd meet.

I am tempted now to say that none of this mattered. In adulthood I am

10

11

12

13

14

15

embarrassed by childhood fears. And, in a way, it didn't matter very much that my parents could not speak English with ease. Their linguistic difficulties had no serious consequences. My mother and father made themselves understood at the county hospital clinic and at government offices. And yet, in another way, it mattered very much—it was unsettling to hear my parents struggle with English. Hearing them, I'd grow nervous, my clutching trust in their protection and power weakened.

There were many times like the night at a brightly lit gasoline station (a blaring white memory) when I stood uneasily, hearing my father. He was talking to a teenaged attendant. I do not recall what they were saying, but I cannot forget the sounds my father made as he spoke. At one point his words slid together to form one word—sounds as confused as the threads of blue and green oil in the puddle next to my shoes. His voice rushed through what he had left to say. And, toward the end, reached falsetto notes, appealing to his listener's understanding. I looked away to the lights of passing automobiles. I tried not to hear anymore. But I heard only too well the calm, easy tones in the attendant's reply. Shortly afterward, walking toward home with my father, I shivered when he put his hand on my shoulder. The very first chance that I got, I evaded his grasp and ran on ahead into the dark, skipping with feigned boyish exuberance. 16

But then there was Spanish. *Español:* my family's language. *Español:* the language that seemed to me a private language. I'd hear strangers on the radio and in the Mexican Catholic church across town speaking in Spanish, but I couldn't really believe that Spanish was a public language, like English. Spanish speakers, rather, seemed related to me, for I sensed that we shared—through our language—the experience of feeling apart from *los gringos*. It was thus a ghetto Spanish that I heard and I spoke. Like those whose lives are bound by a barrio, I was reminded by Spanish of my separateness from *los otros, los gringos* in power. But more intensely than for most barrio children—because I did not live in a barrio— Spanish seemed to me the language of home. (Most days it was only at home that I'd hear it.) It became the language of joyful return. 17

A family member would say something to me and I would feel myself specially recognized. My parents would say something to me and I would feel embraced by the sounds of their words. Those sounds said: *I am speaking with ease in Spanish. I am addressing you in words I never use with* los gringos. *I recognize you as someone special, close, like no one outside. You belong with us. In the family.* 18

(Ricardo.) 19

At the age of five, six, well past the time when most other children no longer easily notice the difference between sounds uttered at home and words spoken in public, I had a different experience. I lived in a world magically compounded of sounds. I remained a child longer than most; I 20 lingered too long, poised at the edge of language—often frightened by the sounds of *los gringos,* delighted by the sounds of Spanish at home. I shared with my family a language that was startlingly different from that used in the great city around us.

For me there were none of the gradations between public and private   21
society so normal to a maturing child. Outside the house was public society; inside the house was private. Just opening or closing the screen door
behind me was an important experience. I'd rarely leave home all alone or
without reluctance. Walking down the sidewalk, under the canopy of tall
trees, I'd warily notice the—suddenly—silent neighborhood kids who
stood warily watching me. Nervously, I'd arrive at the grocery store to
hear there the sounds of the *gringo*—foreign to me—reminding me that in
this world so big, I was a foreigner. But then I'd return. Walking back
toward our house, climbing the steps from the sidewalk, when the front
door was open in summer, I'd hear voices beyond the screen door talking
in Spanish. For a second or two, I'd stay, linger there, listening. Smiling,
I'd hear my mother call out, saying in Spanish (words): "Is that you,
Richard?" All the while her sounds would assure me: *You are home now;*
come closer; inside. With us.

"*Sì,*" I'd reply.   22

Once more inside the house I would resume (assume) my place in the   23
family. The sounds would dim, grow harder to hear. Once more at home,
I would grow less aware of that fact. It required, however, no more than
the blurt of the doorbell to alert me to listen to sounds all over again. The
house would turn instantly still while my mother went to the door. I'd hear
her hard English sounds. I'd wait to hear her voice return to soft-sounding
Spanish, which assured me, as surely as did the clicking tongue of the lock
on the door, that the stranger was gone.

Plainly, it is not healthy to hear such sounds so often. It is not healthy   24
to distinguish public words from private sounds so easily. I remained
cloistered by sounds, timid and shy in public, too dependent on voices at
home. And yet it needs to be emphasized: I was an extremely happy child
at home. I remember many nights when my father would come back from
work, and I'd hear him call out to my mother in Spanish, sounding re-
lieved. In Spanish, he'd sound light and free notes he never could manage
in English. Some nights I'd jump up just at hearing his voice. With *mis*
hermanos I would come running into the room where he was with my
mother. Our laughing (so deep was the pleasure!) became screaming. Like
others who know the pain of public alienation, we transformed the knowledge of our public separateness and made it consoling—the reminder of
intimacy. Excited, we joined our voices in a celebration of sounds. *We are*
speaking now the way we never speak out in public. We are alone—
together, voices sounded, surrounded to tell me. Some nights, no one

seemed willing to loosen the hold sounds had on us. At dinner, we invented new words. (Ours sounded Spanish, but made sense only to us.) We pieced together new words by taking, say, an English verb and giving it Spanish endings. My mother's instructions at bedtime would be lacquered with mock-urgent tones. Or a word like *sí* would become, in several notes, able to convey added measures of feeling. Tongues explored the edges of words, especially the fat vowels. And we happily sounded that military drum roll, the twirling roar of the Spanish *r*. Family language: my family's sounds. The voices of my parents and sisters and brother. Their voices insisting: *You belong here. We are family members. Related. Special to one another. Listen!* Voices singing and sighing, rising, straining, then surging, teeming with pleasure that burst syllables into fragments of laughter. At times it seemed there was steady quiet only when, from another room, the rustling whispers of my parents faded and I moved closer to sleep.

Supporters of bilingual education today imply that students like me 25 miss a great deal by not being taught in their family's language. What they seem not to recognize is that, as a socially disadvantaged child, I consider Spanish to be a private language. What I needed to learn in school was that I had the right—and the obligation—to speak the public language of *los gringos*. The odd truth is that my first-grade classmates could have become bilingual, in the conventional sense of that word, more easily than I. Had they been taught (as upper-middle-class children are often taught early) a second language like Spanish or French, they could have regarded it simply as that: another public language. In my case such bilingualism could not have been so quickly achieved. What I did not believe was that I could speak a single public language.

Without question, it would have pleased me to hear my teachers ad- 26 dress me in Spanish when I entered the classroom. I would have felt much less afraid. I would have trusted them and responded with ease. But I would have delayed—for how long postponed?—having to learn the language of public society. I would have evaded—and for how long could I have afforded to delay?—learning the great lesson of school, that I had a public identity.

Fortunately, my teachers were unsentimental about their responsibility. 27 What they understood was that I needed to speak a public language. So their voices would search me out, asking me questions. Each time I'd hear them, I'd look up in surprise to see a nun's face frowning at me. I'd mumble, not really meaning to answer. The nun would persist, "Richard, stand up. Don't look at the floor. Speak up. Speak to the entire class, not just to me!" But I couldn't believe that the English language was mine to use. (In part, I did not want to believe it.) I continued to mumble. I resisted the teacher's demands. (Did I somehow expect that once I learned the public language my pleasing family life would be changed?) Silent, waiting for the bell to sound, I remained dazed, diffident, afraid.

Because I wrongly imagined that English was intrinsically a public language and Spanish an intrinsically private one, I easily noted the difference between classroom language and the language of home. At school, words were directed to a general audience of listeners. (''Boys and girls.'') Words were meaningfully ordered. And the point was not self-expression alone but to make oneself understood by many others. The teacher quizzed: ''Boys and girls, why do we use that word in this sentence? Could we think of a better word to use there? Would the sentence change its meaning if the words were differently arranged? And wasn't there a better way of saying much the same thing?'' (I couldn't say. I wouldn't try to say.)

Three months. Five. Half a year passed. Unsmiling, ever watchful, my teachers noted my silence. They began to connect my behavior with the difficult progress my older sister and brother were making. Until one Saturday morning three nuns arrived at the house to talk to our parents. Stiffly, they sat on the blue living room sofa. From the doorway of another room, spying the visitors, I noted the incongruity—the clash of two worlds, the faces and voices of school intruding upon the familiar setting of home. I overheard one voice gently wondering. ''Do your children speak only Spanish at home, Mrs. Rodriguez?'' While another voice added, ''That Richard especially seems so timid and shy.''

That Rich-heard!

With great tact the visitors continued, ''Is it possible for you and your husband to encourage your children to practice their English when they are at home?'' Of course, my parents complied. What would they not do for their children's well-being? And how could they have questioned the Church's authority which those women represented? In an instant, they agreed to give up the language (the sounds) that had revealed and accentuated our family's closeness. The moment after the visitors left, the change was observed. *''Ahora,* speak to us *en inglés,''* my father and mother united to tell us.

At first, it seemed a kind of game. After dinner each night, the family gathered to practice ''our'' English. (It was still then *inglés,* a language foreign to us, so we felt drawn as strangers to it.) Laughing, we would try to define words we could not pronounce. We played with strange English sounds, often over-anglicizing our pronunciations. And we filled the smiling gaps of our sentences with familiar Spanish sounds. But that was cheating, somebody shouted. Everyone laughed. In school, meanwhile, like my brother and sister, I was required to attend a daily tutoring session. I needed a full year of special attention. I also needed my teachers to keep my attention from straying in class by calling out, *Rich-heard*—their English voices slowly prying loose my ties to my other name, its three notes,

28
29
30
31
32

Ri-car-do. Most of all I needed to hear my mother and father speak to me in a moment of seriousness in broken—suddenly heartbreaking—English. The scene was inevitable: One Saturday morning I entered the kitchen where my parents were talking in Spanish. I did not realize that they were talking in Spanish however until, at the moment they saw me, I heard their voices change to speak English. Those *gringo* sounds they uttered startled me. Pushed me away. In that moment of trivial misunderstanding and profound insight, I felt my throat twisted by unsounded grief. I turned quickly and left the room. But I had no place to escape to with Spanish. (The spell was broken.) My brother and sisters were speaking English in another part of the house.

Again and again in the days following, increasingly angry, I was   33
obliged to hear my mother and father: "Speak to us *en inglés.*" (*Speak.*)
Only then did I determine to learn classroom English. Weeks after, it happened: one day in school I raised my hand to volunteer an answer. I spoke out in a loud voice. And I did not think it remarkable when the entire class understood. That day, I moved very far from the disadvantaged child I had been only days earlier. The belief, the calming assurance that I belonged in public, had at last taken hold.

QUESTIONS ON CONTENT

1. What does Richard Rodriguez remember about his first day at school? Why was this experience particularly memorable?

2. What, according to Rodriguez, is the stated goal of the supporters of bilingual education? Why is Rodriguez opposed to such a program?

3. Rodriguez distinguishes between "public language" and "private language." What differences does he see?

4. What, did Rodriguez, feel when he heard his parents trying to speak English in public? What difficulties did Rodriguez himself have while trying to learn English? How did his attitude toward the sounds of *los gringos* change over time?

5. What, for Rodriguez, was "the great lesson of school" (26)?

6. What changes occurred in the Rodriguez household after the three nuns from the Catholic school visited one Saturday morning? Why did they want to know what language was spoken in the home?

7. What does Rodriguez mean when he says, "The odd truth is that my first-grade classmates could have become bilingual, in the conventional sense of the word, more easily than I" (25)?

QUESTIONS ON RHETORIC

1. Why is Rodriguez particularly suited to speak on the question of bilingual education?

2. Rodriguez uses a highly personal narrative of his childhood to develop his argument against bilingual education. Did you find this strategy to be effective? Why, or why not?

3. What is the function of the first four paragraphs? How are they related to the essay as a whole?

4. Throughout the essay Rodriguez juxtaposes Spanish words (*los gringos, Ricardo, inglés*) with their English equivalents (the others, Richard, English). How does this device help him establish the separate worlds of his private language and the public language of society in general? How does he use it to show what changes take place as he grows older?

5. In paragraph 23 Rodriguez says, "Once more inside the house I would resume (assume) my place in the family." What does his use of the words "resume" and "assume" reveal about his struggle?

VOCABULARY

endorsed (5)	counterpoint (9)	canopy (21)
intimidated (7)	nasal (12)	diffident (27)
gaudy (8)	barrio (17)	

WRITING TOPICS

1. Think back to your early experiences with language. Did you have problems learning English? What were they? Do you find that you now have greater facility with language? How do you account for any changes?

2. Discuss your own experience learning a foreign language. What are the greatest stumbling blocks, and what are the most effective ways of overcoming them? Were your difficulties at all like those of Rodriguez?

3. Even though we may not have a second language spoken in the home like the Rodriguez family, we are all aware of the differences between the way we talk and write in public or at school and the way we talk at home or among close friends. Write an essay in which you analyze these differences and attempt to explain the reasons for them.

WRITING ASSIGNMENTS FOR "AMERICAN ENGLISH TODAY"

1. Write an essay in which you compare and contrast the view of the state of American English held by Edwin Newman with that of Harvey Daniels.

2. The concept of "Standard English" has caused much misunderstanding and debate. For many Americans, "standard" implies that one variety of English is more correct or more functional than other varieties. Write an essay in which you attempt to define "Standard English" and explain its power or mystique.

3. Bidialectism and bilingualism are highly controversial subjects. Pick one and then prepare a report that (a) presents the opposing views objectively, or (b) supports one particular view over the other. What sociologic and economic factors are important? What issues do not seem to be relevant? From an educational point of view, which argument do you think is strongest? Defend whatever position you take.

4. Each of the following items is normally discussed as a question of usage by usage guides and dictionaries. Consult three or four usage guides in the reference room of your library for information about each item. What advice does each guide offer? How does the advice given by one guide compare with that given by another? What conclusions can you draw about the usefulness of such usage guides?

   a. hopefully
   b. nauseous
   c. imply/infer
   d. contact (as a verb)
   e. ain't
   f. among/between
   g. enthuse
   h. irregardless
   i. lay/lie
   j. uninterested/disinterested

5. In her essay "Black Children, Black Speech," Dorothy Z. Seymour suggests that black children shouldn't have to choose between "black" and "white" English. Instead, she believes a way must be found for these children to learn to speak the basics of Standard English without compromising the vernacular. One solution to the problem, Seymour suggests, is the official adoption of bidialectism. In her words, "The result would be

the ability to use either dialect equally well . . . depending on the time, place, and circumstances.'' With this in mind, reread Jones's essay and in a short paper of your own discuss how you think Jones would react to Seymour's proposition. Give examples from both essays to support your position.

PART III

The Language of Politics and Propaganda

Now, you probably remember the old term "bomb"...

POLITICS AND THE ENGLISH LANGUAGE

George Orwell

An essay usually becomes a classic because it makes an important statement about a subject with unusual effectiveness. Such is the case with this essay, written in the 1940s. Here George Orwell (1903–1950), author of 1984, *discusses the condition of the English language and the ways in which he believes it has seriously deteriorated. He attributes this decline to political and economic causes. Orwell concludes by suggesting a number of remedies to help restore the language to a healthier state.*

Most people who bother with the matter at all would admit that the English language is in a bad way, but it is generally assumed that we cannot by conscious action do anything about it. Our civilization is decadent and our language—so the argument runs—must inevitably share in the general collapse. It follows that any struggle against the abuse of language is a sentimental archaism, like preferring candles to electric light or hansom cabs to aeroplanes. Underneath this lies the half-conscious belief that language is a natural growth and not an instrument which we shape for our own purposes.

Now, it is clear that the decline of a language must ultimately have political and economic causes: it is not due simply to the bad influence of this or that individual writer. But an effect can become a cause, reinforcing the original cause and producing the same effect in an intensified form, and so on indefinitely. A man may take to drink because he feels himself to be a failure, and then fail all the more completely because he drinks. It is rather the same thing that is happening to the English language. It becomes ugly and inaccurate because our thoughts are foolish, but the slovenliness of our language makes it easier for us to have foolish thoughts. The point is that the process is reversible. Modern English, especially written English, is full of bad habits which spread by imitation and which can be avoided if one is willing to take the necessary trouble. If one gets rid of these habits one can think more clearly, and to think clearly is a necessary first step towards political regeneration: so that the fight against bad English is not frivolous and is not the exclusive concern of professional writers. I will come back to this presently, and I hope that by that time the meaning of what I have said here will have become clearer. Meanwhile here are five specimens of the English language as it is now habitually written.

These five passages have not been picked out because they are especially bad—I could have quoted far worse if I had chosen—but because they illustrate various of the mental vices from which we now suffer. They are a little below the average, but are fairly representative samples. I number them so that I can refer back to them when necessary:

> (1) I am not, indeed, sure whether it is not true to say that the Milton who once seemed not unlike a seventeenth-century Shelley had not become, out of an experience ever more bitter in each year, more alien [*sic*] to the founder of that Jesuit sect which nothing could induce him to tolerate.
>
> Professor Harold Laski (Essay in *Freedom of Expression*)

> (2) Above all, we cannot play ducks and drakes with a native battery of idioms which prescribes such egregious collocations of vocables as the Basic *put up with* for *tolerate* or *put at a loss* for *bewilder*.
>
> Professor Lancelot Hogben (*Interglossa*)

> (3) On the one side we have the free personality: by definition it is not neurotic, for it has neither conflict nor dream. Its desires, such as they are, are transparent, for they are just what institutional approval keeps in the forefront of consciousness; another institutional pattern would alter their number and intensity; there is little in them that is natural, irreducible, or culturally dangerous. But *on the other side,* the social bond itself is nothing but the mutual reflection of these self-secure integrities. Recall the definition of love. Is not this the very picture of a small academic? Where is there a place in this hall of mirrors for either personality or fraternity?
>
> Essay on psychology in *Politics* (New York)

> (4) All the "best people" from the gentlemen's clubs, and all the frantic fascist captains, united in common hatred of Socialism and bestial horror of the rising tide of the mass revolutionary movement, have turned to acts of provocation, to foul incendiarism, to medieval legends of poisoned wells, to legalize their own destruction of proletarian organizations, and rouse the agitated petty-bourgeoisie to chauvinistic fervor on behalf of the fight against the revolutionary way out of the crisis.
>
> Communist pamphlet

> (5) If a new spirit *is* to be infused into this old country, there is one thorny and contentious reform which must be tackled, and that is the humanization and galvanization of the B.B.C. Timidity here will bespeak canker and atrophy of the soul. The heart of Britain may be sound and of strong beat, for instance, but the British lion's roar at present is like that of Bottom in Shakespeare's *Midsummer Night's Dream*—as gentle as any sucking dove. A virile new Britain cannot continue indefinitely to be traduced in the eyes or rather ears, of the world by the effete languors of Langham Place, brazenly masquerading as

"standard English." When the voice of Britain is heard at nine o'clock, better far and infinitely less ludicrous to hear aitches honestly dropped than the present priggish, inflated, inhibited, school-ma'amish arch braying of blameless bashful mewing maidens!

Letter in *Tribune*

Each of these passages has faults of its own, but, quite apart from avoidable ugliness, two qualities are common to all of them. The first is staleness of imagery; the other is lack of precision. The writer either has a meaning and cannot express it, or he inadvertently says something else, or he is almost indifferent as to whether his words mean anything or not. This mixture of vagueness and sheer incompetence is the most marked characteristic of modern English prose, and especially of any kind of political writing. As soon as certain topics are raised, the concrete melts into the abstract and no one seems able to think of turns of speech that are not hackneyed: prose consists less and less of *words* chosen for the sake of their meaning, and more and more of *phrases* tacked together like the sections of a prefabricated henhouse. I list below, with notes and examples, various of the tricks by means of which the work of prose-construction is habitually dodged:

DYING METAPHORS. A newly invented metaphor assists thought by evoking a visual image, while on the other hand a metaphor which is technically "dead" (e.g., *iron resolution*) has in effect reverted to being an ordinary word and can generally be used without loss of vividness. But in between these two classes there is a huge dump of worn-out metaphors which have lost all evocative power and are merely used because they save people the trouble of inventing phrases for themselves. Examples are: *Ring the changes on, take up the cudgels for, toe the line, ride roughshod over, stand shoulder to shoulder with, play into the hands of, no axe to grind, grist to the mill, fishing in troubled waters, on the order of the day, Achilles' heel, swan song, hotbed.* Many of these are used without knowledge of their meaning (what is a "rift," for instance?), and incompatible metaphors are frequently mixed, a sure sign that the writer is not interested in what he is saying. Some metaphors now current have been twisted out of their original meaning without those who use them even being aware of the fact. For example, *toe the line* is sometimes written *tow the line.* Another example is the *hammer and the anvil,* now always used with the implication that the anvil gets the worst of it. In real life it is always the anvil that breaks the hammer, never the other way about: a writer who stopped to think what he was saying would be aware of this, and would avoid perverting the original phrase.

OPERATORS OR VERBAL FALSE LIMBS. These save the trouble of picking out   6
appropriate verbs and nouns, and at the same time pad each sentence with
extra syllables which give it an appearance of symmetry. Characteristic
phrases are *render inoperative, militate against, make contact with, be
subjected to, give rise to, give grounds for, have the effect of, play a
leading part (role) in, make itself felt, take effect, exhibit a tendency to,
serve the purpose of,* etc., etc. The keynote is the elimination of simple
verbs. Instead of being a single word, such as *break, stop, spoil, mend,
kill,* a verb becomes a *phrase,* made up of a noun or adjective tacked on
to some general-purposes verb such as *prove, serve, form, play, render.*
In addition, the passive voice is wherever possible used in preference to
the active, and noun constructions are used instead of gerunds (*by examination of* instead of *by examining*). The range of verbs is further cut
down by means of the *-ize* and *de-* formations, and the banal statements
are given an appearance of profundity by means of the *not un-* formation.
Simple conjunctions and prepositions are replaced by such phrases as *with
respect to, having regard to, the fact that, by dint of, in view of, in the
interests of, on the hypothesis that;* and the ends of sentences are saved
from anticlimax by such resounding common-places as *greatly to be desired, cannot be left out of account, a development to be expected in the
near future, deserving of serious consideration, brought to a satisfactory
conclusion,* and so on and so forth.

PRETENTIOUS DICTION. Words like *phenomenon, element, individual* (as   7
noun), *objective, categorical, effective, virtual, basic, primary, promote,
constitute, exhibit, exploit, utilize, eliminate, liquidate,* are used to dress
up simple statements and give an air of scientific impartiality to biased
judgments. Adjectives like *epoch-making, epic, historic, unforgettable,
triumphant, age-old, inevitable, inexorable, veritable,* are used to dignify
the sordid processes of international politics, while writing that aims at
glorifying war usually takes on an archaic color, its characteristic words
being: *realm, throne, chariot, mailed fist, trident, sword, shield, buckler,
banner, jackboot, clarion.* Foreign words and expressions such as *cul de
sac, ancien régime, deus ex machina, mutatis mutandis, status quo, gleich-
schaltung, weltanschauung,* are used to give an air of culture and elegance. Except for the useful abbreviations *i.e., e.g.,* and *etc.,* there is no
real need for any of the hundreds of foreign phrases now current in English. Bad writers, and especially scientific, political and sociological
writers, are nearly always haunted by the notion that Latin or Greek
words are grander than Saxon ones, and unnecessary words like *expedite,
ameliorate, predict, extraneous, deracinated, clandestine, subaqueous*
and hundreds of others constantly gain ground from their Anglo-Saxon

opposite numbers.[1] The jargon peculiar to Marxist writing (*hyena, hangman, cannibal, petty bourgeois, these gentry, lacquey, flunkey, mad dog, White Guard,* etc.) consists largely of words and phrases translated from Russian, German or French; but the normal way of coining a new word is to use a Latin or Greek root with the appropriate affix and, where necessary, the *-ize* formation. It is often easier to make up words of this kind (*deregionalize, impermissible, extramarital, non-fragmentary* and so forth) than to think up the English words that will cover one's meaning. The result, in general, is an increase in slovenliness and vagueness.

MEANINGLESS WORDS. In certain kinds of writing, particularly in art criticism and literary criticism, it is normal to come across long passages which are almost completely lacking in meaning.[2] Words like *romantic, plastic, values, human, dead, sentimental, natural, vitality,* as used in art criticism, are strictly meaningless, in the sense that they not only do not point to any discoverable object, but are hardly ever expected to do so by the reader. When one critic writes, "The outstanding feature of Mr. X's work is its living quality," while another writes, "The immediately striking thing about Mr. X's work is its peculiar deadness," the reader accepts this as a simple difference of opinion. If words like *black* and *white* were involved, instead of the jargon words *dead* and *living,* he would see at once that language was being used in an improper way. Many political words are similarly abused. The word *Fascism* has now no meaning except in so far as it signifies "something not desirable." The words *democracy, freedom, patriotic, realistic, justice,* have each of them several different meanings which cannot be reconciled with one another. In the case of a word like *democracy,* not only is there no agreed definition, but the attempt to make one is resisted from all sides. It is almost universally felt that when we call a country democratic we are praising it: consequently the defenders of every kind of regime claim that it is a democracy, and fear that they might have to stop using the word if it were tied down to any one meaning. Words of this kind are often used in a consciously dishonest way. That is, the person who uses them has his own private definition, but allows his

[1] An interesting illustration of this is the way in which the English flower names which were in use till very recently are being ousted by Greek ones, *snapdragon* becoming *antirrhinum, forget-me-not* becoming *myosotis,* etc. It is hard to see any practical reason for this change of fashion: it is probably due to an instinctive turning-away from the more homely word and a vague feeling that the Greek word is scientific.

[2] Example: "Comfort's catholicity of perception and image, strangely Whitmanesque in range, almost the exact opposite in aesthetic compulsion, continues to evoke that trembling atmospheric accumulative hinting at a cruel, an inexorably serene timelessness. . . . Wrey Gardiner scores by aiming at simple bull's-eyes with precision. Only they are not so simple, and through this contented sadness runs more than the surface bittersweet of resignation." (*Poetry Quarterly*)

hearer to think he means something quite different. Statements like, *Marshal Pétain was a true patriot, The Soviet Press is the freest in the world, The Catholic Church is opposed to persecution,* are almost always made with intent to deceive. Other words used in variable meanings, in most cases more or less dishonestly, are: *class, totalitarian, science, progressive, reactionary, bourgeois, equality.*

Now that I have made this catalogue of swindles and perversions, let   9
me give another example of the kind of writing that they lead to. This time it must of its nature be an imaginary one. I am going to translate a passage of good English into modern English of the worst sort. Here is a well-known verse from *Ecclesiastes:*

> I returned and saw under the sun, that the race is not to the swift, nor the battle to the strong, neither yet bread to the wise, nor yet riches to men of understanding, nor yet favour to men of skill; but time and chance happeneth to them all.

Here it is in modern English: 10

> Objective consideration of contemporary phenomena compels the conclusion that success or failure in competitive activities exhibits no tendency to be commensurate with innate capacity, but that a considerable element of the unpredictable must invariably be taken into account.

This is a parody, but a very gross one. Exhibit (3), above, for instance,   11
contains several patches of the same kind of English. It will be seen that I have not made a full translation. The beginning and ending of the sentence follow the original meaning fairly closely, but in the middle the concrete illustrations—race, battle, bread—dissolve into the vague phrase "success or failure in competitive activities." This had to be so, because no modern writer of the kind I am discussing—no one capable of using phrases like "objective consideration of contemporary phenomena"—would ever tabulate his thoughts in that precise and detailed way. The whole tendency of modern prose is away from concreteness. Now analyse these two sentences a little more closely. The first contains forty-nine words but only sixty syllables, and all its words are those of everyday life. The second contains thirty-eight words of ninety syllables: eighteen of its words are from Latin roots, and one from Greek. The first sentence contains six vivid images, and only one phrase ("time and chance") that could be called vague. The second contains not a single fresh, arresting phrase, and in spite of its ninety syllables it gives only a shortened version of the meaning contained in the first. Yet without a doubt it is the second kind of sentence that is gaining ground in modern English. I do not want to exaggerate. This kind of writing is not yet universal, and outcrops of simplicity will occur here

and there in the worst-written page. Still, if you or I were told to write a few lines on the uncertainty of human fortunes, we should probably come much nearer to my imaginary sentence than to the one from *Ecclesiastes*.

As I have tried to show, modern writing at its worst does not consist in picking out words for the sake of their meaning and inventing images in order to make the meaning clearer. It consists in gumming together long strips of words which have already been set in order by someone else, and making the results presentable by sheer humbug. The attraction of this way of writing is that it is easy. It is easier—even quicker, once you have the habit—to say *In my opinion it is not an unjustifiable assumption that* than to say *I think*. If you use ready-made phrases, you not only don't have to hunt about for words; you also don't have to bother with the rhythms of your sentences, since these phrases are generally so arranged as to be more or less euphonious. When you are composing in a hurry—when you are dictating to a stenographer, for instance, or making a public speech—it is natural to fall into a pretentious, Latinized style. Tags like *a consideration which we should do well to bear in mind* or *a conclusion to which all of us would readily assent* will save many a sentence from coming down with a bump. By using stale metaphors, similes and idioms, you save much mental effort, at the cost of leaving your meaning vague, not only for your reader but for yourself. This is the significance of mixed metaphors. The sole aim of a metaphor is to call up a visual image. When these images clash—as in *The Fascist octopus has sung its swan song, the jackboot is thrown into the melting pot*—it can be taken as certain that the writer is not seeing a mental image of the objects he is naming; in other words he is not really thinking. Look again at the examples I gave at the beginning of this essay. Professor Laski (1) uses five negatives in fifty-three words. One of these is superfluous, making nonsense of the whole passage, and in addition there is the slip *alien* for *akin*, making further nonsense, and several avoidable pieces of clumsiness which increase the general vagueness. Professor Hogben (2) plays ducks and drakes with a battery which is able to write prescriptions, and, while disapproving of the everyday phrase *put up with,* is unwilling to look *egregious* up in the dictionary and see what it means; (3), if one takes an uncharitable attitude towards it, is simply meaningless: probably one could work out its intended meaning by reading the whole of the article in which it occurs. In (4), the writer knows more or less what he wants to say, but an accumulation of stale phrases chokes him like tea leaves blocking a sink. In (5), words and meaning have almost parted company. People who write in this manner usually have a general emotional meaning—they dislike one thing and want to express solidarity with another—but they are not interested in the detail of what they are saying. A scrupulous writer, in every sentence that he writes, will ask himself at least four questions, thus: What am I trying to say? What words will express it? What image or idiom will make it clearer? Is this image fresh enough to have an effect? And he will probably ask himself two more: Could I put it more shortly? Have I said anything that is avoidably ugly? But you are not obliged to go to all this trouble. You can shirk it by simply throwing your mind open and letting the ready-made phrases come crowding in. They will construct your sentences for you—even think your thoughts for you, to a certain extent—and at need they will perform the important service of partially concealing your meaning even from yourself. It is at this point that the special connection between politics and the debasement of language becomes clear.

In our time it is broadly true that political writing is bad writing. Where it is not true, it will generally be found that the writer is some kind of rebel, expressing his private opinions and not a "party line." Orthodoxy, of whatever color, seems to demand a lifeless, imitative style. The political dialects to be found in pamphlets, leading articles, manifestos, White Papers and the speeches of under-secretaries do, of course, vary from party to party, but they are all alike in that one almost never finds in them a fresh, vivid, home-made turn of speech. When one watches some tired hack on the platform mechanically repeating the familiar phrases—*bestial atrocities, iron heel, bloodstained tyranny, free peoples of the world, stand shoulder to shoulder*—one often has a curious feeling that one is not watching a live human being but some kind of dummy: a feeling which suddenly becomes stronger at moments when the light catches the speaker's spectacles and turns them into blank discs which seem to have no eyes behind them. And this is not altogether fanciful. A speaker who uses that kind of phraseology has gone some distance towards turning himself into a machine. The appropriate noises are coming out of his larynx, but his brain is not involved as it would be if he were choosing his words for himself. If the speech he is making is one that he is accustomed to make over and over again, he may be almost unconscious of what he is saying, as one is when one utters the responses in church. And this reduced state of consciousness, if not indispensable, is at any rate favorable to political conformity.

In our time, political speech and writing are largely the defence of the indefensible. Things like the continuance of British rule in India, the Russian purges and deportations, the dropping of the atom bombs on Japan, can indeed be defended, but only by arguments which are too brutal for most people to face, and which do not square with the professed aims of political parties. Thus political language has to consist largely of euphemism, question-begging and sheer cloudy vagueness. Defenceless villages are bombarded from the air, the inhabitants driven out into the countryside, the cattle machine-gunned, the huts set on fire with incendiary bullets: this is called *pacification*. Millions of peasants are robbed of their farms and sent trudging along the roads with no more than they can carry:

13

14

this is called *transfer of population* or *rectification of frontiers*. People are imprisoned for years without trial, or shot in the back of the neck or sent to die of scurvy in Arctic lumber camps: this is called *elimination of unreliable elements*. Such phraseology is needed if one wants to name things without calling up mental pictures of them. Consider for instance some comfortable English professor defending Russian totalitarianism. He cannot say outright, ''I believe in killing off your opponents when you can get good results by doing so.'' Probably, therefore, he will say something like this:

> While freely conceding that the Soviet régime exhibits certain features which the humanitarian may be inclined to deplore, we must, I think, agree that a certain curtailment of the right to political opposition is an unavoidable concomitant of transitional periods, and that the rigors which the Russian people have been called upon to undergo have been amply justified in the sphere of concrete achievement.

The inflated style is itself a kind of euphemism. A mass of Latin words 15
falls upon the facts like soft snow, blurring the outlines and covering up all the details. The great enemy of clear language is insincerity. When there is a gap between one's real and one's declared aims, one turns as it were instinctively to long words and exhausted idioms, like a cuttlefish squirting out ink. In our age there is no such thing as ''keeping out of politics.'' All issues are political issues, and politics itself is a mass of lies, evasions, folly, hatred and schizophrenia. When the general atmosphere is bad, language must suffer. I should expect to find—this is a guess which I have not sufficient knowledge to verify—that the German, Russian and Italian languages have all deteriorated in the last ten or fifteen years, as a result of dictatorship.

But if thought corrupts language, language can also corrupt thought. A 16
bad usage can spread by tradition and imitation, even among people who should and do know better. The debased language that I have been discussing is in some ways very convenient. Phrases like *a not unjustifiable assumption, leaves much to be desired, would serve no good purpose, a consideration which we should do well to bear in mind,* are a continuous temptation, a packet of aspirins always at one's elbow. Look back through this essay, and for certain you will find that I have again and again committed the very faults I am protesting against. By this morning's post I have received a pamphlet dealing with conditions in Germany. The author tells me that he ''felt impelled'' to write it. I open it at random, and here is almost the first sentence that I see: ''[The Allies] have an opportunity not only of achieving a radical transformation of Germany's social and political structure in such a way as to avoid a nationalistic reaction in Germany itself, but at the same time of laying the foundations of a cooperative and

unified Europe.'' You see, he ''feels impelled'' to write—feels, presumably, that he has something new to say—and yet his words, like cavalry horses answering the bugle, group themselves automatically into the familiar dreary pattern. The invasion of one's mind by ready-made phrases (*lay the foundations, achieve a radical transformation*) can only be prevented if one is constantly on guard against them, and every such phrase anaesthetizes a portion of one's brain.

I said earlier that the decadence of our language is probably curable. 17 Those who deny this would argue, if they produced an argument at all, that language merely reflects existing social conditions, and that we cannot influence its development by any direct tinkering with words and constructions. So far as the general tone or spirit of a language goes, this may be true, but it is not true in detail. Silly words and expressions have often disappeared, not through any evolutionary process but owing to the conscious action of a minority. Two recent examples were *explore every avenue* and *leave no stone unturned,* which were killed by the jeers of a few journalists. There is a long list of fly-blown metaphors which could similarly be got rid of if enough people would interest themselves in the job; and it should also be possible to laugh the *not un-* formation out of existence,[3] to reduce the amount of Latin and Greek in the average sentence, to drive out foreign phrases and strayed scientific words, and, in general, to make pretentiousness unfashionable. But all these are minor points. The defence of the English language implies more than this, and perhaps it is best to start by saying what it does *not* imply.

To begin with, it has nothing to do with archaism, with the salvaging 18 of obsolete words and turns of speech, or with the setting up of a ''standard English'' which must never be departed from. On the contrary, it is especially concerned with the scrapping of every word or idiom which has outworn its usefulness. It has nothing to do with correct grammar and syntax, which are of no importance so long as one makes one's meaning clear, or with the avoidance of Americanisms, or with having what is called a ''good prose style.'' On the other hand it is not concerned with fake simplicity and the attempt to make written English colloquial. Nor does it even imply in every case preferring the Saxon word to the Latin one, though it does imply using the fewest and shortest words that will cover one's meaning. What is above all needed is to let the meaning choose the word, and not the other way about. In prose, the worst thing one can do with words is to surrender to them. When you think of a concrete object, you think wordlessly, and then, if you want to describe the thing you have been visualizing you probaby hunt about till you find the exact words that seem to fit it. When you think of something abstract you are

---

[3] One can cure oneself of the *not un-* formation by memorizing this sentence: *A not unblack dog was chasing a not unsmall rabbit across a not ungreen field.*

more inclined to use words from the start, and unless you make a conscious effort to prevent it, the existing dialect will come rushing in and do the job for you, at the expense of blurring or even changing your meaning. Probably it is better to put off using words as long as possible and get one's meaning as clear as one can through pictures or sensations. Afterwards one can choose—not simply *accept*—the phrases that will best cover the meaning, and then switch round and decide what impression one's words are likely to make on another person. This last effort of the mind cuts out all stale or mixed images, all prefabricated phrases, needless repetitions, and humbug and vagueness generally. But one can often be in doubt about the effect of a word or a phrase, and one needs rules that one can rely on when instinct fails. I think the following rules will cover most cases:

1. Never use a metaphor, simile, or other figure of speech which you are used to seeing in print.
2. Never use a long word where a short one will do.
3. If it is possible to cut a word out, always cut it out.
4. Never use the passive where you can use the active.
5. Never use a foreign phrase, a scientific word or a jargon word if you can think of an everyday English equivalent.
6. Break any of these rules sooner than say anything outright barbarous.

These rules sound elementary, and so they are, but they demand a deep change of attitude in anyone who has grown used to writing in the style now fashionable. One could keep all of them and still write bad English, but one could not write the kind of stuff that I quoted in those five specimens at the beginning of this article.

I have not here been considering the literary use of language, but merely language as an instrument for expressing and not for concealing or preventing thought. Stuart Chase and others have come near to claiming that all abstract words are meaningless, and have used this as a pretext for advocating a kind of political quietism. Since you don't know what Fascism is, how can you struggle against Fascism? One need not swallow such absurdities as this, but one ought to recognize that the present political chaos is connected with the decay of language, and that one can probably bring about some improvement by starting at the verbal end. If you simplify your English, you are freed from the worst follies of orthodoxy. You cannot speak any of the necessary dialects, and when you make a stupid remark its stupidity will be obvious, even to yourself. Political language— and with variations this is true of all political parties, from Conservatives to Anarchists—is designed to make lies sound truthful and murder respectable, and to give an appearance of solidity to pure wind. One cannot change this all in a moment, but one can at least change one's own habits, and from time to time one can even, if one jeers loudly enough, send some worn-out and useless phrase—some *jackboot, Achilles' heel, hotbed, melting pot, acid test, veritable inferno* or other lump of verbal refuse—into the dustbin where it belongs.

QUESTIONS ON CONTENT

1. In your own words, summarize Orwell's argument in this essay.

2. It is often said that "mixed metaphors" (for example, "politicians who have their heads in the sand are leading the country over the precipice") are undesirable in either speech or writing because they are inaccurate. For Orwell, a mixed metaphor is symptomatic of a greater problem. What is that problem?

3. Reread paragraph 2 of the essay. What, according to Orwell, is the nature of cause-and-effect relationships?

4. Our world is becoming increasingly prefabricated. What does the concept of prefabrication have to do with Orwell's argument concerning the prevalance of the habitual and trite phrase?

5. Orwell states that he himself in this essay is guilty of some of the errors he is pointing out. Can you detect any of them?

6. According to Orwell, what are four important prewriting questions scrupulous writers ask themselves?

7. Orwell says that one of the evils of political language is "question-begging" (14). What does he mean? Why, according to Orwell, has political language deteriorated? Do you agree with him that "the decadence of our language is probably curable" (17)? Explain.

QUESTIONS ON RHETORIC

1. Why does Orwell present the "five specimens of the English language as it is now habitually written" (2)? What use does he make of these five passages later in his essay?

2. Following are some of the metaphors and similes that Orwell uses in his essay. (Glossary: *Figures of Speech*) Explain how each one works and comment on its effectiveness.

   a. . . . prose consists less . . . of *words* chosen for the sake of their meaning, and more . . . of *phrases* tacked together like the sections of a prefabricated hen-house (4).
   b. But in between these two classes there is a huge dump of worn-out metaphors which have lost all evocative power. . . . (5).
   c. . . . the writer knows . . . what he wants to say, but an accumulation of stale phrases chokes him like tea leaves blocking a sink (12).
   d. A mass of Latin words falls upon the facts like soft snow, blurring the outlines and covering up all the details (15).

   e. When there is a gap between one's real and one's declared aims, one turns
   . . . instinctively to long words and exhausted idioms, like a cuttlefish
   squirting out ink (15).
   f. . . . he . . . feels, presumably, that he has something new to say—and yet
   his words, like cavalry horses answering the bugle, group themselves automatically into the familiar dreary pattern (16).

3. At the end of paragraph 4 Orwell speaks of "the tricks by means of
which the work of prose-construction is habitually dodged," and he then
goes on to classify them. Why is classification a useful rhetorical strategy
in this situation? (Glossary: *Division and Classification*)

4. Point out several terms and concepts that Orwell defines in this essay.
What is his purpose in defining them? How does he go about it in each
instance? (Glossary: *Definition*)

5. In this essay Orwell moves from negative arguments to positive ones.
Where does he make the transition from criticisms to proposals? What is
the effect of his organizing the argument in this way?

6. Orwell describes many of the langauge abuses that he is criticizing as
"habits" or "mental vices." Are these terms consistent with his thesis?
Explain. (Glossary: *Diction*)

7. Orwell suggests that you should never use the passive voice when you
can use the active voice. Consider the following example:

   Passive: It is expected that the welfare budget will be cut by Congress.
   Active: We expect Congress to cut the welfare budget.

Not only is the active version shorter, but it is more precise in that it
properly emphasizes "Congress" as the doer of the action. Rewrite each
of the following sentences in the active voice.

   a. The line-drive single was hit by John.
   b. Two eggs and one stick of butter should be added to the other ingredients.
   c. Information of a confidential nature cannot be released by doctors.
   d. Figures showing that the cost of living rose sharply during the past twelve
   months were released by the administration today.
   e. It was decided that a meeting would be held on each Monday.

Are there any situations in which the passive voice is more appropriate than
the active? Explain. What conclusions can you draw about the active and
passive voices?

VOCABULARY

decadent (1)	impartiality (7)	scrupulous (12)
frivolous (2)	biased (7)	humanitarian (14)
inadvertently (4)	reconciled (8)	evolutionary (17)
implication (5)	pretentious (12)	

WRITING TOPICS

1. Write an essay in which you analyze the language in the following ad, which appeared in *Seventeen* magazine. What do you think Orwell's response to this would be?

SOME STRAIGHT TALK ABOUT SMOKING
FOR YOUNG PEOPLE

We're R.J. Reynolds Tobacco, and we're urging you not to smoke.

We're saying this because, throughout the world, smoking has always been an adult custom. And because today, even among adults, smoking is controversial.

Your first reaction might be to ignore this advice. Maybe you feel we're talking to you as if you were a child. And you probably don't think of yourself that way.

But just because you're no longer a child doesn't mean you're already an adult. And if you take up smoking just to prove you're not a kid, you're kidding yourself.

So please don't smoke. You'll have plenty of time as an adult to decide whether smoking is right for you.

That's about as straight as we can put it.

R.J. Reynolds Tobacco Company[1]

2. Gather five examples of recent American political English that you consider, in Orwell's words, "ugly and inaccurate." You should be able to find more than enough material in current newspapers, magazines, and books. Are the "tricks" used by today's writers the same as those used in Orwell's day? If not, what terms would you invent to describe the "new" tricks?

3. As many of Orwell's examples suggest, language is sometimes used not to express but to conceal meaning. Is this true only of politics? Can you think of any situation in which you or others you know have been under pressure to say something, yet had nothing that you were ready or willing to say? What happened? Write an essay in which you first give some examples of the problem and then suggest ways of handling such situations honestly.

---

[1] © 1985 R.J. REYNOLDS TOBACCO CO.

SELECTION, SLANTING, AND CHARGED LANGUAGE

Newman P. Birk and Genevieve B. Birk

The more we learn about language and how it works, the more abundantly clear it becomes that our language shapes our perceptions of the world. Because we all have the same set of physical organs for perceiving reality—eyes to see, ears to hear, noses to smell, tongues to taste, and skins to feel, reality should be the same for all of us. But we know that it isn't; and language, it seems, is the big difference. Our language, in effect, acts as a filter, heightening certain perceptions, dimming others, and totally voiding still others. In the following selection from their book Understanding and Using English, *Newman and Genevieve Birk discuss how we learn new things, how we put our knowledge into words, and how language can be manipulated to create particular impressions.*

A. THE PRINCIPLE OF SELECTION

Before it is expressed in words, our knowledge, both inside and outside, is influenced by the principle of selection. What we know or observe depends on what we notice; that is, what we select, consciously or unconsciously, as worthy of notice or attention. As we observe, the principle of selection determines which facts we take in.

Suppose, for example, that three people, a lumberjack, an artist, and a tree surgeon, are examining a large tree in a forest. Since the tree itself is a complicated object, the number of particulars or facts about it that one could observe would be very great indeed. Which of these facts a particular observer will notice will be a matter of selection, a selection that is determined by his interests and purposes. A lumberjack might be interested in the best way to cut the tree down, cut it up and transport it to the lumber mill. His interest would then determine his principle of selection in observing and thinking about the tree. The artist might consider painting a picture of the tree, and his purpose would furnish his principle of selection. The tree surgeon's professional interest in the physical health of the tree might establish a principle of selection for him. If each man were now required to write an exhaustive, detailed report on every thing he observed about the tree, the facts supplied by each would differ, for each would report those facts that his particular principle of selection led him to notice.[1]

The principle of selection holds not only for the specific facts that people   3
observe but also for the facts they remember. A student suddenly embarrassed may remember nothing of the next ten minutes of class discussion but may have a vivid recollection of the sensation of the blood mounting, as he blushed, up his face and into his ears. In both noticing and remembering, the principle of selection applies, and it is influenced not only by our special interest and point of view but by our whole mental state of the moment.

The principle of selection then serves as a kind of sieve or screen   4
through which our knowledge passes before it becomes our knowledge. Since we can't notice everything about a complicated object or situation or action or state of our own consciousness, what we do notice is determined by whatever principle of selection is operating for us at the time we gain the knowledge.

It is important to remember that what is true of the way the principle of   5
selection works for us is true also of the way it works for others. Even before we or other people put knowledge into words to express meaning, that knowledge has been screened or selected. Before an historian or an economist writes a book, or before a reporter writes a news article, the facts that each is to present have been sifted through the screen of a principle of selection. Before one person passes on knowledge to another, that knowledge has already been selected and shaped, intentionally or unintentionally, by the mind of the communicator.

B. THE PRINCIPLE OF SLANTING

When we put our knowledge into words, a second process of selection, the   6
process of slanting, takes place. Just as there is something, a rather mysterious principle of selection, which chooses for us what we will notice, and what will then become our knowledge, there is also a principle which operates, with or without our awareness, to select certain facts and feelings from our store of knowledge, and to choose the words and the emphasis

[1] Of course, all three observers would probably report a good many facts in common—the height of the tree, for example, and the size of the trunk. The point we wish to make is that each observer would give us a different impression of the tree because of the different principle of selection that guided his observation.

that we shall use to communicate our meaning.[2] Slanting may be defined as the process of selecting (1) knowledge—factual and attitudinal; (2) words; and (3) emphasis, to achieve the intention of the communicator. Slanting is present in some degree in all communication: one may *slant for* (favorable slanting), *slant against* (unfavorable slanting), or *slant both ways* (balanced slanting). . . .

C. SLANTING BY USE OF EMPHASIS

Slanting by use of the devices of emphasis is unavoidable,[3] for emphasis is simply the giving of stress to subject matter, and so indicating what is important and what is less important. In speech, for example, if we say that Socrates was *a wise old man,* we can give several slightly different meanings, one by stressing *wise,* another by stressing *old,* another by giving equal stress to *wise* and *old,* and still another by giving chief stress to *man.* Each different stress gives a different slant (favorable or unfavorable or balanced) to the statement because it conveys a different attitude toward Socrates or a different judgment of him. Connectives and word order also slant by the emphasis they give: consider the difference in slanting or emphasis produced by *old but wise, old and wise, wise but old.* In writing, we cannot indicate subtle stresses on words as clearly as in speech, but we can achieve our emphasis and so can slant by the use of more complex patterns of word order, by choice of connectives, by underlining heavily stressed words, and by marks of punctuation that indicate short or long pauses and so give light or heavy emphasis. Question marks, quotation marks, and exclamation points can also contribute to slanting.[4] It is impossible either in speech or in writing to put two facts together without giving some slight emphasis or slant. For example, if we have in mind only two facts about a man, his awkwardness and his strength, we subtly slant those facts favorably or unfavorably in whatever way we may choose to join them:

[2] Notice that the "principle of selection" is at work as *we take in* knowledge, and that slanting occurs as *we express* our knowledge in words.

[3] When emphasis is present—and we can think of no instance in the use of language in which it is not—it necessarily influences the meaning by playing a part in the favorable, unfavorable, or balanced slant of the communicator. We are likely to emphasize by voice stress, even when we answer *yes* or *no* to simple questions.

[4] Consider the slanting achieved by punctuation in the following sentences: He called the Senator an honest man? *He* called the Senator an honest man? He called the Senator an honest man! He said one more such "honest" senator would corrupt the state.

More Favorable Slanting	Less Favorable Slanting
He is awkward and strong.	He is strong and awkward.
He is awkward but strong.	He is strong but awkward.
Although he is somewhat awkward, he is very strong.	He may be strong, but he's very awkward.

With more facts and in longer passages it is possible to maintain a delicate balance by alternating favorable emphasis and so producing a balanced effect.

All communication, then, is in some degree slanted by the *emphasis* of the communicator.   8

D. SLANTING BY SELECTION OF FACTS

To illustrate the technique of slanting by selection of facts, we shall ex-   9
amine three passages of informative writing which achieve different effects simply by the selection and emphasis of material. Each passage is made up of true statements or facts about a dog, yet the reader is given three different impressions. The first passage is an example of objective writing or balanced slanting, the second is slanted unfavorably, and the third is slanted favorably.

1. Balanced Presentation

Our dog, Toddy, sold to us a cocker, produces various reactions in various people. Those who come to the back door she usually growls and barks at (a milkman has said that he is afraid of her); those who come to the front door, she whines at and paws; also she tries to lick people's faces unless we have forestalled her by putting a newspaper in her mouth. (Some of our friends encourage these actions; others discourage them. Mrs. Firmly, one friend, slaps the dog with a newspaper and says, "I know how hard dogs are to train.") Toddy knows and responds to a number of words and phrases, and guests sometimes remark that she is a "very intelligent dog." She has fleas in the summer, and she sheds, at times copiously, the year round. Her blonde hairs are conspicuous when they are on people's clothing or on rugs or furniture. Her color and her large brown eyes frequently produce favorable comment. An expert on cockers would say that her ears are too short and set too high and that she is at least six pounds too heavy.

The passage above is made up of facts, verifiable facts,[5] deliberately   10

---

[5] *Verifiable facts* are facts that can be checked and agreed upon and proved to be true by people who wish to verify them. That a particular theme received a failing grade is a verifiable fact; one needs merely to see the theme with the grade on it. That the instructor should have failed the theme is not, strictly speaking, a verifiable fact, but a matter of opinion. That

selected and emphasized to produce a *balanced* impression. Of course not all the facts about the dog have been given—to supply *all* the facts on any subject, even such a comparatively simple one, would be an almost impossible task. Both favorable and unfavorable facts are used, however, and an effort has been made to alternate favorable and unfavorable details so that neither will receive greater emphasis by position, proportion, or grammatical structure.

2. Facts Slanted Against

That dog put her paws on my white dress as soon as I came in the door, and she made so much noise that it was two minutes before she had quieted down enough for us to talk and hear each other. Then the gas man came and she did a great deal of barking. And her hairs are on the rug and on the furniture. If you wear a dark dress they stick to it like lint. When Mrs. Firmly came in, she actually hit the dog with a newspaper to make it stay down, and she made some remark about training dogs. I wish the Birks would take the hint or get rid of that noisy, short-eared, overweight "cocker" of theirs.

This unfavorably slanted version is based on the same facts, but now   11
these facts have been selected and given a new emphasis. The speaker, using her selected facts to give her impression of the dog, is quite possibly unaware of her negative slanting.

Now for a favorably slanted version: 12

3. Facts Slanted For

What a lively and responsive dog! When I walked in the door, there she was with a newspaper in her mouth, whining and standing on her hind legs and wagging her tail all at the same time. And what an intelligent dog. If you suggest going for a walk, she will get her collar from the kitchen and hand it to you, and she brings Mrs. Birk's slippers whenever Mrs. Birk says she is "tired" or mentions slippers. At a command she catches balls, rolls over, "speaks," or stands on her hind feet and twirls around. She sits up and balances a piece of bread on her nose until she is told to take it; then she tosses it up and catches it. If you are eating something, she sits up in front of you and "begs" with those big dark brown eyes set in that light, buff-colored face of hers. When I got up to go and told her I was leaving, she rolled her eyes at me and sat up like a squirrel. She certainly is a lively and intelligent dog.

women on the average live longer than men is a verifiable fact; that they live better is a matter of opinion, *a value judgment.*

Speaker 3, like Speaker 2, is selecting from the "facts" summarized in   14
balanced version 1, and is emphasizing his facts to communicate his impression.

All three passages are examples of *reporting* (i.e., consist only of   15
verifiable facts), yet they give three very different impressions of the same
dog because of the different ways the speakers slanted the facts. Some
people say that figures don't lie, and many people believe that if they have
the "facts," they have the "truth." Yet if we carefully examine the ways
of thought and language, we see that any knowledge that comes to us
through words has been subjected to the double screening of the principle
of selection and the slanting of language. . . .

Wise listeners and readers realize that the double screening that is   16
produced by the principle of selection and by slanting takes place even
when people honestly try to report the facts as they know them. (Speakers
2 and 3, for instance, probably thought of themselves as simply giving
information about a dog and were not deliberately trying to mislead.) Wise
listeners and readers know too that deliberate manipulators of language, by
mere selection and emphasis, can make their slanted facts appear to support almost any cause.

In arriving at opinions and values we cannot always be sure that the   17
facts that sift into our minds through language are representative and relevant and true. We need to remember that much of our information about
politics, governmental activities, business conditions, and foreign affairs
comes to us selected and slanted. More than we realize, our opinions on
these matters may depend on what newspaper we read or what news
commentator we listen to. Worth-while opinions call for knowledge of
reliable facts and reasonable arguments for and against—and such opinions
include beliefs about morality and truth and religion as well as about public
affairs. Because complex subjects involve knowing and dealing with many
facts on both sides, reliable judgments are at best difficult to arrive at. If
we want to be fairminded, we must be willing to subject our opinions to
continual testing by new knowledge, and must realize that after all they *are*
opinions, more or less trustworthy. Their trustworthiness will depend on
the representativeness of our facts, on the quality of our reasoning, and on
the standard of values that we choose to apply.

We shall not give here a passage illustrating the unscrupulous slanting   18
of facts. Such a passage would also include irrelevant facts and false
statements presented as facts, along with various subtle distortions of fact.
Yet to the uninformed reader the passage would be indistinguishable from
a passage intended to give a fair account. If two passages (2 and 3) of
casual and unintentional slanting of facts about a dog can give such contradictory impressions of a simple subject, the reader can imagine what a
skilled and designing manipulation of facts and statistics could do to mis-

lead an uninformed reader about a really complex subject. An example of such manipulation might be the account of the United States that Soviet propaganda has supplied to the average Russian. Such propaganda, however, would go beyond the mere slanting of the facts: it would clothe the selected facts in charged words and would make use of the many other devices of slanting that appear in charged language.

E. SLANTING BY USE OF CHARGED WORDS

In the passages describing the dog Toddy, we were illustrating the technique of slanting by the selection and emphasis of facts. Though the facts selected had to be expressed in words, the words chosen were as factual as possible, and it was the selection and emphasis of facts and not of words that was mainly responsible for the two distinctly different impressions of the dog. In the passages below we are demonstrating another way of slanting—by the use of charged words. This time the accounts are very similar in the facts they contain; the different impressions of the subject, Corlyn, are produced not by different facts but by the subtle selection of charged words.   19

The passages were written by a clever student who was told to choose as his subject a person in action, and to write two descriptions, each using the ''same facts.'' The instructions required that one description be slanted positively and the other negatively, so that the first would make the reader favorably inclined toward the person and the action, and the second would make him unfavorably inclined.   20

Here is the favorably charged description. Read it carefully and form your opinion of the person before you go on to read the second description.   21

Corlyn

Corlyn paused at the entrance to the room and glanced about. A well-cut black dress draped subtly about her slender form. Her long blonde hair gave her chiseled features the simple frame they required. She smiled an engaging smile as she accepted a cigarette from her escort. As he lit it for her she looked over the flame and into his eyes. Corlyn had that rare talent of making every male feel that he was the one man in the world.

She took his arm and they descended the steps into the room. She walked with an effortless grace and spoke with equal ease. They each took a cup of coffee and joined a group of friends near the fire. The flickering light danced across her face and lent an ethereal quality to her beauty. The good conversation, the crackling logs, and the stimulating coffee gave her a feeling of internal warmth. Her eyes danced with each leap of the flames.

Taken by itself this passage might seem just a description of an attrac-   22
tive girl. The favorable slanting by use of charged words has been done so
skillfully that it is inconspicuous. Now we turn to the unfavorable slanted
description of the "same" girl in the "same" actions:

Corlyn

Corlyn halted at the entrance to the room and looked around. A plain black
dress hung on her thin frame. Her stringy bleached hair accentuated her harsh
features. She smiled an inane smile as she took a cigarette from her escort. As
he lit it for her she stared over the lighter and into his eyes. Corlyn had a habit
of making every male feel that he was the last man on earth.

She grasped his arm and they walked down the steps and into the room. Her
pace was fast and ungainly, as was her speech. They each reached for some
coffee and broke into a group of acquaintances near the fire. The flickering light
played across her face and revealed every flaw. The loud talk, the fire, and the
coffee she had gulped down made her feel hot. Her eyes grew more red with
each leap of the flames.

When the reader compares these two descriptions, he can see how   23
charged words influence the reader's attitude. One needs to read the two
descriptions several times to appreciate all the subtle differences between
them. Words, some rather heavily charged, others innocent-looking but
lightly charged, work together to carry to the reader a judgment of a person
and a situation. If the reader had seen only the first description of Corlyn,
he might well have thought that he had formed his "own judgment on the
basis of the facts." And the examples just given only begin to suggest the
techniques that may be used in heavily charged language. For one thing,
the two descriptions of Corlyn contain no really good example of the use
of charged abstractions; for another, the writer was obliged by the assignment to use the same set of facts and so could not slant by selecting his
material.

F. SLANTING AND CHARGED LANGUAGE

. . . When slanting of facts, or words, or emphasis, or any combination of   24
the three *significantly influences* feelings toward, or judgments about, a
subject, the language used is charged language. . . .

Of course communications vary in the amount of charge they carry and   25
in their effect on different people; what is very favorably charged for one
person may have little or no charge, or may even be adversely charged, for
others. It is sometimes hard to distinguish between charged and uncharged

expression. But it is safe to say that whenever we wish to convey any kind of inner knowlege—feelings, attitudes, judgments, values—we are obliged to convey that attitudinal meaning through the medium of charged language; and when we wish to understand the inside knowledge of others, we have to interpret the charged language that they choose, or are obliged to use. Charged language, then, is the natural and necessary medium for the communication of charged or attitudinal meaning. At times we have difficulty in living with it, but we should have even greater difficulty in living without it.

Some of the difficulties in living with charged language are caused by   26
its use in dishonest propaganda, in some editorials, in many political speeches, in most advertising, in certain kinds of effusive salesmanship, and in blatantly insincere, or exaggerated, or sentimental expressions of emotion. Other difficulties are caused by the misunderstandings and misinterpretations that charged language produces. A charged phrase misinterpreted in a love letter; a charged word spoken in haste or in anger; an acrimonious argument about religion or politics or athletics or fraternities; the frustrating uncertainty produced by the effort to understand the complex attitudinal meaning in a poem or play or a short story—these troubles, all growing out of the use of charged language, may give us the feeling that Robert Louis Stevenson expressed when he said, "The battle goes sore against us to the going down of the sun."

But however charged language is abused and whatever misunderstand-   27
ings it may cause, we still have to live with it—and even by it. It shapes our attitudes and values even without our conscious knowledge; it gives purpose to, and guides, our actions; through it we establish and maintain relations with other people and by means of it we exert our greatest influence on them. Without charged language, life would be but half life. The relatively uncharged language of bare factual statement, though it serves its informative purpose well and is much less open to abuse and to misunderstanding, can describe only the bare land of factual knowledge; to communicate knowledge of the turbulencies and the calms and the deep currents of the sea of inner experience we must use charged language.

QUESTIONS ON CONTENT

1. What is the "principle of selection," and how does it work?

2. How is "slanting" different from the "principle of selection"? What devices can a writer or speaker use to slant knowledge?

3. Paragraph 7 is full of examples of slanting by use of emphasis. Explain how each example works.

4. What exactly are "charged words"? Demonstrate your understanding

of charged language by picking good examples from the two descriptions of Corlyn. What are some of the difficulties in living with charged language?

5. Why does a given word—like *lilac, religion,* or *lady*—mean different things to different people?

6. What do the Birks mean when they say, "Without charged language, life would be but half life" (33)?

QUESTIONS ON RHETORIC

1. Did you find the examples about Toddy the dog and Corlyn particularly helpful? What would have been lost had the examples not been included? (Glossary: *Examples*)

2. What is the relationship between paragraphs 1 and 2?

3. How have the Birks organized their essay? Is the organizational pattern appropriate for the subject matter? Explain. (Glossary: *Organization*)

4. What is the Birks's purpose in this essay? Do they seem more intent on explaining or arguing their position? (Glossary: *Purpose*)

VOCABULARY

exhaustive (2)	attitudinal (6)	abstractions (29)
blushed (3)	verifiable (11)	turbulencies (33)
sieve (4)	inconspicuous (26)	

WRITING TOPICS

1. Select an article about a current event from a newspaper or news magazine. Without changing the facts given, rewrite the article so that it makes a different impression on the reader. Hand in the original article, your rewritten version, and your comments about how each version should affect the reader.

2. Following the Birks's example of their dog Toddy, write three descriptions (one balanced, one slanted for, and one slanted against) of one of the following:

    a. your room
    b. your best friend
    c. your favorite coffee cup
    d. a rock star or other celebrity
    e. your school's dining hall
    f. a hamburger
    g. sunglasses
    h. your mother, your father, or a sibling
    i. a video game
    j. a book

3. The following news stories about a Little League World Series appeared in two very different newspapers. Carefully read each article, looking for slanting and charged language. Point out the "verifiable facts." How do you know?

LITTLE LEAGUE SERIES BARS FOREIGNERS

WILLIAMSPORT, PA., NOV. 11 (AP)—The Little League will confine future world series to teams from the continental United States.

This was announced today at the headquarters of the national baseball organization. The effect was to exclude Taiwan, which won the series for boys 8 to 12 years old in the last four years, causing protests in that country. Japan won the two previous years, and Monterrey, Mexico, took the series in 1957 and 1958. The last United States winner was Wayne, N.J., in 1970.

The league said its board of directors had acted after a review of the competition. It said the regional championship series would be continued in Canada, the Far East, Europe and Latin America, and the play-offs for senior (ages 13 to 15) or big league (16 to 18) programs would not be affected.

A spokesman cited travel costs for foreign entries and the nationalistic approach taken abroad as reasons for the change. He described the United States programs as regional in make-up.

Since the Little League expanded in 1957 to include teams outside the continental United States, 20 foreign teams have competed. There are 9,000 teams in the United States.

Robert H. Stirrat, vice president and public relations director, would only say:

"We are standing by the board's resolution and will offer no further details."

The world series will be played next Aug. 19 to 23 at Williamsport, the birthplace of Little League baseball. Only four teams—the United States regional champions—will be entered. There were eight when foreign teams competed.

The ruling eliminates from world series competition children of American servicemen stationed in Europe because, a spokesman said, they are considered "foreign."

The first world series was played in 1947.

Last Aug. 24 Taiwan wrapped up its fourth straight world series with a 12–1 victory in the final over Red Bluff, Calif. The run was the first allowed by the Taiwanese in 46 innings, so complete did they dominate the series.

The team was led by Lin Wen-hsiung, a 12-year-old, right-handed pitcher, who hit two home runs and hurled a two-hitter in the final, striking out 15 of the 21 batters he faced.

The game was shown throughout Taiwan on television via satellite at 3 A.M., but many fans there considered the outcome such a foregone conclusion that they elected to go to sleep rather than watch.

Nevertheless, there were bursts of firecrackers before dawn to celebrate the victory.

So proficient have Taiwanese youngsters become at baseball that they have dominated not only Little League competition, but also divisions for older boys.

This year a Taiwanese team captured the Senior Little League world championship in Gary, Ind., for the third straight time, and the island's Big League team won the title at Fort Lauderdale, Fla., in its first attempt.

LITTLE LEAGUE BANS FOREIGNERS

No More Chinese HRs

Little League Shrinks Map
Limits World Series After Taiwan Romp

After watching Taiwan dominate the Little League World Series at Williamsport, Pa., for four years, the American sponsors found a way yesterday to end that victory streak: they banned foreign entries.

The ban, obviously, will do away with the so-called Chinese home run, a phrase New Yorkers learned about when the upper deck hung out over the playing field at the defunct Polo Grounds where the foul lines were short and homers were plentiful.

Peter J. McGovern, chief executive officer and board chairman of the Little League, said that the series would be restricted to the four regional U.S. champions from now on.

Robert H. Stirrat, vice president and public relations director for the league, said that the organization "is not nationalistic in its point of view." Stirrat said the group feels Little League is basically a community program and it intends returning to the original concept.

"The board took a long view of the international aspects of the program and decided a reassessment of the World Series competition for children aged 12 and under had to be regarded," Stirrat said. "It was their decision to limit the series from here on to the United States."

Stirrat also emphasized the ban on foreign clubs involves only the Little League series at Williamsport. He added that the senior league (13–15) and big league (16–18) are not affected. Those championships will still be waged on an international basis.

"The senior division is the world's largest baseball program," Stirrat said. "But they are unaffected by the decision." The seniors' finale will be played at Gary, Ind., with the big league finals at Fort Lauderdale, Fla.

Japanese Led the Parade

League officials deny the latest ruling was an effort to exclude Taiwan or any other non-U.S. Squad. There are 9,000 little leagues in this country and since the Williamsport brass broadened its program in 1957 to include "outside" teams, 20 foreign clubs have competed.

An American team hasn't been the Little League champ since Wayne, N.J., in 1970. Since then, Japanese representatives won in 1968 and 1969, followed by Taiwan the past four years.

Regional championships will continue to be held in Canada, Latin America, Europe and the Far East, but those winners will not compete in Williamsport.

"The Little League is taken pretty much as a summertime activity for kids in the United States," Stirrat said, "and the World Series is sort of a natural finish of the season for them."

Now, with only four clubs contesting for the 1975 title, which will be decided Aug. 19–23 at Williamsport, Little League brass were undecided as to its new format. They must determine whether sudden-death or a double elimination series will be played.

In any event, the Little League World Series will be an all-American affair.

What kind of newspaper do you think each article appeared in? On what stylistic evidence did you base your decision? Does a knowledge of the kind of newspaper it appeared in help to explain the way in which it was written? In an essay compare and contrast the two reports and your evaluations of their use of slanting and charged language.

GOBBLEDYGOOK

Stuart Chase

*The late Stuart Chase, well-known commentator on the
dynamics of our language and author of* The Power of Words
and The Tyranny of Words, *worked as a consultant for the
federal government to help bureaucrats write "plain"
English. In this now classic essay, Chase examines the world
of obscure language, or gobbledygook, as it has come to be
called. Chase believes "Gobbledygook not only flourishes in
government bureaus but grows wild and lush in the law, the
universities, and sometimes among the literati." He tells us
how to recognize "windy and pretentious language," and
offers some practical advice about "reducing the gobble."*

Said Franklin Roosevelt, in one of his early presidential speeches: "I see   1
one-third of a nation ill-housed, ill-clad, ill-nourished." Translated into
standard bureaucratic prose his statement would read:

> It is evident that a substantial number of persons within the Continental bound-
> aries of the United States have inadequate financial resources with which to
> purchase the products of agricultural communities and industrial establish-
> ments. It would appear that for a considerable segment of the population,
> possibly as much as 33.3333* of the total, there are inadequate housing facil-
> ities, and an equally significant proportion is deprived of the proper types of
> clothing and nutriment.

This rousing satire on gobbledygook—or talk among the bureaucrats—   2
is adapted from a report[1] prepared by the Federal Security Agency is an
attempt to break out of the verbal squirrel cage. "Gobbledygook" was
coined by an exasperated Congressman, Maury Maverick of Texas, and
means using two, or three, or ten words in the place of one, or using a
five-syllable word where a single syllable would suffice. Maverick was
censuring the forbidding prose of executive departments in Washington,
but the term has now spread to windy and pretentious language in general.

"Gobbledygook" itself is a good example of the way a language   3
grows. There was no word for the event before Maverick's invention; one

---

* Not carried beyond four places.
[1] This and succeeding quotations from F.S.A. report by special permission of the author,
Milton Hall.

had to say: "You know, that terrible, involved, polysyllabic language those government people use down in Washington." Now one word takes the place of a dozen.

A British member of Parliament, A. P. Herbert, also exasperated with bureaucratic jargon, translated Nelson's immortal phrase, "England expects every man to do his duty": 4

> England anticipates that, as regards the current emergency, personnel will face up to the issues, and exercise appropriately the functions allocated to their respective occupational groups.

A New Zealand official made the following report after surveying a plot of ground for an athletic field:[2] 5

> It is obvious from the difference in elevation with relation to the short depth of the property that the contour is such as to preclude any reasonable development potential for active recreation.

Seems the plot was too steep.

An office manager sent this memo to his chief: 6

> Verbal contact with Mr. Blank regarding the attached notification of promotion has elicited the attached representation intimating that he prefers to decline the assignment.

Seems Mr. Blank didn't want the job.

> A doctor testified at an English trial that one of the parties was suffering from "circumorbital haematoma."

Seems the party had a black eye.

> In August 1952 the U.S. Department of Agriculture put out a pamphlet entitled: "Cultural and Pathogenic Variability in Single-Condial and Hyphaltip Isolates of Hemlin-Thosporium Turcicum Pass."

Seems it was about corn leaf disease.

On reaching the top of the Finsteraarhorn in 1845, M. Dollfus-Ausset, when he got his breath, exclaimed: 7

> The soul communes in the infinite with those icy peaks which seem to have their roots in the bowels of eternity.

Seems he enjoyed the view.

A governmental department announced: 8

---

[2] This item and the next two are from the piece on gobbledygook by W.E. Farbstein, *New York Times,* March 29, 1953.

Voucherable expenditures necessary to provide adequate dental treatment required as adjunct to medical treatment being rendered a pay patient in in-patient status may be incurred as required at the expense of the Public Health Service.

Seems you can charge your dentist bill to the Public Health Service. Or can you?

LEGAL TALK

Gobbledygook not only flourishes in government bureaus but grows wild   9
and lush in the law, the universities, and sometimes among the literati. Mr.
Micawber was a master of gobbledygook, which he hoped would improve
his fortunes. It is almost always found in offices too big for face-to-face
talk. Gobbledygook can be defined as squandering words, packing a message with excess baggage and so introducing semantic "noise." Or it can
be scrambling words in a message so that meaning does not come through.
The directions on cans, bottles, and packages for putting the contents to
use are often a good illustration. Gobbledygook must not be confused with
double talk, however, for the intentions of the sender are usually honest.

I offer you a round fruit and say, "Have an orange." Not so an expert   10
in legal phraseology, as parodied by editors of *Labor:*

> I hereby give and convey to you, all and singular, my estate and interests, right,
> title, claim and advantages of and in said orange, together with all rind, juice,
> pulp, and pits, and all rights and advantages therein . . . anything hereinbefore
> or hereinafter or in any other deed or deeds, instrument or instruments of whatever nature or kind whatsoever, to the contrary, in any wise, notwithstanding.

The state of Ohio, after five years of work, has redrafted its legal code   11
in modern English, eliminating 4,500 sections and doubtless a blizzard of
"whereases" and "hereinafters." Legal terms of necessity must be closely
tied to their referents, but the early solons tried to do this the hard way, by
adding synonyms. They hoped to trap the physical event in a net of words,
but instead they created a mumbo-jumbo beyond the power of the layman,
and even many a lawyer, to translate. Legal talk is studded with tautologies, such as "cease and desist," "give and convey," "irrelevant, incompetent, and immaterial." Furthermore, legal jargon is a dead language;
it is not spoken and it is not growing. An official of one of the big insurance
companies calls their branch of it "bafflegab." Here is a sample from his
collection.[3]

> One-half to his mother, if living, if not to his father, and one-half to his
> mother-in-law, if living, if not to his mother, if living, if not to his father.

[3] Interview with Clifford B. Reeves by Sylvia F. Porter, New York *Evening Post*, March 14,
1952.

Thereafter payment is to be made in a single sum to his brothers. On the one-half payable to his mother, if living, if not to his father, he does not bring in his mother-in-law as the next payee to receive, although on the one-half to his mother-in-law, he does bring in the mother or father.

You apply for an insurance policy, pass the tests, and instead of a 12 straightforward "here is your policy," you receive something like this:

This policy is issued in consideration of the application therefor, copy of which application is attached hereto and made part hereof, and of the payment for said insurance on the life of the above-named insured.

ACADEMIC TALK

The pedagogues may be less repetitious than the lawyers, but many use 13 even longer words. It is a symbol of their calling to prefer Greek and Latin derivatives to Anglo-Saxon. Thus instead of saying: "I like short clear words," many a professor would think it more seemly to say: "I prefer an abbreviated phraseology, distinguished for its lucidity." Your professor is sometimes right, the longer word may carry the meaning better—but not because it is long. Allen Upward in his book *The New Word* warmly advocates Anglo-Saxon English as against what he calls "Mediterranean" English, with its polysyllables built up like a skyscraper.

Professional pedagogy, still alternating between the Middle Ages and 14 modern science, can produce what Henshaw Ward once called the most repellent prose known to man. It takes an iron will to read as much as a page of it. Here is a sample of what is known in some quarters as "pedageese":

Realization has grown that the curriculum or the experiences of learners change and improve only as those who are most directly involved examine their goals, improve their understandings and increase their skill in performing the tasks necessary to reach newly defined goals. This places the focus upon teacher, lay citizen and learner as partners in curricular improvement and as the individuals who must change, if there is to be curriculum change.

I think there is an idea concealed here somewhere. I think it means: "If 15 we are going to change the curriculum, teacher, parent, and student must all help." The reader is invited to get out his semantic decoder and check on my translation. Observe there is no technical language in this gem of pedageese, beyond possibly the word "curriculum." It is just a simple idea heavily ononverbalized.

In another kind of academic talk the author may display his learning to 16 conceal a lack of ideas. A bright instructor, for instance, in need of prestige may select a common sense proposition for the subject of a learned monograph—say, "Modern cities are hard to live in" and adorn it with imposing polysyllables: "Urban existence in the perpendicular declivities of megalopolis . . ." etc. He coins some new terms to transfix the reader— "mega-decibel" or "strato-cosmopolis"—and works them vigorously. He is careful to add a page or two of differential equations to show the "scatter." And then he publishes, with 147 footnotes and a bibliography to knock your eye out. If the authorities are dozing, it can be worth an associate professorship.

While we are on the campus, however, we must not forget that the technical language of the natural sciences and some terms in the social sciences, forbidding as they may sound to the layman, are quite necessary. Without them, specialists could not communicate what they find. Trouble arises when experts expect the uninitiated to understand the words; when they tell the jury, for instance, that the defendant is suffering from "circumorbital haematoma." 17

Here are two authentic quotations. Which was written by a distinguished modern author, and which by a patient in a mental hospital? You will find the answer at the end of this essay. 18

1. Have just been to supper. Did not knowing what the woodchuck sent me here. How when the blue blue blue on the said anyone can do it that tries. Such is the presidential candidate.

2. No history of a family to close with those and close. Never shall he be alone to be alone to be alone to be alone to be alone to lend a hand and leave it left and wasted.

REDUCING THE GOBBLE

As government and business offices grow larger, the need for doing something about gobbledygook increases. Fortunately the biggest office in the world is working hard to reduce it. The Federal Security Agency in Washington,* with nearly 100 million clients on its books, began analyzing its communication lines some years ago, with gratifying results. Surveys find trouble in three main areas: correspondence with clients about their social security problems, office memos, official reports. 19

Clarity and brevity, as well as common humanity, are urgently needed in this vast establishment which deals with disability, old age, and unemployment. The surveys found instead many cases of long-windedness, foggy meanings, clichés, and singsong phrases, and gross neglect of the reader's point of view. Rather than talking to a real person, the writer was talking to himself. "We often write like a man walking on stilts." 20

* *Ed. note:* Later the Department of Health, Education, and Welfare and subsequently the Department of Health and Human Resources.

Here is a typical case of long-windedness: 21

> *Gobbledygook as found:* "We are wondering if sufficient time has passed so that you are in a position to indicate whether favorable action may now be taken on our recommendation for the reclassification of Mrs. Blank, junior clerk-stenographer, CAF 2, to assistant clerk-stenographer, CAF 3?"
>
> *Suggested improvement:* "Have you yet been able to act on our recommendation to reclassify Mrs. Blank?"

Another case: 22

> Although the Central Efficiency Rating Committee recognizes that there are many desirable changes that could be made in the present efficiency rating system in order to make it more realistic and more workable than it now is, this committee is of the opinion that no further change should be made in the present system during the current year. Because of conditions prevailing throughout the country and the resultant turnover in personnel, and difficulty in administering the Federal programs, further mechanical improvement in the present rating system would require staff retraining and other administrative expense which would seem best withheld until the official termination of hostilities, and until restoration of regular operation.

The F.S.A. invites us to squeeze the gobbledygook out of this statement. Here is my attempt:

> The Central Efficiency Rating Committee recognizes that desirable changes could be made in the present system. We believe, however, that no change should be attempted until the war is over.

This cuts the statement from 111 to 30 words, about one-quarter of the   23
original, but perhaps the reader can do still better. What of importance
have I left out?

Sometimes in a book which I am reading for information—not for   24
literary pleasure—I run a pencil through the surplus words. Often I can cut
a section to half its length with an improvement in clarity. Magazines like
The Reader's Digest have reduced this process to an art. Are long-
windedness and obscurity a cultural lag from the days when writing was
reserved for priests and cloistered scholars? The more words and the deeper
the mystery, the greater their prestige and the firmer the hold on their jobs.
And the better the candidate's chance today to have his doctoral thesis
accepted.

The F.S.A. surveys found that a great deal of writing was obscure   25
although not necessarily prolix. Here is a letter sent to more than 100,000
inquirers, a classic example of murky prose. To clarify it, one needs to *add*
words, not cut them:

In order to be fully insured, an individual must have earned $50 or more in covered employment for as many quarters of coverage as half the calendar quarters elapsing between 1936 and the quarter in which he reaches age 65 or dies, whichever first occurs.

Probably no one without the technical jargon of the office could translate this: nevertheless, it was sent out to drive clients mad for seven years. One poor fellow wrote back: "I am no longer in covered employment. I have an outside job now."

Many words and phrases in officialese seem to come out automatically, as if from lower centers of the brain. In this standardized prose people never *get jobs,* they "secure employment"; *before* and *after* become "prior to" and "subsequent to"; one does not *do,* one "performs"; nobody *knows* a thing, he is "fully cognizant"; one never *says,* he "indicates." A great favorite at present is "implement."   26

Some charming boners occur in this talking-in-one's-sleep. For instance: 27

The problem of extending coverage to all employees, regardless of size, is not as simple as surface appearances indicate.
Though the proportions of all males and females in ages 16–45 are essentially the same. . . .
Dairy cattle, usually and commonly embraced in dairying. . . .

In its manual to employees, the F.S.A. suggests the following: 28

Instead of	Use
give consideration to	consider
make inquiry regarding	inquire
is of the opinion	believes
comes into conflict with	conflicts
information which is of a confidential nature	confidential information

Professional or office gobbledygook often arises from using the passive rather than the active voice. Instead of looking you in the eye, as it were, and writing "This act requires . . ." the office worker looks out of the window and writes: "It is required by this statute that. . . ." When the bureau chief says, "We expect Congress to cut your budget," the message is only too clear; but usually he says, "It is expected that the departmental budget estimates will be reduced by Congress."   29

Gobbled: "All letters prepared for the signature of the Administrator will be single spaced."
Ungobbled: "Single space for all letters for the Administrator." (Thus cutting 13 words to 7.)

ONLY PEOPLE CAN READ

The F.S.A. surveys pick up the point that human communication involves   30
a listener as well as a speaker. Only people can read, though a lot of
writing seems to be addressed to beings in outer space. To whom are you
talking? The sender of the officialese message often forgets the chap on the
other end of the line.

A woman with two small children wrote the F.S.A. asking what she   31
should do about payments, as her husband had lost his memory. "If he
never gets able to work," she said, "and stays in an institution would I be
able to draw any benefits? . . . I don't know how I am going to live and
raise my children since he is disable to work. Please give me some information. . . ."

To this human appeal, she received a shattering blast of gobbledygook,   32
beginning, "State unemployment compensation laws do no provide any
benefits for sick or disabled individuals . . . in order to qualify an individual must have a certain number of quarters of coverage . . ." etc., etc.
Certainly if the writer had been thinking about the poor woman he would
not have dragged in unessential material about old-age insurance. If he had
pictured a mother without means to care for her children, he would have
told her where she might get help—from the local office which handles aid
to dependent children, for instance.

Gobbledygook of this kind would largely evaporate if we thought of   33
our messages as two way—in the above case, if we pictured ourselves
talking on the doorstep of a shabby house to a woman with two children
tugging at her skirts, who in her distress does not know which way to turn.

RESULTS OF THE SURVEY

The F.S.A. survey showed that office documents could be cut 20 to 50   34
percent, with an improvement in clarity and a great saving to taxpayers in
paper and payrolls.

A handbook was prepared and distributed by key officials.[4] They read   35
it, thought about it, and presently began calling section meetings to discuss
gobbledygook. More booklets were ordered, and the local output of documents began to improve. A Correspondence Review Section was established as a kind of laboratory to test murky messages. A supervisor could
send up samples for analysis and suggestions. The handbook is now used
for training new members; and many employees keep it on their desks
along with the dictionary. . . .

[4]By Milton Hall.

The handbook makes clear the enormous amount of gobbledygook 36
which automatically spreads in any large office, together with ways and
means to keep it under control. I would guess that at least half of all the
words circulating around the bureaus of the world are "irrelevant, incompetent, and immaterial"—to use a favorite legalism; or are just plain
"unnecessary"—to ungobble it.

My favorite story of removing the gobble from gobbledygook concerns 37
the Bureau of Standards at Washington. I have told it before but perhaps
the reader will forgive the repetition. A New York plumber wrote the
Bureau that he had found hydrochloric acid fine for cleaning drains, and
was it harmless? Washington replied: "The efficacy of hydrochloric acid is
indisputable, but the chlorine residue is incompatible with metallic perma-
nence."

The plumber wrote back that he was mighty glad the Bureau agreed 38
with him. The Bureau replied with a note of alarm: "We cannot assume
responsibility for the production of toxic and noxious residues with hydrochloric acid, and suggest that you use an alternate procedure." The
plumber was happy to learn that the Bureau still agreed with him.

Whereupon Washington exploded: "Don't use hydrochloric acid; it 39
eats hell out of the pipes!"

NOTE: The second quotation [paragraph 18] comes from Gertrude Stein's *Lucy Church Amiably*.

QUESTIONS ON CONTENT

1. What is gobbledygook? Give three examples of gobbledygook not mentioned by Chase. Why does Chase object to gobbledygook? What does he
mean when he says, "Gobbledygook . . . would largely evaporate if we
thought of our messages as two way . . ." (33).

2. Why do bureaucrats, lawyers, and professors, among others, use gobbledygook? Is its use ever justified? Explain.

3. Do you agree with Chase's paraphrases or translations of bureaucratic
jargon in paragraphs 4 through 10? Try to rewrite the passages differently
from the way Chase has. How effective are Chase's attempts to "reduce
the gobble" in paragraphs 21–22?

4. Chase's statement "It is almost always found in offices too big for
face-to-face talk" (9) emphasizes that gobbledygook goes hand in hand
with the dehumanizing character of most of our institutions. What is the
connection between this statement and George Orwell's recommendation
in "Politics and the English Language" (p. 111) to use concrete terms
when writing?

QUESTIONS ON RHETORIC

1. What is Chase's purpose in this essay? (Glossary: *Purpose*)

2. What methods does Chase use to define gobbledygook? Why is it important for him to establish a defintion for the term? What does Chase see as the main distinction between gobbledygook and doubletalk (sometimes also referred to as *doublespeak*)? (Glossary: *Definition*)

3. What is the function of the many examples and quotations that Chase uses? Why are they important? (Glossary: *Examples*)

4. Chase concludes his essay with the story of the New York plumber. Is this conclusion effective? Why, or why not? What alternatives did Chase have to end his essay? (Glossary: *Beginnings and Endings*)

VOCABULARY

pretentious (2)	tautologies (11)	murky (25)
immortal (4)	advocates (13)	clients (25)
squandering (9)	proposition (16)	

WRITING TOPICS

1. In his essay "The Marks of an Educated Man" (*Context,* Spring 1961), Alan Simpson presents the following example of inflated prose, or, as he aptly dubs it, "verbal smog."

> It is inherent to motivational phenomena that there is a drive for more gratification than is realistically possible, on any level or in any type of personality organization. Likewise it is inherent to the world of objects that not all potentially desirable opportunities can be realized within a human life span. Therefore, any personality must involve an organization that allocates opportunities for gratifications, that systematizes precedence relative to the limited possibilities. The possibilities of gratification, simultaneously or sequentially, of all need dispositions are severely limited by the structure of the object system and by the intrasystemic incompatibility of the consequences of gratifying them all.

What is the author of this passage trying to say? Rewrite the paragraph eliminating the unnecessary verbiage.

2. The following item appeared in the *San Francisco Chronicle.*

STATE MAKES IT PERFECTLY CLEAR

SACRAMENTO For some time the public has wondered what to make of most bureaucratic twaddle—but a new State law has set the record straight at last.

From the revised State code of the Division of Consumer Services, Department of Consumer Affairs, Title 4: subsection 2102, comes the official word:

"Tenses, Gender and Number: For the purpose of the rules and regulations contained in this chapter, the present tense includes the past and future tenses, and the future, the present; the masculine gender includes the feminine, and feminine, the masculine; and the singular includes the plural, and the plural the singular."

Our Correspondent

Comment on this example of gobbledygook. Why is bureaucratic and legal writing particularly prone to gobbledygook?

3. Using examples from Chase's essay and other reading you have done, write an essay in which you discuss the differences between "jargon," "technical language," and "gobbledygook."

PROPAGANDA: HOW NOT TO BE BAMBOOZLED

Donna Woolfolk Cross

While most people are against propaganda in principle, few people know exactly what it is and how it works. In the following essay, Donna Woolfolk Cross, who teaches at Onondaga Community College in New York, takes the mystery out of propaganda. Cross starts by providing a definition of propaganda. She then classifies the tricks of the propagandist into thirteen major categories and discusses each thoroughly. Her essay is chock-full of useful advice on how not to be manipulated by propaganda.

Propaganda. If an opinion poll were taken tomorrow, we can be sure that nearly everyone would be against it because it *sounds* so bad. When we say, "Oh, that's just propaganda," it means, to most people, "That's a pack of lies." But really, propaganda is simply a means of persuasion and so it can be put to work for good causes as well as bad—to persuade people to give to charity, for example, or to love their neighbors, or to stop polluting the environment. 1

For good or evil, propaganda pervades our daily lives, helping to shape our attitudes on a thousand subjects. Propaganda probably determines the brand of toothpaste you use, the movies you see, the candidates you elect when you get to the polls. Propaganda works by tricking us, by momentarily distracting the eye while the rabbit pops out from beneath the cloth. Propaganda works best with an uncritical audience. Joseph Goebbels, Propaganda Minister in Nazi Germany, once defined his work as "the conquest of the masses." The masses would not have been conquered, however, if they had known how to challenge and to question, how to make distinctions between propaganda and reasonable argument. 2

People are bamboozled mainly because they don't recognize propaganda when they see it. They need to be informed about the various devices that can be used to mislead and deceive—about the propagandist's overflowing bag of tricks. The following, then, are some common pitfalls for the unwary. 3

149

1. NAME-CALLING

As its title suggests, this device consists of labeling people or ideas with   4
words of bad connotation, literally, "calling them names." Here the propagandist tries to arouse our contempt so we will dismiss the "bad name"
person or idea without examining its merits.

Bad names have played a tremendously important role in the history of   5
the world. They have ruined reputations and ended lives, sent people to
prison and to war, and just generally made us mad at each other for
centuries.

Name-calling can be used against policies, practices, beliefs and ide-   6
als, as well as against individuals, groups, races, nations. Name-calling is
at work when we hear a candidate for office described as a "foolish
idealist" or a "two-faced liar" or when an incumbent's policies are denounced as "reckless," "reactionary," or just plain "stupid." Some of
the most effective names a public figure can be called are ones that may not
denote anything specific: "Congresswoman Jane Doe is a *bleeding heart!*"
(Did she vote for funds to help paraplegics?) or "The Senator is a *tool of
Washington!*" (Did he happen to agree with the President?) Senator
Yakalot uses name-calling when he denounces his opponent's "radical
policies" and calls them (and him) "socialist," "pinko," and part of a
"heartless plot." He also uses it when he calls small cars "puddle-
jumpers," "can openers," and "motorized baby buggies."

The point here is that when the propagandist uses name-calling, he   7
doesn't want us to think—merely to react, blindly, unquestioningly. So the
best defense against being taken in by name-calling is to stop and ask,
"Forgetting the bad name attached to it, what are the merits of the idea
itself? What does this name really mean, anyway?"

2. GLITTERING GENERALITIES

Glittering generalities are really name-calling in reverse. Name-calling   8
uses words with bad connotations; glittering generalities are words with
good connotations—"virtue words," as the Institute for Propaganda Analysis has called them. The Institute explains that while name-calling tries to
get us to *reject* and *condemn* someone or something without examining the
evidence, glittering generalities try to get us to *accept* and *agree* without
examining the evidence.

We believe in, fight for, live by "virtue words" which we feel deeply   9
about: "justice," "motherhood," "the American way," "our Constitutional rights," "our Christian heritage." These sound good, but when we
examine them closely, they turn out to have no specific, definable mean-

ing. They just make us feel good. Senator Yakalot uses glittering generalities when he says, "I stand for all that is good in America, for our
American way and our American birthright." But what exactly *is* "good
for America"? How can we define our "American birthright"? Just
what parts of the American society and culture does "our American way"
refer to?

We often make the mistake of assuming we are personally unaffected   10
by glittering generalities. The next time you find yourself assuming that,
listen to a political candidate's speech on TV and see how often the use of
glittering generalities elicits cheers and applause. That's the danger of
propaganda; it *works*. Once again, our defense against it is to ask questions: Forgetting the virtue words attached to it, what are the merits of the
idea itself? What does "Americanism" (or "freedom" or "truth") really
mean here? . . .

Both name-calling and glittering generalities work by stirring our emo-   11
tions in the hope that this will cloud our thinking. Another approach that
propaganda uses is to create a distraction, a "red herring," that will make
people forget or ignore the real issues. There are several different kinds of
"red herrings" that can be used to distract attention.

3. PLAIN FOLKS APPEAL

"Plain folks" is the device by which a speaker tries to win our confidence   12
and support by appearing to be a person like ourselves—"just one of the
plain folks." The plain-folks appeal is at work when candidates go around
shaking hands with factory workers, kissing babies in supermarkets, and
sampling pasta with Italians, fried chicken with Southerners, bagels and
blintzes with Jews. "Now I'm a businessman like yourselves" is a plain-
folks appeal, as is "I've been a farm boy all my life." Senator Yakalot
tries the plain-folks appeal when he says, "I'm just a small-town boy like
you fine people." The use of such expressions once prompted Lyndon
Johnson to quip, "Whenever I hear someone say, 'I'm just an old country
lawyer,' the first thing I reach for is my wallet to make sure it's still there."

The irrelevancy of the plain-folks appeal is obvious: even if the man *is*   13
"one of us" (which may not be true at all), that doesn't mean that his ideas
and programs are sound—or even that he honestly has our best interests at
heart. As with glittering generalities, the danger here is that we may
mistakenly assume we are immune to this appeal. But propagandists
wouldn't use it unless it had been proved to work. You can protect yourself
by asking, "Aside from his 'nice guy next door' image, what does this
man stand for? Are his ideas and his past record really supportive of my
best interests?"

4. *ARGUMENTUM AD POPULUM* (STROKING)

Argumentum ad populum means "argument to the people" or "telling the   14
people what they want to hear." The colloquial term from the Watergate
era is "stroking," which conjures up pictures of small animals or children
being stroked or soothed with compliments until they come to like the
person doing the complimenting—and, by extension, his or her ideas.

We all like to hear nice things about ourselves and the group we belong   15
to—we like to be liked—so it stands to reason that we will respond warmly
to a person who tells us we are "hard-working taxpayers" or "the most
generous, free-spirited nation in the world." Politicians tell farmers they
are the "backbone of the American economy" and college students that
they are the "leaders and policy makers of tomorrow." Commercial advertisers use stroking more insidiously by asking a question which invites
a flattering answer: "What kind of a man reads *Playboy?*" (Does he really
drive a Porsche and own $10,000 worth of sound equipment?) Senator
Yakalot is stroking his audience when he calls them the "decent law-
abiding citizens that are the great pulsing heart and the life blood of this,
our beloved country," and when he repeatedly refers to them as "you fine
people," "you wonderful folks."

Obviously, the intent here is to sidetrack us from thinking critically   16
about the man and his ideas. Our own good qualities have nothing to do
with the issue at hand. Ask yourself, "Apart from the nice things he has
to say about me (and my church, my nation, my ethnic group, my neighbors), what does the candidate stand for? Are his or her ideas in my best
interests?"

5. *ARGUMENTUM AD HOMINEM*

Argumentum ad hominem means "argument to the man" and that's exactly   17
what it is. When a propagandist uses *argumentum ad hominem,* he wants
to distract our attention from the issue under consideration with personal
attacks on the people involved. For example, when Lincoln issued the
Emancipation Proclamation, some people responded by calling him the
"baboon." But Lincoln's long arms and awkward carriage had nothing to
do with the merits of the Proclamation or the question of whether or not
slavery should be abolished.

Today *argumentum ad hominem* is still widely used and very effective.   18
You may or may not support the Equal Rights Amendment, but you should
be sure your judgment is based on the merits of the idea itself, and not the
result of someone's denunciation of the people who support the ERA as
"fanatics" or "lesbians" or "frustrated old maids." Senator Yakalot is

using *argumentum ad hominem* when he dismisses the idea of using smaller automobiles with a reference to the personal appearance of one of its supporters, Congresswoman Doris Schlepp. Refuse to be waylaid by *argumentum ad hominem* and ask, "Do the personal qualities of the person being discussed have anything to do with the issue at hand? Leaving him or her aside, how good is the idea itself?"

6. TRANSFER (GUILT OR GLORY BY ASSOCIATION)

In *argumentum ad hominem*, an attempt is made to associate negative   19
aspects of a person's character or personal appearance with an issue or idea he supports. The transfer device uses this same process of association to make us accept or condemn a given person or idea.

A better name for the transfer device is guilt (or glory) by association.   20
In glory by association, the propagandist tries to transfer the positive feelings of something we love and respect to the group or idea he wants us to accept. "This bill for a new dam is in the best tradition of this country, the land of Lincoln, Jefferson, and Washington," is glory by association at work. Lincoln, Jefferson, and Washington were great leaders that most of us revere and respect, but they have no logical connection to the proposal under consideration—the bill to build a new dam. Senator Yakalot uses glory by association when he says full-sized cars "have always been as American as Mom's apple pie or a Sunday drive in the country."

The process works equally well in reverse, when guilt by association is   21
used to transfer our dislike or disapproval of one idea or group to some other idea or group that the propagandist wants us to reject and condemn. "John Doe says we need to make some changes in the way our government operates; well, that's exactly what the Ku Klux Klan has said, so there's a meeting of great minds!" That's guilt by association for you; there's no logical connection between John Doe and the Ku Klux Klan apart from the one the propagandist is trying to create in our minds. He wants to distract our attention from John Doe and get us thinking (and worrying) about the Ku Klux Klan and its politics of violence. (Of course, there are sometimes legitimate associations between the two things; if John Doe had been a *member* of the Ku Klux Klan, it would be reasonable and fair to draw a connection between the man and his group.) Senator Yakalot tries to trick his audience with guilt by association when he remarks that "the words 'Community' and 'Communism' look an awful lot alike!" He does it again when he mentions that Mr. Stu Pott "sports a Fidel Castro beard."

How can we learn to spot the transfer device and distinguish between   22
fair and unfair associations? We can teach ourselves to *suspend judgment* until we have answered these questions: "Is there any legitimate connec-

tion between the idea under discussion and the thing it is associated with? Leaving the transfer device out of the picture, what are the merits of the idea by itself?''

7. BANDWAGON

Ever hear of the small, ratlike animal called the lemming? Lemmings are   23
arctic rodents with a very odd habit: periodically, for reasons no one entirely knows, they mass together in a large herd and commit suicide by rushing into deep water and drowning themselves. They all run in together, blindly, and not one of them ever seems to stop and ask, *"Why* am I doing this? Is this really what I want to do?'' and thus save itself from destruction. Obviously, lemmings are driven to perform their strange mass suicide rites by common instinct. People choose to "follow the herd" for more complex reasons, yet we are still all too often the unwitting victims of the bandwagon appeal.

Essentially, the bandwagon urges us to support an action or an opinion   24
because it is popular—because "everyone else is doing it." This call to "get on the bandwagon" appeals to the strong desire in most of us to be one of the crowd, not to be left out or alone. Advertising makes extensive use of the bandwagon appeal ("join the Pepsi people"), but so do politicians ("Let us join together in this great cause"). Senator Yakalot uses the bandwagon appeal when he says that "More and more citizens are rallying to my cause every day," and asks his audience to "join them—and me—in our fight for America."

One of the ways we can see the bandwagon appeal at work is in the   25
overwhelming success of various fashions and trends which capture the interest (and the money) of thousands of people for a short time, then disappear suddenly and completely. For a year or two in the fifties, every child in North America wanted a coonskin cap so they could be like Davy Crockett; no one wanted to be left out. After that there was the hula-hoop craze that helped to dislocate the hips of thousands of Americans. More recently, what made millions of people rush out to buy their very own "pet rocks"?

The problem here is obvious: just because everyone's doing it doesn't   26
mean that *we* should too. Group approval does not prove that something is true or is worth doing. Large numbers of people have supported actions we now condemn. Just a generation ago, Hitler and Mussolini rose to absolute and catastrophically repressive rule in two of the most sophisticated and cultured countries of Europe. When they came into power they were welled up by massive popular support from millions of people who didn't want to be "left out" at a great historical moment.

Once the mass begins to move—on the bandwagon—it becomes harder   27
and harder to perceive the leader *riding* the bandwagon. So don't be a
lemming, rushing blindly on to destruction because "everyone else is
doing it." Stop and ask, "Where is this bandwagon headed? Never mind
about everybody else, is this what is best for *me*?". . .

As we have seen, propaganda can appeal to us by arousing our emo-   28
tions or distracting our attention from the real issues at hand. But there's
a third way that propaganda can be put to work against us—by the use of
faulty logic. This approach is really more insidious than the other two
because it gives the appearance of reasonable, fair argument. It is only
when we look more closely that the holes in the logical fiber show up. The
following are some of the devices that make use of faulty logic to distort
and mislead.

8. FAULTY CAUSE AND EFFECT

As the name suggests, this device sets up a cause-and-effect relationship   29
that may not be true. The Latin name for this logical fallacy is *post hoc
ergo propter hoc,* which means "after this, therefore because of this." But
just because one thing happened after another doesn't mean that one *caused*
the other.

An example of false cause-and-effect reasoning is offered by the story   30
(probably invented) of the woman aboard the ship *Titanic*. She woke up
from a nap and, feeling seasick, looked around for a call button to summon
the steward to bring her some medication. She finally located a small
button on one of the walls of her cabin and pushed it. A split second later,
the *Titanic* grazed an iceberg in the terrible crash that was to send the entire
ship to its destruction. The woman screamed and said, "Oh, God, what
have I done? What have I done?" The humor of that anecdote comes from
the absurdity of the woman's assumption that pushing the small red button
resulted in the destruction of a ship weighing several hundred tons: "It
happened after I pushed it, therefore it must be *because* I pushed it"—*post
hoc ergo propter hoc* reasoning. There is, of course, no cause-and-effect
relationship there.

The false cause-and-effect fallacy is used very often by political can-   31
didates. "After I came to office, the rate of inflation dropped to 6 percent." But did the person do anything to cause the lower rate of inflation
or was it the result of other conditions? Would the rate of inflation have
dropped anyway, even if he hadn't come to office? Senator Yakalot uses
false cause and effect when he says "our forefathers who made this country
great never had free hot meal handouts! And look what they did for our

country!'' He does it again when he concludes that ''driving full-sized cars means a better car safety record on our American roads today.''

False cause-and-effect reasoning is terribly persuasive because it seems   32
so logical. Its appeal is apparently to experience. We swallowed X product—and the headache went away. We elected Y official and unemployment went down. Many people think, ''There *must* be a connection.'' But causality is an immensely complex phenomenon; you need a good deal of evidence to prove that an event that follows another in time was ''therefore'' caused by the first event.

Don't be taken in by false cause and effect; be sure to ask, ''Is there   33
enough evidence to prove that this cause led to that effect? Could there have been any *other* causes?''

9. FALSE ANALOGY

An analogy is a comparison between two ideas, events, or things. But   34
comparisons can be fairly made only when the things being compared are alike in significant ways. When they are not, false analogy is the result.

A famous example of this is the old proverb ''Don't change horses in   35
the middle of a stream,'' often used as an analogy to convince voters not to change administrations in the middle of a war or other crisis. But the analogy is misleading because there are so many differences between the things compared. In what ways is a war or political crisis like a stream? Is the President or head of state really very much like a horse? And is a nation of millions of people comparable to a man trying to get across a stream? Analogy is false and unfair when it compares two things that have little in common and assumes that they are identical. Senator Yakalot tries to hoodwink his listeners with false analogy when he says, ''Trying to take Americans out of the kind of cars they love is as undemocratic as trying to deprive them of the right to vote.''

Of course, analogies can be drawn that are reasonable and fair. It   36
would be reasonable, for example, to compare the results of busing in one small Southern city with the possible results in another, *if* the towns have the same kind of history, population, and school policy. We can decide for ourselves whether an analogy is false or fair by asking, ''Are the things being compared truly alike in significant ways? Do the differences between them affect the comparison?''

10. BEGGING THE QUESTION

Actually, the name of this device is rather misleading, because it does not   37
appear in the form of a question. Begging the question occurs when, in

discussing a questionable or debatable point, a person assumes as already established the very point that he is trying to prove. For example, "No thinking citizen could approve such a completely unacceptable policy as this one." But isn't the question of whether or not the policy *is* acceptable the very point to be established? Senator Yakalot begs the question when he announces that his opponent's plan won't work "because it is unworkable."

We can protect ourselves against this kind of faulty logic by asking, 38 "What is assumed in this statement? Is the assumption reasonable, or does it need more proof?"

11. THE TWO EXTREMES FALLACY (FALSE DILEMMA)

Linguists have long noted that the English language tends to view reality 39 in sets of two extremes or polar opposites. In English, things are either black or white, tall or short, up or down, front or back, left or right, good or bad, guilty or not guilty. We can ask for a "straightforward yes-or-no answer" to a question, the understanding being that we will not accept or consider anything in between. In fact, reality cannot always be dissected along such strict lines. There may be (usually are) *more* than just two possibilities or extremes to consider. We are often told to "listen to both sides of the argument." But who's to say that every argument has only two sides? Can't there be a third—even a fourth or fifth—point of view?

The two-extremes fallacy is at work in this statement by Lenin, the 40 great Marxist leader: "You cannot eliminate *one* basic assumption, one substantial part of this philosophy of Marxism (it is as if it were a block of steel), without abandoning truth, without falling into the arms of bourgeois-reactionary falsehood." In other words, if we don't agree 100 percent with every premise of Marxism, we must be placed at the opposite end of the political-economic spectrum—for Lenin, "bourgeois-reactionary falsehood." If we are not entirely *with* him, we must be against him; those are the only two possibilities open to us. Of course, this is a logical fallacy; in real life there are any number of political positions one can maintain *between* the two extremes of Marxism and capitalism. Senator Yakalot uses the two-extremes fallacy in the same way as Lenin when he tells his audience that "in this world a man's either for private enterprise or he's for socialism."

One of the most famous examples of the two-extremes fallacy in recent 41 history is the slogan, "America: Love it or leave it," with its implicit suggestion that we either accept everything just as it is in America today without complaint—or get out. Again, it should be obvious that there is a whole range of action and belief between those two extremes.

Don't be duped; stop and ask, "Are those really the only two options   42
I can choose from? Are there other alternatives not mentioned that deserve
consideration?"

12. CARD STACKING

Some questions are so multifaceted and complex that no one can make an   43
intelligent decision about them without considering a wide variety of evidence. One selection of facts could make us feel one way and another
selection could make us feel just the opposite. Card stacking is a device of
propaganda which selects only the facts that support the propagandist's
point of view, and ignores all the others. For example, a candidate could
be made to look like a legislative dynamo if you say, "Representative
McNerd introduced more new bills than any other member of the Congress," and neglect to mention that most of them were so preposterous that
they were laughed off the floor.

Senator Yakalot engages in card stacking when he talks about the   44
proposal to use smaller cars. He talks only about jobs without mentioning
the cost to the taxpayers or the very real—though still denied—threat of
depletion of resources. He says he wants to help his countrymen keep their
jobs, but doesn't mention that the corporations that offer the jobs will also
make large profits. He praises the "American chrome industry," over-
looking the fact that most chrome is imported. And so on.

The best protection against card stacking is to take the "Yes, but . . ."   45
attitude. This device of propaganda is not untrue, but then again it is not
the *whole* truth. So ask yourself, "Is this person leaving something out that
I should know about? Is there some other information that should be
brought to bear on this question?" . . .

So far, we have considered three approaches that the propagandist can   46
use to influence our thinking: appealing to our emotions, distracting our
attention, and misleading us with logic that may appear to be reasonable
but is in fact faulty and deceiving. But there is a fourth approach that is
probably the most common propaganda trick of them all.

13. TESTIMONIAL

The testimonial device consists in having some loved or respected person   47
give a statement of support (testimonial) for a given product or idea. The
problem is that the person being quoted may *not* be an expert in the field;
in fact, he may know nothing at all about it. Using the name of a man who

is skilled and famous in one field to give a testimonial for something in another field is unfair and unreasonable.

Senator Yakalot tries to mislead his audience with testimonial when he   48
tells them that "full-sized cars have been praised by great Americans like John Wayne and Jack Jones, as well as by leading experts on car safety and comfort."

Testimonial is used extensively in TV ads, where it often appears in   49
such bizarre forms as Joe Namath's endorsement of a pantyhose brand. Here, of course, the "authority" giving the testimonial not only is no expert about pantyhose, but obviously stands to gain something (money!) by making the testimonial.

When celebrities endorse a political candidate, they may not be making   50
money by doing so, but we should still question whether they are in any better position to judge than we ourselves. Too often we are willing to let others we like or respect make our decisions *for us,* while we follow along acquiescently. And this is the purpose of testimonial—to get us to agree and accept *without* stopping to think. Be sure to ask, "Is there any reason to believe that this person (or organization or publication or whatever) has any more knowledge or information than I do on this subject? What does the idea amount to on is own merits, without the benefit of testimonial?"

The cornerstone of democratic society is reliance upon an informed and   51
educated electorate. To be fully effective citizens we need to be able to challenge and to question wisely. A dangerous feeling of indifference toward our political processes exists today. We often abandon our right, our duty, to criticize and evaluate by dismissing *all* politicians as "crooked," *all* new bills and proposals as "just more government bureaucracy." But there are important distinctions to be made, and this kind of apathy can be fatal to democracy.

If we are to be led, let us not be led blindly, but critically, intelligently,   52
with our eyes open. If we are to continue to be a government "by the people," let us become informed about the methods and purposes of propaganda, so we can be the masters, not the slaves of our destiny.

QUESTIONS ON CONTENT

1. What is propaganda? Who uses propaganda? Why is it used?

2. Why does Cross feel that people should be informed about propaganda? What is her advice for dealing with it?

3. What is "begging the question"?

4. What, according to Cross, is the most common progaganda trick of them all? Provide some examples of it from your own experience.

5. Why does Cross feel that it is necessary for people in a democratic society to become informed about the methods and practices of propaganda?

QUESTIONS ON RHETORIC

1. Why is classification an appropriate organizational strategy for Cross to use in this essay? (Glossary: *Division and Classification*)

2. How does Cross organize the discussion of each propaganda device she includes in her essay?

3. What use does Cross make of examples in her essay? How effective do you find them? Explain. (Glossary: *Examples*)

4. In her discussion of the bandwagon appeal, Cross uses the analogy of the lemmings. How does this analogy work? Why is it not a "false analogy"? (Glossary: *Analogy*)

VOCABULARY

connotations (8)   colloquial (14)   spectrum (40)
elicits (10)   insidiously (15)

WRITING TOPICS

1. As Cross says in the beginning of her essay, propaganda "can be put to work for good causes as well as bad" (1). Using materials from the Red Cross, United Way, or some other public service organization, write an essay in which you discuss the propaganda used by such organizations. How would you characterize their appeals? Do you ever find such propaganda objectionable? Does the end always justify the means?

2. Using the devices described by Cross, try a piece of propaganda yourself. You can attempt to persuade your classmates to (a) join a particular campus organization, (b) support, either spiritually or financially, a controversial movement or issue on campus, or (c) vote for one candidate and not another in a campus election.

INAUGURAL ADDRESS

John F. Kennedy

*John Fitzgerald Kennedy (1917–1963), the thirty-fifth
president of the United States, was assassinated in Dallas,
Texas, on November 22, 1963. Kennedy, the youngest man
ever elected president, was known both for the youthful and
hopeful image he brought to the White House and for the
eloquence of his speeches. In his inaugural address Kennedy
used powerful rhetoric to urge people both to become
involved in their country's affairs and to join the fight against
the spread of communism.*

We observe today not a victory of party but a celebration of freedom, 1
symbolizing an end as well as a beginning, signifying renewal as well as
change. For I have sworn before you and Almighty God the same solemn
oath our forebears prescribed nearly a century and three-quarters ago.

The world is very different now. For man holds in his mortal hands the 2
power to abolish all forms of human poverty and all forms of human life.
And yet the same revolutionary belief for which our forebears fought is still
at issue around the globe, the belief that the rights of man come not from
the generosity of the state but from the hand of God.

We dare not forget today that we are the heirs of that first revolution. 3
Let the word go forth from this time and place, to friend and foe alike, that
the torch has been passed to a new generation of Americans, born in this
century, tempered by war, disciplined by a hard and bitter peace, proud of
our ancient heritage, and unwilling to witness or permit the slow undoing
of those human rights to which this nation has always been committed, and
to which we are committed today at home and around the world.

Let every nation know, whether it wishes us well or ill, that we shall 4
pay any price, bear any burden, meet and hardship, support any friend,
oppose any foe to assure the survival and the success of liberty.

This much we pledge—and more. 5

To those old allies whose cultural and spiritual origins we share, we 6
pledge the loyalty of faithful friends. United, there is little we cannot do in
a host of co-operative ventures. Divided, there is little we can do, for we
dare not meet a powerful challenge at odds and split asunder.

To those new states whom we welcome to the ranks of the free, we 7
pledge our word that one form of colonial control shall not have passed

away merely to be replaced by a far more iron tyranny. We shall not always expect to find them supporting our view. But we shall always hope to find them strongly supporting their own freedom, and to remember that, in the past, those who foolishly sought power by riding the back of the tiger ended up inside.

To those peoples in the huts and villages of half the globe struggling to   8
break the bonds of mass misery, we pledge our best efforts to help them help themselves, for whatever period is required, not because the Communists may be doing it, not because we seek their votes, but because it is right. If a free society cannot help the many who are poor, it cannot save the few who are rich.

To our sister republics south of our border, we offer a special pledge: 9
to convert our good words into good deeds, in a new alliance for progress, to assist free men and free governments in casting off the chains of poverty. But this peaceful revolution of hope cannot become the prey of hostile powers. Let all our neighbors know that we shall join with them to oppose aggression or subversion anywhere in the Americas. And let every other power know that this hemisphere intends to remain the master of its own house.

To that world assembly of sovereign states, the United Nations, our last   10
best hope in an age where the instruments of war have far outpaced the instruments of peace, we renew our pledge of support: to prevent it from becoming merely a forum for invective, to strengthen its shield of the new and the weak, and to enlarge the area in which its writ may run.

Finally, to those nations who would make themselves our adversary,   11
we offer not a pledge but a request: that both sides begin anew the quest for peace, before the dark powers of destruction unleashed by science engulf all humanity in planned or accidental self-destruction.

We dare not tempt them with weakness. For only when our arms are   12
sufficient beyond doubt can we be certain beyond doubt that they will never be employed.

But neither can two great and powerful groups of nations take comfort   13
from our present course—both sides over-burdened by the cost of modern weapons, both rightly alarmed by the steady spread of the deadly atom, yet both racing to alter that uncertain balance of terror that stays the hand of mankind's final war.

So let us begin anew, remembering on both sides that civility is not a   14
sign of weakness, and sincerity is always subject to proof. Let us never negotiate out of fear, but let us never fear to negotiate.

Let both sides explore what problems unite us instead of belaboring   15
those problems which divide us.

Let both sides, for the first time, formulate serious and precise pro-   16 posals for the inspection and control of arms, and bring the absolute power to destroy other nations under the absolute control of all nations.

Let both sides seek to invoke the wonders of science instead of its   17
terrors. Together let us explore the stars, conquer the deserts, eradicate disease, tap the ocean depths and encourage the arts and commerce.

Let both sides unite to heed in all corners of the earth the command of   18
Isaiah to ''undo the heavy burdens . . . [and] let the oppressed go free.''

And if a beachhead of co-operation may push back the jungle of sus-   19
picion, let both sides join in creating a new endeavor, not a new balance of power, but a new world of law, where the strong are just and the weak secure and the peace preserved.

All this will not be finished in the first one hundred days. Nor will it be   20
finished in the first one thousand days, nor in the life of this Administration, nor even perhaps in our lifetime on this planet. But let us begin.

In your hands, my fellow citizens, more than mine, will rest the final   21
success or failure of our course. Since this country was founded, each generation of Americans has been summoned to give testimony to its national loyalty. The graves of young Americans who answered the call to service surround the globe.

Now the trumpet summons us again—not as a call to bear arms, though   22
arms we need; not as a call to battle, though embattled we are; but a call to bear the burden of a long twilight struggle, year in and year out, ''rejoicing in hope, patient in tribulation,'' a struggle against the common enemies of men: tyranny, poverty, disease and war itself.

Can we forge against these enemies a grand and global alliance, North   23
and South, East and West, that can assure a more fruitful life for all mankind? Will you join in that historic effort?

In the long history of the world, only a few generations have been   24
granted the role of defending freedom in its hour of maximum danger. I do not shrink from this responsibility; I welcome it. I do not believe that any of us would exchange places with any other people or any other generation. The energy, the faith, the devotion which we bring to this endeavor will light our country and all who serve it, and the glow from that fire can truly light the world.

And so, my fellow Americans, ask not what your country can do for   25
you; ask what you can do for your country.

My fellow citizens of the world, ask not what America will do for you,   26
but what together we can do for the freedom of man.

Finally, whether you are citizens of America or citizens of the world,   27
ask of us here the same high standards of strength and sacrifice which we ask of you. With a good conscience our only sure reward, with history that final judge of our deeds, let us go forth to lead the land we love, asking His

blessing and His help, but knowing that here on earth God's work must truly be our own.

QUESTIONS ON CONTENT

1. Kennedy's second paragraph begins with the statement, "The world is very different now." How does Kennedy intend this remark?

2. The president's speech makes promises to several groups, not only to the citizens of the United States, but to groups outside the country as well. Is it clear which groups Kennedy means? See if you can identify a few of these groups; then explain what Kennedy gains by not "naming names."

3. During the most recent presidential campaign, catchy phrases designed to be slotted easily into evening newscasts came to be popularly known by the technical name, "sound bytes." An example of a sound byte was the phrase often used by presidential candidate George Bush, "read my lips." Several of the phrases in Kennedy's speech could be effective sound bytes as well. List a few of them. What makes them stand out? Do they add or detract from the rest of Kennedy's speech?

4. Kennedy makes clear what he wants to accomplish in his tenure as president; however, he doesn't say how he will achieve these goals. Do you find this problematic, or do you feel this inexplicitness is appropriate in a speech of this kind?

QUESTIONS ON RHETORIC

1. Give several examples of Kennedy's use of parallelism. (Glossary: *Parallelism*) Does this rhetorical device add to the strength of his speech?

2. In paragraph 23, Kennedy asks two rhetorical questions. What is his purpose in asking these questions? (Glossary: *Rhetorical Questions*)

3. In his speech, Kennedy addresses other nations as well as the citizens of the United States. How would you characterize his tone in addressing each group? Why do you suppose Kennedy changes his tone in this way?

4. How has Kennedy organized his speech to stress the shift in emphasis from one group to the other? Prepare a scratch outline of his speech to help you answer this question. (Glossary: *Organization*)

5. In paragraph 7, what figure of speech does Kennedy use? What does it mean? Why do you suppose he uses it? (Glossary: *Figures of Speech*)

VOCABULARY

oath (1)   prey (9)   invoke (17)
asunder (6)   subversion (9)   shrink (24)
tyranny (7)   invective (10)

WRITING TOPICS

1. Some political experts say that president Jimmy Carter's biggest mistake was that he forgot the true role of a leader; that is, he should have led the people in their best opinion of themselves instead of holding up to them a mirror reflecting their weaknesses and shortcomings. In this manner the ennobling sentiment expressed by Kennedy in paragraph 25 was paraphrased and entered popular speech as, "And so, my fellow Americans, ask not what your country will do for you, ask what you can do for your country." Camelot and the New Frontier were two other common references used in the Kennedy years. In an essay, discuss what images these last two terms conjure up and what qualities they suggest the Kennedy administration sought to idealize.

2. Taking Kennedy's speech paragraph by paragraph, decide what matters of foreign policy were uppermost in his mind. Where did Kennedy stand on the different issues? Are these issues still matters of national concern? What are some of the major issues facing our country today that had little importance in the early 1960s?

3. Abraham Lincoln was another president renowned for the eloquence and simplicity of his speeches. His Gettysburg Address follows, wherein Lincoln, like Kennedy, urges his fellow countrymen to reach beyond themselves to maintain the greatness of their country. Read the address, then write an essay in which you discuss Lincoln's selection of details and use of language to move his audience.

ABRAHAM LINCOLN'S GETTYSBURG ADDRESS

Four score and seven years ago our fathers brought forth on this continent, a new nation, conceived in Liberty, and dedicated to the proposition that all men are created equal.

Now we are engaged in a great civil war, testing whether that nation, or any nation so conceived and so dedicated, can long endure. We are met on a great battle-field of that war. We have come here to dedicate a portion of that field, as a final resting place for those who here gave their lives that this nation might live. It is altogether fitting and proper that we should do this.

But, in a larger sense, we can not dedicate—we can not consecrate—we can not hallow—this ground. The brave men, living and dead, who struggled here, have consecrated it, far above our poor power to add or detract. The world will little note, nor long remember what we say here, but it can never forget what they did here. It is for us the living, rather, to be dedicated here to the unfinished work which they who fought here have thus far so nobly advanced. It is rather for us to be here dedicated to the great task remaining before us—that from these honored dead we take increased devotion to that cause for which they gave the last full measure of devotion—that we here highly resolve that these dead shall not have died in vain—that this nation, under God, shall have a new birth of freedom—and that government of the people, by the people, for the people, shall not perish from the earth.

THE RONALD REAGAN BASIC 1984 CAMPAIGN SPEECH

The New York Times

In every presidential election year The New York Times
*synthesizes the "basic" campaign speech of each candidate
by combining the material and messages of a number of
the candidate's past speeches. The following is a statement
of the issues and ideas that speech writers developed for
Ronald Reagan to repeat throughout his 1984 presidential
campaign.*

I think there's a new feeling of patriotism in our land, a recognition that   1
by any standard America is a decent and generous place, a force for good
in the world. And I don't know about you but I'm a little tired of hearing
people run her down.

We've come through some tough times but we've come through them   2
together, all of us from every race, every religion and every ethnic background. And we're going forward with values that have never failed us
when we lived up to them: dignity of work, love for family and neighborhood, faith in God, belief in peace through strength, and a commitment to
protect the freedom which is our legacy as Americans.

All that we've done, and all that we mean to do, is to make this country   3
freer still. America's future rests in a thousand dreams inside your hearts.
And helping you make those dreams come true is what this job of mine is
all about.

We hear shrill words from some who were in charge four years ago.   4
But may I suggest that those who gave us double-digit inflation, record
interest rates, tax increases, credit controls, farm embargoes, long lines at
the gas stations, no growth at home, weakness abroad, and told us that it
was our fault that we suffered from a malaise, they're not exactly experts
on the future of growth and fairness in America.

I will say, however, their policies were fair. They didn't discriminate—   5
they made everybody miserable. But I didn't come to dwell on their failures. I came to talk about how, together, we're going to make this great
nation even greater.

ECONOMIC EXPANSION

With your help, we've knocked down inflation from 12.4 to 4.1 percent. 6
And today, from the Jersey shore to San Francisco Bay, economic expansion is carrying America forward. I'd like to ask you some questions, if I
could. I know there are some young people present—some questions about
a certain country. Now, I won't give away the answer by naming the
country, but I will give you a little hint. It has three initials, and its first two
are U.S. Now, of all the great industrialized nations in the world, which
has shown by far the strongest, most sustained economic growth?

AUDIENCE: U.S.A.

THE PRESIDENT: All right, what country can say its investment is 7
up, its productivity is up, its take-home pay is up, and its consumer
spending is up?

A.: U.S.A.

THE PRESIDENT: And what country during the past 20 months cre- 8
ated six million new jobs?

A.: U.S.A.

THE PRESIDENT: And what country created, on an average, more 9
new jobs each month during the past 12—than all the countries of Western
Europe created over the past 19 years, all put together?

A.: U.S.A.

THE PRESIDENT: Now, you get one hundred. You got it right. And 10
my friends, you ain't seen nothing yet.

Today, more of your earnings are staying with your families in your 11
neighborhoods, in your state, where they belong. And we have the rare
opportunity to give our children the gift of peace and prosperity without
inflation. America has worked too hard for this progress to let anybody
destroy it with a massive tax and spending scheme. That would be the
equivalent of about $1,800 more in taxes per household, and it would ruin
the growth and your opportunities for the future.

BLUEPRINT FOR BONDAGE

For them to introduce that blueprint for bondage in Philadelphia, the very 12
birthplace of our liberty, was a betrayal of the American people. Now, they
could have introduced their tax increase in Atlantic City. But, then, that
would have been unfair. The people who go to Atlantic City gamble with
their own money, not yours.

But we don't let them put that ball and chain around America's neck. 13
I don't think that you believe your families were put on this Earth just to
help them make Government bigger. They want to enact a massive tax

increase to put in their new so-called trust fund. We don't want their new Government trust fund; we want a Government that trusts you.

You know, I have to tell you, I'm afraid that the age issue may be a   14
factor in this election after all. My opponent's ideas are just too old.

We're talking about two different worlds. They see America wringing   15
her hands. We see America raising her hands. They see America divided
by envy, each of us challenging our neighbor's success. We see America
inspired by opportunity, all of us challenging the best in ourselves. We
believe in knowing when opportunity knocks. They go out of the way to
knock opportunity. They see an America where every day is April 15th,
tax day. We see an America where every day is the Fourth of July.

Aren't you saying, we want to think big and aim high? And aren't you   16
saying, don't hold us back, give us a chance and see how high we fly?
Well, that's what we want to help you do. So I have some bad news for our
opponents: Our economy will still be healthy come the November election.
But I have some worse news for them: Our economy will still be that way
in November 1988.

FUTURE IS WAITING

Our work isn't done. The future is waiting to be seized, great frontiers in   17
science, in technology, in space waiting to be discovered and pushed back.
And we can do it.

We can do it because, as we saw with our great Olympic athletes, when   18
America goes for the gold, nothing is going to hold her back. And I think
one challenge we're ready to meet as a nation, because it's so crucial to our
future, is to make America's educational system a great center of leadership for excellence.

And we've begun already. The average Scholastic Aptitude Test score,   19
that thing we call "SAT," the college entrance exams, has gone up a full
four points. And that's after nearly 20 years of steady decline of more than
a hundred points. And this is the second increase in three years. And it's
the biggest increase—it doesn't sound like much, four points; but it's the
biggest increase in 21 years. But it's not enough. We've got to do better.

It's time for America to lift her sights. Time for us to resolve that,   20
before this decade is out, we'll raise Scholastic Aptitude Test scores nationwide. We'll make up half of all the ground that was lost over the last 20
years and reduce the dropout rate from 27 percent to 10 percent or less.
And this will require a great national commitment by students, teachers,
administrators and, most certainly, by America's parents.

The challenge isn't easy but my friends we can meet it. Just as we can   21
continue to champion strong economic growth with greater individual op-

portunity. We can simplify our tax system, make it more fair, easier to understand so that we can bring yours and everybody's income tax rates further down, not up.

LOWER TAX RATES

You know when I say make it easier to understand, did you know that 22 Albert Einstein once said that he found the 1040 income tax form too difficult for him to understand?

We can pass an enterprise zones bill that would encourage people 23 through lower tax rates to start up businesses and to train and hire workers in distressed areas. The House Democratic leadership has bottled up that bill for two years in committee.

And we could add to enterprise zones a youth unemployment oppor- 24 tunity wage for teenagers so that employers would be encouraged to hire those who are disadvantaged and members of minority groups and young people who are just starting out with no job experience to get their first job.

We have, as I said, created six million jobs in the last 20 months. 25 That's a good record, better than any other nation, but it's not good enough. I pledge to you I won't rest until every American who wants a job can find a job. Now I propose also that we lift our sights toward a second challenge. By this time next year we must have found ways to simplify that tax system, passed the enterprise zones, passed a youth opportunity wage, and all of us must make this expansion so strong that millions of jobs will be created in distressed areas where our fellow citizens need help the most. This America can and must do.

Our goal is an American opportunity society giving everyone not only 26 an equal chance but a greater chance to pursue that American dream. And we can build that future together if you elect people to the Congress who will not vote for tax increases but vote for growth and economic progress.

To all those Democrats, and I hope there are many here, who have been 27 loyal to the party of F.D.R. and Harry Truman and J.F.K., people who believe in protecting the interests of working people, who are not ashamed or afraid of America's standing for freedom in the world—we say to you: Join us. Come walk with us down that new path of hope and opportunity.

I was a Democrat most of my adult life. I didn't leave my party and 28 we're not suggesting you leave yours. I am telling you that what I felt was that the leadership of the Democratic Party had left me and millions of patriotic Democrats in this country who believed in freedom.

Walk with us down that path of hope and opportunity, and together we 29 can and we will lift America up to meet our greatest days.

QUESTIONS ON CONTENT

1. Reagan's speech defines *patriotism* in the first paragraph. Do you agree with the definition he gives? Why or why not?

2. In paragraph 3 of his speech, Reagan promises to make this country "freer still." Is it clear to you what is meant by this? Explain.

3. Who are the "they" mentioned in paragraph 5? Why doesn't the speech name "them"?

4. Reagan's speech cites several improvements made in the first four years of his presidency. Are the numbers he cites convincing? Can a president reasonably take credit for the improvements mentioned here?

5. What are some of the promises Reagan made in 1984? In your opinion, did Reagan keep those promises?

6. Reagan's speech claims that he never left the Democratic Party. What do you suppose is the strategy behind this statement? Explain your answer.

QUESTIONS ON RHETORIC

1. Reagan is known for his ability to inspire emotions of fierce patriotism. One way he does this is to put everyone on horseback, with the good guys in white hats and the bad guys in black. However, in this generic speech the bad guys are not the Russians, they are the Democrats. Give examples of the words and phrases used in Reagan's speech to characterize "we" and "they" in such a way that the "they" appears nonpatriotic.

2. One reason for Reagan's popularity as a speaker is his ready wit. Identify several passages in which this speech incorporates humor. How does this use of humor influence you?

3. Reagan is known as the Great Communicator as much for his delivery as for the content of his speeches. Read this speech out loud. What do you notice? What identifies this as oral rather than written English? Consider diction, phrasing, and organization of material.

VOCABULARY

patriotism (1)   legacy (2)   malaise (4)

WRITING TOPICS

1. In paragraph 18, Olympic athletes are used as a standard for the American public. In your own words, how does this one example typify the kind of rhetoric employed in Reagan's speeches? Before answering, read and analyze other Reagan speeches, noting the examples and references they most often make and the image of the country they most typically seem to evoke.

2. In an essay earlier in this section, George Orwell claims political speech
is filled with "meaningless words" such as *patriotism*, *democracy*, and
freedom. Choose two of the words Orwell mentions, or two of your own,
and then review the speeches of Kennedy and Reagan with these words in
mind. Does each man define the same words in the same way? In an essay,
discuss any differences you find in Kennedy's and Reagan's use of certain
words and what you think each politician hoped to gain in using these
words in the way he did.

WRITING ASSIGNMENTS FOR "THE LANGUAGE OF POLITICS AND PROPAGANDA"

1. Governments and the news media are prone to using euphemisms, misplaced technical jargon, stock phrases, and connotatively "loaded" words for propaganda purposes. Depending on your position, for example, a "terrorist" and a "freedom fighter" are two very different things. To refer to a group as "self-styled" or as "calling themselves . . ." or to world leaders as "intransigent," "belligerent," "stern," and "forceful" is to use language that embodies strong value judgments. Examine a recent newspaper or news magazine article on a current event for examples of "loaded" words. Then write an analysis of how the writer of the article has attempted to alter your attitudes through biased language.

2. We all have been affected by propaganda at some time in our lives. Think of an experience you have had when you were unwittingly manipulated by propaganda, and write an analysis of the propaganda devices used.

3. In his book *The Second Sin*, psychiatrist Thomas Szasz makes the following observations:

   a. The prevention of parenthood is called "planned parenthood."
   b. Policemen receive bribes; politicians receive campaign contributions.
   c. Homicide by physicians is called "euthanasia."
   d. Marijuana and heroin are sold by pushers; cigarettes and alcohol are sold by businessmen.
   e. Imprisonment by psychiatrists is called "mental hospitalization."

Using Szasz's observations or similar ones of your own, write an essay in which you discuss the way people manipulate words and meanings to suit their particular needs.

4. Using either Orwell's standards of good writing or Cross's list of propaganda devices, write an essay in which you analyze a newspaper editorial, a political speech, a public service advertisement, or a comparable example of contemporary political prose.

5. Orwell says, "As soon as certain topics are raised, the concrete melts into the abstract . . ." (4). One such topic has always been war. Compare the following two war prayers, the first from a Catholic missal and the second by Mark Twain:

O Lord, graciously regard the sacrifice which we offer up: that it may deliver us from all the evil of war, and establish us under Thy sure protection. Through our Lord Jesus Christ, Thy Son, who liveth and reigneth with Thee in the unity of the Holy Ghost.

Oh Lord our God, help us to tear their soldiers to bloody shreds with our shells; help us to cover their smiling fields with their patriot dead; help us to lay waste their humble homes with a hurricane of fire; help us to wring the hearts of their unoffending widows with unavailing grief; help us to turn them out roofless with their little children to wander unfriended the wastes of their desolated land in rags and hunger and thirst. Lord, blast their hopes, blight their lives, protract their bitter pilgrimage, make heavy their steps, water their way with their tears. We ask it, in the spirit of love, of Him Who is the Source of Love, and who is the ever-faithful refuge and friend of all that are sore beset and seek his aid.

How would you characterize the very different effects of these two war prayers? Specifically, how do you account for the differences in effect?

6. Write an essay in which you compare and contrast a national tabloid newspaper (such as the *National Enquirer*) with your local newspaper. You may wish to consider one or more of the following:

    a. intended audience
    b. types of stories covered
    c. placement of stories
    d. formality or informality of writing
    e. amount of visual material
    f. amount and type of advertising

7. Choose an editorial dealing with a controversial issue. Assume that you have been offered equal space in the newspaper in which to present the opposing viewpoint. Write a rebuttal. Hand in both your rebuttal and the original editorial that stimulated it.

8. Write three paragraphs in which you describe the same incident, person, scene, or thing. In the first paragraph, use language that will produce a neutral impression; in the second, language that will produce a favorable impression; and in the third, language that will produce an unfavorable impression. Keep the factual content of each of your paragraphs constant; vary only the language.

9. Reread Kennedy's Inaugural Address (p. 161), Lincoln's Gettysburg Address (p. 165), and Reagan's basic campaign speech (p. 167). Do you think George Orwell would say these speakers have used the language responsibly? Identify any examples of what Orwell would consider their misuse of language. Write an essay in which you discuss your analysis of these three political speeches.

10. In the 1988 presidential campaign, candidate George Bush effectively made the word *liberal* a dirty word. And by referring to his opponent Michael Dukakis as a "card-carrying member of the American Civil Lib-

erties Union," he made Dukakis "un-American" by association. What era in our history was Bush evoking when he employed these strategies? Why do you suppose it was effective in 1988? In an essay, analyze Bush's use of "charged language," as explained by Birk and Birk (p. 125).

PART IV

Advertising
and
Language

*And here's that cozy eat-in kitchen, with that lovely
view of the water!*

THE LANGUAGE OF ADVERTISING CLAIMS

Jeffrey Schrank

*In this essay, Jeffrey Schrank explores the world of
advertising claims. He has classified the most common
techniques that adwriters use to sell products into ten
categories. Schrank, a teacher by profession, challenges each
of us to analyze and evaluate the fairness of the promises and
claims in many ads.*

Students, and many teachers, are notorious believers in their immunity to
advertising. These naive inhabitants of consumerland believe that advertising is childish, dumb, a bunch of lies, and influences only the vast
hordes of the less sophisticated. Their own purchases are made purely on
the basis of value and desire, with advertising playing only a minor supporting role. They know about Vance Packard and his "hidden persuaders" and the adwriter's psychosell and bag of persuasive magic. They are
not impressed.

Advertisers know better. Although few people admit to being greatly
influenced by ads, surveys and sales figures show that a well-designed
advertising campaign has dramatic effects. A logical conclusion is that
advertising works below the level of conscious awareness and it works
even on those who claim immunity to its message. Ads are designed to
have an effect while being laughed at, belittled, and all but ignored.

A person unaware of advertising's claim on him or her is precisely the
one most defenseless against the adwriter's attack. Advertisers delight in
an audience which believes ads to be harmless nonsense, for such an
audience is rendered defenseless by its belief that there is no attack taking
place. The purpose of a classroom study of advertising is to raise the level
of awareness about the persuasive techniques used in ads. One way to do
this is to analyze ads in microscopic detail. Ads can be studied to detect
their psychological hooks, they can be used to gauge values and desires of
the common person, they can be studied for their use of symbols, color,
and imagery. But perhaps the simplest and most direct way to study ads is
through an analysis of the language of the advertising claim. The "claim"
is the verbal or print part of an ad that makes some claim of superiority for

179

the product being advertised. After studying claims, students should be able to recognize those that are misleading and accept as useful information those that are true. A few of these claims are downright lies, some are honest statements about a truly superior product, but most fit into the category of neither bold lies nor helpful consumer information. They balance on the narrow line between truth and falsehood by a careful choice of words.

The reason so many ad claims fall into this category of pseudoinformation is that they are applied to parity products, products in which all or most of the brands available are nearly identical. Since no one superior product exists, advertising is used to create the illusion of superiority. The largest advertising budgets are devoted to parity products such as gasoline, cigarettes, beer and soft drinks, soaps, and various headache and cold remedies.   4

The first rule of parity involves the Alice in Wonderlandish use of the words "better" and "best." In parity claims, "better" means "best" and "best" means "equal to." If all brands are identical, they must all be equally good, the legal minds have decided. So "best" means that the product is as good as the other superior products in its category. When Bing Crosby declares Minute Maid Orange Juice "the best there is" he means it is as good as the other orange juices you can buy.   5

The word "better" has been legally interpreted to be a comparative and therefore becomes a clear claim of superiority. Bing could not have said that Minute Maid is "better than any other orange juice." "Better" is a claim of superiority. The only time "better" can be used is when a product does indeed have superiority over other products in its category or when the better is used to compare the product with something other than competing brands. An orange juice therefore claim to be "better than a vitamin pill," or even "the better breakfast drink."   6

The second rule of advertising claim analysis is simply that if any product is truly superior, the ad will say so very clearly and will offer some kind of convincing evidence of the superiority. If an ad hedges the least bit about a product's advantage over the competition you can strongly suspect it is not superior—maybe equal to but not better. You will never hear a gasoline company say "we will give you four miles per gallon more in your car than any other brand." They would love to make such a claim, but it would not be true. Gasoline is a parity product, and, in spite of some very clever and deceptive ads of a few years ago, no one has yet claimed one brand of gasoline better than any other brand.   7

To create the necessary illusion of superiority, advertisers usually resort to one or more of the following ten basic techniques. Each is common and easy to identify.   8

1. THE WEASEL CLAIM

A weasel word is a modifier that practically negates the claim that follows. [9] The expression "weasel word" is aptly named after the egg-eating habits of weasels. A weasel will suck out the inside of an egg, leaving it appear intact to the casual observer. Upon examination, the egg is discovered to be hollow. Words or claims that appear substantial upon first look but disintegrate into hollow meaninglessness on analysis are weasels. Commonly used weasel words include "helps" (the champion weasel); "like" (used in a comparative sense); "virtual" or "virtually"; "acts" or "works"; "can be"; "up to"; "as much as"; "refreshes"; "comforts"; "tackles"; "fights"; "come on"; "the feel of"; "the look of"; "looks like"; "fortified"; "enriched"; and "strengthened."

Samples of Weasel Claims

"*Helps control* dandruff *symptoms* with *regular use.*" The weasels include "helps control," and possibly even "symptoms" and "regular use." The claim is not "stops dandruff."

"Leaves dishes *virtually* spotless." We have seen so many ad claims that we have learned to tune out weasels. You are supposed to think "spotless," rather than "virtually" spotless.

"Only half the price of *many* color sets." "Many" is the weasel. The claim is supposed to give the impression that the set is inexpensive.

"Tests confirm one mouthwash *best* against mouth odor."

"Hot Nestlés' cocoa is the very *best.*" Remember the "best" and "better" routine.

"Listerine *fights* bad breath." "Fights" not "stops."

"Lots of things have changed, but Hershey's *goodness* hasn't." This claim does not say that Hershey's chocolate hasn't changed.

"Bacos, the crispy garnish that tastes just *like* its name."

2. THE UNFINISHED CLAIM

The unfinished claim is one in which the ad claims the product is better, or [10] has more of something, but does not finish the comparison.

Samples of Unfinished Claims

"Magnavox gives you more." More what?

"Anacin: Twice as much of the pain reliever doctors recommend most." This claim fits in a number of categories but it does not say twice as much of what pain reliever.

"Supergloss does it with more color, more shine, more sizzle, more!"

"Coffee-mate gives coffee more body, more flavor."Also note that "body" and "flavor" are weasels.

"You can be sure of it's Westinghouse." Sure of what?

"Scott makes it better for you."

"Ford LTD—700% quieter."

When the FTC asked Ford to substantiate his claim, Ford revealed that they meant the inside of the Ford was 700% quieter than the outside.

3. THE "WE'RE DIFFERENT AND UNIQUE" CLAIM

This kind of claim states that there is nothing else quite like the product   11
advertised. For example, if Schlitz would add pink food coloring to its beer they could say, "There's nothing like new pink Schlitz." The uniqueness claim is supposed to be interpreted by readers as a claim to superiority.

Samples of the "We're Different and Unique" Claim

"There's no other mascara like it."

"Only Doral has this unique filter system."

"Cougar is like nobody else's car."

"Either way, liquid or spray, there's nothing else like it."

"If it doesn't say Goodyear, it can't be polyglas." "Polyglas" is a trade name copyrighted by Goodyear. Goodrich or Firestone could make a tire exactly identical to the Goodyear one and yet couldn't call it "polyglas"—a name for fiberglass belts.

"Only Zenith has chromacolor." Same as the "polyglas" gambit. Admiral has solarcolor and RCA has accucolor.

4. THE "WATER IS WET" CLAIM

"Water is wet" claims say something about the product that is true for any   12
brand in that product category (for example, "Schrank's water is really

wet''). The claim is usually a statement of fact, but not a real advantage over the competition.

Samples of the "Water Is Wet" Claim

"Mobil: the Detergent Gasoline." Any gasoline acts as a cleaning agent.

"Great Lash greatly increases the diameter of every lash."

"Rheingold, the natural beer." Made from grains and water as are other beers.

"SKIN smells differently on everyone." As do many perfumes.

5. THE "SO WHAT" CLAIM

This is the kind of claim to which the careful reader will react by saing "So What?" A claim is made which is true but which gives no real advantage to the product. This is similar to the "water is wet" claim except that it claims an advantage which is not shared by most of the other brands in the product category. 13

Samples of the "So What" Claim

"Geritol has more than twice the iron of ordinary supplements." But is twice as much beneficial to the body?

"Campbell's gives you tasty pieces of chicken and not one but two chicken stocks." Does the presence of two stocks improve the taste?

"Strong enough for man but made for a woman." This deodorant claim says only that the product is aimed at the female market.

6. THE VAGUE CLAIM

The vague claim is simply not clear. This category often overlaps with others. The key to the vague claim is the use of words that are colorful but meaningless, as well as the use of subjective and emotional opinions that defy verification. Most contain weasels. 14

Samples of the Vague Claim

"Lips have never looked so lucious." Can you imagine trying to either prove or disprove such a claim?

"Lipsavers are fun—they taste good, smell good and feel good."

"Its deep rich lather makes hair feel good again."

"For skin like peaches and cream."

"The end of meatloaf boredom."

"Take a bite and you'll think you're eating on the Champs Elysées."

"Winston tastes good like a cigarette should."

"The perfect little portable for all around viewing with all the features of higher priced sets."

"Fleishman's makes sensible eating delicious."

7. THE ENDORSEMENT OR TESTIMONIAL

A celebrity or authority appears in an ad to lend his or her stellar qualities 15 to the product. Sometimes the people will actually claim to use the product, but very often they don't. There are agencies surviving on providing products with testimonials.

Samples of Endorsements or Testimonials

"Joan Fontaine throws a shot-in-the-dark party and her friends learn a thing or two."

"Darling, have you discovered Masterpiece? The most exciting men I know are smoking it."(Eva Gabor)

"Vega is the best handling car in the U.S." This claim was challenged by the FTC, but GM answered that the claim is only a direct quote from *Road and Track* magazine.

8. THE SCIENTIFIC OR STATISTICAL CLAIM

This kind of ad uses some sort of scientific proof or experiment, very 16 specific numbers, or an impressive sounding mystery ingredient.

Samples of Scientific or Statistical Claims

"Wonder Bread helps build strong bodies 12 ways." Even the weasel "helps" did not prevent the FTC from demanding this ad be withdrawn. But note that the use of the number 12 makes the claim far more believable than if it were taken out.

"Easy-Off has 33% more cleaning power than another popular brand." "Another popular brand" often translates as some other kind of oven cleaner sold somewhere. Also the claim does not say Easy-Off works 33% better.

"Special Morning—33% more nutrition." Also an unfinished claim.

"Certs contain a sparkling drop of Retsyn."

"ESSO with HTA."

"Sinarest. Created by a research scientist who actually gets sinus headaches."

9. THE "COMPLIMENT THE CONSUMER" CLAIM

This kind of claim butters up the consumer by some form of flattery.   17

Samples of the "Compliment the Consumer" Claim

"We think a cigar smoker is someone special."

"If what you do is right for you, no matter what others do, then RC Cola is right for you."

"You pride yourself on your good home cooking. . . ."

"The lady has taste."

"You've come a long way, baby."

10. THE RHETORICAL QUESTION

This technique demands a response from the audience. A question is asked   18
and the viewer or listener is supposed to answer in such a way as to affirm the product's goodness.

Samples of the Rhetorical Question

"Plymouth—isn't that the kind of car America wants?"

"Shouldn't your family be drinking Hawaiian Punch?"

"What do you want most from coffee? That's what you get most from Hills."

"Touch of Sweden: Could your hands use a small miracle?"

QUESTIONS ON CONTENT

1. Schrank introduces the concept "immunity to advertising" in his first paragraph. What does he mean by this phrase? Before reading Schrank's essay did you feel that you were immune to advertising? Explain.

2. In his essay, Schrank quotes the claim that "Only Zenith has chroma-color." Although this statement is true, it is also deceitful. Explain in what way this and other such claims are deceitful. Give examples.

3. "Parity products" are those in which most of the available brands are nearly identical. Do you agree with Schrank that claims of "superiority" among parity products are invalid? Explain using examples from Schrank's essay or your own observations.

4. Schrank says the words *better* and *best* have been redefined for advertisers. What does he claim these words mean when they are used in an ad?

QUESTIONS ON RHETORIC

1. In paragraphs 1 through 3, Schrank introduces his topic. In paragraphs 4 through 7, he discusses parity products. His discussion of ad claims is preceded by a two-sentence transition, after which he uses a brief introduction, followed by a list of examples for each claim. Discuss this change from paragraph form to listing examples.

2. Schrank does not use a concluding paragraph in this essay. Why do you feel he did this? Do you think Schrank's essay would be more effective if he had used a conclusion? Explain your answer.

3. To define the "We're Different and Unique" claim, Schrank uses the analogy "If Schlitz would add pink food coloring to its beer they could say, 'There's nothing like new pink Schlitz.' " Find another analogy in the essay. Do you find these analogies helpful?

4. Schrank has used techniques of division and classification to identify ten advertising plays that he claims are "common and easy to identify." One of these, the vague claim, Schrank says often overlaps with others, but he never explains how or with which other categories vague claims overlap. Would you have benefitted from having this information? Explain.

VOCABULARY

notorious (1)	pseudoinformation (4)	gambit (11)
psychosell (1)	parity (4)	subjective (14)

WRITING TOPICS

1. Schrank describes ten types of claims commonly used by advertisers. Choose five of these claims and in your own words discuss how they work.

Develop an ad of your own for each type of claim you describe. Make sure each ad is an example of just one category.

2. Pay attention to the ads for companies that offer rival products or services (for example, AT&T and MCI, Burger King and McDonald's, Coke and Pepsi). Make note of the ad techniques mentioned in Schrank's essay you see different companies using to compare their product or service to that of their competition. In an essay, discuss what effect you feel these techniques have on each company's intended audience.

3. Ads "can be studied for their use of symbols, color, and imagery," and for their use of unsubstantial claims. Choose three advertisements from your favorite magazine and, in an essay, discuss the visual effects used by the advertisers that support their claims or that detract the reader's attention from recognizing how misleading the claims being made really are.

THE HARD SELL

Ron Rosenbaum

In the following article Ron Rosenbaum, a New York writer, discusses the way advertising agencies sell a company's products by "humiliating" the consumer. This piece was published in Mother Jones, *a consumer advocate magazine that exposes the unfair practices of business, industry, and government.*

Too many viewers, I'm afraid, miss out on the most exciting intellectual challenge offered by television: the commercials. That's right. I said the intellectual challenge of TV commercials and I don't mean just the task of choosing between Stove Top stuffing and potatoes. I mean the pleasure to be found in pitting your intellect against some of the cleverest minds in the country, the Masterminds of Madison Avenue, and trying to figure out how they've figured *you* out.

Too many TV watchers still leave the room during TV commercials for some trivial reason. As a result, they miss some of the best-produced, most skillfully scripted and edited dramas on TV: more thought, more research into human nature and, in some cases, more dollars go into creating those 30- and 60-second ads than into the development of most 30- and 60-minute prime-time programs.

I never leave the room during the commercials. I sit spellbound watching them. I take notes. The highpoint of an evening before the set for me can be discovering a new wrinkle in Mr. Whipple's war on secretive Charmin squeezers, or catching the debut of one of the grand, soaring production numbers the airline or beer people put on to get us in the mood for getting high. I find more intrigue in trying to figure out the mysterious appeal of Mrs. Olsen and Robert Young, those continuing characters in coffee commercials, than in the predictable puzzles of *Masterpiece Theatre*. And I'm convinced that future archaeologists will find more concentrated and reliable clues to the patterns of our culture in one Clorox ad than they could ever find in a week's worth of sit-coms.

Take a look at some of the key trends in TV ads of the 1980s, the changes in tone and technique, and you can see what they tell us about ourselves and consciousness of the new decade.

NO MORE NICE GUYS

The early '80s have witnessed the return of the Hard Sell, or what might
be called the "no more Mr. Nice Guy" school of commercial strategy. If
you had been watching closely you could have picked up an advance
warning, a seismic tremor of the shift to come, in the Buick slogan change.
In the fall of 1979 Buick abruptly yanked its confident slogan, the one that
told us "Make it Buick. After all, life is to enjoy." Then, after that,
everything changed.

The Buick ads of the '80s no longer take a firm position on the meaning
of life. Instead they give us hard numbers and initials: EPA est. MPG.
Which leaves us to wonder; if life is no longer "to enjoy," what is life to?
In the world of the new no-nonsense ads, life is to *struggle,* life is to fight
for survival in a nasty brutish world. "Life got tougher," the makers of
Excedrin tell us, so "we got stronger." And the airways are filled with
new, tougher, hard-edged combative spirit. Little old ladies are seen sav-
agely socking gas pumps in the midsections. Vicious tempers flare into
public displays of anger in Sanka commercials. For years, tough guy
Robert Conrad postured pugnaciously and challenged the unsuspecting
viewer: "I dare you to call this an ordinary battery," threatening by implication to step right out of the tube and commit some assault and battery
right there in our living rooms.

This aggressive stance is echoed by the take-it-or-leave-it approach of
the Italian food canner who declares, "Make it Progresso, or make it
yourself," and was heralded by the Japanese car maker who told us, "If
you can find a better-built small car than Toyota, buy it." This dismissive
imperative tone of voice is the new keynote of ads in the 1980s.

You could see the philosophy of the new no-nonsense school being
formulated by the deep-thinkers of Madison Avenue in the first year of the
new decade. The pages of *Advertising Age* were filled with speculations by
ad people about what to name the period. "The Aching '80s" was one
suggestion. "The Decade of Difficult Decisions," "The Era of Uncertainty," "The Return to Reality" were others. Each sage of the new era
wanted to distinguish the '80s from the previous decade, from what one
advertising agency commentator called "the self-centered, the self-
indulgent, self-gratifying of the Me Decade."

The battle between the old and the new is not confined to the pages of
Ad Age. If you want a quick tour of the combat zone, the best place to start
is with the big-money brokerage battle. You can usually catch the clash on
the Sunday interview shows (*Meet the Press* and the others). Here you can
see four brokerage houses go after their potential client targets with two
totally different advertising strategies. While Paine Webber and Dean Witter try to win hearts and minds with the Late-'70s-Wish-Fulfillment ap-

proach, Merrill Lynch and Smith Barney assault the viewer with the blasted
landscape of Early '80s Angst.

To shift back and forth between the two worlds invites severe disori- 10
entation. Start with Dean Witter's world, where ecstatic customers are
always getting calls and letters from their broker that cause them to burst
with joyful financial fulfillment as a heavenly-sounding choir croons:

"You look like you just heard from Dean Witter." 11

Contrast that with the lead character from another brokerage ad. He's 12
alone. He's lost. There is pain in his big sad eyes; he's cutting his hooves
on icy rocks and crusts of snow as he slowly picks his way in search of
shelter. This harsh winter scene is "today's investment climate," a voice-
over tells us, a time to "protect your assets." We watch the bull finally
find a dark cave in which to shelter his assets (a parable about tax shelters, it seems) just as a terrifying crack of thunder bursts over the frozen
wasteland outside. There hasn't been a storm more fraught with the sheer
terror of existence since the third act of *King Lear*. This is no mere
investment climate; this is all the cold and terror and loneliness of modern
life.

In his most recent appearances, we see the solitary bull wandering a 13
barren desert wasteland beset by the tormenting trickery of a mirage; in
another we see him stepping into a bewildering hedge maze, which conjures up the horror of the hedge maze chase in Stanley Kubrick's *The
Shining* as much as it does the subtle securities offered by hedge funds on
the financial scene. Finally—it was inevitable—the poor beast becomes the
proverbial "bull in the china shop," making his way through a maze of
crystal and making us feel the frightening fragility of the most cloistered of
civilized interiors.

A BULL APART

That lonely bull. He's lonelier than ever now, farther off than ever from 14
any hope of reunion with his herd. Faithful bull-watchers realize that the
'80s have introduced the third major phase in the bull's relation to the
herd. In the original Merrill Lynch ads of the early '70s, when Merrill
Lynch was still unabashedly "bullish on America," he was joyfully
romping with the whole happy herd. In fact, we didn't even single out
any particular bull, such was the togetherness of the big beasts. A late
'70s series of Merrill Lynch ads would open on a lone bull majestically
patrolling scenic outposts on his own but rejoining the herd in the final
shot because, in the modified slogan, Merrill Lynch was "*still* bullish on
America."

Then at the very beginning of the new decade the herd disappeared   15
from the ads completely. (What has become of the other bulls? PBB
poisoning? Cattle mutilations?) Gone too is any attempt to further refurbish
the "bullish on America" slogan. (What could they say—"We're *really,
truly*, still bullish on America"?)

The new slogan, "Merrill Lynch—a breed apart," tells us there's no   16
time to worry about the herd; you have to look after your own assets in
today's cold and nasty economic climate, in which the market falls more
every day.

But wait—ten minutes later, on a break in *Issues and Answers*, for   17
instance, we're suddenly in a whole other America, the kind of place
where everything goes right. We're back not just in civilization but at the
summit of civilized achievements, where we hear the rattle of fine china
teacups and the clink of crystal champagne glasses set to delicate waltz
music. We're in the world of Paine Webber. Grateful clients are acquiring
Renoirs, eating paté or otherwise comforting themselves with the satisfied
obliviousness of the courtiers of Louis XVI. The ad includes a sort of
disclaimer to the effect that while Paine Webber cannot guarantee you
wealth, if you bring your money to them, maybe someday "you might say,
'Thank you, Paine Webber' too."

Ah, yes . . . *maybe someday* . . . It's that old wish-fulfillment witch-   18
craft working.

Another quick flick of the remote control button and the spell of such   19
summery sophistries shatters under the frosty glare with which John Houseman fixes us in the Smith Barney ads. It is a shock, the shift from the plush
carpeted Paine Webber world to the trashy, torn-ticket-tape litter on the
floor of the stock exchange, from the soaring choirs of Dean Witter to the
bare ruined choirs of the Big Board.

Houseman puts on a great performance. Smith Barney has invested   20
wisely in him. "The New York Stock Exchange. The day's trading is
over," he intones ominously in his classic debut spot. "Some tally their
profits," he says with a wintry, dismissive smile that implies: "Fat chance
that's you, fella." "Some," he concludes, impaling us with a veritable
icicle of a glance, "lick their wounds."

Wounds. Suffering. Pain. Insecurity. The tragic view of life. House-   21
man's debut for Smith Barney was the perfect harbinger of the New Hard
Sell. Unlike the old hard sell, with a fast-and-loud-talking salesperson
pitching a product, the new sell portrays the world as cold, brutally tough.
The product isn't pushed so much as the audience is impelled to reach—
reach *hard*—for the hope of security the product offers. The *hope* of
security—that is what the '80s hard sell offers to those of us frozen out by
this brutal era.

THE TOUGH LIFE

A recent editorial in *Ad Age* denounced the new Excedrin "Life got tough- 22
er" ads for "overkill," for giving the impression that "life is now akin to
a forced march to the Gulag Archipelago . . . a kind of doomsday feeling."

Even if life is not getting *that* tough, *tough* is definitely the key word 23
in the world of today's TV commercials. Dodge trucks are "ram tough,"
and the Dodge ads feature hormone-crazed rams smashing horns against
each other. Ford trucks are "built tough," and their promo featured a
grueling tug of war with Toyota.

Then, too, the old-fashioned work ethic has returned to prominence. 24
"They make money the old-fashioned way. They earn it," John Houseman says in a Smith Barney ad. Back to basics. Don't express yourself,
protect yourself. Life is no longer to enjoy. Life is to avoid. The essence
of this new technique is to arouse anxiety and offer relief. It means something, I think, that dollar for dollar Tylenol is the single most frequently
purchased drugstore item in the United States today.

Certainly the older-type commercials, the softer, happier advertising 25
pitches, continue to be the most popular with TV viewers. A look at two
years of polls by Video Storyboards Test Inc. (a market research outfit that
asks a cross section of people what they think is the most outstanding TV
commercial they have seen recently) consistently registers the popularity of
the spiritual, emotional, celebratory ad campaigns. The warmth and emotion of the "Mean Joe Green and the Kid" Coke commercial made it the
most popular in recent years. The stirring musical Americana of the soft
drink spirituals, the lyrical beauty and hearty comaraderie of the beer ads
and the blood-curdling cuteness of cat food commercials consistently push
these upbeat celebrations of humanity, warmth and friendship into the Top
10 of such ad polls.

Whether or not they will continue to be popular with ad people as 26
selling tools is another question. There have been some interesting changes
in the spiritual genre in the new season's ads.

Consider first the very popularity of the word. After a brief appearance 27
and quick death in 1976, the word *spirit* has arisen again. We have the
"catch that Pepsi spirit" campaign; we have the cloud-level soaring "spirit
of Hyatt" and the plucky American Motors gas-saving model, Spirit.

But, hovering over the grand, "Main Street parade" Pepsi spirit spot 28
is an aura of anxiety. We watch the little drum majorette drop her baton in
practice at home. Now it's the Fourth of July parade, and we are treated to
the anxious glances of the parents and friends as they wait to see if their
child will suffer public humiliation. Of course, she catches it; but anxiety
and suspense giving way to relief, and people gulping Pepsi to soothe

throats dry from tension are not the unambiguous hallmarks of joy that
once reigned in soft drink ads. Even they now bode harder times . . .

SOMETHING MORE THAN FEELINGS

Another technique of the late '70s school is the emphasis on feeling. While
this has been a good year for product feelings ("Feelin' 7-Up," "Oh, what
a feeling . . . Toyota"), it has not been a particularly good season for
feelings of love.   29

Why is love slighted? Why did AT&T cancel its love song theme,
"Feelings," and switch to the California hot-tub gestalt "Reach Out and
Touch Someone" theme? What was the flaw for the ad people in "Feel-
ings"?   30

Many to be sure would call it a criminally sentimental piece of trash,
but that never stopped other songs from making it. No, it is the fact that the
Morris Albert classic is specifically a song about feelings of love. And with
love there are always mixed feelings, touchy feelings, fiery feelings, not
the comfortable nonthreatening warmth of reach-out-and-touch feelings.
California closeness is a safer-selling feeling than those volatile feelings of
love.   31

Increasingly, this year we find the notion of love ridiculed and scorned.
In one of those male-bonding, beer-bar get-togethers, a starry-eyed man
bursts in to announce, "I've found *the* woman."   32

"*Again*," some wise guy cracks scornfully to the roar of ridicule from
a crowd clearly disillusioned with the Western Romantic tradition.   33

While some wine commercials celebrate passion and *amore* between
men and women, the most conspicuous instance of love at first sight on
screen these days is between man and car (Mazda's "Just one look . . ."
theme), and the most conspicuous instance of erotic love is between a
woman and herself (the Rive Gauche hard-driving, dawn-watching woman
who "goes it alone," whose "auto-eroticims" as Jeff Greenfield called it
before I got a chance to, is only thinly veiled—we even see the earth move
as she watches the sun also rise).   34

In fact, the one new ad that treated love uncynically celebrated what is
actually pubescent puppy love—the two shy kids in the 1980 "Love's
Baby Soft" teenybopper fragrance ad. It's a brilliant and beguiling piece
of work, but nowhere do you find the equivalent for post-teenagers.   35

The only innovative use of love in the past few years is in the less-
than-romantic name of a cleansing product—"Love My Carpet." (The
most interesting new-product name on the market in recent years has got to
be "Gee, Your Hair Smells Terrific!" Look for more of these exclamatory-
sentence brand names in future TV commercials.)   36

REALM OF NIGHTMARE

In fact, there have been some vicious anti-Romance ads running recently.   37
The most insidious of the genre was the Longines spot that aired last
Christmastime. A cozy marital scene; the man has just given his wife a
watch he worked his heart out to afford. He's gazing at her, brimming over
with loving generosity as she announces, "I love it."

She pauses. Only a microsecond, but one of the most deadly micro-   38
seconds ever aired. "But?" he asks. "No, really," she replies with just a
fleeting smile.

The guy's heart is breaking. She's not even faking enthusiasm.   39
"C'mon, tell me," he pleads weakly.

"I guess I was hoping for a Longines," she says wistfully.   40

This is not Romance but a nasty little murder of it committed right   41
before our eyes.

Here, we have entered the realm of nightmare. Here, other kinds of   42
feelings reign. We are working not with human potential but with human
paranoia. Anxiety. Loss. Fear of loss. Remember that nightmarish classic,
the American Express Lost Traveler's Cheques series. Who can forget the
smug sneer of the French concierge when the frantic young American
couple confess that the traveler's checks they have lost were not American
Express? "Ah," he says, as if gazing down from the frosty remoteness of
Mont Blanc at a particularly distasteful specimen of grape blight. "Most
people carry American Express."

What's shocking here is not the Gallic scorn but the supine response of   43
the American couple. Instead of grabbing the concierge by his starched,
stuffed shirt and reminding him that his mother hadn't asked the Americans
who liberated Paris what kind of bank checks they brought, the couple
turns away in humiliation and self-abasement: We *are* such worms, we
Americans, only good for our virtually worthless dollars, and here we are
too stupid even to do what Most People do and at least avoid inconve-
niencing the concierge with our petty failures.

Certainly this abasement before foreigners must reflect more than the   44
lingering cringe of the colonials before continental civilization. It suggests
a kind of sickening national self-image that masochistically relishes affronts to our representatives abroad.

Consider the slogan for the ad: "American Express Traveler's   45
Cheques—don't leave home without them." Isn't the net effect of that
slogan—which follows portrait after panicked portrait of Americans
robbed, humiliated, traumatized, everything but taken hostage, generally
in foreign lands—isn't the net effect to feed the voice inside our national
psyche, that fearful voice that simply says, "Don't leave home"?

THE HUMILIATION SELL

Humiliation, embarrassment and slovenliness seem to be at the core of not   46
just Miller but Schlitz and other "lite" beer commercials. Ads for full-
bodied beers are still some of the most beautiful, most lyrical, glowingly
lit tributes to the romance of workingpeople, the dignity of the work ethic
and the nobility of adventure and athletic endeavor. But the Lite ads give
us symbols of humiliation, such as comedians Rodney Dangerfield and
malaprop-man Norm Crosby.

And there's Marv Throneberry, who has built a career out of two   47
humiliating seasons as last-place first baseman for the worst team in baseball. It's marvelous that Miller beer has made him a national celebrity—
anybody's better than Bruce Jenner—but what does his popular following
suggest about our new notion of the heroic figure? Rodney Dangerfield, of
course, is famous for "I don't get no respect," but the "lite" beer ethos
seems to play upon our feelings that we don't *deserve* respect.

There are also the repeated small moments of defeat for the nonceleb-   48
rity: the natural cereal eater who is constantly crestfallen at how many
bowls of his brand it would take to equal the vitamins in Total; the shame-
faced jerks ridiculed by their friends for forgetting Prestone, failing to keep
their guard up and stranding them all in the cold; the overachieving,
overtime-working eager beavers who are constantly being whispered about
because they "need a deodorant that works overtime"; the guy in the
Yellow Pages ad who rips the bottom of his pants so embarrassingly that
he has to wait in a telephone booth for a tailor to make him fit to appear in
public again.

The Humiliation Sell goes hand in hand with what's happening in the   49
"real people" genre of TV commercials. The real people being selected to
appear in recent ads are, to put it bluntly, a much stupider, uglier breed
than those of the late '70s. This is not the cute, stupid and ugly urban look
of the late '60s "New York School" of filmic ad realists (the Alka-Seltzer
"No Matter What Shape Your Stomach's In" campaign, for instance).
No, this is a new kind of subhuman suburban subspecies. It is as if the ad
people were saying to the public and the FTC: "You want honesty? You
want truth and reality in ads? O.K. We'll rub your nose in realism! We'll
show you 'real.' "

Someday, bits of this verité material will be recognized as some of the   50
most accurate journalism of our time. Nothing captures the bleak reality of
the suburban teen-ager better than the picture of the "real kid" in a laundry
detergent ad, staring vacantly with what looks like angel-dust-blasted eyes
at two piles of white linen and grunting, "I'm not into wash, but like, that
one's cleaner."

Not only do these real people look vacant, they seem totally cut off   51
from the people closest to them; they exhibit not merely mistaken product
identification responses but an almost pathological failure to know the
world around them.

After all these years, how is it possible for a real person in a super-   52
market aisle, approached by a man with a microphone, not to know that he
or she ought to pick Stove Top stuffing instead of potatoes? And how could
all those mothers in the Proctor & Gamble ads fail to know their sons and
husbands prefer clean clothes to dingy? Are ad people trying to rub the
noses of real people in their nitty-gritty griminess?

And talk about rubbing it in: have you seen the latest Charmin toilet   53
paper ad with Mr. Whipple? It's a remarkable example of ad people boasting shamelessly about their manipulative trickery to the very people they
have successfully hoodwinked.

This crown jewel of the epic Charmin campaign (first begun a decade   54
ago, it transformed Charmin from a minor regional brand into the No. 1
product of its kind) takes place outside Whipple's supermarket. He has
taken down his old Don't Squeeze the Charmin signs and is ushering in a
new era, during which there will be no more silly prohibitions on squeezing. As he does so, he reflects on the whole ''Don't Squeeze'' theme of the
campaign and confides at last the true motive behind the gimmick.
''Squeezing the Charmin wasn't so bad after all,'' Whipple confesses. His
''Don't Squeeze'' prissiness was just a trick to provoke and then co-opt
your rebelliousness. Hence, the brand-new Charmin slogan: ''The squeezing gets you. The softness keeps you.''

In other words, Whipple is virtually coming out and saying, ''We   55
tricked you into buying it.'' You can almost hear the triumphant crowing
of the ad people—you laughed at us for putting on such a ridiculous
campaign, but, Mr. and Mrs. America, the joke's on you: you bought it
anyway.

Perhaps the final, most insulting touch to top off this trend was the   56
reappearance of ventriloquists' dummies in place of real people in some
campaigns. We have had one ventriloquist's dummy mouthing ''ring
around the collar'' in a Wisk ad and another saying ''butter'' in the Parkay
margarine spots. Real people are so malleable, so willing to say whatever
the ad people want them to, they might as well be ventriloquists' dummies
as far as the ad people are concerned. This explains, perhaps, the birth of
the dummy trend and the displacement of their flesh-and-blood counter-
parts.

One gets the feeling that these commercials are expressing a certain   57
impatience with the consumer on the part of ad people, perhaps even a
subconscious hostility. Industry has become tired of trying to persuade us,
seduce us, flatter us, indulge our fantasies. The Me Decade is over on

Madison Avenue, and from now on it's no more Mr. Nice Guy. Tough times are here, even for advertising.

Advertising is going through a period during which precipitous agency- 58 client shifts have raised cries of disloyalty and betrayal in some quarters. Product "positioning" wars and head-to-head comparison ad conflicts grow more fierce, even vicious. "ANOTHER ROUND IN COLA WARS"; "GF SENDS 'MASTER BLEND' INTO BATTLE"—the images in the trade paper headlines are grimly warlike. Even in the sweet little candy world, big battles are erupting: "LIFE-SAVERS, CHICLE READY FOR CANDY ROLL MARKET CLASH" proclaimed one front page battle dispatch in *Ad Age*.

There are signs of even tougher times to come, both on the screen and 59 in the offices of Madison Avenue. The trade papers are reporting with increasing frequency the problems ad agencies are having with slow-paying buyers. Credit problems are cropping up and forcing the creation of a new get-tough policy toward debtors.

It was around the turn of the decade that I first spotted a notice in *Ad* 60 *Age* for an outfit that said it specialized in "advertising debt-collection problems." Their slogan: "We're gentlemen."

Were they hinting with that line that there are nongentlemen working 61 the suites of Madison Avenue, tough guys who specialize in more forceful, no-nonsense ways of dealing with advertising debt collection? One cannot help but imagine a *Rocky* type in a gray flannel suit visiting a Creative Director and delivering the ultimatum, "Pay up or we'll mangle the syntax of your slogan." Perhaps the only satisfaction we can get from all this is that if ads are getting tougher on life, life is certainly getting tougher on advertising.

QUESTIONS ON CONTENT

1. Rosenbaum states that, initially, there was the Hard Sell era of the fast-talking salesmen. This, he says, turned into the Hard Life era of bitter reality. Rosenbaum then discusses the Humiliation Sell and Love in advertising. What does Rosenbaum say about these topics? Why does he make repeated comparisons to sincere emotional ads such as the "Mean Joe Greene and the Kid" Coke commercial, while only devoting one paragraph to a discussion of these ads?

2. Adwriters for Excedrin explain that "Life got tough, so we got stronger." Why do you think advertisers exploit the idea that life is tough? Is life, in your opinion, really as tough as advertisements would lead us to believe?

3. What are the different ways in which love is portrayed in ads, according to Rosenbaum?

4. Rosenbaum's attitude toward advertisements is generally negative. Which types of ads does Rosenbaum dislike most? Are there any ads Rosenbaum likes? Based on the attitudes Jeffrey Schrank expresses in the previous reading, how do you think he would respond to these ads?

QUESTIONS ON RHETORIC

1. Rosenbaum's word choice is generally more sophisticated than Jeffrey Schrank's. Because diction should be suited to the author's audience, who do you think Rosenbaum intended his audience to be?

2. Rosenbaum discusses the effects of ads on "us" as "we" watch "our" television sets. Why do you think he uses first person plural rather than second person (you) or third person (they)?

3. Rosenbaum places a good deal of emphasis on the style of the advertisements of brokerage firms. What is the significance of this? What else does Rosenbaum emphasize to make his point?

4. What do you believe is Rosenbaum's purpose in writing this essay: to teach, to inform, to persuade, or to entertain? Explain your answer.

VOCABULARY

pugnaciously (6)	bode (28)	crestfallen (48)
cloistered (13)	gestalt (30)	hoodwinked (53)
sophistries (19)	malaprop (46)	malleable (56)
intones (20)	ethos (47)	precipitous (58)
harbinger (21)		

WRITING TOPICS

1. Society has tended to give nicknames to decades, the way people do to friends, to describe the characteristics and tendencies that distinguish them. For instance, the Roaring Twenties were so called for their wild impetuosity, while the seventies were called the "Me Decade." Judging by the social tendencies you see around you, what predictions can you make about names society might bestow on the '90s? In an essay, discuss the ways you think advertising might reflect and play up to these priorities.

2. Over the course of a week, pay close attention to the television commercials aired in a variety of different time slots. How many of the selling tactics Rosenbaum describes do you see used in any one evening? In an essay, describe the commercials and label them according to the selling tactic each employs.

THE PRESENCE OF
THE WORD IN TV
ADVERTISING

Jay Rosen

Jay Rosen, who is an assistant professor of journalism and mass communications at New York University and a contributing editor of Channels *magazine, has taken a particular interest in television ads. In the following essay, Rosen proposes that watching TV with the sound turned off is the best way to find out what commercials are really "saying."*

It is safe to say that most inquiries into the language of television adver- 1
tising would look at the sort of language actually used in the ads. I could imagine, for example, a rather interesting article on how an advertising slogan like "Where's the Beef?" became almost instantly part of the American language in the summer of 1984. Indeed, in a journal like *Et cetera* there could easily be an entire issue devoted to the "Where's the Beef?" For cultural observers, then, there is quite a lot of material in the language employed by television advertising. But that is not the direction I want to take in this article.

I would like to begin by observing the following fact. All over America 2
there are people who have discovered a new way of watching television. The advertising industry calls them "flippers," people who drift restlessly around the dial by remote control, changing the channel at the slightest provocation—the appearance on screen of Angie Dickinson, for example. I know one man—not an academic, as it turns out—who says he hits the button as soon as he feels the smallest hint of content coming on. My own habits are not quite so severe, but I am, I confess, a flipper. (By the way, most flippers are male, something no one has thought to study yet.) If the advertising industry is concerned about flippers, it would be doubly con- cerned about me. For I am not only a flipper, but I often flip with the sound off. I find it easier to recognize patterns that way, and pattern recognition is, so to speak, my profession.

Now, flipping with the sound off is a good way of investigating tele-   3
vision ads. Frequently I find myself asking, "what is this ad about?" as I
watch the images float by. "What is this ad about?" is a different question,
of course, from "what *product* is this an ad for?" To ask what an ad is
"about" is to inquire into the underlying message of the ad. . . . Deodorant ads, as almost everyone knows, are about shame and the body, no
matter what they seem to be saying. The art of flipping makes it easier to
recognize such things, and I recommend it to everyone as an inexpensive
research tool.

You don't have to be a flipper to recognize that one trend in television   4
advertising is toward increasing visualization—more images, arriving at a
faster clip, and packing more of a punch. Often they are accompanied by
music, and frequently this music is borrowed or adapted from hit songs on
the radio. MTV is thus an obvious influence on this sort of advertising, but
there's an important difference. A certain vagueness or incoherence is
possible, even desirable, in a music video. As a result, it is often impossible to say what music videos are really about, despite the presence of a
lot of striking images. In advertising there is not as much license. The
images must succeed, not only in grabbing attention, but in communicating
a single concept or theme which can then be linked to the product. This is
what I mean by "deep structure" in TV advertising.

A good example is a new series of ads for Michelob beer. You may   5
recall that Michelob's slogan used to be "Weekends Were Made For
Michelob." In the new campaign the line is, "The Night Belongs to
Michelob," suggesting that by the 1990s, Michelob will have colonized
the entire week. In any event, the ads now feature a series of images, very
well shot, all of which vivify life in the big city at night. Well-dressed
women step out of cabs, skylines twinkle and glow, performers take the
stage in smoky nightclubs, couples kiss on the street, backlit by the head-
lights of cars. These are not only images *of* the night; they are *about* the
night as an idea or myth. Their goal is to create a swirl of associations
around the word "night," which is actually heard in the ad if you have the
sound on. Phil Collins of the rock band Genesis sings a song in which the
word "tonight" is repeated over and over.

But what's interesting about the ads is that neither the lyrics of Phil   6
Collins nor the slogan, "The Night Belongs to Michelob" are necessary to
get the message. The word "night" comes through in the very texture of
the images. It's there even when the sound is off and no language is being
heard. What Walter Ong once called "the presence of the word" does not,
in this case, depend on the presence of language. For example, a singer is
shown silhouetted in a spotlight on stage at a nightclub. This is not merely
a picture *taken* at night, in a place associated *with* the night. It is almost an
abstract diagram of the concept of night. The beam of the spotlight, be-

cause it is visible, demonstrates the presence of darkness all around. The singer appears as a silhouette, a black shape who is in, of, and surrounded by the night. The spotlight, then, is the very principle of intelligibility at work: It lights up the night, not in order to obliterate it, but to give it form, to demonstrate what "night" is, almost like a Sesame Street vocabulary lesson. This giving of form to an abstract concept is the logic behind a number of ads on television.

Levi's, for example, has created a series of ads about the idea of "blue." Naturally they are shot in blue tones on city streets. They also feature blues songs being strummed in the background. And, of course, the actors are all wearing blue jeans. But blue is communicated on a deeper level, as well. The feeling of blue—the meaning blue has taken on in popular culture—is brought out in the way a girl walks wistfully down the street, blowing soap bubbles into the air. In these ads, blue would come through without the sound of blues songs or the product name— Levi's 501 blues. Indeed, I am tempted to say that blue would come through even on a black and white set. Why? Because the director has found images which "mean" blue at the deepest cultural level. It is not the surfaced presence of the *color* blue that matters, but a kind of inner architecture of blue, on top of which blue scenes, blue jeans and blues songs have been placed.   7

This may seem easy enough with a concept, like blue, that is primarily visual. But what about notions that are essentially verbal? The Hewlett-Packard company has attempted something along these lines. It is now running a series of ads whose slogan is "What if . . .?" In these ads, Hewlett-Packard people are seen pondering difficult problems, hitting upon a possible answer, and rushing to their colleagues to announce, "I've got it: What if . . ." and the sound fades out.   8

Of course, if you turn the sound off, there is no "what if" to be heard and no fade out. And yet the idea of "what if" is not necessarily gone. Picture this: An intelligent-looking woman in glasses is shown alone in her office, tapping a pencil and sort of looking skyward, as if contemplating a majestic possibility. Here the attempt is to produce a visual image of "what-if–ness," a notion ordinarily expressed in words or mathematical symbols. It has often been said that pictures have no tense. But Hewlett-Packard is attempting to prove that a tense—in this case, the conditional— can in fact be a visual idea—borrowed from language, but expressed in images. Perhaps we will soon see ads visualizing a host of ideas we ordinarily think of as linguistic. How about a series of pictures about the concept of "nevertheless" or "because"?   9

What I am trying to point out is a certain irony in the trend toward increased visualization. As TV ads become shorter, they become more visual, as a way of saying more in a smaller amount of time. But as they   10 become more visual, the ads seem to be about concepts which are inescapably verbal. Advertising may appear to be relying less on language, but language is simply functioning on a deeper level. It has not, in any sense, gone away. And a final irony is this: In order to discover this deeper level of language it is necessary to ignore the language on the surface. In a strange way, turning the sound off allows you to hear what's really being said.

QUESTIONS ON CONTENT

1. Rosen states that "as they become more visual, the ads seem to be about concepts which are inescapably verbal." In your own words, explain what Rosen means by this statement.

2. What are some of the techniques advertisers use to make ads "convincing" without using the spoken word?

3. While he discusses celebrity endorsements (such as Phil Collins's lyrics playing throughout a commercial), Rosen downplays the celebrity's role in the commercial. Is he saying the "presence of the word" and not Phil Collins's voice is selling Michelob? Do you agree?

4. Rosen finds the use of visual persuasion interesting for two reasons. What are they?

QUESTIONS ON RHETORIC

1. Who do you think Rosen intends his audience to be? What specific examples from his essay lead you to this conclusion?

2. Rosen suggests that advertising is full of irony. In his conclusion, Rosen points to what he calls the "final irony." What "irony" is he talking about? Discuss irony as it applies to this essay.

3. Reread the opening sentence in each of Rosen's paragraphs. What do they have in common? How do they work to move his argument forward?

VOCABULARY

provocation (2)   license (4)   obliterate (6)
visualization (4)

WRITING TOPICS

1. Describe in words the following abstract concepts: *although, never again, improved, inexpensive, more, unique.* Choose one of these words and devise a short, silent ad conveying the idea of this word for a product of your choice.

2. Watch television one evening with the sound turned down. Look for (1) ads whose true meaning comes through with the sound off; (2) ads that mean something very different with the sound off; and (3) ads whose visual presentation is so blatant that sound and text are not necessary. In an essay, discuss which kind of ad you find most convincing. Why do you feel this way?

GETTIN' RICH BY DROPPIN' THE G

Edwin Newman

Edwin Newman, television journalist, author of Strictly Speaking *and* A Civil Tongue, *and a well-known advocate for good speech, says that in spite of a national effort to raise education's standards, advertisers continue to make money by using bad grammar.*

It has been estimated, by people who spend their time estimating this sort of thing, that American boys and girls, on reaching the age of eighteen, have seen, on the average, 350,000 television commercials. Whatever the number may be—and the feeling sometimes takes hold that we see that many in a day—too many are ungrammatical, usually deliberately so. When a national effort is under way to raise standards of education, the country is not helped by the glorification of semiliteracy.

It is, for example, an article of faith among some advertisers that dropping the *g* on words ending in *ing* is the sure path to riches. Where *g*'s are not dropped, profit-making is often thought to rest on double negatives, on the use of "ain't," on never saying "I" where "me" can be worked in. In the same way, "as" rather than "like," and "well" rather than "good," are thought to lead in no time at all to the bankruptcy courts.

Over the years, with the same devotion to duty that once led me to listen to John Madden for an entire NFL playoff game to count his "Y'know"'s (fifty-six), I have made a list of some of the more offensive misuses of English in advertising on the air and in print. The misuses are not interesting, just obvious, and childish. A tiny sample:

"Ain't nothing like the real thing," proclaims a hamburger chain. "Me and my buddies," says a retired football player as he begins an automobile commercial. ("My buddies and I" would be considered by advertisers and their agencies to be fatally "elitist.") "Works in as quick as twenty-two minutes," says a product that eases stomach upset.

"Get major credit cards easy," so we are urged. "That works good," says a mouthwash. "You won't believe how great it holds your dentures," says something that holds dentures great. "There ain't nothing like it nowhere," says a car dealer. "I don't have to give up taste or freshness, or nothin'," simpers a model for a breath deodorant. Another model explains why she chooses a particular brand of underwear: "Makes me look like I'm not wearin' nothin'."

"It looks as good as it performs," boasts a motorcycle. "Tastes as good as it works," says a mouthwash that works good. "Frank, me, and the kids want a reliable laxative," declares a housewife.

Is it believable that "Ain't no" will sell more hamburgers than "There is no"? Or that a shampoo will earn higher profits because it claims to be for "bouncin' and behavin' hair," or an appliance manufacturer because it makes "good things for livin' "? And even if they will, which seems doubtful, should these companies be promoting sloppiness and semiliteracy?

There is, moreover, no need for intentional mistakes. There are enough of the other kind. A hotel claimed to be "among the two or three very best hotels in the country between either coast." Given the choice, which coast would you rather be between? In that hotel, it might have been appropriate to use the toothpaste that "cleans beautifully in between each tooth." Unless you preferred the one that "gives like a shine" to your teeth.

A brokerage house promises to build up clients' investments: "Nobody can help you do that better than us." Here is a message from a computer manufacturer: "If the following pages can't convince you what to do with a home computer, maybe you belong in another age." Convince you what to do. Who writes this stuff? Who passes it?

My favorite? It's grammatical but otherwise irresistible: "I never buy any product out on the market that wouldn't shrink hemorrhoidal tissues." What does he eat?

QUESTIONS ON CONTENT

1. In his opening paragraph, Newman claims that advertisers employ bad grammer and in other ways generally misuse the English language. However, he does not give a rationale for this misuse of English. What reasons could you give?

2. Choose four or five of Newman's examples of the misuse of language in an advertisement and correct them. What is the effect? Do you think the adwriter in each case broke a rule conciously or simply did not know better?

QUESTIONS ON RHETORIC

1. Newman gives twenty different examples of advertisements, yet never mentions a brand name or manufacturer. How effective is this technique? Would this essay be more convincing if Newman included examples of particular brands? Explain.

2. Newman bestows human traits on the products he discusses to imply that they "sell themselves." What other uses does Newman make of personification? Use examples from the text to support your answer. (Glossary: *Personification*)

3. Newman is sometimes vague in his writing and seems to assume that the reader knows what he is talking about without a full explanation. For example, Newman says, "There is, moreover, no need for intentional mistakes. There are enough of the other kind." What is the effect of such a writing style?

VOCABULARY

semiliteracy (1)   elitist (4)   simpers (5)

WRITING TOPICS

1. Newman places a lot of blame on advertisers for their contribution to the misuse of language. However, essayists, too, can be guilty of inventing words and using cliches and idioms to convince their readers. Reread Newman's essay, as well as the essays of the other writers in this section. In an essay of your own, discuss the writing "tricks" each uses to convince the reader that his point of view is the right one.

2. Newman writes that advertisers seem to believe "dropping the *g* on words ending in *ing* is the sure path to riches." Other writers in this section accuse advertisers of additional faults as well. Discuss these accusations. Write an essay exploring some of the arguments advertisers might use in their own self-defense. Are advertisers "guilty" as the writers in this section say they are?

IT'S NATURAL! IT'S ORGANIC! OR IS IT?

Consumers Union

"Natural" and "organic" are two advertising buzz words of the 1980s, products of the health and fitness movement that is sweeping the country. But these two words have the Consumers Union worried because products labeled "natural" and/or "organic" often don't deliver what customers expect. In the following essay, the Consumers Union, a nonprofit organization that provides "consumers with information and counsel on consumer goods and services," examines the words "natural" and "organic" and how they are being used by advertisers. To educate consumers, the Union classifies a number of the deceptive advertising techniques used by manufacturers and advertising agencies.

"No artificial flavors or colors!" reads the Nabisco advertisement in *Progressive Grocer*, a grocery trade magazine. "And research shows that's exactly what consumers are eager to buy."

The ad, promoting Nabisco's *Sesame Wheats* as "a natural whole wheat cracker," might raise a few eyebrows among thoughtful consumers of Nabisco's *Wheat Thins* and *Cheese Nips,* which contain artificial colors, or of its *Ginger Snaps* and *Oreo Cookies,* which have artificial flavors. But Nabisco has not suddenly become a champion of "natural" foods. Like other giants of the food industry, the company is merely keeping its eye on what will produce a profit.

Nabisco's trade ad, which was headlined "A Natural for Profits," is simply a routine effort by a food processor to capitalize on the concerns that consumers have about the safety of the food they buy.

Supermarket shelves are being flooded with "natural" products, some of them containing a long list of chemical additives. And some products that never did contain additives have suddenly sprouted "natural" or "no preservative" labels. Along with the new formulations and labels have come higher prices, since the food industry has realized that consumers are willing to pay more for products they think are especially healthful.

The mass merchandising of "natural" foods is a spillover onto super-   5
market shelves of a phenomenon once confined to health-food stores, as major food manufacturers enter what was once the exclusive territory of small entrepreneurs. Health-food stores were the first to foster and capitalize on the growing consumer interest in nutrition and are still thriving. Along with honey-sweetened snacks, "natural" vitamins, and other "natural" food products, the health-food stores frequently feature "organic" foods.

Like the new merchandise in supermarkets, the products sold at health-   6
food stores carry the implication that they're somehow better for you— safer or more nutritious. In this report, we'll examine that premise, looking at both "natural" foods, which are widely sold, and "organic" foods, which are sold primarily at health-food stores. While the terms "natural" and "organic" are often used loosely, "organic" generally refers to the way food is grown (without pesticides or chemical fertilizers) and "natural" to the character of the ingredients (no preservatives or artificial additives) and to the fact that the food product has undergone minimal processing.

Langendorf Natural Lemon Flavored Creme Pie contains no cream. It   7
does contain sodium propionate, certified food colors, sodium benzoate, and vegetable gum.

That's natural?   8

Yes indeed, says L.A. Cushman, Jr., chairman of American Bakeries   9
Co., the Chicago firm that owns Langendorf. The word "natural," he explains, modifies "lemon flavored," and the pie contains oil from lemon rinds. "The lemon flavor," Cushman states "comes from the natural lemon flavor as opposed to artificial lemon flavor, assuming there is such a thing as artificial lemon flavor."

Welcome to the world of natural foods.   10

You can eat your "natural" way from one end of the supermarket to   11
the other. Make yourself a sandwich of *Kraft Cracker Barrel Natural Cheddar Cheese* on *Better Way Natural Whole Grain Wheat Nugget Bread* spread with *Autumn Natural Margarine*. Wash it down with *Anheuser-Busch Natural Light Beer* or *Rich-Life Natural Orange Nutri-Pop*. Snack on any number of brands of "natural" potato chips and "natural" candy bars. And don't exclude your pet: Feed your dog *Gravy Train Dog Food With Natural Beef Flavor* or, if it's a puppy, try *Blue Mountain Natural Style Puppy Food*.

The "natural" bandwagon doesn't end at the kitchen. You can bathe in   12
Batherapy Natural Mineral Bath (sodium sesquicarbonate, isopropyl myristate, fragrance, D & C Green No. 5, D & C Yellow No. 10 among

its ingredients), using *Queen Helene "All-Natural" Amino Peptide Shampoo* (propylene glycol, hydroxyethyl cellulose, methylparaben, D & C Red No. 3, D & C Brown No. 1) and *Organic Aid Natural Clear Soaps.* Then, if you're so inclined, you can apply *Naturade Conditioning Mascara with Natural Protein* (stearic acid, PVP, butylene glycol, sorbitan sesquioleate, triethanolamine, imidazolidinyl urea, methylparaben, propylparaben).

At its ridiculous extreme, the "natural" ploy extends to furniture, cigarettes, denture adhesives, and shoes.   13

The word "natural" does not have to be synonymous with "ripoff."   14
Over the years, the safety of many food additives has been questioned. And a consumer who reads labels carefully can in fact find some foods in supermarkets that have been processed without additives.

But the word "natural" does not guarantee that. All too often, as the   15
above examples indicate, the word is used more as a key to higher profits. Often, it implies a health benefit that does not really exist.

Co-op News, the publication of the Berkeley Co-op, the nation's larg-   16
est consumer-cooperative store chain, reported on "two fifteen-ounce cans of tomato sauce, available side-by-side" at one of its stores. One sauce, called *Health Valley,* claimed on its label to have "no citric acid, no sugars, no preservatives, no artificial colors or flavors." There were none of those ingredients in the Co-op's house brand, either, but their absence was hardly worth noting on the label, since canned tomato sauce almost never contains artificial colors or flavors and doesn't need preservatives after being heated in the canning process. The visible difference between the two products was price, not ingredients. The *Health Valley* tomato sauce was selling for 85 cents; the Co-op house brand, for only 29 cents.

One supermarket industry consultant estimates that 7 percent of all   17
processed food products now sold are touted as "natural." And that could be just the beginning. A Federal Trade Commission report noted that 63 percent of people polled in a survey agreed with the statement, "Natural foods are more nutritious than other foods." Thirty-nine percent said they regularly buy food because it is "natural," and 47 percent said they were willing to pay 10 percent more for a food that is "natural."

According to those who have studied the trend, the consumer's desire   18
for "natural" foods goes beyond the fear of specific chemicals. "There is a mistrust of technology," says Howard Moskowitz, a taste researcher and consultant to the food industry. "There is a movement afoot to return to simplicity in all aspects of life." A spokeswoman for Lever Bros., one of the nation's major food merchandisers, adds: " 'Natural' is a psychological thing of everyone wanting to get out of the industrial world."

Because consumers are acting out of such vague, undefined feelings,   19
they aren't sure what they should be getting when they buy a product labeled "natural." William Wittenberg, president of Grandma's Food Inc.,

comments: "Manufacturers and marketers are making an attempt to appeal to a consumer who feels he should be eating something natural, but doesn't know why. I think the marketers of the country in effect mirror back to the people what they want to hear. People have to look to themselves for their own protection." Grandma's makes a *Whole Grain Date Filled Fruit 'n' Oatmeal Bar* labeled "naturally Good Flavor." The ingredients include "artificial flavor."

"Natural" foods are not necessarily preferable nor, as we have seen, necessarily natural. 20

Consider "natural" potato chips. They are often cut thick from un- 21 peeled potatoes, packaged without preservatives in heavy foil bags with fancy lettering, and sold at a premium price. Sometimes, such chips include "sea salt," a product whose advantage over conventional "land" salt has not been demonstrated. The packaging is intended to give the impression that "natural" potato chips are less of a junk food than regular chips. But nutritionally there is no difference. Both are made from the same food, the potato, and both have been processed so that they are high in salt and in calories.

Sometimes the "natural" products may have ingredients you'd prefer 22 to avoid. *Quaker 100% Natural* cereal, for example, contains 24 percent sugars, a high percentage, considering it's not promoted as a sugared cereal. (*Kellogg's Corn Flakes* has 7.8 percent sugar.) Many similar "natural" granola-type cereals have oil added, giving them a much higher fat content than conventional cereals.

Taste researcher Moskowitz notes that food processors are "trying to 23 signal to the consumer a sensory impact that can be called natural." Two of the most popular signals, says Moskowitz, are honey and coconut. But honey is just another sugar, with no significant nutrients other than calories, and coconut is especially high in saturated fats.

While many processed foods are less nutritious than their fresh coun- 24 terparts, processing can sometimes help foods: Freezing preserves nutrients that could be lost if fresh foods are not consumed quickly; pasteurization kills potentially dangerous bacteria in milk. Some additives are also both safe and useful. Sorbic acid, for instance, prevents the growth of potentially harmful molds in cheese and other products, and sodium benzoate has been used for more than 70 years to prevent the growth of microorganisms in acidic foods.

"Preservative" has become a dirty word, to judge from the number of 25 "no preservative" labels on food products. Calcium propionate might sound terrible on a bread label, but this mildew-retarding substance occurs naturally in both raisins and Swiss cheese. "Bread without preservatives could well cost you more than bread with them," says Vernal S. Packard Jr., a University of Minnesota nutrition professor. "Without preservatives, the bread gets stale faster; it may go moldy with the production of hazardous aflatoxin. And already we in the United States return [to producers] 100 million pounds of bread each year—this in a world nagged by hunger and malnutrition.''

Nor are all ''natural'' substances safe. Sassafras tea was banned by the U.S. Food and Drug Administration several years ago because it contains safrole, which has produced liver cancer in laboratory animals. Kelp, a seaweed that is becoming increasingly fashionable as a dietary supplement, can have a high arsenic content. Aflatoxin, produced by a mold that can grow on improperly stored peanuts, corn, and grains, is a known carcinogen.

To complicate matters, our palates have become attuned to many unnatural tastes. ''We don't have receptors on our tongues that signal ''natural,'' says taste researcher Moskowitz. He points out, for instance, that a panel of consumers would almost certainly reject a natural lemonade ''in favor of a lemonade scientifically designed to taste natural. If you put real lemon, sugar, and water together, people would reject it as harsh. They are used to flavors developed by flavor houses.'' Similarly, Moskowitz points out, many consumers say that for health reasons they prefer less salty food—but the results of various taste tests have contradicted this, too.

In the midst of all this confusion, it's not surprising that the food industry is having a promotional field day. Companies are using various tactics to convince the consumer that a food product is ''natural''—and hence preferable. Here are some of the most common:

THE INDETERMINATE MODIFIER. Use a string of adjectives and claim that ''natural'' modifies only the next adjective in line, not the product itself. Take *Pillsbury Natural Chocolate Flavored Chocolate Chip Cookies.* Many a buyer might be surprised to learn from the fine print that these cookies contain artificial flavor, as well as the chemical antioxidant BHA. But Pillsbury doesn't bat an eyelash at this. ''We're not trying to mislead anybody,'' says a company representative, explaining that the word ''natural'' modifies only ''chocolate flavored,'' while the artificial flavoring is vanilla. Then why not call the product ''Chocolate Chip Cookies with Natural Chocolate Flavoring''? ''From a labeling point of view, we're trying to use a limited amount of space'' was the answer.

INNOCENCE BY ASSOCIATION. Put nature on your side. *Life Cinnamon Flavor High Protein Cereal,* a Quaker Oats Co. product, contains BHA and artificial color, among other things. How could the company imply the cereal was ''natural'' and still be truthful? One series of *Life* boxes solves the problem neatly. The back panel has an instructional lesson for children entitled ''Nature.'' The box uses the word ''Nature'' four times and ''natural'' once—but never actually to describe the cereal inside. Other products surround themselves with a ''natural'' aura by picturing outdoor or farm scenes on their packages.

THE ''PRINTER'S ERROR.'' From time to time, readers send us food wrappers 31 making a ''natural'' claim directly contradicted by the ingredients list. We have, for example, received a batch of individually wrapped *Devonsheer* crackers with a big red label saying: ''A Natural Product, no preservatives.'' The ingredients list includes ''calcium propionate (to retard spoilage).''

How could a manufacturer defend that? ''At a given printing, the 32 printer was instructed to remove 'no preservatives, natural product' when we changed ingredients, but he didn't do it,'' says Curtis Marshall, vice president for operations at Devonsheer Melba Corp.

THE BEST DEFENSE. Don't defend yourself; attack the competition. Some- 33 times the use of the word ''natural'' is, well, just plain unnatural. Take the battle that has been brewing between the nation's two largest beer makers, Miller Brewing Co. and Anheuser-Busch. The latter's product, *Anheuser-Busch Natural Light Beer,* has been the object of considerable derision by Miller.

Miller wants the word ''natural'' dropped from Anheuser-Busch's ad- 34 vertisements because beers are ''highly processed, complex products, made with chemical additives and other components not in their natural form.''

Anheuser-Busch has responded only with some digs at Miller, charging 35 Miller with using artificial foam stabilizer and adding an industrial enzyme instead of natural malt to reduce the caloric content of its *Miller Lite* beer.

No victor has yet emerged from the great beer war, but the industry is 36 obviously getting edgy.

''Other brewers say it's time for the two companies to shut up,'' the 37 *Wall Street Journal* reported. ''One thing they [the other brewers] are worried about, says William T. Elliot, president of C. Schmidt & Sons, a Philadelphia brewery, is all the fuss over ingredients. Publicity about that issue is disclosing to beer drinkers that their suds include sulfuric acid, calcium sulfate, alginic acid, or amyloglucosidase.''

THE NEGATIVE PITCH. Point out in big letters on the label that the product 38 doesn't contain something it wouldn't contain anyway. The ''no artificial preservatives'' label stuck on a jar of jam or jelly is true and always has been—since sugar is all the preservative jams and jellies need. Canned goods, likewise, are preserved in their manufacture—by the heat of the canning process. Then there is the ''no cholesterol'' claim of vegetable oils, margarines, and even (in a radio commercial) canned pineapple. Those are also true, but beside the point, since cholesterol is found only in animal products.

What can be done about such all-but-deceptive practices? One might [39] suggest that the word "natural" is so vague as to be inherently deceptive, and therefore should not be available for promotional use. Indeed, the FTC staff suggested precisely that a few years ago but later backed away from the idea. The California legislature last year passed a weak bill defining the word "organic," but decided that political realities argued against tackling the word "natural."

"If we had included the word 'natural' in the bill, it most likely would [40] not have gotten out of the legislature," says one legislative staff member. "When you've got large economic interests in certain areas, the tendency is to guard those interests very carefully."

Under the revised FTC staff proposal, which had not been acted on by [41] the full commission as we went to press, the word "natural" can be used if the product has undergone only minimal processing and doesn't have artificial ingredients. That would eliminate the outright frauds, as well as the labeling of such products as Lever Bros.' *Autumn Natural Margarine,* which obviously has been highly processed from its original vegetable-oil state. But the FTC proposal might run into difficulty in defining exactly what "minimal processing" means. And it would also allow some deceptive implications. For instance, a product containing honey might be called "natural," while a food with refined sugar might not, thus implying that honey is superior to other sugars, which it is not.

A law incorporating similar regulations went into effect in Maine at the [42] beginning of this year. If a product is to be labeled "natural" and sold in Maine, it must have undergone only minimal processing and have no additives, preservatives, or refined additions such as white flour and sugar.

So far, according to John Michael, the state legislator who sponsored [43] the bill, food companies have largely ignored the law, but he expects the state to start issuing warnings this summer.

QUESTIONS ON CONTENT

1. Why are Americans eager to purchase "natural" foods? Are foods that carry the label *natural* a ripoff? Explain.

2. Why are more manufacturers getting into the natural-food business? Why do they use the term *natural* in their products' names and in advertising for these products?

3. What relationship, if any, exists between natural and nutritious?

MADE OF THE FINEST FIBER

If you're like most people who eat right, you probably give high fiber high priority.

And like most people, when you think of fiber, you probably automatically think of bran cereals.

Well, there's another good source of dietary fiber you should know about. Delicious Campbell's® Bean with Bacon Soup.

In fact, Campbell's has four soups that are high in fiber.

And you can see from the chart that follows exactly how each one measures up to bran cereals.

So now when you think of fiber, you don't have to think about

having it just at breakfast.

Instead, you can do your body good any time during the day. With a hot, hearty bowl of one of these Campbell's Soups.

You just might feel better for it—right to the very fiber of your being.

FIBER IN A SUGGESTED SERVING		
CAMPBELL'S SOUP	BRAN CEREALS	
Bean with Bacon 9g	100% Brans	11g
Split Pea with Ham 6g	40% Brans	6g
Green Pea 5g	Raisin Brans	5g
Low Sodium Green Pea 7g	Others	5–10g
This comparison includes soluble and insoluble fiber		

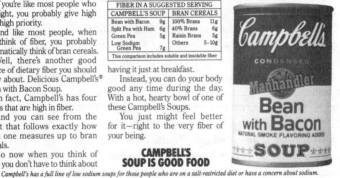

CAMPBELL'S SOUP IS GOOD FOOD

Campbell's has a full line of low sodium soups for those people who are on a salt-restricted diet or have a concern about sodium.

4. Many people believe that the processing of foods is necessarily bad. What, according to the Consumers Union, are some benefits of processing?

5. How, according to taste researcher Howard Moskowitz, have consumers' tastes complicated the issue of natural and artificial flavors?

6. What are the various tactics that companies use to convince potential consumers that their products are ''natural''? How does each tactic work?

7. What regulations does Consumers Union believe ought to be imposed on current ''all-but-deceptive'' advertising practices?

8. The latest buzz word of the ''health-food'' market is *fiber*. Analyze the

Campbell's ad on page 214. How do you suppose the Consumers Union would respond?

QUESTIONS ON RHETORIC

1. What is Consumers Union's purpose in this essay? (Glossary: *Purpose*)

2. In paragraph 6 Consumers Union defines both *natural* and *organic.* Why is it necessary for them to give these definitions?

3. The writers use examples both to illustrate and to support their generalizations about the use of the words *natural* and *organic* in the advertisements. How effective did you find these examples? Which ones seemed to work best? Why?

4. How is this essay organized? You may find it helpful to make a scratch outline of the essay so that you can see the overall structure.

VOCABULARY

trade (1)	bandwagon (12)	palates (27)
foster (5)	ploy (13)	derision (33)
implication (6)	touted (17)	
premise (6)	carcinogen (26)	

WRITING TOPICS

1. What, for you, are the connotations of the words *natural* and *organic?* Do you believe, as some have claimed, that these words are inherently deceptive? Write an essay in which you argue for or against the banning of these words from advertising.

2. Collect five or six print advertisements that use the word *natural,* and analyze each one carefully. Which of the Consumers Union's "tactics of deception" do they employ? What benefits are implied in each ad? Do you think the advertisers are trying to deceive you? Write an essay in which you present your analysis and state your conclusions.

3. Spend some time in your local supermarket looking at the messages printed on a variety of products. Do you find other words that manufacturers and advertisers are using in much the same way they use *natural* and *organic?* Write an essay in which you discuss your findings.

ADVERTISING'S FIFTEEN BASIC APPEALS

Jib Fowles

Jib Fowles, instructor of advertising and mass media at the University of Houston, discusses the basic emotions appealed to in advertisements. Fowles suggests it is no accident that the list parallels a "hierarchy of needs" described by several leading psychologists. The following article was published in Et Cetera, *a magazine of general semantics, focusing on how words and their meanings influence the behavior of society.*

EMOTIONAL APPEALS

The nature of effective advertisements was recognized full well by the late media philosopher Marshall McLuhan. In his *Understanding Media*, the first sentence of the section on advertising reads, "The continuous pressure is to create ads more and more in the image of audience motives and desires."

By giving form to people's deep-lying desires, and picturing states of being that individuals privately yearn for, advertisers have the best chance of arresting attention and affecting communication. And that is the immediate goal of advertising: to tug at our psychological shirt sleeves and slow us down long enough for a word or two about whatever is being sold. We glance at a picture of a solitary rancher at work, and "Marlboro" slips into our minds.

Advertisers (I'm using the term as a shorthand for both the products' manufacturers, who bring the ambition and money to the process, and the advertising agencies, who supply the know-how) are ever more compelled to invoke consumers' drives and longings; this is the "continuous pressure" McLuhan refers to. Over the past century, the American marketplace has grown increasingly congested as more and more products have entered into the frenzied competition after the public's dollars. The economies of other nations are quieter than ours since the volume of goods being hawked does not so greatly exceed demand. In some economies, consumer wares are scarce enough that no advertising at all is necessary.

But in the United States, we go to the other extreme. In order to stay in business, an advertiser must strive to cut through the considerable commercial hub-bub by any means available—including the emotional appeals that some observers have held to be abhorrent and underhanded.

The use of subconscious appeals is a comment not only on conditions among sellers. As time has gone by, buyers have become stoutly resistant to advertisements. We live in a blizzard of these messages and have learned to turn up our collars and ward off most of them. A study done a few years ago at Harvard University's Graduate School of Business Administration ventured that the average American is exposed to some 500 ads daily from television, newspapers, magazines, radio, billboards, direct mail, and so on. If for no other reason than to preserve one's sanity, a filter must be developed in every mind to lower the number of ads a person is actually aware of—a number this particular study estimated at about seventy-five ads per day. (Of these, only twelve typically produced a reaction—nine positive and three negative, on the average.) To be among the few messages that do manage to gain access to minds, advertisers must be strategic, perhaps even a little underhanded at times.

There are assumptions about personality underlying advertisers' efforts to communicate via emotional appeals, and while these assumptions have stood the test of time, they still deserve to be aired. Human beings, it is presumed, walk around with a variety of unfulfilled urges and motives swirling in the bottom half of their minds. Lusts, ambitions, tendernesses, vulnerabililties—they are constantly bubbling up, seeking resolution. These mental forces energize people, but they are too crude and irregular to be given excessive play in the real world. They must be capped with the competent, sensible behavior that permits individuals to get along well in society. However, this upper layer of mental activity, shot through with caution and rationality, is not receptive to advertising's pitches. Advertisers want to circumvent this shell of consciousness if they can, and latch on to one of the lurching, subconscious drives.

In effect, advertisers over the years have blindly felt their way around the underside of the American psyche, and by trial and error have discovered the softest points of entree, the places where their messages have the greatest likelihood of getting by consumers' defenses. As McLuhan says elsewhere, "Gouging away at the surface of public sales resistance, the ad men are constantly breaking through into the *Alice in Wonderland* territory behind the looking glass, which is the world of subrational impulses and appetites."

An advertisement communicates by making use of a specially selected image (of a supine female, say, or a curly-headed child, or a celebrity) which is designed to stimulate "subrational impulses and desires" even when they are at ebb, even if they are unacknowledged by their possessor.

Some few ads have their emotional appeal in the text, but for the greater number by far the appeal is contained in the artwork. This makes sense, since visual communication better suits more primal levels of the brain. If the viewer of an advertisement actually has the importuned motive, and if the appeal is sufficiently well-fashioned to call it up, then the person can be hooked. The product in the ad may then appear to take on the semblance of gratification for the summoned motive. Many ads seem to be saying, "If you have this need, then this product will help satisfy it." It is a primitive equation, but not an ineffective one for selling.

Thus, most advertisements appearing in national media can be under- 8 stood as having two orders of content. The first is the appeal to deep-running drives in the minds of consumers. The second is information regarding the good[s] or service being sold: its name, its manufacturer, its picture, its packaging, its objective attributes, its functions. For example, the reader of a brassiere advertisement sees a partially undraped but blandly unperturbed woman standing in an otherwise commonplace public setting, and may experience certain sensations; the reader also sees the name "Maidenform," a particular brassiere style, and, in tiny print, words about the material, colors, price. Or, the viewer of a television commercial sees a demonstration with four small boxes labelled 650, 650, 650, and 800; something in the viewer's mind catches hold of this, as trivial as thoughtful consideration might reveal it to be. The viewer is also exposed to the name "Anacin," its bottle, and its purpose.

Sometimes there is an apparently logical link between an ad's emo- 9 tional appeal and its product information. It does not violate common sense that Cadillac automobiles be photographed at country clubs, or that Japan Air Lines be associated with Orientalia. But there is no real need for the linkage to have a bit of reason behind it. Is there anything inherent to the connection between Salem cigarettes and mountains, Coke and a smile, Miller Beer and comradeship? The link being forged in minds between product and appeal is a pre-logical one.

People involved in the advertising industry do not necessarily talk in 10 the terms being used here. They are stationed at the sending end of this communications channel, and may think they are up to any number of things—Unique Selling Propositions, explosive copywriting, the optimal use of demographics or psychographics, ideal media buys, high recall ratings, or whatever. But when attention shifts to the receiving end of the channel, and focuses on the instant of reception, then commentary becomes much more elemental: an advertising message contains something primary and primitive, an emotional appeal, that in effect is the thin end of the wedge, trying to find its way into a mind. Should this occur, the product information comes along behind.

When enough advertisements are examined in this light, it becomes 11 clear that the emotional appeals fall into several distinguishable categories, and that every ad is a variation on one of a limited number of basic appeals. While there may be several ways of classifying these appeals, one particular list of fifteen has proven to be especially valuable.

Advertisements can appeal to:

1. The need for sex
2. The need for affiliation
3. The need to nurture
4. The need for guidance
5. The need to aggress
6. The need to achieve
7. The need to dominate
8. The need for prominence
9. The need for attention
10. The need for autonomy
11. The need to escape
12. The need to feel safe
13. The need for aesthetic sensations
14. The need to satisfy curiosity
15. Physiological needs: food, drink, sleep, etc.

MURRAY'S LIST

Where does this list of advertising's fifteen basic appeals come from? Several years ago, I was involved in a research project which was to have as one segment an objective analysis of the changing appeals made in post-World War II American advertising. A sample of magazine ads would have their appeals coded into the categories of psychological needs they seemed aimed at. For this content analysis to happen, a complete roster of human motives would have to be found. 12

The first thing that came to mind was Abraham Maslow's famous four-part hierarchy of needs. But the briefest look at the range of appeals made in advertising was enough to reveal that they are more varied, and more profane, than Maslow had cared to account for. The search led on to the work of psychologist Henry A. Murray, who together with his colleagues at the Harvard Psychological Clinic had constructed a full taxonomy of needs. As described in *Explorations in Personality*, Murray's team 13 had conducted a lengthy series of depth interviews with a number of subjects in order to derive from scratch what they felt to be the essential variables of personality. Forty-four variables were distinguished by the Harvard group, of which twenty were motives. The need for achievement ("to overcome obstacles and obtain a high standard") was one, for instance; the need to defer was another; the need to aggress was a third; and so forth.

Murray's list had served as the groundwork for a number of subsequent   14 projects. Perhaps the best-known of these was David C. McClelland's extensive study of the need for achievement, reported in his *The Achieving Society*. In the process of demonstrating that a people's high need for achievement is predictive of later economic growth, McClelland coded achievement imagery and references out of a nation's folklore, songs, legends, and children's tales.

Following McClelland, I too wanted to cull the motivational appeals   15 from a culture's imaginative product—in this case, advertising. To develop categories expressly for this purpose, I took Murray's twenty motives and added to them others he had mentioned in passing in *Explorations in Personality* but not included on the final list. The extended list was tried out on a sample of advertisements, and motives which never seemed to be invoked were dropped. I ended up with eighteen of Murrays' motives, into which 770 print ads were coded. The resulting distribution is included in the 1976 book *Mass Advertising as Social Forecast*.

Since that time, the list of appeals has undergone refinements as a result   16 of using it to analyze television commercials. A few more adjustments have stemmed from the efforts of students in my advertising classes to decode appeals; tens of term papers surveying thousands of advertisements have caused some inconsistencies in the list to be hammered out. Fundamentally, though, the list remains the creation of Henry Murray. In developing a comprehensive, parsimonious inventory of human motives, he pinpointed the subsurface mental forces that are the least quiescent and the most susceptible to advertising's entreaties.

FIFTEEN APPEALS

1. *Need for sex.* Let's start with sex, because this is the appeal which   17 seems to pop up first whenever the topic of advertising is raised. Whole books have been written about this one alone, to find a large audience of mildly titillated readers. Lately, due to campaigns to sell blue jeans, concern with sex in ads has redoubled.

The fascinating thing is not how much sex there is in advertising, but   18 how little. Contrary to impressions, unambiguous sex is rare in these

messages. Some of this surprising observation may be a matter of definition: the Jordache ads with the lithe, blouse-less female astride a similarly
clad male is clearly an appeal to the audience's sexual drives, but the same
cannot be said about Brooke Shields in the Calvin Klein commercials.
Directed at young women and their credit-card carrying mothers, the image
of Miss Shields instead invokes the need to be looked at. Buy Calvins and
you'll be the center of much attention, just as Brooke is, the ads imply;
they do not primarily inveigle their target audience's need for sexual intercourse.

In the content analysis reported in *Mass Advertising as Social Fore-*   19
cast, only two percent of ads were found to pander to this motive. Even
Playboy ads shy away from sexual appeals: a recent issue contained eighty-
three full-page ads, and just four of them (or less than five percent) could
be said to have sex on their minds.

The reason this appeal is so little used is that it is too blaring and tends   20
to obliterate the product information. Nudity in advertising has the effect of
reducing brand recall. The people who do remember the product may do so
because they have been made indignant by the ad; this is not the response
most advertisers seek.

To the extent that sexual imagery is used, it conventionally works   21
better on men than women; typically a female figure is offered up to the
male reader. A Black Velvet liquor advertisement displays an attractive
woman wearing a tight black outfit, recumbent under the legend, "Feel the
Velvet." The figure does not have to be horizontal, however, for the
appeal to be present, as National Airlines revealed in its "Fly me" campaign. Indeed, there does not even have to be a female in the ad: "Flick my
Bic" was sufficient to convey the idea to many.

As a rule, though, advertisers have found sex to be a tricky appeal, to   22
be used sparingly. Less controversial and equally fetching are the appeals
to our need for affectionate human contact.

2. *Need for affiliation.* American mythology upholds autonomous in-   23
dividuals, and social statistics suggest that people are ever more going it
alone in their lives, yet the high frequency of affiliative appeals in ads
belies this. Or maybe it does not: maybe all the images of companionship
are compensation for what Americans privately lack. In any case, the need
to associate with others is widely invoked in advertising and is probably the
most prevalent appeal. All sorts of goods and services are sold by linking
them to our unfulfilled desires to be in good company.

According to Henry Murray, the need for affiliation consists of desires   24
"to draw near and enjoyably cooperate or reciprocate with another; to
please and win affection of another; to adhere and remain loyal to a friend."
The manifestations of this motive can be segmented into several different
types of affiliation, beginning with romance.

Courtship may be swifter nowadays, but the desire for pair-bonding is   25
far from satiated. Ads reaching for this need commonly depict a youngish
male and female engrossed in each other. The head of the male is usually
higher than the female's, even at this late date; she may be sitting or
leaning while he is standing. They are not touching in the Smirnoff vodka
ads, but obviously there is an intimacy, sometimes frolicsome, between
them. The couple does touch for Martell Cognac when "The moment was
Martell." For Wind Song perfume they have touched, and "Your Wind
Song stays on his mind."

Depending on the audience, the pair does not absolutely have to be   26
young—just together. He gives her a DeBeers diamond, and there is a tear
in her laugh lines. She takes Geritol and preserves herself for him. And
numbers of consumers, wanting affection too, follow suit.

Warm family feelings are fanned in ads when another generation is   27
added to the pair. Hallmark Cards brings grandparents into the picture, and
Johnson and Johnson Baby Powder has Dad, Mom, and baby, all fresh
from the bath, encircled in arms and emblazoned with "Share the Feeling." A talc has been fused to familial love.

Friendship is yet another form of affiliation pursued by advertisers.   28
Two women confide and drink Maxwell House coffee together; two men
walk through the woods smoking Salem cigarettes. Miller Beer promises
that afternoon "Miller Time" will be staffed with three or four good
buddies. Drink Dr. Pepper, as Mickey Rooney is coaxed to do, and join in
with all the other Peppers. Coca-Cola does not even need to portray the
friendliness; it has reduced this appeal to "a Coke and a smile."

The warmth can be toned down and disguised, but it is the same   29
affiliative need that is being fished for. The blonde has a direct gaze and her
friends are firm businessmen in appearance, but with a glass of Old Bush-
mill you can sit down and fit right in. Or, for something more upbeat, sing
along with the Pontiac choirboys.

As well as presenting positive images, advertisers can play to the need   30
for affiliation in negative ways, by invoking the fear of rejection. If we
don't use Scope, we'll have the "Ugh! Morning Breath" that causes the
male and female models to avert their faces. Unless we apply Ultra-Brite
or Close-Up to our teeth, it's good-bye romance. Our family will be cursed
with "House-a-tosis" if we don't take care. Without Dr. Scholl's anti-
perspirant foot spray, the bowling team will keel over. There go all the
guests when the supply of Dorito's nacho cheese chips is exhausted. Still
more rejection if our shirts have ring-around-the-collar, if our car needs to
be Midasized. But make a few purchases, and we are back in the bosom of
human contact.

As self-directed as Americans pretend to be, in the last analysis we   31
remain social animals, hungering for the positive, endorsing feelings that

only those around us can supply. Advertisers respond, urging us to "Reach out and touch someone," in the hopes our monthly bills will rise.

3. *Need to nurture.* Akin to affiliative needs is the need to take care of 32 small, defenseless creatures—children and pets, largely. Reciprocity is of less consequence here, though; it is the giving that counts. Murray uses synonyms like "to feed, help, support, console, protect, comfort, nurse, heal." A strong need it is, woven deep into our genetic fabric, for if it did not exist we could not successfully raise up our replacements. When advertisers put forth the image of something diminutive and furry, something that elicits the word "cute" or "precious," then they are trying to trigger this motive. We listen to the childish voice singing the Oscar Mayer weiner song, and our next hot-dog purchase is prescribed. Aren't those darling kittens something, and how did this Meow Mix get into our shopping cart?

This pitch is often directed at women, as Mother Nature's chief nur- 33 turers. "Make me some Kraft macaroni and cheese, please," says the elfin preschooler just in from the snowstorm, and mothers' hearts go out, and Kraft's sales go up. "We're cold, wet, and hungry," whine the husband and kids, and the little woman gets the Manwiches ready. A facsimile of this need can be hit without children or pets: the husband is ill and sleepless in the television commercial, and the wife grudgingly fetches the NyQuil.

But it is not women alone who can be touched by this appeal. The 34 father nurses his son Eddie through adolescence while the John Deere lawn tractor survives the years. Another father counts pennies with his young son as the subject of New York Life Insurance comes up. And all over America are businessmen who don't know why they dial Qantas Airlines when they have to take a trans-Pacific trip; the koala bear knows.

4. *Need for guidance.* The opposite of the need to nurture is the need 35 to be nurtured: to be protected, shielded, guided. We may be loath to admit it, but the child lingers on inside every adult—and a good thing it does, or we would not be instructable in our advancing years. Who wants a nation of nothing but flinty personalities?

Parent-like figures can successfully call up this need. Robert Young 36 recommends Sanka coffee, and since we have experienced him for twenty-five years as television father and doctor, we take his word for it. Florence Henderson as the expert mom knows a lot about the advantages of Wesson oil.

The parent-ness of the spokesperson need not be so salient; sometimes 37 pure authoritativeness is better. When Orson Welles scowls and intones, "Paul Masson will sell no wine before its time," we may not know exactly what he means, but we still take direction from him. There is little maternal about Brenda Vaccaro when she speaks up for Tampax, but there is a certainty to her that many accept.

A celebrity is not a necessity in making a pitch to the need for guid- 38 ance, since a fantasy figure can serve just as well. People accede to the Green Giant, or Betty Crocker, or Mr. Goodwrench. Some advertisers can get by with no figure at all: "When E.F. Hutton talks, people listen."

Often it is tradition or custom that advertisers point to and consumers take guidance from. Bits and pieces of American history are used to sell whiskeys like Old Crow, Southern Comfort, Jack Daniels. We conform to traditional male/female roles and age-old social norms when we purchase Barclay cigarettes, which informs us "The pleasure is back."   39

The product itself, if it has been around for a long time, can constitute a tradition. All those old labels in the ad for Morton salt convince us that we should continue to buy it. Kool-Aid says, "You loved it as a kid. You trust it as a mother," hoping to get yet more consumers to go along.   40

Even when the product has no history at all, our need to conform to tradition and to be guided are strong enough that they can be invoked through bogus nostalgia and older actors. Country-Time lemonade sells because consumers want to believe it has a past they can defer to.   41

So far the needs and the ways they can be invoked which have been looked at are largely warm and affiliative; they stand in contrast to the next set of needs, which are much more egoistic and assertive.   42

5. *Need to aggress.* The pressures of the real world create strong retaliatory feelings in every functioning human being. Since these impulses can come forth as bursts of anger and violence, their display is normally tabooed. Existing as harbored energy, aggressive drives present a large, tempting target for advertisers. It is not a target to be aimed at thoughtlessly, though, for few manufacturers want their products associated with destructive motives. There is always the danger that, as in the case of sex, if the appeal is too blatant, public opinion will turn against what is being sold.   43

Jack-in-the-Box sought to abruptly alter its marketing by going after older customers and forgetting the younger ones. Their television commercials had a seventy-ish lady command, "Waste him," and the Jack-in-the-Box clown exploded before our eyes. So did public reaction, until the commercials were toned down. Print ads for Club cocktails carried the faces of octogenarians under the headline, "Hit me with a Club"; response was contrary enough to bring the campaign to a stop.   44

Better disguised aggressive appeals are less likely to backfire: Triumph cigarettes has models making a lewd gesture with their uplifted cigarettes, but the individuals are often laughing and usually in the close company of others. When Exxon said, "There's a Tiger in your tank," the implausibility of it concealed the invocation of aggressive feelings.   45

Depicted arguments are a common way for advertisers to tap the audience's needs to aggress. Don Rickles and Lynda Carter trade gibes, and   46 consumers take sides as the name of Seven-Up is stitched on minds. The Parkay tub has a difference of opinion with the user; who can forget it, or who (or what) got the last word in?

6. *Need to achieve.* This is the drive that energizes people, causing them to strive in their lives and careers. According to Murray, the need for achievement is signalled by the desires "to accomplish something difficult. To overcome obstacles and attain a high standard. To excel one's self. To rival and surpass others." A prominent American trait, it is one that advertisers like to hook on to because it identifies their product with winning and success.

The Cutty Sark ad does not disclose that Ted Turner failed at his latest attempt at yachting's America Cup; here he is represented as a champion on the water as well as off in his television enterprises. If we drink this whiskey, we will be victorious alongside Turner. We can also succeed with O.J. Simpson by renting Hertz cars, or with Reggie Jackson by bringing home some Panasonic equipment. Cathy Rigby and Stayfree Maxipads will put people out front.

Sports heroes are the most convenient means to snare consumers' needs to achieve, but they are not the only one. Role models can be established, ones which invite emulation, as with the profiles put forth by Dewar's scotch. Successful, tweedy individuals relate they have "graduated to the flavor of Myer's rum." Or the advertiser can establish a prize: two neighbors play one-on-one basketball for a Michelob beer in a television commercial, while in a print ad a bottle of Johnnie Walker Black Label has been gilded like a trophy.

Any product that advertises itself in superlatives—the best, the first, the finest—is trying to make contact with our needs to succeed. For many consumers, sales and bargains belong in this category of appeals, too; the person who manages to buy something at fifty percent off is seizing an opportunity and coming out ahead of others.

7. *Need to dominate.* This fundamental need is the craving to be powerful—perhaps omnipotent, as in the Xerox ad where Brother Dominic exhibits heavenly powers and creates miraculous copies. Most of us will settle for being just a regular potentate, though. We drink Budweiser because it is the King of Beers, and here come the powerful Clydesdales to prove it. A taste of Wolfschmidt vodka and "The spirit of the Czar lives on."

The need to dominate and control one's environment is often thought of as being masculine, but as close students of human nature advertisers know, it is not so circumscribed. Women's aspirations for control are suggested in the campaign theme, "I like my men in English Leather, or nothing at all." The females in the Chanel No. 19 ads are "outspoken" and wrestle their men around.

Male and female, what we long for is clout; what we get in its place is   53
Mastercard.

8. *Need for prominence.* Here comes the need to be admired and   54
respected, to enjoy prestige and high social status. These times, it appears,
are not so egalitarian after all. Many ads picture the trappings of high
position; the Oldsmobile stands before a manorial doorway, the Volvo is
parked beside a steeplechase. A book-lined study is the setting for Dewar's
12, and Lenox China is displayed in a dining room chock full of antiques.

Beefeater gin represents itself as "The Crown Jewel of England" and   55
uses no illustrations of jewels or things British, for the words are sufficient
indicators of distinction. Buy that gin and you will rise up the prestige
hierarchy, or achieve the same effect on yourself with Seagram's 7 Crown,
which unambiguously describes itself as "classy."

Being respected does not have to entail the usual accoutrements of   56
wealth: "Do you know who I am?" the commercials ask, and we learn that
the prominent person is not so prominent without his American Express
card.

9. *Need for attention.* The previous need involved being *looked up to*,   57
while this is the need to be *looked at*. The desire to exhibit ourselves in
such a way as to make others look at us is a primitive, insuppressible
instinct. The clothing and cosmetic industries exist just to serve this need,
and this is the way they pitch their wares. Some of this effort is aimed at
males, as the ads for Hathaway shirts and Jockey underclothes. But the
greater bulk of such appeals is targeted singlemindedly at women.

To come back to Brooke Shields: this is where she fits into American   58
marketing. If I buy Calvin Klein jeans, consumers infer, I'll be the object
of fascination. The desire for exhibition has been most strikingly played to
in a print campaign of many years duration, that of Maidenform lingerie.
The woman exposes herself, and sales surge. "Gentlemen prefer Hanes"
the ads dissemble, and women who want eyes upon them know what they
should do. Peggy Fleming flutters her legs for L'eggs, encouraging females who want to be the star in their own lives to purchase this product.

The same appeal works for cosmetics and lotions. For years, the little   59
girl with the exposed backside sold gobs of Coppertone, but now the
company has picked up the pace a little: as a female, you are supposed to
"Flash 'em a Coppertone tan." Food can be sold the same way, especially
to the diet-conscious; Angie Dickinson poses for California avocadoes and
says, "Would this body lie to you?" Our eyes are too fixed on her for us
to think to ask if she got that way by eating mounds of guacomole.

10. *Need for autonomy.* There are several ways to sell credit card   60
services, as has been noted: Mastercard appeals to the need to dominate,
and American Express to the need for prominence. When Visa claims,
"You can have it the way you want it," yet another primary motive is

being beckoned forward—the need to endorse the self. The focus here is upon the independence and integrity of the individual; this need is the antithesis of the need for guidance and is unlike any of the social needs. "If running with the herd isn't your style, try ours," says Rotan-Mosle, and many Americans feel they have finally found the right brokerage firm.

The photo is of a red-coated Mountie on his horse, posed on a snow-   61
covered ledge; the copy reads, "Windsor—One Canadian stands alone." This epitome of the solitary and proud individual may work best with male customers, as may Winston's man in the red cap. But one-figure advertisements also strike the strong need for autonomy among American women. As Shelly Hack strides for Charlie perfume, females respond to her obvious pride and flair; she is her own person. The Virginia Slims' tale is of people who have come a long way from subservience to independence. Cachet perfume feels it does not need a solo figure to work this appeal, and uses three different faces in its ads; it insists, though, "It's different on every woman who wears it."

Like many psychological needs, this one can also be appealed to in a   62
negative fashion, by invoking the loss of independence or self-regard. Guilt and regrets can be stimulated: "Gee, I could have had a V-8." Next time, get one and be good to yourself.

11. *Need to escape.* An appeal to the need for autonomy often co-   63
occurs with one for the need to escape, since the desire to duck out of our social obligations, to seek rest or adventure, frequently takes the form of one-person flight. The dashing image of a pilot, in fact, is a standard way of quickening this need to get away from it all.

Freedom is the pitch here, the freedom that every individual yearns for   64
whenever life becomes too oppressive. Many advertisers like appealing to the need for escape because the sensation of pleasure often accompanies escape, and what nicer emotional nimbus could there be for a product? "You deserve a break today," says McDonalds, and Stouffer's frozen foods chime in, "Set yourself free."

For decades men have imaginatively bonded themselves to the Marl-   65
boro cowboy who dwells untarnished and unencumbered in Marlboro Country some distance from modern life; smokers' aching needs for autonomy and escape are personified by that cowpoke. Many women can identify with the lady ambling through the woods behind the words, "Benson and Hedges and mornings and me."

But escape does not have to be solitary. Other Benson and Hedges ads,   66
part of the same campaign, contain two strolling figures. In Salem cigarette advertisements, it can be several people who escape together into the mountaintops. A commercial for Levi's pictured a cloudbank above a city through which ran a whole chain of young people.

There are varieties of escape, some wistful like the Boeing "Some-   67 day'' campaign of dream vacations, some kinetic like the play and parties in soft drink ads. But in every instance, the consumer exposed to the advertisement is invited to momentarily depart his everyday life for a more carefree experience, preferably with the product in hand.

12. *Need to feel safe.* Nobody in their right mind wants to be intimi- 68
dated, menaced, battered, poisoned. We naturally want to do whatever it takes to stave off threats to our well-being, and to our families'. It is the instinct of self-preservation that makes us responsive to the ad of the St. Bernard with the keg of Chivas Regal. We pay attention to the stern talk of Karl Malden and the plight of the vacationing couples who have lost all their funds in the American Express travelers cheques commercials. We want the omnipresent stag from Hartford Insurance to watch over us too.

In the interest of keeping failure and calamity from our lives, we like 69
to see the durability of products demonstrated. Can we ever forget that Timex takes a licking and keeps on ticking? When the American Tourister suitcase bounces all over the highway and the egg inside doesn't break, the need to feel safe has been adroitly plucked.

We take precautions to diminish future threats. We buy Volkswagen 70
Rabbits for the extraordinary mileage, and MONY insurance policies to avoid the tragedies depicted in their black-and-white ads of widows and orphans.

We are careful about our health. We consume Mazola margarine be- 71
cause it has ''corn goodness'' backed by the natural food traditions of the American Indians. In the medicine cabinet is Alka-Seltzer, the ''home remedy''; having it, we are snug in our little cottage.

We want to be safe and secure; buy these products, advertisers are 72
saying, and you'll be safer than you are without them.

13. *Need for aesthetic sensations.* There is an undeniable aesthetic 73
component to virtually every ad run in the national media: the photography or filming or drawing is near-perfect, the type style is well chosen, the layout could scarcely be improved upon. Advertisers know there is little chance of good communication occurring if an ad is not visually pleasing. Consumers may not be aware of the extent of their own sensitivity to artwork, but it is undeniably large.

Sometimes the aesthetic element is expanded and made into an ad's 74
primary appeal. Charles Jordan shoes may or may not appear in the ac-companying avant-garde photographs; Kohler plumbing fixtures catch attention through the high style of their desert settings. Beneath the slightly out of focus photograph, languid and sensuous in tone, General Electric feels called upon to explain, ''This is an ad for the hair dryer.''

This appeal is not limited to female consumers: J and B scotch says ''It 75
whispers'' and shows a bucolic scene of lake and castle.

14. *Need to satisfy curiosity.* It may seem odd to list a need for infor- 76

mation among basic motives, but this need can be as primal and compelling as any of the others. Human beings are curious by nature, interested in the world around them, and intrigued by tidbits of knowledge and new developments. Trivia, percentages, observations counter to conventional wisdom—these items all help sell products. Any advertisement in a question-and-answer format is strumming this need.

A dog groomer has a question about long distance rates, and Bell   77
Telephone has a chart with all the figures. An ad for Porsche 911 is replete with diagrams and schematics, numbers and arrows. Lo and behold, Anacin pills have 150 more milligrams than its competitors; should we wonder if this is better or worse for us?

15. *Physiological needs.* To the extent that sex is solely a biological   78
need, we are now coming around full circle, back toward the start of the list. In this final category are clustered appeals to sleeping, eating, drinking. The art of photographing food and drink is so advanced, sometimes these temptations are wondrously caught in the camera's lens: the crab meat in the Red Lobster restaurant ads can start us salivating, the Quarterpounder can almost be smelled, the liquor in the glass glows invitingly. Imbibe, these ads scream.

STYLES

Some common ingredients of advertisements were not singled out for   79
separate mention in the list of fifteen because they are not appeals in and of themselves. They are stylistic features, influencing the way a basic appeal is presented. The use of humor is one, and the use of celebrities is another. A third is time imagery, past and future, which goes to several purposes.

For all of its employment in advertising, humor can be treacherous,   80
because it can get out of hand and smother the product information. Supposedly, this is what Alka-Seltzer discovered with its comic commercials of the late sixties; "I can't believe I ate the whole thing," the sad-faced husband lamented, and the audience cackled so much it forgot the antacid. Or, did not take it seriously.

But used carefully, humor can punctuate some of the softer appeals and   81
soften some of the harsher ones. When Emma says to the Fruit-of-the-Loom fruits, "Hi, cuties. Whatcha doing in my laundry basket?" we smile as our curiosity is assuaged along with hers. Bill Cosby gets consumers tickled about the children in his Jell-O commercials, and strokes the need to nurture.

An insurance company wants to invoke the need to feel safe, but does   82
not want to leave readers with an unpleasant aftertaste; cartoonist Rowland

Wilson creates an avalanche about to crush a gentleman who is saying to
another, "My insurance company? New England Life, of course. Why?"
The same tactic of humor undercutting threat is used in the cartoon commercials for Safeco when the Pink Panther wanders from one disaster to
another. Often humor masks aggression: comedian Bob Hope in the outfit
of a boxer promises to knock out the knock-knocks with Texaco; Rodney
Dangerfield, who "can't get no respect," invites aggression as the comic
relief in Miller Lite commercials.

Roughly fifteen percent of all advertisements incorporate a celebrity,   83
almost always from the fields of entertainment or sports. This approach can
also prove troublesome for advertisers, for celebrities are human beings too,
and fully capable of the most remarkable behavior; if anything distasteful
about them emerges, it is likely to reflect on the product. The advertisers
making use of Anita Bryant and Billy Jean King suffered several anxious
moments. An untimely death can also reflect poorly on a product. But advertisers are willing to take risks because celebrities can be such a good link
between producers and consumers, perfoming the social role of introducer.

There are several psychological needs these middlemen can play upon.   84
Let's take the product class of cameras and see how different celebrities
can hit different needs. The need for guidance can be invoked by Michael
Landon, who plays such a wonderful dad on "Little House on the Prairie";
when he says to buy Kodak equipment, many people listen. James Garner
for Polaroid cameras is put in a similar authoritative role, so defined by a
mocking spouse. The need to achieve is summoned up by Tracy Austin and
other tennis stars for Canon AE-1; the advertiser first makes sure we see
these athletes playing to win. When Cheryl Tiegs speaks up for Olympus
cameras, it is the need for attention that is being targeted.

The past and future, being outside our grasp, are exploited by adver-   85
tisers as locales for the projection of needs. History can offer up heroes
(and call up the need to achieve) or traditions (need for guidance) as well
as art objects (need for aesthetic sensations). Nostalgia is a kindly version
of personal history and is deployed by advertisers to rouse needs for affiliation and for guidance; the need to escape can come in here, too. The
same need to escape is sometimes the point of futuristic appeals, but
picturing the avant-garde can also be a way to get at the need to achieve.

ANALYZING ADVERTISEMENTS

When analyzing ads yourself for their emotional appeals, it takes a bit of   86
practice to learn to ignore the product information (as well as one's own
experience and feelings about the product). But that skill comes soon
enough, as does the ability to quickly sort out from all the non-product

aspects of an ad the chief element which is the most striking, the most likely to snag attention first and penetrate brains farthest. The key to the appeal, this element usually presents itself centrally and forwardly to the reader or viewer.

Another clue: the viewing angle which the audience has on the ad's 87
subjects is informative. If the subjects are photographed or filmed from below and thus are looking down at you much as the Green Giant does, then the need to be guided is a good candidate for the ad's emotional appeal. If, on the other hand, the subjects are shot from above and appear deferential, as is often the case with children or female models, then other needs are being appealed to.

To figure out an ad's emotional appeal, it is wise to know (or have a 88
good hunch about) who the targeted consumers are; this can often be inferred from the magazine or television show it appears in. This piece of information is a great help in determining the appeal and in deciding between two different interpretations. For example, if an ad features a partially undressed female, this would typically signal one appeal for readers of *Penthouse* (need for sex) and another for readers of *Cosmopolitan* (need for attention).

It would be convenient if every ad made just one appeal, were aimed 89
at just one need. Unfortunately, things are often not that simple. A cigarette ad with a couple at the edge of a polo field is trying to hit both the need for affiliation and the need for prominence; depending on the attitude of the male, dominance could also be an ingredient in this. An ad for Chimere perfume incorporates two photos: in the top one the lady is being commanding at a business luncheon (need to dominate), but in the lower one she is being bussed (need for affiliation). Better ads, however, seem to avoid being too diffused; in the study of post-World War II advertising described earlier, appeals grew more focused as the decades passed. As a rule of thumb, about sixty percent have two conspicuous appeals; the last twenty percent have three or more. Rather than looking for the greatest number of appeals, decoding ads is most productive when the loudest one or two appeals are discerned, since those are the appeals with the best chance of grabbing people's attention.

Finally, analyzing ads does not have to be a solo activity and probably 90
should not be. The greater number of people there are involved, the better chance there is of transcending individual biases and discovering the essential emotional lure built into an advertisement.

DO THEY OR DON'T THEY?

Do the emotional appeals made in advertisements add up to the sinister 91
manipulation of consumers?

It is clear that these ads work. Attention is caught, communication   92
occurs between producers and consumers, and sales result. It turns out to
be difficult to detail the exact relationship between a specific ad and a
specific purchase, or even between a campaign and subsequent sales figures, because advertising is only one of a host of influences upon con-
sumption. Yet no one is fooled by this lack of perfect proof; everyone
knows that advertising sells. If this were not the case, then tight-fisted
American businesses would not spend a total of fifty billion dollars annually on these messages.

But before anyone despairs that advertisers have our number to the   93
extent that they can marshall us at will and march us like automatons to the
check-out counters, we should recall the resiliency and obduracy of the
American consumer. Advertisers may have uncovered the softest spots in
minds, but that does not mean they have found truly gaping apertures.
There is no evidence that advertising can get people to do things contrary
to their self-interests. Despite all the finesse of advertisements, and all the
subtle emotional tugs, the public resists the vast majority of the petitions.
According to the marketing division of the A.C. Nielsen Company, a
whopping seventy-five percent of all new products die within a year in the
marketplace, the victims of consumer disinterest which no amount of advertising could overcome. The appeals in advertising may be the most
captivating there are to be had, but they are not enough to entrap the wiley
consumer.

The key to understanding the discrepancy between, on the one hand,   94
the fact that advertising truly works, and, on the other, the fact that it
hardly works, is to take into account the enormous numbers of people
exposed to an ad. Modern-day communications permit an ad to be displayed to millions upon millions of individuals; if the smallest fraction of
that audience can be moved to buy the product, then the ad has been
successful. When one percent of the people exposed to a television advertising campaign reach for their wallets, that could be one million sales,
which may be enough to keep the product in production and the advertisements coming.

In arriving at an evenhanded judgment about advertisements and their   95
emotional appeals, it is good to keep in mind that many of the purchases
which might be credited to these ads are experienced as genuinely gratifying to the consumer. We sincerely like the goods or service we have
bought, and we may even like some of the emotional drapery that an ad
suggests comes with it. It has sometimes been noted that the most avid
students of advertisements are the people who have just bought the product; they want to steep themselves in the associated imagery. This may be
the reason that Americans, when polled, are not negative about advertising
and do not disclose any sense of being misused. The volume of advertising

may be an irritant, but the product information as well as the imaginative material in ads are partial compensation.

A productive understanding is that advertising messages involve costs and benefits at both ends of the communications channel. For those few ads which do make contact, the consumer surrenders a moment of time, has the lower brain curried, and receives notice of a product; the advertiser has given up money and has increased the chance of sales. In this sort of communications activity, neither party can be said to be the loser.

₉₆

QUESTIONS ON CONTENT

1. In his essay, Fowles states that "As time has gone by, buyers have become stoutly resistant to advertisements. We live in a blizzard of these messages and have learned to turn up our collars and ward off most of them." Do you agree with this statement? Give examples from your own experiences to support your answer.

2. Unlike the other authors in this section, Fowles suggests that "emotional appeal is contained in the artwork" of an ad. Choose a familiar ad from among those Fowles mentions in his essay. What emotion(s) is the artwork appealing to in your opinion? What makes you think so?

3. Fowles says that the endorsement of Wesson Oil by Florence Henderson satisfies our need for guidance. He also states that consumers buy Country-Time lemonade because they want to believe the drink "has a past they can defer to." How do you feel about Fowles's assessment of these ads? Does it offend you? Why or why not?

4. "Response was contrary enough to bring the [Club Cocktails'] campaign to a stop," writes Fowles, with respect to their "Hit me with a Club" commercials featuring elderly people. What type of opposition do you think it would take to halt an ad campaign?

QUESTIONS ON RHETORIC

1. What is the thesis advanced by Fowles in his essay? Is it implied or directly stated?

2. Fowles is making a very different statement from that of the other writers in this section. He claims that in addition to their use of unsubstantiated facts and their misleading claims, advertisers also appeal to the emotions of the viewer. What kinds of evidence does Fowles offer to support his argument? Is he convincing? Explain your answer.

3. Is the tone of Fowles's essay angry, supportive, or objective in your opinion? Use examples of Fowles's diction and attitude to support your answer. Compare the tone of this essay with that of Rosenbaum. In what way is the tone of the two essays similar? (Glossary: *Diction, Tone*)

VOCABULARY

hawked (3)	titillated (17)	aesthetic (73)
abhorrent (3)	inveigle (18)	avant-garde (85)
circumvent (5)	facsimile (33)	avid (95)
importuned (7)	gibes (46)	curried (96)
profane (13)	nimbus (64)	

WRITING TOPICS

1. Fowles suggests that an advertiser can be successful by using psychology in writing ads. One topic Fowles does not discuss however, is *subliminal advertising*, the technique that attempts to convince the public to buy by "hiding" a message in an ad. For example, in a hypothetical ad for Krunchy Kookie Cereal one frame, moving too fast for the viewer to notice it consciously, will flash the message "Buy Krunchy Kookie Cereal." The viewer won't remember seeing the message, but the mind will get it. In an essay, discuss your position on the use of subliminal advertising. You may want to research this topic in some detail.

2. Evaluate the following syllogism:

Advertising leads to adequate consumer information.
Adequate consumer information leads to an informed buying decision.
An informed buying decision leads to a personal buying preference.
Therefore, advertising leads to a personal buying preference.

Does this kind of logic negate Fowles's ideas?

INTENSIFY/DOWNPLAY

Hugh Rank

Hugh Rank, professor of literature at Governors State University in Park Forest, Illinois, is a member of the Committee on Public Doublespeak (National Council of Teachers of English). His schema "Intensify/Downplay" was developed to help people deal with public persuasion. As Rank explains, "INTENSIFY/DOWNPLAY is a pattern useful to analyze communication, persuasion, and propaganda. All people intensify *(commonly by* repetition, association, composition) *and downplay (commonly by* omission, diversion, confusion) *as they communicate in words, gestures, numbers, etc. But, 'professional persuaders' have more training, technology, money, and media access than the average citizen. Individuals can better cope with organized persuasion by recognizing the common ways* how communication is intensified or downplayed, and by considering *who is saying what to whom, with what intent and what result."*

The Committee on Public Doublespeak gave Rank's schema the George Orwell Award for 1976. The following is a schematic set of questions that Rank developed, based on his "Intensify/Downplay" schema, to help you analyze advertisements on radio and television and in newspapers and magazines.

QUESTIONS you can ask about any ad

INTENSIFY

Repetition

How often have you seen the ad? On TV? In print? Do you recognize the **brand name? trademark? logo? company? package?** What key words or images repeated within ad? Any repetition patterns *(alliteration, anaphora, rhyme)* used? Any **slogan?** Can you hum or sing the **musical theme** or **jingle?** How long has this ad been running? How old were you when you first heard it? (For information on frequency, duration, and costs of ad campaigns, see *Advertising Age.)*

1

Association

What **"good things"** - already loved or desired by the intended audience - are associated with the product? Any links with basic needs *(food, activity, sex, security)?* With an appeal to save or gain money? With desire for certitude or outside approval (from *religion, science,* or the *"best," "most,"* or *"average" people)?* With desire for a sense of space *(neighborhood, nation, nature)?* With desire for love and belonging *(intimacy, family, groups)?* With other human desires *(esteem, play, generosity, curiosity, creativity, completion)?* Are **"bad things"** - things already hated or feared - stressed, as in a **"scare-and-sell"** ad? Are *problems* presented, with products as *solutions?* Are the speakers (models, endorsers) **authority figures:** people you respect, admire? Or **friend figures:** people you'd like as friends, identify with, or would like to be?

2

Composition

Look for the basic strategy of "the pitch": Hi . . . TRUST ME . . . YOU NEED . . . HURRY . . . BUY. What are the **attention-getting (HI)** words, images, devices? What are the **confidence-building (TRUST ME)** techniques: words, images, smiles, endorsers, brand names? Is the main **desire-stimulation (YOU NEED)** appeal focused on our benefit-seeking *to get* or *to keep* a *"good,"* or *to avoid* or *to get rid of* a *"bad"?* Are you the **"target audience"?** If not, who is? Are you part of an unintended audience ? When and where did the ads appear? Are **product claims** made for: *superiority, quantity, beauty, efficiency, scarcity, novelty, stability, reliability, simplicity, utility, rapidity,* or *safety?* Are any **"added values"** suggested or implied by using any of the association techniques (see above)? Is there any **urgency-stressing (HURRY)** by words, movement, pace? Or is a "soft sell" conditioning for *later* purchase? Are there specific **response-triggering** words **(BUY):** to buy, to do, to call? Or is it conditioning (image building or public relations) to make us *"feel good"* about the company, to get favorable public opinion on *its* side *(against government regulations. laws, taxes)?* **Persuaders seek some kind of response!**

3

based on Hugh Rank's INTENSIFY/DOWNPLAY schema:

Omission

What "bad" aspects, disadvantages, drawbacks, hazards, have been **omitted** from the ad? Are there some unspoked assumptions? An unsaid story? Are some things implied or suggested, but not explicitly stated? Are there concealed problems concerning the **maker,** the **materials,** the **design,** the **use,** or the **purpose of the product? Are there any unwanted or harmful side effects:** *unsafe, unhealthy, uneconomical, inefficient, unneeded?* Does any **"disclosure law"** exist (or is needed) requiring public warning about a concealed hazard? In the ad, what gets less time, less attention, smaller print? *(Most ads are true, but incomplete.)*

4

Diversion

What benefits (low cost, high speed, etc.) get high priority in the ad's claim and promises? Are these **your** priorities? Significant, important to you? Is there any **"bait-and-switch"**? *(Ad stresses low cost, but the actual seller switches buyer's priority to high quality.)* Does ad divert focus from **key issues,** important things *(e.g., nutrition, health, safety)*? Does ad focus on **side-issues,** unmeaningful trivia *(common in parity products)*? Does ad divert attention from your other choices, other options: buy something else, use less, use less often, rent, borrow, share, do without? *(Ads need not show other choices, but you should know them.)*

5

Confusion

Are the words clear or ambiguous? Specific or vague? Are claims and promises absolute, or are there qualifying words *("may help," "some")*? Is the claim measurable? Or is it **"puffery"**? *(Laws permit most "sellers's talk" of such general praise and subjective opinions.)* Are the words common, understandable, familiar? Uncommon? Jargon? Any parts difficult to "translate" or explain to others? Are analogies clear? Are comparisons within the same kind? Are examples related? Typical? Adequate? Enough examples? Any contradictions? Inconsistencies? Errors? Are there frequent changes, variations, revisions *(in size, price, options, extras, contents, packaging)*? Is it too complex: too much, too many? Disorganized? Incoherent? Unsorted? Any confusing statistics? Numbers? Do you know exact costs? Benefits? Risks? Are **your own goals,** priorities, and desires clear or vague? Fixed or shifting? Simple or complex? *(Confusion can also exist within us as well as within an ad. If any confusion exists: slow down, take care.)*

6

DOWNPLAY

QUESTIONS ON CONTENT

1. What does Rank mean by "professional persuaders"?

2. What are the three ways persuaders intensify? Explain with examples how each way works.

3. What are the three ways persuaders downplay? Explain with examples how each way works.

4. Is it possible for someone to intensify and downplay at the same time? Explain.

QUESTIONS ON RHETORIC

1. Why did Rank develop his "Intensify/Downplay" schema?

2. How has he used classification to achieve his purpose? (Glossary: *Division and Classification, Purpose*)

3. No other writer in this section has discussed the value of the size, position, and contrast of words in ad copy as a means of convincing the reader. What does Rank's analysis of these attention-getting devices add to your understanding of the language of advertising? Explain your answer.

VOCABULARY

logo (1)   assumptions (4)   certitude (2)
slogan (1)   explicitly (4)   analogies (6)

WRITING TOPICS

1. Study the ads that appear on pp. 239–241 (or other ads, if your instructor wishes). Find examples of intensifying and of downplaying in each. In a brief essay, describe your findings.

2. Real estate advertisements are often deliberately designed to manipulate potential buyers. For example, one language analyst noted that in his home town "adorable" meant "small," "eat-in kitchen" meant "no dining room," "handyman's special" meant "portion of building still standing," "by appointment only" meant "expensive," and "starter home" meant "cheap." Analyze the language used in the real estate advertisements in your local newspaper. Does the real estate that one company offers sound better to you than that offered by another company?

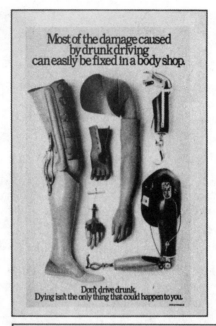

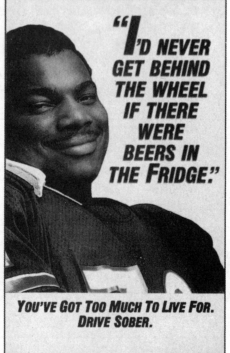

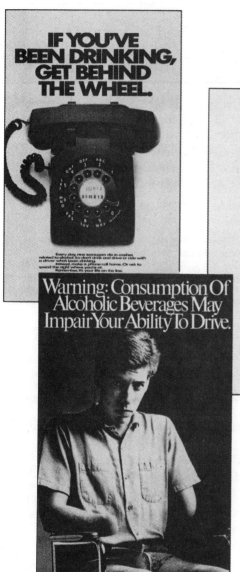

WRITING ASSIGNMENTS FOR "ADVERTISING AND LANGUAGE"

1. Think of a product that you have used but that has failed to live up to advertising claims. Write and send a letter to the company explaining why you feel its advertisements have been misleading.

2. Many advertisers seem to believe that by manipulating language they can make any product appeal to consumers. Here is how a very common item might be made to appear desirable by means of advertising:

New! Convenient!
Strike-Ups

The latest scientific advance for smokers since the cigarette lighter. Inexpensive and lightweight, you'll never want to be caught without Strike-Ups.

Why tolerate heavy, expensive cigarette lighters? Why run the risk of soiling your clothes with dangerous lighter fluid? Why be hassled by the technicalities of replacing flints? Why be embarrassed by a lighter that fails when it means everything to you?

Strike-Ups Has a Better Way

Lightweight, 100% reliable, Strike-Ups gives 20, that's right 20, or more lights. Each booklet has its own handy striking surface, right where you need it—up front. A striking surface so large you'll be able to get quick and easy lights even in the darkest places. Strike-Ups comes with a handsome decorator cover. An added feature, at no extra cost, is the plain white surface inside the cover, useful for phone numbers or doodling.

Once you use Strike-Ups, you'll agree, as many Americans have, that you simply can't do without them.

Ask for Strike-Ups at All Stores Where
Quality Smoking Accessories Are Sold.

Write an advertisement for any one of the items listed below; use as many of the advertising tricks or persuasive techniques as you can in order to sell your product.

paper clips
dental floss
toothpicks
rubber bands
salt shakers
staples
bottle caps

3. As more and more of our basic material needs are satisfied, the advertisers must create and push new ''needs'' so the buying process on which

our consumer culture is based can continue. Many of these new "needs" are created by exploitative appeals to values we all cherish or even hold sacred. For example, the Gino's fast-food chain used the word *freedom* to sell its food: "Freedom of Choice—French Fries or Onion Rings." The word *love* is another highly exploited device of advertisers.

Jerry Rubin once said, "How can I say 'I love you' when 'Cars love Shell'?" Here are some other examples:

> "Canada Dry tastes like love."
>
> "Hello. I'm Catherine Denueve. When somebody loves me, I'm always surprised. But I don't want to be told. I prefer gestures. Like—Chanel No. 5."
>
> Olympic Gold Medal winner Mark Spitz: "You know what's a great feeling? Giving someone you love a gift. The Schick Flexamatic is a great gift."
>
> A beautiful woman in a trench coat stands alone in the fog on a waterfront. She says, "I like men. Even when they're unkind to me. But men are men. They need love. They need understanding. And they need English Leather."
>
> A good-looking man says, "I know what girls need. They need love. And love's a little color." A girl appears and the man starts applying makeup to her face. The announcer says, "Love's a Little Color isn't makeup. It's only a little color."
>
> "Love is being a nurse. Learn all about professional nursing by writing to. . . ."

In each of these ads, a product is being sold by using the affective connotations of the word *love*—in other words, the word *love* (which ought to be sacred) is being exploited for profits.

Collect examples of other words like *health, success,* or *power* being used for commercial or promotional purposes. Write an essay in which you discuss the ways the word is being used as well as the possible effects on its meaning that this widespread usage may have.

4. Some people believe that advertising performs a useful service to consumers, and that most consumers know enough not to be taken in by half-truths and exaggerations. Do you agree? Why, or why not? If you agree, what benefits do we receive either directly or indirectly from advertising? Write an essay in which you clearly support your position on this issue.

5. Many product names are chosen because of their connotative or suggestive values. For example, the name *Tide* for the detergent suggests the power of the ocean tides and the rhythmic surge of cleansing waters, the name *Pride* for the wax suggests how the user will feel after using the product. Write an essay in which you discuss how the connotations of the brand names in one of the following categories enhance the appeal of the various products: cosmetics, deodorants, candy, paint, car batteries, motorcycles, fast-food sandwiches, and so on.

6. The advertising industry is governed by the Federal Trade Commission, specifically the Wheeler-Lea amendment to the FTC act. Check your encyclopedia for what this amendment says. Discuss the roles of the FTC and its implications on the ad industry.

7. *Adweek*, an advertising trade journal, annually accepts nominations for the year's worst ads. Contributors to the "BADvertising" feature select ads they dislike for one reason or another. Nominate five ads that "irritate" you and another five you consider to be ineffective. Then in an essay, explain how each ad is qualified for an award in its category.

8. John Kenneth Galbraith, a prominent economist, has stated that ads result in "a control of consumer reactions which, though imperfect and greatly complicated by the rivalry, is still far more secure than would be the ungoverned responses of consumers in the absence of such effort." What do you think Galbraith means by this statement? Do you agree? In an essay, compare and contrast Galbraith's point of view to that of the other authors in this section.

9. In order to be effective, advertising must define social values; it must tell the public what the public wants and needs. But in doing so is advertising, in your opinion, merely reflecting values already current in society or is it setting standards to which the public is expected to live up? In an essay, discuss your point of view based on your own observations and experiences.

PART V

Prejudice
and
Stereotypes

Jerry, this is Winthrop Dumble III, my accountant.

THE LANGUAGE
OF PREJUDICE

Gordon Allport

In this selection from The Nature of Prejudice, *Gordon
Allport examines the connection between language and
prejudice. Language plays a major role in the development
and continuation of prejudice because human thinking is
intimately linked to language. Allport identifies and explains
some of the specific ways in which language, often very
subtly and inadvertently, induces and shapes prejudice. Of
particular interest to Allport are the labels—Jew, reactionary,
jock, cripple—that we use to categorize people.
Unfortunately, such labels tend to magnify one attribute while
masking many other perhaps equally important ones.*

Without words we should scarcely be able to form categories at all. A   1
dog perhaps forms rudimentary generalizations, such as small-boys-are-
to-be avoided—but this concept runs its course on the conditioned reflex
level, and does not become the object of thought as such. In order to hold
a generalization in mind for reflection and recall, for identification and for
action, we need to fix it in words. Without words our world would be, as
William James said, an "empirical sand-heap."

NOUNS THAT CUT SLICES

In the empirical world of human beings there are some two and a half   2
billion grains of sand corresponding to our category "the human race."
We cannot possibly deal with so many separate entities in our thought, nor
can we individualize even among the hundreds whom we encounter in our
daily round. We must group them, form clusters. We welcome, therefore,
the names that help us to perform the clustering.

The most important property of a noun is that it brings many grains of   3
sand into a single pail, disregarding the fact that the same grains might
have fitted just as appropriately into another pail. To state the matter
technically, a noun *abstracts* from a concrete reality some one feature and

assembles different concrete realities only with respect to this one feature. The very act of classifying forces us to overlook all other features, many of which might offer a sounder basis than the rubric we select. Irving Lee gives the following example:

> I knew a man who had lost the use of both eyes. He was called a "blind man." He could also be called an expert typist, a conscientious worker, a good student, a careful listener, a man who wanted a job. But he couldn't get a job in the department store order room where employees sat and typed orders which came over the telephone. The personnel man was impatient to get the interview over. "But you're a blind man," he kept saying, and one could almost feel his silent assumption that somehow the incapacity in one aspect made the man incapable in every other. So blinded by the label was the interviewer that he could not be persuaded to look beyond it.

Some labels, such as "blind man," are exceedingly salient and pow-   4
erful. They tend to prevent alternative classification, or even cross-classification. Ethnic labels are often of this type, particularly if they refer to some highly visible feature, e.g., Negro, Oriental. They resemble the labels that point to some outstanding incapacity—*feeble-minded, cripple, blind man.* Let us call such symbols "labels of primary potency." These symbols act like shrieking sirens, deafening us to all finer discriminations that we might otherwise perceive. Even though the blindness of one man and the darkness of pigmentation of another may be defining attributes for some purposes, they are irrelevant and "noisy" for others.

Most people are unaware of this basic law of language—that every   5
label applied to a given person refers properly only to one aspect of his nature. You may correctly say that a certain man is *human, a philanthropist, a Chinese, a physician, an athlete.* A given person may be all of these; but the chances are that *Chinese* stands out in your mind as the symbol of primary potency. Yet neither this nor any other classificatory label can refer to the whole of a man's nature. (Only his proper name can do so.)

Thus each label we use, especially those of primary potency, distracts   6

LABELS OF PRIMARY POTENCY

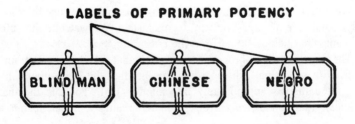

our attention from concrete reality. The living, breathing, complex individual—the ultimate unit of human nature—is lost to sight. As in the figure, the label magnifies one attribute out of all proportion to its true significance, and masks other important attributes of the individual. . . .

A category, once formed with the aid of a symbol of primary potency, tends to attract more attributes than it should. The category labeled *Chinese* comes to signify not only ethnic membership but also reticence, impassivity, poverty, treachery. To be sure, . . . there may be genuine ethnic-linked traits, making for a certain *probability* that the member of an ethnic stock may have these attributes. But our cognitive process is not cautious. The labeled category, as we have seen, includes indiscriminately the defining attribute, probable attributes, and wholly fanciful, nonexistent attributes.

Even proper names—which ought to invite us to look at the individual person—may act like symbols of primary potency, especially if they arouse ethnic associations. Mr. Greenberg is a person, but since his name is Jewish, it activates in the hearer his entire category of Jews-as-a-whole. An ingenious experiment performed by Razran shows this point clearly, and at the same time demonstrates how a proper name, acting like an ethnic symbol, may bring with it an avalanche of stereotypes.

Thirty photographs of college girls were shown on a screen to 150 students. The subjects rated the girls on a scale from one to five for *beauty, intelligence, character, ambition, general likability.* Two months later the same subjects were asked to rate the same photographs (and fifteen additional ones introduced to complicate the memory factor). This time five of the original photographs were given Jewish surnames (Cohen, Kantor, etc.), five Italian (Valenti, etc.), and five Irish (O'Brien, etc); and the remaining girls were given names chosen from the signers of the Declaration of Independence and from the Social Register (Davis, Adams, Clark, etc.).

When Jewish names were attached to photographs there occurred the following changes in ratings:

decrease in liking
decrease in character
decrease in beauty
increase in intelligence
increase in ambition

For those photographs given Italian names there occurred:

decrease in liking
decrease in character
decrease in beauty
decrease in intelligence

Thus a mere proper name leads to prejudgments of personal attributes. The individual is fitted to the prejudice ethnic category, and not judged in his own right.

While the Irish names also brought about depreciated judgment, the depreciation was not as great as in the case of the Jews and Italians. The falling of likability of the ''Jewish girls'' was twice as great as for ''Italians'' and five times as great as for ''Irish.'' We note, however, that the ''Jewish'' photographs caused higher ratings in *intelligence* and in *ambition*. Not all stereotypes of out-groups are unfavorable.

The anthropologist, Margaret Mead, has suggested that labels of primary potency lose some of their force when they are changed from nouns into adjectives. To speak of a Negro soldier, a Catholic teacher, or a Jewish artist calls attention to the fact that some other group classifications are just as legitimate as the racial or religious. If George Johnson is spoken of not only as a Negro but also as a *soldier,* we have at least two attributes to know him by, and two are more accurate than one. To depict him truly as an individual, of course, we should have to name many more attributes. It is a useful suggestion that we designate ethnic and religious membership where possible with *adjectives* rather than *nouns*.   9

EMOTIONALLY TONED LABELS

Many categories have two kinds of labels—one less emotional and one more emotional. Ask yourself how you feel, and what thoughts you have, when you read the words *school teacher,* and then *school marm.* Certainly the second phrase calls up something more strict, more ridiculous, more disagreeable than the former. Here are four innocent letters: m-a-r-m. But they make us shudder a bit, laugh a bit, and scorn a bit. They call up an image of a spare, humorless, irritable old maid. They do not tell us that she is an individual human being with sorrows and troubles of her own. They force her instantly into a rejective category.   10

In the ethnic sphere even plain labels such as Negro, Italian, Jew, Catholic, Irish-American, French-Canadian may have emotional tone for a reason that we shall soon explain. But they all have their higher key equivalents: nigger, wop, kike, papist, harp, canuck. When these labels are employed we can be almost certain that the speaker *intends* not only to characterize the person's membership, but also to disparage and reject him.   11

Quite apart from the insulting intent that lies behind the use of certain labels, there is also an inherent (''physiognomic'') handicap in many terms designating ethnic membership. For example, the proper names characteristic of certain ethnic memberships strike us as absurd. (We compare them, of course, with what is familiar and therefore ''right.'') Chinese names are short and silly; Polish names intrinsically difficult and outlandish. Unfamiliar dialects strike us as ludicrous. Foreign dress (which, of course, is a visual ethnic symbol) seems unnecessarily queer.   12

But of all these "physiognomic" handicaps the reference to color, 13
clearly implied in certain symbols, is the greatest. The word Negro comes
from the Latin *niger* meaning black. In point of fact, no Negro has a black
complexion, but by comparison with other blonder stocks, he has come to
be known as a "black man." Unfortunately *black* in the English language
is a word having a preponderance of sinister connotations: the outlook is
black, blackball, blackguard, black-hearted, black death, blacklist, black-
mail, Black Hand. In his novel *Moby Dick,* Herman Melville considers at
length the remarkably morbid connotations of black and the remarkably
virtuous connotations of white.

Nor is the ominous flavor of black confined to the English language. A 14
cross-cultural study reveals that the semantic significance of black is more
or less universally the same. Among certain Siberian tribes, members of a
privileged clan call themselves "white bones," and refer to all others as
"black bones." Even among Uganda Negroes there is some evidence for
a white god at the apex of the theocratic hierarchy; certain it is that a white
cloth, signifying purity, is used to ward off evil spirits and disease.

There is thus an implied value-judgment in the very concept of *white* 15
race and *black race.* One might also study the numerous unpleasant connotations of *yellow,* and their possible bearing on our conception of the
people of the Orient.

Such reasoning should not be carried too far, since there are undoubt- 16
edly, in various contexts, pleasant associations with both black and yellow.
Black velvet is agreeable, so too are chocolate and coffee. Yellow tulips
are well liked; the sun and moon are radiantly yellow. Yet it is true that
"color" words are used with chauvinistic overtones more than most people
realize. There is certainly condescension indicated in many familiar
phrases: dark as a nigger's pocket, darktown strutters, white hope (a term
originated when a white contender was sought against the Negro heavy-
weight champion, Jack Johnson), the white man's burden, the yellow
peril, black boy. Scores of everyday phrases are stamped with the flavor of
prejudice, whether the user knows it or not.

We spoke of the fact that even the most proper and sedate labels for 17
minority groups sometimes seem to exude a negative flavor. In many
contexts and situations the very terms *French-Canadian, Mexican,* or *Jew,*
correct and nonmalicious though they are, sound a bit opprobrious. The
reason is that they are labels of social deviants. Especially in a culture
where uniformity is prized, the name of *any* deviant carries with it *ipso*
facto a negative value-judgment. Words like *insane, alcoholic, pervert* are
presumably neutral designations of a human condition, but they are more:
they are finger-pointing at a deviance. Minority groups are deviants, and
for this reason, from the very outset, the most innocent labels in many
situations imply a shading of disrepute. When we wish to highlight the

deviance and denigrate it still further we use words of a higher emotional key: crackpot, soak, pansy, greaser, Okie, nigger, harp, kike.

Members of minority groups are often understandably sensitive to   18
names given them. Not only do they object to deliberately insulting epithets, but sometimes see evil intent where none exists. Often the word Negro is spelled with a small *n*, occasionally as a studied insult, more often from ignorance. (The term is not cognate with white, which is not capitalized, but rather with Caucasian, which is.) Terms like "mulatto," or "octoroon" cause hard feeling because of the condescension with which they have often been used in the past. Sex differentiations are objectionable, since they seem doubly to emphasize ethnic difference: why speak of Jewess and not of Protestantess, or of Negress and not of whitess? Similar overemphasis is implied in the terms like Chinamen or Scotchman; why not American man? Grounds for misunderstanding lie in the fact that minority group members are sensitive to such shadings, while majority members may employ them unthinkingly.

THE COMMUNIST LABEL

Until we label an out-group it does not clearly exist in our minds. Take the   19
curiously vague situation that we often meet when a person wishes to locate responsibility on the shoulders of some out-group whose nature he cannot specify. In such a case he usually employs the pronoun "they" without an antecedent. "Why don't they make these sidewalks wider?" "I hear they are going to build a factory in this town and hire a lot of foreigners." "I won't pay this tax bill; they can just whistle for their money." If asked "who?" the speaker is likely to grow confused and embarrassed. The common use of the orphaned pronoun *they* teaches us that people often want and need to designate out-groups (usually for the purpose of venting hostility) even when they have no clear conception of the out-group in question. And so long as the target of wrath remains vague and ill-defined specific prejudice cannot crystallize around it. To have enemies we need labels.

Until relatively recently—strange as it may seem—there was no agreed-   20
upon symbol for *communist*. The word, of course, existed but it had no special emotional connotation, and did not designate a public enemy. Even when, after World War I, there was a growing feeling of economic and social menace in this country, there was no agreement as to the actual source of the menace.

A content analysis of the Boston *Herald* for the year 1920 turned up the   21
following list of labels. Each was used in a content implying some threat. Hysteria had overspread the country, as it did after World War II. Someone

must be responsible for the postwar malaise, rising prices, uncertainty. There must be a villain. But in 1920 the villain was impartially designated by reporters and editorial writers with the following symbols:

> alien, agitator, anarchist, apostle of bomb and torch, Bolshevik, communist, communist laborite, conspirator, emissary of false promise, extremist, foreigner, hyphenated-American, incendiary, IWW, parlor anarchist, parlor pink, parlor socialist, plotter, radical, red, revolutionary, Russian agitator, socialist, Soviet, syndicalist, traitor, undesirable.

From this excited array we note that the *need* for an enemy (someone   22
to serve as a focus for discontent and jitters) was considerably more apparent than the precise *identity* of the enemy. At any rate, there was no clearly agreed upon label. Perhaps partly for this reason the hysteria abated. Since no clear category of "communism" existed there was no true focus for the hostility.

But following World War II this collection of vaguely interchangeable   23
labels became fewer in number and more commonly agreed upon. The out-group menace came to be designated almost always as *communist* or *red*. In 1920 the threat, lacking a clear label, was vague; after 1945 both symbol and thing became more definite. Not that people knew precisely what they meant when they said "communist," but with the aid of the term they were at least able to point consistently to *something* that inspired fear. The term developed the power of signifying menace and led to various repressive measures against anyone to whom the label was rightly or wrongly attached.

Logically, the label should apply to specifiable defining attributes, such   24
as members of the Communist Party, or people whose allegiance is with the Russian system, or followers, historically, of Karl Marx. But the label came in for far more extensive use.

What seems to have happened is approximately as follows. Having   25
suffered through a period of war and being acutely aware of devastating revolutions abroad, it is natural that most people should be upset, dreading to lose their possessions, annoyed by high taxes, seeing customary moral and religious values threatened, and dreading worse disasters to come. Seeking an explanation for this unrest, a single identifiable enemy is wanted. It is not enough to designate "Russia" or some other distant land. Nor is it satisfactory to fix blame on "changing social conditions." What is needed is a human agent near at hand: someone in Washington, someone in our schools, in our factories, in our neighborhood. If we *feel* an immediate threat, we reason, there must be a near-lying danger. It is, we conclude, communism, not only in Russia but also in America, at our doorstep, in our government, in our churches, in our colleges, in our neighborhood.

Are we saying that hostility toward communism is prejudice? Not   26 necessarily. There are certainly phases of the dispute wherein realistic social conflict is involved. American values (e.g., respect for the person) and totalitarian values as represented in Soviet practice are intrinsically at odds. A realistic opposition in some form will occur. Prejudice enters only when the defining attributes of *communist* grow imprecise, when anyone who favors any form of social change is called a communist. People who fear social change are the ones most likely to affix the label to any persons or practices that seem to them threatening.

For them the category is undifferentiated. It includes books, movies, 27 preachers, teachers who utter what for them are uncongenial thoughts. If evil befalls—perhaps forest fires or a factory explosion—it is due to communist saboteurs. The category becomes monopolistic, covering almost anything that is uncongenial. On the floor of the House of Representatives in 1946, Representative Rankin called James Roosevelt a communist. Congressman Outland replied with psychological acumen, "Apparently everyone who disagrees with Mr. Rankin is a communist."

When differentiated thinking is at a low ebb—as it is in times of social 28 crises—there is a magnification of two-valued logic. Things are perceived as either inside or outside a moral order. What is outside is likely to be called communist. Correspondingly—and here is where damage is done— whatever is called communist (however erroneously) is immediately cast outside the moral order.

This associative mechanism places enormous power in the hands of a 29 demagogue. For several years Senator McCarthy managed to discredit many citizens who thought differently from himself by the simple device of calling them communist. Few people were able to see through this trick and many reputations were ruined. But the famous senator has no monopoly on the device. As reported in the Boston *Herald* on November 1, 1946, Representative Joseph Martin, Republican leader in the House, ended his election campaign against his Democratic opponent by saying, "The people will vote tomorrow between chaos, confusion, bankruptcy, state socialism or communism, and the preservation of our American life, with all its freedom and its opportunities." Such an array of emotional labels placed his opponent outside the accepted moral order. Martin was reelected. . . .

Not everyone, of course, is taken in. Demagogy, when it goes too far, 30 meets with ridicule. Elizabeth Dilling's book, *The Red Network,* was so exaggerated in its two-valued logic that it was shrugged off by many people with a smile. One reader remarked, "Apparently if you step off the sidewalk with your left foot you're a communist." But it is not easy in times of social strain and hysteria to keep one's balance, and to resist the tendency of a verbal symbol to manufacture large and fanciful categories of prejudiced thinking.

VERBAL REALISM AND SYMBOL PHOBIA

Most individuals rebel at being labeled, especially if the label is uncom-   31
plimentary. Very few are willing to be called *fascistic, socialistic,* or
anti-Semitic. Unsavory labels may apply to others; but not to us.

An illustration of the craving that people have to attach favorable   32
symbols to themselves is seen in the community where white people banded
together to force out a Negro family that had moved in. They called
themselves "Neighborly Endeavor" and chose as their motto the Golden
Rule. One of the first acts of this symbol-sanctified band was to sue the
man who sold property to Negroes. They then flooded the house which
another Negro couple planned to occupy. Such were the acts performed
under the banner of the Golden Rule.

Studies made by Stagner and Hartmann show that a person's political   33
attitudes may in fact entitle him to be called a fascist or a socialist, and yet
he will emphatically repudiate the unsavory label, and fail to endorse any
movement or candidate that overtly accepts them. In short, there is a
symbol phobia that corresponds to *symbol realism.* We are more inclined
to the former when we ourselves are concerned, though we are much less
critical when epithets of "fascist," "communist," "blind man," "school
marm" are applied to others.

When symbols provoke strong emotions they are sometimes regarded   34
no longer as symbols, but as actual things. The expressions "son of a
bitch" and "liar" are in our culture frequently regarded as "fighting
words." Softer and more subtle expressions of contempt may be accepted.
But in these particular cases, the epithet itself must be "taken back." We
certainly do not change our opponent's attitude by making him take back
a word, but it seems somehow important that the word itself be eradicated.

Such verbal realism may reach extreme length.   35

The City Council of Cambridge, Massachusetts, unanimously passed a resolution (December, 1939) making it illegal "to possess, harbor, sequester,
introduce or transport, within the city limits, any book, map, magazine, newspaper, pamphlet, handbill or circular containing the words Lenin or Lenin-
grad."

Such naiveté in confusing language with reality is hard to comprehend
unless we recall that word-magic plays an appreciable part in human thinking. The following examples, like the one preceding, are taken from Hayakawa.

The Malagasy soldier must eschew kidneys, because in the Malagasy language
the word for kidney is the same as that for "shot"; so shot he would certainly
be if he ate a kidney.

In May, 1937, a state senator of New York bitterly opposed a bill for the control of syphilis because "the innocence of children might be corrupted by a widespread use of the term. . . . This particular word creates a shudder in every decent woman and decent man."

This tendency to reify words underscores the close cohesion that exists   36 between category and symbol. Just the mention of "communist," "Negro," "Jew," "England," "Democrats," will send some people into a panic of fear or a frenzy of anger. Who can say whether it is the word or the thing that annoys them? The label is an intrinsic part of any monopolistic category. Hence to liberate a person from ethnic or political prejudice it is necessary at the same time to liberate him from *word fetishism*. This fact is well known to students of general semantics who tell us that prejudice is due in large part to verbal realism and to symbol phobia. Therefore any program for the reduction of prejudice must include a large measure of semantic therapy.

QUESTIONS ON CONTENT

1. Allport quotes William James's statement that without words our lives would be an "empirical sand-heap" (1). What did James mean by the phrase? What are the implications of a world in which we could not determine categories?

2. Nouns or names provide an essential service in making categorization possible. Yet, according to Allport, nouns are also words that "cut slices." What does he mean by "cut slices"? What is inherently unfair about nouns?

3. What does Allport mean by the "orphaned pronoun *they*" (19)? Why is it used so often?

4. What are "labels of primary potency" (4)? Why are they so important? Can and should we avoid the use of such labels?

5. Why may "labels of primary potency lose some of their force when they are changed from nouns into adjectives" (9)? Do you agree that "it is a useful suggestion that we designate ethnic and religious membership where possible with *adjectives* rather than with *nouns*" (9)? Why, or why not?

6. Allport wrote "The Language of Prejudice" in the early 1950s. Does this help explain why he devotes paragraphs 19–30 to a discussion of the label *communist?* How do Americans react to the label *communist* today?

7. What do the terms *reify* (36), *verbal realism* (35), *symbol phobia* (33), *word fetishism* (36), and *symbol realism* (33) mean? Why does Allport believe that "any program for the reduction of prejudice must include a large measure of semantic therapy" (36)?

QUESTIONS ON RHETORIC

1. What is Allport's thesis, and where is it stated? (Glossary: *Thesis*)

2. The first three paragraphs of Allport's essay become progressively concrete. Explain how these paragraphs logically narrow our focus to the noun and how it functions. (Glossary: *Concrete/Abstract*)

3. Allport includes six fairly lengthy quotations in his essay. What is the function of each one? Do you think each quotation is effective? Why, or why not? (Glossary: *Examples*)

4. In paragraph 17, identify the topic sentence. What method is used to develop the paragraph? (Glossary: *Topic Sentence* and *Examples*)

VOCABULARY

rudimentary (1)	sinister (13)	array (29)
ethnic (4)	morbid (13)	cohesion (36)
inherent (12)	sedate (17)	intrinsic (36)
ludicrous (12)		

WRITING TOPICS

1. Read the following newspaper article. Write an essay in which you attack or defend the UN recommendations.

UN GROUP URGES DROPPING OF WORDS WITH RACIST TINGE

In an effort to combat racial prejudice, a group of United Nations experts is urging sweeping revision of the terminology used by teachers, mass media and others dealing with race.

Words such as *Negro, primitive, savage, backward, colored, bushman* and *uncivilized* would be banned as either "contemptuous, unjust or inadequate." They were described as aftereffects of colonialism.

The report said that the terms were "so charged with emotive potential that their use, with or without conscious pejorative intent, to describe or characterize certain ethnic, social or religious groups, generally provoked an adverse reaction on the part of these groups."

The report said further that even the term *race* should be used with particular care since its scientific validity was debatable and that it "often served to perpetuate prejudice." The experts suggested that the word *tribe* should be used as sparingly as possible, since most of the "population groups" referred to by this term have long since ceased to be tribes or are losing their tribal character. A *native* should be called *inhabitant*, the group advised, and instead of *paganism* the words *animists, Moslems, Brahmans* and other precise words should be used. The word *savanna* is preferable to *jungle*, and the new countries should be described as *developing* rather than *underdeveloped*, the experts said.

2. Make an extensive list of the labels that have been or could be applied to you. Write an essay in which you discuss the labels that you find "truly offensive," those you can "live with," and those that you "like to be associated with." Explain your reasons for putting labels in each of these categories.

WORDS WITH
BUILT-IN JUDGMENTS

S. I. Hayakawa

In Language in Thought and Action, *from which the
following selection is taken, general semanticist S. I.
Hayakawa explores the complex relationships that exist
between reality and the language we use to describe it. He
explains the power that some words—especially those
associated with "race, religion, political heresy, and
economic dissent"—have to evoke strong emotional responses
and how an awareness of this power can help one both to stir
up traditional prejudices and unintentionally to give offense.*

The fact that some words arouse both informative and affective conno- 1
tations simultaneously gives a special complexity to discussions involving
religious, racial, national, and political groups. To many people, the word
"communist" means simultaneously "one who believes in communism"
(informative connotations) *and* "one whose ideals and purposes are altogether repellent" (affective connotations). Words applying to occupations
of which one disapproves ("pickpocket," "racketeer," "prostitute"), like
those applying to believers in philosophies of which one may disapprove
("atheist," "heretic," "materialist," "Holy Roller," "radical," "liberal"), likewise often communicate *simultaneously* a fact and a judgment
on the fact.

In some parts of the southwestern United States there is strong preju- 2
dice against Mexicans, both immigrant and American-born. The strength
of this prejudice is indirectly revealed by the fact that newspapers and
polite people have stopped using the word "Mexican" altogether, using
the expression "Spanish-speaking person" instead. "Mexican" has been
used with contemptuous connotations for so long that it has become, in the
opinion of many people in the region, unsuitable for polite conversation. In
some circles, the word is reserved for lower-class Mexicans, while the
"politer" term is used for the upper class. There are also terms, such as
"chicano" and "Latino," that Mexican-American and Spanish-speaking
groups have chosen to describe themselves.

In dealing with subjects about which strong feelings exist, we are 3
compelled to talk in roundabout terms if we wish to avoid traditional
prejudices, which hinder clear thinking. Hence we have not only such
terms as "Spanish-speaking persons" but also, in other contexts, "problem drinkers" instead of "drunkards," and "Hansen's disease" instead of
"leprosy."

These verbal stratagems are necessitated by the strong affective con- 4
notations as well as by the often misleading implications of their blunter
alternatives; they are not merely a matter of giving things fancy names in
order to fool people, as the simple-minded often believe. Because the old
names are "loaded," they dictate traditional patterns of behavior toward
those to whom they are applied. When everybody "knew" what to do
about "little hoodlums," they threw them in jail and "treated 'em rough."
Once in jail, little hoodlums showed a marked tendency to grow up into big
hoodlums. When thoughtful people began to observe such facts, they
started rethinking the problem, using different terminologies. What is the
best way of describing these troubled and troublesome youths? Shall they
be described as "defectives" or "psychopathic personalities"? Or as
"maladjusted" or "neurotic"? Shall we say they are "deprived," "disadvantaged," "frustrated," or "socially displaced"? Shall we say they
are "troubled by problems of identity"? Are they in need of "confine-
ment," "punishment," "treatment," "education," or "rehabilitation"?
It is through trying out many, many possible terms such as these that new
ways of dealing with the problem are discovered and devised.

The meaning of words, as we have observed, changes from speaker to 5
speaker and from context to context. The words "Japs" and "niggers,"
for instance, although often used both as a designation and an insult, are
sometimes used with no intent to offend. In some classes of society and in
some geographical areas, there are people who know no other words for
Japanese, and in other areas there are people who know no other words for
Blacks. Ignorance of regional and class differences of dialect often results
in feelings being needlessly hurt. Those who believe that the meaning of a
word is *in the word* often fail to understand this simple point of differences
in usage. For example, an elderly Japanese woman of my acquaintance
used to squirm at the mention of the word "Jap," even when used in an
innocuous or complimentary context. "Whenever I hear the word," she
used to say, "I feel dirty all over."

The word "nigger" has a similar effect on most Blacks. A distin- 6
guished Black sociologist tells of an incident in his adolescence when he
was hitchhiking far from home in regions where Blacks are hardly ever
seen. He was befriended by an extremely kindly white couple who fed him
and gave him a place to sleep in their home. However, they kept calling
him "little nigger"—a fact which upset him profoundly, even while he

was grateful for their kindness. He finally got up courage to ask the man not to call him by that "insulting term."

"Who's insultin' you, son?" said the man.
"You are, sir—that name you're always calling me."
"What name?"
"Uh . . . you know."
"I ain't callin' you no names, son."
"I mean your calling me 'nigger.' "
"Well, what's insultin' about that? You are a nigger, ain't you?"

As the sociologist says now in telling the story, "I couldn't think of an 7
answer then, and I'm not sure I can now."

In case the sociologist reads this book, we are happy to provide him 8
with an answer, although it may be twenty-five years late. He might have said to his benefactor, "Sir, in the part of the country I come from, white people who treat colored people with respect call them Blacks, while those who wish to show their contempt for colored people call them niggers. I hope the latter is not your intention." And the man might have replied, had he been kindly in thought as he was in deed, "Well, you don't say! Sorry I hurt your feelings, son, but I didn't know." And that would have been that. Many black people now have rejected the term "Negro" as itself an insulting term and prefer to be called Blacks or Afro-Americans. Some "hip" terms that they use for themselves are "moulenjam," "splib," "member," "blood," and "boots."

Blacks, having for a long time been victims of unfair persecution 9
because of race, are often even more sensitive about racial appellations than the Japanese woman previously mentioned. It need hardly be said that Blacks suffer from the confusion or informative and affective connotations just as often as white people—or Japanese. Such Blacks, and those white sympathizers with their cause who are equally naive in linguistic matters, tend to feel that the entire colored "race" is vilified whenever and wherever the word "nigger" occurs. They bristle even when it occurs in such expressions as "niggertoe" (the name of an herb; also a dialect term for Brazil nut), "niggerhead" (a type of chewing tobacco), "niggerfish" (a kind of fish found in West Indian and Floridan waters)—and even the word "niggardly" (of Scandinavian origin, unrelated, of course, to "Negro") has to be avoided before some audiences.

Such easily offended people sometimes send delegations to visit dic- 10
tionary offices to demand that the word "nigger" be excluded from future editions, being unaware that dictionaries . . . perform a historical, rather than legislative, function. To try to reduce racial discrimination by getting dictionaries to stop including the word "nigger" is like trying to cut down the birth rate by shutting down the office of the county register of births.

When racial discrimination against Blacks is done away with, the word will either disappear or else lose its present connotations. By losing its present connotations, we mean, first, that people who need to insult their fellow men will have found more interesting grounds on which to base their insults and, second, that people who are called "niggers" will no longer fly off the handle any more than a person from New England does at being called a "Yankee."

One other curious fact needs to be recorded about words applied to   11
such hotly debated issues as race, religion, political heresy, and economic dissent. Every reader is acquainted with certain people who, according to their own flattering descriptions of themselves, "believe in being frank" and like to "tell it like [sic] it is." By "telling it like it is," they usually mean calling anything or anyone by the term which has the strongest and most disagreeable affective connotations. Why people should pin medals on themselves for "candor" for performing this nasty feat has often puzzled me. Sometimes it is necessary to violate verbal taboos as an aid to clearer thinking, but more often "calling a spade a spade" is to provide our minds with a greased runway down which we may slide back into old *and discredited* patterns of evaluation and behavior.

QUESTIONS ON CONTENT

1. What is the distinction Hayakawa draws between "informative connotations" and "affective connotations"?

2. Why, according to Hayakawa, have many people in the American Southwest stopped using the term "Mexican"?

3. How can names, as Hayakawa asserts, "dictate traditional patterns of behavior toward those to whom they are applied" (4)?

4. On what basis does Hayakawa argue that "verbal stratagems" (4) are often a necessity?

5. Why is it important to realize that the meanings of words may change "from speaker to speaker and from context to context" (5)? Explain how the Black sociologist's story in paragraph 6 serves to illustrate this point.

6. In what ways are Hayakawa's "words with built-in judgments" similar to Allport's "labels of primary potency" (Allport, paragraph 4)?

QUESTIONS ON RHETORIC

1. Most of the paragraphs in Hayakawa's essay are organized in the same way. Explain how they are organized, paying particular attention to the topic sentences. (Glossary: *Topic Sentence* and *Examples*)

2. What technique does Hayakawa use to define both informative and affective connotations? (Glossary: *Definition*) Did you find his definitions clear and easy to understand? Why, or why not?

3. Discuss Hayakawa's use of transitions between paragraphs. What transitions does he use? What effect does each transition have? (Glossary: *Transitions*)

4. How effective is the metaphor of the ''greased runway'' in the final paragraph? Explain. (Glossary: *Figures of Speech*)

VOCABULARY

simultaneously (1)	psychopathic (4)	benefactor (8)
repellent (1)	rehabilitation (4)	dissent (11)
contemptuous (2)	innocuous (5)	candor (11)

WRITING TOPICS

1. Hawakawa lists a number of terms (*pickpocket, racketeer, prostitute, atheist, heretic, materialist, Holy Roller, radical, liberal, Mexican, drunkard, leprosy, hoodlums, Japs, niggers*) that evoke simultaneously both affective connotations and informative connotations. Think of at least three other terms that also do this. Write an essay in which you explain the affective and informative connotations of each term.

2. Using examples from your own experiences, write an essay in which you show that it is better ''to talk in roundabout terms if we wish to avoid traditional prejudices, which hinder clear thinking'' (3). Can you think of any situations in which it would be ''necessary to violate verbal taboos as an aid to clearer thinking'' (11)?

THE ETYMOLOGY OF THE INTERNATIONAL INSULT

Charles F. Berlitz

More than any other form of prejudiced language, racial slurs are intended to wound and to disgrace. In the following essay, Charles F. Berlitz, founder of the Berlitz School of Languages, examines the origins of some of these words in hope of getting to the root of racial misunderstanding. Strangely, he discovers that in many cases the original meaning of these words was anything but hateful and unkind.

"What is a kike?" Disraeli once asked a small group of fellow po- 1
liticans. Then, as his audience shifted nervously, Queen Victoria's great Jewish Prime Minister supplied the answer himself. "A kike," he observed, "is a Jewish gentleman who has just left the room."

The word kike is thought to have derived from the ending *-ki* or *-ky* 2
found in many names borne by the Jews of Eastern Europe. Or, as Leo Rosten suggests, it may come from *kikel*, Yiddish for a circle, the preferred mark for name signing by Jewish immigrants who could not write. This was used instead of an *X*, which resembles a cross. Kikel was not originally pejorative, but has become so through use.

Yid, another word for Jew, has a distinguished historic origin, coming 3
from the German *Jude* (through the Russian *zhid*.) *Jude* itself derives from the tribe of Judah, a most honorable and ancient appellation. The vulgar and opprobrious word "Sheeny" for Jew is a real inversion, as it derives from *shaine* (Yiddish) or *schön* (German), meaning "beautiful." How could beautiful be an insult? The answer is that it all depends on the manner, tone or facial expression or sneer (as our own Vice President has trenchantly observed) with which something is said. The opprobrious Mexican word for an American—*gringo*, for example, is essentially simply a sound echo of a song the American troops used to sing when the Americans were invading Mexico—"Green Grow the Lilacs." Therefore the Mexicans began to call the Americans something equivalent to "los greengrows" which became Hispanicized to *gringo*. But from this innocent

264

beginning to the unfriendly emphasis with which many Mexicans say *gringo* today there is a world of difference—almost a call to arms, with unforgettable memories of past real or fancied wrongs, including "lost" Texas and California.

The pejorative American word for Mexicans, Puerto Ricans, Cubans   4
and other Spanish-speaking nationals is simply *spik*, excerpted from the useful expression "No esspick Englitch." Italians, whether in America or abroad, have been given other more picturesque appellations. *Wop*, an all-time pejorative favorite, is curiously not insulting at all by origin, as it means, in Neapolitan dialect, "handsome," "strong" or "good looking." Among the young Italian immigrants some of the stronger and more active—sometimes to the point of combat—were called *guappi,* from which the first syllable, "wop," attained an "immediate insult" status for all Italians.

"Guinea" comes from the days of the slave trade and is derived from   5
the African word for West Africa. This "guinea" is the same word as the British unit of 21 shillings, somehow connected with African gold profits as well as New Guinea, which resembled Africa to its discoverers. Dark or swarthy Italians and sometimes Portuguese were called *Guineas* and this apparently spread to Italians of light complexion as well.

One of the epithets for Negroes has a curious and tragic historic origin,   6
the memory of which is still haunting us. The word is *"coons."* It comes from *baracoes* (the o gives a nasal *n* sound in Portuguese), and refers to the slave pens or barracks (*"baracoons"*) in which the victims of the slave trade were kept while awaiting transshipment. Their descendants, in their present emphasizing of the term "black" over "Negro," may be in the process of upgrading the very word "black," so often used pejoratively, as in "blackhearted," "black day," "black arts," "black hand," etc. Even some African languages use "black" in a negative sense. In Hausa "to have a black stomach" means to be angry or unhappy.

The sub-Sahara African peoples, incidentally, do not think that they are   7
black (which they are not, anyway). They consider themselves a healthy and attractive "people color," while whites to them look rather unhealthy and somewhat frightening. In any case, the efforts of African Americans to dignify the word "black" may eventually represent a semantic as well as a socio-racial triumph.

A common type of national insult is that of referring to nationalities by   8
their food habits. Thus "Frogs" for the French and "Krauts" for the Germans are easily understandable, reflecting on the French addition to *cuisses de grenouilles* (literally "thighs of frogs") and that of the Germans for various kinds of cabbage, hot or cold. The French call the Italians *"les macaronis"* while the German insult word for Italians is *Katzenfresser* (Cateaters), an unjust accusation considering the hordes of cats among the

Roman ruins fed by individual cat lovers—unless they are fattening them up? The insult word for an English person is "limey" referring to the limes distributed to seafaring Englishmen as an antiscurvy precaution in the days of sailing ships and long periods at sea.

At least one of these food descriptive appellations has attained a per-   9
manent status in English. The word "Eskimo" is not an Eskimo word at all but an Algonquin word unit meaning "eaters-of-flesh." The Eskimos naturally do not call themselves this in their own language but, with simple directness, use the word *Inuit*—"the men" or "the people."

Why is it an insult to call Chinese "Chinks"? Chink is most probably   10
a contraction of the first syllables of *Chung-Kuo-Ren*—"Middle Country Person." In Chinese there is no special word for China, as the Chinese, being racially somewhat snobbish themselves (although *not* effete, accord- ing to recent reports), have for thousands of years considered their land to be the center or middle of the world. The key character for China is therefore the word *chung* of "middle" which, added to *kuo*, becomes "middle country" or "middle kingdom"—the complete Chinese expres- sion for "China" being *Chung Hwa Min Kuo* ("Middle Flowery People's Country"). No matter how inoffensive the origin of "Chink" is, however, it is no longer advisable for everyday or anyday use now.

Jap, an insulting diminutive that figured in the . . . [1968] national   11
U.S. election (though its use in the expression "fat Jap" was apparently meant to have an endearing quality by our Vice President) is a simple contraction of "Japan," which derives from the Chinese word for "sun." In fact the words "Jap" and "Nip" both mean the same thing. "Jap" comes from Chinese and "Nip" from Japanese in the following fashion: *Jihpen* means "sun origin" in Chinese, while *Ni-hon* (Nippon) gives a like meaning in Japanese, both indicating that Japan was where the sun rose. Europeans were first in contact with China, and so originally chose the Chinese name for Japan instead of the Japanese one.

The Chinese "insult" words for whites are based on the observations   12
that they are too white and therefore look like ghosts or devils, *fan kuei* (ocean ghosts), or that their features are too sharp instead of being pleas- antly flat, and that they have enormous noses, hence *ta-bee-tsu* (great- nosed ones). Differences in facial physiognomy have been fully reciprocated by whites in referring to Asians as "Slants" or "Slopes."

Greeks in ancient times had an insult word for foreigners too, but one   13
based on the sound of their language. This word is still with us, though its original meaning has changed. The ancient Greeks divided the world into Greeks and "Barbarians"—the latter word coming from a description of the ridiculous language the stranger was speaking. To the Greeks it sounded like the "baa-baa" of a sheep—hence "Barbarians!"

The black peoples of South Africa are not today referred to as Negro or   14

Black but as Bantu—not in itself an insult but having somewhat the same effect when you are the lowest man on the totem pole. But the word means simply "the men," *ntu* signifying "man" and *ba* being the plural prefix. This may have come from an early encounter with explorers or missionaries when Central or South Africans on being asked by whites who they were may have replied simply "men"—with the implied though probably unspoken follow-up questions, "And who are you?"

This basic and ancient idea that one's group are the only people—at   15 least the only friendly or non-dangerous ones—is found among many tribes throughout the world. The Navajo Indians call themselves *Diné*—"the people"—and qualify other tribes generally as "the enemy." Therefore an Indian tribe to the north would simply be called "the northern enemy," one to the east "the eastern enemy," etc., and that would be the *only* name used for them. These ancient customs, sanctified by time, of considering people who differ in color, customs, physical characteristics and habits— and by enlargement all strangers—as potential enemies is something mankind can no longer afford, even linguistically. Will man ever be able to rise above using insult as a weapon? It may not be possible to love your neighbor, but by understanding him one may be able eventually to tolerate him. Meanwhile, if you stop calling him names, he too may eventually learn to dislike *you* less.

QUESTIONS ON CONTENT

1. What do the words *kike, Jude, wop, schon, guappi,* and *Chung-Kuo-Ren* have in common? Can you name others that are similarly related?

2. Most people are probably unaware that the word *Eskimo* is a racial slur. How do you explain their ignorance of this fact?

3. In paragraph 7, Berlitz predicts that "the efforts of African-Americans to dignify the word 'black' may eventually represent a semantic and socio-racial triumph." What are some of the semantic and socio-racial obstacles to be overcome?

4. Many tribal peoples refer to themselves as "the people" and others as "the enemy." How does this tendency relate to the origin and purpose of racial insults?

QUESTIONS ON RHETORIC

1. For the most part, Berlitz presents his information in an unemotional, objective tone. (Glossary: *Tone*) Yet in order to cover his material, he has to mention several highly charged, offensive terms. What effect does Berlitz's use of these words have on you? Do you think Berlitz intended to

shock his readers? What evidence can you offer of Berlitz's attitude toward racial slurs?

2. Berlitz gives examples of several kinds of insults and their original meanings. What different groups can you identify? Can you think of any others?

3. Berlitz waits until the final paragraph of his essay to present his thesis. What is that thesis? What does Berlitz gain by not presenting his thesis earlier?

VOCABULARY

pejorative (2)	opprobious (3)	swarthy (5)
appellation (3)	trenchantly (3)	epithets (6)
vulgar (3)	picturesque (4)	sanctified (15)

WRITING TOPICS

1. Make a list of racial slurs you are familiar with. Research their meanings and write an essay about your findings. Include in your essay answers to the following: What is the origin of the word? Was the word originally intended to insult? How does the word relate to that people's image of themselves? In summary, were you surprised at your findings? How did the research add to your perception of racial misunderstanding?

2. In his final paragraph, Berlitz says, "These ancient customs, sanctified by time, of considering people who differ in color, customs, physical characteristics and habits—and by enlargement all strangers—as potential enemies is something mankind can no longer afford, even linguistically." Write an essay explaining what you think Berlitz may have meant in this statement. Do you agree with him?

3. The Eskimos Berlitz mentions are only one example of a people who have been named by someone other than themselves. Are there any groups in your geographic area who are commonly referred to by a name someone else has given them? What effect do you think this has on a people? Write an essay on the importance of "self-identification," as contrasted with having names imposed on one by others.

WHAT IT MEANS TO BE BLACK

William Raspberry

The word black *is a source of pride in the world of music, athletics, or sexual performance, says William Raspberry, a respected syndicated columnist for the* Washington Post. *In all other areas of endeavor it is expected that blacks will not live up to white standards. In his essay, Raspberry urges blacks to develop ethnic traditions of achievement that will enable them to understand they are "capable of doing whatever they put their minds to."*

I know all about bad schools, mean politicians, economic deprivation and racism. Still, it occurs to me that one of the heaviest burdens black Americans—and black children in particular—have to bear is the handicap of definition: the question of what it means to be black.

Let me explain quickly what I mean. If a basketball fan says that the Boston Celtics' Larry Bird plays "black," the fan intends it—and Bird probably accepts it—as a compliment. Tell pop singer Tom Jones he moves "black" and he might grin in appreciation. Say to Teena Marie or The Average White Band that they sound "black" and they'll thank you.

But name one pursuit, aside from athletics, entertainment or sexual performance in which a white practitioner will feel complimented to be told he does it "black." Tell a white broadcaster he talks "black" and he'll sign up for diction lessons. Tell a white reporter he writes "black" and he'll take a writing course. Tell a white lawyer he reasons "black" and he might sue you for slander.

What we have here is a tragically limited definition of blackness, and it isn't only white people who buy it.

Think of all the ways black children can put one another down with charges of "whiteness." For many of these children, hard study and hard work are "white." Trying to please a teacher might be criticized as acting "white." Speaking correct English is "white." Scrimping today in the interest of tomorrow's goals is "white." Educational toys and games are "white."

An incredible array of habits and attitudes that are conducive to success   6
in business, in academia, in the non-entertainment professions are likely to
be thought of as somehow "white." Even economic success, unless it
involves such "black" undertakings as numbers banking, is defined as
"white."

And the results are devastating. I wouldn't deny that blacks often are   7
better entertainers and athletes. My point is the harm that comes from too
narrow a definition of what is black.

One reason black youngsters tend to do better at basketball, for in-   8
stance, is that they assume they can learn to do it well, and so they practice
constantly to prove themselves right.

Wouldn't it be wonderful if we could infect black children with the   9
notion that excellence in math is "black" rather than white, or possibly
Chinese? Wouldn't it be of enormous value if we could create the myth that
morality, strong families, determination, courage and love of learning are
traits brought by slaves from Mother Africa and therefore quintessentially
black?

There is no doubt in my mind that most black youngsters could develop   10
their mathematical reasoning, their elocution and their attitudes the way
they develop their jump shots and their dance steps: by the combination of
sustained, enthusiastic practice and the unquestioned belief that they can
do it.

In one sense, what I am talking about is the importance of developing   11
positive ethnic traditions. Maybe Jews have an innate talent for communication; maybe the Chinese are born with a gift for mathematical reasoning; maybe blacks are naturally blessed with athletic grace. I doubt it.
What is at work, I suspect, is assumption, inculcated early in their lives,
that this is a thing our people do well.

Unfortunately, many of the things about which blacks make this as-   12
sumption are things that do not contribute to their career success—except
for that handful of the truly gifted who can make it as entertainers and
athletes. And many of the things we concede to whites are the things that
are essential to economic security.

So it is with a number of assumptions black youngsters make about   13
what it is to be a "man": physical aggressiveness, sexual prowess, the
refusal to submit to authority. The prisons are full of people who, by this
perverted definition, are unmistakably men.

But the real problem is not so much that the things defined as "black"   14
are negative. The problem is that the definition is much too narrow.

Somehow, we have to make our children understand that they are   15
intelligent, competent people, capable of doing whatever they put their
minds to and making it in the American mainstream, not just in a black
subculture.

What we seem to be doing, instead, is raising up yet another generation of young blacks who will be failures—by definition. 16

QUESTIONS ON CONTENT

1. In paragraph 2, Raspberry suggests three occasions when it is a compliment for white people to be told they are doing something "black." In each case, what does the compliment mean?

2. Black children insult each other with charges of acting "white." According to Raspberry, what is wrong with wanting to be unlike whites?

3. In paragraph 11, Raspberry dismisses the possibility of "innate" talent. What explanation does he offer for ethnic gifts? Do you agree? Why or why not?

4. According to Raspberry, what is the real problem with the definitions he gives of the word *black*? Do you think he is right? Explain your answer.

QUESTIONS ON RHETORIC

1. In several instances throughout his essay, Raspberry uses the words *black* and *white* without defining them. What assumption does he make in doing so? Is this an effective strategy? Why or why not?

2. In paragraphs 2 and 3, Raspberry contrasts positive and negative uses of the word *black*. What point is he trying to make? Is he convincing? Explain.

3. Raspberry poses several questions in his essay. What is his reason for asking these questions? What reaction do you suppose he is looking for? In your opinion, does he succeed in eliciting such a response? Explain your answer.

VOCABULARY

racism (1)   quintessentially (9)   inculcated (11)
conducive (6)   elocution (10)   concede (12)

WRITING TOPICS

1. At the end of his essay, Raspberry says, "Somehow, we have to make our children understand that they are intelligent, competent people, capable of doing whatever they put their minds to and making it in the American mainstream, not just in a black subculture." Raspberry talks elsewhere in his essay about developing positive ethnic traditions, but he doesn't suggest how these goals might be achieved. Based on your own studies of history, consider the ways in which a culture fosters a people's good opinion of itself. To what degree would you say a minority group is at the

mercy of the majority's opinion? In an essay offer some of your own insights into this issue.

2. Look up the words *black* and *white* in your dictionary. What are the connotations of most phrases and metaphors that include the word *black*? the word *white*? Why do you suppose the word *black* has more negative connotations? Is it for racist reasons? Discuss your opinions in an essay.

WRITING ASSIGNMENTS FOR "PREJUDICE AND STEREOTYPES"

1. Members of a group often have different perceptions of the characteristics of that group from those held by outsiders. What is your own image of the racial, national, religious, and social groups to which you belong? How do nonmembers view these groups? Write an essay in which you compare the two images and attempt to account for the differences.

2. Write an essay in which you compare and/or contrast the discussions of prejudice and language by Allport and Hayakawa.

3. Since the early 1960s black Americans have sought a self-identifying label for themselves. After suffering for years under the labels *nigger, colored,* and *Negro* imposed by the dominant white society, they have experimented with such labels as *Afro-American, black,* and *people of color.* Write an essay in which you trace the shifts that have taken place and construct a reasonable linguistic explanation for these shifts.

4. Write an essay in which you discuss what your name means to you. Some questions you might consider include: How did your parents decide on your name? How do you like your name? What does your name mean? How do others respond to your name? Are there any stereotypes associated with your first name? Are there any racial or ethnic stereotypes associated with your last name?

5. Show-business people often change their names. Here are the professional names and the original names of a number of celebrities.

Professional Name	Original Name
Tony Curtis	Bernard Schwartz
Mick Jagger	Michael Philip
Simone Signoret	Simone Kaminker
Roy Rogers	Leonard Slye
Raquel Welch	Raquel Tejada
James Garner	James Bumgarner
Bob Dylan	Robert Zimmerman
Doris Day	Doris von Kappelhoff
Fred Astaire	Frederick Austerlitz
John Wayne	Marion Michael Morrison
Cyd Charisse	Tula Finklea
Anne Bancroft	Annemaria Italiano
Michael Caine	Maurice J. Micklewhite

David Bowie	David Jones
Redd Foxx	John Elroy Sanford
Ringo Starr	Richard Starkey
Elizabeth Arden	Florence Nightingale Graham

Write an essay in which you speculate about the reasons for these name changes. Why, do you think, such changes are less common among younger performers?

6. CBS news commentator Charles Osgood once wrote, "To hate somebody, to hate them enough to kill them, you must first dehumanize them in your mind. . . . That is why racial and religious epithets are so evil. To call somebody a nigger or a kike or a spic or wop is to rob a human being of his humanity. It is a form of hate, a form of murder." Write an essay in which you discuss the dehumanizing effects of racial, ethnic, and religious labels.

7. The following news item appeared in the Burlington (Vt.) *Free Press* on June 4, 1977:

'NIGGER' CAN BE ERASED IN MAINE

AUGUSTA, Maine (AP)—Names such as Nigger Hill and Nigger Island could be erased from the Maine map under a new law approved Friday by Gov. James B. Longley.

Longley signed a measure into law which allows people to complain to the Maine Human Rights Commission when they feel that the use of the term "nigger" in the name of a geographic site is offensive.

About 10 geographic features in Maine—hills, brooks and islands—include the term.

Rep. Gerald Talbot, D-Portland, the state's only black lawmaker, introduced the bill after he said he tried in vain to have the names changed by other means.

His measure originally called for banning the use of any name which is offensive to a nationality or racial group, but lawmakers amended the bill when they said it was too broad.

They said the original plan could have been extended to include terms such as "squaw."

The law will take effect in the fall.

In an essay discuss whether this is an example of censorship or a sincere attempt to eradicate prejudice. In your opinion, was the law as originally proposed "too broad"? Why, or why not?

8. Almost every area of the country has its share of racial or ethnic slurs. What slurs are used in your area? Have you ever been the object of a racial, ethnic, or religious slur? How did it feel? In an essay, discuss how a group (of which you are a member) perceives itself in a way that differs from how outsiders perceive it.

PART VI

Sexism and Language

. . . And I resent being referred to as a stubborn and tiresome freshman. I'm a <u>first-year student</u>, *thank you!*

SEXISM IN ENGLISH: A 1990s UPDATE

Alleen Pace Nilsen

Twenty years ago, Alleen Pace Nilsen, an English professor and assistant vice-president for academic affairs at Arizona State University, began a card catalog of sexist language. What began as a study of language grew into a commitment to social change. Twenty years later, Nilsen concludes that sexism will not disappear from our language until it is erased from our minds.

Twenty years ago I embarked on a study of the sexism inherent in American English. I had just returned to Ann Arbor, Michigan, after living for two years (1967–69) in Kabul, Afghanistan, where I had begun to look critically at the role society assigned to women. The Afghan version of the *chaderi* prescribed for Moslem women was particularly confining. Afghan jokes and folklore were blatantly sexist, such as this proverb: "If you see an old man, sit down and take a lesson; if you see an old woman, throw a stone."

But it wasn't only the native culture that made me question women's roles, it was also the American community.

Most of the American women were like myself—wives and mothers whose husbands were either career diplomats, employees of USAID, or college professors who had been recruited to work on various contract teams. We were suddenly bereft of our traditional roles: some of us became alcoholics, others got very good at bridge, while still others searched desperately for ways to contribute either to our families or to the Afghans. The local economy provided few jobs for women and certainly none for foreigners; we were isolated from former friends and the social goals we had grown up with.

When I returned in the fall of 1969 to the University of Michigan in Ann Arbor, I was surprised to find that many other women were also questioning the expectations they had grown up with. In the spring of 1970, a women's conference was announced. I hired a babysitter and attended, but I returned home more troubled than ever. The militancy of these women frightened me. Since I wasn't ready for a revolution, I decided I would have my own feminist movement. I would study the English language and see what it could tell me about sexism. I started reading a desk dictionary and making notecards on every entry that seemed to tell something about male and female. I soon had a dog-eared dictionary, along with a collection of note cards filling two shoe boxes.

Ironically, I started reading the dictionary because I wanted to avoid   5
getting involved in social issues, but what happened was that my notecards brought me right back to looking at society. Language and society are as intertwined as a chicken and an egg. The language a culture uses is telltale evidence of the values and beliefs of that culture. And because there is a lag in how fast a language changes—new words can easily be introduced, but it takes a long time for old words and usages to disappear—a careful look at English will reveal the attitudes that our ancestors held and that we as a culture are therefore predisposed to hold. My notecards revealed three main points. Friends have offered the opinion that I didn't need to read the dictionary to learn such obvious facts. Nevertheless, it was interesting to have linguistic evidence of sociological observations.

WOMEN ARE SEXY; MEN ARE SUCCESSFUL

First, in American culture a woman is valued for the attractiveness and   6
sexiness of her body, while a man is valued for his physical strength and accomplishments. A woman is sexy. A man is successful.

A persuasive piece of evidence supporting this view are the eponyms—   7
words that have come from someone's name—found in English. I had a two-and-a-half-inch stack of cards taken from men's names but less than a half-inch stack from women's names, and most of those came from Greek mythology. In the words that came into American English since we separated from Britain, there are many eponyms based on the names of famous American men: *Bartlett pear, boysenberry, diesel engine, Franklin stove, Ferris wheel, Gatling gun, mason jar, sideburns, sousaphone, Schick test,* and *Winchester rifle.* The only common eponyms taken from American women's names are *Alice blue* (after Alice Roosevelt Longworth), *bloomers* (after Amelia Jenks Bloomer), and *Mae West jacket* (after the buxom actress). Two out of the three feminine eponyms relate closely to a woman's physical anatomy, while the masculine eponyms (except for *sideburns* after General Burnsides) have nothing to do with the namesake's body but, instead, honor the man for an accomplishment of some kind.

Although in Greek mythology women played a bigger role than they   8
did in the biblical stories of the Judeo-Christian cultures and so the names of goddesses are accepted parts of the language in such place names as

Pomona from the goddess of fruit and Athens from Athena and in such common words as *cereal* from Ceres, *psychology* from Psyche, and *arachnoid* from Arachne, the same tendency to think of women in relation to sexuality is seen in the eponyms *aphrodisiac* from Aphrodite, the Greek name for the goddess of love and beauty, and *veneral disease* from Venue, the Roman name for Aphrodite.

Another interesting word from Greek mythology is *Amazon*. According-   9
ing to Greek folk etymology, the *a* means "without" as in *atypical* or *amoral,* while *mazon* comes from *mazos* meaning "breast" as still seen in *mastectomy.* In the Greek legend, Amazon women cut off their right breasts so that they could better shoot their bows. Apparently, the story-tellers had a feeling that for women to play the active, "masculine" role the Amazons adopted for themselves, they had to trade in part of their femininity.

This preoccupation with women's breasts is not limited to ancient   10
stories. As a volunteer for the University of Wisconsin's *Dictionary of American Regional English (DARE)*, I read a western trapper's diary from the 1930s. I was to make notes of any unusual usages or language patterns. My most interesting finding was that the trapper referred to a range of mountains as *The Teats,* a metaphor based on the similarity between the shapes of the mountains and women's breasts. Because today we use the French wording, *The Grand Tetons,* the metaphor isn't as obvious, but I wrote to mapmakers and found the following listings: *Nippletop* and *Little Nipple Top* near Mount Marcy in the Adirondacks; *Nipple Mountain* in Archuleta County, Colorado; *Nipple Peak* in Coke County, Texas; *Nipple Butte* in Pennington, South Dakota; *Squaw Peak* in Placer County, Cali-fornia (and many other locations); *Maiden's Peak* and *Squaw Tit* (they're the same mountain) in the Cascade Range in Oregon; *Mary's Nipple* near Salt Lake City, Utah; and *Jane Russell Peaks* near Stark, New Hampshire.

Except for the movie star Jane Russell, the women being referred to are   11
anonymous—it's only a sexual part of their body that is mentioned. When topographical features are named after men, it's probably not going to be to draw attention to a sexual part of their bodies but instead to honor individuals for an accomplishment. For example, no one thinks of a part of the male body when hearing a reference to Pike's Peak, Colorado, or Jackson Hole, Wyoming.

Going back to what I learned from my dictionary cards, I was surprised   12
to realize how many pairs of words we have in which the feminine word has acquired sexual connotations while the masculine word retains a seri-ous businesslike aura. For example, a *callboy* is the person who calls actors when it is time for them to go on stage, but a *callgirl* is a prostitute. Compare *sir* and *madam. Sir* is a term of respect, while *madam* has acquired the specialized meaning of a brothel manager. Something similar

has happened to *master* and *mistress*. Would you rather have a painting by an *old master* or an *old mistress?*

It's because the word *woman* had sexual connotations, as in "She's   13
his woman," that people began avoiding its use, hence such terminology as *ladies' room, lady of the house,* and *girls' school* or *school for young ladies.* Feminists, who ask that people use the term *woman* rather than *girl* or *lady,* are rejecting the idea that *woman* is primarily a sexual term. They have been at least partially successful in that today *woman* is commonly used to communicate gender without intending implications about sexuality.

I found two hundred pairs of words with masculine and feminine forms,   14
e.g., *heir-heiress, hero-heroine, steward-stewardess, usher-usherette.* In nearly all such pairs, the masculine word is considered the base, with some kind of a feminine suffix being added. The masculine form is the one from which compounds are made, e.g., from *king-queen* comes *kingdom* but not *queendom,* from *sportsman-sportslady* comes *sportsmanship* but not *sportsladyship.* There is one—and only one—semantic area in which the masculine word is not the base or more powerful word. This is in the area dealing with sex and marriage. When someone refers to a *virgin,* a listener will probably think of a female, unless the speaker specifies *male* or uses a masculine pronoun. The same is true for *prostitute.*

In relation to marriage, there is much linguistic evidence showing that   15
weddings are more important to women than to men. A woman cherishes the wedding and is considered a bride for a whole year, but a man is referred to as a groom only on the day of the wedding. The word *bride* appears in *bridal attendant, bridal gown, bridesmaid, bridal shower,* and even *bridegroom. Groom* comes from the Middle English *grom,* meaning "man," and in the sense is seldom used outside of the wedding. With most pairs of male/female words, people habitually put the masculine word first, *Mr. and Mrs., his and hers, boys and girls, men and women, kings and queens, brothers and sisters, guys and dolls,* and *host and hostess,* but it is the *bride and groom* who are talked about, not the *groom and bride.*

The importance of marriage to a woman is also shown by the fact that   16
when a marriage ends in death, the woman gets the title of *widow.* A man gets the derived title of *widower.* This term is not used in other phrases or contexts, but *widow* is seen in *widowhood, widow's peak,* and *widow's walk.* A *widow* in a card game is an extra hand of cards, while in typesetting it is an extra line of type.

How changing cultural ideas bring changes to language is clearly vis-   17
ible in this semantic area. The feminist movement has caused the differences between the sexes to be downplayed, and since I did my dictionary study two decades ago, the word *singles* has largely replaced such sex specific and value-laden terms as *bachelor, old maid, spinster, divorcee,*

widow, and *widower.* And in 1970 I wrote that when a man is called *a professional* he is thought to be a doctor or a lawyer, but when people hear a woman referred to as *a professional* they are likely to think of a prostitute. That's not as true today because so many women have become doctors and lawyers that it's no longer incongruous to think of women in those professional roles.

Another change that has taken place is in wedding announcements. They used to be sent out from the bride's parents and did not even give the name of the groom's parents. Today, most couples choose to list either all or none of the parents' names. Also it is now much more likely that both the bride and groom's picture will be in the newspaper, while a decade ago only the bride's picture was published on the "Women's" or the "Society" page. Even the traditional wording of the wedding ceremony is being changed. Many officials now pronounce the couple "husband and wife" instead of the old "man and wife," and they ask the bride if she promises "to love, honor, and cherish," instead of "to love, honor, and obey." **18**

WOMEN ARE PASSIVE; MEN ARE ACTIVE

The wording of the wedding ceremony also relates to the second point that my cards showed, which is that women are expected to play a passive or weak role while men play an active or strong role. In the traditional ceremony, the official asks, "Who gives the bride away?" and the father answers, "I do." Some fathers answer, "Her mother and I do," but that doesn't solve the problem inherent in the question. The idea that a bride is something to be handed over from one man to another bothers people because it goes back to the days when a man's servants, his children, and his wife were all considered to be his property. They were known by his name because they belonged to him, and he was responsible for their actions and their debts. **19**

The grammar used in talking or writing about weddings as well as other sexual relationships shows the expectation of men playing the active role. Men *wed* women while women *become* brides of men. A man *possesses* a woman; he *deflowers* her; he *performs;* he *scores;* he *takes away* her virginity. Although a woman can *seduce* a man, she cannot offer him her virginity. When talking about virginity, the only way to make the woman the actor in the sentence is to say that "She lost her virginity," but people lose things by accident rather than by purposeful actions, and so she's only the grammatical, not the real-life, actor. **20**

The reason that women tried to bring the term *Ms.* into the language to replace *Miss* and *Mrs.* relates to this point. Married women resent being identified only under their husband's names. For example, when Susan **21**

Glascoe did something newsworthy, she would be identified in the news-paper only as Mrs. John Glascoe. The dictionary cards showed what ap-peared to be an attitude on the part of the editors that it was almost indecent to let a respectable woman's name march unaccompanied across the pages of a dictionary. Women were listed with male names whether or not the male contributed to the woman's reason for being in the dictionary or in his own right was as famous as the woman. For example, Charlotte Brontë was identified as Mrs. Arthur B. Nicholls, Amelia Earhart as Mrs. George Palmer Putnam, Helen Hayes as Mrs. Charles MacArthur, Jenny Lind as Mme. Otto Goldschmit, Cornelia Otis Skinner as the daughter of Otis, Harriet Beecher Stowe as the sister of Henry Ward Beecher, and Edith Sitwell as the sister of Osbert and Sacheverell. A very small number of women got into the dictionary without the benefit of a masculine escort. They were rebels and crusaders: temperance leaders Frances Elizabeth Caroline Willard and Carry Nation, women's rights leaders Carrie Chap-man Catt and Elizabeth Cady Stanton, birth control educator Margaret Sanger, religious leader Mary Baker Eddy, and slaves Harriet Tubman and Phillis Wheatley.

Etiquette books used to teach that if a woman had *Mrs.* in front of her name, then the husband's name should follow because *Mrs.* is an abbre-viated form of *Mistress* and a woman couldn't be a mistress of herself. As with many arguments about "correct" language usage, this isn't very logical because *Miss* is also an abbreviation of *Mistress.* Feminists hoped to simplify matters by introducing *Ms.* as an alternative to both *Mrs.* and *Miss,* but what happened is that *Ms.* largely replaced *Miss,* to became a catch-all business title for women. Many married women still prefer the title *Mrs.,* and some resent being addressed with the term *Ms.* As one frustrated newspaper reporter complained, "Before I can write about a woman, I have to know not only her marital status but also her political philosophy." The result of such complications may contribute to the de-mise of titles, which are already being ignored by many computer pro-grammers who find it more efficient to simply use names, for example in a business letter: "Dear Joan Garcia," instead of "Dear Mrs. Joan Gar-cia," "Dear Ms. Garcia," or "Dear Mrs. Louis Garcia." 22

The titles given to royalty provide an example of how males can be disadvantaged by the assumption that they are always to play the more powerful role. In British royalty, when a male holds a title, his wife is automatically given the feminine equivalent. But the reverse is not true. For example, a *count* is a high political officer with a *countess* being his wife. The same is true for a *duke* and a *duchess* and a *king* and a *queen.* But when a female holds the royal title, the man she marries does not automatically acquire the matching title. For example, Queen Elizabeth's husband has the title of *prince* rather than *king,* but if Prince Charles should 23 become king while he is still married to Lady or Princess Diana, she will be known as the queen. The reasoning appears to be that since masculine words are stronger, they are reserved for true heirs and withheld from males coming into the royal family by marriage. If Prince Phillip were called *King Phillip,* it would be much easier for British subjects to forget where the true power lies.

The names that people give their children show the hopes and dreams   24
they have for them, and when we look at the differences between male and female names in a culture, we can see the cumulative expectations of that culture. In our culture girls often have names taken from small, aesthetically pleasing items, e.g., *Ruby, Jewel,* and *Pearl. Esther* and *Stella* mean "star," *Ada* means "ornament," and *Vanessa* means "butterfly." Boys are more likely to be given names with meanings of power and strength, e.g., *Neil* means "champion," *Martin* is from Mars, the God of War, *Raymond* means "wise protection," *Harold* means "chief of the army," *Ira* means "vigilant," *Rex* means "king," and *Richard* means "strong king."

We see similar differences in food metaphors. Food is a passive sub-   25
stance just sitting there waiting to be eaten. Many people have recognized this and so no longer feel comfortable describing women as "delectable morsels." However, when I was a teenager, it was considered a compliment to refer to a girl (we didn't call anyone a *woman* until she was middle-aged) as a *cute tomato,* a *peach,* a *dish,* a *cookie, honey, sugar,* or *sweetie-pie.* When being affectionate, women will occasionally call a man *honey* or *sweetie,* but in general, food metaphors are used much less often with men than with women. If a man is called *a fruit,* his masculinity is being questioned. But it's perfectly acceptable to use a food metaphor if the food is heavier and more substantive than that used for women. For example pin-up pictures of women have long been known as *cheesecake,* but when Burt Reynolds posed for a nude centerfold the picture was immediately dubbed *beefcake,* c.f., *a hunk of meat.* That such sexual references to men have come into the language is another reflection of how society is beginning to lessen the differences between their attitudes toward men and women.

Something similar to the *fruit* metaphor happens with references to   26
plants. We insult a man by calling him a *pansy,* but it wasn't considered particularly insulting to talk about a girl being a *wallflower,* a *clinging vine,* or a *shrinking violent,* or to give girls such names as *Ivy, Rose, Lily, Iris, Daisy, Camellia, Heather,* and *Flora.* A plant metaphor can be used with a man if the plant is big and strong, for example, Andrew Jackson's nickname of *Old Hickory.* Also, the phrases *blooming idiots* and *budding geniuses* can be used with either sex, but notice how they are based on the most active thing a plant can do which is to bloom or bud.

Animal metaphors also illustrate the different expectations for males   27
and females. Men are referred to as *studs, bucks,* and *wolves* while women
are referred to with such metaphors as *kitten, bunny, beaver, bird, chick,*
and *lamb.* In the 1950s we said that boys went *tomcatting,* but today it's
just *catting around* and both boys and girls do it. When the term *foxy,*
meaning that someone was sexy, first became popular it was used only for
girls, but now someone of either sex can be described as *a fox.* Some
animal metaphors that are used predominantly with men have negative
connotations based on the size and/or strength of the animals, e.g., *beast,*
bullheaded, jackass, rat, loanshark, and *vulture.* Negative metaphors used
with women are based on smaller animals, e.g., *social butterfly, mousy,*
catty, and *vixen.* The feminine terms connote action, but not the same kind
of large scale action as with the masculine terms.

WOMEN ARE CONNECTED WITH NEGATIVE
CONNOTATIONS; MEN WITH POSITIVE CONNOTATIONS

The final point that my notecards illustrated was how many positive con-   28
notations are associated with the concept of masculine, while there are
either trivial or negative connotations connected with the corresponding
feminine concept. An example from the animal metaphors makes a good
illustration. The word *shrew* taken from the name of a small but especially
vicious animal was defined in my dictionary as "an ill-tempered scolding
woman," but the word *shrewd* taken from the same root was defined as
"marked by clever, discerning awareness" and was illustrated with the
phrase "a shrewd businessman."

Early in life, children are conditioned to the superiority of the mascu-   29
line role. As child psychologists point out, little girls have much more
freedom to experiment with sex roles than do little boys. If a little girl acts
like a *tomboy,* most parents have mixed feelings, being at least partially
proud. But if their little boy acts like a *sissy* (derived from *sister*), they call
a psychologist. It's perfectly acceptable for a little girl to sleep in the crib
that was purchased for her brother, to wear his hand-me-down jeans and
shirts, and to ride the bicycle that he has outgrown. But few parents would
put a boy baby in a white and gold crib decorated with frills and lace, and
virtually no parents would have their little boys wear his sister's hand-
me-down dresses, nor would they have their son ride a girl's pink bicycle
with a flower-bedecked basket. The proper names given to girls and boys
show this same attitude. Girls can have "boy" names—*Cris, Craig, Jo,*
Kelly, Shawn, Teri, Toni, and *Sam*—but it doesn't work the other way
around. A couple of generations ago, *Beverley, Frances, Hazel, Marion,*
and *Shirley* were common boys' names. As parents gave these names to

more and more girls, they fell into disuse for males, and some older men who have these names prefer to go by their initials or by such abbreviated forms as *Haze* or *Shirl.*

When a little girl is told to *be a lady,* she is being told to sit with her 30 knees together and to be quiet and dainty. But when a little boy is told to *be a man* he is being told to be noble, strong, and virtuous—to have all the qualities that the speaker looks on as desirable. The concept of manliness has such positive connotations that it used to be a compliment to call someone a *he-man,* to say that he was doubly a man. Today many people are more ambivalent about this term and respond to it much as they do to the word *macho.* But calling someone a *manly man* or a *virile man* is nearly always meant as a compliment. *Virile* comes from the Indo-European *vir* meaning "man," which is also the basis of *virtuous.* Contrast the positive connotations of both *virile* and *virtuous* with the negative connotations of *hysterical.* The Greeks took this latter word from their name for *uterus* (as still seen in *hysterectomy*). They thought that women were the only ones who experienced uncontrolled emotional outbursts, and so the condition must have something to do with a part of the body that only women have.

Differences in the connotations between positive male and negative 31 female connotations can be seen in several pairs of words that differ denotatively only in the matter of sex. *Bachelor* as compared to *spinster* or *old maid* has such positive connotations that women try to adopt them by using the term *bachelor-girl* or *bachelorette. Old maid* is so negative that it's the basis for metaphors: pretentious and fussy old men are called *old maids,* as are the leftover kernels of unpopped popcorn, and the last card in a popular children's game.

Patron and *matron* (Middle English for *father* and *mother*) have such 32 different levels of prestige that women try to borrow the more positive masculine connotations with the word *patroness,* literally "female father." Such a peculiar term came about because of the high prestige attached to *patron* in such phrases as *a patron of the arts* or *a patron saint. Matron* is more apt to be used in talking about a woman in charge of a jail or a public restroom.

When men are doing jobs that women often do, we apparently try to 33 pay the men extra by giving them fancy titles, for example, a male cook is more likely to be called a *chef* while a male seamstress will get the title of *tailor.* The armed forces have a special problem in that they recruit under such slogans as "The Marine Corps builds men!" and "Join the Army! Become a Man." Once the recruits are enlisted, they find themselves doing much of the work that has been traditionally thought of as "women's work." The solution to getting the work done and not insulting anyone's masculinity was to change the titles as shown below:

waitress	orderly
nurse	medic or corpsman
secretary	clerk-typist
assistant	adjutant
dishwasher or kitchen helper	KP (kitchen police)

Compare *brave* and *squaw*. Early settlers in America truly admired   34
Indian men and hence named them with a word that carried connotations
of youth, vigor, and courage. But they used the Algonquin's name for
"woman" and over the years it developed almost opposite connotations to
those of *brave*. *Wizard* and *witch* contrast almost as much. The masculine
wizard implies skill and wisdom combined with magic, while the feminine
witch implies evil intentions combined with magic. Part of the unattrac-
tiveness of both *witch* and *squaw* is that they have been used so often to
refer to old women, something with which our culture is particularly uncomfortable, just as the Afghans were. Imagine my surprise when I ran
across the phrases *grandfatherly advice* and *old wives' tales* and realized
that the underlying implication is the same as the Afghan proverb about old
men being worth listening to while old women talk only foolishness.

Other terms that show how negative we view old women as compared   35
to young women are *old nag* as compared to *filly, old crow* or *old bat* as
compared to *bird,* and of being *catty* as compared to being *kittenish.* There
is no matching set of metaphors for men. The chicken metaphor tells the
whole story of a woman's life. In her youth she is a *chick.* Then she
marries and begins *feathering her nest.* Soon she begins feeling *cooped up,*
so she goes to *hen parties* where she *cackles* with her friends. Then she has
her *brood,* begins to *henpeck* her husband, and finally turns into an *old
biddy.*

I embarked on my study of the dictionary not with the intention of   36
prescribing language change but simply to see what the language would tell
me about sexism. Nevertheless I have been both surprised and pleased as
I've watched the changes that have occurred over the past two decades. I'm
one of those linguists who believes that new language customs will cause
a new generation of speakers to grow up with different expectations. This
is why I'm happy about people's efforts to use inclusive language, to say
he or she or *they* when speaking about individuals whose names they do
not know. I'm glad that leading publishers have developed guidelines to
help writers use language that is fair to both sexes, and I'm glad that most
newspapers and magazines list women by their own names instead of only
by their husbands' names and that educated and thoughtful people no
longer begin their business letters with "Dear Sir" or "Gentlemen," but
instead use a memo form or begin with such salutations as "Dear Colleagues," "Dear Reader," or "Dear Committee Members." I'm also glad

that such words as *poetess, authoress, conductress,* and *aviatrix* now sound quaint and old-fashioned and that *chairman* is giving way to *chair* or *head, mailman* to *mail carrier, clergyman* to *clergy,* and *stewardess* to *flight attendant.* I was also pleased when the National Oceanic and Atmospheric Administration bowed to feminist complaints and in the late 1970s began to alternate men's and women's names for hurricanes. However, I wasn't so pleased to discover that the change did not immediately erase sexist thoughts from everyone's mind, as shown by a headline about Hurricane David in a 1979 New York tabloid, "David Rapes Virgin Islands." More recently a similar metaphor appeared in a headline in the *Arizona Republic* about Hurricane Charlie, "Charlie Quits Carolinas, Flirts with Virginia."

What these incidents show is that sexism is not something existing   37 independently in American English or in the particular dictionary that I happened to read. Rather, it exists in people's minds. Language is like an X ray in providing visible evidence of invisible thoughts. The best thing about people being interested in and discussing sexist language is that as they make conscious decisions about what pronouns they will use, what jokes they will tell or laugh at, how they will write their names, or how they will begin their letters, they are forced to think about the underlying issue of sexism. This is good because as a problem that begins in people's assumptions and expectations, it's a problem that will be solved only when a great many people have given it a great deal of thought.

QUESTIONS ON CONTENT

1. What precipitated Nilsen's investigation of sexism in the English language? How did her private "feminist movement" differ from the feminist movement of others? Why was she unable to avoid facing social issues head on?

2. What point does Nilsen make about each of the following:

   a. English words derived from the name of a person
   b. geographical names
   c. pairs of words, one masculine and the other feminine
   d. the use of words referring to foods, plants, and animals in connection with women
   e. the first names given to male and female infants
   f. the use of *Ms.*
   g. dictionary entries concerning famous women
   h. positive and negative connotations connected with the concepts "masculine" and "feminine."

3. Most dictionary makers try to describe accurately the ways in which speakers of English use the language. Can we, therefore, reasonably fault them for reflecting cultural attitudes in word definitions?

4. According to Nilsen, in what two areas does the English language reveal the importance of women?

5. Nilsen states she has seen many changes in the language since she began her study twenty years ago. List these changes and discuss what Nilsen says they reveal to her about the nature of sexist language. In what ways, for example, has the pronoun *Ms.* proven unsatisfactory?

QUESTIONS ON RHETORIC

1. What techniques does Nilsen use to support her conclusions? Is her evidence convincing? Why, or why not? (Glossary: *Examples*)

2. How has Nilsen organized her essay? (Glossary: *Organization*) You may find it helpful to make a scratch outline of her main ideas.

3. What is the tone of this essay? How does Nilsen maintain this tone? Is her tone appropriate for her subject and audience? (Glossary: *Tone*)

4. In essays of substantial length such as this one, short transitional paragraphs are often used to link the main sections of the essay. Identify two such paragraphs in Nilsen's article. Are they effective? When would you use a transitional paragraph? When would you avoid doing so? (Glossary: *Transition*)

5. Nilsen uses a simile in her concluding paragraph. (Glossary: *Figures of Speech*) Identify the simile and explain how it works to make Nilsen's point. Did you like it? Why, or why not?

VOCABULARY

inherent (1)	semantic (14)	ambivalent (30)
eponyms (7)	temperance (21)	quaint (36)
gender (13)	trivial (28)	

WRITING TOPICS

1. Nilsen provides us with an extensive catalogue of words that reveal a disparaging attitude toward women. It is not her purpose, however, to offer any solutions to the problem of bias in the language. Write an essay in which you discuss the possible improvements that you as a user of the language, lexicographers as makers of dictionaries, and women and men as leaders of the equal rights movement can bring about.

2. Like any attempt to change the status quo, women's attempts to change language have aroused a great deal of opposition. Who is the opposition? To what do they seem to be reacting? Does the opposition seem justified in any of its objections? What techniques does the opposition employ?

REAL MEN DON'T: ANTI-MALE BIAS IN ENGLISH

Eugene R. August

Bias against women is not the only form of sexist language evident in English according to Eugene R. August, an English professor at the University of Dayton. Men are also the victims of insulting and dehumanizing language. In this essay and in this book, Men's Studies: A Selected and Annotated Interdisciplinary Bibliography, *August challenges us to examine English with fresh insights in order to purge it of all sexist language—anti-male as well as anti-female.*

Despite numerous studies of sex bias in language during the past fifteen years, only rarely has anti-male bias been examined. In part, this neglect occurs because many of these studies have been based upon assumptions which are questionable at best and which at worst exhibit their own form of sex bias. Whether explicitly or implicitly many of these studies reduce human history to a tale of male oppressors and female victims or rebels. In this view of things, all societies become *patriarchal societies,* a familiar term used to suggest that for centuries males have conspired to exploit and demean females. Accordingly, it is alleged in many of these studies that men control language and that they use it to define women and women's roles as inferior.

Despite the popularity of such a view, it has received scant support from leading social scientists, including one of the giants of modern anthropology, Margaret Mead. Anticipating current ideology, Mead in *Male and Female* firmly rejected the notion of a "male conspiracy to keep women in their place," arguing instead that

> the historical trend that listed women among the abused minorities . . . lingers on to obscure the issue and gives apparent point to the contention that this is a man-made world in which women have always been abused and must always fight for their rights.
>
> It takes considerable effort on the part of both men and women to reorient

ourselves to thinking—when we think basically—that this is a world not made
by men alone, in which women are unwilling and helpless dupes and fools or
else powerful schemers hiding their power under their ruffled petticoats, but a
world made by mankind for human beings of both sexes. (298, 299–300)

The model described by Mead and other social scientists shows a world in
which women and men have lived together throughout history in a symbiotic relationship, often mutually agreeing upon the definition of gender
roles and the distribution of various powers and duties.

More importantly for the subject of bias in speech and writing,   3
women—as well as men—have shaped language. As Walter J. Ong reminds us,

Women talk and think as much as men do, and with few exceptions we all . . .
learn to talk and think in the first instance largely from women, usually and
predominantly our mothers. Our first tongue is called our "mother tongue" in
English and in many other languages. . . . There are no father tongues. . . .
(36)

Feminists like Dorothy Dinnerstein agree: "There seems no reason to
doubt that the baby-tending sex contributed at least equally with the history-
making one to the most fundamental of all human inventions: language"
(22). Because gender roles and language are shaped by society in general—
that is, by both men and women—anti-male bias in language is as possible
as anti-female bias.

To say this, however, is emphatically not to blame women alone, or   4
even primarily, for anti-male usage. If guilt must be assigned, it would
have to be placed upon sexist people, both male and female, who use
language to manipulate gender role behavior and to create negative social
attitudes towards males. But often it is difficult to point a finger of blame:
except where prejudiced gender stereotypes are deliberately fostered, most
people evidently use sex-biased terminology without clearly understanding
its import. In the long run, it is wiser to concentrate not on fixing blame,
but on heightening public awareness of anti-male language and on discouraging its use. In particular, teachers and writers need to become aware
of and to question language which denigrates or stereotypes males.

In modern English, three kinds of anti-male usage are evident: first,   5
gender-exclusive language which omits males from certain kinds of consideration; second, gender-restrictive language which attempts to restrict
males to an accepted gender role, some aspects of which may be outmoded, burdensome, or destructive; and third, negative stereotypes of
males which are insulting, dehumanizing, and potentially dangerous.

Although gender-exclusive language which excludes females has often   6
been studied, few students of language have noted usage which excludes
males. Those academics, for example, who have protested *alumnus* and

alumni as gender-exclusive terms to describe a university's male and female graduates have failed to notice that, by the same logic, *alma mater* (nourishing mother) is an equally gender-exclusive term to describe the university itself. Those who have protested *man* and *mankind* as generic terms have not begun to question *mammal* as a term of biological classification, but by categorizing animals according to the female's ability to suckle the young through her mammary glands, *mammal* clearly omits the male of the species. Consequently, it is as suspect as generic *man*.

In general, gender-exclusive usage in English excludes males as parents and as victims. Until recently, the equating of *mother* with *parent* in the social sciences was notorious: a major sociological study published in 1958 with the title *The Changing American Parent* was based upon interviews with 582 mothers and no fathers (Roman and Haddad 87). Although no longer prevalent in the social sciences, the interchangeability of *mother* and *parent* is still common, except for *noncustodial parent* which is almost always a synonym for *father*. A recent ad for *Parents* magazine begins: "To be the best mother you can be, you want practical, reliable answers to the questions a mother must face." Despite the large number of men now seen pushing shopping carts, advertisers still insist that "Choosy mothers choose Jif" and "My Mom's a Butternut Mom." Frequently, children are regarded as belonging solely to the mother, as in phrases like *women and their children*. The idea of the mother as primary parent can be glimpsed in such expressions as *mother tongue, mother wit, mother lode, mother of invention,* and *mothering* as a synonym for *parenting*.

The male as victim is ignored in such familiar expressions as *innocent women and children*. In June 1985, when President Reagan rejected a bombing strike to counter terrorist activities, newspapers reported that the decision had been made to prevent "the deaths of many innocent women and children in strife-torn Lebanon" (Glass). Presumably, strife-torn Lebanon contained no innocent men. Likewise, *rape victim* means females only, an assumption made explicit in the opening sentences of this newspaper article on rape: "Crime knows no gender. Yet, there is one offense that only women are prey to: rape" (Mougey). The thousands of males raped annually, in addition to the sexual assaults regularly inflicted upon males in prison, are here entirely overlooked. (That these males have been victimized mostly by other males does not disqualify them as victims of sexual violence, as some people assume.) Similarly, the term *wife and child abuse* conceals the existence of an estimated 282,000 husbands who are battered annually (O'Reilly et al. 23). According to many expressions in English, males are not parents and they are never victimized.

Unlike gender-exclusive language, gender-restrictive language is usually applied to males only, often to keep them within the confines of a socially prescribed gender role. When considering gender-restrictive language, one must keep in mind that—as Ruth E. Hartley has pointed out—the masculine gender role is enforced earlier and more harshly than the feminine role in (235). In addition, because the boy is often raised primarily by females in the virtual absence of close adult males, his grasp of what is required of him to *be a man* is often unsure. Likewise, prescriptions for male behavior are usually given in the negative, leading to the "Real Men Don't" syndrome, a process which further confuses the boy. Such circumstances leave many males extremely vulnerable to language which questions their sense of masculinity.

Furthermore, during the past twenty years an increasing number of men   10
and women have been arguing that aspects of our society's masculine gender role are emotionally constrictive, unnecessarily stressful, and potentially lethal. Rejecting "the myth of masculine privilege," psychologist Herb Goldberg reports in *The Hazards of Being Male* that "every critical statistic in the area of [early death], disease, suicide, crime, accidents, childhood emotional disorders, alcoholism, and drug addiction shows a disproportionately higher male rate" (5). But changes in the masculine role are so disturbing to so many people that the male who attempts to break out of familiar gender patterns often finds himself facing hostile opposition which can be readily and powerfully expressed in a formidable array of sex-biased terms.

To see how the process works, let us begin early in the male life cycle.   11
A boy quickly learns that, while it is usually acceptable for girls to be *tomboys,* God forbid that he should be a *sissy.* In *Sexual Signatures: On Being a Man or a Woman* John Money and Patricia Tucker note:

> The current feminine stereotype in our culture is flexible enough to let a girl behave "boyishly" if she wants to without bringing her femininity into question, but any boy who exhibits "girlish" behavior is promptly suspected of being queer. There isn't even a word corresponding to "tomboy" to describe such a boy. "Sissy" perhaps comes closest, or "artistic" and "sensitive," but unlike "tomboy," such terms are burdened with unfavorable connotations. (72)

Lacking a favorable or even neutral term to describe the boy who is quiet, gentle, and emotional, the English language has long had a rich vocabulary to insult and ridicule such boys—*mamma's boy, mollycoddle, milksop, muff, twit, softy, creampuff, paintywaist, weenie, Miss Nancy,* and so on. Although sometimes used playfully, the currently popular *wimp* can be used to insult males from childhood right into adulthood.

Discussion of words like *sissy* as insults have been often one-sided: 12
most commentators are content to argue that the female, not the male, is being insulted by such usage. "The implicit sexism" in such terms, writes one commentator, "disparages the woman, not the man" (Sorrels 87).

Although the female is being slurred indirectly by these terms, a moment's reflection will show that the primary force of the insult is being directed against the male, specifically the male who cannot differentiate himself from the feminine. Ong argues in *Fighting for Life* that most societies place heavy pressure on males to differentiate themselves from females because the prevailing environment of human society is feminine (70–71). In English-speaking societies, terms like *sissy* and *weak sister*, which have been used by both females and males, are usually perceived not as insults to females but as ridicule of males who have allegedly failed to differentiate themselves from the feminine.

Being *all boy* carries penalties, however: for one thing, it means being   13
less lovable. As the nursery rhyme tells children, little girls are made of "sugar and spice and all that's nice," while little boys are made of "frogs and snails and puppy-dogs' tails." Or, as an American version of the rhyme puts it:

> *Girls are dandy,*
> *Made of candy—*
> *That's what little girls are made of.*
> *Boys are rotten,*
> *Made of cotton—*
> *That's what little boys are made of.*

(Baring-Gould 176n116)

When not enjoined to *be all boy,* our young lad will be urged to *be a big boy, be a brave soldier,* and (the ultimate appeal) *be a man.* These expressions almost invariably mean that the boy is about to suffer something painful or humiliating. The variant—*take it like a man*—provides the clue. As Paul Theroux defines it, *be a man* means: "Be stupid, be unfeeling, obedient and soldierly, and stop thinking."

Following our boy further into the life cycle, we discover that in school   14
he will find himself in a cruel bind: girls his age will be biologically and socially more mature than he is, at least until around age eighteen. Until then, any ineptness in his social role will be castigated by a host of terms which are reserved almost entirely for males. "For all practical purposes," John Gordon remarks, "the word 'turkey' (or whatever the equivalent is now) can be translated as 'a boy spurned by influential girls' " (141). The equivalents of *turkey* are many: *jerk, nerd, clod, klutz, schmuck, dummy, goon, dork, square, dweeb, jackass, meathead, geek, zero, reject, goofball, drip,* and numerous others, including many obscene terms. Recently, a Michigan high school decided to do away with a scheduled "Nerd Day" after a fourteen-year-old male student, who apparently had been so harassed as a nerd by other students, committed suicide (" 'Nerd' day"). In this case, the ability of language to devastate the emotionally vulnerable young male is powerfully and pathetically dramatized.

As our boy grows, he faces threats and taunts if he does not take risks   15
or endure pain to prove his manhood. *Coward,* for example, is a word
applied almost exclusively to males in our society, as are its numerous
variants—*chicken, chickenshit, yellow, yellow-bellied, lily-livered, weak-
kneed, spineless, squirrelly, fraidy cat, gutless wonder, weakling, butterfly, jellyfish,* and so on. If our young man walks away from a stupid
quarrel or prefers to settle differences more rationally than with a swift jab
to the jaw, the English language is richly supplied with these and other
expressions to call his masculinity into question.

Chief among the other expressions that question masculinity is a   16
lengthy list of homophobic terms such as *queer, pansy, fag, faggot, queen,
queeny, pervert, bugger, deviant, fairy, tinkerbell, puss, priss, flamer,
feller, sweet, precious, fruit, sodomite,* and numerous others, many obscene. For many people, *gay* is an all-purpose word of ridicule and con-
demnation. Once again, although homosexuals are being insulted by these
terms, the primary target is more often the heterosexual male who fails or
refuses to live up to someone else's idea of masculinity. In "Homophobia
Among Men" Gregory Lehne explains, "Homophobia is used as a technique of social control . . . to enforce the norms of male sex-role behavior. . . . [H]omosexuality is not the real threat, the real threat is change in
the male sex-role" (77).

Nowhere is this threat more apparent than in challenges to our society's   17
male-only military obligation. When a young man and a young woman
reach the age of eighteen, both may register to vote; only the young man
is required by law to register for military service. For the next decade at
least, he must stand ready to be called into military service and even into
combat duty in wars, "police actions," "peace-keeping missions," and
"rescue missions," often initiated by legally dubious means. Should he
resist this obligation, he may be called a *draft dodger, deserter, peacenik,
traitor, shirker, slacker, malingerer,* and similar terms. Should he declare
himself a conscientious objector, he may be labeled a *conchy* or any of the
variants of *coward.*

In his relationships with women, he will find that the age of equality   18
has not yet arrived. Usually, he will be expected to take the initiative, do
the driving, pick up the tab, and in general show a deferential respect for
women that is a leftover from the chivalric code. Should he behave in an
ungentlemanly fashion, a host of words—which are applied almost always
to males alone—can be used to tell him so: *louse, rat, creep, sleaze, scum,
stain, worm, fink, heel, stinker, animal, savage, bounder, cad, wolf, gig-
olo, womanizer, Don Juan, pig, rotter, boor,* and so on.

In sexual matters he will usually be expected to take the initiative and   19
to *perform.* If he does not, he will be labeled *impotent.* This word, writes
Goldberg, "is clearly sexist because it implies a standard of acceptable

masculine sexual performance that makes a man abnormal if he can't live up to it'' (*New Male* 248). Metaphorically, *impotent* can be used to demean any male whose efforts in any area are deemed unacceptable. Even if our young man succeeds at his sexual performance, the sex manuals are ready to warn him that if he reaches orgasm before a specified time he is guilty of *premature ejaculation.*

When our young man marries, he will be required by law and social custom to support his wife and children. Should he not succeed as bread-winner or should he relax in his efforts, the language offers numerous terms to revile him: *loser, deadbeat, bum, freeloader, leech, parasite, goldbrick, sponch, mooch, ne'er-do-well, good for nothing,* and so on. If women in our society have been regarded as sex objects, men have been regarded as success objects, that is, judged by their ability to provide a standard of living. The title of a recent book—*How to Marry a Winner*—reveals immediately that the intended audience is female (Collier). 20

When he becomes a father, our young man will discover that he is a second-class parent, as the traditional interchangeability of *mother* and *parent* indicates. The law has been particularly obtuse in recognizing fathers as parents, as evidenced by the awarding of child custody to mothers in ninety percent of divorce cases. In 1975 a father's petition for custody of his four-year-old son was denied because, as the family court judge said, ''Fathers don't make good mothers'' (qtd. in Levine 21). The judge apparently never considered whether *fathers* make good *parents.* 21

And so it goes throughtout our young man's life: if he deviates from society's gender role norm, he will be penalized and he will hear about it. 22

The final form of anti-male bias to be considered here is negative stereotyping. Sometimes this stereotyping is indirectly embedded in the language, sometimes it resides in people's assumptions about males and shapes their response to seemingly neutral words, and sometimes it is overtly created for political reasons. It is one thing to say that some aspects of the traditional masculine gender role are limiting and hurtful; it is quite another to gratuitously suspect males in general of being criminal and evil or to denounce them in wholesale fashion as oppressors, exploiters, and rapists. The *The New Male* Goldberg writes, ''Men may very well be the last remaining subgroup in our society that can be blatantly, negatively and vilely stereotyped with little objection or resistance'' (103). As our language demonstrates, such sexist stereotyping, whether unintentional or deliberate, is not only familiar but fashionable. 23

In English, crime and evil are usually attributed to the male. As an experiment I have compiled lists of nouns which I read to my composition students, asking them to check whether the words suggest ''primarily females,'' ''primarily males,'' or ''could be either.'' Nearly all the words for law-breakers suggest males rather than females to most students. These 24

words include *murderer, swindler, crook, criminal, burglar, thief, gang-
ster, mobster, hood, hitman, killer, pickpocket, mugger,* and *terrorist.*
Accounting for this phenomenon is not always easy. *Hitman* may obviously suggest "primarily males," and the *-er* in *murderer* may do the
same, especially if it reminds students of the word's feminine form, *mur-
deress.* Likewise, students may be aware that most murders are committed
by males. Other words—like *criminal* and *thief*—are more clearly
gender-neutral in form, and it is less clear why they should be so closely
linked with "primarily males." Although the dynamics of the association
may be unclear, English usage somehow conveys a subtle suggestion that
males are to be regarded as guilty in matters of law-breaking.

This hint of male guilt extends to a term like *suspect.* When the per-   25
son's gender is unknown, the suspect is usually presumed to be a male. For
example, even before a definite suspect had been identified, the perpetrator
of the 1980–1981 Atlanta child murders was popularly known as *The Man.*
When a male and female are suspected of a crime, the male is usually
presumed the guilty party. In a recent murder case, when two suspects—
Debra Brown and Alton Coleman—were apprehended, police discovered
Brown's fingerprint in a victim's car and interpreted this as evidence of
Coleman's guilt. As the Associated Press reported:

> Authorities say for the first time they have evidence linking Alton Coleman
> with the death of an Indianapolis man.
> A fingerprint found in the car of Eugene Scott has been identified as that of
> Debra Brown, Coleman's traveling companion . . ." ("Police")

Nowhere does the article suggest that Brown's fingerprint found in the
victim's car linked Brown with the death: the male suspect was presumed
the guilty party, while the female was only a "traveling companion."
Even after Brown had been convicted of two murders, the Associated Press
was still describing her as "the accused accomplice of convicted killer
Alton Coleman" ("Indiana").

In some cases, this presumption of male guilt extends to crimes in   26
which males are not the principal offenders. As noted earlier, a term like
wife and child abuse ignores battered husbands, but it does more: it suggests that males alone abuse children. In reality most child abuse is committed by mothers (Straus, Gelles, Steinmetz 71). Despite this fact, a 1978
study of child abuse bears the title *Sins of the Fathers* (Inglis).

The term *rape* creates special problems. While the majority of rapes are   27
committed by males and the number of female rape victims outdistances
the number of male rape victims, it is widely assumed—as evidenced by
the newspaper article cited above—that rape is a crime committed only by
males in which only females are victims. Consequently, the word *rape* is

often used as a brush to tar all males. In *Against Our Will* Susan Brown-miller writes: "From prehistoric times to the present, I believe, rape . . . is nothing more or less than a conscious process of intimidation by which *all men* keep *all women* in a state of fear" (15; italics in original). Making the point explicitly, Marilyn French states, "All men are rapists and that's all they are" (qtd. in Jenness 33). Given this kind of smear tactic, *rape* can be used metaphorically to indict males alone and to exonerate females, as in this sentence: "The rape of nature—and the ecological disaster it presages—is part and parcel of a dominating masculinity gone out of control" (Hoch 137). The statement neatly blames males alone even when the damage to the environment has been caused in part by females like Anne Gorsuch Burford and Rita Lavelle.

Not only crimes but vices of all sorts have been typically attributed to   28
males. As Muriel R. Schulz points out, "The synonyms for *inebriate . . .* seem to be coded primarily 'male': for example, *boozer, drunkard, tippler, toper, swiller, tosspot, guzzler, barfly, drunk, lush, boozehound, souse, tank, stew, rummy,* and *bum*" (126). Likewise, someone may be *drunk as a lord* but never *drunk as a lady.*

Sex bias or sexism itself is widely held to be a male-only fault. When   29
sexism is defined as "contempt for women"—as if there were no such thing as contempt for men—the definition of *sexism* is itself sexist (Bard-wick 34).

Part of the reason for this masculinization of evil may be that in the   30
Western world the source of evil has long been depicted in male terms. In the Bible the Evil One is consistently referred to as *he,* whether the reference is to the serpent in the Garden of Eden, Satan as Adversary in Job, Lucifer and Beelzebub in the gospels, Jesus' tempter in the desert, or the dragon in Revelations. *Beelzebub,* incidentally, is often translated as *lord of the flies,* a term designating the demon as masculine. So masculine is the word *devil* that the female prefix is needed, as in *she-devil,* to make a feminine noun of it. The masculinization of evil is so unconsciously accepted that writers often attest to it even while attempting to deny it, as in this passage:

> From the very beginning, the Judeo-Christian tradition has linked women and evil. When second-century theologians struggled to explain the Devil's origins, they surmised that Satan and his various devils had once been angels. (Gerzon 224)

If the Judeo-Christian tradition has linked women and evil so closely, why is the writer using the masculine pronoun *his* to refer to Satan, the source of evil according to that tradition? Critics of sex-bias in religious language seldom notice or mention its masculinization of evil: of those objecting to

God the Father as sexist, no one—to my knowledge—has suggested that designating Satan as the *Father of Lies* is equally sexist. Few theologians talk about Satan and her legions.

The tendency to blame nearly everything on men has climaxed in   31
recent times with the popularity of such terms as *patriarchy, patriarchal society,* and *male-dominated society.* More political than descriptive, these terms are rapidly becoming meaningless, used as all-purpose smear words to conjure up images of male oppressors and female victims. They are a linguistic sleight of hand which obscures the point that, as Mead has observed (299–300), societies are largely created by both sexes for both sexes. By using a swift reference to *patriarchal structures* or *patriarchal attitudes,* a writer can absolve females of all blame for society's flaws while fixing the onus solely on males. The give-away of this ploy can be detected when *patriarchy* and its related terms are never used in a positive or neutral context, but are always used to assign blame to males alone.

Wholesale denunciations of males as oppressors, exploiters, rapists,   32
Nazis, and slave-drivers have become all too familiar during the past fifteen years. Too often the academic community, rather than opposing this sexism, has been encouraging it. All too many scholars and teachers have hopped on the male-bashing bandwagon to disseminate what John Gordon calls "the myth of the monstrous male." While increasing frequency, this academically fashionable sexism can also be heard echoing from our students. "A white upper-middle-class straight male should seriously consider another college," declares a midwestern college student in *The New York Times Selective Guide to Colleges.* "You [the white male] are the bane of the world. . . . Ten generations of social ills can and will be strapped upon your shoulders" (qtd. in Fiske 12). It would be comforting to dismiss this student's compound of misinformation, sexism, racism, and self-righteousness as an extreme example, but similar yahooisms go unchallenged almost everywhere in modern academia.

Surely it is time for men and women of good will to reject and protest   33
such bigotry. For teachers and writers, the first task is to recognize and condemn forms of anti-male bias in language, whether they are used to exclude males from equal consideration with females, to reinforce restrictive aspects of the masculine gender role, or to stereotype males callously. For whether males are told that *fathers don't make good mothers,* that *real men don't cry,* or that *all men are rapists,* the results are potentially dangerous: like any other group, males can be subtly shaped into what society keeps telling them they are. In *Why Men Are the Way They Are* Warren Farrell puts the matter succinctly: "The more we make men the enemy, the more they will have to behave like the enemy" (357).

Works Cited

Bardwick, Judith. *In Transition: How Feminism, Sexual Liberation, and the Search for Self-Fulfillment Have Altered Our Lives.* NY: Holt, 1979.

Baring-Gould, William S., and Ceil Baring-Gould. *The Annotated Mother Goose: Nursery Rhymes Old and New, Arranged and Explained.* NY: Clarkson N. Potter, 1962.

Brownmiller, Susan. *Against Our Will: Men, Women and Rape.* NY: Simon, 1975.

Collier, Phyllis K. *How to Marry a Winner.* Englewood Cliffs, NJ: Prentice, 1982.

Dinnerstein, Dorothy. *The Mermaid and the Minotaur: Sexual Arrangements and Human Malaise.* NY: Harper, 1976.

Farrell, Warren. *Why Men Are the Way They Are: The Male-Female Dynamic.* NY: McGraw-Hill, 1986.

Fiske, Edward B. *The New York Times Selective Guide to Colleges.* NY: Times Books, 1982.

Gerzon, Mark. *A Choice of Heroes: The Changing Faces of American Manhood.* Boston: Houghton, 1982.

Glass, Andrew J. "President wants to unleash military power, but cannot." *Dayton Daily News* 18 June 1985: 1.

Goldberg, Herb. *The Hazards of Being Male: Surviving the Myth of Masculine Privilege.* 1976. NY: NAL, 1977.

———. *The New Male: From Self-Destruction to Self-Care.* 1979. NY: NAL, 1980.

Gordon, John. *The Myth of the Monstrous Male, and Other Feminist Fables.* NY: Playboy P, 1982.

Hartley, Ruth E. "Sex-Role Pressures and the Socialization of the Male Child." *The Forty-Nine Percent Majority: The Male Sex Role.* Ed. Deborah S. David and Robert Brannon. Reading, MA: Addison-Wesley, 1976. 235–44.

Hoch, Paul. *White Hero, Black Beast: Racism, Sexism and the Mask of Masculinity.* London: Pluto P, 1979.

"Indiana jury finds Brown guilty of murder, molesting." *Dayton Daily News* 18 May 1986: 7A.

Inglis, Ruth. *Sins of the Fathers: A Study of the Physical and Emotional Abuse of Children.* NY: St. Martin's, 1978.

Jennes, Gail. "All Men Are Rapists." *People* 20 Feb. 1978: 33–34.

Lehne, Gregory. "Homophobia Among Men." *The Forty-Nine Percent Majority: The Male Sex Role.* Ed. Deborah S. David and Robert Brannon. Reading, MA: Addison-Wesley, 1976. 66–88.

Levine, James A. *Who Will Raise the Children? New Options for Fathers (and Mothers).* Philadelphia: Lippincott, 1976.

Mead, Margaret. *Male and Female: A Study of the Sexes in a Changing World.* NY: Morrow, 1949, 1967.

Money, John, and Patricia Tucker. *Sexual Signatures: On Being a Man or a Woman.* Boston: Little, 1976.

Mougey, Kate. "An act of confiscation: Rape." *Kettering-Oakwood* [OH] *Times* 4 Feb. 1981: 1b.

" 'Nerd' day gets a boot after suicide." *Dayton Daily News* 34 Jan. 1986: 38.

Ong, Walter J. *Fighting for Life: Contest, Sexuality, and Consciousness.* Ithaca, NY: Cornell UP, 1981.

O'Reilly, Jane, et al. "Wife-Beating: The Silent Crime." *Time* 5 Sept. 1983: 23–4, 26.

"Police: Print links Coleman, death." *Dayton Daily News* 31 Aug. 1984: 26.

Roman, Mel, and William Haddad. *The Disposable Parent: The Case for Joint Custody.* 1978. NY: Penguin, 1979.

Schulz, Muriel R. "Is the English Language Anybody's Enemy?" *Speaking of Words: A Language Reader.* Ed. James MacKillop and Donna Woolfolk Cross. 3rd ed. NY: Holt, 1986. 125–27.

Sorrels, Bobbye D. *The Nonsexist Communicator: Solving the Problems of Gender and Awkwardness in Modern English.* Englewood Cliffs, NJ: Prentice 1983.

Straus, Murray A., Richard J. Gelles, and Suzanne K. Steinmetz. *Behind Closed Doors: Violence in the American Family.* 1980. Garden City, NY: Doubleday, 1981.

Theroux, Paul. "The Male Myth." *New York Times Magazine* 27 Nov. 1983: 116.

QUESTIONS ON CONTENT

1. Language studies have failed to examine anti-male bias in English because of one basic assumption. What is that assumption? According to August, what is the flaw in this assumption?

2. August identifies three kinds of anti-male bias evident in the English language. Name them and offer examples of each.

3. Feminists argue that words such as *sissy, mama's boy,* and *weak sister* ultimately disparage the woman not the man. August disagrees. What is his central argument? Is he convincing? Explain.

4. Starting in boyhood and continuing throughout their lives, males are told to "be a man." What demands does this injunction make on a male? What are the consequences to him if he should fail? Name some of the terms of expectation the author gives for each stage of a man's life. What are some others with which you are familiar?

5. The ultimate disparagment of the male, according to August, is the masculinization of evil. How in August's terms, did evil come to be associated with the male? What are some of the ways he feels this association of the masculine with evil is manifested in attitudes about crime and vice?

6. August calls for "men and women of good will to reject and protest such bigotry." What does he say are the dangers of ignoring the problem of sexual bigotry?

QUESTIONS ON RHETORIC

1. In paragraph 3, August quotes two thinkers who support his thesis that there has been no male conspiracy to keep women in their place. Why do you suppose August chose these particular examples? How is August's use of these examples especially effective?

2. Beginning in paragraph 11, August makes extensive use of examples to support the idea that gender-restrictive language usually is aimed at males. Into what different classes of nouns does he group these examples? (Glossary: *Classification and Division*) Which group is the largest? What does this suggest to you?

3. How does August's choice of a title for this essay help make his point? What other titles can you suggest that might have had a similar effect?

4. At the beginning of his essay, August challenges established notions of sexist language. How does this challenge set the tone of the essay? (Glossary: *Tone*)

VOCABULARY

symbiotic (2)	slurred (12)	deferential (18)
denigrates (4)	enjoined (13)	obtuse (21)
notorious (7)	castigated (14)	bane (32)
virtual (9)	homophobic (16)	yahooisms (32)

WRITING TOPICS

1. August describes an experiment he did with his class in which he read them a list of nouns and asked them to decide which of them were "primarily female," which "primarily male," and which "could be either." In your own class try the experiment August conducted with his students. In a short essay discuss the results. Were they similar to those August achieved? How did they differ? What do you conclude from these results?

2. In an essay titled "We're Not Really 'Equal,' " Thomas Sowell argues that we may be muddying the waters when we insist on *equality* without defining our terms. "When we speak of 'equal justice under the law,' " he says, "we simply mean applying the same rules to everybody. That has

nothing whatsoever to do with whether everyone performs equally.'' Yet, Sowell claims, in recent years some people have insisted that if outcomes are different, then the rules must have been applied differently: ''It would destroy my last illusion to discover that Willie Mays didn't really play better baseball than everybody else, but that the umpires and sportswriters just conspired to make it look that way.'' This insistence that everyone be ''equal'' by demanding equal outcome is extended to the notion of equality of the sexes; but, Sowell asks, ''When women have children and men don't, how can they be either equal or unequal?'' Write an essay discussing your own point of view on these issues.

GENDER BENDERS

Jack Rosenthal

Jack Rosenthal begins his essay with a question: Of the two terms, chicken soup *and* beef soup, *which is masculine and which is feminine? The answer he says is almost always the same, the chicken soup is feminine and the beef is masculine. Rosenthal says this explains why ridding language of sexist terms is merely a superficial effort. We need to go deeper. For in assigning gender to gender-free words, "we expose attitudes so deeply embedded in our culture that most of us, male or female, macho or feminist, share them. We turn values into gender and gender into communication."*

Chicken soup and beef soup. Which is masculine and which is feminine? 1
In English, neither chicken nor beef nor soup has formal gender. Yet most people find the question easy to answer: chicken soup is feminine and beef soup is masculine, and that unanimity demonstrates how vast is the task of stamping out sexist words. That effort, while constructive, remains superficial; deep within language lurks the powerful force of Hidden Gender.

Many languages use formal gender to categorize nouns and pronouns 2
as masculine, feminine, and neuter. There's not much logic in these categories. "In German," Mark Twain once wrote, "a young lady has no sex, while a turnip has. Think what overwrought reverence that shows for the turnip and what callous disrespect for the girl." A Spanish butterfly is aptly feminine: *la mariposa.* A French butterfly is masculine, but at least the word sounds delicate: *le papillon.* A German butterfly is, as an old linguistic's joke observes, masculine and sounds it: *der Schmetterling.*

Beyond formal gender, societies observe a ceremonial gender. A na- 3
tion is a "she." So is a ship, an invention, an engine. Think of "Star Trek": one can just hear Scotty down in the engine room calling Captain Kirk: "I canna' get her into warp drive, Capt'n!"

Women's liberation has brought a new turn toward neutering 4
language—using firefighter instead of fireman and generalizing with "they" instead of "he." This process, generally positive, can be carried to extremes. When someone once denounced *yeoman* as sexist and urged *yeoperson* instead, The *Times* groaned in an editorial, fearing the ultimate

absurdity—*woperson*. Nonsense, several letter writers promptly responded. The ultimate absurdity, they observed, would be *woperdaughter*.

Hidden Gender, compared with such questions of surface gender, rolls   5
beneath the language like the tide. The chicken soup/beef soup question is just one illustration. Consider some variations on the idea, which began as a children's game and has been elaborated by Roger W. Shuy and other sociologists at Georgetown University.

Which of the following is masculine and which is feminine: 6

Ford and Chevrolet
Chocolate and vanilla
Salt and pepper
Pink and purple

From English speakers, the answers usually come back the same, re-   7
gardless of age, race, class, region—or sex. Some people see no gender at all in any of the terms. But those who do usually say that Ford, chocolate, pepper and purple are masculine.

The consensus is not limited to these pairs. You can get the same   8
predictability by making up other combinations—coffee and tea, shoes and boots, skis and skates, plane and train.

Why does almost everybody label chicken soup feminine? One obvious   9
explanation is that beef connotes cattle—big, solid, stolid animals. Chickens are small, frail, agile. Why does almost everybody label Chevrolet feminine? Perhaps for reasons of sound. Ford ends in a tough, blunt consonant, almost as masculine-sounding as *Mack truck*. By comparison, Chevro-lay seems graceful and flexible.

Why do so many people label vanilla feminine? Sound is probably part   10
of it, but so also is color and character. Chocolate, being darker and with a more pronounced taste, is masculine in this pairing. Likewise for pepper and purple.

Consider the attributes associated with masculine: solid, blunt, more   11
pronounced, and those associated with feminine: frail, graceful, light. They do not arise from the words themselves but from the pairings. What the game exposes is that Hidden Gender is relative.

In assigning gender to one word or the other, we expose attributes so   12
deeply embedded in our culture that most of us, male or female, macho or feminist, share them. We turn values into gender and gender into communication.

Try playing the game with single words instead of pairs. When you ask   13
people the gender of fork, you'll get blank looks. Hidden Gender only shows up when people are asked to give relative importance to two words.

Which is masculine and which is feminine: knife or fork? Usually, the   14
answer is that fork is feminine. But why? There's nothing inherently fem-

inine about the word fork. The answer is obvious when you try a different pair. Which is masculine and which is feminine: fork or spoon?

Purging language of sexist terms is worth doing for its own sake, but the superficiality of the effort should also be recognized. Whether one refers to ocean liners or God as "she" is a cosmetic matter. Hidden Gender endures, and the only way to alter it is to alter the culture on which it feeds.

QUESTIONS ON CONTENT

1. Rosenthal insists on the danger of "Hidden Gender." What is Hidden Gender? Is Rosenthal's definition stated or implied?

2. In paragraph 6, Rosenthal describes a game of word pairing used to test perception of gender in gender-free words. How does he say most people react to the questions? What happens, according to Rosenthal, when the game is played with single nouns? What does this suggest to Rosenthal? What does it suggest to you?

3. What explanations does Rosenthal offer for labeling nouns male or female? Do you agree? Can you think of any others?

4. Many cultures use formal gender to label a noun female, male, or neuter. Name the other kind of gender Rosenthal says societies observe. Can you offer examples of your own of this other gender?

5. Name one success women's lib has had in combating sexist language. How has antisexism in language been taken to the extreme? What examples of your own can you give?

QUESTIONS ON RHETORIC

1. Rosenthal begins his essay with a question. What effect did this question have on you? Why was it an effective beginning?

2. Reread the opening sentences in paragraphs 9, 10, 11, 13, 14, and 15. Each of them involves the reader in the essay. How do they accomplish this? Do you think involving the reader is an effective strategy? Why or why not?

3. Prepare a scratch outline of Rosenthal's essay. How has Rosenthal organized his argument? What is the function of paragraphs 3, 4, and 5? Could he have done without them? What happens to the flow of the essay if these three paragraphs are deleted?

VOCABULARY

formal (1)	callous (2)	purging (15)
superficial (1)	inherently (14)	cosmetic (15)

WRITING TOPICS

1. Rosenthal tries to explain the feminine and masculine qualities we associate with certain nouns that would cause them to be labeled as one gender or another. For example, he uses the word *frail* to describe the qualities of some of the nouns people said sounded "feminine," while he uses words such as *blunt* and *more pronounced* to describe nouns labeled "masculine." Could Rosenthal have chosen more neutral adjectives that would as reasonably have maintained the findings of the language experts? Explain your answer.

2. Gather some of your friends together and play the word game Rosenthal describes in paragraphs 5 and 6. What were the results? Did your friends assign gender to neutral nouns? Could they explain their responses? In an essay discuss what playing the game taught you about Hidden Gender.

ONE SMALL STEP FOR GENKIND

Casey Miller and Kate Swift

Casey Miller and Kate Swift's articles on language and sexism have appeared nationwide in magazines and newspapers. In this 1972 essay they examine the ways that sexist attitudes reveal themselves, not only in our everyday speech, but in the language of textbooks, dictionaries, religion, and the media.

A riddle is making the rounds that goes like this: A man and his young son were in an automobile accident. The father was killed and the son, who was critically injured, was rushed to a hospital. As attendants wheeled the unconscious boy into the emergency room, the doctor on duty looked down at him and said, "My God, it's my son!" What was the relationship of the doctor to the injured boy?

If the answer doesn't jump to your mind, another riddle that has been around a lot longer might help: The blind beggar had a brother. The blind beggar's brother died. The brother who died had no brother. What relation was the blind beggar to the blind beggar's brother?

As with all riddles, the answers are obvious once you see them: The doctor was the boy's mother and the beggar was her brother's sister. Then why doesn't everyone solve them immediately? Mainly because our language, like the culture it reflects, is male oriented. To say that a woman in medicine is an exception is simply to confirm that statement. Thousands of doctors are women, but in order to be seen in the mind's eye, they must be called women doctors.

Except for words that refer to females by definition (mother, actress, Congresswoman), and words for occupations traditionally held by females (nurse, secretary, prostitute), the English language defines everyone as male. The hypothetical person ("If a man can walk 10 miles in two hours . . ."), the average person ("the man in the street") and the active person ("the man on the move") are male. The assumption is that unless otherwise identified, people in general—including doctors and beggars—are men. It is a semantic mechanism that operates to keep women invisible: *man* and *mankind* represent everyone; *he* in generalized use refers to either

sex; the "land where our fathers died" is also the land of our mothers—
although they go unsung. As the beetle-browed and mustachioed man in a
Steig cartoon says to his two male drinking companions, "When I speak
of mankind, one thing I *don't* mean is womankind."

Semantically speaking, woman is not one with the species of man, but 5
a distinct subspecies. "Man," says the 1971 edition of the Britannica
Junior Encyclopedia, "is the highest form of life on earth. His superior
intelligence, combined with certain physical characteristics, have enabled
man to achieve things that are impossible for other animals." (The prose
style has something in common with the report of a research team describing its studies on "the development of the uterus in rats, guinea pigs and
men.") As though quoting the Steig character, still speaking to his friends
in McSorley's, the Junior Encyclopedia continues: "Man must invent most
of his behavior, because he lacks the instincts of lower animals. . . . Most
of the things he learns have been handed down from his ancestors by
language and symbols rather than by biological inheritance."

Considering that for the last 5,000 years society has been patriarchal, 6
that statement explains a lot. It explains why Eve was made from Adam's
rib instead of the other way around, and who invented all those Adam-rib
words like *fe*male and *wo*man in the first place. It also explains why, when
it is necessary to mention woman, the language makes her a lower caste,
a class separate from the rest of man; why it works to "keep her in her
place."

This inheritance through language and other symbols begins in the 7
home (also called a man's castle) where man and wife (not husband and
wife, or man and woman) live for a while with their children. It is reinforced by religious training, the educational system, the press, government, commerce and the law. As Andrew Greeley wrote not long ago in
his magazine, "Man is a symbol-creating animal. He orders the interprets
his reality by his symbols, and he uses the symbols to reconstruct their
reality."

Consider some of the reconstructed realities of American history. When 8
schoolchildren learn from their textbooks that the early colonists gained
valuable experience in governing themselves, they are not told that the
early colonists who were women were denied the privilege of self-
government; when they learn that in the 18th century the average man had
to manufacture many of the things he and his family needed, they are not
told that this "average man" was often a woman who manufactured much
of what she and her family needed. Young people learn that intrepid
pioneers crossed the country in covered wagons with their wives, children
and cattle; they do not learn that women themselves were intrepid pioneers
rather than part of the baggage.

In a paper published this year in Los Angeles as a guide for authors and   9
editors of social-studies textbooks, Elizabeth Burr, Susan Dunn and Norma
Farquhar document unintentional skewings of this kind that occur either
because women are not specifically mentioned as affecting or being affected by historical events, or because they are discussed in terms of
outdated assumptions. "One never sees a picture of women captioned
simply 'farmers' or 'pioneers,' " they point out. The subspecies nomenclature that requires a caption to read "women farmers" or "women
pioneers" is extended to impose certain jobs on women by definition. The
textbook guide gives as an example the word *housewife,* which it says not
only "suggests that domestic chores are the exclusive burden of females,"
but gives "female students the idea that they were born to keep house and
teaches male students that they are automatically entitled to laundry, cooking and housecleaning services from the women in their families."

Sexist language is any language that expresses such stereotyped atti-   10
tudes and expectations, or that assumes the inherent superiority of one sex
over the other. When a woman says of her husband, who had drawn up
plans for a new bedroom wing and left out closets, "Just like a man," her
language is as sexist as the man's who says, after his wife has changed her
mind about needing the new wing after all, "Just like a woman."

Male and female are not sexist words, but masculine and feminine   11
almost always are. Male and female can be applied objectively to individual people and animals and, by extension, to things. When electricians and
plumbers talk about male and female couplings, everyone knows or can
figure out what they mean. The terms are graphic and culture free.

Masculine and feminine, however, are as sexist as any words can be,   12
since it is almost impossible to use them without invoking cultural stereotypes. When people construct lists of "masculine" and "feminine" traits
they almost always end up making assumptions that have nothing to do
with innate differences between the sexes. We have a friend who happens
to be going through the process of pinning down this very phenomenon. He
is 7 years old and his question concerns why his coats and shirts button left
over right while his sister's button the other way. He assumes it must have
something to do with the differences between boys and girls, but he can't
see how.

What our friend has yet to grasp is that the way you button your coat,   13
like most sex-differentiated customs, has nothing to do with real differences but much to do with what society wants you to feel about yourself as
a male or a female person. Society decrees that it is appropriate for girls to
dress differently from boys, to act differently, and to think differently.
Boys must be masculine, whatever that means, and girls must be feminine.

*   *   *

Unabridged dictionaries are a good source for finding out what society   14
decrees to be appropriate, though less by definition than by their choice of
associations and illustrations. Words associated with males—*manly, virile*
and *masculine,* for example—are defined through a broad range of positive
attributes like strength, courage, directness and independence, and they are
illustrated through such examples of contemporary usage as "a manly
determination to face what comes," "a virile literary style," "a masculine
love of sports." Corresponding words associated with females are defined
with fewer attributes (though weakness is often one of them) and the
examples given are generally negative if not clearly pejorative: "feminine
wiles," "womanish tears," "a womanlike lack of promptness," "convinced that drawing was a waste of time, if not downright womanly."

Male-associated words are frequently applied to females to describe   15
something that is either incongruous ("a mannish voice") or presumably
commendable ("a masculine mind," "she took it like a man"), but
female-associated words are unreservedly derogatory when applied to
males, and are sometimes abusive to females as well. The opposite of
"masculine" is "effeminate," although the opposite of "feminine" is
simply "unfeminine."

One dictionary, after defining the word *womanish* as "suitable to or re-   16
sembling a woman," further defines it as "unsuitable to a man or to a
strong character of either sex." Words derived from "sister" and "brother"
provide another apt example, for whereas "sissy," applied either to a male
or female, conveys the message that sisters are expected to be timid and
cowardly, "buddy" makes clear that brothers are friends.

The subtle disparagement of females and corresponding approbation of   17
males wrapped up in many English words is painfully illustrated by "tomboy." Here is an instance where a girl who likes sports and the out-
of-doors, who is curious about how things work, who is adventurous and
bold instead of passive, is defined in terms of something she is not—a boy.
By denying that she can be the person she is and still be a girl, the word
surreptitiously undermines her sense of identity: it says she is unnatural. A
"tomboy," as defined by one dictionary, is a "girl, especially a young
girl, who behaves like a spirited boy." But who makes the judgment that
she is acting like a spirited boy, not a spirited girl? Can it be a coincidence
that in the case of the dictionary just quoted the editor, executive editor,
managing editor, general manager, all six members of the Board of Linguists, the usage editor, science editor, all six general editors of definitions, and 94 out of the 104 distinguished experts consulted on usage—are
men?

It isn't enough to say that any invidious comparisons and stereotypes   18
lexicographers perpetuate are already present in the culture. There are
ways to define words like womanly and tomboy that don't put women

down, though the tradition has been otherwise. Samuel Johnson, the lexicographer, was the same Dr. Johnson who said, "A woman preaching is like a dog's walking on his hind legs. It is not done well; but you are surprised to find it done at all."

Possibly because of the negative images associated with womanish and   19
womanlike, and with expressions like "woman driver" and "woman of the street," the word *woman* dropped out of fashion for a time. The women at the office and the women on the assembly line and the women one first knew in school all became ladies or girls or gals. Now a countermovement, supported by the very term *women's liberation*, is putting back into words like *woman* and *sister* and *sisterhood* the meaning they were losing by default. It is as though, in the nick of time, women had seen that the language itself could destroy them.

Some long-standing conventions of the news media add insult to in-   20
jury. When a woman or girl makes news, her sex is identified at the beginning of a story, if possible in the headline or its equivalent. The assumption, apparently is that whatever event or action is being reported, a woman's involvement is less common and therefore more newsworthy than a man's. If the story is about achievement, the implication is: "pretty good for a woman." And because people are assumed to be male unless otherwise identified, the media have developed a special and extensive vocabulary to avoid the constant repetition of "woman." The results, "Grandmother Wins Nobel Prize," "Blonde Hijacks Airliner," "Housewife to Run for Congress," convey the kind of information that would be ludicrous in comparable headlines if the subjects were men. Why, if "Unsalaried Husband to Run for Congress" is unacceptable to editors, do women have to keep explaining that to describe them through external or superficial concerns reflects a sexist view of women as decorative objects, breeding machines and extensions of men, not real people?

Members of the Chicago chapter of the National Organization for   21
Women recently studied the newspapers in their area and drew up a set of guidelines for the press. These include cutting out descriptions of the "clothes, physical features, dating life and marital status of women where such references would be considered inappropriate if about men": using language in such a way as to include women in copy that refers to homeowners, scientists and business people where "newspaper descriptions often convey the idea that all such persons are male"; and displaying the same discretion in printing generalizations about women as would be shown toward racial, religious and ethnic groups. "Our concern with what we are called may seem trivial to some people," the women said, "but we regard the old usages as symbolic of women's position within this society."

The assumption that an adult woman is flattered by being called a girl   22
is matched by the notion that a woman in a menial or poorly paid job finds
compensation in being called a lady. Ethel Strainchamps has pointed out
that since *lady* is used as an adjective with nouns designating both high and
low occupations (lady wrestler, lady barber, lady doctor, lady judge),
some writers assume they can use the noun form without betraying value
judgments. Not so, Strainchamp says, rolling the issue into a spitball:
"You may write, 'He addressed the Republican ladies,' or 'The Democratic ladies convened' . . . but I have never seen 'the Communist ladies'
or 'the Black Panther ladies' in print."

Thoughtful writers and editors have begun to repudiate some of the old   23
usages. "Divorcée," "grandmother" and "blonde," along with "viva-
cious," "pert," "dimpled" and "cute," were dumped by the *Washington
Post* in the spring of 1970 by the executive editor, Benjamin Bradlee. In a
memo to his staff, Bradlee wrote, "The meaningful equality and dignity of
women is properly under scrutiny today . . . because this equality has
been less than meaningful and the dignity not always free of stereotype and
condescension."

What women have been called in the press—or at least the part that   24
operates above ground—is only a fraction of the infinite variety of alternatives to "women" used in the subcultures of the English-speaking world.
Beyond "chicks," "dolls," "dames," "babes," "skirts" and "broads"
are the words and phrases in which women are reduced to their sexuality
and nothing more. It would be hard to think of another area of language in
which the human mind has been so fertile in devising and borrowing
abusive terms. In *The Female Eunuch*, Germaine Greer devotes four pages
to anatomical terms and words for animals, vegetables, fruits, baked goods,
implements and receptacles, all of which are used to dehumanize the
female person. Jean Faust, in an article aptly called "Words That Op-
press," suggests that the effort to diminish women through language is
rooted in a male fear of sexual inadequacy. "Woman is made to feel guilty
for and akin to natural disasters," she writes; "hurricanes and typhoons are
named after her. Any negative or threatening force is given a feminine
name. If a man runs into bad luck climbing up the ladder of success (a
male-invented game), he refers to the 'bitch goddess' success."

The sexual overtones in the ancient and no doubt honorable custom of   25
calling ships "she" have become more explicit and less honorable in an
age of air travel: "I'm Karen. Fly me." Attitudes of ridicule, contempt and
disgust toward female sexuality have spawned a rich glossary of insults and
epithets not found in dictionaries. And the usage in which four-letter words
meaning copulate are interchangeable with *cheat*, *attack* and *destroy* can
scarcely be unrelated to the savagery of rape.

In her updating of Ibsen's *A Doll's House,* Clare Booth Luce has Nora   26
tell her husband she is pregnant—"In the way only men are supposed to
get pregnant." "Men, pregnant?" he says, and she nods; "With ideas.
Pregnancies there [*she taps his head*] are masculine. And a very superior
form of labor. Pregnancies here [*taps her tummy*] are feminine—a very
inferior form of labor."

Public outcry followed a revised translation of the New Testament   27
describing Mary as "pregnant" instead of "great with child." The objections were made in part on esthetic grounds: there is no attractive adjective
in modern English for a woman who is about to give birth. A less obvious
reason was that replacing the euphemism with a biological term under-
mined religious teaching. The initiative and generative power in the conception of Jesus are understood to be God's; Mary, the mother, was a
vessel only.

Whether influenced by this teaching or not, the language of human   28
reproduction lags several centuries behind scientific understanding. The
male's contribution to procreation is still described as though it were the
entire seed from which a new life grows: the initiative and generative
power involved in the process are thought of as masculine, receptivity and
nurturance as feminine. "Seminal" remains a synonym for "highly original," and there is no comparable word to describe the female's equivalent
contribution.

An entire mythology has grown from this biological misunderstanding   29
and its semantic legacy; its embodiment in laws that for centuries made
women nonpersons was a key target of the 19th-century feminist movement. Today, more than 50 years after women finally won the basic democratic right to vote, the word "liberation" itself, when applied to women,
means something less than when used of other groups of people. An
advertisement for the N.B.C. news department listed Women's Liberation
along with crime in the streets and the Vietnam War as "bad news."
Asked for his views on Women's Liberation, a highly placed politician was
quoted as saying, "Let me make one thing perfectly clear. I wouldn't want
to wake up next to a lady pipe-fitter."

One of the most surprising challenges to our male-dominated culture is   30
coming from within organized religion, where the issues are being stated,
in part, by confronting the implications of traditional language. What a
growing number of theologians and scholars are saying is that the myths of
the Judeo-Christian tradition, being the products of patriarchy, must be
reexamined, and that the concept of an exclusively male ministry and the
image of a male god have become idolatrous.

Women are naturally in the forefront of this movement, both in their   31
efforts to gain ordination and full equality and through their contributions

to theological reform, although both these efforts are often subtly diminished. When the Rev. Barbara Anderson was ordained by the American Lutheran Church, one newspaper printed her picture over a caption headed "Happy Girl." *Newsweek*'s report of a protest staged last December by women divinity students at Harvard was jocular ("another tilt at the windmill") and sarcastic: "Every time anyone in the room lapsed into what [the students] regarded as male chauvinism—such as using the word 'mankind' to describe the human race in general—the outraged women . . . drowned out the offender with earpiercing blasts from party-favor kazoos . . . What annoyed the women most was the universal custom of referring to God as 'He.' "

The tone of the report was not merely unfunny; it missed the connection between increasingly outmoded theological language and the accelerating number of women (and men) who are dropping out of organized religion, both Jewish and Christian. For language, including pronouns, can be used to construct a reality that simply mirrors society's assumptions. To women who are committed to the reality of religious faith, the effect is doubly painful. Professor Harvey Cox, in whose classroom the protest took place, stated the issue directly: The women, he said, were raising the "basic theological question of whether God is more adequately thought of in personal or suprapersonal terms."

Toward the end of Don McLean's remarkable ballad "American Pie," a song filled with the imagery of abandonment and disillusion, there is a stanza that must strike many women to the quick. The church bells are broken, the music has died; then:

And the three men I admire most,
The Father, Son and the Holy Ghost,
They caught the last train for the Coast—
The day the music died.

Three men I admired most. There they go, briefcases in hand and topcoats buttoned left over right, walking down the long gold platform under the city, past the baggage wagons and the hissing steam onto the Pullman. Bye, bye God—all three of you—made in the image of male supremacy. Maybe out there in L.A. where the weather is warmer, someone can believe in you again.

The Roman Catholic theologian Elizabeth Farian says "the bad theology of an overmasculinized church continues to be one of the root causes of women's oppression." The definition of oppression is "to crush or burden by abuse of power or authority; burden spiritually or mentally as if by pressure."

*   *   *

When language oppresses, it does so by any means that disparage and   36
belittle. Until well into the 20th century, one of the ways English was
manipulated to disparage women was through the addition of feminine
endings to nonsexual words. Thus a woman who aspired to be a poet was
excluded from the company of real poets by the label poetess, and a
woman who piloted an airplane was denied full status as an aviator by
being called an aviatrix. At about the time poetess, aviatrix, and similar
Adam-ribbisms were dropping out of use, H. W. Fowler was urging that
they be revived. ''With the coming expansion of women's vocations,'' he
wrote in the first edition (1926) of *Modern English Usage*, ''feminines for
vocation-words are a special need of the future.'' There can be no doubt
he subconsciously recognized the relative status implied in the -*ess* designations. His criticism of a woman who wished to be known as an author
rather than an authoress was that she had no need ''to raise herself to the
level of the male author by asserting her right to his name.''

Who has the prior right to a name? The question has an interesting   37
bearing on words that were once applied to men alone, or to both men and
women, but now, having acquired abusive associations, are assigned to
women exclusively. Spinster is a gentle case in point. Prostitute and many
of its synonyms illustrate the phenomenon better. If Fowler had chosen to
record the changing usage of harlot from hired man (in Chaucer's time)
through rascal and entertainer to its present definition, would he have
maintained that the female harlot is trying to raise herself to the level of the
male harlot by asserting her right to his name? Or would he have plugged
for harlotress?

The demise of most -*ess* endings came about before the start of the new   38
feminist movement. In the second edition of *Modern English Usage*, published in 1965, Sir Ernest Gowers frankly admitted what his predecessors
had been up to. ''Feminine designations,'' he wrote, ''seem now to be
falling into disuse. Perhaps the explanation of this paradox is that it symbolizes the victory of women in their struggle for equal rights; it reflects the
abandonment by men of those ideas about women in the professions that
moved Dr. Johnson to his rude remark about women preachers.''

If Sir Ernest's optimism can be justified, why is there a movement back   39
to feminine endings in such words as chairwoman, councilwoman and
congresswoman? Betty Hudson, of Madison, Conn., is campaigning for
the adoption of ''selectwoman'' as the legal title for a female member of
that town's executive body. To have to address a woman as ''Selectman,''
she maintains, ''is not only bad grammar and bad biology, but it implies
that politics is still, or should be, a man's business.'' A valid argument,
and one that was, predictably, countered by ridicule, the surefire weapon
for undercutting achievement. When the head of the Federal Maritime

Commission, Helen D. Bentley, was named "Man of the Year" by an association of shipping interests, she wisely refused to be drawn into light-hearted debate with interviewers who wanted to make the award's name a humorous issue. Some women, of course, have yet to learn they are invisible. An 8-year-old who visited the American Museum of Natural History with her Brownie scout troop went through the impressive exhibit on pollution and overpopulation called "Can Man Survive?" Asked afterward, "Well, can he?" she answered, "I don't know about him, but we're working on it in Brownies."

Nowhere are women rendered more invisible by language than in politics. The United States Constitution, in describing the qualifications for Representative, Senator and President, refers to each as *he*. No wonder Shirley Chisholm, the first woman since 1888 to make a try for the Presidential nomination of a major party, has found it difficult to be taken seriously. 40

The observation by Andrew Greeley already quoted—that "man" used "his symbols" to reconstruct "his reality"—was not made in reference to the symbols of language but to the symbolic impact that "nomination of a black man for the Vice-Presidency" would have on race relations in the United States. Did the author assume the generic term "man" would of course be construed to include "woman"? Or did he deliberately use a semantic device to exclude Shirley Chisholm without having to be explicit? 41

Either way, his words construct a reality in which women are ignored. As much as any other factor in our language, the ambiguous meaning of *man* serves to deny women recognition as people. In a recent magazine article, we discussed the similar effect on women of the generic pronoun *he*, which we proposed to replace by a new common gender pronoun *tey*. We were immediately told, by a number of authorities, that we were dabbling in the serious business of linguistics, and the message that reached us from these scholars was loud and clear: It-is-absolutely-impossible-for-anyone-to-introduce-a-new-word-into-the-language-just-because-there-is-a-need-for-it, so-stop-wasting-your-time. 42

When words are suggested like "herstory" (for history), "sportsoneship" (for sportsmanship) and "mistresspiece" (for the work of a Virginia Woolf) one suspects a not-too-subtle attempt to make the whole language problem look silly. But unless Alexander Pope, when he wrote "The proper study of mankind is man," meant that women should be relegated to the footnotes (or, as George Orwell might have put it, "All men are equal, but men are more equal than women"), viable new words will surely someday supersede the old. 43

*   *   *

Without apologies to Freud, the great majority of women do not wish in their hearts that they were men. If having grown up with a language that tells them they are at the same time men and not men raises psychic doubts for women, the doubts are not of their sexual identity but of their human identity. Perhaps the present unrest surfacing in the Women's Movement is part of an evolutionary change in our particular form of life—the one form of all in the animal and plant kingdoms that orders and interprets its reality by symbols. The achievements of the species called man have brought us to the brink of self-destruction. If the species survives into the next century with the expectation of going on, it may only be because we have become part of what Harlow Shapley calls the psychozoic kingdom, where brain overshadows brawn and rationality has replaced superstition.

Searching the roots of Western civilization for a word to call this new 44 species of man and woman, someone might come up with *gen*, as in genesis and generic. With such a word, *man* could be used exclusively for males as *woman* is used for females, for gen would include both sexes. Like the words deer and bison, gen would be both plural and singular. Like progenitor, progeny, and generation, it would convey continuity. *Gen* would express the warmth and generalized sexuality of generous, gentle, and genuine; the specific sexuality of genital and genetic. In the new family of gen, girls and boys would grow to genhood, and to speak of genkind would be to include all the people of the earth.

QUESTIONS ON CONTENT

1. According to the authors, the English language is built upon the assumption that everyone is male. Why do they find that notion harmful?

2. How do the authors define sexist language? In their opinion, are men the only ones guilty of using sexist language?

3. In paragraph 11, the authors assert that "Male and female are not sexist words, but masculine and feminine almost always are." How do they distinguish between *male* and *female* and *masculine* and *feminine*? Miller and Swift offer only one example of male and female words. Can you offer some others? What kinds of examples do they give of masculine and feminine words?

4. What are some of the ways the media works to demean women? What guideline for the press has one women's group developed?

5. The authors say that religion has produced a "surprising challenge to our male-dominated culture. . . ." In what areas have women come to the forefront of the movement to reexamine the Judeo-Christian traditions? How has the press dealt with these efforts?

QUESTIONS ON RHETORIC

1. What is the figure of speech used in the title of this essay? How does it relate to the authors' argument?

2. The authors begin their essay with two familiar riddles. (Glossary: *Beginnings and Endings*). How do these riddles function to launch the essay? Do you think them effective? Explain.

3. Miller and Swift make liberal use of examples throughout their essay. Choose several of these examples to show how they strengthen the authors' point of view. Do any of them fail to support the authors' argument? Explain.

4. Would you define the tone of this essay as argumentative, angry, or ironic? Use examples of the authors' diction and phrasing to support your answer. Is the tone appropriate to the authors' point and subject? (Glossary: *Diction, Tone*)

5. The word *genkind* does not appear until paragraph 45. Why do you suppose the authors waited until the end of their essay to include it? How does this strategy help to support their argument?

VOCABULARY

riddle (1)	approbation (17)	euphemism (27)
intrepid (8)	surreptitiously (17)	supersede (43)
skewings (9)	invidious (18)	progenitor (45)
nomenclature (9)	lexicographer (18)	progeny (45)
invoking (12)	repudiate (23)	
incongruous (15)		

WRITING TOPICS

1. The authors refer to the word *tomboy* as a "subtle disparagement of females." They add that dictionaries have the choice to define words without putting women down. Look up some of the words the authors mention in their essay to determine for yourself the extent to which the dictionary perpetuates sexist attitudes. What do you find?

2. Miller and Swift say they are grateful that words with the suffix "ess," as in poetess and authoress, are fading from use, while words such as selectperson are gaining respect. Reread paragraphs 36–39. How do the authors distinguish between a legitimate and artificial ways of rendering nouns feminine? In your opinion is the distinction important? Why or why not?

3. In paragraph 20, Miller and Swift report that "because people are assumed to be male unless otherwise identified, the media have developed a special and extensive vocabulary to avoid the constant repetition of

"woman." Read your local newspaper over several days. Are women referred to any differently than men? Do articles routinely substitute words such as "wife," or "mother" for the word *woman* in cases in which the word *man* would not be replaced with "husband," or "father?" Write an essay discussing what you discovered about these and other examples of sexist speech in print.

IN DEFENSE
OF GENDER

Cyra McFadden

*For almost two decades now, feminist linguists have
spearheaded the movement against language that
discriminates against women. Although their attempts to
eradicate sexism have been largely applauded, some people
do not like what has happened to English in the process.
Such a person is novelist and columnist Cyra McFadden. In
the following essay, she argues that the "neutering" of
English is both awkward and ludicrous.*

So pervasive is the neutering of the English language on the progressive   1
West Coast, we no longer have people here, only persons: male persons
and female persons, chairpersons and doorpersons, waitpersons,
mailpersons—who may be either male or female mailpersons—and refuse-
collection persons. In the classified ads, working mothers seek childcare
persons, though one wonders how many men (archaic for "male person")
take care of child persons as a full-time occupation. One such ad, fusing
nonsexist language and the most popular word in the California growth
movement, solicits a "nurtureperson."

Dear gents and ladies, as I might have addressed you in less troubled   2
times, this female person knows firsthand the reasons for scourging
sexist bias from the language. God knows what damage was done me, at
fifteen, when I worked in my first job—as what is now known as a newspaper copyperson—and came running to the voices of men barking,
"Boy!"

No aspirant to the job of refuse-collection person myself, I nonetheless   3
take off my hat (a little feathered number, with a veil) to those of my own
sex who may want both the job and a genderless title with it. I argue only
that there must be a better way, and I wish person or persons unknown
would come up with one.

Defend it on any grounds you choose; the neutering of spoken and   4
written English, with its attendant self-consciousness, remains ludicrous.
In print, those "person" suffixes and "he/she's" jump out from the page,
as distracting as a cloud of gnats, demanding that the reader note the

writer's virtue. "Look what a nonsexist writer person I am, voiding the use of masculine forms for the generic."

Spoken, they leave conversation fit only for the Coneheads on "Saturday Night Live." "They have a daily special," a woman at the next table told her male companion in Perry's, a San Francisco restaurant. "Ask your waitperson." In a Steig cartoon, the words would have marched from her mouth in the form of a computer printout.

In Berkeley, Calif., the church to which a friend belongs is busy stripping its liturgy of sexist references. "They've gone berserk," she writes, citing a reading from the pulpit of a verse from 1 Corinthians. Neutered, the once glorious passage becomes "Though I speak with the tongues of persons and of angels. . . ." So much for sounding brass and tinkling cymbals.

The parson person of the same church is now referring to God as "He/She" and changing all references accordingly—no easy undertaking if he intends to be consistent. In the following, the first pronoun would remain because at this primitive stage of human evolution, male persons do not give birth to babies: "And she brought forth her firstborn son/daughter, and wrapped him/her in swaddling clothes, and laid him/her in a manger; because there was no room for them in the inn. . . ."

As the after-dinner speaker at a recent professional conference, I heard a text replete with "he/she's" and "his/her's" read aloud for the first time. The hapless program female chairperson stuck with the job chose to render these orally as "he-slash-she" and "his-slash-her," turning the following day's schedule for conference participants into what sounded like a replay of the Manson killings.

Redress may be due those of us who, though female, have answered to masculine referents all these years, but slashing is not the answer; violence never is. Perhaps we could right matters by using feminine forms as the generic for a few centuries, or simply agree on a per-woman lump-sum payment.

Still, we would be left with the problem of referring, without bias, to transpersons. These are not bus drivers or Amtrak conductors but persons in transit from one gender to the other—or so I interpret a fund-drive appeal asking me to defend their civil rights, along with those of female and male homosexuals.

Without wishing to step on anyone's civil rights, I hope transpersons are not the next politically significant pressure group. If they are, count on it, they will soon want their own pronouns.

In the tradition of the West, meanwhile, feminists out here wrestle the language to the ground, plant a foot on its neck and remove its masculine appendages. Take the local art critic Beverly Terwoman.

She is married to a man surnamed Terman. She writes under "Terwoman," presumably in the spirit of *vive la différence*. As a letter to the editor of the paper for which she writes noted, however, "Terwoman" is not ideologically pure. It still contains "man," a syllable reeking of all that is piggy and hairy-chested.

Why not Beverly Terperson? Or better, since "Terperson" contains "son," Terdaughter"? Or a final refinement, Beverly Ter?   14

Beverly Terwoman did not dignify this sexist assault with a reply. The writer of the letter was a male person, after all, probably the kind who leaves his smelly sweat socks scattered around the bedroom floor.   15

No one wins these battles anyway. In another letter to the same local weekly, J. Seibert, female, lets fire at the printing of an interview with Phyllis Schlafly. Not only was the piece "an offense to everything that Marin County stands for," but "it is even more amusing that your interview was conducted by a male.   16

"This indicates your obvious assumption that men understand women's issues better than women since men are obviously more intelligent (as no doubt Phyllis would agree)."   17

A sigh suffuses the editor's note that follows: "The author of the article, Sydney Weisman, is a female."   18

So the war of the pronouns and suffixes rages, taking no prisoners except writers. Neuter your prose with all those clanking "he/she's," and no one will read you except Alan Alda. Use masculine forms as the generic, and you have joined the ranks of the oppressor. None of this does much to encourage friendly relations between persons, transpersons or—if there are any left—people.   19

I also have little patience with the hyphenated names more and more California female persons adopt when they marry, in the interests of retaining their own personhood. These accomplish their intention of declaring the husband separate but equal. They are hell on those of us who have trouble remembering one name, much less two. They defeat answering machines, which can't handle "Please call Gwendolyn Grunt-Messerschmidt." And in this culture, they retain overtones of false gentility.   20

Two surnames, to me, still bring to mind the female writers of bad romances and Julia Ward Howe.   21

It's a mug's game, friends, this neutering of a language already fat, bland and lethargic, and it's time we decide not to play it. This female person is currently writing a book about rodeo. I'll be dragged behind a saddle bronc before I will neuter the text with "cowpersons."   22

QUESTIONS ON CONTENT

1. Why does McFadden object to the "neutering" of English? Does she think that this neutering process is just another language fad? How do you know?

2. How does McFadden react to "person" suffixes and "he/she's" in print? In speech? Do you have similar reactions?

3. On what grounds does McFadden object to hyphenated names? Do you share her objections? Why, or why not?

4. What does McFadden mean when she says "so the war of the pronouns and suffixes rages, taking no prisoners except writers" (19)?

5. McFadden believes there must be a "better way" to eliminate sexism than to "slash" English to death. Does she offer any solutions? Can you think of any solutions?

QUESTIONS ON RHETORIC

1. What is McFadden's thesis? (Glossary: *Thesis*) Where is it stated? How does she support it?

2. How would you describe McFadden's tone in this essay? (Glossary: *Tone*) Is it appropriate given her subject and purpose?

3. In paragraph 2 McFadden says that "this female person knows firsthand the reasons for scourging sexist bias from the language." How does this claim function in the context of her argument? Did you find it effective? Why, or why not?

4. Identify several metaphors and similes that McFadden uses and explain how each one works. (Glossary: *Figures of Speech*)

5. McFadden claims that "person" suffixes and "he/she's" are both awkward and ridiculous. In what ways does her essay itself illustrate this point?

6. Why do you think McFadden chose to use the word "neuter" to describe the process of eliminating sexism from English? What are the connotations of this word? (Glossary: *Connotation*) Is it an appropriate choice? Explain.

VOCABULARY

fusing (1)	replete (8)	appendages (12)
scourging (2)	render (8)	suffuses (18)
aspirant (3)	generic (9)	lethargic (22)
liturgy (6)		

 the

WRITING TOPICS

1. When McFadden wrote her essay in 1981, she believed that the neutering of English was largely a West Coast phenomenon. How widespread is it today? Do you come into contact with neutered English on a daily basis? Or, has such usage started to die out? Write an essay in which you discuss neutering as a language fad or as a "here-to-stay" change. Feel free to take issue with McFadden and show the serious intent of the changes that have occurred. You might also want to consider other negative reactions to feminist "over-zealousness."

2. Select a passage from the *Bible,* an essay in this book, or a legal document and rewrite it so as to eliminate all sexist language. What do you think of the revised version? What has been lost in the rewriting? Which version do you prefer?

GIRL TALK-BOY TALK

John Pfeiffer

*John Pfeiffer is a science writer whose works have appeared
in many popular science magazines. In the following essay,
he discusses the results of studies to examine the differences
between male and female speech patterns in conversation and
the ways they reflect our culture's image of the two sexes.
The findings show that women ask the most questions while
men do most of the interrupting. However, he points out that
slowly, as our attitudes about men and women change, the
way we talk to each other changes too.*

An investigator, pencil in hand, is transcribing two minutes of an "un- 1
obtrusively" recorded coffee-shop conversation between two university
students, male and female—listening intently, making out words and pronunciations, noting hesitations, timing utterances. The tape whirs in reverse for a replay and then again, eight replays in all. Part of the final

> *Andrew: It's about time uh that my family really went on a vacation* (pause)
> *y'know my father goes places all the time* (prolonged syllable) *but he
> y'know goes on business like he'll go ta' Tokyo for the afternoon 'n
> he'll get there at* (stammer) *at ten in the morning 'n catch a nine
> o'clock flight leaving . . .* (two-second pause)

> *Betsy: That sounds fantastic* (pause) *not everybody can jus' spend a day in
> someplace—*(interruption)

> *Andrew: Well, we've already established the fact that um y'know he's not just*
> anyone. (eight-second pause)

> *Betsy: Don't you I* (stammer) *well it seems to me you you you probably have
> such an um interesting background that you must y'know have trouble
> finding um people uh like to talk to if you—*(interruption)

> *Andrew: Most definitely . . .*

Candace West and Don Zimmerman, the researchers who analyzed these 2
recordings, were particularly interested in the interruptions. The pattern is
typical. According to these University of California sociologists, it held

for all 11 two-person, cross-sex conversations recorded mainly in public places: Males accounted for some 96 percent of the interruptions. In same-sex conversations males also cut off males and females cut off females, but in 20 recorded encounters, interruptions were equally distributed between the speakers.

This study is part of an active and rapidly expanding field of language   3
research—the role of gender in speech, with the accent primarily on how, under what conditions, and why the sexes talk differently. A 1983 bibliography of relevant publications includes some 800 titles, compared with about 150 titles in a bibiliography published eight years before. The boom started little more than a decade ago, inspired by the women's movement. A new generation of investigators began taking hard looks at some of the things that had been written about women's talk by earlier investigators, mainly male. They encountered a number of statements like the following from Otto Jespersen, a Danish linguist who has earned a prominent place in the feminist rogues' gallery: "[W]omen much more often than men break off without finishing their sentences, because they start talking without having thought out what they are going to say."

Such belittlement of female conversation may be somewhat less fre-   4
quent nowadays. But it lives on in everyday contexts, hardly surprising since it involves attitudes imbedded in thinking that get passed on like bad genes from generation to generation. The latest issue of a women-and-language newsletter notes items involving sexism in everything from the *New England Journal of Medicine* and Maidenform bra ads to campaign speeches and government offices in Japan.

Work focused on interruption contributes to understanding who con-   5
trols conversations and how. To check on their original observations in a more casual context, West and Zimmerman conducted an experiment in which students meeting for the first time were told to "relax and get to know one another," with familiar results. Males again turned out to be the chief culprits, although they made only 75 percent of the interruptions, compared with that 96 percent figure for previously acquainted pairs— perhaps because they were more restrained among new acquaintances.

Men not only do the lion's share of the interrupting (and the talking)   6
but often choose what to talk about. This can be seen in a study conducted by public relations consultant Pamela Fishman. Her subjects were three couples, a social worker and five graduate students, who consented to having tape recorders in their apartments, providing some 52 hours of conversation, 25 of which have been transcribed.

Fishman's first impression: "At times I felt that all the women did was   7
ask questions . . . I attended to my own speech and discovered the same pattern." In fact, the women asked more than 70 percent of the questions. Dustin Hoffman put this speech pattern to use in the motion picture *Tootsie*,

using the questioning intonation frequently when impersonating a woman and rather less frequently when acting unladylike.

In her study, Fishman discovered that a particular question was used with great frequency: "D'ya know what?" Research by other investigators had described how children frequently use this phrase to communicate with their elders. It serves as a conversation opener, calling for an answer like "What?" or "No, tell me," a go-ahead signal that they may speak up and that what they have to say will be heeded. **8**

Pursuing this lead, Fishman found out why women need such reassurances when she analyzed the 76 efforts in taped conversations to start conversations or keep them going. Men tried 29 times and succeeded 28 times. That is, in all but a single case the outcome was some discussion of the topic broached. Women tried 47 times, sometimes for as long as five minutes, with dead-end results 30 times, an unimpressive .362 batting average. (It could have been worse. Each of the male subjects in this experiment professed sympathy for the women's movement.) **9**

Other actions that control conversation (and often power) are more complicated, less open to statistical analysis. Cheris Kramarae, professor of speech communication at the University of Illinois in Urbana-Champaign, tells what happened when, as the only woman member of an important policy-shaping committee, she tried to communicate with the chairman before the start of a meeting. She suggested that certain items be added to the agenda, apparently to no effect. "He paid no attention to me, and I gave up." Once the meeting got under way, however, he featured her ideas in a review of the agenda and, turning to a male colleague, commented: "I don't remember who suggested these changes. I think it was Dick here." **10**

Kramarae cites such instances of being heard but not listened to, "as if you were speaking behind a glass," as the sort of thing women must cope with every day. Other examples of everyday difficulties include being first-named by people who address males by last names plus "Mr." or "Dr.," hearing men discuss hiring a "qualified" woman, and looking a block ahead to see whether men are around who might make catcalls or pass out unwanted compliments. **11**

These sorts of affronts lead women to a guarded way of life that fosters sensitivity to biases in the King's English. There is the intriguing record of efforts to abolish the generic masculine where *man* means not just males but all humans (as in "Man is among the few mammals in which estrus has disappeared entirely," from *Emergence of Man* by John Pfeiffer, 1978). *Woman* is used only in reference to a female, a rule established by male grammarians some 250 years ago. **12**

At first the move to a more generalized language was widely opposed, mainly on the grounds of triviality and the inviolability of language. Critics **13** included some feminists, the linguistic faculty at Harvard, and *Time* magazine, the latter exhibiting its usual delicate touch in an essay entitled "Sispeak: A Msguided Attempt to Change Herstory." Then a number of psychologists, among them Donald MacKay and Wendy Martyna of the University of California, ran tests showing that, whatever the speaker or writer intended, most people associate *man* and the matching pronoun *he* with a male image and that the generic masculine could hurt the way *boy* hurts blacks. Today it is common practice to edit such references out of textbook manuscripts and other writings.

Meanwhile research continues along a widening front, trying to cope   14
with unconscious attitudes, sexist and otherwise, which distinguish women and men—"two alien cultures, oddly intertwined," in the words of Barrie Thorne of Michigan State University. Recent studies of the American male culture by and large support previous findings. Men spend considerable time playing the dominance game, either at a joking level or for real. The telling of a tall tale, followed by a still taller tale in an I-can-top-that atmosphere, seems to be typically male.

In this game, keeping cool commands the respect of the other players,   15
with an occasional flash of emotion commended, providing it has to do with politics or sports or shop talk—practically anything but personal feelings. Elizabeth Aries of Amherst College, who has recorded 15 hours of conversation among newly acquainted male students, reports that certain males consistently dominated the conversation. Her subjects addressed the entire group rather than individuals at least a third of the time, nearly five times more often than women interacting under similar conditions.

Detailed studies of women's conversations are rare, mainly conducted   16
in the past few years. Aries discovered that leaders in all-female groups tend to assume a low profile and encourage others to speak, while leaders among men tend to resist the contributions of others. Mercilee Jenkins of San Francisco State University studied the conversation of mothers in a discussion group over a five-month period. She was interested in subject matter as well as conversational style. She found that the young mothers discussed a broad range of subjects—much beyond domestic problems.

Storytelling makes up a large proportion of conversational encounters,   17
with narrative styles that reflect other gender differences. "The universe is made of stories, not atoms," said poet Muriel Rukeyser, and linguistic analysis confirms her insight. As a rule, the women in the Jenkins' study avoided first-person narratives. In 26 out of 57 transcribed stories, the narrator played no role at all, while men frequently shine in their own stories. The women listening became heavily involved in the incidents recounted and chimed in with stories supporting the narrator, challenging the preceding story in only five percent of the cases.

Mixing sexes conversationally produces some interesting reactions, at   18 least among newly acquainted Harvard students in the Aries study. The men softened, competing less among themselves and talking more about their personal lives. (This may be a kind of instinctive mating or courting display, an attracting mechanism discarded upon closer acquaintance when the male usually reassumes his impersonal ways.) Women students responded with a pattern of their own, becoming more competitive. Aries notes that "the social significance of women for one another in a mixed group was low." They maintained a supportive style in talking with men, but it was every woman for herself as they spoke disproportionately more to the men than to each other.

The "music" of conversation may be as meaningful as the words. [19] Women not only have higher voices, but the pitch is notably higher than can be explained solely by the anatomy of the female vocal apparatus. Moreover, Sally McConnell-Ginet of Cornell University finds that women's voices are more colorful—they vary more in pitch and change pitch more frequently than do men's voices. In one experiment, women immediately assumed a monotone style when asked to imitate men's speech. McConnell-Ginet regards speaking tunefully as an effective strategy for getting and holding attention, a strategy used more often by women than men, perhaps because they are more often ignored.

No one has a workable theory that accounts for all these differences. [20] Even the longest running, most thorough searches for the root causes of differences between the sexes raise more questions than they answer. Carol Nagy Jacklin of the University of Southern California and Eleanor Maccoby of Stanford University have been tracking the development of 100 children from birth to age six. These children have been observed at several stages, in various settings. When this group reached 45 months of age, the researchers focused on how 58 of them interacted with their parents during playtime.

A surprising conclusion emerged: Discrimination by gender originates [21] mainly outside the home. "Mothers do little behavior stereotyping," Jacklin summarizes. "They appear to treat [their own] little boys and little girls much the same." (While fathers tend to treat their children in more gender-sterotyped ways during playtimes, they ordinarily have less influence on childbearing and on actually creating the home environment.)

The implication is intriguing. If it is true that outsiders are largely [22] responsible, and since most outsiders are also parents, it follows that parents have gender-based preconceptions more often about other people's children than about their own. In any event, school is one place where highly significant changes take place. In the beginning, teacher is "home base," a surrogate parent to whom children come for reassurance and support, and that holds for all children—until second grade.

At that point boys but not girls begin increasingly to turn away from [23] teacher and toward one another. The stress is more and more on hierarchy, jockeying for position in speech as well as action, in talking as well as playing cowboy, soldier, Star Wars, and so on. All this is part of a constellation of changes. In playgrounds girls tend to go around in pairs, usually near teachers and the school building; boys form groups of half a dozen or so, usually as far away as possible. Boys may get more attention than girls because they are often more disruptive.

In discussing such patterns Thorne cites the classic psychoanalytic theory that boys, being raised mainly by women at home, feel the need at school to assert themselves as "not female." Also, teachers may have biased expectations about boys. But, according to Raphaela Best of the Montgomery County school system in Maryland, a high price may be paid for early male-male competition. She suggests that the resulting tensions may help account for the fact that reading disabilities are at least five times more frequent among boys than among girls. 24

Though the study of gender-based differences is relatively new, significant steps have been taken. Furthermore—a totally unexpected development—gender-related work has helped spark renewed interest in general language use. The ways in which men talk to men and women talk to women have come under scrutiny, as have the speech differences between people of different cultures and professional backgrounds. 25

West, for example, is currently interested in exchanges between doctors and patients. This work demands looking as well as listening, analyzing a kind of choreography of nonverbal as well as verbal behavior. Her raw data consist of videotapes complete with sound tracks. So far she has spent more than 550 hours transcribing seven hours of conversation in 21 patient-physician meetings at a family-practice center in the southern United States. Preliminary analysis indicates that doctors out-interrupt their patients, male and female, by a two-to-one margin—except when the doctor is a woman. In that case, the situation is reversed, with patients—both male and female—out-interrupting by the same margin. 26

Similar studies are tuning in on the finer points of speech and behavior. An outstanding and continuing analysis by Marjorie Harness Goodwin of the University of South Carolina shows that girls as well as boys form social groups, except that the girls tend to form exclusive "coalitions," whereas boys form all-inclusive hierarchies. With the girls not everyone gets to play, while with the boys everyone, even the nerds, can play as long as they respect rank. Girls also are far less direct in arguing with one another, and their debates may simmer for weeks, in contrast to male arguments, which generally end within a few minutes. 27

These findings are based on taped observations of black children at play in an urban setting. Other observations hint that the same points might apply more widely, a possibility that remains to be probed. What holds true 28 for one culture or society may not for another. Male dominance in speech seems to be a global phenomeon. But the most notable exception cries for analysis: Sexism is probably at a lower level in Bali, where to vote or be otherwise active as a citizen, one must be part of a couple.

While most of the recent research has revealed conflict between the sexes, Carole Edelsky of Arizona State University has discovered a trend worth noting. She has studied five "very informal" meetings of a standing faculty committee consisting of seven women and four men—7.5 hours of taped conversation. It started as a "fishing expedition" project—a search for sexisms, and there were plenty. As usual, men talked longer and interrupted more, appearing to hold the floor longer.   29

But Edelsky also recognized a second method of holding the floor. She identified short interludes, between the more formal addresses, that featured mutual support and "greater discourse equality." (These episodes were most informal and laughter-filled.) At first Edelsky had the impression that the women were doing most of the talking during these periods. But actual counts of words and time per turn revealed an equal-time situation (thus supporting the observation that a "talkative" woman is one who talks as much as the average man). These episodes made up less than 20 percent of total talk time, but such encounters as these may reflect a change in communication between the sexes.   30

The future may see great change in our current perception of a conversational gap between the sexes. It may also see a correction of imbalance in present-day research—a shift in the gender composition of the researchers. Today in the United States there are about 200 investigators of language and gender, and all but a dozen of them are women. Many of the researchers believe that as more men enter the field the "two alien cultures" will draw closer together.   31

QUESTIONS ON CONTENT

1. How does Pfeiffer define the newest branch of language research? What is its goal? When did it begin? What attitudes inspired it?

2. In paragraph 4, Pfeiffer points out that the belittlement of female conversation is still prevalent in spite of changing attitudes toward women. What do these lingering attitudes reveal about the nature of sexism? Where are some of the different places this kind of thinking shows up?

3. List some of the differences between male and female styles of conversation. What do you find the most indicative of sex-bias attitudes?

4. Pfeiffer describes the results of several gender differentiation studies in his essay. The Aires's study, conducted among Harvard students, pro-

duced results that Pfeiffer found particularly interesting. Briefly describe the results. Did you find the results interesting? Why or why not?

5. What other areas of "language use" have begun to interest researchers as a result of the studies into gender-based differences in language?

6. At the end of his essay, Pfeiffer suggests that conversational habits among men and women are changing. What do you think accounts for these changes? Are they borne out by your own personal experience?

QUESTIONS ON RHETORIC

1. Pfeiffer uses comparison and contrast (Glossary: *Comparison and Contrast*) to present the information for his argument. How effective is his use of this method? He also quotes experts in the field of language study. Is his use of this information convincing? Why or why not?

2. Paragraphs 12 and 13 could be seen as "interruptions" in Pfeiffer's essay. Why do you suppose he included these paragraphs? In your opinion, do they need to be included? Explain your answer.

3. At times, Pfeiffer adopts a sarcastic, almost angry tone. (Glossary: *Tone*) Who are the targets of his sarcasm? Give examples from the text to support your answer.

4. In paragraph 31, Pfeiffer discloses that those involved in the field of gender-based differences in language are almost exclusively women. Does this strike you as ironic? What are the implications of this fact? Why do you suppose Pfeiffer saves this information until the end?

VOCABULARY

unobtrusively (1)	intonation (7)	constellation (23)
rogues' gallery (3)	agenda (10)	coalitions (27)
culprits (5)	affronts (12)	phenomenon (28)

WRITING TOPICS

1. Pay attention to conversation in your school dining hall or some other campus hangout. What gender-based patterns do you hear? Listen to yourself (being aware that a self-conscious observer affects the outcome of his or her data). In an essay describe the ways your own habits compare to the "norms" for your sex that Pfeiffer discusses in his essay.

2. Pfeiffer points out that women ask 70 percent of the questions in a conversation. Does this necessarily strike you as a sign of weakness? If so, on what basis? What points could you make in favor of this trait? Using examples from your own experience and observation, discuss in an essay what you think of this tendency of women to ask questions?

3. Discuss in class what male and female students believe their conversational habits to be, then ask for permission to tape the class one day during a period of class discussion. It is important that the class not know when it is being taped. Discuss and write up the results of your findings.

THE "F" WORD

Catharine R. Stimpson

In this essay taken from Ms. *magazine, Catharine R.
Stimpson, dean of the Graduate School at Rutgers University
and chair of the* Ms. *Board of Scholars, lists six basic
attitudes that have turned feminism into a dirty word. To
quiet these "voices" she suggests a counterattack that
includes humor and a willingness to repeat the word over
and over until it loses its mystique: "The more we say it the
more reasonable it will become and then it will be G rated."*

F*eminism* entered the English language in 1895, *X ray* in 1896. Femi-   1
nism was to film our behavior as sharply as X rays did our bones. However, nearly a century later, people say X rays without spluttering.
Feminism is an X-rated word.

I understand some distrust of feminism. We have made wild claims in   2
our day, insisting, for example, that all women are the same, despite
differences of class, race, or age.

However, much of the X-rating is vicious, fearful, or irrational. At its   3
most zany, the resistance to feminism lurches into phobia. Where a reasonable person sees walls, the claustrophobe sees walls collapsing. Where
a reasonable person sees change, the feminaphobe, female or male, sees a
world collapsing if women change.

The fear of feminism, in mild or phobic form, wells up, whether   4
feminism seems puny or powerful. In many ways, it is both. We still lack
influence in certain areas: podium, pulpit, TV studio, White House briefing
room. But feminism offers three potent gifts: a moral vision of women, in
all their diversity, and social justice; political and cultural organizations
(like shelters for battered women) that translate the vision into action; and
psychological processes that enable men and women to re-experience and
re-form themselves.

Inevitably, as feminism has grown and become more diverse, as it   5
has become feminisms, the forms of resistance to it have also altered. I now hear at least six voices that choke on the sentence, "I am a
feminist."

TYPE A—THE NEOCONSERVATIVE

Type A labels feminism a violation of the laws of God, man, and nature.   6
The conservative man who dreads the loss of women's cheap labor is a
familiar example; the conservative woman is not so well understood. She
may have translated her fear of economic insecurity, and her ardent devotion to family as a source of security, into a fear of feminism. Or she
may simply disregard the feminine role when it suits her purposes. ("I can
work outside the home, but if all those other women do, too—watch out!")

TYPE B—THE SCAPEGOATER

Every society creates boundaries. Every society also creates scapegoats,   7
pushes them beyond the boundaries, and then punishes them for being out
there. Women have often been malleable candidates for scapegoathood.
Around 1486, two papal inquisitors named Heinrich and James labeled
certain women witches. Witches raise hailstorms and tempests instead of
children; killed the children they did have; sterilized men and beasts; and
flew through the air to copulate with devils. Today, we still hear echoes of
Heinrich and James—except now they're saying that feminists sleep with
each other instead of warlocks.

TYPE C—"I'M NOT A FEMINIST, I'M A RUGGED INDIVIDU-
ALIST"

Americans traditionally, if self-deceptively, think of themselves as indi-   8
viduals, not as ideologues. Ironically, feminism, which is ideological,
urges each woman to think of herself as an individual as well as a citizen
of a community. Women who really ought to consider themselves feminists can still do things like ask their sons to wash the dishes without being
called "libbers"—they simply call themselves individualists.

TYPE D—"I WANT MOMMY"

Most of us want to be special, showered with care, bathed in nurture—no   9
matter how fiercely we might repress these longings. Symbolically, the
"good mother" provides these blissful services. Feminists may disagree
about a biological mother's natural right to her baby, but we agree on many
other points: that fathers can mother; that parents deserve real rewards; that
men and women need new child-care systems; and that women other than

Mother Teresa can refuse to bear children. Many people misinterpret these positions and think of feminism as the ax murderer of the Good Mother.

TYPE E—THE LANGUID HEIRESS

In 1937, the first woman to get tenure on the graduate facilities of Colum-   10
bia University, Majorie Hope Nicolson, decided that the professional women of her generation occupied a unique position. Born in the last decade of the 19th century, they were old enough to "escape the self-consciousness and belligerence" of the feminist pioners and young enough to escape the constrictions society placed on white women after the fight for suffrage was over. Some postfeminists are a 1980s equivalent. Born in the years between *The Second Sex* (1953) and *Sexual Politics* (1970), they are the beneficiaries of the will of the active feminists of the 1960s and 1970s. They are now living on a trust fund from history. Like many children with inherited money, they heedlessly spend the income and refuse to add to the principal.

TYPE F—THE FEMINIST MYSTIQUE

Feminism, like other movements for social justice, is demanding. Erasing   11
the images of Betty Crocker or Aunt Jemima and generating new models is much harder than whipping up a waffle. Even feminists fear feminism. We underestimated how difficult it would be to wipe out the psychological residue of the feminine mystique. Many of us still carry within ourselves a conflict about what gender and change mean. We say, "I am a feminist," but we often whisper, with irritation, guilt, and ennui, "I wish I did not have to be."

If all women's lives continue to change as they have been changing,   12
many people will be able to say "feminist" as casually as they now say "wife" or "kid" or "snack." The feminist analyses of injustice—of domestic violence or of women's incomes—are too compelling to ignore. The feminist remedies—social support for child care, for example—are too appealing. Ultimately, the X-raters and feminaphobes will lose their power.

Until then, those of us who call ourselves feminists might revise our   13
strategy. First of all, let's just take to calling it the F word. It might deflect a little of that hostility back to where it came from. And it will help us to remember how long it has taken all of us to learn to say "feminist" without stammering. Next, we need even more audacity, more humor, when we speak of feminism. We are strong enough to know that self-satire does not

THE "F" WORD   337

signify self-contempt. Finally, we must be aware that the sentence, "I am a feminist," translates into many social languages, each with its own rhythm, idioms, and nuance. The more we say it, the more reasonable it will become—and then it will be G rated.

QUESTIONS ON CONTENT

1. When did the word *feminism* enter the English language, according to Stimpson? Are you surprised by this fact?

2. Stimpson states that "The fear of feminism, in mild or phobic form, wells up, whether feminism seems puny or powerful" (4). What are the "puny" and the "powerful" aspects of feminism Stimpson names? What are feminism's three potent gifts according to Stimpson? For whom or what does Stimpson imply these "gifts" are intended?

3. In your own words, summarize the main features of the six voices Stimpson says choke on the sentence, "I am a feminist."

4. Stimpson says, "Even feminists fear feminism" (11). Why? What does Stimpson gain by admitting it? In your own words, how would you describe the feminine mystique?

5. What strategy does Stimpson offer to bring about a change in attitude toward the word *feminism?* Will this strategy work, in your opinion? Why is Stimpson confident that the word *feminism* is likely to become commonplace of its own accord?

QUESTIONS ON RHETORIC

1. What is Stimpson's purpose in writing this essay? (Glossary: *Purpose*) Stimpson obviously intended her readers to expect something different when they read the title of her essay. How do you think she wanted you to react upon reading the first few words of her essay? How does this anticipated reaction serve Stimpson's purpose?

2. Stimpson never quotes experts in her essay. Instead, she relies on her readers' knowledge of the issue. Is this a proper assumption to make of readers of *Ms.* magazine? Why or why not? What might Stimpson have gained by quoting famous feminists?

3. What is the figure of speech Stimpson uses in paragraph 10? (Glossary: *Figure of Speech*) Why do you think she chose it? Identify other figures of speech Stimpson uses. How do they work in the context of her essay?

4. Stimpson is writing on a very emotional controversial subject without the militant tone sometimes present in other feminist writing. How would you describe her tone: angry, conciliatory, humorous? What does Stimpson gain by using this tone? Point to examples from the text to support your answer.

VOCABULARY

feminism (1)	ideologues (8)	mystique (11)
zany (3)	repress (9)	compelling (12)
lurches (3)	belligerence (10)	nuance (13)

WRITING TOPICS

1. In her opening paragraph, Stimpson says the word *feminism* entered the English language in 1895. Do some digging to find out more about the word *feminism:* who coined it, how it was defined, what the state of the women's movement was at the time, how it was received, etc. In what ways has the original attitude toward the word *feminism* been altered by the six voices Stimpson describes in her essay?

2. In her essay, Stimpson divides the different forms of resistance to the word *feminism* into "six voices." Choose one of these voices and write an essay describing your own encounters with this attitude, whether your own inner voice, the voice of a friend or relative, or the voice you hear most often on campus.

3. In discussing the Type C voice, Stimpson suggests that women who call themselves individualists ought to call themselves feminists, because except for fear of the word *feminist,* there are no important differences between the two. Do you agree? Write an essay in which you compare and contrast the words *feminist* and *individualist,* using examples from your own experience.

WRITING ASSIGNMENTS FOR "SEXISM AND LANGUAGE"

1. Find twenty-five words in your desk dictionary that have some relation to males and females, and study the words in the way Alleen Nilsen studied her words. (Try to avoid overlapping her examples.) Using Nilsen's article as a model, write a short paper in which you discuss the biases, if any, that you see in the language.

2. Since its beginning, the feminist movement has been surrounded with controversy. One commentator, for example, in a recent essay in *Time,* said, "The feminist attack on social crimes [sex discrimination, etc.] may be as legitimate as it was inevitable. But the attack on words is only another social crime—one against the means and the hope of communication." Write an essay in which you agree or disagree with this writer's view of women's attempts to change language. Be sure to use examples to support your position.

3. It has been said that the words Americans use to describe old women are more derisive than those of old men because the words for women represent them as thoroughly repugnant and disgusting. Compile a list of words that you use or that you have heard used to refer to old people. Are the words for women more derogatory and demeaning? Write an essay in which you discuss the words on your list.

4. Write an essay in which you analyze Cyra McFadden's arguments in "In Defense of Gender." Does she ever seem to have missed the point of the language changes? Which of her objections seem to you valid?

5. Write an essay in which you consider one or more of the following potentially sexist words or groups of words in English:

    a. feminine suffixes *-ess* or *-trix*
    b. fellow
    c. old wives' tale
    d. coed
    e. salutations in letters
    f. *Ms, Miss,* and *Mrs.*
    g. *girl* and *gal*

6. Consider the language used to describe the institution of marriage. Write an essay in which you discuss any sexist attitudes that are revealed in the words we use to write and talk about marriage.

7. John Pfeiffer discusses some of the ways sexist language hurts women: "These sorts of affronts lead to a guarded way of life that fosters sensitivity

to biases in the King's English. There is the intriguing record of efforts to abolish the generic masculine where *man* means not just males but all humans.'' In an essay, discuss the ways in which sex-biased language has hurt you or others around you. If possible, talk with someone older who was growing up before current attitudes about men and women became popular. How do they handle these affronts? How do you handle these affronts? Do you both perceive them as affronts in the same way?

8. Catharine R. Stimpson chairs the board of scholars at *Ms.* magazine, one of the most popular of feminist publications. Read through a couple of issues from several years ago and compare them with more recent issues. Look over the table of contents, the ads, and the covers. In what ways do you find the publication has changed over the years? What conclusions can you draw about the feminist movement from these changes? In an essay discuss your observations.

9. Carefully read the following letter to the editor of *The New York Times*. In it the author, president of a small Manhattan advertising agency, argues against using the word *guys* to address women.

WOMEN AREN'T GUYS

By Nancy Stevens

A young woman, a lawyer, strides into a conference room. Already in attendance, at what looks to be the start of a high-level meeting, are four smartly dressed women in their 20's and 30's. The arriving woman plunks her briefcase down at the head of the polished table and announces, "O.K., guys, let's get started."

On "Kate and Allie," a television show about two women living together with Kate's daughter and Allie's daughter and son, the dialogue often runs to such phrases as, "Hey, you guys, who wants pizza?" All of the people addressed are female, except for Chip, the young son. "Come on, you guys, quit fighting," pleads one of the daughters when there is a tiff between the two women.

Just when we were starting to be aware of the degree to which language affects people's perceptions of women and substitute "people working" for "men working" and "humankind" for "mankind," this "guy" thing happened. Just when poeople have started becoming aware that a 40-year-old woman shouldn't be called a girl, this "guy" thing has crept in.

Use of "guy" to mean "person" is so insidious that I'll bet most women don't notice they are being called "guys," or, if they do, find it somehow flattering to be one of them.

Sometimes, I find the courage to pipe up when a bunch of us are assembled and are called "guys" by someone of either gender. "We're not guys," I say. Then everyone looks at me funny.

One day, arriving at a business meeting where there were five women and one man, I couldn't resist. "Hello, ladies," I said. Everyone laughed embarrassedly for the blushing man until I added, "and gent." Big sigh of relief. Wouldn't want to call a guy a "gal" now, would we?

Why is it not embarrassing for a woman to be called "guy?" We know why. It's the same logic that says women look sexy and cute in a man's shirt, but did you ever try your silk blouse on your husband and send him to the deli? It's the same mentality that holds that anything male is worthy (and to be aspired toward) and anything female is trivial.

We all sit around responding, without blinking, "black with one sugar, please," when anyone asks, "How do you guys like your coffee?"

What's all that murmuring I hear?

"Come on, lighten up."

"Be a good guy."

"Nobody means anything by it."

Nonsense.

Whatever our different opinions may be about anti-male and anti-female bias in the language, the examples of the man's shirt and the woman's silk blouse in Stevens's letter rings true in our experience. What does it reveal about our perceptions of men and women? Do you agree that this example reveals the same biases that allow even women to use the word *guy* when they refer to women? Write an essay supporting your conclusions.

PART VII

Euphemism
and
Taboos

What do you mean, ''did we go moo-moo in our dipe-dipes?''

EUPHEMISM

Neil Postman

In the following essay taken from his book Crazy Talk,
Stupid Talk, *Neil Postman, professor of media ecology at
New York University, defines* euphemism *and explains the
often disapproved process of euphemizing. He believes that
"euphemisms are a means through which a culture may alter
its imagery and by so doing subtly change its style, its
priorities, and its values." There are those people, however,
for whom all euphemisms are bad. Postman argues that many
euphemisms serve worthwhile social purposes.*

A euphemism is commonly defined as an auspicious or exalted term 1
(like "sanitation engineer") that is used in place of a more down-to-earth
term (like "garbage man"). People who are partial to euphemisms stand
accused of being "phony" or of trying to hide what it is they are talking
about. And there is no doubt that in some situations the accusation is
entirely proper. For example, one of the more detestable euphemisms I
have come across in recent years is the term "Operation Sunshine," which
is the name the U.S. Government gave to some experiments it conducted
with the hydrogen bomb in the South Pacific. It is obvious that the government, in choosing this name, was trying to expunge the hideous imagery that the bomb evokes and in so doing committed, as I see it, an
immoral act. This sort of process—giving pretty names to essentially ugly
realities—is what has given euphemizing such a bad name. And people
like George Orwell have done valuable work for all of us in calling attention to how the process works. But there is another side to euphemizing
that is worth mentioning, and a few words here in its defense will not be
amiss.

To begin with, we must keep in mind that things do not have "real" 2
names, although many people believe that they do. A garbage man is not
"really" a "garbage man," any more than he is really a "sanitation
engineer." And a pig is not called a "pig" because it is so dirty, nor a
shrimp a "shrimp" because it is so small. There are things, and then there
are the names of things, and it is considered a fundamental error in all

branches of semantics to assume that a name and a thing are one and the same. It is true, of course, that a name is usually so firmly associated with the thing it denotes that it is extremely difficult to separate one from the other. That is why, for example, advertising is so effective. Perfumes are not given names like "Bronx Odor," and an automobile will never be called "The Lumbering Elephant." Shakespeare was only half right in saying that a rose by any other name would smell as sweet. What we call things affect how we will perceive them. It is not only harder to sell someone a "horse mackerel" sandwich than a "tuna fish" sandwich, but even though they are the "same" thing, we are likely to enjoy the taste of the tuna more than that of the horse mackerel. It would appear that human beings almost naturally come to *identify* names with things, which is one of our more fascinating illusions. But there is some substance to this illusion. For if you change the names of things, you change how people will regard them, and that is as good as changing the nature of the thing itself.

Now, all sorts of scoundrels know this perfectly well and can make us 3 love almost anything by getting us to transfer the charm of a name to whatever worthless thing they are promoting. But at the same time and in the same vein, euphemizing is a perfectly intelligent method of generating new and useful ways of perceiving things. The man who wants us to call him a "sanitation engineer" instead of a "garbage man" is hoping we will treat him with more respect than we presently do. He wants us to see that he is of some importance to our society. His euphemism is laughable only if we think that he is not deserving of such notice or respect. The teacher who prefers us to use the term "culturally different children" instead of "slum children" is euphemizing, all right, but is doing it to encourage us to see aspects of a situation that might otherwise not be attended to.

The point I am making is that there is nothing in the process of eu- 4 phemizing itself that is contemptible. Euphemizing is contemptible when a name makes us see something that is not true or diverts our attention from something that is. The hydrogen bomb kills. There is nothing else that it does. And when you experiment with it, you are trying to find out how widely and well it kills. Therefore, to call such an experiment "Operation Sunshine" is to suggest a purpose for the bomb that simply does not exist. But to call "slum children" "culturally different" is something else. It calls attention, for example, to legitimate reasons why such children might feel alienated from what goes on in school.

I grant that sometimes such euphemizing does not have the intended 5 effect. It is possible for a teacher to use the term "culturally different" but still be controlled by the term "slum children" (which the teacher may believe is their "real" name). "Old people" may be called "senior citizens," and nothing might change. And "lunatic asylums" may still be filthy, primitive prisons though they are called "mental institutions." Nonetheless, euphemizing may be regarded as one of our more important intellectual resources for creating new perspectives on a subject. The *attempt* to rename "old people" "senior citizens" was obviously motivated by a desire to give them a political identity, which they not only warrant but which may yet have important consequences. In fact, the fate of euphemisms is very hard to predict. A new and seemingly silly name may replace an old one (let us say, "chairperson" for "chairman") and for years no one will think or act any differently because of it. And then, gradually, as people begin to assume that "chairperson" is the "real" and proper name (or "senior citizen" or "tuna fish" or "sanitation engineer"), their attitudes begin to shift, and they will approach things in a slightly different frame of mind. There is a danger, of course, in supposing that a new name can change attitudes quickly or always. There must be some authentic tendency or drift in the culture to lend support to the change, or the name will remain incongruous and may even appear ridiculous. To call a teacher a "facilitator" would be such an example. To eliminate the distinction between "boys" and "girls" by calling them "childpersons" would be another.

But to suppose that such changes never "amount to anything" is to   6
underestimate the power of names. I have been astounded not only by how rapidly the name "blacks" has replaced "Negroes" (a kind of euphemizing in reverse) but also by how significantly perceptions and attitudes have shifted as an accompaniment to the change.

The key idea here is that euphemisms are a means through which a   7
culture may alter its imagery and by so doing subtly change its style, its priorities, and its values. I reject categorically the idea that people who use "earthy" language are speaking more directly or with more authenticity than people who employ euphemisms. Saying that someone is "dead" is not to speak more plainly or honestly than saying he has "passed away." It is, rather, to suggest a different conception of what the event means. To ask where the "shithouse" is, is no more to the point than to ask where the "restroom" is. But in the difference between the two words, there is expressed a vast difference in one's attitude toward privacy and propriety. What I am saying is that the process of euphemizing has no moral content. The moral dimensions are supplied by what the words in question express, what they want us to value and see. A nation that calls experiments with bombs "Operation Sunshine" is very frightening. On the other hand, a people who call "garbage men" "sanitation engineers" can't be all bad.

QUESTIONS ON CONTENT

1. If, as Postman says, "there is nothing in the process of euphemizing itself that is contemptible" (4), why do euphemisms have such a bad name?

2. Postman states, "There are things, and then there are the names of things, and it is considered a fundamental error in all branches of semantics to assume that a name and a thing are one and the same" (2). What does he mean? What happens when people think that a name and a thing are the same?

3. Postman believes that "euphemizing may be regarded as one of our more important intellectual resources for creating new perspectives on a subject" (5) How can you change people's perception of something by simply changing its name? Give several examples of your own which substantiate Postman's claim.

4. What does Postman mean when he says that the change from "Negroes" to "blacks" is "a kind of euphemizing in reverse" (6)?

5. Why does Postman "reject categorically the idea that people who use 'earthy' language are speaking more directly or with more authenticity than people who employ euphemisms" (7)? Do you agree with him?

QUESTIONS ON RHETORIC

1. What is Postman arguing for in this essay?

2. Postman presents a dictionary definition of *euphemism* in the first sentence of the essay. Why is it appropriate that he begin with a definition of the term? (Glossary: *Beginnings*)

3. What would be lost if Postman hadn't used all the examples that he includes? (Glossary: *Examples*) Are they all functional and necessary? Explain.

4. In what ways has Postman used transitions to make paragraph 2 coherent? (Glossary: *Transitions*)

5. Why are Postman's last two sentences an appropriate conclusion to his essay? (Glossary: *Beginnings and Endings*)

VOCABULARY

auspicious (1)	evokes (1)	illusions (2)
exalted (1)	amiss (1)	contemptible (4)
expunge (1)	semantics (2)	categorically (7)
hideous (1)		

WRITING TOPICS

1. Postman says, "Euphemizing is contemptible when a name makes us see something that is not true or diverts our attention from something that is" (4). Which of the euphemisms listed below do you find contemptible? Why are they contemptible? Why are the others not contemptible?

pre-owned ("used")
broadcast journalist ("news reporter")
Internal Revenue Service ("tax collector")
nervous wetness ("sweat")
facial blemishes ("pimples")
orderly withdrawal ("retreat")
resources control program ("defoliation")
health alteration committee ("assassination team")
convenient terms ("18 percent annual interest")
queen-size ("large")

Write an essay discussing the uses to which euphemisms can be put. Be sure to include some examples of your own.

2. Several years ago, the editors of *Time* said that "despite its swaggering sexual candor, much contemporary speech still hides behind that traditional enemy of plain talk, the euphemism." Using examples from your own experience or observation, write an essay in which you agree or disagree with the editors of *Time*.

VERBAL TABOO

S. I. Hayakawa

S. I. Hayakawa, formerly president of San Francisco State University and United States Senator from California, is one of the leading semanticists in this country. In this excerpt from Language in Thought and Action, *Hayakawa examines the verbal taboo, the phenomenon that occurs in almost all languages when the distinction between languages and reality becomes confused.*

In every language there seem to be certain "unmentionables"—words of such strong affective connotations that they cannot be used in polite discourse. In English, the first of these to come to mind are, of course, words dealing with excretion and sex. We ask movie ushers and filling-station attendants where the "lounge" or "rest room" is, although we usually have no intention of lounging or resting. "Powder room" is another euphemism for the same facility, also known as "toilet," which itself is an earlier euphemism. Indeed, it is impossible in polite society to state, without having to resort to baby talk or medical vocabulary, what a "rest room" is for. (It is "where you wash your hands.") Another term is "John." There is now a book on the best "Johns" in New York.

Money is another subject about which communication is in some ways inhibited. It is all right to mention *sums* of money, such as $10,000 or $2.50. But it is considered in bad taste to inquire directly into other people's financial affairs, unless such an inquiry is really necessary in the course of business. When creditors send bills, they almost never mention money, although that is what they are writing about. There are many circumlocutions: "We beg to call your attention to what might be an oversight on your part." "We would appreciate your early attention to this matter." "May we look forward to an early remittance?"

The fear of death carries over, quite understandably in view of the widespread confusion of symbols with things symbolized, into fear of the *words* having to do with death. Many people, therefore, instead of saying "died," substitute such expressions as "passed away," "went to his reward," "departed," and "went west." In Japanese, the word for death, *shi,* happens to have the same pronunciation as the word for the number four. This coincidence results in many linguistically awkward situations, since people avoid *"shi"* in the discussion of numbers and prices, and use *"yon,"* a word of different origin, instead.

Words having to do with anatomy and sex—and words even vaguely suggesting anatomical or sexual matters—have, especially in American culture, remarkable affective connotations. Ladies of the nineteenth century could not bring themselves to say "breast" or "leg"—not even of chicken—so that the terms "white meat" and "dark meat" were substituted. It was thought inelegant to speak of "going to bed," and "to retire" was used instead. In rural America there are many euphemisms for the word "bull"; among them are "he-cow," "cow-critter," "male cow," "gentleman cow." But Americans are not alone in their delicacy about such matters. When D. H. Lawrence's first novel, *The White Peacock* (1911), was published, the author was widely and vigorously criticized for having used (in innocuous context) the word "stallion." "Our hearts are warm, our bellies are full" was changed to "Our hearts are warm, and we are full" in a 1962 presentation of the Rodgers and Hammerstein musical *Carousel* before the British Royal Family.

These verbal taboos, although sometimes amusing, also produce serious problems, since they prevent frank discussion of sexual matters. Social workers, with whom I have discussed this question, report that young people of junior high school and high school age who contact venereal disease, become pregnant out of wedlock, and get into other serious trouble of this kind are almost always profoundly ignorant of the most elementary facts about sex and procreation. Their ignorance is apparently due to the fact that neither they nor their parents have a vocabulary with which to discuss such matters: the nontechnical vocabulary of sex is to them too coarse and shocking to be used, while the technical, medical vocabulary is unknown to them. The social workers find, therefore, that the first step in helping these young people is usually a linguistic one: the students have to be taught a vocabulary in which they can talk about their problems before they can be helped further.

The stronger verbal taboos have, however, a genuine social value. When we are extremely angry and we feel the need of expressing our anger in violence, uttering these forbidden words provides us with a relatively harmless verbal substitute for going beserk and smashing furniture; that is, the words act as a kind of safety valve in our moments of crisis.

It is difficult to explain why some words should have such powerful affective connotations while others with the same informative connotations do not. Some of our verbal reticences, especially the religious ones, have the authority of the Bible: "Thou shalt not take the name of the Lord thy God in vain; for the Lord will not hold him guiltless that taketh his name in vain" (Exodus 21:7). "Gee," "gosh almighty," and "gosh darn" are ways to avoid saying, "Jesus," "God Almighty," and "God damn"; and carrying the biblical injunction one step further, we also avoid taking the name of the Devil in vain by means of such expressions as "the deuce," "the dickens," and "Old Nick." It appears that among all the people of the world, among the civilized as well as the primitive, there is a feeling that the names of the gods are too holy, and the names of evil spirits too terrifying, to be spoken lightly.

The primitive confusion of word with thing, of symbol with thing 8
symbolized, manifests itself in some parts of the world in a belief that the name of a person is *part of* that person. To know someone's name, therefore, is to have power over him. Because of this belief, it is customary among some peoples for children to be given at birth a "real name" known only to the parents and never used, as well as a nickname or public name to be called by in society. In this way the child is protected from being put in anyone's power. The story of Rumpelstiltskin is a European illustration of this belief in the power of names. . . .

QUESTIONS ON CONTENT

1. Into what categories does Hayakawa classify taboo words? Give an example of each subject area.

2. What does Hayakawa mean when he says that taboo words have "strong affective connotations"(1)? How do affective connotations differ from informative connotations?

3. According to Hayakawa, what problems result from the existence of verbal taboos?

4. Hayakawa says that the "stronger verbal taboos have . . . a genuine social value" (6). What is it?

5. What does Hayakawa mean when he says there is "widespread confusion of symbols with things symbolized" (3)?

6. What is the relationship between taboo words and euphemisms? Provide several examples to illustrate your answer.

QUESTIONS ON RHETORIC

1. Which sentence in paragraph 4 is the topic sentence? How does Hayakawa support this idea? (Glossary: *Topic Sentence*)

2. How does Hayakawa make the transition between paragraphs 5 and 6? What other transitional devices does he use in this essay? (Glossary: *Transitions*)

3. Hayakawa assumes that his readers are familiar with the story of

Rumpelstiltskin, a children's classic, and therefore does not retell the story to make his point. Is Hayakawa's assumption correct? Do you know the story?

4. In what ways do Hayakawa's numerous examples function in this essay? (Glossary: *Examples*) Which ones are most effective for you? Why?

VOCABULARY

inhibited (2)   coincidence (3)   ignorant (5)
symbols(3)   anatomical (4)

WRITING TOPICS

1. There is an important distinction between symbols and the things they stand for, that is, their referents. For example, a person should not confuse an actual chair (physical object) with the word *chair* (symbol). Nevertheless, as Hayakawa observes, there is "widespread confusion of symbols with things symbolized" (3). In this connection, discuss the following episode in which a small child is talking to her mother: "Mommy! I'm scared of *death*. I don't like to hear that word. It frightens me! If only it were called something else, like *looma*." What in your opinion would happen if the word were changed? Can you suggest other examples to support your view?

2. In recent years "concerned citizens" across the country have attempted to remove the *Dictionary of American Slang* as well as certain desk dictionaries from schools and libraries. They have done so to keep their children from being exposed to taboo language. What underlying assumption about the relationship between words and things do such efforts reflect? If these citizens were successful in removing these books, would their children be protected? Why, or why not?

FOUR-LETTER WORDS
CAN HURT YOU

Barbara Lawrence

*Barbara Lawrence was born in Hanover, New Hampshire,
and graduated from Connecticut College. Before becoming a
professor of humanities at the State University of New York
at Old Westbury, she worked as an editor at* McCall's,
Redbook, *and the* New Yorker. *In the following essay,
published in* The New York Times *in 1973, she defines
"obscenity" and explains why she finds the obscene language
some people use to be "implicitly sadistic or denigrating to
women."*

W hy should any words be called obscene? Don't they all describe   1
natural human functions? Am I trying to tell them, my students demand,
that the "strong, earthy, gut-honest"—or, if they are fans of Norman
Mailer, the "rich, liberating, existential"—language they use to describe
sexual activity isn't preferable to "phony-sounding, middle-class words
like 'intercourse' and 'copulate'?" "Cop You Late!" they say with fancy
inflections and gagging grimaces. "Now, what is *that* supposed to mean?"

Well, what is it supposed to mean? And why indeed should one group   2
of words describing human functions and human organs be acceptable in
ordinary conversations and another, describing presumably the same organs and functions, be tabooed—so much so, in fact, that some of these
words still cannot appear in print in many parts of the English-speaking
world?

The argument that these taboos exist only because of "sexual hang-   3
ups" (middle-class, middle-age, feminist), or even that they are a result of
class oppression (the contempt of the Norman conquerors for the language
of their Anglo-Saxon serfs), ignores a much more likely explanation, it
seems to me, and that is the sources and functions of the words themselves.

The best known of the tabooed sexual verbs, for example, comes from   4
the German *ficken,* meaning "to strike"; combined, according to Partridge's etymological dictionary *Origins,* with the Latin sexual verb *futu-*

ere; associated in turn with the Latin *fustis,* "a staff or cudgel"; the Celtic *buc,* "a point, hence to pierce"; the Irish *bot,* "the male member"; the Latin *battuere,* "to beat"; the Gaelic *batair,* "a cudgeller"; the Early Irish *bualaim,* "I strike"; and so forth. It is one of what etymologists sometimes call "the sadistic group of words for the man's part in copulation."

The brutality of this word, then, and its equivalents ("screw," "bang," etc.), is not an illusion of the middle class or a crotchet of Women's Liberation. In their origins and imagery these words carry undeniably painful, if not sadistic, implications, the object of which is almost always female. Consider, for example, what a "screw" actually does to the wood it penetrates; what a painful, even mutilating, activity this kind of analogy suggests. "Screw" is particularly interesting in this context, since the noun, according to Partridge, comes from words meaning "groove," "nut," "ditch," "breeding sow," "scrofula" and "swelling," while the verb, besides its explicit imagery, has antecedent associations to "write on," "scratch," "scarify," and so forth—a revealing fusion of a mechanical or painful action with an obviously denigrated object.

Not all obscene words, of course, are as implicitly sadistic or denigrating to women as these, but all that I know seem to serve a similar purpose: to reduce the human organism (especially the female organism) and human functions (especially sexual and procreative) to their least organic, most mechanical dimension; to substitute a trivializing or deforming resemblance for the complex human reality of what is being described.

Tabooed male descriptives, when they are not openly denigrating to women, often serve to divorce a male organ or function from any significant interaction with the female. Take the word "testes," for example, suggesting "witnesses" (from the Latin *testis*) to the sexual and procreative strengths of the male organ; and the obscene counterpart of this word, which suggests little more than a mechanical shape. Or compare almost any of the "rich," "liberating" sexual verbs, so fashionable today among male writers, with that much-derided Latin word "copulate" ("to bind or join together") or even that Anglo-Saxon phrase (which seems to have had no trouble surviving the Norman Conquest) "make love."

How arrogantly self-involved the tabooed words seem in comparison to either of the other terms, and how contemptuous of the female partner. Understandably so, of course, if she is only a "skirt," a "broad," a "chick," a "pussycat" or a "piece." If she is, in other words, no more than her skirt, or what her skirt conceals; no more than a breeder, or the broadest part of her; no more than a piece of a human being or a "piece of tail."

The most severely tabooed of all the female descriptives, incidentally, are those like a "piece of tail," which suggest (either explicitly or through antecedents) that there is no significant difference between the female channel through which we are all conceived and born and the anal outlet common to both sexes—a distinction that pornographers have always enjoyed obscuring.

This effort to deny women their biological identity, their individuality, their humanness, is such an important aspect of obscene language that one can only marvel at how seldom, in an era preoccupied with definitions of obscenity, this fact is brought to our attention. One problem, of course, is that many of the people in the best position to do this (critics, teachers, writers) are so reluctant today to admit that they are angered or shocked by obscenity. Bored, maybe, unimpressed, aesthetically displeased, but—no matter how brutal or denigrating the material—never angered, never shocked.   10

And yet how eloquently angered, how piously shocked many of these same people become if denigrating language is used about any minority group other than women; if the obscenities are racial or ethnic, that is, rather than sexual. Words like "coon," "kike," "spic," "wop," after all, deform identity, deny individuality and humanness in almost exactly the same way that sexual vulgarisms and obscenities do.   11

No one that I know, least of all my students, would fail to question the values of a society whose literature and entertainment rested heavily on racial or ethnic pejoratives. Are the values of a society whose literature and entertainment rest as heavily as ours on sexual pejoratives any less questionable?   12

QUESTIONS ON CONTENT

1. How does Lawrence explain the existence of taboos? What other explanations does she mention and then dismiss?

2. Why does Lawrence, as a woman, object to obscene language? Could men object to obscene language on the same grounds?

3. Do you agree with Lawrence's argument? Why, or why not? Would it be fair to consider Lawrence's view of obscenity as strictly feminist?

4. In paragraph 4 Lawrence details the origin of "the best known of the tabooed sexual verbs." In what way is this presentation of the word's etymology related to her central argument? How did you respond to this paragraph? Why?

QUESTIONS ON RHETORIC

1. Lawrence begins her essay with a series of questions. What functions do these questions serve? (Glossary: *Beginnings* and *Rhetorical Questions*)

2. Lawrence consciously avoids using "obscene" words. What, in your opinion, is gained or lost as a result of this strategy? Explain.

3. Comment on the connotations of the words which have been italicized in the following sentence: (Glossary: *Connotation*)

> And yet how *eloquently* angered, how *piously* shocked many of these same people become if denigrating language is used about any minority group other than women. . . .(11)

4. Should paragraphs 11 and 12 have been combined? Why do you feel Lawrence has made separate paragraphs?

5. What is the effect of Lawrence's final question? How would you answer it?

VOCABULARY

preferable (1)	analogy (5)	contemptuous (8)
grimaces (1)	antecedent (5)	pejoratives (12)
oppression (3)	implicity (6)	

WRITING TOPICS

1. Discuss the pros and cons of the proposition that women's use of "liberated" language is self-defeating. Why, in your opinion, do some women make a point of using such language?

2. Do you commonly use sexual obscenities and feel justified in doing so? Or do such words offend you? How would you describe your feelings about obscenities? Defend your feelings to someone who does not share them.

3. Lawrence observes that "some of these words still cannot appear in print in many parts of the English-speaking world" (2)—and books that contain these words, including some dictionaries, are banned from many school libraries and bookstores. What reasons can be given for and against censoring obscene words, or banning publications in which they appear? Does such action really eradicate the problem, or merely force it underground? What is your position? How would you support it?

THE LANGUAGE OF NUCLEAR WAR STRATEGISTS

Stephen Hilgartner, Richard C. Bell, and Rory O'Connor

What are the ramifications of nuclear capability? How might nuclear warfare be triggered and fought? Who would survive? What are the consequences of "thinking the unthinkable"? Because the threat of full-scale nuclear war is real, our military analysts must deal with that possibility and make predictions accordingly. The following essay offers a view of the "reality" of nuclear warfare suggested by the highly specialized language of nuclear war strategists.

The world of nuclear warfare is a world of doublethink, a hall of mirrors, where *peace* is preserved through the constant threat of war, *security* is obtained through mutual insecurity, and nuclear war planners "think about the *unthinkable*," holding millions of civilians hostage to the most powerful death machines in history.

Nuclear war strategists have developed an esoteric, highly specialized vocabulary. In their ultrarational world, they talk in cool, clinical language about *megatons* and *megadeaths*. Cities are *bargaining chips;* they are not destroyed, they are *taken out* with *clean, surgical strikes*—as if they were tumors.

Since there is no way to defend cities and industry against nuclear attack, *global stability* is now preserved through a system called the *balance of terror*. The balance of terror is based upon the principle of *deterrence*. Nuclear deterrence is, in effect, a mutual suicide pact: if you attack me, it may kill me, but I will kill you before I die. The civilian population of each superpower is held hostage by the opposite power. The same is true of the allies covered by the *nuclear umbrellas* of the superpowers. If either side attacks, all the hostages will be destroyed.

The U.S. Department of *Defense* (known as the War Department until   4
1948) is incapable of defending the United States against a nuclear attack
by the USSR. But it is capable of killing many millions of Russian citizens
at the push of a button, and the Russians are incapable of doing anything
to prevent the carnage. If the Russians were to attack the U.S. or its allies
with nuclear weapons, the U.S. would retaliate by attacking the USSR.
Since the Russians know this, the reasoning goes, they will be deterred
from striking first. A mirror-image argument describes how Russia deters
the U.S. from striking its people.

Military analysts classify nuclear attacks as either *counterforce* or *coun-*   5
tervalue attacks. A counterforce attack is one that is directed primarily
against the other side's military forces; countervalue attacks are directed
against cities and industry.

That a counterforce attack is directed primarily against military forces   6
does not mean that there would be few civilian casualties. On the contrary,
counterforce attacks could leave millions of civilians dead from the fallout
produced by attacks on missile silos. A large airport might be construed as
a military target because it could serve as a base for military planes. A
naval base situated in a metropolitan area is another example of a target
that could be interpreted as either counterforce or countervalue. The difference between a counterforce and a countervalue attack is not whether
civilians die, but whether this is the main goal or a side effect. The deaths
of civilians and the destruction of nonmilitary property in a counterforce
attack is called *collateral damage.*

Nuclear war planners have always been afraid that the other side might   7
try to launch a *preemptive first strike* (also known as a *splendid first strike*),
that is, a counterforce attack designed to cripple the enemy's ability to
retaliate. The reasoning behind a preemptive first-strike strategy goes as
follows: If country X can destroy a large enough number of country Y's
missiles in a first-strike attack, then X can also threaten to destroy Y's
remaining cities in a second *nuclear salvo* if Y retaliates with any remaining missiles. It is assumed that Y will be *rational* and surrender to X rather
than ensure its total destruction by launching an attack for revenge. X can
then impose its will on Y, thus *winning* the nuclear war.

In its public statements, the USSR has renounced the *first use* of nu-   8
clear weapons; the United States has not. Nevertheless, military planners
in both countries prepare for *worst-case* situations and tend not to believe
verbal declarations. In war, the argument goes, *capabilities* count more
than *intentions,* since intentions change without warning.

As a result of this perception of the possibility of an enemy attempting   9
a splendid first strike, the two superpowers have engaged in a massive
arms race, reaching higher and higher levels of destructive power. Some
years ago, each superpower attained *overkill,* the ability to kill every

citizen on the other side more than once. Nevertheless, the arms race continues, and each side continues to expand and *modernize* its nuclear arsenal.

The driving force behind the arms race is a treacherous double-bind   10
known as the *security dilemma*. Since X is afraid of Y's weapons. X adds to its arsenal. X's arms buildup, which is conceived of as *defensive* by X, is perceived as *offensive* by Y, prompting Y to build more weapons to deter an attack by X. X looks at this and concludes that Y must be planning to attack; otherwise Y would not have expanded its arsenal. X therefore decides to build still more weapons, and the cycle continues.

The security dilemma has led to the creation of huge military estab-   11
lishments in both the U.S. and the USSR. The superpowers' *hawks* watch each other closely, passing what they see through the gloomy filter of worst-case *scenarios*. The hawks of one nation contribute to the prestige and power of the hawks of the other, and arms budgets climb.

The arms race has produced a wide array of nuclear weapons and   12
delivery systems for getting them to their targets. The weapons are designed for use in different situations and vary considerably in explosive power. Nuclear warriors generally divide these weapons into three categories: strategic, tactical, and theater.

Strategic nuclear weapons have high-yield warheads; each warhead   13
may be hundreds of times as powerful as the bomb that destroyed Hiroshima. The Hiroshima bomb had a *yield* of 13,000 tons of TNT, or 13 *kilotons;* strategic weapons often have a yield measured in *megatons*—millions of tons of TNT. Strategic weapons are capable of striking targets many thousands of miles away. Both superpowers have deployed their strategic weapons in bombers, in land-based missiles, and in submarines. In the U.S., this three-legged war machine is called the *strategic TRIAD*. Bombers armed with nuclear weapons wait for the *go code*. Land-based *Intercontinental Ballistic Missiles* (*ICBMs*) are ready to strike at the push of a button. Submarines bearing nuclear-armed missiles are *on-station,* waiting for a transmission that would order them to launch their cargo. Radar systems scan the sky for incoming missiles or bombers. At least one of the *Strategic Air Command's* flying command posts, officially called the *Looking Glass Planes* and unofficially known as the *Doomsday Planes,* is in the air at all times. And overhead, a network of satellites circles the earth, watching Soviet ICBM fields and maintaining *command, control and communications,* or C^3 (C *cubed*)—the capability to transmit and receive information and orders.

Tactical nuclear weapons are designed for use on the *nuclear battle-*   14
field. They have much smaller yields than strategic weapons; their yields usually range from as low as one kiloton to several times the yield of the Hiroshima bomb. Tactical nuclear weapons are designed for use in con-

junction with *conventional military forces*. In a land war, tactical nuclear weapons might be used to *take out* enemy tank columns. On the sea, they could be used to sink enemy warships. They can be shot from artillery, dropped from planes, shot in short-range missiles, used in depth charges or torpedoes, or placed in land mines.

Theater nuclear weapons have powerful warheads like those of strategic weapons. They do not have intercontinental range, however, and are designed for use in a *limited theater of operations*—like Europe, for example. These weapons include bombers and missiles with medium to long ranges. They are *deployed* on land and on aircraft carriers.   15

The U.S. government has also developed a new kind of nuclear weapon called the *neutron bomb* or *enhanced radiation warhead*. Neutron bombs produce less explosive blast than other nuclear weapons, releasing a greater fraction of their energy in a deadly burst of neutron radiation. Neutron bombs purportedly make it possible to kill enemy troops while reducing blast damage to the surrounding countryside. In its war games, the Defense Department envisions using neutron bombs to stop Soviet tank attacks in western Europe.   16

Equipped with this array of armaments, nuclear warriors are ready to play the game of *escalation,* using threats and counterthreats to deter, influence, coerce, and block their opponents.   17

The theory of *limited war*—war which the combatant nations limit in scope or intensity by tacit or explicit agreement—is important to escalation strategy. This theory holds that war can be limited by restricting the geographic region in which it is conducted, by limiting the kinds of weapons used, or by limiting the kinds of targets attacked.   18

Nuclear war strategist Herman Kahn outlined a theory of escalation and limited war in a 1965 book called *On Escalation: Metaphors and Scenarios*. Kahn developed an *escalation ladder* with forty-four rungs, or levels of conflict. The rungs Kahn described range from "Political, Economic and Diplomatic *Gestures*" through "Nuclear '*Ultimatums*' " and limited evacuation of cities, before crossing the "*No Nuclear Use Threshold*." From "*Local Nuclear War*," the ladder rises to "*Exemplary Attacks*" on property and population, before reaching "*Slow-Motion Countercity War*." As the intensity of the conflict climbs, the level of "*Countervalue Salvo*" is reached, and finally, the orgasmic release of "*Spasm or Insensate War*," as everyone lets loose with everything they have got.   19

Escalation strategy is a complex game of *nuclear chicken*. Opposing strategists, like two drivers headed on a collision course, try to force each other to back down by threatening terrible consequences for both unless somebody backs down. A disagreement might escalate into a crisis, a crisis into a conventional war. The use of tactical nuclear weapons would escalate conventional war into *limited nuclear war*. If this happens, no one   20 knows whether the use of nuclear force could be neatly contained. Some analysts fear that crossing the *no-nuclear-use threshold* would ultimately lead to a *spasm war.*

Escalation strategy, also known as *brinksmanship,* is ripe with para- 21
dox. Survival depends on everyone being *rational,* yet it is hard to tell what the word *rational* means. Sometimes it seems rational to pretend to be irrational, even to act irrationally, making the illusion more credible by making it more real. In a game of chicken, the driver who throws his steering wheel out the window has won control of the road. Similarly, the nuclear warrior can seize the advantage by throwing away options, or by convincing the opponent he is willing to plunge over the brink. President Nixon, for example, developed a strategy he called the *"Madman Theory"* to try to force the North Vietnamese to negotiate. According to Nixon operative H. R. Haldeman, convicted in the Watergate coverup, Nixon said:

> I want the North Vietnamese to believe I've reached the point where I might do *anything* [original emphasis] to stop the war. We'll just slip the word to them that "for God's sake, you know Nixon is obsessed about Communism. We can't restrain him when he's angry—and he has his hand on the *nuclear button''*—and Ho Chi Minh himself will be in Paris in two days begging for peace.

Over the years, the U.S. government has developed a number of the- 22
ories about how to maintain deterrence; these are known as *strategic doctrines.* The best known is the strategy of *mutually assured destruction (MAD),* developed by Robert McNamara, Secretary of Defense during the Kennedy and Johnson administrations. Under this strategy, nuclear war is deterred by the threat that any attack would promptly lead to a *nuclear exchange* that would destroy both superpowers.

For the balance of terror to remain *stable,* nuclear war strategists must 23
keep escalation under control. Each side must believe that everyone's nuclear forces have *survivability,* the ability to survive a counterforce attack and still deliver a crippling retaliatory blow. Both sides must believe that the *costs of striking* would be greater than the *costs of not striking.*

If the survivability of either side's forces is in question, the whole 24
situation becomes a hall of mirrors. What if X thinks Y thinks X could take out Y's weapons in a preemptive first strike? Should X strike? If X doesn't, Y might strike first, because X thinks Y might think it has nothing to lose. And what might Y think about all this? A terrifying web of perceptions and misperceptions is possible. *Spiraling tensions* could start a thermonuclear war even if no one wanted it.

During the late 1960s and the early 1970s, the survivability of each 25
superpower's nuclear forces was not in question. In the past decade, how-

ever, improvements in weapons technology have made the survivability of land-based missiles less certain. This erosion of survivability is the result of what is known as *technological creep,* improvements in weapons technology that seem to have a momentum of their own.

One of the most *destabilizing* technological developments of the 1970s   26
was the deployment of *MIRVs, multiple independently targetable reentry vehicles.* MIRVs make it possible for a single missile to carry a number of nuclear warheads, each of which can be aimed at a separate target. The U.S. began deploying MIRVs in 1970, and the Soviet Union began in 1975.

MIRVs tend to give the advantage to the side which strikes first in a   27
nuclear exchange. A quick look at the following example will illustrate why this is so. Imagine a situation in which each side has 1,000 missiles with 10 MIRVed warheads on each missile. By striking first with 100 missiles—MIRVed with 1,000 warheads—the attacker could eliminate all of the other side's missiles. This would leave the attacker 900 missiles to use as a deterrent against retaliation. While this example is hypothetical, the message is clear; MIRVs are destablizing.

A second case of technological creep has occurred in the area of missile   28
accuracy. Extreme accuracy is not important for *city-busting,* since the target is large and *soft*—unprotected and easily destroyed. Accuracy is important for counterforce attacks, however. Underground missile silos, with their heavy shieldings, and very *hard* targets, and to destroy them, it is necessary to make a *direct hit.* Over the past decade, each superpower has greatly improved the accuracy of its missiles, so much so that they can now land within a few hundred feet of their targets. Weapons specialists refer to this increase in accuracy as a decrease in the *CEP,* or the *circular error probable,* which is the radius of the circle in which a missile has a 50 percent chance of landing if aimed at its center. As a result of the increase in accuracy, land-based missiles in both the U.S. and the USSR are vulnerable to counterforce attack.

No one has developed *antisubmarine warfare (ASW)* technology capa-   29
ble of threatening the survivability of either U.S. or USSR submarines, and the subs remain a *credible* deterrent. Work to *improve* antisubmarine warfare is under way in both countries, however.

The C^3 systems both superpowers depend on to coordinate their nuclear   30
forces might be vulnerable to nuclear attack. This could provide a *strong incentive* to strike first. As the newsletter of the Federation of American Scientists (FAS) noted in October 1980,

> A nation that strikes first with strategic forces does so with its command structure, control mechanisms, and communications devices wholly intact, alerted, and ready. Each and every telephone line, satellite, and antenna is functioning and every relevant person is alive and well. By contrast, the nation

which seeks to launch a retaliatory attack may find its chain of command highly disrupted, its telephone lines dead, its satellites inoperative, its radio signals interfered with, and its communications officers out of action.

The FAS called attacks on C^3 "a kind of supercounterforce and correspondingly destabilizing." The Federation predicted: "Should either side carry out deliberate efforts to attack the C^3 of the other, it appears almost certain that a spasm war would result in which the attacked nation gave its military commanders either by prior agreement or by last desperate message, the authority to *fire at will*. As its ability to communicate gave out, it could and would do no less than use its last communications channel for *the final order*. [31]

Another threat to the stability of deterrence is the possibility that a system failure in either superpower's nuclear-war-fighting computers could trigger an accidental nuclear war. Three recent *alerts* caused by computer errors show that this threat may not be as insignificant as the Department of Defense claims: [32]

> In November of 1979, data from a computer *war game* accidentally flowed into a live warning and command network, triggering a low-level alert. The computer's mistake was not detected for six minutes. In the meantime, B-52 pilots were told to man their planes, and the launch officers in ICBM silos unlocked a special strong box, removed the *attack verification codes,* and inserted the *keys* into their slots. When two keys ten feet apart are turned within two seconds of each other, the missiles blast off.

> In June, 1980, on two separate occasions, a computer error caused by a faulty circuit chip worth 46¢ sent out false signals that the USSR had launched missiles headed for the U.S. In both cases, some of the B-52 fleet started its engines before the error was detected.

The Pentagon maintains that there is *"no chance that any irretrievable actions would be taken on the basis of ambiguous computer information,"* noting that the computers do not make decisions alone and that *human intervention* has always detected the errors. [33]

Nevertheless, there is little time for the people involved to read the signals properly and make decisions. Land-based missiles can reach the U.S. in about thirty minutes, while submarine-launched missiles might take only half that time. Moreover, the threat exists that an erroneous alert could generate a nuclear attack as if by a trick of mirrors. If in response to a computer error the B-52s were suddenly to take off from their air bases, the Russians would immediately detect the maneuver. Soviet officers would have even less time to reach a judgment about how to respond, since their *early warning systems* are not as sophisticated as those of the U.S. If the Soviets dispatched their bombers, the U.S. warning system would in [34] turn detect the planes, and the computer's message, though originally erroneous, would be *confirmed.*

The Pentagon claims that such a *chain reaction is a "highly unlikely* 35 *scenario."* A full public discussion of the issues involved is impossible because most of the relevant information is classified.

QUESTIONS ON CONTENT

1. What do the authors mean when they state that "the world of nuclear warfare is a world of doublethink"(1)? Explain how the image of a "hall of mirrors" works in this essay.

2. The authors describe the language of nuclear war strategist as "cool" and "clinical." Do you agree with their assessment? Why do you suppose war strategists choose to use such language? How is their language related to the War Department's name change in 1948?

3. Explain the principle of "deterrence." Why are nuclear war planners afraid of a "preemptive first strike"? And how is the threat of a preemptive first strike related to what we know as the "arms race"?

4. What is the difference between a neutron bomb and a conventional nuclear bomb?

5. What developments in the 1970s destabilized the situation between the United States and the USSR? What other threats to deterrence exist?

6. Choose a paragraph or two from the essay and try to substitute words for those italicized. What is the effect?

QUESTIONS ON RHETORIC

1. What seems to be the authors' purpose in this essay—to explain the highly specialized vocabulary of the nuclear strategies or to argue against the use of such language? Explain your answer with examples from the essay. (Glossary: *Purpose*)

2. Identify passages in which the authors make use of the strategies of classification and analyzing cause and effect. (Glossary: *Division and Classification* and *Cause and Effect*)

3. In paragraphs 20 and 21 the authors use the analogy of two drivers competing in a game of chicken to explain "escalation strategy." Explain how the analogy works. How helpful did you find it in understanding the complexities of escalation strategy? (Glossary: *Analogy*)

4. In paragraphs 21, 30, and 32, the authors use examples. Explain the function of each example within the context of its paragraph. (Glossary: *Examples*)

VOCABULARY

esoteric (2)	conjunction (14)	orgasmic (19)
carnage (4)	purportedly (16)	insensate (19)
retaliate (4)	arrray (17)	hypothetical (27)
construed (6)	tacit (18)	vulnerable (28)
arsenal (9)		

WRITING TOPICS

1. Using examples from the essay you've just read and examples of your own if you have them, write an essay in which you argue that the language of the nuclear war strategists gives us an inaccurate picture of the realities of nuclear warfare.

2. How would you describe the language of nuclear war strategists, particularly the words italicized by Hilgartner and his coauthors? How much of this language is jargon, and how much is legitimate technical vocabulary? How much would you call euphemism?

3. Is it acceptable to use euphemisms to deal with matters, such as nuclear warfare, that pose psychological difficulties? Or is such action simply immoral? How do you think Neil Postman (pp. 345–347) would react to the language of the nuclear war strategists?

WRITING ASSIGNMENTS FOR "EUPHEMISM AND TABOOS"

1. Linguist Benjamin Lee Whorf has pointed out that "the structure of a given language determines, in part, how the society that speaks it views reality." Explain how our use of euphemisms affects both our behavior and our opinion of our behavior. Consider, for example, the following expressions and the euphemisms for them:

    false teeth ("dental appliance")
    typist ("data processor")
    bombing raid ("limited duration protective reaction strike")
    lie ("inoperative statement")
    rerun ("encore telecast")
    fire ("terminate")
    constipation ("occasional irregularity")

List other euphemisms used by government, big business, and professions. How may the use of such euphemisms influence behavior?

2. Write an essay in which you use the following quote from *Time* magazine as your thesis: "Like stammers or tears, euphemisms will be created whenever men doubt, or fear, or do not know."

3. In an article called "Public Doublespeak," Terence Moran presented the following list of recommendations given to the faculty of an elementary school in Brooklyn:

FOR PARENT INTERVIEWS AND REPORT CARDS

Harsh Expression (Avoid)	Acceptable Expression (Use)
Does all right if pushed	Accomplishes tasks when interest is stimulated.
Too free with fists	Resorts to physical means of winning his point or attracting attention.
Lies (Dishonest)	Shows difficulty in distinguishing between imaginary and factual material.
Cheats	Needs help in learning to adhere to rules and standards of fair play.
Steals	Needs help in learning to respect the property rights of others.
Noisy	Needs to develop quieter habits of communication.
Lazy	Needs ample supervision in order to work well.

Is a bully	Has qualities of leadership but needs help in learning to use them democratically.
Associates with "gangs"	Seems to feel secure only in group situations; needs to develop sense of independence.
Disliked by other children	Needs help in learning to form lasting friendships.

After reading Neil Postman's essay on euphemisms, write an essay in which you discuss what this list recommends and the possible effects of its use on teachers, students, and parents.

4. Write an essay in which you compare and contrast the analyses of taboo words by Hayakawa and Lawrence.

5. Write an essay in which you argue that the euphemism, when used honestly, is "a handy verbal tool to avoid making enemies needlessly or shocking friends."

6. People use euphemisms when they want to avoid talking directly about subjects that make them uncomfortable, although what makes people uncomfortable changes. For example, we have been able to mention the words *legs* and *breasts* for quite a while and *venereal disease* for a shorter time, but many people still avoid the words *die* and *death*. Identify some other subjects for which euphemisms are still prevalent, and list several euphemisms for each. Do you use the same euphemisms as your parents? As your grandparents?

7. The following news item, first published in *Time* (December 11, 1972), is another example of efforts to "clean-up" our language.

BOWDLER IN OREGON

Some American place names have a unique resonance about them—places like Maggie's Nipples, Wyo., or Greasy Creek, Ark., Lickskillet, Ky., or Scroungeout, Ala. Collectors of Americana also savor Braggadocio, Mo., the Humptulips River in Washington, Hen Scratch, Fla., Dead Irishman Gulch, S. Dak., Cut 'N Shoot, Texas, Helpmejack Creek, Ark., Bastard Peak, Wyo., Goon Dip Mountain, Ark., Tenstrike, Minn., Laughing Pig, Wyo., Two Teats, Calif., or Aswaguscawadic, Me.

Not the least flavorsome was a sylvan place called Whorehouse Meadows, outside of Ontario, Ore. The meadow was named, with admirable directness, for some local women who once profitably entertained sheepherders there. But last week, the Oregon Geographic Names Board filed an official objection to a bit of bowdlerization by the Federal Bureau of Land Management. It discovered that the bureau, in drawing up a map of the area, had changed the name from Whorehouse Meadows to Naughty Girl Meadows. The bureau also cleaned up a nearby spot, deftly retitling it Bullshirt Springs, a change so small that the natives see no reason to contest it.

Write an essay in which you discuss the way name changes reflect Americans' perceptions of themselves and their culture. You may use examples from "Bowdler in Oregon" as well as other name changes that you know about in writing your essay.

8. Dr. Joyce Brothers says that the words we consider offensive change from generation to generation. Pay attention to television drama for a week. What do you notice about the language? What words are spoken that would have been considered offensive on television as recently as five years ago? What other "unmentionables," such as homosexuality, menstruation, and venereal disease, are now regular subjects of television advertising and drama? In an essay, discuss your reaction to the changing attitudes reflected in the use of these words and topics.

PART VIII

Media
and
Language

"NOW ... THIS"

Neil Postman

In the following essay from his book Amusing Ourselves to
Death, *Neil Postman examines the ways in which the format
for broadcast news has trivialized the news itself. Postman, a
professor of media ecology at New York University, warns
that the effort to keep the news hour entertaining not only
keeps the public ignorant, it ultimately puts the entire culture
at risk of extinction.*

The American humorist H. Allen Smith once suggested that of all the   1
worrisome words in the English language, the scariest is "uh oh," as when
a physician looks at your X rays and with knitted brow says, "Uh oh." I
should like to suggest that the words which are the title of this chapter are
as ominous as any, all the more so because they are spoken without knitted
brow—indeed, with a kind of idiot's delight. The phrase, if that's what it
may be called, adds to our grammar a new part of speech, a conjunction
that does not connect anything to anything but does the opposite: separates
everything from everything. As such, it serves as a compact metaphor for
the discontinuities in so much that passes for public discourse in present-
day America.

"Now . . . this" is commonly used on radio and television newscasts   2
to indicate that what one has just heard or seen has no relevance to what
one is about to hear or see, or possibly to anything one is ever likely to hear
or see. The phrase is a means of acknowledging the fact that the world as
mapped by the speeded-up electronic media has no order or meaning and
is not to be taken seriously. There is no murder so brutal, no earthquake so
devastating, no political blunder so costly—for that matter, no ball score so
tantalizing or weather report so threatening—that it cannot be erased from
our minds by a newscaster saying, "Now . . . this." The newscaster
means that you have thought long enough on the previous matter (approximately forty-five seconds), that you must not be morbidly preoccupied
with it (let us say, for ninety seconds), and that you must now give your
attention to another fragment of news or a commercial.

Television did not invent the "Now . . . this" world view. . . . It is   3
the offspring of the intercourse between telegraphy and photography. But
it is through television that it has been nurtured and brought to a perverse
maturity. For on television, nearly every half hour is a discrete event,

separated in content, context, and emotional texture from what precedes and follows it. In part because television sells its time in seconds and minutes, in part because television must use images rather than words, in part because its audience can move freely to and from the television set, programs are structured so that almost each eight-minute segment may stand as a complete event in itself. Viewers are rarely required to carry over any thought or feeling from one parcel of time to another.

Of course, in television's presentation of the "news of the day," we   4
may see the "Now . . . this" mode of discourse in its boldest and most embarrassing form. For there, we are presented not only with fragmented news but news without context, without consequences, without value, and therefore without essential seriousness; that is to say, news as pure entertainment.

Consider, for example, how you would proceed if you were given the   5
opportunity to produce a television news show for any station concerned to attract the largest possible audience. You would, first, choose a cast of players, each of whom has a face that is both "likable" and "credible." Those who apply would, in fact, submit to you their eight-by-ten glossies, from which you would eliminate those whose countenances are not suitable for nightly display. This means that you will exclude women who are not beautiful or who are over the age of fifty, men who are bald, all people who are overweight or whose noses are too long or whose eyes are too close together. You will try, in other words, to assemble a cast of talking hair-do's. At the very least, you will want those whose faces would not be unwelcome on a magazine cover.

Christine Craft has just such a face, and so she applied for a co-anchor   6
position on KMBC-TV in Kansas City. According to a lawyer who represented her in a sexism suit she later brought against the station, the management of KMBC-TV "loved Christine's look." She was accordingly hired in January 1981. She was fired in August 1981 because research indicated that her appearance "hampered viewer acceptance." What exactly does "hampered viewer acceptance" mean? And what does it have to do with the news? Hampered viewer acceptance means the same thing for television news as it does for any television show: Viewers do not like looking at the performer. It also means that viewers do not believe the performer, that she lacks credibility. In the case of a theatrical performance, we have a sense of what that implies: The actor does not persuade the audience that he or she is the character being portrayed. But what does lack of credibility imply in the case of a news show? What character is a co-anchor playing? And how do we decide that the performance lacks verisimilitude? Does the audience believe that the newscaster is lying, that what is reported did not in fact happen, that something important is being concealed?

It is frightening to think that this may be so, that the perception of the   7
truth of a report rests heavily on the acceptability of the newscaster. In the
ancient world, there was a tradition of banishing or killing the bearer of bad
tidings. Does the television news show restore, in a curious form, this
tradition? Do we banish those who tell us the news when we do not care
for the face of the teller? Does television countermand the warnings we
once received about the fallacy of the ad hominem argument?

If the answer to any of these questions is even a qualified "Yes," then   8
here is an issue worthy of the attention of epistemologists. Stated in its
simplest form, it is that television provides a new (or, possibly, restores an
old) definition of truth: The credibility of the teller is the ultimate test of the
truth of a proposition. "Credibility" here does not refer to the past record
of the teller for making statements that have survived the rigors of reality-
testing. It refers only to the impression of sincerity, authenticity, vulnerability or attractiveness (choose one or more) conveyed by the actor/
reporter.

This is a matter of considerable importance, for it goes beyond the   9
question of how truth is perceived on television news shows. If on television, credibility replaces reality as the decisive test of truth-telling, political leaders need not trouble themselves very much with reality provided
that their performances consistently generate a sense of verisimilitude. I
suspect, for example, that the dishonor that now shrouds Richard Nixon
results not from the fact that he lied but that on television he looks like a
liar. Which, if true, should bring no comfort to anyone, not even veteran
Nixon-haters. For the alternative possibilities are that one may look like a
liar but be telling the truth; or even worse, look like a truth-teller but in fact
be lying.

As a producer of a television news show, you would be well aware of   10
these matters and would be careful to choose your cast on the basis of
criteria used by David Merrick and other successful impresarios. Like
them, you would then turn your attention to staging the show on principles
that maximize entertainment value. You would, for example, select a
musical theme for the show. All television news programs begin, end, and
are somewhere in between punctuated with music. I have found very few
Americans who regard this custom as peculiar, which fact I have taken as
evidence for the dissolution of lines of demarcation between serious public
discourse and entertainment. What has music to do with the news? Why is
it there? It is there, I assume, for the same reason music is used in the
theater and films—to create a mood and provide a leitmotif for the entertainment. If there were no music—as is the case when any television
program is interrupted for a news flash—viewers would expect something
truly alarming, possibly life-altering. But as long as the music is there as
a frame for the program, the viewer is comforted to believe that there is

nothing to be greatly alarmed about; that, in fact, the events that are reported have as much relation to reality as do scenes in a play.

This perception of a news show as a stylized dramatic performance   11
whose content has been staged largely to entertain is reinforced by several other features, including the fact that the average length of any story is forty-five seconds. While brevity does not always suggest triviality, in this case it clearly does. It is simply not possible to convey a sense of seriousness about any event if its implications are exhausted in less than one minute's time. In fact, it is quite obvious that TV news has no intention of suggesting that any story *has* any implications, for that would require viewers to continue to think about it when it is done and therefore obstruct their attending to the next story that waits panting in the wings. In any case, viewers are not provided with much opportunity to be distracted from the next story since in all likelihood it will consist of some film footage. Pictures have little difficulty in overwhelming words and short-circuiting introspection. As a television producer, you would be certain to give both prominence and precedence to any event for which there is some sort of visual documentation. A suspected killer being brought into a police station, the angry face of a cheated consumer, a barrel going over Niagara Falls (with a person alleged to be in it), the President disembarking from a helicopter on the White House lawn—these are always fascinating or amusing and easily satisfy the requirements of an entertaining show. It is, of course, not necessary that the visuals actually document the point of a story. Neither is it necessary to explain why such images are intruding themselves on public consciousness. Film footage justifies itself, as every television producer well knows.

It is also of considerable help in maintaining a high level of unreality   12
that the newscasters do not pause to grimace or shiver when they speak their prefaces or epilogs to the film clips. Indeed, many newscasters do not appear to grasp the meaning of what they are saying, and some hold to a fixed and ingratiating enthusiasm as they report on earthquakes, mass killings and other disasters. Viewers would be quite disconcerted by any show of concern or terror on the part of newscasters. Viewers, after all, are partners with the newscasters in the "Now . . . this" culture, and they expect the newscaster to play out his or her role as a character who is marginally serious but who stays well clear of authentic understanding. The viewers, for their part, will not be caught contaminating their responses with a sense of reality, any more than an audience at a play would go scurrying to call home because a character on stage has said that a murderer is loose in the neighborhood.

The viewers also know that no matter how grave any fragment of news   13
may appear (for example, on the day I write a Marine Corps general has declared that nuclear war between the United States and Russia is inevi-

table), it will shortly be followed by a series of commercials that will, in an instant, defuse the import of the news, in fact render it largely banal. This is a key element in the structure of a news program and all by itself refutes any claim that television news is designed as a serious form of public discourse. Imagine what you would think of me, and this book, if I were to pause here, tell you that I will return to my discussion in a moment, and then proceed to write a few words in behalf of United Airlines or the Chase Manhattan Bank. You would rightly think that I had no respect for you and, certainly, no respect for the subject. And if I did this not once but several times in each chapter, you would think the whole enterprise unworthy of your attention. Why, then, do we not think a news show similarly unworthy? The reason, I believe, is that whereas we expect books and even other media (such as film) to maintain a consistency of tone and a continuity of content, we have no such expectation of television, and especially television news. We have become so accustomed to its discontinuities that we are no longer struck dumb, as any sane person would be, by a newscaster who having just reported that a nuclear war is inevitable goes on to say that he will be right back after this word from Burger King; who says, in other words, "Now . . . this." One can hardly overestimate the damage that such juxtapositions do to our sense of the world as a serious place. The damage is especially massive to youthful viewers who depend so much on television for their clues as to how to respond to the world. In watching television news, they, more than any other segment of the audience, are drawn into an epistemology based on the assumption that all reports of cruelty and death are greatly exaggerated and, in any case, not to be taken seriously or responded to sanely.

I should go so far as to say that embedded in the surrealistic frame of   14
a television news show is a theory of anticommunication, featuring a type of discourse that abandons logic, reason, sequence and rules of contradiction. In aesthetics, I believe the name given to this theory is Dadaism; in philosophy, nihilism; in psychiatry, schizophrenia. In the parlance of the theater, it is known as vaudeville.

For those who think I am here guilty of hyperbole, I offer the following   15
description of television news by Robert MacNeil, executive editor and co-anchor of the "MacNeil-Lehrer Newshour." The idea, he writes, "is to keep everything brief, not to strain the attention of anyone but instead to provide constant stimulation through variety, novelty, action, and movement. You are required . . . to pay attention to no concept, no character, and no problem for more than a few seconds at a time." He goes on to say that the assumptions controlling a news show are "that bite-sized is best, that complexity must be avoided, that nuances are dispensible, that qualifications impede the simple message, that visual stimulation is a substitute for thought, and that verbal precision is an anachronism."

Robert MacNeil has more reason than most to give testimony about the   16
television news show as vaudeville act. The "MacNeil-Lehrer Newshour"
is an unusual and gracious attempt to bring to television some of the
elements of typographic discourse. The program abjures visual stimulation, consists largely of extended explanations of events and in-depth interviews (which even there means only five to ten minutes), limits the
number of stories covered, and emphasizes background and coherence.
But television has exacted its price for MacNeil's rejection of a show
business format. By television's standards, the audience is minuscule, the
program is confined to public-television stations, and it is a good guess that
the combined salary of MacNeil and Lehrer is one-fifth of Dan Rather's or
Tom Brokaw's.

If you were a producer of a television news show for a commercial   17
station, you would not have the option of defying television's requirements. It would be demanded of you that you strive for the largest possible
audience, and, as a consequence and in spite of your best intentions, you
would arrive at a production very nearly resembling MacNeil's description. Moreover, you would include some things MacNeil does not mention. You would try to make celebrities of your newscasters. You would
advertise the show, both in the press and on television itself. You would do
"news briefs," to serve as an inducement to viewers. You would have a
weatherman as comic relief, and a sportscaster whose language is a touch
uncouth (as a way of his relating to the beer-drinking common man). You
would, in short, package the whole event as any producer might who is in
the entertainment business.

The result of all this is that Americans are the best entertained and quite   18
likely the least well-informed people in the Western world. I say this in the
face of the popular conceit that television, as a window to the world, has
made Americans exceedingly well informed. Much depends here, of
course, on what is meant by being informed. I will pass over the now
tiresome polls that tell us that, at any given moment, 70 percent of our
citizens do not know who is the Secretary of State or the Chief Justice of
the Supreme Court. Let us consider, instead, the case of Iran during the
drama that was called the "Iranian Hostage Crisis." I don't suppose there
has been a story in years that received more continuous attention from
television. We may assume, then, the Americans know most of what there
is to know about this unhappy event. And now, I put these questions to
you: Would it be an exaggeration to say that not one American in a hundred
knows what language the Iranians speak? Or what the word "Ayatollah"
means or implies? Or knows any details of the tenets of Iranian religious
beliefs? Or the main outlines of their political history? Or knows who the
Shah was, and where he came from?

Nonetheless, everyone had an opinion about this event, for in America   19 everyone is entitled to an opinion, and it is certainly useful to have a few when a pollster shows up. But these are opinions of a quite different order from eighteenth- or nineteenth-century opinions. It is probably more accurate to call them emotions rather than opinions, which would account for the fact that they change from week to week, as the pollsters tell us. What is happening here is that television is altering the meaning of "being informed" by creating a species of information that might properly be called *disinformation*. I am using this word almost in the precise sense in which it is used by spies in the CIA or KGB. Disinformation does not mean false information. It means misleading information—misplaced, irrelevant, fragmented or superficial information—information that creates the illusion of knowing something but which in fact leads one away from knowing. In saying this, I do not mean to imply that television news deliberately aims to deprive Americans of a coherent, contextual understanding of their world. I mean to say that when news is packaged as entertainment, that is the inevitable result. And in saying that the television news show entertains but does not inform, I am saying something far more serious than that we are being deprived of authentic information. I am saying we are losing our sense of what it means to be well informed. Ignorance is always correctable. But what shall we do if we take ignorance to be knowledge?

Here is a startling example of how this process bedevils us. A *New* 20 *York Times* article is headlined on February 15, 1983:

REAGAN MISSTATEMENTS GETTING LESS ATTENTION

The article begins in the following way:

> President Reagan's aides used to become visibly alarmed at suggestions that he had given mangled and perhaps misleading accounts of his policies or of current events in general. That doesn't seem to happen much anymore.
>
> Indeed, the President continues to make debatable assertions of fact but news accounts do not deal with them as extensively as they once did. In the view of White House officials, the declining news coverage mirrors a *decline in interest by the general public.* (my italics)

This report is not so much a news story as a story about the news, and 21 our recent history suggests that it is not about Ronald Reagan's charm. It is about how news is defined, and I believe the story would be quite astonishing to both civil libertarians and tyrants of an earlier time. Walter Lippmann, for example, wrote in 1920: "There can be no liberty for a community which lacks the means by which to detect lies." For all of his pessimism about the possibilities of restoring an eighteenth- and nineteenth-century level of public discourse, Lippmann assumed, as did Thomas Jefferson before him, that with a well-trained press functioning as a lie-detector, the public's interest in a President's mangling of the truth would be piqued, in both senses of that word. Given the means to detect lies, he believed, the public could not be indifferent to their consequences.

But this case refutes his assumption. The reporters who cover the   22 White House are ready and able to expose lies, and thus create the grounds for informed and indignant opinion. But apparently the public declines to take an interest. To press reports of White House dissembling, the public has replied with Queen Victoria's famous line: "We are not amused." However, here the words mean something the Queen did not have in mind. They mean that what is not amusing does not compel their attention. Perhaps if the President's lies could be demonstrated by pictures and accompanied by music the public would raise a curious eyebrow. If a movie, like *All the President's Men,* could be made from his misleading accounts of government policy, if there were a break-in of some sort or sinister characters laundering money, attention would quite likely be paid. We do well to remember that President Nixon did not begin to come undone until his lies were given a theatrical setting at the Watergate hearings. But we do not have anything like that here. Apparently, all President Reagan does is *say* things that are not entirely true. And there is nothing entertaining in that.

But there is a subtler point to be made here. Many of the President's   23 "misstatements" fall in the category of contradictions—mutually exclusive assertions that cannot possibly both, in the same context, be true. "In the same context" is the key phrase here, for it is context that defines contradiction. There is no problem in someone's remarking that he prefers oranges to apples, and also remarking that he prefers apples to oranges— not if one statement is made in the context of choosing a wallpaper design and the other in the context of selecting fruit for dessert. In such a case, we have statements that are opposites, but not contradictory. But if the statements are made in a single, continuous, and coherent context, then they are contradictions, and cannot both be true. Contradiction, in short, requires that statements and events be perceived as interrelated aspects of a continuous and coherent context. Disappear the context, or fragment it, and contradiction disappears. This point is nowhere made more clear to me than in conferences with my younger students about their writing. "Look here," I say. "In this paragraph you have said one thing. And in that you have said the opposite. Which is it to be?" They are polite, and wish to please, but they are as baffled by the question as I am by the response. "I know," they will say, "but that is *there* and this is *here.*" The difference between us is that I assume "there" and "here," "now" and "then," one paragraph and the next to be connected, to be continuous, to be part of the same coherent world of thought. That is the way of typographic discourse, and typography is the universe I'm "coming from,"; as they say. But they are coming from a different universe of discourse altogether: the "Now

. . . this" world of television. The fundamental assumption of that world is not coherence but discontinuity. And in a world of discontinuities, contradiction is useless as a test of truth or merit, because contradiction does not exist.

My point is that we are by now so thoroughly adjusted to the "Now . . . this" world of news—a world of fragments, where events stand alone, stripped of any connection to the past, or to the future, or to other events— that all assumptions of coherence have vanished. And so, perforce, has contradiction. In the context of *no context,* so to speak, it simply disappears. And in its absence, what possible interest could there be in a list of what the President says *now* and what he said *then?* It is merely a rehash of old news, and there is nothing interesting or entertaining in that. The only thing to be amused about is the bafflement of reporters at the public's indifference. There is an irony in the fact that the very group that has taken the world apart should, on trying to piece it together again, be surprised that no one notices much, or cares.

For all his perspicacity, George Orwell would have been stymied by this situation; there is nothing "Orwellian" about it. The President does not have the press under his thumb. *The New York Times* and *The Washington Post* are not *Pravda;* the Associated Press is not Tass. And there is no Newspeak here. Lies have not been defined as truth nor truth as lies. All that has happened is that the public has adjusted to incoherence and been amused into indifference. Which is why Aldous Huxley would not in the least be surprised by the story. Indeed, he prophesied its coming. He believed that it is far more likely that the Western democracies will dance and dream themselves into oblivion than march into it, single file and manacled. Huxley grasped, as Orwell did not, that it is not necessary to conceal anything from a public insensible to contradiction and narcoticized by technological diversions. Although Huxley did not specify that television would be our main line to the drug, he would have no difficulty accepting Robert MacNeil's observation that "Television is the *soma* of Aldous Huxley's *Brave New World.*" Big Brother turns out to be Howdy Doody.

I do not mean that the trivialization of public information is all accomplished *on* television. I mean that television is the paradigm for our conception of public information. As the printing press did in an earlier time, television has achieved the power to define the form in which news must come, and it has also defined how we shall respond to it. In presenting news to us packaged as vaudeville, television induces other media to do the same, so that the total information environment begins to mirror television.

For example, America's newest and highly successful national newspaper, *USA Today,* is modeled precisely on the format of television. It is sold on the street in receptacles that look like television sets. Its stories are uncommonly short, its design leans heavily on pictures, charts and other graphics, some of them printed in various colors. Its weather maps are a visual delight; its sports section includes enough pointless statistics to distract a computer. As a consequence, *USA Today,* which began publication in September 1982, has become the third largest daily in the United States (as of July 1984, according to the Audit Bureau of Circulations), moving quickly to overtake the *Daily News* and the *Wall Street Journal.* Journalists of a more traditional bent have criticized it for its superficiality and theatrics, but the paper's editors remain steadfast in their disregard of typographic standards. The paper's Editor-in-Chief, John Quinn, has said: "We are not up to undertaking projects of the dimensions needed to win prizes. They don't give awards for the best investigative paragraph." Here is an astonishing tribute to the resonance of television's epistemology: In the age of television, the paragraph is becoming the basic unit of news in print media. Moreover, Mr. Quinn need not fret too long about being deprived of awards. As other newspapers join in the transformation, the time cannot be far off when awards will be given for the best investigative sentence.

It needs also to be noted here that new and successful magazines such   28
as *People* and *Us* are not only examples of television-oriented print media but have had an extraordinary "ricochet" effect on television itself. Whereas television taught the magazines that news is nothing but entertainment, the magazines have taught television that nothing but entertainment is news. Television programs, such as "Entertainment Tonight," turn information about entertainers and celebrities into "serious" cultural content, so that the circle begins to close: Both the form and content of news become entertainment.

Radio, of course, is the least likely medium to join in the descent into   29
Huxleyan world of technological narcotics. It is, after all, particularly well suited to the transmission of rational, complex language. Nonetheless, and even if we disregard radio's captivation by the music industry, we appear to be left with the chilling fact that such language as radio allows us to hear is increasingly primitive, fragmented, and largely aimed at invoking visceral response; which is to say, it is the linguistic analogue to the ubiquitous rock music that is radio's principal source of income. As I write, the trend in call-in shows is for the "host" to insult callers whose language does not, in itself, go much beyond humanoid grunting. Such programs have little content, as this word used to be defined, and are merely of archeological interest in that they give us a sense of what a dialogue among Neanderthals might have been like. More to the point, the language of radio newscasts has become, under the influence of television, increasingly decontextualized and discontinuous, so that the possibility of anyone's knowing about the world, as against merely knowing *of* it, is effectively

blocked. In New York City, radio station WINS entreats its listeners to "Give us twenty-two minutes and we'll give you the world." This is said without irony, and its audience, we may assume, does not regard the slogan as the conception of a disordered mind.

And so, we move rapidly into an information environment which may 30 rightly be called trivial pursuit. As the game of that name uses facts as a source of amusement, so do our sources of news. It has been demonstrated many times that a culture can survive misinformation and false opinion. It has not yet been demonstrated whether a culture can survive if it takes the measure of the world in twenty-two minutes. Or if the value of its news is determined by the number of laughs it provides.

QUESTION OF CONTENT

1. Postman assigns great importance to the words "Now . . . this" not for themselves alone but for what they represent. What for Postman makes these two little words so frightening? What concept of the world does he suggest they imply?

2. In your own words, how does the division of time on television provide a nurturing atmosphere for what Postman calls the "Now . . . this" world view?

3. What do the words "hampered viewer acceptance" mean? How does Postman relate this phrase to a theatrical performance?

4. How does Postman distinguish between the two kinds of truth he mentions in paragraph 8?

5. What are some of the features of a news show that contribute to its dramatic performance?

6. In your own words, define the term *contradiction*. How does the "Now . . . this" world view make the concept of contradiction extinct?

QUESTIONS ON RHETORIC

1. In paragraph 13, Postman illustrates his point that commercial breaks "defuse the import of the news." Did you find his illustration convincing? Why or why not?

2. Postman asks several questions in his essay. Locate a few of the questions he poses, and explain the different ways Postman uses questions to engage the reader.

3. In paragraph 14, Postman uses comparison to support his idea that "embedded in the surrealistic frame of a television news show is a theory of anticommunication." What effect did these illustrations have on you?

Do you think Postman has placed them in any particular order? Explain your answer. (Glossary: *Illustration*)

4. What do you think is Postman's attitude toward television news and the public that tolerates it? (Glossary: *Attitude*) Choose examples of Postman's diction to support your answer. (Glossary: *Diction*)

5. In the final paragraph, Postman makes a subtle prediction. What is it, and how well do you think it works as a conclusion to Postman's essay? (Glossary: *Beginnings and Endings*)

VOCABULARY

tantalizing(2)	leitmotif (10)	conceit (18)
perverse (3)	juxtapositions (13)	perspicacity (25)
discrete (3)	nuances (15)	paradigm (26)
epistemologists (8)	anachronism (15)	analogue (29)
versimilitude (9)	abjures (16)	ubiquitous (29)

WRITING TOPICS

1. Postman says "Americans are the best entertained and quite likely the least well-informed people in the Western world." What evidence does he give to support his statement? In a brief essay, use examples from your own observations to argue for or against Postman's point of view.

2. Postman expresses his dread over the growing popularity of call-in shows. What is his fear? Listen to some of these shows in your area. Do you think his fear is valid? Why or why not? In a brief essay, discuss your conclusions.

3. In paragraph 18, Postman discusses the public's lack of knowledge about Iran and Islam despite there not having "been a story in years that received more attention from television" than the Iran hostage crisis. What are some of the "facts" we never got from watching that news story on television? Choose several other significant news events of recent times. In an essay, discuss any points you know of relevant to those events that the television news never mentioned. Would you have been interested in knowing more than the television news provided?

THE MESSAGES BEHIND
THE NEWS

Herbert J. Gans

*Herbert J. Gans, from the Center for Policy Research and
from Columbia University, studies the mass media from the
sociologist's point of view. In the following essay, first
published in 1979 in the* Columbia Journalism Review *and
later published in his book* Deciding What's News: A Study
of CBS Evening News, NBC Nightly News, Newsweek, and
Time, *Gans theorizes that the nightly news is anything but
"neutral." Instead, by the stories it selects and the way it
chooses to tell them, television news projects value judgments
in the form of "a picture of nation and society as it ought to
be."*

Journalism is, like sociology, an empirical discipline. Like other empir-   1
ical disciplines, the news does not limit itself to reality judgments; it also
contains values, or preference statements. This in turn makes it possible to
suggest that there is, underlying the news, a picture of nation and society
as it ought to be.

The values in the news are rarely explicit and must be found between   2
the lines—in which actors and activities are reported or ignored, and in
how they are described. Because journalists do not, in most instances,
deliberately insert values into the news, these values must be inferred.

I shall employ a narrow definition of values, examining only preference   3
statements about nation and society, and major national or societal issues.
I also distinguish between two types of values, which I call topical and
enduring, and I will analyze only the latter. Enduring values are values
which can be found in many different types of news stories over a long
period of time; often, they affect what events become news and even help
define the news.

The list that follows is limited to the enduring values I have found in   4
the news over the last two decades, although all are probably of far more
venerable vintage; obviously, it includes those which this inferrer, bringing
his own values to the task, has found most visible and important. The
methods by which I identified the values were impressionistic; the values

really emerged from continual scrutiny of the news. Some came from the ways actors and activities are described, the tones in which stories are written, told, or filmed, and the connotations that accrue to commonly used verbs, nouns, and adjectives, especially if neutral terms are available but not used. When years ago the news reported that Stokely Carmichael has "turned up" somewhere, while the president had, on the same day, "arrived" somewhere else, or when another story pointed out that a city was "plagued by labor problems," the appropriate values were not difficult to discern, if only because neutral terms were available but were not used. However, sometimes neutral terms are simply not available. The news could have called the young men who refused to serve in the Vietnam War draft evaders, dodgers, or resisters, but it rarely used the last term.

The enduring values I want to discuss can be grouped into eight clus-   5
ters: ethnocentrism, altruistic democracy, responsible capitalism, small-town pastoralism, individualism, moderatism, order, and national leadership.

ETHNOCENTRISM

Like the news of other countries, American news values its own nation   6
above all others, even though it sometimes disparages blatant patriotism. This ethnocentrism is most explicit in foreign news, which judges other countries by the extent to which they live up to or imitate American practices and values, but it also underlies domestic news. While the news contains many stories that are critical of domestic conditions, they are almost always treated as deviant cases, with the implication that American ideals, at least, remain viable. The Watergate scandals were usually ascribed to a small group of power-hungry politicians, and beyond that, to the "imperial presidency"—but with the afterthought, particularly following Nixon's resignation, that nothing was fundamentally wrong with American democracy even if reforms were needed.

The clearest expression of ethnocentrism, in all countries, appears in   7
war news. While reporting the Vietnam War, the news media described the North Vietnamese and the National Liberation Front as "the enemy," as if they were the enemy of the news media. Similarly, weekly casualty stories reported the number of Americans killed, wounded, or missing, and the number of South Vietnamese killed; but the casualties on the other side were impersonally described as "the Communist death toll" or the "body count."

Again, as in war reporting everywhere, atrocities, in this case by Americans, did not often get into the news, and then only toward the end of the   8
war. Seymour Hersh, the reporter credited with exposing the Mylai mas-

sacre, had considerable difficulty selling the story until the evidence was incontrovertible. The end of the war was typically headlined as "the fall of South Vietnam," with scarcely a recognition that, by other values, it could also be considered a liberation, or, neutrally, a change in governments.

ALTRUISTIC DEMOCRACY

While foreign news suggests quite explicity that democracy is superior to dictatorship, and the more so if it follows American forms, domestic news is more specific, indicating how American democracy should perform by its frequent attention to deviations from an unstated ideal, evident in stories about corruption, conflict, protest, and bureaucratic malfunctioning. That ideal may be labeled altruistic democracy because, above all, the news implies that politics should be based on the public interest and service. 9

Although the news has little patience for losers, it insists that both winners and losers should be scrupulously honest, efficient, and dedicated to acting in the public interest. Financial corruption is always news, as is nepotism, patronage appointments, logrolling, and "deals" in general. Decisions based, or thought to be based, on either self-interest or partisan concerns thus continue to be news whenever they occur, even though they long ago ceased to be novel. 10

Politicians, politics, and democracy are also expected to be merito-cratic; the regular activities of political machines are regularly exposed, and "machine" itself is a pejorative term. Although the news therefore regards civil-service officials more highly than "political appointees," the former are held to a very high standard of efficiency and performance; as a result, any deviant bureaucratic behavior becomes newsworthy. "Waste" is always an evil; the mass of paperwork created by bureaucracy is a frequent story, and the additional paperwork generated by attempts to reduce the amount of paperwork is a humorous item that has appeared in the news regularly. 11

The news keeps track of the violations of official norms, but it does so selectively. Over the years, the news has been perhaps most concerned with freedom of the press and related civil liberties; even recurring local violations, school boards that censor libraries, say, have often become national news. Violations of the civil liberties of radicals, of due process, habeas corpus, and other constitutional protections, particularly for crim-inals, are less newsworthy. Another official norm observed by the news is racial integration. Because citizens are expected to live up to these norms altruistically and because the norms are viewed as expressions of the public interest, the violations of the legal and political rights of blacks in the 12

South were news even before supporters of the civil-rights movement began to demonstrate.

While—and perhaps because—the news consistently reports political   13
and legal failures to achieve altruistic and official democracy, it concerns itself much less with the economic barriers that obstruct the realization of the ideal. Of course, the news is aware of candidates who are millionaires or who obtain substantial amounts of corporate or union campaign money, but it is less conscious of the relationship between poverty and powerlessness, or of the difficulty that Americans of median income have in gaining political access.

The relative inattention to economic obstacles to democracy stems   14
from the assumption that the policy and the economy are separate and independent of each other. Under ideal conditions, one is not supposed to affect or interfere with the other, although, typically, government intervention in the economy is more newsworthy and serious than private industry's intervention in government. Accordingly, the news rarely notes the extent of public subsidy of private industry, and it continues to describe firms and institutions which are completely or partly subsidized by government funds as private—for example, Lockheed, many charities, and most privately run universities.

RESPONSIBLE CAPITALISM

The underlying posture of the news toward the economy resembles that   15
taken toward the polity: an optimistic faith that, in the good society, businessmen and women will compete with each other in order to create increased prosperity for all, but that they will refrain from unreasonable profits and gross exploitation of workers or customers. While monopoly is clearly evil, there is little explicit or implicit criticism of the oligopolistic nature of much of today's economy. Unions and consumer organizations are accepted as countervailing pressures on business (the former less so than the latter), and strikes are frequently judged negatively, especially if they inconvenience "the public," contribute to inflation, or involve violence.

Economic growth is always a positive phenomenon, unless it brings   16
about inflation or environmental pollution, leads to the destruction of a historical landmark, or puts craftsmen or craftswomen out of work. In the past, when anchormen gave the stock market report, even the most detached ones looked cheerful when the market had had a good day, assuming this to be of universal benefit to the nation.

Like politicians, business officials are expected to be honest and effi-   17
cient; but while corruption and bureaucratic misbehavior are as undesirable

in business as in government, they are nevertheless tolerated to a somewhat greater extent in the former. For example, the January 2, 1978, issue of *Time* included a three-page critique of government bureaucracy, titled "Rage Over Rising Regulation: To Autocratic Bureaucrats, Nothing Succeeds Like Excess"; but a business-section story reporting that General Motors had sent refunds to the purchasers of Oldsmobiles equipped with Chevrolet engines was only one column long and was headed "End of the Great Engine Flap."

It is now accepted that the government must help the poor, but only the   18
deserving poor, for "welfare cheaters" are a continuing menace and are more newsworthy than people, other than the very rich, who cheat on their taxes. Public welfare agencies are kept under closer scrutiny than others, so that although the news reported on the "welfare mess" in the 1960s, it did not describe equivalent situations in other government agencies in the same way. There was, for example, no "defense mess," and what is "waste" in H.E.W. programs are "cost overruns" in Pentagon programs.

SMALL-TOWN PASTORALISM

The rural and anti-industrial values which Thomas Jefferson is usually   19
thought to have invented can also be found in the news, which favors small towns (agricultural or market) over other types of settlements. At one time, this preference was complemented by a celebration of the large city and of the vitality of its business and entertainment districts; but the end of this period can be dated almost exactly by *Life*'s special issue on the cities, which appeared in December 1965.

For the last ten years cities have been in the news almost entirely as   20
problematic, with the major emphasis on racial conflict, crime, and fiscal insolvency. Suburbs are not often newsworthy, despite the fact that a near majority of Americans now live in them, and they, too, have generally received a bad press. During the 1950s and 1960s, suburbs were viewed as breeding grounds of homogeneity, boredom, adultery, and other evils; since then, they have come into the news because they are suffering increasingly from "urban" problems, particularly crime, or because they keep out racial minorities.

The small town continues to reign supreme, not only in Charles Kuralt's   21
"On the Road" reports for CBS News, but also in television and magazine stories about "the good life" in America. Stories about city neighborhoods judge them by their ability to retain the cohesiveness, friendliness, and slow pace ascribed to small towns, and during the period of journalistic interest in ethnicity, to the ethnic enclaves of the past.

Needless to say, the pastoral values underlying the news are romantic;   22 they visualize rural and market towns as they were imagined to have existed in the past.

Small-town pastoralism is, at the same time, a specification of two   23
more general values: the desirability both of nature and of smallness *per se.*
The news dealt with the conflict between the preservation of nature and the activities of developers long before the environment and ecology became political issues; and, more often than not, the news took at least an implicit stand against the developers. The postwar developers of suburbia were seen as despoiling the land in their rapacious search for profits; that they were concurrently providing houses for people was rarely noted.

The virtue of smallness comes through most clearly in stories that deal   24
with the faults of bigness, for in the news, big government, big labor, and big business rarely have virtues. Bigness is feared, among other things, as impersonal and inhuman. In the news as well as in architecture, the ideal social organization should reflect a "human scale." The fear of bigness also reflects a fear of control, of privacy and individual freedom being ground under by organizations too large to notice, much less to value, the individual. As such, bigness is a major threat to individualism.

INDIVIDUALISM

It is no accident that many of the characters in Kuralt's pastoral features are   25
"rugged individualists," for one of the most important enduring news values is the preservation of the freedom of the individual against the encroachments of nation and society. The good society of the news is populated by individuals who participate in it, but on their own terms, acting in the public interest, but as they define it.

The ideal individual struggles successfully against adversity and over-   26
comes more powerful forces. The news looks for people who act heroically during disasters, and it pays attention to people who conquer nature without hurting it: explorers, mountain climbers, astronauts, and scientists. "Self-made" men and women remain attractive, as do people who overcome poverty or bureaucracy.

The news often contains stories about new technology that endangers   27
the individual—notably the computer, which is viewed anthropomorphically, either as a robot that will deprive human beings of control over their own lives or as a machine endowed with human failings, which is therefore less of a threat. In any case, there is always room for a gleeful story about computers that break down. The news has, however, always paid attention to the dangers of new technology; when television sets were first mass-produced, they were viewed as dehumanizing because they robbed people

of the art of conversation; similar fears were expressed at the time of the institution of digit-dialing in telephones.

Conversely, the news celebrates old technology and mourns its passing, partly because it is tied to an era when life was thought to have been simpler, partly because it is viewed as being under individual control. 28

MODERATISM

The idealization of the individual could result in praise for the rebel and the 29 deviant, but this possiblity is neutralized by an enduring value that discourages excess or extremism. Individualism that violates the law, the dominant mores, and enduring values is suspect; equally important, what is valued in individuals is discouraged in groups. Thus, groups that exhibit what is seen as extreme behavior are criticized in the news through pejorative adjectives or a satirical tone.

For example, the news treats atheists as extremists and uses the same 30 approach, if more gingerly, with religious fanatics. People who consume conspicuously are criticized, but so are people such as hippies, who turn their backs entirely on consumer goods. The news is scornful both of the overly academic scholar and the oversimplifying popularizer: it is kind neither to highbrows nor to lowbrows, to users of jargon or users of slang.

The same value applies to politics. Political ideologists are suspect, but 31 so are completely unprincipled politicians. The totally self-seeking are thought to be consumed by excessive ambition, but the complete do-gooders are not believed. Political candidates who talk only about issues may be described as dull; those who avoid issues entirely evoke doubts about their fitness for office. Poor speakers are thought to be unelectable, while demogogues are taken to be dangerous. Those who regularly follow party lines are viewed as hacks, and those who never do are called mavericks or loners—although these terms are pejorative only for the politically unsuccessful; the effective loner becomes a hero.

ORDER

The frequent appearance of stories about disorder suggests that order is an 32 important value in the news, but order is a meaningless term unless one specifies what order and whose order is being valued. Social disorder is generally defined as disorder in the public areas of the society. A protest march in which three people die would be headline national news, whereas a family murder that claimed three victims would be a local story. Disorders in affluent areas or elite institutions are more likely to be reported than their occurrence elsewhere. In the 1960s, the looting of a handful of stores on New York's Fifth Avenue received as much attention as a much larger spree taking place in a ghetto area that same day. Peaceful demonstrations on college campuses, especially elite ones, are usually more newsworthy than those in factories or prisons. But the major public area is the seat of government; thus, a trouble-free demonstration in front of a city hall or a police station is news, whereas that in front of a store is not.

Still, the most important criterion of worthiness is the target of a 33 demonstration. The anti-war demonstrations of the past decade were covered as disorder stories because they were aimed at presidents. Likewise, the 1978 coal strike did not become a magazine cover story until it involved the president.

Beneath the concern for political order lies another, perhaps even 34 deeper concern for social cohesion, which reflects fears that not only the official rules of the political order but also the informal rules of the social order are in danger of being disobeyed. Hippies and college dropouts of the 1960s were newsworthy in part because they rejected the so-called Protestant work ethic; even now, drug use by the young, and its consequences, is in the news more than alcohol use because it signifies a rejection of traditional methods of seeking oblivion or mind expansion. Indeed, the news evaluates the young almost entirely in terms of the adult rules they are in the process of rejecting.

Moral disorder stories are, in the end, cued to much the same concern 35 for social cohesion, particularly those stories which report violations of the mores rather than the laws. Such stories are based on the premise that the activities of public officials, public agencies, and corporations should derive from the same moral and ethical values that are supposed to apply to personal, familial, and friendship relations. Even if every political reporter knows that politicians cannot operate with the same ideal of honesty as friends, the failure of politicians to do so continues to be news. In the last analysis, the values underlying social and moral disorder news are the same, although the two types of news differ in subject and object: social disorder news monitors the repsect of citizens for authority, while moral disorder stories evaluate whether authority figures respect the rules of the citizenry.

With some oversimplification, it would be fair to say that the news 36 supports the social order of public, business and professional, upper-middle-class, middle-aged, and white-male sectors of society. Because the news emphasizes people over groups, it pays less attention to the institutionalized social order, except as reflected in its leaders; but obviously the news is also generally supportive of governments and their agencies, private enterprise, the prestigious professions, and a variety of other national institutions, including the quality universities. But here, too, always with a proviso: obedience to the relevant enduring values.

Nevertheless, the news is not subservient to powerful individuals or   37
groups, for it measures their behavior against a set of values that is assumed to transcend them. Moral disorder stories can bid the elites to relinquish, or at least hide, their moral deficiencies. To be sure, the values invoked in moral disorder stories are themselves often set by and shared by these elites. The president's policies are not often viewed from the perspectives of, or judged by, the values of low-income and moderate-income citizens; corporate officials are even less rarely judged by the values of employees or customers; or university presidents, by the values of students or campus janitors. Instead, the values in the news derive largely from reformers and reform movements, which are themselves elites. Still, the news is not simply a complaint supporter of elites, or the establishment, or the ruling class; rather, it views nation and society through its own set of values and with its own conception of the good social order.

LEADERSHIP

If the news values moral and social order, it also suggests how to maintain   38
them, primarily through the availability of morally and otherwise competent leadership. The news focuses on leaders; and, with some exceptions, public agencies and private organizations are represented by their leaders. In the past, magazine cover stories often reported national topics or issues in relation to an individual who played an instrumental or symbolic leadership role in them. When necessary, the news even helps to create leaders; in the 1960s, radical and black organizations functioning on the basis of participatory democracy sometimes complained that journalists would pick out one spokesperson on whom they would lavish most of their attention, thereby making a leader out of him or her.

Although several practical considerations encourage the news media to   39
emphasize leaders, the news is also based on a theory of society that would argue, were it made explicit, that the social process, above all others, is shaped by leaders—people who, either because of their political or managerial skills, or personal attributes which inspire others, move into positions of authority and make things happen. A lengthy 1974 *Time* cover story that surveyed existing definitions of leadership concluded that most "emphasize honesty, candor, and vision, combined with sheer physical stamina and courage"; to which the magazine added that "courage without brains was [not] sufficient." A leader must also be strong and able to control subordinates; their moral failings and inefficiencies are a sign of weak leadership.

The foremost leader in America is the president, who is viewed as the   40
ultimate protector of order. He is the final backdrop for domestic tranquil-
ity and the principal guardian of national security, his absence from the
White House due to resignation or death evoking fears of an enemy attack
or possible panic by a now leaderless populace. Through his own behavior
and the concern he shows for the behavior of others, the president also
becomes the nation's moral leader. He sets an example that might be
followed by others: should he permit or condone corruption among his
associates or appointees, he is suspected of moral disorder. Finally, he is
the person who states and represents the national values and he is the agent
of the national will.

NEWS VALUES AND IDEOLOGY

If the news includes values, it also contains ideology. That ideology,   41
however, is an aggregate of only partly thought-out values which are
neither entirely consistent nor well integrated; and since it changes somewhat over time, it is also flexible on some issues. I call this aggregate of
values and the reality judgments associated with it para-ideology, partly to
distinguish it from the deliberate, integrated, and more doctrinaire set of
values usually defined as ideology; it is ideology nevertheless.

The para-ideology can itself be placed on the conventional spectrum,   42
but not easily, since journalists are not much interested in ideology or
aware that they, too, promulgate ideology. As a result, individual stories
and journalists can span various parts of the spectrum, although their
values rarely coincide with those on the far right or the far left. Even the
news media as a whole, and the news, analyzed over time, are not easily
classified.

In its advocacy of altruistic and official democracy, the news defends   43
a mixture of liberal and conservative values, but its conception of responsible capitalism comes closest to what I would call right-leaning liberalism.
On the other hand, in its respect for tradition and its nostalgia for pastoralism and rugged individualism, the news is unabashedly conservative, as
it is also both in its defense of the social order and its faith in leadership.
If the news has to be pigeonholed ideologically, it is right-liberal or left-
conservative.

In reality, the news is not so much conservative or liberal as it is   44
reformist; indeed, the enduring values are very much like the values of the
Progressive movement of the early twentieth century. The resemblance is
often uncanny, as in the common advocacy of honest, meritocratic, and
anti-bureaucratic government, and in the shared antipathy to political machines and demagogues, particularly of populist bent. Altruistic democracy

is, in other words, close to the Progressive ideal of government. The notion of responsible capitalism is also to be found in Progressivism, as is the dislike of bigness, the preference for craftsmanship over technology, the defense of nature, and the celebration of anti-urban pastoral society. Journalistic para-ideology and Progressivism are further akin in their mutual support of individualism, their uneasiness about collective solutions, other than at the grassroots level, and their opposition to socialism. Moreover, the preservation of an upper-class and upper-middle-class social order, like the need for morally and otherwise competent national leadership, has its equivalents in Progressive thought.

The Progressive movement is long dead, but many of its basic values 45 and its reformist impulses have persisted. The news is reformist and its being so helps explain why it is not easily fitted into the conventional ideological spectrum. Of course, Progressive thought can be placed on the spectrum, although historians have not yet agreed whether the movement was liberal, conservative, or both. In any case, the news may be marching to a somewhat different drummer; and when journalists are unwilling to describe themselves as liberal or conservative, and prefer to see themselves as independents, they may be sensing, if not with complete awareness, that they are, as a profession, Progressive reformers.

QUESTIONS ON CONTENT

1. In the beginning of his essay, Gans says he will "distinguish between two types of values, which I call topical and enduring, and I will analyze only the latter." After reading his essay, what would you infer Gans means by "topical" values? Give examples of both topical and enduring values. Do you agree with the distinction Gans makes between the two kinds of values?

2. What is ethnocentrism? How, according to Gans, does it manifest itself in newscasting?

3. Gans says that domestic news is more specific than foreign news in its definition of the ways American democracy ought to perform. What is the term Gans uses for the ideal of democracy held forth in domestic newscasting? How does he define it? What expectations does Gans say this ideal places on politicians?

4. Thomas Jefferson is thought to have invented the rural and anti-industrial values that declare "small is better," according to Gans. In contrast, what are some of the perceived ills Gans mentions that account for the "bad press" given to big cities and suburban neighborhoods? In what kinds of stories does the implied virtue of "smallness" come through most clearly, according to Gans? Give some examples.

5. How does Gans think the ideal of the individual finds expression in the news? What "enduring value" does he say neutralizes the notion of the individual somewhat? What forms of individualism does he see as a threat to this enduring value?

6. How does the news tend to "evaluate the young," according to Gans? Do your observations confirm this? Explain.

7. In your own words, what is the ideology that best describes television news reporting, according to Gans?

QUESTIONS ON RHETORIC

1. What do you think is Gans's purpose in writing this essay? (Glossary: *Purpose*) Does he want to persuade readers, warn them, or amuse them? Use examples of Gans's rhetoric to support your answer.

2. Reread Gans's essay. What system of organization does he use? (Glossary: *Organization*) Does this pattern work well as a means of presenting his information? Would another method have worked just as well? Why or why not?

3. Gans uses a rich vocabulary in his essay. Did it hamper your reading of the essay or enhance it? Did you look up unfamiliar words as you went along? What does Gans's diction tell you about his intended audience? (Glossary: *Diction*)

4. What kinds of evidence does Gans use to support his theory about the values being projected in the news? (Glossary: *Evidence*) Choose a few of the examples he uses in the essay, and explain in what ways they are or are not convincing evidence.

5. Gans makes the point that by its choice of stories the news projects certain values. Is Gans neutral? Show how by his use of words Gans projects his own value judgments on news topics and broadcast news. (Glossary: *Diction*)

6. In paragraph 36, Gans explains who it is that determines the shared values projected in the news. Did you have any trouble understanding him? Is his evaluation expressed clearly? Why or why not?

VOCABULARY

inferred (2)	habeas corpus (12)	anthropomorphically (27)
scrutiny (4)	countervailing (15)	proviso (36)
disparages (6)	pastoral (22)	promulgate (42)
scrupulously (10)	rapacious (23)	antipathy (44)

WRITING TOPICS

1. Gans says a reverence for the virtues of small-town life was "complemented by a celebration of the large city and of the vitality of its business

and entertainment districts.'' However, he says this attitude has changed and now big cities are depicted as ''problematic.'' Watch and read the news for a week. What kinds of references are made to big cities and small towns? In your opinion, is news reporting with regard to small towns really more favorable? In an essay, discuss the kinds of problems and the virtues the news attaches to both small towns and large cities.

2. Gans cites one news story as reporting that black activist Stokely Carmichael ''turned up'' somewhere, while on the same day the president is said to have ''arrived'' someplace else. Clearly, says Gans, the words *turned up* are value-laden while the term *arrived* is not. Listen to the news, paying close attention to the choice of words used to describe events. Now make a list of what words three different networks used to report the same story. For added interest, listen also to the public television station in your area. In your opinion, do newscasters really use value-laden language, or are they as neutral as the language permits? Write an essay to report your findings.

3. Look up the word *reformist* in your dictionary. Compare that definition to the description of the Progressive movement of the early twentieth century that Gans offers at the end of his essay. Are they similar? How do these two definitions compare to the ideology explicit in the reporting of the news as described by Gans?

WHEN NICE PEOPLE BURN BOOKS

Nat Hentoff

Nat Hentoff is a columnist for the Washington Post *who also writes for liberal publications such as* The Progressive, *from which this piece was taken. In this essay he offers evidence that totalitarian tendencies to limit free speech and a free press are not confined to the far right; they are beginning to show up in groups to the left. Hentoff wonders about "liberals" who have championed the cause of civil rights and yet can justify censorship to protect their idea of what is right.*

It happened one splendid Sunday morning in a church. Not Jerry Fal-   1
well's Baptist sanctuary in Lynchburg, Virginia, but rather the First Uni-
tarian Church in Baltimore. On October 4, 1981, midway through the 11
A.M. service, pernicious ideas were burned at the altar.

As reported by Frank P. L. Somerville, religion editor of the *Baltimore*   2
Sun, "Centuries of Jewish, Christian, Islamic, and Hindu writings were
'expurgated'—because of sections described as 'sexist.'

"Touched off by a candle and consumed in a pot on a table in front of   3
the altar were slips of paper containing 'patriarchal' excerpts from Martin
Luther, Thomas Aquinas, the Koran, St. Augustine, St. Ambrose, St. John
Chrysostom, the Hindu Code of Manu V, an anonymous Chinese author,
and the Old Testament." Also hurled into the purifying fire were works by
Kierkegaard and Karl Barth.

The congregation was much exalted: "As the last flame died in the pot,   4
and the organ pealed, there was applause," Somerville wrote.

I reported that news of the singed holy spirit to a group of American   5
Civil Liberties Union members in California, and one woman was furious.
At me.

"We did the same thing at our church two Sundays ago," she said.   6
"And long past time, too. Don't you understand it's just *symbolic?*"

I told this ACLU member that when the school board in Drake, North   7
Dakota, threw thirty-four copies of Kurt Vonnegut's *Slaughterhouse Five*

into the furnace in 1973, it wasn't because the school was low on fuel. That burning was symbolic, too. Indeed, the two pyres—in North Dakota and in Baltimore—were witnessing to the same lack of faith in the free exchange of ideas.

What an inspiring homily for the children attending services at a liberated church: They now know that the way to handle ideas they don't like is to set them on fire.

The stirring ceremony in Baltimore is just one more illustration that the spirit of the First Amendment is not being savaged only by malign forces of the Right, whether private or governmental. Campaigns to purge school libraries, for example, have been conducted by feminists as well as by Phyllis Schlafly. Yet, most liberal watchdogs of our freedom remain fixed on the Right as *the* enemy of free expression.

For a salubrious change, therefore, let us look at what is happening to freedom of speech and press in certain enclaves—some colleges, for instance—where the New Right has no clout at all. Does the pulse of the First Amendment beat more vigorously in these places than where the Yahoos are?

Well, consider what happened when Eldridge Cleaver came to Madison, Wisconsin, last October to savor the exhilarating openness of dialogue at the University of Wisconsin. Cleaver's soul is no longer on ice; it's throbbing instead with a religious conviction that is currently connected financially, and presumably theologically, to the Reverend Sun Myung Moon's Unification Church. In Madison, Cleaver never got to talk about his pilgrim's progress from the Black Panthers to the wondrously ecumenical Moonies. In the Humanities Building—*Humanities*—several hundred students and others outraged by Cleaver's apostasy shouted, stamped their feet, chanted "Sieg Heil," and otherwise prevented him from being heard.

After ninety minutes of the din, Cleaver wrote on the blackboard, "I regret that the totalitarians have deprived us of our constitutional rights to free assembly and free speech. Down with communism. Long live democracy."

And, raising a clenched fist while blowing kisses with his free hand, Cleaver left. Cleaver says he'll try to speak again, but he doesn't know when.

The University of Wisconsin administration, through Dean of Students Paul Ginsberg, deplored the behavior of the campus totalitarians of the Left, and there was a fiercely denunciatory editorial in the Madison *Capital Times:* "These people lack even the most primitive appreciation of the Bill of Rights."

It did occur to me, however, that if Eldridge Cleaver had not abandoned his secularist rage at the American Leviathan and had come to Madison as the still burning spear of black radicalism, the result might have been quite different if he had been shouted down that night by young apostles of the New Right. That would have made news around the country, and there would have been collectively signed letters to the *New York Review of Books* and *The Nation* warning of the prowling dangers to free speech in the land. But since Cleaver has long since taken up with bad companions, there is not much concern among those who used to raise bail for him as to whether he gets to speak freely or not.

A few years ago, William F. Buckley Jr., invited to be commencement 16
speaker at Vassar, was told by student groups that he not only would be shouted down if he came but might also suffer some contusions. All too few liberal members of the Vassar faculty tried to educate their students about the purpose of a university, and indeed a good many faculty members joined in the protests against Buckley's coming. He finally decided not to appear because, he told me, he didn't want to spoil the day for the parents. I saw no letters on behalf of Buckley's free-speech rights in any of the usual liberal forums for such concerns. After all, he had not only taken up with bad companions; he was an original bad companion.

During the current academic year, there were dismaying developments 17
concerning freedom for bad ideas in the college press. The managing editor of *The Daily Lobo,* the University of New Mexico's student newspaper, claimed in an editorial that Scholastic Aptitude Test scores show minority students to be academically inferior. Rather than rebut his facile misinterpretation of what those scores actually show—that class, not race, affects the results—black students and their sympathizers invaded the newspaper's office.

The managing editor prudently resigned, but the protesters were not sat- 18
isfied. They wanted the head of the editor. The brave Student Publications Board temporarily suspended her, although the chairman of the journalism department had claimed the suspension was a violation of her First Amendment rights. She was finally given her job back, pending a formal hearing, but she decided to quit. The uproar had not abated, and who knew what would happen at her formal hearing before the Student Publications Board?

When it was all over, the chairman of the journalism department ob- 19
served that the confrontation had actually reinforced respect for First Amendment rights on the University of New Mexico campus because infuriated students now knew they couldn't successfully insist on the firing of an editor because of what had been published.

What about the resignations? Oh, they were free-will offerings. 20

I subscribe to most of the journalism reviews around the country, but 21
I saw no offer of support to those two beleaguered student editors in New Mexico from professional journalists who invoke the First Amendment at almost any public opportunity.

Then there was a free-speech war at Kent State University, as summa- 22 rized in the November 12, 1982, issue of *National On-Campus Report*. Five student groups at Kent State are vigorously attempting to get the editor of the student newspaper fired. They are: "gay students, black students, the undergraduate and graduate student governments, and a progressive student alliance."

Not a reactionary among them. Most are probably deeply concerned   23
with the savaging of the free press in Chile, Uruguay, Guatemala, South Africa, and other such places.

What had this editor at Kent State done to win the enmity of so hu-   24
manistic a grand alliance? He had written an editorial that said that a gay student group should not have access to student-fee money to sponsor a Hallowe'en dance. Ah, but how had he gone about making his point?

"In opening statements," says the *National On-Campus Report*, "he   25
employed words like 'queer' and 'nigger' to show that prejudice against any group is undesirable." Just like Lenny Bruce. Lenny, walking on stage in a club, peering into the audience, and asking, "Any spics here tonight? Any kikes? Any niggers?"

Do you think Lenny Bruce could get many college bookings today? Or   26
write a column for a college newspaper?

In any case, the rest of the editorial went on to claim that the proper use   27
of student fees was for educational, not social, activities. The editor was not singling out the Kent Gay/Lesbian Foundation. He was opposed to *any* student organization using those fees for dances.

Never mind. He had used impermissible words: Queer. Nigger. And   28
those five influential cadres of students are after his head. The editor says that university officials have assured him, however, that he is protected at Kent State by the First Amendment. If that proves to be the case, those five student groups will surely move to terminate, if not defenestrate, those university officials.

It is difficult to be a disciple of James Madison on campus these days.   29
Take the case of Phyllis Schlafly and Wabash College. The college is a small, well-regarded liberal arts institution in Crawfordsville, Indiana. In the spring of 1981, the college was riven with discord. Some fifty members of the ninety-odd faculty and staff wrote a stiff letter to the Wabash Lecture Series Committee, which had displayed the exceedingly poor taste to invite Schlafly to speak on campus the next year.

The faculty protesters complained that having the Sweetheart of the   30
Right near the Wabash River would be "unfortunate and inappropriate." The dread Schlafly is "an ERA opponent . . . a far-right attorney who travels the country, being highly paid to tell women to stay at home fulfilling traditional roles while sending their sons off to war."

Furthermore, the authors wrote, "The point of view she represents is   31
that of an ever-decreasing minority of American women and men, and is

based in sexist mythology which promulgates beliefs inconsistent with those held by liberally educated persons, and this does not merit a forum at Wabash College under the sponsorship of our Lecture Series.''

This is an intriguing document by people steeped in the traditions of academic freedom. One of the ways of deciding who gets invited to a campus is the speaker's popularity. If the speaker appeals only to a "decreasing minority of American women and men," she's not worth the fee. So much for Dorothy Day, were she still with us. 32

And heaven forfend that anyone be invited whose beliefs are "inconsistent with those held by liberally educated persons." Mirror, mirror on the wall. . . . 33

But do not get the wrong idea about these protesting faculty members: "We subscribe," they emphasized, "to the principles of free speech and free association, of course." 34

All the same, "it does not enhance our image as an all-male college to endorse a well-known sexist by inviting her to speak on our campus." If Phyllis Schlafly is invited nonetheless, "we intend not to participate in any of the activities surrounding Ms. Schlafly's visit and will urge others to do the same." 35

The moral of the story: If you don't like certain ideas, boycott them. 36

The lecture committee responded to the fifty deeply offended faculty members in a most unkind way. The committee told the signers that "William Buckley would endorse your petition. No institution of higher learning, he told us on a visit here, should allow to be heard on its campus any position that it regards as detrimental or 'untrue.' 37

"Apparently," the committee went on, "error is to be refuted not by rational persuasion, but by censorship." 38

Phyllis Schlafly did come to Wabash and she generated a great deal of discussion—most of it against her views—among members of the all-male student body. However, some of the wounded faculty took a long time to recover. One of them, a tenured professor, took aside at a social gathering the wife of a member of the lecture committee that had invited Schlafly. Both were in the same feminist group on campus. 39

The professor cleared her throat, and said to the other woman, "You are going to leave him, aren't you?" 40

"My husband? Why should I leave him?" 41

"Really, how can you stay married to someone who invited Phyllis Schlafly to this campus?" 42

And really, should such a man even be allowed visitation rights with the children? 43

Then there is the Ku Klan Klan. As Klan members have learned in recent months, both in Boston and in Washington, their First Amendment 44 right peaceably to assemble—let alone actually to speak their minds—can only be exercised if they are prepared to be punched in the mouth. Klan members get the same reception that Martin Luther King Jr. and his associates used to receive in Bull Conner's Birmingham.

As all right-thinking people know, however, the First Amendment isn't just for anybody. That presumably is why the administration of the University of Cincinnati has refused this year to allow the KKK to appear on campus. Bill Wilkerson, the Imperial Wizard of the particular Klan faction that has been barred from the University of Cincinnati, says he's going to sue on First Amendment grounds.   45

Aside from the ACLU's, how many *amicus* briefs do you think the Imperial Wizard is likely to get from liberal organizations devoted to academic freedom?   46

The Klan also figures in a dismaying case from Vancouver, Washington. There, an all-white jury awarded $1,000 to a black high school student after he had charged the Battle Ground School District (including Prairie High School) with discrimination. One of the claims was that the school had discriminated against this young man by permitting white students to wear Ku Klux Klan costumes to a Hallowe'en assembly.   47

Symbolic speech, however, is like spoken or written speech. It is protected under the First Amendment. If the high school administration had originally forbidden the wearing of the Klan costumes to the Hallowe'en assembly, it would have spared itself that part of the black student's lawsuit, but it would have set a precedent for censoring symbolic speech which would have shrunken First Amendment protections at Prairie High School.   48

What should the criteria be for permissible costumes at a Hallowe'en assembly? None that injure the feelings of another student? So a Palestinian kid couldn't wear a PLO outfit. Or a Jewish kid couldn't come as Ariel Sharon, festooned with maps. And watch out for the wise guy who comes dressed as that all-around pain-in-the-ass, Tom Paine.   49

School administrators might say the best approach is to have no costumes at all. That way, there'll be no danger of disruption. But if there were real danger of physical confrontation in the school when a student wears a Klan costume, is the school so powerless that it can't prevent a fight? And indeed, what a compelling opportunity the costumes present to teach about the Klan, to ask those white kids who wore Klan costumes what they know of the history of the Klan. To get black and white kids *talking* about what the Klan represents, in history—and right now.   50

Such teaching is too late for Prairie High School. After that $1,000 award to the black student, the white kids who have been infected by Klan demonology will circulate their poison only among themselves, intensify-   51 ing their sickness of spirit. There will be no more Klan costumes in that school, and so no more Klan costumes to stimulate class discussion.

By the way, in the trial, one offer of proof that the school district had   52
been guilty of discrimination was a photograph of four white boys wearing Klan costumes to that Hallowe'en assembly. It's a rare picture. It was originally printed in the school yearbook but, with the lawsuit and all, the picture was cut out of each yearbook before it was distributed.

That's the thing about censorship, whether good liberals or bad com-   53
panions engage in it. Censorship is like a greased pig. Hard to confine. You start trying to deal with offensive costumes and you wind up with a blank space in the yearbook. Isn't that just like the Klan? Causing decent people to do dumb things.

QUESTIONS ON CONTENT

1. Hentoff describes two book burnings in the beginning of his essay. In what ways were they different? How were they similar, according to Hentoff?

2. One member of a liberated church justified the burning of books at her church, according to Hentoff, by saying the burning was only "symbolic." In your own words, what does Hentoff consider to be the flaw in this reasoning? Does the fact that "slips of paper" were burned rather than actual books make a difference to Hentoff? Does it make a difference to you?

3. In paragraphs 15 and 16, Hentoff refers to "bad companions." What does he mean by "bad"? Can you give examples of the kind of people Hentoff is referring to?

4. Hentoff's essay offers a host of examples of persons and groups on the political Left who have in one way or another denied freedom of speech to people with whom they disagree. If you had to choose one sentence from his essay that best sums up the attitude Hentoff thinks these acts embody, in your opinion which one would it be? Why?

5. In paragraph 48, Hentoff explains what he calls "symbolic speech." What precisely is symbolic speech? How does Hentoff compare it to spoken or written speech? What does Hentoff seem to think are the dangers in suppressing such speech?

QUESTIONS OF RHETORIC

1. Hentoff drops names throughout his essay. For instance, he refers to Jerry Falwell, St. Augustine, the ACLU, Phyllis Schlafly, William F. Buckley Jr., Tom Paine, and several other people and organizations without identifying them. What assumptions is Hentoff making about his au-

dience? Who do you think reads *The Progressive* (the magazine from which this article was taken)? What in particular makes Hentoff a convincing advocate for freedom of speech in this case?

2. Hentoff includes in his essay many examples of left-wing violations of the First Amendment. Did he need to include so many? Explain your answer.

3. Hentoff uses specific language to reveal his attitude toward people from the Left who violate the principles of the First Amendment. (Glossary: *Attitude*) In your opinion what is Hentoff's attitude? Choose a few examples from the text to support your answer.

VOCABULARY

pernicious (1)	salubrious (10)	riven (29)
expurgated (2)	apostasy (11)	promulgates (31)
homily (8)	secularist (15)	

WRITING TOPICS

1. In the last sentence of his essay Hentoff says, "Isn't that just like the Klan? Causing decent people to do dumb things." Is Hentoff serious? Why does he end his essay with this remark? In an essay, discuss the real targets of Hentoff's criticism and his feelings toward them.

2. Following his query, "What should the criteria be for permissible costumes at a Hallowe'en assembly? None that injure the feelings of another student?" (49), Hentoff responds to his own question, airing the point of view that free expression of this kind prevents more serious consequences. In your own experience, have you ever been "offended" by the appearance of someone who stands in extreme opposition to your beliefs? Do you agree with Hentoff that such expression might prevent other, more serious, consequences? In an essay, discuss where, if anywhere, you think the line has to be drawn.

3. Hentoff alludes to "the purpose of a university" (16) in relation to students refusing freedom of speech to speakers they despise. In a brief essay, discuss what you think Hentoff believes the purpose of a university to be.

NOW YOU TAKE "BAMBI" OR "SNOW WHITE" —THAT'S SCARY!

Stephen King

In the following article written for TV Guide *in 1981, Stephen King, the author of popular horror novels such as* Carrie, The Shining, *and* Pet Sematery, *offers his opinion on what kind of "scary" television viewing is suitable for small children. Although he agrees that some programs are too violent or horrifying for young minds, King warns that scarier still is the specter of programming censorship. The "element of Big Brotherism" inherent in such censoring makes him both uneasy and angry.*

Read the story synopsis below and ask yourself if it would make the sort   1
of film you'd want your kids watching on the Friday- or Saturday-night movie:

A good but rather weak man discovers that, because of inflation, re-   2
cession and his second wife's fondness for overusing his credit cards, the family is tottering on the brink of financial ruin. In fact, they can expect to see the repossession men coming for the car, the almost new recreational vehicle and the two color TVs any day; and a pink warning-of-foreclosure notice has already arrived from the bank that holds the mortgage on their house.

The wife's solution is simple but chilling: kill the two children, make   3
it look like an accident and collect the insurance. She browbeats her husband into going along with this homicidal scheme. A wilderness trip is arranged, and while wifey stays in camp, the father leads his two children deep into the Great Smoky wilderness. In the end, he finds he cannot kill them in cold blood; he simply leaves them to wander around until, presumably, they will die of hunger and exposure.

The two children spend a horrifying three days and two nights in the   4
wilderness. Near the end of their endurance, they stumble upon a back-country cabin and go to it, hoping for rescue. The woman who lives alone there turns out to be a cannibal. She cages the two children and prepares to roast them in her oven as she has roasted and eaten other wanderers

before them. The boy manages to get free. He creeps up behind the woman as she stokes her oven and pushes her in, where she burns to death in her own fire.

You're probably shaking your head no, even if you have already rec-   5
ognized the origin of this bloody little tale (and if you didn't, ask your kids: they probably will) as "Hansel and Gretel," a so-called "fairy tale" that most kids are exposed to even before they start kindergarten. In addition to this story, with its grim and terrifying images of child abandonment, children lost in the woods and imprisoned by an evil woman, cannibalism and justifiable homicide, small children are routinely exposed to tales of mass murder and mutilation ("Bluebeard"), the eating of a loved one by a monster ("Little Red Riding-Hood"), treachery and deceit ("Snow White") and even the specter of a little boy who must face a black-hooded, ax-wielding headsman (*The 500 Hats of Bartholomew Cubbins,* by Dr. Seuss).

I'm sometimes asked what I allow my kids to watch on the tube, for   6
two reasons: first, my three children, at 10, 8 and 4, are still young enough to be in the age group that opponents of TV violence and horror consider to be particularly impressionable and at risk; and second, my seven novels have been popularly classified as "horror stories." People tend to think those two facts contradictory. But . . . I'm not sure that they are.

Three of my books have been made into films, and at this writing, two   7
of them have been shown on TV. In the cases of "Salem's Lot," a made-for-TV movie, there was never a question of allowing my kids to watch it on its first run on CBS; it began at 9 o'clock in our time zone, and all three children go to bed earlier than that. Even on a weekend, and even for the oldest, an 11 o'clock bedtime is just not negotiable. A previous *TV Guide* article about children and frightening programs mentioned a 3-year-old who watched "Lot" and consequently suffered night terrors. I have no wish to question any responsible parent's judgment—all parents raise their children in different ways—but it did strike me as passingly odd that a 3-year-old should have been allowed to stay up that late to get scared.

But in my case, the hours of the telecast were not really a factor,   8
because we have one of those neat little time-machines, a videocassette recorder. I taped the program and, after viewing it myself, decided my children could watch it if they wanted to. My daughter had no interest; she's more involved with stories of brave dogs and loyal horses these days. My two sons, Joe, 8, and Owen, then 3, did watch. Neither of them seemed to have any problems either while watching it or in the middle of the night—when those problems most likely turn up.

I also have a tape of "Carrie," a theatrical film first shown on TV   9 about two and a half years ago. I elected to keep this one on what my kids call "the high shelf" (where I put the tapes that are forbidden to them), because I felt that its depiction of children turning against other children, the lead character's horrifying embarrassment at a school dance and her later act of matricide would upset them. "Lot," on the contrary, is a story that the children accepted as a fairy tale in modern dress.

Other tapes on my "high shelf" include "Night of the Living Dead" (cannibalism), "The Brood" (David Cronenberg's film of intergenerational breakdown and homicidal "children of rage" who are set free to murder and rampage) and "The Exorcist." They are all up there for the same reason: they contain elements that I think might freak the kids out. 10

Not that it's possible to keep kids away from everything on TV (or in the movies, for that matter) that will freak them out; the movies that terrorized my own nights most thoroughly as a kid were not those through which Frankenstein's monster or the Wolfman lurched and growled, but the Disney cartoons. I watched Bambi's mother shot and Bambi running frantically to escape being burned up in a forest fire. I watched, appalled, dismayed and sweaty with fear, as Snow White bit into the poisoned apple while the old crone giggled in evil ecstasy. I was similarly terrified by the walking brooms in "Fantasia" and the big, bad wolf who chased the fleeing pigs from house to house with such grim and homicidal intensity. More recently, Owen, who just turned 4, crawled into bed with my wife and me, "Cruella DeVille is in my room," he said. Cruella DeVille is, of course, the villainess of "101 Dalmatians," and I suppose Owen had decided that a woman who would want to turn puppies into dogskin coats might also be interested in little boys. All these films would certainly get G-ratings if they were produced today, and frightening excerpts of them have been shown on TV during "the children's hour." 11

Do I believe that all violent or horrifying programming should be banned from network TV? No, I do not. Do I believe it should be telecast only in the later evening hours, TV's version of the "high shelf"? Yes, I do. Do I believe that children should be forbidden all violent or horrifying programs? No, I do not. Like their elders, children have a right to experience the entire spectrum of drama, from such warm and mostly unthreatening programs as *Little House on the Prairie* and *The Waltons* to scarier fare. It's been suggested again and again that such entertainment offers us a catharsis—a chance to enter for a little while a scary and yet controllable world where we can express our fears, aggressions and possibly even hostilities. Surely no one would suggest that children do not have their own fears and hostilities to face and overcome; those dark feelings are the basis of many of the fairy tales children love best. 12

Do I think a child's intake of violent or horrifying programs should 13 be limited? Yes, I do, and that's why I have a high shelf. But the pressure groups who want to see all horror (and anything smacking of sex, for that matter) arbitrarily removed from television make me both uneasy and angry. The element of Big Brotherism inherent in such an idea causes the unease; the idea of a bunch of people I don't even know presuming to dictate what is best for my children causes the anger. I feel that deciding such things myself is my right—and my responsibility.

Responsibility is the bottom line, I guess. If you are going to have that   14
magic window in your living room, you have to take a certain amount of responsibility for what it will show kids when they push the ON button. And when your children ask to stay up to watch something like "The Shining" (when it is shown on cable TV this month), here are some ideas on how you might go about executing your responsibility to your children—from a guy who's got kids of his own and who also wears a fright wig from time to time.

If it's a movie you've seen yourself, you should have no problem. It is   15
not possible to know *everything* that will frighten a child—particularly a small one—but there are certain plot elements that can be very upsetting. These include physical mutilation, the death of an animal the child perceives as "good," the murder of a parent, a parent's treachery, blood in great quantities, drowning, being locked in a tight place and endings that offer no hope—and no catharsis.

If it's a movie you haven't seen, check the listings carefully for the   16
elements listed above, or for things you know upset your children in particular (if, for instance, you have a child who was once lost and was badly shaken by the experience, you may want to skip even such a mild film as "Mountain Family Robinson").

If you're not getting a clear fix on the program from the listings, call   17
the station. They'll be happy to help you; in fact, the station managers I queried said they fall all over themselves trying to help parents who request such information, but usually end up fielding complaints from adults who couldn't be bothered to call until after the offending program.

If the listing is marked *Meant for mature audiences only,* don't auto-   18
matically give up. What may not be suitable for some families (or for some younger children) may be perfectly OK for your children.

If you do elect to let your children watch a frightening TV program,   19
discuss it with them afterward. Ask them what frightened them and why. Ask them what made them feel good and why. In most cases, you'll find that kids handle frightening make-believe situations quite well; most of them can be as tough as they need to be. And "talking it through" gives a parent a better idea of where his or her child's private fear button is

located—which means a better understanding of the child and the child's mind.

If you think it's too scary, don't let them watch it. Period. The end. Remind yourself that you are bigger than they are, if that's what it takes. Too much frightening programming is no good for anyone, child or adult.   20

Most of all, try remembering that television spreads out the most incredible smorgasbord of entertainment in the history of the world, and it does so *every day*. Your child wants to taste a little of everything, even as you do yourself. But it would be wrong to let him or her eat only one single dish, particularly one as troublesome and as potentially dangerous as this one. Parenting presumes high shelves of all kinds, and that applies to some TV programs as well as to dangerous machines or household cleaners.   21

One last word: when the scary program comes and you've decided that your children may watch, try to watch *with* them. Most children have to walk through their own real-life version of Hansel and Gretel's "dark wood" from time to time, as we did ourselves. The tale of terror can be a dress rehearsal for those dark times.   22

But if we remember our own scary childhood experiences, we'll probably remember that it was easier to walk through that dark wood with a friend.   23

QUESTIONS ON CONTENT

1. What plots does King consider too scary for most children? What do these plots have in common?

2. King says he puts certain movie tapes on what he calls the "high shelf." What is the high shelf? How does King extend the meaning of this term later in his essay?

3. Why does King disapprove of the censoring of television programming for children? Who in his opinion has the right to decide what children may watch on television?

4. What steps does King suggest parents can take to ensure their children are watching suitable television programs?

QUESTIONS ON RHETORIC

1. Is King's choice of a title for this essay a good one? Why or why not? What other names might have worked better?

2. What do you think is King's purpose in writing this essay? (Glossary: *Purpose*) Is it stated or implied?

3. King makes a distinction between stories that belong on the "high

shelf" and those that don't. Do you find his distinctions useful? Explain your answer.

VOCABULARY

matricide (9)   arbitrarily (13)   queried (17)
catharsis (12)

WRITING TOPICS

1. Check your dictionary for the definition of *fairy tale*. Why do you suppose King's modern plot line of "Hansel and Gretel" sounds so gory? Did the original strike you that way when you heard it as a child? Choose another fairy tale and try modernizing it the way King did. What, if anything, seems to get lost in the translation?

2. King says horror stories will frighten a child if they "offer no hope— and no catharsis" (15). Consider any of King's novels that you have read or seen as films. Discuss in an essay the ways his stories do or do not offer "hope" and a "catharsis" at the end. Do you agree that for children these are important elements of a horror story? Explain why you feel this way.

ADVERTISING IN DISGUISE

Consumer Reports

Desiring greater credibility and wishing to avoid the high cost of advertising, some American businesses and their public-relations agencies now provide "canned news" stories to television stations and newspapers throughout the country. In this essay, the editors of Consumer Reports, *a consumer advocacy publication, expose "product plugs" that are being passed off as news.*

Last year, Procter & Gamble Co. launched a special promotion for Spic   1
and Span. Cubic zirconia—fake diamonds—were inserted in more than 2 million boxes of the powdered cleaner. But five hundred boxes contained real diamonds, worth about six hundred dollars each. You could tell which type of stone was in your package by taking it to a participating jeweler for a free evaluation.

The promotion got plenty of exposure on television. That might not   2
seem surprising, since Procter & Gamble is the nation's largest television advertiser, spending more than half a billion dollars a year on network and local television.

But in this case, the air time didn't cost the company a cent. Hill &   3
Knowlton, the large public-relations firm that represents Procter & Gamble, sent a package of materials to some 200 TV stations. It featured a ninety-second videotape designed to be inserted into local news broadcasts. There was also supporting footage, prominently featuring the Spic and Span assembly line.

The story line ostensibly was that cubic zirconia are difficult to distin-   4
guish from diamonds without special test equipment, and that sales of the low-priced diamond mimics were growing fast. But blended in were plenty of snippets about the Procter & Gamble promotion.

Hill & Knowlton says that its materials were used by stations in at least   5
twenty-seven cities nationwide, including San Francisco (KPIX), Dallas (WFAA), Boston (WBZ), and New York City (WCBS).

For Hill & Knowlton, the Spic and Span campaign proved a resounding   6
success. But consumers have no reason to rejoice over such campaigns. By

blurring the distinction between news and advertising, such activities imperil an important function of the media: providing consumers with accurate, unbiased information about the marketplace.

Passing out corporate handouts as news is nothing new. It's gone on for   7
as long as there have been public-relations firms—and lazy journalists. In recent years, though, the techniques used to insert product plugs in the media under the guise of news have become more sophisticated.

For corporations, insinuating product plugs into news articles or news   8
broadcasts can produce more impact than advertising can buy. "People like to think they're very savvy and hip to ads," says Hill & Knowlton broadcast specialist Colleen Growe. But, she says, "when it comes in the form of a news story, it has a lot more truth to the average viewer."

IN THE CAN

The public-relations crowd has lately enjoyed a good deal of success plac-   9
ing product plugs on television. Many stations have introduced expanded newscasts; with more time to fill, they jump at the opportunity for free material.

PR people have honed their technique for preparing canned video news   10
stories. Hill & Knowlton, for example, offers local TV stations a choice. They can run the report just as it's received or they can use narration by their own reporter over additional silent footage, called "B-Roll," that the public-relations firm supplies. For Spic and Span, Hill & Knowlton even suggested the following lead-in script that the local anchorperson could read:

"Diamonds are a personal gift. Very personal. Now a low-cost version   11
is making its debut—in a soap box. [Blank] has the story."

Nor is the possible local angle overlooked. In the Spic and Span pro-   12
motion, the public-relations firm supplied names of local participating supermarkets and jewelers in case the TV stations wanted to do its own interviews.

To make the fare look fresh instead of canned, PR firms use a trick that   13
you might call "the vanishing interviewer." A PR person will interview an expert on some subject. When the footage is given to the TV stations, it's formatted so that a station can dub in the face or voice of its own newspeople asking the prepackaged questions. In effect, the reporter serves as an actor in a commercial.

The canned news is packaged neatly. A TV station can take the ma-   14
terial in familiar videocassette form. Or it can have the footage beamed in by satellite.

ON THE PAGE

On the newspaper side, such "canned news" is most often seen in special   15
sections, such as those devoted to real estate, automobiles, travel, and
food. The company that wants to promote its products will frequently hire
a distribution service that devotes itself entirely to canned news. One such
firm, Chicago-based Associated Release Service Inc., each month distrib-
utes between forty and one hundred articles to more than three thousand
newspapers. "We send out original-quality proofs that are already type-
set," says Ted Hathorn, Associated's president. "If they like the material,
they can put it right into their page layout."

Hathorn finds that canned editorials—an oil company, for instance,   16
might prepare an editorial advocating offshore drilling—don't have a very
large market. What the newspapers mainly want, he says, "is anything that
deals with the consumer. We send out a lot of food releases, a lot of
consumer tips. For instance, All-State might have insurance ideas to help
the consumer."

A skilled PR person will bury the commercial plug so that the reader   17
won't easily guess the source of the story. As one example, Associated
recently distributed a nine paragraph article headlined "Heartburn—A Peril
in the Night." Not until the story's eighth paragraph does the name of
Associated's client pop up: "Another option is an over-the-counter antacid
that works even when the nighttime heartburn sufferer is lying down.
Gaviscon, a unique foaming antacid, is physician recommended and has
been proven effective in relieving nighttime heartburn for many years."

In some cases, the "consumer information" can be extraordinarily   18
self-serving. In a newspaper column called "Winter Driving Tips," we
learn that "According to the experts, one cold start produces that equivalent of two thousand miles of over-the-road engine wear. . . . This means
that the family vehicle could rack up over two hundred thousand miles in
engine wear in a just one average twenty-week cold season, with one cold
start per day." But a worried reader quickly finds out that help is available.
"A practical and economical solution to the problem of cold engine starts,"
the article continues, "is offered by Temro, a major Canadian manufacturer of automotive heating and starting aids." (CU's auto experts say that,
while cold starts are indeed hard on your car, the mileage equivalency
figures are "absurd.")

WHO'S USING IT?

Who uses this sort of stuff? When Sun Color Service, another distribution   19
agency, polled newspapers on the subject, only 25 percent said they didn't

want to receive its releases. Dorothy Rabb, a Sun Color executive, says that "the large papers, with two hundred thousand circulation and up, for the most part do their own articles. Most of our material is accepted by papers with less than eighty thousand circulation."

Still, big papers are not immune. In January, *The New York Times* ran   20
a special supplement on health, in the format known as an "advertorial." In size and general appearance, it resembled *The New York Times Magazine*. Conventional advertisements for health products alternated with other material that looked like editorial matter. In fact, the entire supplement was advertising. But while the supplement was labeled as advertising in small, light print, *The New York Times* logo appeared on the cover, and the reader would have had to read carefully to discern that *The New York Times* news staff played no role in preparing it.

The number of papers willing to run advertisements in news stories'   21
clothing rises when the sponsor is a big advertiser. "If we do something for Kraft's, we know it's going to go well," says Rabb. "For Kraft's, we'd expect to have from 150 to 180 newspapers, totaling anywhere from 4 to 6 million circulation.

One such Kraft-sponsored page of recipes, sent out by Sun Color last   22
summer, featured salads to take to picnics. Not surprisingly, all the recipes included Miracle Whip or other Kraft dressings.

GROUND THAT EAGLE

On days with lots of news space to fill because of heavy ad volume, a   23
newspaper can brim with canned news. Last Thanksgiving, for example, the Wyoming *Tribune-Eagle,* the newspaper of Cheyenne, the state capital, carried fifteen canned news articles—thirteen of them mentioning specific brand names and two plugging generic products. The paper advised its readers to use Blistex, a lip ointment, "on the mistletoe circuit," to fill their Christmas stockings with Hazel Bishop Moisture Gloss Stick, and to install "the watchful eye" of the Sony WatchCam security system, which "helps to make certain it's just Santa stirring in the house and out."

Isn't it deceptive to use this canned copy alongside legitimate news   24
articles? "I've asked a number of times to label the copy advertising," says *Tribune-Eagle* editor Don Hurlburt, who notes that the Wyoming paper's canned articles are selected by the advertising department. "My voice has fallen on deaf ears. I don't like it; I don't like the way they do it, but it's not my decision to make."

A *Tribune-Eagle* advertising executive, who asked not to be identified,   25
insists that the canned news is justified. "Products that are usable by the

public are news," he contends. "It's the economics of the retail business that keeps all of us going."

PLUGS FOR DRUGS

When the product plugged by a disguised advertisement is a drug, the 26 issues involved are more serious than usual. Under the law, a company can't advertise a prescription drug without including a full and accurate account of potential hazards and side effects. But drug companies can accomplish the same end if they hook the press into serving as middleman.

"The area of press releases and videos gets a bit messy," says Ken 27 Feather, an official in the Drug Advertising Regulation Branch of the U.S. Food and Drug Administration. "If they produce a pseudonews kind of blurb, which they pass out for the press to use, we would object if it were inconsistent with the labeling. However, we have little opportunity to find out about these things."

To see how a canned video news report on a drug works, consider the 28 case of Augmentin, manufactured by Beecham Laboratories. It combines a penicillin derivative with a compound that breaks down bacterial resistance to penicillin. In some instances, Augmentin can be prescribed when penicillin alone wouldn't be effective.

In late 1984, Beecham received FDA approval to market Augmentin, 29 and turned to Hill & Knowlton to prepare a video news report. The public-relations firm prepared the usual arsenal: a press kit, a videotape news report, and additional footage that stations could use with their own narration. Hill & Knowlton also sent the stations telexes with suggestions for interviews with local doctors who had participated in testing Augmentin.

In some cases, local television stations prepared their own news reports 30 on Augmentin, and when they used Beecham-supplied material, they noted that fact on the screen. But the station-prepared material and the Beecham film clip sometimes seemed like fraternal twins.

The narrator of the Beecham video release said, "Infectious bacteria, 31 doubling their numbers every twenty minutes. And these are some of the victims: children." The screen showed bacteria growing, followed by a scene of children playing. Viewers of WNEW-TV in New York City saw those same two scenes, only superimposed on the screen was, "Dr. Max Gomez, 'The 10 O'Clock News,' Ch. 5." The voice was that of scientist-reporter Gomez saying, "Unchecked they can double their number in twenty minutes. And these are some of the victims: young children."

We asked Gomez, who holds a Ph.D in neurosciences and is now 32 health-and-science editor of KYW-TV in Philadelphia, about taking his narration from a script by publicity agents. "I can't say I'm not guilty of that," he notes, "but it would be unusual of me to do that."

In the Augmentin video news release, Dr. Richard Wallace, associate   33 professor of research and clinical medicine at the University of Texas Health Center at Tyler, spoke about the drug. "We studied between twenty and twenty-five patients who were infected with these organisms," he said, "and all these patients were treated successfully with this agent Augmentin."

But the news clip didn't mention that twenty-five patients is a small-   34 scale study, or that the study lacked a control group.

Dr. Wallace says that Hill & Knowlton paid him one thousand dollars   35 to participate in the video clip, but that his comments were his own and not from a script. He says he put the money into a research fund as "my way of getting around any sense of obligation."

Is it proper for a doctor to be paid to appear in a film that will later   36 appear on TV newscasts? Looking back on it, Dr. Wallace has some serious doubts. "I'm a scientist and am supposed to be separate from the company," he says. "They're selling a product; they want to package this so it sells to newspapers, radio, and television. I probably would not do it again."

For Kenneth Rabin, who heads Hill & Knowlton's health unit, the   37 Augmentin video clip was a total success. "It would not be an exaggeration to estimate that fifty to one hundred TV stations used that clip in one part or another," he said. Rabin adds that "any time someone reads something in a magazine as news content or sees it on a TV news show, it carries a certain weight it doesn't in an ad."

THE ORAFLEX CASE

On May 19, 1982, Eli Lilly & Co. released news of its antiarthritic drug   38 Oraflex. Press kits went to news organizations all over the country, and a video news clip was prepared for use by television networks.

The Lilly material had omitted a key fact: On May 8, the *British*   39 *Medical Journal* had published several articles about severe adverse reactions to Oraflex. According to the FDA, news of these articles had become widely known in the medical community by May 16.

The FDA found, however, that many TV and radio stations apparently   40 took their reports on Oraflex directly from the Lilly material. According to an FDA internal memorandum dated July 10, 1982, "These broadcasts were of a uniform character: i.e. they all described Oraflex as being a potential remittive agent and as having a minimal potential for side effects.

In fact, several broadcasts over different networks used nearly identical wording to these descriptions.''

Oraflex, which had been approved by the FDA in April 1982, was 41 pulled from the market that August. During that time, Federal investigators maintain it was a factor in the deaths of at least twenty-six Americans. Last summer, Lilly pleaded guilty to criminal charges for not having informed Federal officials that Oraflex had been linked to deaths and illnesses in foreign countries.

The FDA's internal memorandum takes particular note of a report on 42 ABC-TV network news on May 19. The report, the memorandum says, ''included a statement that physicians regard side effects related to Oraflex as being minor when compared to aspirin.''

ABC science editor Jules Bergman, who prepared the Oraflex news 43 report, says he now consults a panel of doctors before doing any similar report.

THE WAY OUT

Much of what businesses do is news. Certainly, we'd be the last to dis- 44 courage reports that name brands and companies, so long as the reporting is done with vigor and objectivity. But thinly disguised product plugs are not news and shouldn't be passed off as such.

Companies and their public-relations agencies certainly aren't going to 45 stop playing the disguised ad game. For them, the appeal of canned news is understandable. It commands far more credibility than advertising—and it does it at a much lower cost. Sun Color Service, for instance, says that it can reach as many people by spending one dollar on canned news as it can by spending twenty-three dollars on advertising. Given that motivation, public relations people will keep trying to get the media to serve as shills.

It's up to the news media to avoid parroting plugs. When some news 46 reports are really ads in disguise, it casts doubt on everything presented as news.

QUESTIONS ON CONTENT

1. What, according to *Consumer Reports,* is the advantage to a corporation of plugging its products in a news story? In what way does this practice imperil the function of the media?

2. In paragraphs 10–14, *Consumer Reports* lists the ways that corporations have "honed their technique" for preparing canned video news stories. Briefly describe those techniques.

3. *Consumer Reports* claims that newspapers usually use canned news in what sections of the paper? How do PR firms play down the fact that this material is really advertising?

4. Who buys this form of advertising according to *Consumer Reports?* What factor do they say encourages larger papers to buy canned news? When are papers most likely to brim with prepackaged news?

5. The PR firms who prepare the canned news appear to be remarkably candid about their work. How did that strike you as you read this article?

QUESTIONS ON RHETORIC

1. What would you say is the thesis of this article by *Consumer Reports?* Where is it stated?

2. *Consumer Reports* includes two lengthy examples of PR campaigns that were turned into news stories. Do you think it was necessary to include such extensive evidence? Could the same point have been made in fewer words? Explain.

3. *Consumer Reports* moves quickly and is easy to read. Who is its audience? Give examples of diction and organization to support your conclusion.

VOCABULARY

imperil (6)   savvy (8)   blurb (27)
guise (7)   formatted (13)   vigor (44)
insinuating (8)

WRITING TOPICS

1. *Consumer Reports* says, "[W]e'd be the last to discourage reports that name brands and companies so long as the reporting is done with vigor and objectivity" (44). Watch television for a week and pay close attention to the way some reporting permits advertising of products while others are real news stories. What distinctions can you make between the two? Write an essay showing you understand the meanings of the words *vigor* and *objectivity* as used in *Consumer Reports*.

2. Reread the two cases of ads-as-news recounted in detail in *Consumer Reports;* then prepare an essay in which you describe what you believe is the harm, if any, of advertising disguised as news.

PIGSKIN ENGLISH

Robert MacNeil

In this essay, Robert MacNeil recounts his investigation into the language of sportscasters. MacNeil, who with Robin Lehrer co-anchors the "MacNeil-Lehrer Newshour" on public television and is also the author of The Story of English, *expected to discover that popular football commentators such as John Madden were mangling English grammar and setting a poor example for viewers. Instead, he found that sportscasters really don't speak any worse than anyone else, including many news reporters.*

When I sat down recently to assess football commentators' English, I thought it would be a snap. Not a big football fan, I assumed all I had to do was turn on the television, watch a little football and fill a notebook with mangled grammar. After all, wasn't this the frontline for the decline of the English language? Hadn't the Gothic hordes captured sports television, driving frail civilization before them—burning, pillaging and raping the language as they came? And the Super Bowl! The Visigoths festival! Language vandalism on an epic scale!

No, even grander than epic—universal, because the Super Bowl is now seen around the world. People in 59 countries watched last year, seven million in Britain, God knows how many millions in the People's Republic of China. This year the penguins in Antarctica will watch the clash of the titans on CBS and hear Pat Summerall and John Madden describe it.

English is already the world's most widely used language; the first or second language of almost a billion people. Countless millions are studying it avidly—250 million people in China alone. Events like the Super Bowl are watched hypnotically not only as sport but as lessons in American culture—and English. So, what do they hear?

First, sheer verbal energy; energy in decibels—a relentless barrage of words; a collision of words as fierce as the crunch of linesmen, when the smack of their action occasionally interrupts the torrential talk. Words shouted, words bellowed, words screamed; voices raised to be heard above a crowd the commentators can't hear because they are inside a glass booth—in short a pandemonium of words.

The game may be dull. Football can be dull and television has made it duller by stretching a game into hours and hours of fragments to accommodate commercials and promotions. Tex Schramm, the Cowboys' owner, said: "I think it's wrong to confuse dullness with length." It may be wrong, but it is human nature, Tex. Things interesting for two hours may be intolerable for four. Television knows that. So to compensate for the dullness TV has imposed on the game, the sportscasters keep up the verbal razzle-dazzle.

It is like colorizing old movies to make them compelling, after chopping them into seven-minute segments to insert the commercials and then arguing that people won't watch them in black and white.   6

They talk so hard and so fast at each other—often in the two-shots so comically close together that you wonder about bad breath—there must be a competition for Most Valuable Mouth (MVM). *USA Today* fosters that by devoting a special column to TV sports coverage, rating commentators for "best lines," "best fact," "worst line," etc.   7

One way to win MVM is to have a handy supply of reach-for-it metaphors, and John Madden of CBS is the clear MVM in that league. As recorded by *USA Today,* here is John Madden waiting for an instant-replay decision: "It's like paying alimony and then waiting for the rabbit to die''; Madden on Jim McMahon: "He doesn't worry about the horse being blind. He's going to load the wagon"; or, "Randy White is like an all-day sucker. You never get it licked.''   8

It is bizarre to think what those metaphors tell a football fan in China about American life and morals. More important, how does football language affect American fans? When I and my colleagues worked on the television series and the book, *The Story of English,* we found an interesting paradox. Despite the vast influence of television, people do not talk like television.   9

American broadcasters—radio and television—have grown their own variety of English: Linguists call it Network Standard, an accent drawn from the Midwest, generally admired for its clarity, intelligibility and neutrality. Consciously or unconsciously, broadcasters adopted it early in their careers, ironing out their own regional speech patterns. Dan Rather told us he took speech lessons to rid his speech of his Texas "tin" for "ten." Although Rather is enormously admired, his fellow Texans still say "tin."   10

In short, despite its impact on the rest of American life, television is not leveling out regional dialects. Football commentators are even more popular than television newsmen, yet they do not seem to be creating the speech of their fans but *reflecting* it.   11

To begin with, football commentators do not mangle the language nearly to the extent I believed. You have to go out of your way to look for really glaring examples. Here are some—Musburger (CBS): A player "was to have been the intended receiver." Trumpy (NBC): "It appears Miami's   12 weakness is defensing the run." Vermeil (CBS): "It's hard on young players technique-wise and mentally-wise," and, "In college football you teach people to be a team guy."

Much more common is that these commentators speak very regular, colloquial American, filled with "lotsa," "gotta," "musta," "woulda." It is nonstandard in grammar but often used informally by Americans who use standard grammar otherwise. It is the language of the beer commercials that sustain the games. Speaking it is like hanging up the business suit and putting on jeans for the weekend. [13]

It is very much the language you will hear from John Madden in the Super Bowl: "All this guy does is get open . . . It seems like for years anytime they need yardage, they use Joe Jacoby . . . There are thing you have to like about Schroeder . . . This Gary Clark is something . . . I'll guarantee ya' he's loosenin' up this defense . . . That what it's all about." [14]

Leaving anxious language students in Singapore aside for the moment, is such language influencing American speech, corrupting standard usage, undoing the work of our schools? Edwin Newman thinks so. Citing Madden's repeated misuse of "like," as well as using "I tell ya" 11 times and "y'know" 39 times in the second half of one NFL game, Newman says: "That sets a fairly deplorable example for those listening." Perhaps. [15]

But the English Madden speaks so colorfully is already a widely used variety, something to relax with, like the act of watching football itself. It is a way of crossing the lines of economic class and finding fellow feeling. There is still in this culture a residue of the frontier suspicion that a man too finicky with words, who talks like the schoolmarm, is not quite masculine. Relaxed, untutored speech is associated with outdoor jobs that seem more virile. Football is an easy way to bridge the gap. [16]

The truth is that we all move up- and down-market, so to speak, in our language. Language is the great excluder and includer and most of us unconsciously play it both ways; keeping some people at a distance with one form of talk, ingratiating ourselves with others by adopting theirs. [17]

Madden's is not the only style. There are football voices that would please the prickliest English teacher: NBC's Ahmad Rashad talking about "the consummate tight end," and Dick Enberg talking about "this penchant for the close game" are using elegant English. So is Madden's co-worker on the Super Bowl, Pat Summerall, when he says: "The interception at which we'll take another look in a minute." How about that, Edwin Newman? [18]

Newsmen tend to look down a little on the sportscasters. But to be honest I doubt the network football commentators are much harder on the language than a lot of TV newsmen left to ad-lib for more than a few minutes. Besides, the football guys have the added advantage of knowing what they are talking about. [19]

QUESTIONS ON CONTENT

1. Robert MacNeil confesses that he brought a basic assumption to his assessment of sportscasters' English. What did he expect to find? What was his fear about the effect sportscasters' English might have on the listening audience?

2. What does MacNeil say is the function of the sportscaster? What qualities, in his opinion, make John Madden one of the best?

3. What distinctions does MacNeil make between the speech of news and sports broadcasters? List some of the characteristics of each he mentions.

4. In the course of his investigation, MacNeil changed his attitude toward sportscasters. In what ways did he find Madden's style to be appropriate for sportscasting? Do you agree? Explain.

QUESTIONS ON RHETORIC

1. MacNeil's essay is made lively by the use of several different kinds of figures of speech. (Glossary: *Figures of Speech*) Identify a few of the ones you find most appropriate and give your reasons.

2. In paragraph 13, MacNeil says sportscasters' speech reflects the relaxed, informal speech of Americans who use standard grammar otherwise. Speaking it, he says, is like "hanging up the business suit and putting on jeans for the weekend." MacNeil himself is generally known for his impeccable speech. Choosing examples from his essay, show how he has used diction here to, in his own words, "put on jeans for the weekend." (Glossary: *Diction*)

3. MacNeil quotes Edwin Newman in paragraph 15. Who is Edwin Newman? Why would MacNeil expect Newman's point of view on the subject of language to carry weight with his readers? Explain your answer.

4. MacNeil ends his essay with a point of view that is opposite to the one with which he begins. (Glossary: *Beginnings and Endings*) How does this device help to persuade the reader? How does MacNeil organize his evidence to support his shift of opinion?

VOCABULARY

epic (1)	glaring (12)	ingratiating (17)
pandemonium (4)	colloquial (13)	consummate (18)
compelling (6)	deplorable (15)	penchant (18)
paradox (9)	finicky (16)	

WRITING TOPICS

1. John Madden is the hapless target of criticism from lovers of the language, yet MacNeil manages to defend him. In a brief essay, express your

own feelings on the state of the language in television sportscasting. Do you agree with MacNeil or with Newman?

2. A great portion of broadcast time is devoted to a variety of sports. Watch a few different sportscasts over a period of a few weeks. Are there significant differences in the way different sports are reported? For example, are football sportscasters more outrageous in their reporting than tennis commentators? What, if any, are the differences? How do you think these differences reflect differences among audiences for these various events? Discuss your findings in an essay.

3. Newscasters speak what is know as Network Standard, "an accent drawn from the Midwest, generally admired for its clarity, intelligibility and neutrality" (10). Yet according to MacNeil, in spite of the vast number of hours most people spend in front of the television set, Americans are not losing their regional dialects. In a brief essay, explain why you think this is true.

WRITING ASSIGNMENTS FOR "MEDIA AND LANGUAGE"

1. Asked whether it's deceptive to use canned news in the same section as legitimate news articles, *Tribune-Eagle* editor Don Hurlbutt replied that he had asked repeatedly that such canned news be labeled as advertising, according to the article from *Consumer Reports*. He added that such material is chosen, not by the editorial department, but by the advertising department. An ad executive of the paper, on the other hand, insisted that canned news is "justified." "Products that are usable by the public are news," he contends. "It's the economics of the retail business that keeps all of us going." What is your reaction to this remark? Who at the *Tribune-Eagle* makes final decisions about what ads appear in the paper and where, according to editor Don Hurlbutt? What does this reveal about the real balance of power in print journalism at that paper? Call your local daily. What is the policy there? Write an essay in which you discuss your reaction to the story in *Consumer Reports*. Include your findings about the paper in your town.

2. "Football commentators are even more popular than television newsmen, yet they do not seem to be creating the speech of their fans but *reflecting* it," says Robert MacNeil in his essay. Read through a week's worth of the sports section of your local newspapers. If you live in a small town include articles from a big city paper in your study. What kind of diction and phrasing does each use? How does it differ from other news writing in diction and tone? What do you learn about the audiences each is addressing? Write an essay to support your conclusions.

3. In "Now . . . This," Neil Postman compares the predictions of George Orwell, author of *1984,* to those of Aldous Huxley, author of *Brave New World.* Reread Postman's description of the two men's fears for the future of society and then in your own words discuss why Postman agrees with Huxley's world view. Do you agree with it? Why or why not? In an essay, describe your own vision of the future as you see it reflected in the attitudes those around you have toward the news.

4. In his essay, Herbert J. Gans says the news media projects a "picture of nation and society as it ought to be." This is accomplished, he says, not only by the choice of certain stories over others, but also by the way in which the stories are presented. Reread Gans's essay, keeping in mind that he wrote it ten years ago. What stories were most important then, according to Gans? What values did he think they revealed? In your opinion, have

there been any changes since then? Has the news media in recent months reported the same kinds of stories and attached the similar values to them? Discuss your findings in an essay.

5. Write an essay discussing the main points of agreement presented in the different essays in this section. What are the chief concerns these writers have about the state of news reporting? How do they think those concerns relate to the state of the culture? In your opinion, is their concern justified? Explain your answer using examples from your own experiences with the news.

6. In his essay, "When Nice People Burn Books," Nat Hentoff refers to "good liberals" and "bad companions" to make an important point, that point being that once we have labeled people and nations "good" and "bad," we then justify or condemn their behavior accordingly. What do Hentoff and the other writers see as the dangers inherent in such preconceived notions of right and wrong? In an essay, explore the implications of this kind of thinking and the ways it threatens the First Amendment.

7. In early 1989, the novel *The Satanic Verses* by Indian Muslim Salman Rushdie was published in the West. In the book, Rushdie depicted the prophet Mohammed in situations that many Moslems found offensive, spurring Iran's late fundamentalist ruler, the Ayatollah Khomaini, to offer a reward for Rushdie's assassination. Fearing terrorist revenge, booksellers worldwide pulled the book from their shelves. While the author went underground in London, writers around the world read chapters of the book in public to protest its censoring. In an essay, discuss your reaction to this story. Do you think censorship is ever justified? How else might the bookstores have handled this situation? Choose one or two writers from this section and argue what their position might be on this issue.

PART IX

Writing Well: Using Language Responsibly

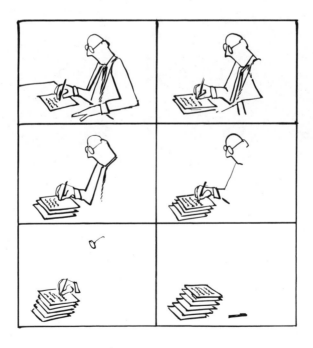

HOW TO SAY NOTHING IN 500 WORDS

Paul Roberts

Paul Roberts wrote this essay thirty years ago, but his point is still relevant for modern students. Good writing is not simply a matter of filling up a page. . . . The words have to hold the reader's interest and they have to say something. Roberts, author of the book Understanding English, *from which this essay was taken, offers students a bag of writing tricks that are good advice to anyone who wishes to write well.*

NOTHING ABOUT SOMETHING

It's Friday afternoon, and you have almost survived another week of classes. You are just looking forward dreamily to the weekend when the English instructor says, "For Monday you will turn in a five-hundred-word composition on college football." 1

Well, that puts a good big hole in the weekend. You don't have any strong views on college football one way or the other. You get rather excited during the season and go to all the home games and find it rather more fun than not. On the other hand, the class has been reading Robert Hutchins in the anthology and perhaps Shaw's "Eighty-Yard Run," and from the class discussion you have got the idea that the instructor thinks college football is for the birds. You are no fool, you. You can figure out what side to take. 2

After dinner you get out the portable typewriter that you got for high school graduation. You might as well get it over with and enjoy Saturday and Sunday. Five hundred words is about two double-spaced pages with normal margins. You put in a sheet of paper, think up a title, and you're off: 3

WHY COLLEGE FOOTBALL SHOULD BE ABOLISHED
College football should be abolished because it's bad for the school and also bad for the players. The players are so busy practicing that they don't have any time for their studies.

This, you feel, is a mighty good start. The only trouble is that it's only thirty-two words. You still have four hundred and sixty-eight to go, and you've pretty well exhausted the subject. It comes to you that you do your best thinking in the morning, so you put away the typewriter and go to the movies. But the next morning you have to do your washing and some math problems, and in the afternoon you go to the game. The English instructor turns up too, and you wonder if you've taken the right side after all. Saturday night you have a date, and Sunday morning you have to go to church. (You shouldn't let English assignments interfere with your religion.) What with one thing and another, it's ten o'clock Sunday night before you get out the typewriter again. You make a pot of coffee and start to fill out your views on college football. Put a little meat on the bones.

WHY COLLEGE FOOTBALL SHOULD BE ABOLISHED

In my opinion, it seems to me that college football should be abolished. The reason why I think this to be true is because I feel that football is bad for the colleges in nearly every respect. As Robert Hutchins says in his article in our anthology in which he discusses college football, it would be better if the colleges had race horses and had races with one another, because then the horses would have had to attend classes. I firmly agree with Mr. Hutchins on this point, and I am sure that many other students would agree too.

One reason why it seems to me that college football is bad is that it has become too commercial. In the olden times when people played football just for the fun of it, maybe college football was all right, but they do not play football just for the fun of it now as they used to in the old days. Nowadays college football is what you might call a big business. Maybe this is not true at all schools, and I don't think it is especially true here at State, but certainly this is the case at most colleges and universities in America nowadays, as Mr. Hutchins points out in his very interesting article. Actually the coaches and alumni go around to the high schools and offer the high school stars large salaries to come to their colleges and play football for them. There was one case where a high school star was offered a convertible if he would play football for a certain college.

Another reason for abolishing college football is that it is bad for the players. They do not have time to get a college education, because they are so busy playing football. A football player has to practice every afternoon from three to six, and then he is so tired that he can't concentrate on his studies. He just feels like dropping off to sleep after dinner, and then the next day he goes to his classes without having studied and maybe he fails the test.

(Good ripe stuff so far, but you're still a hundred and fifty-one words from home. One more push.)

Also I think college football is bad for the colleges and the universities because not very many students get to participate in it. Out of a college of ten thousand students only seventy-five or a hundred play football, if that many.

Football is what you might call a spectator sport. That means that most people go to watch it but do not play it themselves.

(Four hundred and fifteen. Well, you still have the conclusion and when you retype it, you can make the margins a little wider.)

These are the reasons why I agree with Mr. Hutchins that college football should be abolished in American colleges and universities.

On Monday you turn it in, moderately hopeful, and on Friday it comes back marked "weak in content" and sporting a big D.   4

This essay is exaggerated a little, not much. The English instructor will recognize it as reasonably typical of what an assignment on college football will bring in. He knows that nearly half of the class will contrive in five hundred words to say that college football is too commercial and bad for the players. Most of the other half will inform him that college football builds character and prepares one for life and brings prestige to the school. As he reads paper after paper all saying the same thing in almost the same words, all bloodless, five hundred words dripping out of nothing, he wonders how he allowed himself to get trapped into teaching English when he might have had a happy and interesting life as an electrician or a confidence man.   5

Well, you may ask, what can you do about it? The subject is one on which you have few convictions and little information. Can you be expected to make a dull subject interesting? As a matter of fact, this is precisely what you are expected to do. This is the writer's essential task. All subjects, except sex, are dull until somebody makes them interesting. The writer's job is to find the argument, the approach, the angle, the wording that will take the reader with him. This is seldom easy, and it is particularly hard in subjects that have been much discussed: College Football, Fraternities, Popular Music, Is Chivalry Dead?, and the like. You will feel that there is nothing you can do with such subjects except repeat the old bromides. But there are some things you can do that will make your papers, if not throbbingly alive, at least less insufferably tedious than they might otherwise be.   6

AVOID THE OBVIOUS CONTENT

Say the assignment is college football. Say that you've decided to be against it. Begin by putting down the arguments that come to mind: it is too commercial, it takes the students' minds off their studies, it is hard on the players, it makes the university a kind of circus instead of an intellectual center, for most schools it is financially ruinous. Can you think of any   7 more arguments just off hand? All right. Now when you write your paper, *make sure that you don't use any of the material on this list.* If these are the points that leap to your mind, they will leap to everyone else's too, and whether you get a C or a D may depend on whether the instructor reads your paper early when he is fresh and tolerant or late, when the sentence, "In my opinion, college football has become too commercial," inexorably repeated, has brought him to the brink of lunacy.

Be against college football for some reason or reasons of your own. If   8
they are keen and perceptive ones, that's spendid. But even if they are trivial or foolish or indefensible, you are still ahead so long as they are not everybody else's reasons too. Be against it because the colleges don't spend enough money on it to make it worthwhile, because it is bad for the characters of the spectators, because the players are forced to attend classes, because the football stars hog all the beautiful women, because it competes with baseball and is therefore un-American and possibly Communist inspired. There are lots of more or less unused reasons for being against college football.

Sometimes it is a good idea to sum up and dispose of the trite and   9
conventional points before going on to your own. This has the advantage of indicating to the reader that you are going to be neither trite nor conventional. Something like this:

> We are often told that college football should be abolished because it has become too commercial or because it is bad for the players. These arguments are no doubt very cogent, but they don't really go to the heart of the matter.

Then *you* go to the heart of the matter.

TAKE THE LESS USUAL SIDE

One rather simple way of getting interest into your paper is to take the side   10
of the argument that most of the citizens will want to avoid. If the assignment is an essay on dogs, you can, if you choose, explain that dogs are faithful and lovable companions, intelligent, useful as guardians of the house and protectors of children, indispensable in police work—in short, when all is said and done, man's best friends. Or you can suggest that those big brown eyes conceal, more often than not, a vacuity of mind and an inconstancy of purpose; that the dogs you have known most intimately have been mangy, ill-tempered brutes, incapable of instruction; and that only your nobility of mind and fear of arrest prevent you from kicking the flea-ridden animals when you pass them on the street.

Naturally, personal convictions will sometimes dictate your approach.   11
If the assigned subject is "Is Methodism Rewarding to the Individual?"

and you are a pious Methodist, you have really no choice. But few assigned subjects, if any, will fall in this category. Most of them will lie in broad areas of discussion with much to be said on both sides. They are intellectual exercises, and it is legitimate to argue now one way and now another, as debaters do in similar circumstances. Always take the side that looks to you hardest, least defensible. It will almost always turn out to be easier to write interestingly on that side.

This general advice applies where you have a choice of subjects. If you 12 are to choose among "The Value of Fraternities" and "My Favorite High School Teacher" and "What I Think About Beetles," by all means plump for the beetles. By the time the instructor gets to your paper, he will be up to his ears in tedious tales about the French teacher at Bloombury High and assertions about how fraternities build character and prepare one for life. Your views on beetles, whatever they are, are bound to be a refreshing change.

Don't worry too much about figuring out what the instructor thinks 13 about the subject so that you can cuddle up with him. Chances are his views are no stronger than yours. If he does have convictions and you oppose them, his problem is to keep from grading you higher than you deserve in order to show he is not biased. This doesn't mean that you should always cantankerously dissent from what the instructor says; that gets tiresome too. And if the subject assigned is "My Pet Peeve" do not begin. "My pet peeve is the English instructor who assigns papers on 'My Pet Peeve.' " This was still funny during the War of 1812, but it has sort of lost its edge since then. It is generally good manners to avoid personalities.

SLIP OUT OF ABSTRACTION

If you will study the essay on college football in section 239, you will 14 perceive that one reason for its appalling dullness is that it never gets down to particulars. It is just a series of not very glittering generalities: "Football is bad for the colleges," "It has become too commercial," "Football is a big business," "It is bad for the players," and so on. Such round phrases thudding against the reader's brain are unlikely to convince him, though they may well render him unconscious.

If you want the reader to believe that college football is bad for the 15 players, you have to do more than say so. You have to display the evil. Take your roommate, Alfred Simkins, the second-string center. Picture poor old Alfy coming home from football practice every evening, bruised and aching, agonizingly tired, scarcely able to shovel the mashed potatoes into his mouth. Let us see him staggering up to the room, getting out his econ textbook, peering desperately at it with his good eye, falling asleep and failing the test in the morning. Let us share his unbearable tension as Saturday draws near. Will he fail, be demoted, lose his monthly allowance, be forced to return to the coal mines? And if he succeeds, what will be his reward? Perhaps a slight ripple of applause when the third-string center replaces him, a moment of elation in the locker room if the team wins, of despair if it loses. What will he look back on when he graduates from college? Toil and torn ligaments. And what will be his future? He is not good enough for pro football, and he is too obscure and weak in econ to succeed in stocks and bonds. College football is tearing the heart from Alfy Simkins and, when it finishes with him, will callously toss aside the shattered hulk.

This is no doubt a weak enough argument for the abolition of college football, but it is a sight better than saying, in three or four variations, that college football (in your opinion) is bad for the players. 16

Look at the work of any professional writer and notice how constantly he is moving from the generality, the abstract statement, to the concrete example, the facts and figures, the illustration. If he is writing on juvenile delinquency, he does not just tell you that juveniles are (it seems to him) delinquent and that (in his opinion) something should be done about it. He shows you juveniles being delinquent, tearing up movie theatres in Buffalo, stabbing high school principals in Dallas, smoking marijuana in Palo Alto. And more than likely he is moving toward some specific remedy, not just a general wringing of the hands. 17

It is no doubt possible to be *too* concrete, too illustrative or anecdotal, but few inexperienced writers err this way. For most the soundest advice is to be seeking always for the picture, to be always turning general remarks into seeable examples. Don't say, "Sororities teach girls the social graces." Say, "Sorority life teaches a girl how to carry on a conversation while pouring tea, without sloshing the tea into the saucer." Don't say, "I like certain kinds of popular music very much." Say, "Whenever I hear Gerber Spinklittle play 'Mississippi Man' on the trombone, my socks creep up my ankles." 18

GET RID OF OBVIOUS PADDING

The student toiling away at his weekly English theme is too often tormented by a figure: five hundred words. How, he asks himself, is he to achieve this staggering total? Obviously by never using one word when he can somehow work in ten. 19

He is therefore seldom content with a plain statement like "Fast driving 20 is dangerous.'' This has only four words in it. He takes thought, and the sentence becomes:

> In my opinion, fast driving is dangerous.

Better, but he can do better still:

> In my opinion, fast driving would seem to be rather dangerous.

If he is really adept, it may come out:

> In my humble opinion, though I do not claim to be an expert on this compli-
> cated subject, fast driving, in most circumstances, would seem to be rather
> dangerous in many respects, or at least so it would seem to me.

Thus four words have been turned into forty, and not an iota of content has been added.

Now this is a way to go about reaching five hundred words, and if you are content with a D grade, it is as good a way as any. But if you aim higher, you must work differently. Instead of stuffing your sentences with straw, you must try steadily to get rid of the padding, to make your sentences lean and tough. If you are really working at it, you first draft will greatly exceed the required total, and then you will work it down, thus:

> It is thought in some quarters that fraternities do not contribute as much as
> might be expected to campus life.
> Some people think that freaternities contribute little to campus life.

> The average doctor who practices in small towns or in the country must toil
> night and day to heal the sick.
> Most country doctors work long hours.

> When I was a little girl, I suffered from shyness and embarrassment in the
> presence of others.
> I was a shy little girl.

> It is absolutely necessary for the person employed as a marine fireman to
> give the matter of steam pressure his undivided attention at all times.
> The fireman has to keep his eye on the steam gauge.

You may ask how you can arrive at five hundred words at this rate. Simply. You dig up more real content. Instead of taking a couple of obvious points off the surface of the topic and then circling warily around them for six paragraphs, you work in and explore, figure out the details. You illustrate. You say that fast driving is dangerous, and then you prove it. How long does it take to stop a car at forty and at eighty? How far can you see at night? What happens when a tire blows? What happens in a head-on collision at fifty miles an hour? Pretty soon your paper will be full of broken glass and blood and headless torsos, and reaching five hundred words will not really be a problem.

CALL A FOOL A FOOL

Some of the padding in freshman themes is to be blamed not on anxiety   23
about the word minimum but on excessive timidity. The student writes,
"In my opinion, the principal of my high school acted in ways that I
believe every unbiased person would call foolish." If he was a fool, call
him a fool. Hedging the thing about with "in my opinions" and "it seems
to me's" and "as I see it's" and "at least from my point of view's" gains
you nothing. Delete these phrases whenever they creep into your paper.

The student's tendency to hedge stems from a modesty that in other   24
circumstances would be commendable. He is, he realizes, young and inexperienced, and he half suspects that he is dopey and fuzzy-minded beyond the average. Probably only too true. But it doesn't help to announce
your incompetence six times in every paragraph. Decide what you want to
say and say it as vigorously as possible, without apology and in plain
words.

Linguistic diffidence can take various forms. One is what we call   25
euphemism. This is the tendency to call a spade "a certain garden implement" or women's underwear "unmentionables." It is stronger in some
eras than others and in some people than others but it always operates more
or less insubjects that are touchy or taboo: death, sex, madness, and so on.
This we shrink from saying, "He died last night," but say instead "passed
away," "left us," "joined his Maker," "went to his reward." Or we try
to take off the tension with a lighter cliché: "kicked the bucket," "cashed
in his chips," "handed in his dinner pail." We have likewise found all
sorts of ways to avoid saying *mad:* "mentally ill," "touched," "not quite
right upstairs," "feeble-minded," "innocent," "simple," "off his trol-
ly," "not in his right mind." Even such a now plain word as *insane* began
as a euphemism with the meaning "not healthy."

Modern science, particularly psychology, contributes many polysylla-   26
bles in which we can wrap out thoughts and blunt their force. To many
writers there is no such thing as a bad schoolboy. Schoolboys are maladjusted or unoriented or misunderstood or in need of guidance or lacking in
continued success toward satisfactory integration of the personality as a
social unit, but they are never bad. Psychology no doubt makes us better
men and women, more sympathetic and tolerant, but it doesn't make
writing any easier. Had Shakespeare been confronted with psychology,
"To be or not to be" might have come out, "To continue as a social unit
or not to do so. That is the personality problem. Whether 'tis a better sign
of integration at the conscious level to display a psychic tolerance toward
the maladjustments and repressions induced by one's lack of orientation in
one's environment or—" But Hamlet would never have finished the so-
liloquy.

Writing in the modern world, you cannot altogether avoid modern 27
jargon. Nor, in an effort to get away from euphemism, should you salt your
paper with four-letter words. But you can do much if you will mount guard
against those roundabout phrases, those echoing polysyllables that tend to
slip into your writing to rob it of its crispness and force.

BEWARE OF THE PAT EXPRESSION

Other things being equal, avoid phrases like "other things being equal." 28
Those sentences that come to you whole, or in two or three doughy lumps,
are sure to be bad sentences. They are no creation of yours but pieces of
common thought floating in the community soup.

Pat expressions are hard, often impossible, to avoid, because they 29
come too easily to be noticed and seem too necessary to be dispensed with.
No writer avoids them altogether, but good writers avoid them more often
than poor writers.

By "pat expressions" we mean such tags as "to all practical intents 30
and purposes," "the pure and simple truth," "from where I sit," "the
time of his life," "to the ends of the earth," "in the twinkling of an eye,"
"as sure as you're born," "over my dead body," "under cover of darkness," "took the easy way out," "when all is said and done," "told him
time and time again," "parted the best of friends," "stand up and be
counted," "gave him the best years of her life," "worked her fingers to
the bone." Like other clichés, these expressions were once forceful. Now
we should use them only when we can't possibly think of anything else.

Some pat expressions stand like a wall between the writer and thought. 31
Such a one is "the American way of life." Many student writers feel that
when they have said that something accords with the American way of life
or does not they have exhausted the subject. Actually, they have stopped
at the highest level of abstraction. The American way of life is the complicated set of bonds between a hundred and eighty million ways. All of us
know this when we think about it, but the tag phrase too often keeps us
from thinking about it.

So with many another phrase dear to the politician: "this great land of 32
ours," "the man in the street," "our national heritage." These may prove
our patriotism or give a clue to our political beliefs, but otherwise they add
nothing to the paper except words.

COLORFUL WORDS

The writer builds with words, and no builder uses a raw material more 33
slippery and elusive and treacherous. A writer's work is a constant struggle

to get the right word in the right place, to find that particular word that will convey his meaning exactly, that will persuade the reader or soothe him or startle or amuse him. He never succeeds altogether—sometimes he feels that he scarcely succeeds at all—but such successes as he has are what make the thing worth doing.

COLORFUL WORDS

There is no book of rules for this game. One progresses through everlasting 34 experiment on the basis of ever-widening experience. There are few useful generalizations that one can make about words as words, but there are perhaps a few.

Some words are what we call "colorful." By this we mean that they 35 are calculated to produce a picture or induce an emotion. They are dressy instead of plain, specific instead of general, loud instead of soft. Thus, in place of "Her heart beat," we may write, "Her heart *pounded, throbbed, fluttered, danced.*" Instead of "He sat in his chair," we may say, "He *lounged, sprawled, coiled.*" Instead of "It was hot," we may say, "It was *blistering, sultry, muggy, suffocating, steamy, wilting.*"

However, it should not be supposed that the fancy word is always 36 better. Often it is as well to write "Her heart beat" or "It was hot" if that is all it did or all it was. Ages differ in how they like their prose. The nineteenth century liked it rich and smoky. The twentieth has usually preferred it lean and cool. The twentieth century writer, like all writers, is forever seeking the exact word, but he is wary of sounding feverish. He tends to pitch it low, to understate it, to throw it away. He knows that if he gets too colorful, the audience is likely to giggle.

See how this strikes you: "As the rich, golden glow of the sunset died 37 away along the eternal western hills, Angela's limpid blue eyes looked softly and trustingly into Montague's flashing brown ones, and her heart pounded like a drum in time with the joyous song surging in her soul." Some people like that sort of thing, but most modern readers would say, "Good grief," and turn on the television.

COLORED WORDS

Some words we would call not so much colorful as colored—that is, loaded 38 with associations, good or bad. All words—except perhaps structure words—have associations of some sort. We have said that the meaning of a word is the sum of the contexts in which it occurs. When we hear a word, we hear with it an echo of all the situations in which we have heard it before.

In some words, these echoes are obvious and discussable. The word 39 *mother*, for example, has, for most people, agreeable associations. When you hear *mother* you probably think of home, safety, love, food, and various other pleasant things. If one writes, "She was like a mother to me," he gets an effect which he would not get in "She was like an aunt to me." The advertiser makes use of the associations of *mother* by working it in when he talks about his product. The politician works it in when he talks about himself.

So also with such words as *home, liberty, fireside, contentment, patriot, tenderness, sacrifice, childlike, manly, bluff, limpid.* All of these words are loaded with associations that would be rather hard to indicate in a straightforward definition. There is more than a literal difference between "They sat around the fireside" and "They sat around the stove, but *fireside* suggests leisure, grace, quiet tradition, congenial company, and *stove* does not.   40

Conversely, some words have bad associations. *Mother* suggests pleasant things, but *mother-in-law* does not. Many mothers-in-law are heroically lovable and some mothers drink gin all day and beat their children insensible, but these facts of life are beside the point. The point is that *mother* sounds good and *mother-in-law* does not.   41

Or consider the word *intellectual.* This would seem to be a complimentary term, but in point of fact it is not, for it has picked up associations of impracticality and ineffectuality and general dopiness. So also such words as *liberal, reactionary, Communist, socialist, capitalist, radical, schoolteacher, truckdriver, undertaker, operator, salesman, huckster, speculator.* These convey meaning on the literal level, but beyond that—sometimes, in some places—they convey contempt on the part of the speaker.   42

The question of whether to use loaded words or not depends on what is being written. The scientist, the scholar, try to avoid them; for the poet, the advertising writer, the public speaker, they are standard equipment. But every writer should take care that they do not substitute for thought. If you write, "Anyone who thinks that is nothing but a Socialist (or Communist or capitalist)" you have said nothing except that you don't like people who think that, and such remarks are effective only with the most naive readers. It is always a bad mistake to think your readers more naive than they really are.   43

COLORLESS WORDS

But probably most student writers come to grief not with words that are colorful or those that are colored but with those that have no color at all. A pet example is *nice*, a word we would find it hard to dispense with in casual conversation but which is no longer capable of adding much to a description. Colorless words are those of such general meaning that in a   44 particular sentence they mean nothing. Slang adjectives like *cool* ("That's real cool") tend to explode all over the language. They are applied to everything, lose their original force, and quickly die.

Beware also of nouns of very general meaning, like *circumstances,* *cases, instances, aspects, factors, relationships, attitudes, eventualities,* etc. In most circumstances you will find that those cases of writing which contain too many instances of words like these will in this and other aspects have factors leading to unsatisfactory relationships with the reader resulting in unfavorable attitudes on his part and perhaps other eventualities, like a grade of "D." Notice also what *etc.* means. It means "I'd like to make this list longer, but I can't think of any more examples." 45

QUESTIONS FOR STUDY AND DISCUSSION

1. What does Roberts say is the job of a writer? How in particular does he say the task is made difficult for college English students? Discuss how your own college experiences lead you to agree or disagree with Roberts.

2. Roberts offers several "tricks" of good writing. What are they? Are some better than others? Explain.

3. A good writer never uses unnecessary words, according to Roberts. What does he give as legitimate ways for a student to reach a goal of five hundred words?

4. How has modern psychology made it more difficult to write well, according to Roberts?

5. Make a scratch outline of Roberts's essay. Do you see any similarities between his organization of material and the steps he advises students to take? Explain.

6. Roberts has a writing style well suited to his student audience. In fact, he is a perfect example of a writer who practices what he preaches. How would you describe Roberts's style? What are some of the ways he uses humor, diction, and illustration to hold his readers' interest?

7. What kind of information does the title of Roberts's essay lead you to expect? Does he deliver what he promises? Why do you think he chose this title?

8. Roberts wrote his essay thirty years ago. Is there anything in his diction that gives this away? In your opinion, does Roberts sound contemporary? Choose examples of his diction to support your answer. (Glossary: *Diction*)

WRITING HONESTLY

Donald Hall

*Donald Hall is a poet, essayist, and teacher of writing. After
graduating from Harvard and Oxford Universities, he taught
at the University of Michigan until 1976, when he moved to
his farm in New Hampshire to devote all his time to his
writing. In the following essay, taken from his college
textbook* Writing Well, *Hall discusses the importance of the
interrelationship of sincerity, inspiration, and discipline for
the writer.*

Writing well is the art of clear thinking and honest feeling. The phrase   1
honest feeling implies an opposite, dishonest feeling, which no one admits
to but which we sometimes see clearly in others. We are all aware of
honest and dishonest expression. We have grown up on the false laughter
of television, the fake enthusiasm of advertising, the commercial jollity
and condolences of greeting cards, and the lying assertions of politicians.
If some falsity has not entered our prose, we are made of aluminum.

We can be false in a thousand ways. We do it with handshakes and we   2
do it with grunts. We do it by saying outright lies and we do it by keeping
silent. But in these examples we understand our own falsity. When we fool
ourselves we are in more trouble. We fool ourselves with words that can
mean almost anything. How much have we said when we call someone
liberal? We fool ourselves when we avoid blame by leaving *I* out of the
sentence, as when we knock over a lamp and claim that "The lamp was
knocked over" or that "The lamp fell," as if it acted by itself. We also
fool ourselves by using clichés, trite expressions that have become meaningless substitutes for feeling and thought.

impressionable age	bottom line
startling conclusion	name of the game
a vital part of our future	get a point across
made it what it is today	a changing society

Clichés are little cinder blocks of crushed and reprocessed experience.
When we use them in writing, we violate our agreement to construct
sentences in order to reach someone else. We appear to make contact, but

the appearance is not a reality. Clichés are familiar and comfortable; they *seem* to mean something, but when I reach the *startling conclusion* that the *bottom line* is the *name of the game* in a *changing society,* I say nothing to anyone. Clichés prevent true contact by making false contact in its place.

Every profession—medicine, law, theater, business—has its own clichés. We call the clichés that belong to a profession its *jargon.* One set of clichés appears especially at graduations, from primary school through graduate school.   3

The future belongs to you.
The challenge of new . . .
In today's world . . .
Responsibility, good citizenship, service to the community . . .

The university, in fact, is one of the great sources of jargon. Here are two paragraphs from a letter addressed by a newly elected college president to his faculty.

> Dear Members of the State College Community:
>
> I am deeply honored and challenged by the opportunity to join State College as its seventh president. The hospitality and spontaneous warmth of everyone we have met has made both Barbara and me feel very welcome. We look forward to making State our home as quickly as we can arrange an orderly transition from our current responsibilities.
>
> State College is rich in tradition: it is an institution with a past, and, more importantly, it is a College with a future. Building on its heritage, and maximizing its resources, State College can continue to achieve distinction by providing educational opportunities for young men and women.

Not all college presidents write this sort of thing, but many do. It is the language we expect from officials—from politicians and bureaucrats, from the presidents of colleges and the presidents of corporations. It says nothing, and it says it with maximum pomposity. It took this man years to learn the trick of empty jargon, the style of interlocking cliché. Every phase is trite, and the phrases are stuck together with mortar like *is* and *and* and *with.* The edifice is reprocessed garbage.

deeply honored
challenged by the opportunity
spontaneous warmth
making . . . our home
orderly transition
current responsibilities
rich in tradition
Building on its heritage
maximizing its resources

achieve distinction
providing educational opportunities

One should mention as well the trite and meaningless contrast between the past, as in *heritage*—a word as hokey as *home*—and *a college with a future*. The contrast says nothing. Unless the collegiate doors are closing tomorrow, of course it has *a future*. The word *future*—like *heritage* and *home*—carries vaguely positive connotations. A candidate for president of the United States used as a slogan, *The future lies before us,* trying to associate himself with this positive connotation; no one found the slogan offensive, but he lost.

In the college president's letter, the smoothness of the masonry is   4
exceptional, but the passage is without content and without feeling. The paragraphs are insincere because they do not represent a person's feelings. Of course the author did not *intend* insincerity, nor did he feel that he was lying.

We must look closely at the notion of sincerity; otherwise, we might   5
use it to justify its opposite. The worst liars sincerely say, to themselves and to the world, that they are the most honest. Yet sincerity can be a valuable idea if we think clearly about it, and sincerity has everything to do with the reasons for writing well. Peter Elbow, quoted in Ken Macrorie's book *Uptaught,* says:

> I warn against defining sincerity, as telling true things about oneself. It is more accurate to define it functionally as the sound of a writer's voice or self on paper—a general sound of authenticity in words. The point is that self-revelation . . . is an easy route in our culture and therefore can be used as an evasion: it can be functionally insincere even if substantially true and intimate. To be precise, *sincerity is the absence of "noise" or static—the ability or courage not to hide the real message.*

The static is the distance between what the words say and what we   6
sense lies behind them. The person with a pose of sincerity fixes us with his eyes, saying, "I am going to be wholly honest with you. I am a bastard. I cheat on my girlfriend and I steal my roommate's toothpaste." The real message: "Love me, I'm so *honest.*"

The distance between the meaning (the apparently stated) and the ex-   7
pression (the really implied) ruins the statement and prevents real communication between people. In the college president's letter, the meaning has something to do with expressing pleasure in a new task; the expression is an exhibition of academic smoothness; it is a little dance performed by a well-trained educationist seal. It says, "Look at me. Admit me to your ranks. I am one of you."

We cannot accept sincerity as a standard if we are going to take the   8
writer's word for it. We can take it seriously if we listen to his *words* for

it. Sincerity is *functional* (Elbow's word) if we believe it, if we hear the voice of a real person speaking forth in the prose—whether of speech or of the written word. The reader must feel that the prose is sincere. And sincerity comes from the self-knowledge we earn by self-exploration. When we express self-knowledge in our writing, we speak in a voice which sounds natural and which reaches the ears of other people. Finding this voice is not easy. It requires self-examination and hard thinking or analysis. It is worth it. Socrates made the commitment: the life which is unexamined is not worth living.

EXAMINING THE WORDS

By learning to write well, we learn methods of self-discovery and techniques for self-examination. Understanding the self allows us to move outside the self, to read, to analyze, to define, and thus to make contact outside the self, with others. Writing well can be a starting point for all thinking. Self-examination finds what we have inside us that is our own. Of course we are stuffed with clichés—we have been exposed to them all our lives—but clichés are not "our own." We have swallowed everything that has ever happened to us: we dropped the bottle to the floor at the age of eight weeks and cried for the lack of it; the telephone did not ring last week, and we cried for the lack of it; the toy shines under the tree, the toy rusts behind the garage; the smell of bacon, the smell of roses, the smell of kittens that have been careless, the flowers and the beer cans emerging from the snow. Everything that ever happened to us remains on file in our heads. As a professor at MIT put it: the human brain is a big computer made of meat. 9

If the brain is a computer, we are all engaged in learning how to operate it. For the college president quoted above, the task of writing was simple; he was programmed to write that kind of prose; he pushed the right keys and his brain computer turned out preassembled units of academic jargon. The commencement speaker, or the student writing home for money, presses other keys for printouts of ready-made pseudothoughts and pseudofeelings. But let us suppose that we are interested in something genuine, the voice without static, the utterance in which expression and meaning are the same. We must learn new ways to use the accumulation of words, sense impressions, and ideas that we keep in the floppy discs of the brain. Our words must not make rows of identical houses like the subdivision prose of cliché. "New" is fresh, genuine, ourselves, our own experience. Making it new, we make contact with the reader. 10

Freshness is not, however, the inevitable result of spontaneity. Writing freely, without pausing for correction, is a good way to practice writing, to 11 learn to flow, and to uncover material you didn't know was in you. It can be important to develop a sense of freedom in writing. But then there is the second half of genuine expression, the half that applies the map maker's self-examination to the new country of self-exploration. This self-examination, leading to revision, allows the writer to communicate with other human beings. Revising the map, we think of the reader; we revise to make contact with the reader.

REVISING THE MAP

Almost all writers, almost all the time, need to revise. We need to revise   12
because spontaneity is never adequate. Writing that is merely emotional release for the writer becomes emotional chaos for the reader. Even when we write as quickly as our hand can move, we slide into emotional falsity, into cliché or other static. And we make leaps by private association that leave our prose unclear. And we often omit steps in thinking or use a step that we later recognize as bad logic. Sometimes we overexplain the obvious. Or we include irrelevant detail. First drafts remain first drafts. They are the material that we must shape, a marble block that the critical brain chisels into form. We must shape this material in order to pass it from mind to mind; we shape our material into a form that allows other people to receive it. This shaping often requires us, in revising, to reorganize whole paragraphs, both the order of sentences and the sentences themselves. We must drop sentences and clauses that do not belong; we must expand or supply others necessary to a paragraph's development. Often we must revise the order of paragraphs; often we must write new paragraphs to provide coherent and orderly progress.

Good writing is an intricate interweaving of inspiration and discipline.   13
A student may need one strand more than the other. Most of us continually need to remember both sides of writing: *we must invent, and we must revise*. In these double acts, invention and revision, we are inventing and revising not just our prose style but our knowledge of ourselves and of the people around us. When Confucius recommended "Make it new," he told us to live what Socrates called "the examined life." It was a moral position. By our language, we shall know ourselves—not once and for all, by a breakthrough, but continually, all our lives. Therefore, the necessity to write well arises from the need to understand and to discriminate, to be genuine and to avoid what is not genuine, in ourselves and in others. By understanding what our words reveal, we can understand ourselves; by changing these words until we arrive at our own voices, we change ourselves; by arriving at our own voices, we are able to speak to others and be heard.

QUESTIONS FOR STUDY AND DISCUSSION

1. What is Hall's thesis in this essay, and where is it stated? (Glossary: *Thesis*)

2. How, according to Hall, do people fool themselves by using the passive voice, personification, clichés, and jargon?

3. What does Hall mean when he says, "We must look closely at the notion of sincerity; otherwise, we might use it to justify its opposite"(5)? Explain Peter Elbow's definition of sincerity, which Hall quotes in paragraph 5.

4. Explain Hall's use of the computer analogy in paragraph 10. Is the analogy effective? Why, or why not? (Glossary: *Analogy*)

5. What role does Hall believe spontaneity plays in writing? What does he believe are its benefits? Its limitations?

6. In what ways is Hall's final paragraph an appropriate conclusion for his essay? (Glossary: *Endings*)

7. To what extent would you say that Hall practices what he preaches? Explain.

WRITING FOR AN AUDIENCE

Linda Flower

Linda Flower is an Associate Professor of English at Carnegie-Mellon University, where she directed the Business Communication program for a number of years. Her widely recognized research on the composing process resulted in the textbook Problem-Solving Strategies for Writing *(2nd edition, 1985). In the following selection taken from that text, Flower discusses the importance of defining your audience of readers before you start writing.*

The goal of the writer is to create a momentary common ground between the reader and the writer. You want the reader to share your knowledge and your attitude toward that knowledge. Even if the reader eventually disagrees, you want him or her to be able for the moment to *see things as you see them.* A good piece of writing closes the gap between you and the reader.

ANALYZE YOUR AUDIENCE

The first step in closing that gap is to gauge the distance between the two of you. Imagine, for example, that you are a student writing your parents, who have always lived in New York City, about a wilderness survival expedition you want to go on over spring break. Sometimes obvious differences such as age or background will be important, but the critical differences for writers usually fall into three areas: the reader's *knowledge* about the topic; his or her *attitude* toward it, and his or her personal or professional *needs.* Because these differences often exist, good writers do more than simply express their meaning; they pinpoint the critical differences between themselves and their reader and design their writing to reduce those differences. Let us look at these three areas in more detail.

KNOWLEDGE This is usually the easiest difference to handle. What does your reader need to know? What are the main ideas you hope to teach?

Does your reader have enough background knowledge to really understand you? If not, what would he or she have to learn?

ATTITUDES When we say a person has knowledge, we usually refer to his   4
conscious awareness of explicit facts and clearly defined concepts. This kind of knowledge can be easily written down or told to someone else. However, much of what we "know" is not held in this formal, explicit way. Instead it is held as an attitude or image—as a loose cluster of associations. For instance, my image of lakes includes associations many people would have, including fishing, water skiing, stalled outboards, and lots of kids catching night crawlers with flashlights. However, the most salient or powerful parts of my image, which strongly color my whole attitude toward lakes, are thoughts of cloudy skies, long rainy days, and feeling generally cold and damp. By contrast, one of my best friends has a very different cluster of associations: to him a lake means sun, swimming, sailing, and happily sitting on the end of a dock. Needless to say, our differing images cause us to react quite differently to a proposal that we visit a lake. Likewise, one reason people often find it difficult to discuss religion and politics is that terms such as "capitalism" conjure up radically different images.

As you can see, a reader's image of a subject is often the source of   5
attitudes and feelings that are unexpected and, at times, impervious to mere facts. A simple statement that seems quite persuasive to you, such as "Lake Wampago would be a great place to locate the new music camp," could have little impact on your reader if he or she simply doesn't visualize a lake as a "great place." In fact, many people accept uncritically any statement that fits in with their own attitudes—and reject, just as uncritically, anything that does not.

Whether your purpose is to persuade or simply to present your per-   6
spective, it helps to know the image and attitudes that your reader already holds. The more these differ from your own, the more you will have to do to make him or her *see* what you mean.

NEEDS When writers discover a large gap between their own knowledge   7
and attitudes and those of the reader, they usually try to change the reader in some way. Needs, however, are different. When you analyze a reader's needs, it is so that you, the writer, can adapt to him. If you ask a friend majoring in biology how to keep your fish tank from clouding, you don't want to hear a textbook recitation on the life processes of algae. You expect the friend to adapt his or her knowledge and tell you exactly how to solve your problem.

The ability to adapt your knowledge to the needs of the reader is   8
often crucial to your success as a writer. This is especially true in writing done on a job. For example, as producer of a public affairs program

for a television station, 80 percent of your time may be taken up planning the details of new shows, contacting guests, and scheduling the taping sessions. But when you write a program proposal to the station director, your job is to show how the program will fit into the cost guidelines, the FCC requirements for relevance, and the overall programming plan for the station. When you write that report your role in the organization changes from producer to proposal writer. Why? Because your reader needs that information in order to make a decision. He may be *interested* in your scheduling problems and the specific content of the shows, but he *reads* your report because of his own needs as station director of that organization. He has to act.

In college, where the reader is also a teacher, the reader's needs are   9
a little less concrete but just as important. Most papers are assigned as a way to teach something. So the real purpose of a paper may be for you to make connections between two historical periods, to discover for yourself the principle behind a laboratory experiment, or to develop and support your own interpretation of a novel. A good college paper doesn't just rehash the facts; it demonstrates what your reader, as a teacher, needs to know—that you are learning the thinking skills his or her course is trying to teach.

Effective writers are not simply expressing what they know, like a   10
student madly filling up an examination bluebook. Instead they are *using* their knowledge: reorganizing, maybe even rethinking their ideas to meet the demands of an assignment or the needs of their reader.

QUESTIONS FOR STUDY AND DISCUSSION

1. What, for Flower, should be the goal of the writer?

2. What does Flower mean by the "distance" between the writer and the reader? How, according to Flower, do writers close the gap between themselves and their readers?

3. What does Flower see as the three critical differences between writers and readers? Why do you suppose she devotes so little attention to "knowledge" and so much more to both "attitude" and "needs"?

4. What is the difference between "knowledge" and "attitude"? Why is it important to know the difference?

5. Why is it so important for writers to adapt their knowledge to their readers' needs? How do you determine what your reader's needs are? Explain.

6. What, according to Flower, does a good college paper do? What does she mean when she says that effective writers do not simply express what they know, they *use* their knowledge?

7. Flower wrote this selection for college students. How well did she assess your knowledge, attitude, and needs about the subject of a writer's audience?

SIMPLICITY

William Zinsser

The following essay is taken from William Zinsser's On
Writing Well: An Informal Guide to Writing Nonfiction. *In it
Zinsser, a longtime writer, editor, critic, and teacher of
writing, advises and demonstrates that self-discipline and
hard work are necessary to achieve clear, simple prose. No
matter what your experience as a writer has been, you will
find Zinsser's observations sound and his advice practical.*

Clutter is the disease of American writing. We are a society strangling   1
in unnecessary words, circular constructions, pompous frills and meaningless jargon.

Who can understand the viscous language of everyday American com-   2
merce and enterprise: the business letter, the interoffice memo, the corporation report, the notice from the bank explaining its latest "simplified"
statement? What member of an insurance or medical plan can decipher the
brochure that tells him what his costs and benefits are? What father or
mother can put together a child's toy—on Christmas Eve or any other
eve—from the instructions on the box? Our national tendency is to inflate
and thereby sound important. The airline pilot who announces that he is
presently anticipating experiencing considerable precipitation wouldn't
dream of saying that it may rain. The sentence is too simple—there must
be something wrong with it.

But the secret of good writing is to strip every sentence to its cleanest   3
components. Every word that serves no function, every long word that
could be a short word, every adverb that carries the same meaning that's
already in the verb, every passive construction that leaves the reader unsure
of who is doing what—these are the thousand and one adulterants that
weaken the strength of a sentence. And they usually occur, ironically, in
proportion to education and rank.

During the late 1960s the president of a major university wrote a letter   4
to mollify the alumni after a spell of campus unrest. "You are probably
aware," he began, "that we have been experiencing very considerable
potentially explosive expressions of dissatisfaction on issues only partially
related." He meant that the students had been hassling them about different
things. I was far more upset by the president's English than by the stu-

dents' potentially explosive expressions of dissatisfaction. I would have preferred the presidential approach taken by Franklin D. Roosevelt when he tried to convert into English his own government's memos, such as this blackout order of 1942:

> Such preparations shall be made as will completely obscure all Federal buildings and non-Federal buildings occupied by the Federal government during an air raid for any period of time from visibility by reason of internal or external illumination.

"Tell them," Roosevelt said, "that in buildings where they have to   5
keep the work going to put something across the windows."

Simplify, simplify. Thoreau said it, as we are so often reminded, and   6
no American writer more consistently practiced what he preached. Open *Walden* to any page and you will find a man saying in a plain and orderly way what is on his mind:

> I love to be alone. I never found the companion that was so companionable as solitude. We are for the most part more lonely when we go abroad among men than when we stay in our chambers. A man thinking or working is always alone, let him be where he will. Solitude is not measured by the miles of space that intervene between a man and his fellows. The really diligent student in one of the crowded hives of Cambridge College is as solitary as a dervish in the desert.

How can the rest of us achieve such enviable freedom from clutter? The   7
answer is to clear our heads of clutter. Clear thinking becomes clear writing: one can't exist without the other. It is impossible for a muddy thinker to write good English. He may get away with it for a paragraph or two, but soon the reader will be lost, and there is no sin so grave, for he will not easily be lured back.

Who is this elusive creature the reader? He is a person with an attention   8
span of about twenty seconds. He is assailed on every side by forces competing for his time: by newspapers and magazines, by television and radio, by his stereo and videocassettes, by his wife and children and pets, by his house and his yard and all the gadgets that he has bought to keep them spruce, and by that most potent of competitors, sleep. The man snoozing in his chair with an unfinished magazine open on his lap is a man who was being given too much unnecessary trouble by the writer.

It won't do to say that the snoozing reader is too dumb or too lazy to   9
keep pace with the train of thought. My sympathies are with him. If the reader is lost, it is generally because the writer has not been careful enough to keep him on the path.

This carelessness can take any number of forms. Perhaps a sentence is   10
so excessively cluttered that the reader, hacking his way through the ver-

biage, simply doesn't know what it means. Perhaps a sentence has been so shoddily constructed that the reader could read it in any of several ways. Perhaps the writer has switched pronouns in mid-sentence, or has switched tenses, so the reader loses track of who is talking or when the action took place. Perhaps Sentence B is not a logical sequel to Sentence A—the writer, in whose head the connection is clear, has not bothered to provide the missing link. Perhaps the writer has used an important word incorrectly by not taking the trouble to look it up. He may think that "sanguine" and "sanguinary" mean the same thing, but the difference is a bloody big one. The reader can only infer (speaking of big differences) what the writer is trying to imply.

Faced with these obstacles, the reader is at first a remarkably tenacious 11
bird. He blames himself—he obviously missed something, and he goes back over the mystifying sentence, or over the whole paragraph, piecing it out like an ancient rune, making guesses and moving on. But he won't do this for long. The writer is making him work too hard, and the reader will look for one who is better at his craft.

The writer must therefore constantly ask himself: What am I trying to 12
say? Surprisingly often, he doesn't know. Then he must look at what he has written and ask: Have I said it? Is it clear to someone encountering the subject for the first time? If it's not, it is because some fuzz has worked its way into the machinery. The clear writer is a person clear-headed enough to see this stuff for what it is: fuzz.

I don't mean that some people are born clear-headed and are therefore 13
natural writers, whereas others are naturally fuzzy and will never write well. Thinking clearly is a conscious act that the writer must force upon himself, just as if he were embarking on any other project that requires logic: adding up a laundry list or doing an algebra problem. Good writing doesn't come naturally, though most people obviously think it does. The professional writer is forever being bearded by strangers who say that they'd like to "try a little writing sometime" when they retire from their real profession. Or they say, "I could write a book about that." I doubt it.

Writing is hard work. A clear sentence is no accident. Very few sen- 14
tences come out right the first time, or even the third time. Remember this as a consolation in moments of despair. If you find that writing is hard, it's because it *is* hard. It's one of the hardest things that people do.

QUESTIONS FOR STUDY AND DISCUSSION

1. What is the relationship that Zinsser sees between thinking and writing?

2. What is clutter? How does Zinsser think that we can free ourselves of clutter?

3. What assumptions does Zinsser make about readers? According to Zinsser, what responsibilities do writers have to readers?

4. What questions should the writer constantly ask? Why are these questions so important?

5. What does Zinsser mean by "simplicity"? Would you agree with him that "our national tendency is to inflate and thereby sound important"(2)? Why, or why not?

6. Zinsser uses short sentences (seven or fewer words) effectively in his essay. Locate several examples of short sentences, and explain the function of each within its paragraph.

7. The following two pages show a passage from the final manuscript for this essay. Carefully study the manuscript, and then discuss the ways in which Zinsser has been able to eliminate clutter.

5 --

is too dumb or too lazy to keep pace with the ~~writer's~~ train
of thought. My sympathics are ~~entirely~~ with him.) ~~He's not~~
~~so dumb.~~ (If the reader is lost, it is generally because the
writer ~~of the article~~ has not been careful enough to keep
him on the ~~proper~~ path.

This carelessness can take any number of ~~different~~ forms.
Perhaps a sentence is so excessively ~~long and~~ cluttered that
the reader, hacking his way through ~~all~~ the verbiage, simply
doesn't know what it ~~the writer~~ means. Perhaps a sentence has
been so shoddily constructed that the reader could read it in
any of several ~~two or three different~~ ways. ~~He thinks he knows what~~
~~the writer is trying to say, but he's not sure.~~ Perhaps the
writer has switched pronouns in mid-sentence, or ~~perhaps he~~
has switched tenses, so the reader loses track of who is
talking ~~to whom,~~ or ~~exactly~~ when the action took place. Perhaps Sentence B is not a logical sequel to Sentence A -- the
writer, in whose head the connection is ~~perfectly~~ clear, has
not bothered to provide ~~given enough thought to providing~~ the missing link. Perhaps the writer has used an important word incorrectly by not
taking the trouble to look it up ~~and make sure.~~ He may think
that "sanguine" and "sanguinary" mean the same thing, but)
~~I can assure you that~~ (the difference is a bloody big one ~~to the~~
~~reader.~~ The reader ~~He~~ can only ~~try to~~ infer ~~what~~ (speaking of big differences) what the writer is trying to imply.

Faced with these ~~such a variety of~~ obstacles, the reader
is at first a remarkably tenacious bird. He ~~tends to~~ blames
himself ~~He~~ obviously missed something, ~~he thinks,~~ and he goes
back over the mystifying sentence, or over the whole paragraph,

6 --

piecing it out like an ancient rune, making guesses and moving
on. But he won't do this for long. ~~He will soon run out of
patience.~~ The writer is making him work too hard ~~-- harder
than he should have to work --~~ and the reader will look for
~~a writer~~ one who is better at his craft.

The writer must therefore constantly ask himself: What am
I trying to say, ~~in this sentence?~~ Surprisingly often, he
doesn't know. ~~And~~ Then he must look at what he has ~~just~~
written and ask: Have I said it? Is it clear to someone
~~who is coming upon~~ encountering the subject for the first time? If it's
not, ~~clear,~~ it is because some fuzz has worked its way into the
machinery. The clear writer is a person ~~who is~~ clear-headed
enough to see this stuff for what it is: fuzz.

I don't mean ~~to suggest~~ that some people are born
clear-headed and are therefore natural writers, whereas
~~other people~~ others are naturally fuzzy and will ~~therefore~~ never write
well. Thinking clearly is ~~an entirely~~ a conscious act that the
writer must force ~~keep forcing~~ upon himself, just as if he were
~~starting out~~ embarking on any other ~~kind of~~ project that ~~calls for~~ requires logic:
adding up a laundry list or doing an algebra problem ~~or playing
chess.~~ Good writing doesn't ~~just~~ come naturally, though most
people obviously think ~~it's as easy as walking.~~ it does. The professional

THE MAKER'S EYE: REVISING YOUR OWN MANUSCRIPTS

Donald M. Murray

*Donald M. Murray is a writer who recently taught writing at
the University of New Hampshire. He served as an editor at
Time magazine and won the Pulitzer Prize in 1954 for
editorials that appeared in the Boston Globe. His works
include poetry, novels, short stories, and sourcebooks for
teachers of writing, like A Writer Teaches Writing and
Learning by Teaching, where he explores aspects of the
writing process. In the following essay, first published in The
Writer, Murray discusses the importance of revision to the
work of a writer.*

When students complete a first draft, they consider the job of writing   1
done—and their teachers too often agree. When professional writers complete a first draft, they usually feel that they are at the start of the writing
process. When a draft is completed, the job of writing can begin.

That difference in attitude is the difference between amateur and pro-   2
fessional, inexperience and experience, journeyman and craftsman. Peter
F. Drucker, the prolific business writer, calls his first draft "the zero
draft"—after that he can start counting. Most writers share the feeling that
the first draft, and all of those which follow, are opportunities to discover
what they have to say and how best they can say it.

To produce a progression of drafts, each of which says more and says   3
it more clearly, the writer has to develop a special kind of reading skill. In
school we are taught to decode what appears on the page as finished
writing. Writers, however, face a different category of possibility and
responsibility when they read their own drafts. To them the words on the
page are never finished. Each can be changed and rearranged, can set off
a chain reaction of confusion or clarified meaning. This is a different kind
of reading which is possibly more difficult and certainly more exciting.

Writers must learn to be their own best enemy. They must accept the   4
criticism of others and be suspicious of it; they must accept the praise of

others and be even more suspicious of it. Writers cannot depend on others. They must detach themselves from their own pages so that they can apply both their caring and their craft to their own work.

Such detachment is not easy. Science-fiction writer Ray Bradbury sup- 5
posedly puts each manuscript away for a year to the day and then rereads it as a stranger. Not many writers have the discipline or the time to do this. We must read when our judgment may be at its worst, when we are close to the euphoric moment of creation.

Then the writer, counsels novelist Nancy Hale, "should be critical of 6
everything that seems to him most delightful in his style. He should excise what he most admires, because he wouldn't thus admire it if he weren't . . . in a sense protecting it from criticism." John Ciardi, the poet, adds, "The last act of the writing must be to become one's own reader. It is, I suppose, a schizophrenic process, to begin passionately and to end critically, to begin hot and to end cold; and, more important, to be passion-hot and critic-cold at the same time."

Most people think that the principal problem is that writers are too 7
proud of what they have written. Actually, a greater problem for most professional writers is one shared by the majority of students. They are overly critical, think everything is dreadful, tear up page after page, never complete a draft, see the task as hopeless.

The writer must learn to read critically but constructively, to cut what 8
is bad, to reveal what is good. Eleanor Estes, the children's book author, explains: "The writer must survey his work critically, coolly, as though he were a stranger to it. He must be willing to prune, expertly and hard-heartedly. At the end of each revision, a manuscript may look . . . worked over, torn apart, pinned together, added to, deleted from, words changed and words changed back. Yet the book must maintain its original freshness and spontaneity."

Most readers underestimate the amount of rewriting it usually takes to 9
produce spontaneous reading. This is a great disadvantage to the student writer, who sees only a finished product and never watches the craftsman who takes the necessary step back, studies the work carefully, returns to the task, steps back, returns, steps back, again and again. Anthony Burgess, one of the most prolific writers in the English-speaking world, admits, "I might revise a page twenty times." Roald Dahl, the popular children's writer, states, "By the time I'm nearing the end of a story, the first part will have been reread and altered and corrected at least 150 times. . . . Good writing is essentially rewriting. I am positive of this."

Rewriting isn't virtuous. It isn't something that ought to be done. It is 10
simply something that most writers find they have to do to discover what they have to say and how to say it. It is a condition of the writer's life.

There are, however, a few writers who do little formal rewriting, 11 primarily because they have the capacity and experience to create and review a large number of invisible drafts in their minds before they approach the page. And some writers slowly produce finished pages, performing all the tasks of revision simultaneously, page by page, rather than draft by draft. But it is still possible to see the sequence followed by most writers most of the time in rereading their own work.

Most writers scan their drafts first, reading as quickly as possible to catch the larger problems of subject and form, then move in closer and closer as they read and write, reread and rewrite. 12

The first thing writers look for in their drafts is *information*. They know that a good piece of writing is built from specific, accurate, and interesting information. The writer must have an abundance of information from which to construct a readable piece of writing. 13

Next writers look for *meaning* in the information. The specifics must build to a pattern of significance. Each piece of specific information must carry the reader toward meaning. 14

Writers reading their own drafts are aware of *audience*. They put themselves in the reader's situation and make sure that they deliver information which a reader wants to know or needs to know in a manner which is easily digested. Writers try to be sure that they anticipate and answer the questions a critical reader will ask when reading the piece of writing. 15

Writers make sure that the *form* is appropriate to the subject and the audience. Form, or genre, is the vehicle which carries meaning to the reader, but form cannot be selected until the writer has adequate information to discover its significance and an audience which needs or wants that meaning. 16

Once writers are sure the form is appropriate, they must then look at the *structure,* the order of what they have written. Good writing is built on a solid framework of logic, argument, narrative, or motivation which runs through the entire piece of writing and holds it together. This is the time when many writers find it most effective to outline as a way of visualizing the hidden spine by which the piece of writing is supported. 17

The element on which writers may spend a majority of their time is *development*. Each section of a piece of writing must be adequately developed. It must give readers enough information so that they are satisfied. How much information is enough? That's as difficult as asking how much garlic belongs in a salad. It must be done to taste, but most beginning writers underdevelop, underestimating the reader's hunger for information. 18

As writers solve development problems, they often have to consider questions of *dimension*. There must be a pleasing and effective proportion among all the parts of the piece of writing. There is a continual process of subtracting and adding to keep the piece of writing in balance. 19

Finally, writers have to listen to their own voices. *Voice* is the force 20 which drives a piece of writing forward. It is an expression of the writer's authority and concern. It is what is between the words on the page, what glues the piece of writing together. A good piece of writing is always marked by a consistent, individual voice.

As writers read and reread, write and rewrite, they move closer and closer to the page until they are doing line-by-line editing. Writers read their own pages with infinite care. Each sentence, each line, each clause, each phrase, each word, each mark of punctuation, each section of white space between the type has to contribute to the clarification of meaning. 21

Slowly the writer moves from word to word, looking through language to see the subject. As a word is changed, cut, or added, as a construction is rearranged, all the words used before that moment and all those that follow that moment must be considered and reconsidered. 22

Writers often read aloud at this stage of the editing process, muttering or whispering to themselves, calling on the ear's experience with language. Does this sound right—or that? Writers edit, shifting back and forth from eye to page to ear to page. I find I must do this careful editing in short runs, no more than fifteen or twenty minutes at a stretch, or I become too kind with myself. I begin to see what I hope is on the page, not what actually is on the page. 23

This sounds tedious if you haven't done it, but actually it is fun. Making something right is immensely satisfying, for writers begin to learn what they are writing about by writing. Language leads them to meaning, and there is the joy of discovery, of understanding, of making meaning clear as the writer employs the technical skills of language. 24

Words have double meanings, even triple and quadruple meanings. Each word has its own potential for connotation and denotation. And when writers rub one word against the other, they are often rewarded with a sudden insight, an unexpected clarification. 25

The maker's eye moves back and forth from word to phrase to sentence to paragraph to sentence to phrase to word. The maker's eye sees the need for variety and balance, for a firmer structure, for a more appropriate form. It peers into the interior of the paragraph, looking for coherence, unity, and emphasis, which make meaning clear. 26

I learned something about this process when my first bifocals were prescribed. I had ordered a larger section of the reading portion of the glass because of my work, but even so, I could not contain my eyes within this new limit of vision. And I still find myself taking off my glasses and bending my nose toward the page, for my eyes unconsciously flick back and forth across the page, back to another page, forward to still another, as I try to see each evolving line in relation to every other line. 27

When does this process end? Most writers agree with the great Russian writer Tolstoy, who said, ''I scarcely ever reread my published writings, 28 if by chance I come across a page, it always strikes me: all this must be rewritten; this is how I should have written it.''

The maker's eye is never satisfied, for each word has the potential to   29 ignite new meaning. This article has been twice written all the way through the writing process, and it was published four years ago. Now it is to be republished in a book. The editors made a few small suggestions, and then I read it with my maker's eye. Now it has been re-edited, re-revised, re-read, re-re-edited, for each piece of writing to the writer is full of potential and alternatives.

A piece of writing is never finished. It is delivered to a deadline, torn   30 out of the typewriter on demand, sent off with a sense of accomplishment and shame and pride and frustration. If only there were a couple more days, time for just another run at it, perhaps then. . . .

QUESTIONS FOR STUDY AND DISCUSSION

1. Why does Murray see revision as such an important element in the process of writing?

2. What is Murray's purpose in writing this essay? (Glossary: *Purpose*)

3. What, according to Murray, are the eight things a writer must be conscious of in the process of revision? Describe the process you generally go through when you revise your writing. How does your process compare with Murray's?

4. What does Murray mean when he says, ''Writers must learn to be their own best enemy''(4)?

5. What does Murray gain from frequently quoting professional writers? What seems to be the common message from the professionals?

6. How do professionals view first drafts? Why is it important for you to adopt a similar attitude?

7. What does Murray see as the connection between reading and writing? How does reading help the writer?

8. When, according to Murray, does revision end? Why do you suppose he concludes his essay in mid-sentence?

THE QUALITIES OF
GOOD WRITING

Jacqueline Berke

Jacqueline Berke teaches writing at Drew University in New Jersey and is the author of the textbook Twenty Questions for the Writer. *In the following article, drawn from the third edition of that text, Berke describes the basics of good, memorable writing.*

Even before you set out, you come prepared by instinct and intuition to make certain judgments about what is "good." Take the following familiar sentence, for example: "I know not what course others may take, but as for me, give me liberty or give me death." Do you suppose this thought of Patrick Henry's would have come ringing down through the centuries if he had expressed this sentiment not in one tight, rhythmical sentence but as follows:

> It would be difficult, if not impossible, to predict on the basis of my limited information as to the predilections of the public, what the citizenry at large will regard as action commensurate with the present provocation, but after arduous consideration I personally feel so intensely and irrevocably committed to the position of social, political, and economic independence, that rather than submit to foreign despotic control which is anathema to me, I will make the ultimate sacrifice of which humanity is capable—under the aegis of personal honor, ideological conviction, and existential commitment, I will sacrifice my own mortal existence.

How does this rambling, "high-flown" paraphrase measure up to the bold "Give me liberty or give me death"? Who will deny that something is "happening" in Patrick Henry's rousing challenge that not only fails to happen in the paraphrase but is actually negated there? Would you bear with this long-winded, pompous speaker to the end? If you were to judge this statement strictly on its rhetoric (its choice and arrangement of words), you might aptly call it more boring than brave. Perhaps a plainer version will work better:

> Liberty is a very important thing for a person to have. Most people—at least the people I've talked to or that other people have told me about—know this and

462

therefore are very anxious to preserve their liberty. Of course I can't be absolutely sure about what other folks are going to do in this present crisis, what with all these threats and everything, but I've made up my mind that I'm going to fight because liberty is really a very important thing to me; at least that's the way I feel about it.

This flat, "homely" prose, weighted down with the Flaubert called "fatty deposits," is grammatical enough. As in the pompous paraphrase, every verb agrees with its subject, every comma is in its proper place; nonetheless it lacks the qualities that make a statement—of one sentence or one hundred pages—pungent, vital, moving, memorable.

Let us isolate these qualities and describe them briefly. . . . The first quality of good writing is *economy*. In an appropriately slender volume entitled *The Elements of Style,* authors William Strunk and E. B. White stated concisely the case for economy: "A sentence should contain no unnecessary words, a paragraph no unnecessary sentences, for the same reason that a drawing should have no unnecessary lines and a machine no unnecessary parts. This requires not that the writer make all his sentences short or that he avoid all detail . . . but that every word tell." In other words, economical writing is *efficient* and *aesthetically satisfying.* While it makes a minimum demand on the energy and patience of readers, it returns to them a maximum of sharply compressed meaning. You should accept this as your basic responsibility as a writer: that you inflict no unnecessary words on your readers—just as a dentist inflicts no unnecessary pain, a lawyer no unnecessary risk. Economical writing avoids strain and at the same time promotes pleasure by producing a sense of form and right proportion, a sense of words that fit the ideas that they embody—with not a line of "deadwood" to dull the reader's attention, not an extra, useless phrase to clog the free flow of ideas, one following swiftly and clearly upon another.

Another basic quality of good writing is *simplicity.* Here again this does not require that you make all your sentences primerlike or that you reduce complexities to bare bone, but rather that you avoid embellishment or embroidery. The natural, unpretentious style is best. But, paradoxically, simplicity or naturalness does not come naturally. By the time we are old enough to write, most of us have grown so self-conscious that we stiffen, sometimes to the point of rigidity, when we are called upon to make a statement in speech or in writing. It is easy to offer the kindly advice "Be yourself," but many people do not feel like themselves when they take a pencil in hand or sit down at a typewriter. Thus during the early days of the Second World War, when air raids were feared in New York City, and blackouts were instituted, an anonymous writer—probably a young civil service worker at City Hall—produced and distributed to stores throughout the city the following poster:

Illumination
is Required
to be
Extinguished
on These Premises
After Nightfall

What this meant, of course, was simply "Lights Out After Dark"; but   6
apparently that direct imperative—clear and to the point—did not sound
"official" enough; so the writer resorted to long Latinate words and involved syntax (note the awkward passives "*is* Required" and "*to be*
Extinguished") to establish a tone of dignity and authority. In contrast,
how beautifully simple are the words of the translators of the King James
Version of the Bible, who felt no need for flourish, flamboyance, or gran-
diloquence. The Lord did not loftily or bombastically proclaim that universal illumination was required to be instantaneously installed. Simply but
majestically "God said, Let there be light: and there was light. . . . And
God called the light Day, and the darkness he called Night."

Most memorable declarations have been spare and direct. Abraham   7
Lincoln and John Kennedy seemed to "speak to each other across the span
of a century," notes French author André Maurois, for both men embodied
noble themes in eloquently simple terms. Said Lincoln in his second Inaugural Address: "With malice towards none, with charity for all, with
firmness in the right as God gives us the right, let us strive on to finish the
work we are in. . . ." One hundred years later President Kennedy made
his Inaugural dedication: "With a good conscience our only sure reward,
with history the final judge of our deeds, let us go forth to lead the land we
love. . . ."

A third fundamental element of good writing is *clarity*. Some people   8
question whether it is always possible to be clear; after all, certain ideas are
inherently complicated and inescapably difficult. True enough. But the
responsible writer recognizes that writing should not add to the complications nor increase the difficulty; it should not set up an additional roadblock
to understanding. Indeed, the German philosopher Wittgenstein went so
far as to say that "whatever can be said can be said clearly." If you
understand your own idea and want to convey it to others, you are obliged
to render it in clear, orderly, readable, understandable prose—else why
bother writing in the first place? Actually, obscure writers are usually
confused, uncertain of what they want to say or what they mean; they have
not yet completed that process of thinking through and reasoning into the
heart of the subject.

Suffice it to say here that whatever the topic, whatever the occasion,   9
expository writing should be readable, informative, and, wherever possible, engaging. At its best it may even be poetic, as Nikos Kazantzakis

suggests in *Zorba the Greek,* where he draws an analogy between good prose and a beautiful landscape:

> To my mind the Cretan countryside resembled good prose, carefully ordered, sober, free from superfluous ornament, powerful and restrained. It expressed all that was necessary with the greatest economy. It had no flippancy nor artifice about it. It said what it had to say with a manly austerity. But between the severe lines one could discern an unexpected sensitiveness and tenderness; in the sheltered hollows the lemon and orange trees perfumed the air, and from the vastness of the sea emanated an inexhaustible poetry.

Even in technical writing, where the range of styles is necessarily limited (and poetry is neither possible nor appropriate), you must always be aware of "the reader over your shoulder." Take such topics as how to follow postal regulations for overseas mail, how to change oil in an engine, how to produce aspirin from salicylic acid. Here are technical expository descriptions that defy a memorable turn of phrase; here is writing that is of necessity cut and dried, dispassionate, and bloodless. But it need not be difficult, tedious, confusing, or dull to those who want to find out about mailing letters, changing oil, or making aspirin. Those who seek such information should have reasonably easy access to it, which means that written instructions should be clear, simple, spare, direct, and most of all, *human:* for no matter how technical a subject, all writing is done *for* human beings *by* human beings. Writing, in other words, like language itself, is a strictly human enterprise. Machines may stamp letters, measure oil, and convert acids, but only human beings talk and write about these procedures so that other human beings may better understand them. It is always appropriate, therefore, to be human in one's statement. 10

Part of this humanity must stem from your sense of who your readers are. You must assume a "rhetorical stance." Indeed this is a fundamental principle of rhetoric: *nothing should ever be written in a vacuum.* You should identify your audience, hypothetical or real, so that you may speak to them in an appropriate voice. A student, for example, should never "just write," without visualizing a definite group of readers—fellow students, perhaps, or the educated community at large (intelligent nonspecialists). Without such definite readers in mind, you cannot assume a suitable and appropriate relationship to your material, your purpose, and your audience. A proper rhetorical stance, in other words, requires that you have an active sense of the following: 11

1. Who you are as a writer.
2. Who your readers are.
3. Why you are addressing them and on what occasion.
4. Your relationship to your subject matter.
5. How you want your readers to relate to the subject matter.

QUESTIONS FOR STUDY AND DISCUSSION

1. Berke says there is more to good writing than good grammar. What are the qualities she considers basic to good writing? What additional quality does she claim is present in writing at its best?

2. Berke says the best style is a natural unpretentious one. Paradoxically, she adds, such a style does not come "naturally." Why not? In your experience is it difficult to write the way you talk?

3. According to Berke, what two writers does French author André Maurois cite as embodying the qualities of memorable writing? Reread the work of these two authors presented in a previous section of this book (pp. 161–166). Do you agree with Maurois's assessment as quoted by Berke? Can you offer other examples of this kind of writing?

4. What, according to Berke, does obscure writing reveal about an author?

5. In paragraph 10, Berke insists that even technical writing has to be "human." What does she intend the word *human* to mean in this context?

6. Berke gets to the point of her essay in her first paragraph by the use of comparison and contrast. (Glossary: *Comparison and Contrast*) What is she comparing? How does Berke use this device throughout her essay to support her point? Explain.

7. Berke's paragraphs are long and filled with information. What kinds of information does she include in each? In your opinion, does Berke herself sacrifice clarity and simplicity by using long paragraphs? Would short, punchier paragraphs have served her point better? Why or why not?

8. In paragraph 9, Berke includes an analogy, written by Nikos Kazantzakis, between good prose and a beautiful countryside. In your opinion, how effective is the analogy? Can you think of an analogy of your own for good prose?

9. Berke uses several metaphors in her article. Choose a couple of these, explain them, and discuss how well they work.

WRITING ASSIGNMENTS FOR "WRITING WELL: USING LANGUAGE RESPONSIBLY"

1. Each of the essays in this section is concerned with the importance of writing well, of using language responsibly. Write an essay in which you discuss the common themes that are emphasized in two or more of the essays.

2. Write an essay in which you discuss the proposition that honesty, while it does not guarantee good writing, is a prerequisite of good writing.

3. Philosopher Ludwig Wittgenstein once said, "The limits of my language are the limits of my world." What do you think he meant? Write an essay in which you support Wittgenstein's generalization with carefully selected examples from your own experience.

4. In her essay, Jacqueline Berke says a writer has to identify his or her audience "so that you may speak to them in an appropriate voice." Choose a topic close to your heart, such as the benefits of living away from home or how well your diet is going. Write an essay designed for reading by your best friend. Now write an essay on the same subject to be read by your instructor. How does your voice differ from essay to essay? Which voice comes more easily? Why?

5. We are often told that writing is an important means of communication. But the more writing we do, the more we realize that writing is important in other ways as well. Write an essay in which you discuss the particular reasons why you value writing.

6. Some of our most pressing social issues depend for their solutions upon a clear statement of the problem and the precise definition of critical terms. For example, the increasing number of people kept alive by machines has brought worldwide attention to the legal and medical definitions of the word *death*. Debates continue about the meanings of other controversial words, such as *morality, minority* (ethnic), *alcoholism, life* (as in the abortion issue), *pornography, kidnapping, drugs, censorship, remedial, insanity, monopoly* (business), and *literacy*. Select one of these words, and write an essay in which you discuss the problems associated with the term and its definition.

RHETORICAL TABLE OF CONTENTS

The essays in *LANGUAGE AWARENESS* are arranged in nine sections according to their subjects. The following alternate table of contents, which is certainly not exhaustive, classifies the essays according to the rhetorical strategies they exemplify.

ANALOGY

Bergen Evans, "The Power of Words"   **29**
Donald Hall, "Writing Honestly"   **441**

ARGUMENT AND PERSUASION

Edwin Newman, "Language on the Skids"   **59**
Bergen Evans, "The Power of Words"   **29**
Harvey Daniels, "Is There Really a Language Crisis?"   **63**
S.I. Hayakawa, "Why English Should Be Our Official Language"   **71**
Alice Roy, "The English Only Movement"   **75**
Dorothy Z. Seymour, "Black Children, Black Speech"   **84**
Rachel Jones, "What's Wrong with Black English"   **93**
George Orwell, "Politics and the English Language"   **111**
John F. Kennedy, "Inaugural Address"   **161**
The New York Times, "The Ronald Reagan Basic 1984 Campaign Speech"   **167**
Eugene R. August, "Real Men Don't: Anti-Male Bias in English"   **289**
Cyra McFadden, "In Defense of Gender"   **320**
Stephen King, "Now, You Take 'Bambi' or 'Snow White'—*That's* Scary!"   **406**

CAUSE AND EFFECT ANALYSIS

Donald V. Mehus, "Contemporary American Graffiti"   **37**
Edward T. Hall and Mildred Read Hall, "The Sounds of Silence"   **42**
Harvey Daniels, "Is There Really a Language Crisis?"   **63**
Dorothy Z. Seymour, "Black Children, Black Speech"   **84**
George Orwell, "Politics and the English Language"   **111**
Jay Rosen, "The Presence of the Word in TV Advertising"   **199**
Consumers Union, "It's Natural! It's Organic! Or Is It?"   **207**

Barbara Lawrence, "Four-Letter Words Can Hurt You"   354
Stephen Hilgartner, Richard C. Bell, and Rory O'Connor,
  "The Language of Nuclear War Strategists"   358
Neil Postman, "Now . . . This"   373
Herbert J. Gans, "The Message Behind the News"   385
Consumer Reports, "Advertising in Disguise: How the Hid-
  den Hand of a Corporate Ghostwriter Can Turn a News
  Report into a Commercial"   412

COMPARISON AND CONTRAST

Paul Roberts, "A Brief History of English"   17
Dorothy Z. Seymour, "Black Children, Black Speech"   84
Richard Rodriquez, "Caught Between Two Languages"   97
Newman P. Birk and Genevieve B. Birk, "Selection, Slant-
  ing, and Charged Language"   125
John Pfeiffer, "Girl Talk-Boy Talk,"   325
Robert MacNeil, "Pigskin English"   420

DEFINITION

Donald V. Mehus, "Contemporary American Graffiti"   37
Newman P. Birk and Genevieve B. Birk, "Selection, Slant-
  ing, and Charged Language"   125
Stuart Chase, "Gobbledygook"   138
Donna Woolfolk Cross, "Propaganda: How Not to Be Bam-
  boozled"   149
Consumers Union, "It's Natural! It's Organic! Or Is It?"   207
S. I. Hayakawa, "Words with Built-in Judgments"   259
William Raspberry, "What It Means to Be Black"   269
Neil Postman, "Euphemism"   345
Barbara Lawrence, "Four-Letter Words Can Hurt You"   354
William Zinsser, "Simplicity"   451
Jacqueline Berke, "The Qualities of Good Writing"   462

DESCRIPTION

Paul Roberts, "A Brief History of English"   17
Dorothy Z. Seymour, "Black Children, Black Speech"   84
Ron Rosenbaum, "The Hard Sell"   188

DIVISION AND CLASSIFICATION

Donna Woolfolk Cross, "Propaganda: How Not to Be Bam-
  boozled"   149
Jeffrey Schrank, "The Language of Advertising Claims"   179
Jib Fowles, "Advertising's Fifteen Basic Appeals"   216
Hugh Rank, "Intensify/Downplay"   235
Alleen Pace Nilsen, "Sexism in English"   277
Catharine T. Stimpson, "The 'F' Word"   334
S. I. Hayakawa, "Verbal Taboo"   350

Stephen Hilgartner, Richard C. Bell, and Rory O'Connor,
"The Language of Nuclear War Strategists"   358

EXAMPLE AND ILLUSTRATION
Edwin Newman, "Language on the Skids"   59
Bergen Evans, "The Power of Words"   29
Donald V. Mehus, "Contemporary American Graffiti"   37
Edward T. Hall and Mildred Read Hall, "The Sounds of
   Silence"   42
Rachel Jones, "What's Wrong with Black English"   93
Newman P. Birk and Genevieve B. Birk, "Selection, Slant-
   ing, and Charged Language"   125
Stuart Chase, "Gobbledygook"   138
John F. Kennedy, "Inaugural Address"   161
The New York Times, "The Ronald Reagan Basic 1984
   Campaign Speech"   167
Jeffrey Schrank, "The Language of Advertising Claims"   179
Ron Rosenbaum, "The Hard Sell"   188
Jay Rosen, "The Presence of the Word in TV Advertising"   199
Edwin Newman, "Gettin' Rich by Droppin' the G"   204
Consumers Union, "It's Natural! It's Organic! Or Is It?"   207
Jib Fowles, "Advertising's Fifteen Basic Appeals"   216
Gordon Allport, "The Language of Prejudice"   247
Charles F. Berlitz, "The Etymology of the International
   Insult"   264
William Raspberry, "What It Means to Be Black"   269
Alleen Pace Nilsen, "Sexism in English"   227
Eugene R. August, "Real Men Don't: Anti-Male Bias in
   English"   289
Casey Miller and Kate Swift, "One Small Step for Gen-
   kind"   307
Jack Rosenthal, "Gender Benders"   303
Neil Postman, "Euphemism"   345
S.I. Hayakawa, "Verbal Taboo"   350
Nat Hentoff, "When Nice People Burn Books"   398
William Zinsser, "Simplicity"   451
Jacqueline Berke, "The Qualities of Good Writing"   460

NARRATION
Malcolm X, "Coming to an Awareness of Language"   9
Helen Keller, "The Day Language Came into My Life"   13
Paul Roberts, "A Brief History of English"   17
Richard Rodriquez, "Caught Between Two Languages"   97

PROCESS ANALYSIS
Stuart Chase, "Gobbledygook"   138
Gordon Allport, "The Language of Prejudice"   247

Consumer Reports, "Advertising in Disguise: How the Hidden Hand of a Corporate Ghostwriter Can Turn a News Report into a Commercial"   **412**
Paul Roberts, "How to Say Nothing in 500 Words"   **429**
Donald Hall, "Writing Honestly"   **441**
Linda Flower, "Writing for an Audience"   **447**
Donald M. Murray, "The Maker's Eye: Revising Your Own Manuscripts"   **457**

GLOSSARY OF
RHETORICAL TERMS

Abstract   See *Concrete/Abstract.*

Allusion   An allusion is a passing reference to a familiar person, place, or thing drawn from history, the Bible, mythology, or literature. An allusion is an economical way for a writer to capture the essence of an idea, atmosphere, emotion, or historical era, as in "The scandal was his Watergate," or "He saw himself as a modern Job," or "Everyone there held those truths to be self-evident." An allusion should be familiar to the reader, for if it is not, it will add nothing to the meaning.

Analogy   Analogy is a special form of comparison in which the writer explains something complex or unfamiliar by comparing it to something familiar: "A transmission line is simply a pipeline for electricity. In the case of a water pipeline, more water will flow through the pipe as water pressure increases. The same is true of a transmission line for electricity." When a subject is unobservable, complex, or abstract—when it is so generally unfamiliar that readers may have trouble understanding it—analogy is particularly useful.

Argument   Argument is one of the four basic types of prose. (Narration, description, and exposition are the other three.) To argue is to attempt to convince a reader to agree with a point of view, to make a given decision, or to pursue a particular course of action. Logical argument is based upon reasonable explanations and appeals to the reader's intelligence. See also *Persuasion, Logical Fallacies, Deduction,* and *Induction.*

Attitude   A writer's attitude reflects his or her opinion of a subject. For example, a writer can think very positively or very negatively about a subject. In most cases the writer's attitude falls somewhere between these two extremes. See also *Tone.*

Audience   An audience is the intended readership for a piece of writing. For example, the readers of a national weekly news magazine come from all walks of life and have diverse opinions, attitudes, and educational experiences. In contrast, the readership for an organic chemistry journal is made up of people whose interests and educations are quite similar. The essays in this book are intended for general readers, intelligent people who may lack specific information about the subjects being discussed.

Beginnings/Endings   A *beginning* is that sentence, group of sentences, or section that introduces the essay. Good beginnings usually identify the thesis or controlling idea, attempt to interest the reader, and establish a tone. Some effective ways in which writers begin essays include (1) telling an anecdote that illustrates the thesis, (2) providing a controversial statement or opinion that engages the reader's interest, (3) presenting startling statistics or facts, (4) defining a term that is central to the discussion that follows, (5) asking thought-provoking questions, (6) providing a quotation that illustrates the thesis, (7) referring to a current event that helps to establish the thesis, or (8) showing the significance of the subject or stressing its importance to the reader.

An *ending* is that sentence or group of sentences that brings an essay to closure. Good endings are purposeful and well planned. Endings satisfy readers when they are the natural outgrowths of the essays themselves and give the readers a sense of finality or completion. Good essays do not simply stop; they conclude.

Cause and Effect Analysis   Cause and effect analysis is one of the types of exposition. (Process analysis, definition, division and classification, and comparison and contrast are the others.) Cause and effect analysis answers the question *why*. It explains the reasons for an occurrence or the consequences of an action. Whenever a question asks *why*, answering it will require discovering a *cause* or series of causes for a particular *effect*; whenever a question asks *what if*, its answer will point out the effect or effects that can result from a particular cause.

Classification   See *Division and Classification*.

Cliché   A cliché is an expression that has become ineffective through overuse. Expressions such as *quick as a flash, dry as dust, jump for joy,* and *slow as molasses* are all clichés. Writers normally avoid such trite expressions and seek instead to express themselves in fresh and forceful language. See also *Figures of Speech*.

Coherence   Coherence is a quality of good writing that results when all sentences, paragraphs, and longer divisions of an essay are naturally connected. Coherent writing is achieved through (1) a logical sequence of ideas (arranged in chronological order, spatial order, order of importance, or some other appropriate order), (2) the thoughtful repetition of key words and ideas, (3) a pace suitable for your topic and your reader, and (4) the use of transitional words and expressions. Coherence should not be confused with unity. See also *Unity* and *Transitions*.

Colloquial Expressions   A colloquial expression is characteristic of or appropriate to spoken language or to writing that seeks its effect. Colloquial expressions are informal, as *chem, gym, come up with, be at loose ends, won't,* and *photo* illustrate. Thus, colloquial expressions are acceptable in formal writing only if they are used purposefully.

Comparison and Contrast   Comparison and contrast make up one of the types of exposition. (Process analysis, definition, division and classification, and cause and effect analysis are the others.) In comparison and contrast, the writer points out the similarities and differences between two or more subjects in the same class or category. The function of any comparison and contrast is to clarify—to reach some conclusion about the items being compared and contrasted. An effective comparison and contrast will not dwell on obvious similarities or differences; it will tell readers something significant that they may not already know.

Conclusions See *Beginnings/Endings*

Concrete/Abstract A concrete word names a specific object, person, place, or action that can be directly perceived by the senses: *car, bread, building, book, John F. Kennedy, Chicago,* or *hiking.* An abstract word, in contrast, refers to general qualities, conditions, ideas, actions, or relationships which cannot be directly perceived by the senses: *bravery, dedication, excellence, anxiety, stress, thinking,* or *hatred.*

Although writers must use both concrete and abstract language, good writers avoid too many abstract words. Instead, they rely on concrete words to define and illustrate abstractions. Because concrete words affect the senses, they are easily comprehended by a reader.

Connotation/Denotation Both connotation and denotation refer to the meanings of words. Denotation is the dictionary meaning of a word, the literal meaning. Connotation, on the other hand, is the implied or suggested meaning of a word. For example, the denotation of *lamb* is "a young sheep." The connotations of lamb are numerous: *gentle, docile, weak, peaceful, blessed, sacrificial, blood, spring, frisky, pure, innocent,* and so on. Good writers are sensitive to both the denotations and the connotations of words and use these meanings to advantage in their writing.

Deduction Deduction is the process of reasoning from stated premises to a conclusion that follows necessarily. This form of reasoning moves from the general to the specific. See also *Syllogism.*

Definition Definition is one of the types of exposition. (Process analysis, division and classification, comparison and contrast, and cause and effect analysis are the others.) Definition is a statement of the meaning of a word. A definition may be either brief or extended, part of an essay or an entire essay itself.

Denotation See *Connotation/Denotation.*

Description Description is one of the four basic types of prose. (Narration, exposition, and argument are the other three.) Description tells how a person, place, or thing is perceived by the five senses. Objective description reports these sensory qualities factually, whereas subjective description gives the writer's interpretation of them.

Diction Diction refers to a writer's choice and use of words. Good diction is precise and appropriate—the words mean exactly what the writer intends, and the words are well suited to the writer's subject, intended audience, and purpose in writing. The word-conscious writer knows that there are differences among *aged, old,* and *elderly; blue, navy,* and *azure;* and *disturbed, angry,* and *irritated.* Furthermore, this writer knows in which situation to use each word. See also *Connotation/Denotation.*

Division and Classification Division and classification make up one of the types of exposition. (Process analysis, definition, comparison and contrast, and cause and effect analysis are the others.) Division involves breaking down a single large unit into smaller subunits, or separating a group of items into discrete categories. Classification, on the other hand, involves arranging or sorting people, places, or things into categories according to their differing characteristics, thus making them more manageable for the writer and more understandable for the reader. Division, then, takes apart, while classification groups together.

Although the two processes can operate separately, most often they work hand in hand.

Endings   See *Beginnings/Endings.*

Essay   An essay is a relatively short piece of nonfiction in which the writer attempts to make one or more closely related points. A good essay is purposeful, informative, and well organized.

Evidence   Evidence is the data on which a judgment or argument is based or by which proof or probability is established. Evidence usually takes the form of statistics, facts, names, examples or illustrations, and opinions of authorities.

Examples   Examples illustrate a larger idea or represent something of which they are a part. An example is a basic means of developing or clarifying an idea. Furthermore, examples enable writers to show and not simply to tell readers what they mean. The terms *example* and *illustration* are sometimes used interchangeably. An example may be anything from a statistic to a story; it may be stated in a few words or go on for several pages. What is required of an example is that it be closely *relevant* to the idea or generalization it is meant to illustrate. To be most effective, an example should be *representative.* The story it tells or the fact it presents should be typical of many others that readers are sure to be familiar with.

Exposition   Exposition is one of the four basic types of prose. (Narration, description, and argument are the other three.) The purpose of exposition is to clarify, explain, and inform. The methods of exposition are process analysis, definition, division and classification, comparison and contrast, and cause and effect analysis. For a detailed discussion of each of these methods of exposition, see the appropriate entries in this glossary.

Fallacy   See *Logical Fallacies.*

Figures of Speech   Figures of speech are brief, imaginative comparisons which highlight the similarities between things that are basically dissimilar. They make writing vivid and interesting and therefore more memorable. The most common figures of speech are:

Simile: An implicit comparison introduced by *like* or *as.* "The fighter's hands were like stone."

Metaphor: An implied comparison which uses one thing as the equivalent of another. "All the world's a stage."

Personification: A special kind of simile or metaphor in which human traits are assigned to an inanimate object. "The engine coughed and then stopped."

Idiom   An idiom is a word or phrase that is used habitually with a particular meaning in a language. The meaning of an idiom is not always readily apparent to nonnative speakers of that language. For example, *catch cold, hold a job, make up your mind,* and *give them a hand* are all idioms in English.

Illustration   See *Examples.*

Induction   Induction is the process of reasoning to a conclusion about all members of a class through an examination of only a few members of the class. This form of reasoning moves from a set of specific examples to a general statement or principle. As long as the evidence is accurate, pertinent, complete, and sufficient to represent the assertion, the conclusion of the inductive argument can be regarded as valid; if, however, you can spot inaccuracies in the evidence or point to contrary evidence, you have good reason to doubt the assertion as it stands. Inductive reasoning is the most common of argumentative structures. See also *Deduction*.

Introductions   See *Beginnings/Endings*.

Irony   The use of words to suggest something different from their literal meaning. A writer can use irony to establish a special relationship with the reader and to add an extra dimension or twist to the meaning.

Jargon   See *Technical Language*.

Logical Fallacies   A logical fallacy is an error in reasoning that renders an argument invalid. Some of the more common logical fallacies are:

Oversimplification: The tendency to provide simple solutions to complex problems. "The reason we have inflation today is that OPEC has unreasonably raised the price of oil."

Non sequitur ("It does not follow"): An inference or conclusion that does not follow from established premises or evidence. "It was the best movie I saw this year, and it should get an Academy Award."

Post hoc, ergo propter hoc ("After this, therefore because of this"): Confusing chance or coincidence with causation. Because one event comes after another one, it does not necessarily mean that the first event caused the second. "I won't say I caught cold at the hockey game, but I certainly didn't have it before I went there."

Begging the question: Assuming in a premise that which needs to be proven. "If American autoworkers built a better product, foreign auto sales would not be so high."

False analogy: Making a misleading analogy between logically unconnected ideas. "He was a brilliant basketball player; therefore, there's no question in my mind that he will be a fine coach."

Either/or thinking: The tendency to see an issue as having only two sides. "Used car salesmen are either honest or crooked."

Logical Reasoning   See *Deduction* and *Induction*.

Metaphor   See *Figures of Speech*.

Narration   One of the four basic types of prose. (Description, exposition, and argument are the other three.) To narrate is to tell a story, to tell what happened. While narration is most often used in fiction, it is also important in nonfiction, either by itself or in conjunction with other types of prose. A good narrative essay has four essential features. The first is *context*: the writer makes clear when the action happened, where it happened, and to whom. The second is *point of view*: the writer establishes and maintains a consistent relationship to the action, either as a participant or as a reporter simply looking on. The third is *selection of detail*: the writer carefully chooses what to include, focusing on those actions and details that are most important to the story while merely mentioning or actually eliminating others. The fourth is *organization*: the writer organizes the events of the narrative into an appropriate sequence, often a strict chronology with a clear beginning, middle, and end.

Objective/Subjective   Objective writing is factual and impersonal, whereas subjective writing, sometimes called impressionistic, relies heavily on personal interpretation.

Organization   In writing, organization is the thoughtful arrangement and presentation of one's points or ideas. Narration is often organized chronologically. Exposition may be organized from simplest to most complex or from most familiar to least familiar. Argument may be organized from least important to most important. There is no single correct pattern of organization for a given piece of writing, but good writers are careful to discover an order of presentation suitable for their subject, their audience, and their purpose.

Paradox   A paradox is a seemingly contradictory statement that may nonetheless be true. For example, *we little know what we have until we lose it* is a paradoxical statement.

Paragraph   The paragraph, the single most important unit of thought in an essay, is a series of closely related sentences. These sentences adequately develop the central or controlling idea of the paragraph. This central or controlling idea, usually stated in a topic sentence, is necessarily related to the purpose of the whole composition. A well-written paragraph has several distinguishing characteristics: a clearly stated or implied topic sentence, adequate development, unity, coherence, and an appropriate organizational strategy.

Personification   See *Figures of Speech.*

Persuasion   Persuasion, or persuasive argument, is an attempt to convince readers to agree with a point of view, to make a given decision, or to pursue a particular course of action. Persuasion heavily appeals to the emotions whereas logical argument does not. See *Argument, Induction,* and *Deduction.*

Point of View   Point of view refers to the grammatical person of the speaker in an essay. For example, a first-person point of view uses the pronoun *I* and is commonly found in autobiography and the personal essay; a third-person point of view uses the pronouns *he, she,* or *it* and is commonly found in objective writing.

Process Analysis   Process analysis is a type of (Definition, division and classification, comparison and contrast, and cause and effect analysis are others.) Process analysis answers the question *how* and explains how something works or gives step-by-step directions for doing something.

Purpose   Purpose is what the writer wants to accomplish in a particular piece of writing. Purposeful writing seeks to *relate* or *tell* (narration), to *describe* (description), to *explain* (process analysis, definition, division and classification, comparison and contrast, and cause and effect analysis), or to *convince* (argument).

Rhetorical Questions   A rhetorical question is asked but requires no answer from the reader. "When will nuclear proliferation end?" is such a question. Writers use rhetorical questions to introduce topics they plan to discuss or to emphasize important points.

Simile   See *Figures of Speech.*

Slang   Slang is the unconventional, very informal language of particular subgroups in our culture. Slang, such as *zonk, coke, split, rap, cop,* and *stoned,* is acceptable in formal writing only if it is used purposefully.

Specific/General   General words name groups or classes of objects, qualities, or actions. Specific words, on the other hand, name individual objects, qualities, or actions within a class or group. To some extent the terms *general* and *specific* are relative. For example, *dessert* is a class of things. *Pie,* however, is more specific than *dessert* but more general than *pecan pie* or *chocolate cream pie.*

Good writing judiciously balances the general with the specific. Writing with too many general words is likely to be dull and lifeless. General words do not create vivid responses in the reader's mind as concrete specific words can. On the other hand, writing that relies exclusively on specific words may lack focus and direction, the control that more general statements provide.

Style   Style is the individual manner in which a writer expresses his or her ideas. Style is created by the author's particular selection of words, construction of sentences, and arrangement of ideas.

Subjective   See *Objective/Subjective.*

Syllogism   A syllogism is an argument that utilizes deductive reasoning and consists of a major premise, a minor premise, and a conclusion. For example,

All trees that lose leaves are deciduous. (major premise)

Maple trees lose their leaves. (minor premise)

Therefore, maple trees are deciduous. (conclusion)

See also *Deduction.*

Symbol   A symbol is a person, place, or thing that represents something beyond itself. For example, the eagle is a symbol of America, and the bear, a symbol of Russia.

Syntax   Syntax refers to the way in which words are arranged to form phrases, clauses, and sentences as well as to the grammatical relationship among the words themselves.

Technical Language   Technical language is the special vocabulary of a trade or profession. Writers who use technical language do so with an awareness of their audiences. If the audience is a group of peers, technical language may be used freely. If the audience is a more general one, technical language should be used sparingly and carefully so as not to sacrifice clarity. Technical language that is used only to impress, hide the truth, or cover insecurities is termed *jargon* and is not condoned. See *Diction.*

Thesis   A thesis is a statement of the main idea of an essay. Also known as the controlling idea, a thesis may sometimes be implied rather than stated directly.

Tone   Tone is the manner in which a writer relates to an audience, the "tone of voice" used to address readers. Tone may be described as friendly, serious, distant, angry, cheerful, bitter, cynical, enthusiastic, morbid, resentful, warm, playful, and so forth. A particular tone results from a writer's diction, sentence structure, purpose, and attitude toward the subject. See also *Attitude.*

Topic Sentence   The topic sentence states the central idea of a paragraph and thus limits and controls the subject of the paragraph. Although the topic sentence normally appears at the beginning of the paragraph, it may appear at any other point, particularly if the writer is trying to create a special effect. Also see *Paragraph.*

Transitions   Transitions are words or phrases that link sentences, paragraphs, and larger units of a composition in order to achieve coherence. These devices include parallelism, pronoun references, conjunctions, and the repetition of key ideas, as well as the many unconventional transitional expressions such as *more-*

over, on the other hand, in addition, in contrast, and *therefore.* Also see *Coherence.*

Unity   Unity is achieved in an essay when all the words, sentences, and paragraphs contribute to its thesis. The elements of a unified essay do not distract the reader. Instead, they all harmoniously support a single idea or purpose.

Acknowledgments (continued)

"Is There Really a Language Crisis?" from *Famous Last Words: The American Language Crisis Reconsidered*, by Harvey A. Daniels. Copyright © 1983 by Southern Illinois University Board of Trustees. Reprinted by permission of Southern Illinois University Press.

"Why English Should Be Our Official Language" by S.I. Hayakawa from the May 1987 issue of *The Education Digest*. Reprinted by permission.

"The English Only Movement" by Alice Roy first appeared in *The Writing Instructor*, Fall, 1987. Permission to reprint granted by *The Writing Instructor*, 1989.

"Black Children, Black Speech" by Dorothy Z. Seymour. Reprinted by permission of Commonweal Foundation.

"What's Wrong with Black English" by Rachel L. Jones. Reprinted by permission of the author. Rachel L. Jones is a feature writer for the St. Petersburg Times.

"Caught Between Two Languages" from *Hunger of Memory* by Richard Rodriguez. Copyright © 1981 by Richard Rodriguez. Reprinted by permission of David R. Godine, Publisher, Boston, MA.

III THE LANGUAGE OF POLITICS AND PROPAGANDA

"Politics and the English Language" by George Orwell. Copyright © 1946 by Sonia Brownell Orwell and renewed 1974 by Sonia Orwell. Reprinted from *Shooting an Elephant and Other Essays* by George Orwell by permission of Harcourt Brace Jovanovich, Inc.

"Selection, Slanting, and Charged Language" from *Understanding and Using English* by Newman P. Birk and Genevieve B. Birk. Reprinted with permission of Macmillan Publishing Company from *Understanding and Using English*. Copyright © 1972 by Macmillan Publishing Company.

"Gobbledygook" from *Power of Words*, copyright © 1954, 1982 by Stuart Chase. Reprinted by permission of Harcourt Brace Jovanovich, Inc.

"Propaganda: How Not To Be Bamboozled" by Donna Woolfolk Cross. From *Speaking of Words: A Language Reader*. Reprinted by permission of Donna Woolfolk Cross.

"The Ronald Reagan Basic 1984 Campaign Speech." Copyright © 1984 by The New York Times Company. Reprinted by permission.

IV ADVERTISING AND LANGUAGE

"The Language of Advertising Claims" by Jeffrey Schrank. From *Media and Methods*, March 1974. Reprinted by permission.

"The Hard Sell" by Ron Rosenbaum from *Mother Jones*, December 1981. Copyright © 1981 by Ron Rosenbaum. Reprinted by permission of the author.

"The Presence of the Word in TV Advertising" by Jay Rosen. Reprinted from *ETC*. Volume 44, Number 2 by permission of the International Society for General Semantics.

"Gettin' Rich by Droppin' the G" by Edwin Newman. Reprinted by permission of Warner Books/New York. From *I Must Say*. Copyright © 1988 by Edwin Newman.

"It's Natural! It's Organic! Or Is It?" from Consumers Union. Copyright 1980 by Consumers Union of United States, Inc., Mount Vernon, N.Y. 10553. Introduction and Part I reprinted by permission from *Consumer Reports*, July 1980.

"Advertising's Fifteen Basic Appeals" by Jib Fowles. Reprinted from *ETC*. Volume 39, Number 3 by permission of the International Society for General Semantics.

"Intensify/Downplay" by Hugh Rank, from *Teaching about Doublespeak*, edited by Daniel Dietrich (NCTE, 1976). Copyright © 1976 by the National Council of Teachers of English. Reprinted by permission of the publisher and the author. "Intensify/Downplay" schema, copyright © 1976, by Hugh Rank. Reprinted by permission of the author.

V. PREJUDICE AND STEREOTYPES

"The Language of Prejudice" by Gordon Allport. From *The Nature of Prejudice*, copyright © 1979, Addison-Wesley Publishing Co., Inc., Reading, Massachusetts. Reprinted with permission.

a Commercial.'' Copyright 1986 by Consumers Union of United States, Inc., Mount Vernon, NY 10553. Reprinted by permission from *Consumer Reports*, March 1986.

"Pigskin English'' by Robert MacNeil. From *Sport* Magazine, February 1987. Reprinted by permission from Sport Magazine, Copyright © 1987.

IX WRITING WELL: USING LANGUAGE RESPONSIBLY

"How to Say Nothing in 500 Words'' from *Understanding English* by Paul Roberts. Copyright © 1958 by Paul Roberts. Reprinted by permission of Harper & Row, Publishers, Inc.

"Writing Honestly'' from *Writing Well*, 2/e by Donald Hall. Copyright © 1976, 1973 by Donald Hall. Reprinted by permission of Scott, Foresman and Company.

"Writing for an Audience'' from *Problem Solving Strategies for Writing*, Second Edition, by Linda Flower. Copyright © 1985 by Harcourt Brace Jovanovich, Inc. Reprinted by permission of the publisher.

"Simplicity'' from *On Writing Well*, Second Edition by William Zinsser. Copyright © 1980 by William K. Zinsser. Reprinted by permission of the author.

"The Maker's Eye: Revising Your Own Manuscript'' by Donald M. Murray. Reprinted by permission of International Creative Management. Copyright © 1973 by Donald Murray.

"The Qualities of Good Writing'' from *Twenty Questions for the Writer*, Second Edition. Copyright © 1976 by Harcourt Brace Jovanovich, Inc. Reprinted by permission of the publisher.

ADDITIONAL CREDITS:

Drunk driving advertisements reprinted by permission of the Reader's Digest Foundation; "Women Aren't Guys'' by Nancy Stevens. Copyright © 1988 by The New York Times Company. Reprinted by permission.

Instructor's Manual to Accompany

Language Awareness

FIFTH EDITION

PAUL ESCHHOLZ
ALFRED ROSA
VIRGINIA CLARK
EDITORS

Instructor's Manual to Accompany

Language Awareness

Fifth Edition

Editors

PAUL ESCHHOLZ

ALFRED ROSA

VIRGINIA CLARK

St. Martin's Press
New York

Manufactured in the United States of America.
4 3 2 1 0
f e d c b a

For information, write:
St. Martin's Press, Inc.
175 Fifth Avenue
New York, NY 10010

ISBN: 0-312- 02080-5

PREFACE

How a teacher uses a textbook is a highly individual matter. In this manual we have indicated how we use the materials and ideas in *Language Awareness* in our own classes, and we hope that the manual suggests possibilities or alternatives that will be useful to you. Although *Language Awareness* might be assigned in various courses, we use it in a composition course; for such a purpose it can readily be complemented by a handbook or handbook/rhetoric.

In suggesting answers to the "Questions on Content" and "Questions on Rhetoric," we have tried to assist you by (1) indicating central themes or issues, (2) explaining and describing rhetorical strategies, (3) suggesting expected student responses to the questions, (4) anticipating problems that students might experience, (5) citing additional readings to enrich or develop a particular topic, and (6) offering additional questions when appropriate. As in the text, quotations and vocabulary words are followed by paragraph numbers in parentheses to indicate their locations in a given essay. In addition, we have often included cross-references to related selections. The overall intent has been to save you time, not to dictate directions or answers. There are no substitutes for your own experience with the text and your sense of what will work most successfully for your students.

For the "Writing Assignments" we have tried to give some background material about each assignment. We have (1) provided when necessary an explanation of the purpose of the assignment, (2) suggested preparatory readings or discussion material, (3) pointed out specific prewriting activities, (4) offered guidelines for altering or limiting the assignment, or (5) previewed what you might expect from students.

One of our most successful projects has been to have our students keep a "language journal," in which, in addition to making a daily record of their own responses to their language environment, they keep a "scrapbook" of newspaper and magazine articles that have to do with language and advertisements that exemplify interesting uses of language. It is truly amazing how many of these items a student can collect during a single semester, and most students seem to enjoy this project once they become aware of the abundance of material around them.

Finally, if you have suggestions or questions about the contents of either *Language Awareness* or this manual, we would like very much to hear from you. We can be reached at the English Department, 315 Old Mill, The University of Vermont 05405.

PAUL ESCHHOLZ
ALFRED ROSA
VIRGINIA CLARK

TABLE OF CONTENTS

I. DISCOVERING LANGUAGE   1

Malcolm X, COMING TO AN AWARENESS OF LANGUAGE   1
Helen Keller, THE DAY LANGUAGE CAME INTO MY LIFE   2
Paul Roberts, A BRIEF HISTORY OF ENGLISH   4
Bergen Evans, THE POWER OF WORDS   6
Donald V. Mehus, CONTEMPORARY AMERICAN GRAFFITI   7
Edward T. Hall and Mildred Reed Hall, THE SOUNDS OF SILENCE   9

II. AMERICAN ENGLISH TODAY   12

Edwin Newman, LANGUAGE ON THE SKIDS   12
Harvey Daniels, IS THERE REALLY A LANGUAGE CRISIS?   13
S.I. Hayakawa, WHY ENGLISH SHOULD BE OUR OFFICIAL LAN-
    GUAGE   16
Alice Roy, THE ENGLISH ONLY MOVEMENT   18
Dorothy Z. Seymour, BLACK CHILDREN, BLACK SPEECH   20
Rachel L. Jones, WHAT'S WRONG WITH BLACK ENGLISH   23
Richard Rodriguez, CAUGHT BETWEEN TWO LANGUAGES   24

III. THE LANGUAGE OF POLITICS AND PROPAGANDA   27

George Orwell, POLITICS AND THE ENGLISH LANGUAGE   27
Newman P. Birk and Genevieve B. Birk, SELECTION, SLANTING, AND
    CHARGED LANGUAGE   30
Stuart Chase, GOBBLEDYGOOK   33
Donna Woolfolk Cross, PROPAGANDA: HOW NOT TO BE BAM-
    BOOZLED   36
John F. Kennedy, INAUGURAL ADDRESS   37
New York Times, THE RONALD REAGAN BASIC 1984 CAMPAIGN
    SPEECH   39

IV. ADVERTISING AND LANGUAGE   41

Jeffrey Schrank, THE LANGUAGE OF ADVERTISING CLAIMS   41
Ron Rosenbaum, THE HARD SELL   43
Jay Rosen, THE PRESENCE OF THE WORD IN TV ADVERTISING   45
Edwin Newman, GETTIN' RICH BY DROPPIN' THE G   46
Consumers Union, IT'S NATURAL! IT'S ORGANIC! OR IS IT?   47

Jib Fowles, ADVERTISING'S FIFTEEN BASIC APPEALS   49
Hugh Rank, INTENSIFY/DOWNPLAY   50

V. PREJUDICE AND STEREOTYPES   53

Gordon Allport, THE LANGUAGE OF PREJUDICE   53
S.I. Hayakawa, WORDS WITH BUILT-IN JUDGMENTS   55
Charles F. Berlitz, THE ETYMOLOGY OF THE INTERNATIONAL INSULT   57
William Raspberry, WHAT IT MEANS TO BE BLACK   59

VI. SEXISM AND LANGUAGE   61

Alleen Pace Nilsen, SEXISM IN ENGLISH: A 1990's UPDATE   61
Eugene R. August, REAL MEN DON'T: ANTI-MALE BIAS IN ENGLISH   63
Jack Rosenthal, GENDER BENDERS   65
Casey Miller and Kate Swift, ONE SMALL STEP FOR GENKIND   67
Cyra McFadden, IN DEFENSE OF GENDER   69
John Pfeiffer, GIRL TALK–BOY TALK   72
Catharine R. Stimpson, THE "F" WORD   74

VII. EUPHEMISM AND TABOOS   76

Neil Postman, EUPHEMISM   76
S.I. Hayakawa, VERBAL TABOO   77
Barbara Lawrence, FOUR-LETTER WORDS CAN HURT YOU   79
Stephen Hilgartner, Richard C. Bell, and Rory O'Connor, THE LANGUAGE OF
   NUCLEAR WAR STRATEGISTS   80

VIII. MEDIA AND LANGUAGE   83

Neil Postman,"NOW... THIS"   83
Herbert J. Gans, THE MESSAGES BEHIND THE NEWS   85
Nat Hentoff, WHEN NICE PEOPLE BURN BOOKS   88
Stephen King, NOW YOU TAKE "BAMBI" OR "SNOW WHITE"—THAT'S
   SCARY!   90
Consumer Reports, ADVERTISING IN DISGUISE   91
Robert MacNeil, PIGSKIN ENGLISH   92

IX. WRITING WELL: USING LANGUAGE RESPONSIBLY   95

Paul Roberts, HOW TO SAY NOTHING IN 500 WORDS   95
Donald Hall, WRITING HONESTLY   96
Linda Flower, WRITING FOR AN AUDIENCE   97

William Zinsser, SIMPLICITY 97
Donald M. Murray, THE MAKER'S EYE: REVISING YOUR OWN
  MANUSCRIPTS 98
Jacqueline Berke, THE QUALITIES OF GOOD WRITING 99

I. DISCOVERING LANGUAGE

COMING TO AN AWARENESS OF LANGUAGE, Malcolm X   (p. 9)

Questions on Content

1. Malcolm X's explanation of his motivation is in paragraph 8: "I became increasingly frustrated at not being able to express what I wanted to convey in letters that I wrote...."
2. By this Malcolm X means that, although he read all the pages of a book, he had to skip over so many words that were unknown to him that he had little comprehension of what he was "reading." To overcome this problem he decided to study a dictionary, word by word.
3. When Malcolm X refers to himself as having been an articulate hustler he defines articulate as "commanding attention" when he said something. He describes functional, on the other hand, as being able to speak or write in a plain manner merely to convey meaning. Outside the world of the streets, Malcolm X discovered that he was neither articulate nor functional in his ability to express himself in speech or writing.
4. *Aardvark* was one of the first words in the dictionary and was accompanied by a picture. The description and picture of the strange animal intrigued Malcolm X, and an awareness of this word taught him something about his African heritage.
5. In this simile Malcolm X compares the dictionary to an encyclopedia because, like an encyclopedia, a dictionary contains a vast amount of information.
6. Malcolm X implies that although he is still in prison, his mind has been liberated by his ability to read and to write.

Questions on Rhetoric

1. The first-person narrator lends immediacy and believability to this very personal experience. A third-person narrator, either participant or omniscient, would sacrifice this personal tone.
2. This essay is organized as a chronological narrative. Malcolm X traces the development of his language skills by first discussing how his letter writing in prison led to his "homemade education" (7). Then, after briefly explaining his frustration at not being able to express himself adequately, and a short flashback describing how the envy of knowledge was first instilled in him, he details his experiences in acquiring language skills through reading and copying pages of the dictionary.
3. The short sentences that introduce paragraphs 1 and 2 arrest the reader's attention and, as dramatic assertions, call for more information. For these reasons they are especially effective.
4. Paragraphs 12, 13, and 14 could be combined, but something would be lost.
   The shortness of these paragraphs emphasizes the initial hesitant and painful steps

1

Malcolm X took in studying the dictionary. The sense of drama associated with Malcolm X's uncertain efforts at fashioning a homemade education would be lost if the paragraphs were combined.

5. It is appropriate that Malcolm X narrate these early experiences in acquiring a homemade education in simple language. To do otherwise would destroy the drama and realism of the narrative.

Vocabulary

frustrated (8): prevented from accomplishing a purpose or fulfilling a desire.
articulate (8): characterized by clear, expressive language.
functional (8): capable of performing.
emulate (10): to strive to equal or excel, especially through imitation.
inevitable (17): incapable of being avoided or prevented.

Writing Topics

1. This writing assignment will help students become more aware of their language. It is an important tone-setting exercise and should be presented relatively early in the course. Since some students may be apprehensive about sharing experiences in which they felt that their command of language was inadequate, you may wish to get things started by narrating one or two such experiences of your own. Students should be encouraged to include a number of details in order to communicate their impression of the experience effectively. You may want to ask students to volunteer to read their narratives.

2. Most students will find the notion of studying the dictionary a long and tedious way to combat the problem of illiteracy, and will also find it impractical since most people do not have the time to devote to such study that being in prison afforded Malcolm X. To get students to consider other alternatives ask them what they would do if all the members of their families, besides themselves, were illiterate. This may elicit some responses that they can use in developing their essays on this topic.

THE DAY LANGUAGE CAME INTO MY LIFE, Helen Keller (p. 13)

Questions on Content

1. Keller defines her most important day as the day Anne Sullivan came into her life because Sullivan would eventually "reveal all things" to her through language. Keller was also awed by the "immeasurable contrast between the two lives it (that first day) connects."

2. Keller experienced anger, bitterness and a deep languor brought on by her frustrated attempts to understand the world around her. One the day language came to her, Keller was able to understand that she had destroyed her doll. For the first time in her life, she experienced feelings of repentance and sorrow.

3. That day at the well-house, Keller finally understood that words are more than a scribbled line on a hand or on a page; words are the names we give to the things in our world, and when

we speak those names we bring our world to life in our minds. For Keller, the connection between the things we name and the names we give them is essential to the creation of new thoughts and ideas.

Questions On Rhetoric

1. Sullivan is loving while Keller is not. In paragraph 4, Keller describes her first meeting with Sullivan. She (Keller) was "caught up and held close in the arms of her who had come to reveal all things to me, and more than all things, to love me." By contrast, in paragraph 6, Keller shows no remorse at breaking her doll: "I had not loved the doll. In the still, dark world in which I lived there was no strong sentiment or tenderness."

   Sullivan is persistent, patient, self-assured and kind. In paragraph 6 Keller explains that although Sullivan dropped the attempt to help Keller see the difference between m-u-g and w-a-t-e-r, she renewed the effort at the first opportunity. Throughout the article, Sullivan reveals an unrelenting patience in her effort to get through to Keller, who is impatient, cross, and vengeful. The girl considers the endless hand-spelling to be a game that, however charming, should not be bothersome. In a temper tantrum over an unsuccessful lesson, Keller deliberately breaks her new doll, and is gratified when the cause of her "discomfort" has been removed. By contrast, Sullivan does not fly into a rage of her own. Instead, after sweeping the debris aside, she gives Keller her hat and takes her outside for a stroll.

2. Keller's first words were nouns and verbs. These words are the basic units of thought, because they name the things in our world and describe the way those things move. The building blocks of writing are the names we give to things. The writer faces the same challenge Keller's teacher faced, to describe the world bluntly, in its simplest terms and then to shade it in with ideas that cannot be named in a word. As hard as it is for us to express our ideas, we can only wonder at how Keller came to understand words such as "beauty," "goodness," "justice," and "truth."

3. Narrative was probably the most effective way for Keller to make her point. In her opening paragraph Keller characterizes her relationship with Sullivan, not as merely one between a teacher and student, but as one that proved to be loving and intimate. The narrative, or story form, lends itself to a more personal, intimate portrayal of Keller's discovery of language than any other form would have.

Vocabulary

languor (2) lethargy; lassitude.
tangible (3) perceptible by the sense of touch.
plummet (3) a line with a plumb (lead weight) at one end, used to measure how deep water is.
confounding (6) mixing up; confusing.

Writing Topics

1. Sighted and hearing readers are imaginatively guided into Keller's experience in a sightless and soundless world by her use of metaphor and simile. For students to similarly express their feelings over an inability to communicate, ask them to consider those situations in which they were so overwhelmed by an emotion—joy, fear, frustration, amazement, etc.— that they could not speak. Because of the strong emotion(s) present, the situation should be memorable and fairly easy to reconstruct. Did—or does—a particular metaphor suggest

3

itself, as with Keller's metaphor of being lost in a fog? Connecting the experience to metaphors or similes can be a confusing (but stimulating) task because of the many choices and possibilities before the writer: informal peer evaluation may prove useful. Review the narratives in class (perhaps allowing the writers to remain anonymous) to examine the effectiveness, suitability, and originality of the figurative language employed.

2. Keller found that comprehending and using words affected her thoughts, feelings, and behavior, for indeed, all are inextricably connected. Language not only allows us to share our feelings, but, as Keller realized, it can shape them as well (Later sections, such as "The Language of Politics and Propaganda" and "Prejudice and Stereotypes" will further explore this phenomenon.) Because words permit close and specific identification of everything they name, they exact certain amounts of purpose and responsibility from their users. Keller probably felt remorse for destroying an object that had been given to her by the woman who had just taught her how to think and communicate with language.

A BRIEF HISTORY OF ENGLISH, Paul Roberts (p. 17)

Questions on Content

1. The three major periods in the history of English are Old English (600-1100), Middle English (1100-1500), and Modern English (1500–present).
2. Most changes in any language can be explained by historical events. The relationship is usually a causal one: historical changes cause changes in the language. Among the historical changes Roberts discusses in regard to the development of English are the following:
   a. The decline and departure from England of the Roman Empire in the fifth century made way for the Anglo-Saxon invasions and the introduction of "English" into England.
   b. In the ninth century, the Viking invasions led to an influx of Norse linguistic characteristics.
   c. The Norman conquest in 1066 introduced many French features into English.
   d. Perhaps the most profound change of the Modern English era was the invention of printing in 1475, which unified languages, arrested the development of dialect differences, and hastened the standardization of spelling.
3. In paragraph 26 Roberts explains why French did not replace English as the language of the people: "The reason is that the Conquest was not a national migration, as the earlier Anglo-Saxon invasion had been."
4. In social terms, French was the language of the court, and the French words that came into English were the words of this class.

   In paragraph 29, Roberts provides examples of words that were borrowed from the French in the following areas: government, church, food, colors, household, play, literary, and learning.
5. In paragraphs 35 and 36 Roberts explains the changes that occurred as a result of the Great Vowel Shift.

   Roberts says that the Great Vowel Shift affected thousands of words and gave us different symbols for vowel sounds.

4

6. According to Roberts, schoolchildren tend not to be interested in the study of the English language because they have been taught English grammar on the Latin model. This, he feels, has obscured the real features of English structure.

Questions on Rhetoric

1. Roberts's thesis is presented in the first sentence of his essay.
2. Because the purpose of the essay is to show historical and developmental changes, a chronological organization is only natural.
3. Roberts uses many examples in this essay to illustrate the various points that he is making as well as to establish himself as an authority on the subject.
4. In paragraphs 20 through 24, Roberts contrasts Old English with Modern English. By showing us how Old English differs from present-day English, he is better able to show us what Old English was.
5. Roberts's use of the pronouns *we*, *our*, and *us* identifies him as a member of his own audience, an audience for whom he is acting as spokesperson. This makes it seem as though he is participating in the unraveling of the history of English right along with his readers rather than lecturing "at" them, and helps sustain interest for them.

Vocabulary

forays (6): quick raids for the purpose of taking plunder.
siphoned (8): drained off.
conversion (11): a change in belief or attitudes.
impunity (15): exemption from punishment.
facilitated (25): helped or assisted the progress of.
zealously (28): ardently or actively.
linger (39): remain in existence or use while waning in importance or strength.

Writing Topics

1. The following list identifies the language from which each word was borrowed.

barbecue: Spanish	*casino*: Italian
buffalo: Latin	*decoy*: Dutch
ditto: Italian	*orangutan*: Malay
fruit: Old French	*posse*: Middle Latin
hustle: Middle Dutch	*raccoon*: Algonquian
marmalade: Portuguese	*veranda*: Spanish

   To emphasize the extent to which borrowed words are used in English, have students look up the origin of words associated with a hobby or skill that they are familiar with to find out how many of the terms have been taken from other languages. This may provide a context from which they can develop their essays.
2. If you wish to help students generate supporting information for this writing assignment, list the various topic headings (Vietnam War, NASA, etc.) on the board or overhead, as well as any other historical influences that you or your students can devise, and then spend 20 minutes or so brainstorming to find examples that fit the categories.

   You may also want to review the organizing principle of division and classification since many students will find it appropriate for their essays.

THE POWER OF WORDS, Bergen Evans (p. 29)

Questions on Content

1. As Evans says in paragraph 2: "The more words we know, the closer we can come to expressing precisely what we want to."
2. In paragraphs 4-6, Evans explains that misunderstandings are the result of confusion over the meanings of words—when general terms mean one thing to the person speaking but another to the person(s) spoken to. The chances of misunderstanding can therefore be reduced if the speaker "will take the trouble to use specific terms instead of doubtful ones" (7).
3. Evans discusses the relationship between vocabulary and intelligence in paragraphs 27 and 28. He equates the ability to increase one's vocabulary with intellectual progress and establishes words as important to adjusting to life's situations.
4. According to Evans, a large vocabulary makes a person more aware of what is going on because he will understand more—difficult books will become readable and he will be able to share the thoughts of poets, philosophers, historians, essayists, etc., "and in sharing their thoughts [his] own world will expand" (16).
5. One of the principal means Americans use for classifying other Americans is language. Because we do not have titles and because ancestry is less important here than in many countries, we rely on possessions—houses, cars, clothes—and, increasingly, on speech to provide information about people we meet. Many Americans worry about whether or not their language is "correct" because we tend to use language and words as status symbols. Examples of "vocabulary building" features taken from local papers will facilitate class discussion.
6. Here is an opportunity to discuss the idea that "words do not have meanings; people have meanings for words" (W. Nelson Francis, *The English Language: An Introduction* [New York: Norton, 1965], p 119). Four-letter words, for example, are not objectionable in themselves; it is what people associate with them that arouses strong reactions, though reactions to the same words change from generation to generation. See also Neil Postman's "Euphemism" and Barbara Lawrence's "Four-Letter Words Can Hurt You." The association that each student makes for *dinner, money, Thanksgiving, fear,* and *success* will depend upon his or her own experiences.

Questions on Rhetoric

1. Evans states his thesis in the last sentence of paragraph 2: "The more words we know, the closer we can come to expressing precisely what we want to"
2. The words-as-a-tool analogy is useful, but the comparison is in some respects limited; words, for example, affect their users; tools usually do not.
   In paragraphs 18-20, Evans uses the analogy of the human mind as a filing system.
3. Evans refers to Caliban in paragraph 10 in order to make a point in paragraph 11 about our use of language: namely, that as infants we all begin as "Calibans," for without language we do not, and cannot, know ourselves or our world.
4. Evans uses the technique of exemplification—in particular making use of the language employed during the 1962 Cuban missile crisis (13 and 14)—to support his generalization.
5. Evans's tone is informal; he seems to be talking directly to the reader.

Vocabulary

futile (4): having no useful result.
exasperation (6): the state of being annoyed or irritated.
communicable (14): able to be transmitted.
inevitably (16): unavoidably
subconscious (17): not conscious; beneath consciousness.
perverse (18): directed away from what is right or good.
intricate (20): involved or complex.
muddle (22): to mix confusedly; jumble.
correlation (27): a causal, complementary, parallel, or reciprocal relationship.

Writing Topics

1. Another way to define a term is to use a synonym, but remind your students that not only is a true synonym impossible but that even the same word is never used more than once with exactly the same meaning. Before students define the four terms in this exercise, ask them to define *clock* and *lexicography* and to differentiate them from *watch* and *semantics*. After they have written their definitions, you may wish to duplicate and distribute representative definitions for class discussion.
2. To prepare students for this assignment you can discuss instances when they have noticed a limited vocabulary in people they have encountered. Ask the students to describe these experiences and explain how or why they recognized an "impoverished vocabulary" in someone else. Then find out how they responded, internally and externally, to these situations. Your discussion may stimulate students to analyze their own vocabularies thoroughly, as well as their attitudes about them, as they prepare their written assignments.
3. Reading has always been considered essential to developing a large vocabulary. As a prewriting activity for this assignment, find out if this precept is borne out by the students' experiences in acquiring vocabularies. Survey the class to discover which students have made it a practice to read a lot outside of school assignments. Then ask these students how they feel about the range of their vocabulary. Do the same with those who do little or no outside reading, and see how the two groups' perceptions compare. After you've discussed individual attitudes about the connection between reading and vocabulary see if you can draw any general conclusions. This activity can demonstrate one approach for generating and developing material related to this topic.

CONTEMPORARY AMERICAN GRAFFITI, Donald V. Mehus (p. 37)

Questions on Content

1. Mehus defines graffiti in paragraph 2 as "the ancient art of anonymous, unauthorized wall writing."
2. Graffiti became more visible and more creative in the late sixties than it had been previously.

7

That flowering coincided with an era of expression and rebellion (most blatantly expressed in opposition to the Vietnam War). The timing suggests that graffiti can be an expression of frustration, rage, and cynicism brought on by feelings of powerlessness in the face of war and other perceived inequities. However, this style of expression also shows a spirit of individualism that refuses to be ignored: whatever the sentiment, whatever the tone, graffiti by its nature declares, "I will be heard."

3. It is obvious to Mehus that graffiti is now being taken seriously in the United States because it has received "respectful recognition" from publications such as The New York Times and Newsweek, and from playwrights and authors.

4. As American graffiti flowered it became, according to Mehus, "more pointed and articulate, more socially conscious, much more vitriolic." The best of it seems to speak out against, rather than in favor of, something.

5. Mehus names the four major groups responsible for graffiti. Men, students, hippies, and young business people created most of the graffiti when Mehus wrote his article in the late seventies. Typically, graffiti is about religion, sex, advertising, and America's racial troubles. The best graffiti is found mostly on university campuses, and in the restrooms of bars and coffeehouses expressing opinions, voicing insults, joking, asserting one's individuality, and protesting social and political conditions. However, graffiti can also express feelings of love, such as, "John loves Sue," and much restroom graffiti becomes a "dialogue" among patrons as they add on to each others' comments.

6. Pseudo-graffiti "lacks the apparent spontaneity of true graffiti," according to Mehus. His cited example is more along the lines of bumper-sticker humor than it is a heartfelt, individual belief.

Questions on Rhetoric

1. Mehus uses specific examples of the various purposes graffiti serves. They recall for the reader the various graffiti we have all seen for ourselves and in some cases recall for us emotions we have felt like expressing ourselves from time to time. Words such as "heartfelt," (1) "witty," "provocative," (3) "vividly imaginative writing," (4) are only a few of the many words Mehus uses throughout his essay that indicate a sympathetic attitude toward graffiti. However, words such as "vitriolic," "cynical," and "bitter," indicate that as sympathetic as he may be, Mehus perceives a real anger among some of the graffiti writers.

2. Each of Mehus' beginning sentences is also his topic sentence, which is to say that it introduces the central idea of the paragraph.

3. In each paragraph, after the topic sentence, Mehus elaborates on the idea and then offers several examples. For example, in paragraph 3 Mehus begins by stating that American graffiti has flowered, goes on to explain that it takes several forms (such as "humorous" and "vitriolic"), and then further breaks down graffiti into topics such as war, peace, government, the individual and society.

4. The words Mehus uses to characterize graffiti and those who create it are a mix of positive and negative: "lightly humorous," "witty," "plaintive," "virulent," "socially conscious," "striking back," "sharing," "obscene," "insulting," "asserting," "protesting," "intellectual," "romantic," "articulate," "perceptive," "vitriolic," "cynical," "bitter," "sophisticated," "misanthropic," "caustic," and "provocative," to name a few. Mehus's even representation of the spectrum of emotions, intellects, and purposes behind graffiti shows that he has carefully observed and studied attitudes toward graffiti and the people who write it. Mehus himself seems happily intrigued by, and accepting of, graffiti, even of its creators as people

who simply have something to express. However, he does note that graffiti (and hence its writers) can disturb, sadden, worry, frighten, and otherwise dismay people.

Vocabulary

alleviate (1) mitigate; lighten.
plaintive (1) expressive of suffering or woe.
vitriolic (3) caustic or biting.
conundrum (4) riddle.
cynical (5) attributing all actions to selfish motives.
caustically (6) sharply; incisively.
pithy (9) brief and to the point.
abstruse (9) hard to understand.
altruistic (11) unselfishly interested in the welfare of others.
virulent (12) bitterly hostile.
misanthropic (12) hating humankind.
pregnant (13) rich in significance.
injuction (15) order; admonition.

Writing Topics

1. As students are turning in their essays, take a quick survey to find out about your campus's graffiti. Where does graffiti appear? What is it about? Note locations and issues on the chalkboard. Then note students' responses to the question, "What are some of the advantages and disadvantages of campus graffiti?" With student approval, survey, results, the list of advantages and disadvantages, comments from class discussion, and (excerpts from) student essays may be submitted to campus and local newspaper.
2. In order to begin this assignment, students need to have a clear idea of the distinctions Mehus makes between the three types of graffiti. Take a few minutes in class to review his essay. Ask for specific examples of true and pseudo-graffiti (meaningless obscenities should be self-explanatory). To provide such an example, you might wear, or ask students to wear to this class session, a T-shirt that proclaims a message.

THE SOUNDS OF SILENCE, Edward T. Hall and Mildred Reed Hall (p. 42)

Questions on Content

1. The Halls discuss pupillary reflex in paragraph 12. When people are very interested in what they are looking at, their pupils tend to dilate.
2. The Halls attribute differences in eye and walking behavior, territoriality, and the use of time to differences in cultural background.

Their examples suggest the many social, business, and political situations in which these differences may be important.

3. The bubble that the Halls describe is "a kind of mobile territory that [each of us] will defend against intrusion" (17).

   The bubble expands or contracts at any given time depending on the person's emotional state, the activity he or she is performing, and his or her cultural background.

4. The four zones are:
   a. intimate (see paragraph 23)
   b. personal (see paragraph 24)
   c. social (see paragraph 25)
   d. public (see paragraph 26)

5. The Halls discuss both male and female preening gestures in paragraphs 34 and 35. Preening gestures are specific gestures used to attract those of the opposite sex.

6. Students generally like this activity because it gives them a chance to show what they have learned about body language and how well they can interpret it. Some feel awkward at first, but they soon get used to playing the assigned roles.

Questions on Rhetoric

1. The first four paragraphs function as an introduction to the essay. They give four specific examples of body language, each showing a different aspect of the topic. Because these examples show us body language in action, they are engaging for the reader.

2. The diction in this essay is generally informal.

   The Halls use second-person pronouns, the active voice, contractions, loose sentences, and dashes. The treatment of the subject is serious, but the tone is informal enough to appeal to the readership of *Playboy*, where the piece was first published.

3. The Halls use comparison and contrast throughout to point out ethnic and cultural differences in body language. In paragraph 10, the Halls use classification in discussing eye behavior, and in paragraphs 23 through 26 they use classification to discuss the four main distances used by middle-class Americans in business and social relations.

4. The Halls use rhetorical questions to begin paragraphs 32, 34, and 36. These questions further the progress of the essay by closing previous discussions and beginning new ones.

Vocabulary

savors (1): enjoys by taste or smell.
proximity (3): nearness in place.
cordial (4): courteous and gracious.
congruity (5): agreement or harmony.
dilated (12): made wider or larger.
vehemence (19): violence or fury.
melee (21): a confused general hand-to-hand fight.
inhibitions (28): psychological restraints.
volatile (30): easily aroused.
precarious (46): uncertain or unstable.

Writing Topics

1. One of the difficulties in assessing nonverbal communication is that we are not always aware of having misunderstood the signals we encounter. It may be helpful, therefore, to have

students offer examples of instances when they were made to feel uncomfortable because of an apparent nonverbal trespass or misinterpretation. Then discuss what the communicator in each example may have been attempting to convey, and why the receiver misinterpreted. This can help prepare students for their writing assignment on the cultural differences reflected in nonverbal communication.

2. Students may find it helpful, before they begin this assignment, to discuss some of the silent "communications" that are transmitted when someone is late. Ask them to consider the nonverbal messages that might be conveyed when a person arrives late for the following:

> picking someone up for a date
> meeting someone for lunch or dinner
> a class or lecture
> a day at work
> a religious worship service
> a concert, movie, or play

Discussion will help students recognize how quickly and seriously we ascribe meaning to nonverbal communication situations as well as their own and others' feelings about the importance of being on time.

3. For this writing topic it may be fun to conduct a class analysis of the relation between your students' feelings about "space" and their geographical or ethnic backgrounds. First find out which students feel they have a strong sense of territoriality and which feel they are more at ease with intrusions into their personal space. Then see if there is a connection between the geographical origins or the nationalities of each type and the nonverbal communication they associate with their personal space, as the Halls contend there is. Your analysis, in addition to putting one of the Halls' conclusions to the test, may generate material that students can incorporate into their essays.

II. AMERICAN ENGLISH TODAY

LANGUAGE ON THE SKIDS, Edwin Newman   (p. 59)

Questions on Content

1. In each of these cases the problem is redundancy: "unique" means "singularly"; "proliferation" means "the spread of"; and "stole second" implies that it was done "successfully."
2. Newman feels that Americans are extravagant with words because they believe "that an idea is more effective if it is repeated and reinforced" (3), they fail "to understand what words mean" (4), and they "desire to make what is being done, however simple and routine it may be, sound grand and complicated" (5).
3. According to Newman, language that promotes self-importance is used "because it serves as a fence that keeps others outside and respectful, or it leads them to ignore what is going on inside because it is too much trouble to find out" (6).
   Students' opinions as to whether such language is appropriate or legitimate may vary. If there are any who feel it is appropriate, ask them to explain and justify their opinions.
4. Because the language belongs to everyone in society, those who abuse it abuse something that is their own. That is, if we abuse the medium through which we communicate, we abuse our own effectiveness as human beings.
5. Newman believes that we could improve our use of the language by demanding "that our leaders speak better English, so that we know what they are talking about and, incidentally, so that they do" (12).
6. When discussing this question, have students consider how they react to the use, or abuse, of language. Ask them, for instance, whether they have had instructors who were obscure or redundant when lecturing. If so, how did they react? Were they amused? Did they get angry or frustrated? Their responses may offer a better perspective on Newman's point of view.

Questions on Rhetoric

1. Newman's thesis is stated in paragraph 13: "Our language should be specific and concrete, eloquent where possible, playful where possible, and personal so that we don't all sound alike."
2. The topic sentence in paragraph 4 is the first sentence: "Another cause is a failure to understand what words mean." The sentences that follow demonstrate how people use words without understanding what they mean.
3. Though Newman's tone makes it clear that he is irritated by the misuse of language, his essay does not seem "cranky and pedantic" because he is also able to see the humor in the misuses he exposes. For example, after presenting an example, in paragraph 3, that illustrates the tendency to repeat and reinforce, Newman finishes the paragraph with a humorous remark. Many of his paragraphs end in this light-hearted manner.

4. Newman does not really mean that we should use these terms. His irony lets us share in his ridicule of overblown language.
5. Newman's examples give substance and authority to the essay. Without them the essay would be much less persuasive.

   Students may disagree on the need for more examples. Some may feel that more examples would obscure the points Newman wishes to make by using them, while others may feel that the examples do such a good job of clarifying Newman's ideas that more would be helpful, especially in the closing paragraphs.
6. The question that begins paragraph 6 is pivotal. It allows Newman to move from a description of the problem to an analysis of it.

Vocabulary

unique (1): having no like or equal; one of a kind.
redundancy (2): superfluous repetition of words; verbosity.
extolled (4): praised highly or lauded.
plummet (4): to drop precipitously.
turgid (11): inflated; ponderous.
ponderous (11): dull; labored.

Writing Topics

1. This assignment is intended to give students the experience of examining for themselves actual sports jargon. They will probably find some examples of sports writing that Newman would consider trite or ungrammatical. Some students will argue that jargon has a place in sports writing, that it is largely ritualistic. For a more detailed discussion of Newman's assessment of sports jargon, see "Is Your Team Hungry Enough, Coach?" in his book *Strictly Speaking* (Indianapolis: Bobbs-Merrill, 1974), pp. 149–170.
2. Class discussion of #3 in "Questions on Content" can serve as a prewriting activity for this assignment. Students should analyze their own attitudes toward the misuse of language by sharing memorable encounters with such language and their reactions to them. They can then apply the issues discussed in class to the development of their essays.

IS THERE REALLY A LANGUAGE CRISIS?, Harvey Daniels   (p. 63)

Questions on Content

1. In Daniels's view, the normal condition of American English is for it to be filled with so-called misuses and abuses. He is not concerned about this, however, because he sees language as a neutral instrument and believes "the illnesses, the abuses, the wounds, the sufferings of a language reside in the minds and hearts of its users" (4).
2. As Daniels reveals in paragraph 7, the story of the Chicago fire "reminds us that our attitudes about the speechways of other people are as much a part of the linguistic environment as nouns, verbs, and adjectives—and that today these attitudes appear unusually harsh and

unforgiving." Daniels traces the roots of this episode of linguistic intolerance to the prevailing sense of panic over the "literacy crisis," a crisis created and fostered by pop grammarians and language critics.

3. The most commonly suggested remedies for the so-called literacy crisis are "strong doses of 'The Basics'" and a rebirth of grammar instruction coupled with a general toughening of standards and a firm resolve not to coddle inadequate speakers. Daniels's negative response to these remedies is evident in the tone (evoked through his selection of vocabulary) of his statements referring to them: "Astute educational publishers *crank out old-fangled* grammar books. English professors offer *convoluted* explanations of the crisis and its causes..." (10).

4. Daniels states that language critics are often concerned with the following: (1) ridiculing poor speakers and praising good ones; (2) ranking various languages according to their supposed superiority in expressing literary or scientific concepts; (3) defending the Mother Tongue from real or imagined assaults (16).

   Daniels sees linguists, on the other hand, as being concerned with understanding and explaining "the complex mechanisms which allow human beings to communicate with each other" (16). He sums up the difference between critics and linguists by stating that the former's main business is evaluative and prescriptive while the latter's is explanatory and descriptive.

5. According to Daniels, there are three basic ways that pop grammarians and language critics actually contribute to language problems rather than help solve them: (1) they promulgate and reinforce ideas about language that are wrong; (2) their inaccurate notions about language can inspire teaching curricula and techniques that hinder children's development of communication skills; (3) they trivialize language—through their preoccupation with form they deflect attention from meaning.

   Your students' own learning experiences with communication skills will no doubt influence how they react to Daniels's analysis.

6. The gravest problem that Daniels sees with the "language crisis" is that it reinforces and glorifies the hatreds and prejudices that already exist in American society by "using minor differences in language as ways of identifying, classifying, avoiding, or punishing anyone whom we choose to consider our social or intellectual inferior" (21).

Questions on Rhetoric

1. Daniels's writing is informal and, at times, even colloquial—"Is it really, uh, terminal?" (1). This approach suits his attitude and subject matter since his whole point is that pop language critics are too rigid and superficial in their analyses of the current state of American English.

2. The argument that American English is *not* diseased can be divided into two major sections. In the first half of the essay, Daniels discusses the nature of the current "literacy crisis" as it has been conveyed by pop grammarians and language critics, and includes the attitudes and reactions it has helped foster. Then, beginning with paragraph 13, he presents his own analysis of the state of American English today, using the findings of linguistic research as a springboard for his refutation and denunciation of the so-called literacy crisis.

3. Daniels conveys a sense of impatience and controlled hostility toward the evaluative and prescriptive assumptions of the pop grammarians, while calmly and rationally disputing the notion that a crisis in language exists.

4. Paragraph 13 serves as a transition between Daniels's presentation of the language crisis (as perceived by pop grammarians) and his own interpretation of the elements discussed in that presentation.

5. The Richard Mitchell quotation in paragraph 14 allows Daniels to use the words of one of the pop grammarians who have falsely created the "language crisis" to support his own contention that such a crisis does not, and never did, exist.

   Daniels uses the quotation effectively by first agreeing with its general intent and then letting his disagreement with its specific application serve as the lead-in to a discussion of language history and linguistic research.
6. Daniels finds medical metaphors unsatisfactory for describing the language crisis because he views language as a neutral instrument—the only life (and, therefore, susceptibility to illness) it has "resides in the minds and hearts of its users" (4).

Vocabulary

somber (1): melancholy; sad.
bereaved (1): those left saddened by someone's death.
prognosis (2): prediction or forecast, especially as to the future course of a disease.
cant (3): specialized or esoteric vocabulary.
argot (3): specialized or secret language peculiar to a class or a group.
inveigh (5): to utter vehement censure or invective.
succinct (6): reduced to a minimum number of words; concise.
obfuscation (8): the act of obscuring the clarity or meaning of.
convoluted (10): coiled or twisted around so that one part turns inward upon another.
coddling (12): pampering.
inadvertent (21): unintentional.

Writing Topics

1. As you discuss students' reactions to these two essays, consider the characteristics that distinguish language critics from linguists, as they are described in paragraph 16 of Daniels's essay. Ask students to locate evidence, in either essay, of the distinctions Daniels has set forth.
2. As part of your discussion of the "back to basics" movement, be sure students are aware of some of the alternatives to strict grammar instruction and an emphasis on form over content. In some cases, "basics" may be the only kind of instruction students have known and your discussion can acquaint them with learning strategies that other class members have been exposed to in their development of language skills.

   Your discussion should also address some of the issues that the back to basics movement has raised in regard to curriculum-competency-based programs for students and for teachers, increased emphasis on teacher accountability, lack of freedom in curriculum development, etc. Your analysis of these issues will provide students with more information to consider for completing this writing assignment.
3. Another way you can demonstrate the connection between language and prejudice is to have students consider whether the language they use changes depending on the person or persons they are speaking to. Do they, for instance, speak to an instructor any differently than to a friend? Do they use different "languages" to correspond with relatives and business acquaintances? Does their language change at all when they address total strangers?

   As they consider these questions, have them also evaluate *why* they alter their language in certain situations (if indeed they do) and what connection this might have to being perceived as "socially or intellectually inferior." They may discover that they sense and fear that they are being judged by these various people just as they themselves judge others in the same situations.

WHY ENGLISH SHOULD BE OUR OFFICIAL LANGUAGE,
S. I. Hayakawa (p. 71)

Questions on Content

1. Hayakawa's definition of the melting pot seems accurate, as far as it goes. However, it does not take into account that the integration of various ethnic groups sometimes takes decades. For example, Blacks, Jews, Hispanics and other ethnic groups continue to live in separate neighborhoods in cities across the United States. In the earlier decades of our country, Irish, Italian, German and other immigrant groups lived in ghettos from which their culture seeped very slowly into the mainstream. Thus the effect was at any given time less one of homogeneity than of different cultures coexisting under one flag.
2. Bilingual education is a key element of the salad bowl that holds as its ideal the mixing of different ethnic groups without destroying their individual cultures.
3. In paragraph 7, Hayakawa identifies those responsible for the move toward bilingualism as Hispanic political leaders, bilingual education teachers, and Hispanic lobbying organizations. These groups list three changes that will be necessary to reflect the growing influence of the Spanish population in American culture. They are (1) the implementation of bilingual education, (2) the inclusion of Spanish in commercials shown nationwide, and (3) the legal implementation of both English and Spanish as the official United States languages.
4. Hayakawa is adamant that a bilingual education might be used to further the education of a native child, but only if that kind of education was chosen freely by the school district and if it was "truly transitional, preparing the student for transfer into a standard English classroom after one or not more than two years."

Questions on Rhetoric

1. In paragraph 11 Hayakawa most directly states the central idea of his thesis that English must be the official language of the United States.
2. As proof that "a move is afoot to split the U.S.," Hayakawa runs through a few of the changes suggested by proponents of bilingualism. This is the strongest evidence he offers to any of the claims he makes in his essay. At the end of his essay, Hayakawa defends himself from the charges of racism leveled at him by reminding readers that, like the Hispanic-American, he himself is a nonwhite immigrant. While this background information suggests that Hayakawa is sensitive to, and fair-minded about, the acculturation difficulties of nonwhite immigrants—including Hispanic-Americans—the mere fact of being a nonwhite immigrant does not preclude one from harboring racist sentiments. Of the three claims Hayakawa makes in his essay, the weakest is that we must escape binationalism. Perhaps his assertion is true, but Hayakawa does not support it with any concrete examples of the consequences of binationalism.
3. Hayakawa sounds almost angry in places, but overall his essay is forceful in tone. This is evident in his choice of words such as: "so-called bilingual education," (2) "salad bowl agenda." (2) "it is not we who attempt to segregate children," (10) "must be chosen freely," (12) "must be truly transitional," (12) "condenscending" (13) and "insulting" (13).
4. Hayakawa's opening sentences are all strong, emotional statements of his beliefs and fears about the bilingual movement and as such are effective in making his argument more persuasive.

Vocabulary

truism (1): an undoubted or self-evident truth
enclaves (1): a territorial or culturally distinct unit
ethnic (1): of or relating to races or large groups of people classed according to common traits and customs.
pluralistic (4): characterized by systems in which minority groups participate in dominant society while maintaining their cultural differences.
specter (8): ghost
referendum (9): the principle or practice of referring legislative measures to the voters for approval or rejection.
xenophobia (10): fear and hatred of strangers and foreigners.

Writing Topics

1. As recommended in the textbook, discuss the consequences of making both English and Spanish the official languages of the United States. Ask students if any among them have grown up bilingual, or if any have traveled to multilingual areas or countries. Do they feel that bilingualism is valuable for everyone? Necessary for everyone? Can a community— or nation—be unified if all of its members do not speak the same language? Who is to determine or measure the degree of unity? How do speakers of English only respond to these questions? Hayakawa's essay may be supplemented with recent newspaper and magazine articles that raise practical considerations on the theories and ideals your class will uncover.
2. Ask those students who have studied a foreign language to describe the specific difficulties they encountered in doing so. (What was the learning environment—a classroom, a home, their neighborhood, or a place far away? Was the student willing to learn a foreign or second language? How would they rate their instruction in that language? What elements or aspects of the language were stressed? Ignored?)
   Students who have never studied a second language may focus on the first part of this writing topic. "Forced" is the key word in the question. Before this group of students begins writing, ask them to consider the question, "How do you think most English-speaking students would react if they were *forbidden* to learn Spanish in school?" This framing of extremes may help students think through the issue and encourage them to present their views in a balanced, thoughtful manner.
3. The juxtaposition of the national purity issue in Israel with the English Only movement in America serves to counter the blind defensiveness some American students may feel as they think about the English Only movement and observe one of its proponents labeled a xenophobe; the forced comparison with a related situation in another country provides distance and permits better objectivity as students ask themselves why they think the way they do about the English Only (and similar) movements. In reviewing students' essays, check to see that they have focused on the definition of "xenophobia." If they make claims of xenophobia present in one or both issues, do they offer examples of "hatred" and "fear" on the part of those involved? (Examples may come from the readings or personal experience.) Do any students note the defining or descriptive activity on the one hand (Israel), and the prescriptive activity on the other (English Only)? Do they trace developments and follow conclusions into the next generation of Israeli and American citizens?

THE ENGLISH ONLY MOVEMENT, Alice Roy (p. 75)

Questions on Content

1. Roy believes that the stated goal of keeping English the official language of the United States is a smoke-screen for "anti-immigrant and divisive sentiments that rest on economic fears." She expands this statement with a briefly stated, reasonable sounding theory of the effects of economic conditions on social attitudes. She then supports her theory by pointing to the kinds of goals the English Only movement is avoiding. For instance, Roy says the movement has no desire to interfere with bilingual advertising: "Bilingual is all right if it makes money."
2. English Only legislation could mandate the use of English in all official proceedings, publications, and education.
3. One myth is that all immigrants to America learn English immediately. Another myth describes the melting pot metaphor, in which "all immigrant groups arrived, jumped into the common cauldron, and came out homogenized." A third myth holds that language can be taught outside the social context, and a fourth myth insists that the English language can be preserved against change.

   Answering the first myth, Roy says the issue of immigrants failing to learn the mother tongue right away is as old as our country. "Benjamin Franklin worried about the Germans—they had little knowledge of English." as for the melting pot, Roy says, it has proven homogeneous for Northern Protestant Europeans. But for other groups, the process has been slow and sometimes painful. The third myth is exploded with statistics showing that a second language is not learned with a "head–on assault," but that we most easily learn a language when we have the chance to use it. The fourth myth ignores the reality, Roy says, that languages are constantly changing, that change is the norm, not the exception. Roy describes the ways in which Monterey Park is supposed to be an example of perfect racial harmony. Yet, even there, Roy says citizens work behind closed doors to ensure that new immigrants do not cross the border. However, this one example, although poignant, does not serve as proof of her argument.
4. Roy suggests the use of tutors to reinforce diverse cultures among students and to include non-English speaking parents in the school and community environment. Another effort would oppose the English Only movement so that non-English speaking children and adults can continue to have access to classes conducted in their own languages. Third, Roy suggests that the public can be educated as to the ways that immigrant groups enrich industry and consumerism. Finally, Roy says students must learn to respect cultural and linguistic diversity. Her goals are impractical only to the degree that funding of them is difficult. It would seem that communities who face language and immigrant problems would be open to solutions that effected change without costing them too much. A few of her suggestions could be implemented on a volunteer basis.

Questions on Rhetoric

1. Roy's thesis that the English Only movement is really an anti-immigrant effort is stated directly in paragraph 6.
2. Roy might have begun her essay by stating her thesis or by describing various reasons for combatting the English Only movement. Her beginning is effective because by the time readers know that Roy opposes the English Only movement, they have a strong idea of how mighty the "enemy" is.

3. Roy comes at the reader with a rich assortment of examples, statistics, quotations and illustrations, ample and diverse enough to be very convincing.
4. Roy's position as a writing teacher would indicate that she has expertise in both language and education. However, her knowledge of socio-economic issues and her talent as a writer also add authority to her article.

Vocabulary

explicitly (5): clearly and precisely.
chauvinism (6): excessive or blind patriotism.
exacerbate (6): to make more violent, bitter, or severe.
implicitly (8): understood though not directly stated.
assimilation (10): to absorb into a cultural tradition.
inequity (10): unfairness; favoritism or bias.
exploitation (10): the unfair use of something or someone else for one's own advantage.
influx (11): a flowing in.
euphorically (12): in a manner showing a feeling of well-being or elation.
polarized (12): concentrated at opposing extremes.

Writing Topics

1. Class discussions of the Roy and Hayakawa articles will likely touch on the questions for this writing topic. Select one or two of Roy's sub-arguments and ask students to point out *how* she backs them up. In other words, guide students back into Roy's essay to uncover examples of her strategies and methods (this will show them how to examine Hayakawa's essay, too, if they have not already done so). As students write about their perceptions of Hayakawa and Roy, remind them to examine their own methods: are they more similar to those of Hayakawa, or to those of Roy? Why? Stress that while both authors have written persuasive articles, the styles and methods each employs will be of unequal use and credibility for different writers, and of varying influence upon different audiences (academic versus expressly political, for example).
2. Hayakawa's essay, in its brevity, acts as a more personal, emotional message from its author than does Roy's longer piece, with its wide coverage of facts and viewpoints. The reader of "Why English Should Be Our Official Language" must respond to the author's personal opinions, selective facts and quotes, and the emotional force of his argument, for these are largely what comprise his article. This sense of Hayakawa's immediacy effectively grabs the reader; it is somewhat flattering and interesting to have a former U.S. Senator (or anyone else, for that matter) address one so excitedly yet informally. Roy, on the other hand, can transmit a wealth of useful facts and thoroughly examine several important aspects of bilingualism and the English Only movement because of her article's greater length. (Students' outlines of the two articles will illustrate the formal, more objective nature of Roy's "The English Only Movement.")
3. Present mainstream American culture *is* drifting away from some of its traditional standards; a more careful, precise use of English is one of these. Yoder points out the hypocrisy and irony of efforts to ensconce English as the official language of the United States, even as its native speakers show less and less pride and interest in it. Perhaps, Yoder thinks, if the mainstream culture valued its language and literature more highly, there would be no thought of forcing English upon non-native speakers (and no hypocrisy, either). Note students' interest in this question—how serious are their responses? Are some written more

19

carefully, more precisely, more earnestly than usual? Do others have an angry, dismissive, or apathetic tone? Report your findings to the class, and allow discussion.

BLACK CHILDREN, BLACK SPEECH, Dorothy Z. Seymour (p. 84)

Questions on Content

1. Seymour defines Black English as "a dialect characteristic of many inner-city Negroes" (8), which has a form and structure of its own (10).
2. In Seymour's view, the specialization in sounds, structure, and vocabulary establishes Black English as a distinct dialect. The consistent substitutions and omissions of Black English sounds for those of Standard English; the meaningful alterations in indicating tense, time, plurality, gender, and negatives; and a unique vocabulary all characterize Black English as a distinct dialect rather than just a careless way of speaking Standard English.

   Seymour accounts for these differences by noting that whenever anyone learns a new language he will try to speak it with the sounds and structure of his native speech and, as Seymour explains, "if a person's first language does not happen to have a particular sound needed in the language he is learning, he will tend to substitute a similar or related sound from his native language and use it to speak the new one" (31). In the case of Black English, then, Seymour traces the changes in sounds, structure, and vocabulary to the West African languages that were ancestors to the Black English spoken today.
3. Seymour believes it is necessary for black children to learn Standard English as well as Black dialect so they can deal with society on its own terms. She goes on to quote Professor Toni Cade of Rutgers: "If you want to get ahead in this country, you must master the language of the ruling class," and finishes by stating that this has always been the case for minority groups (38).
4. Seymour points to the stance taken by some modern linguists that no dialect is intrinsically good or bad and concludes, therefore, that "a non-standard speech style is not defective speech but different speech" (13). The only way a language can be judged deficient is in comparison to another language and, as Seymour demonstrates in paragraph 13, such a comparison is relative, depending upon whose point of view is considered.

   It is important for Seymour to make this point because before she can present her argument in favor of bidialectism she needs to dispel the notion that Black dialect is inferior to Standard English, otherwise it would appear as though she supports the proposition that black children should be encouraged to learn and use a deficient language system.
5. Seymour lists the deficiencies of Standard English from the West African point of view in paragraph 33:
   a. It lacks certain language sounds.
   b. It has a couple of unnecessary language sounds for which others may serve as good substitutes.
   c. It doubles and drawls some of its vowel sounds in sequences that are unusual and difficult to imitate.
   d. It lacks a method for forming an important tense.

e. It requires an unnecessary number of ways to indicate tense, plurality, and gender.

f. It doesn't mark negatives sufficiently for the result to be a good strong negative statement.

6. In Seymour's view, bidialectism can give children the ability to use Standard English while at the same time help to eliminate the devastating effects that the denigration of Black English can instill in those who use it. This, in turn, can reduce the feelings of alienation and the number of dropouts in the black community.

To accomplish this goal students would have to learn and use two language systems; teachers would have to learn enough about Black dialect to understand and accept it as a viable form of English; and parents would have to be receptive to the belief that Black English is merely a *different* language pattern, not a *deficient* one, and that it can be beneficial to a child's development.

Questions on Rhetoric

1. The ultimate purpose of Seymour's essay is to persuade her readers to accept the need for bidialectism in public schools. However, to accomplish this she must first explain the issue in an effort to dispel the notion that Black English is defective and indicates deficiency in those who use it.

Students' opinions on whether Seymour's purpose is accomplished may vary, but they will probably agree that her essay at least provides a better understanding of Black English and therefore a more knowledgeable basis from which to consider the issue of bidialectism.

2. There are at least three ways in which the first seven paragraphs are an appropriate introduction for Seymour's essay. First, the conversation between the two boys is a good illustrative example of the dialect she refers to throughout her essay. Second, the content of the boys' conversation reveals the difficulties black children often face when confronted with Standard English in school. And third, this opening allows readers to consider their own judgments about the boys' use of Black dialect before reading the rest of Seymour's essay.

3. An inductive pattern of organization is appropriate for Seymour's essay because the majority of her readers will probably be initially hostile to the idea of bidialectism. By examining the evidence before she presents her conclusion, Seymour hopes to diffuse some of that hostility, thereby getting readers to consider her conclusion more rationally and favorably. If she had presented her conclusion—that bidialectism should be established in public schools-early in her essay, she might have lost many readers before they had even considered the evidence she has to offer, or they might have considered that evidence after already forming the conviction that Seymour is wrong.

4. Seymour cites authorities to lend importance and credibility to her argument. Her continual references to noted authors, linguists, and educators suggest that the analysis of Black English is an important area of study and therefore worthy of consideration by public schools. These references also allow Seymour to substantiate her claims about Black English and its role as a dialect with a form and structure of its own.

5. Most of the descriptions and explanations of the linguistic qualities of Black English are fairly easy to understand because Seymour *does* accommodate those readers who do not have a linguistics background. For instance, at the outset of her discussion of the sounds of Black English, she provides a parenthetical note that explains the use of slashes to indicate language sounds. In some cases, Seymour presents a full explanation of her use of a linguistic term, as with the "glided or dipthongized vowel sound" in paragraph 20. And finally, she also provides specific examples to illustrate each of her explanations so that readers can "see" what she means.

6. Seymour's tone can be characterized as "earnest." She is very straightforward and serious as she presents her information. This tone is appropriate since it conveys a sense of seriousness and sincerity and reflects the importance Seymour attaches to her subject matter and the presentation of her argument.
7. Paragraph 34 could be joined to the one preceding it since it is the conclusion to the ideas raised in paragraph 33. Using this one sentence as a paragraph in itself, however, places more emphasis on Seymour's point about the relative nature of so-called language deficiency.
8. The questions presented in paragraphs 34-36 reveal the points of argument that Seymour will address in her remaining paragraphs. They form the basis for her argument in support of bidialectism. The information preceding paragraph 34 is explanation and clarification of Black English—necessary before Seymour can present the thrust of her argument. The series of questions mark the transition from explanation to persuasion.

Vocabulary

stigmatized (8): characterized as disgraceful.
devastating (9): overwhelming, in a negative way.
eminent (10): outstanding; distinguished.
repudiated (12): not accepted as valid; rejected.
intrinsically (13): characterized by belonging to the nature of a thing or person; inherently.
assimilated (29): absorbed into the main social or cultural body.
autonomous (37): functioning or existing independently.
stratagem (38): a maneuver or plan.
denigrating (39): slandering; defaming.
vernacular (39): the common daily speech of a particular group of people.

Writing Topics

1. Before students begin writing about how their attitudes toward others are affected by the way they speak, ask them to look back at Seymour's introductory paragraphs and evaluate their own responses to the language used by the boys in the opening example. They should consider what kinds of opinions they formed about the speakers when they first read this conversation, and whether those opinions were altered any by the contents of Seymour's essay. Their analyses will give students a jumping-off point for considering the relationship between language and self-worth in their essays.
2. As a prewriting activity for this assignment, discuss with students what they learned about Black English from reading Seymour's essay, and then ask them to evaluate what effect this knowledge has had on their own attitudes toward Black dialect. Their evaluations may suggest advantages to be considered in their essays as they address the importance of understanding the characteristics of nonstandard dialects.
3. In her discussion of bidialectism Seymour focuses on those aspects that support her point of view and that demonstrate the positive effects of such a program. As a prelude to students developing their own argument on the issue, discuss both the pros and cons of bidialectism. Some students may have firsthand experience with a bilingual curriculum and can offer opinions on its benefits or its drawbacks. The point of your discussion should be to generate information on both sides of the issue, from which students can draw their own conclusions and select material to support their points of view.

Questions on Content

1. Jones first realized that she "talked white," when she was nine years old and the class bully accused her of getting good grades because she "talked white."

2. Jones has deduced that when people accuse her of talking white they are accusing her of being "articulate and well-versed." Years of observation have "confirmed the depressing reality that for many blacks, standard English is not only unfamiliar, it is socially unacceptable."

3. In paragraph 2 Jones says she spoke proper English long before she was aware it was unacceptable to many blacks, and long before she was exposed to white culture, in other words at a time when she was an integral member if a black culture. At that time it never occurred to her that she was not as "black" as any one else because of the way she spoke. Jones also quotes famous black leaders who spoke standard English at the same time that they were inspiring blacks to a sense of pride in their own culture. These references will be particularly convincing to readers who are familiar with these leaders and their strong sense of black identity, which clearly was not compromised by speaking standard English.

4. Jones defines black English in paragraph 1 as that "colorful, grammar-to-the-winds patois."

5. In the last three paragraphs of her essay Jones expresses concern that blacks who cannot speak standard English will be at a disadvantage in the job market and in the educational system. She also says they will be excluded "from full participation in the world we live in." This would include exclusion from participation in the political arena and the inability to express oneself in everyday situations such as complaining to a store manager about a purchase that does not work as promised.

Questions on Rhetoric

1. The quote from William Labov sets up the problem as Jones sees it, which is to convince whites and blacks that speaking standard English is not a betrayal of blackness. Her tone throughout the essay is one of annoyance more than of anger. In order to convey that annoyance Jones sometimes uses polite sarcasm. She describes herself as lower-middle class, "which in my mind is a polite way of describing a condition only slightly better than poverty." (2) "I was reminded once again of my "white pipes" problem while apartment hunting in Evanston, Illinois, last winter." (4) "But how heart-warming is (black dialect) when they hit the pavement searching for employment?" (8)

2. Jones offers brief narratives of her experiences with the misunderstanding about standard English such as the ones in paragraphs (3,) (4) and (5). She quotes black leaders in paragraph (7) and in the same paragraph contrasts standard English with black patois to make her point that even blacks concerned with civil rights did not compromise their use of standard English. The variety of examples Jones uses is in itself convincing. By including episodes with her peers, the speech of black leaders and prevalent attitudes among whites, Jones convinces her reader of the scope of the misunderstanding of what it means to be black.

3. Jones is not only articulate, she is a talented writer. "It is almost Jekyll and Hyde-ish the way I can slip out of academic abstractions into a long, lean double-negative-filled dialogue," (6) "I'd be lying if I said that the rhythms of my people caught up in "some serious rap" don't

sound natural and right to me sometimes." (8) "I don't think I talk white, I think I talk right." (10)

4. By ending with this reference Jones comes full circle in her dialogue with those who misunderstand what it means to "talk right." It is effective because by the time she has completed her argument, the reader has had the opportunity to weigh the opening quote against the implications of Jones's evidence.

Vocabulary

linguist (1): one who studies human speech.
patois (1): a dialect other than the standard or literary dialect.
doggedly (4): in a stubbornly determined manner.
deduced (5): derived by reasoning.
articulate (6): expressing oneself effectively and readily.
staples (6): the main parts of some thing; chief items.
dialect (10): a regional variety of a language.

Writing Topics

1. Even if your campus does have a Black Studies program, vital excerpts from students' essays might be submitted to the campus newspaper: professors, deans, and other students should be kept informed of student opinion on this issue.
2. Jones has a sensitivity to the plight of those whose black English has a negative effect on potential employers. She is concerned about the difficulty some black students have understanding their teachers and professors. Her no-nonsense, realistic outlook on life (seen in her personal asides and mild disclaimers) reflects her awareness of the many hurdles and labels black speakers of standard English encounter. Finally, Jones has a dignity that allows her to believe in her language abilities as a person first, above any other character-istics. Jones might argue that, as a minority group, blacks have a collective, ever-changing framework of concerns, hopes, and self-images; Jones is defined by, and also sensitively and intelligently helps define, that framework.

CAUGHT BETWEEN TWO LANGUAGES, Richard Rodriguez   (p. 97)

Questions on Content

1. Rodriguez remembers the nun calling out his name his first day at school. It was a memorable experience because it was the first time he heard anyone name him in English.
2. According to Rodriguez, the goal of the supporters of bilingual education is to "permit non-English-speaking children, many from lower-class homes, to use their family language as the language of school." Rodriguez opposes such a program because he does not believe it is possible for a child to use his family's language at school and that "not to understand this is to misunderstand the public uses of schooling and to trivialize the nature of family life" (5).

3. Rodriguez describes public language as that which demonstrates that a person belongs in public society, while private language reveals a shared feeling of being apart from "los gringos," of being *home*. He also presents, in paragraph 28, the characteristics he noticed as a child that distinguished public, classroom language from the private language of his home: (1) It was directed to a general audience of listeners; (2) Its words were meaningfully ordered; (3) The point of it was not self-expression alone but to make oneself understood by many others.

4. Rodriguez found his parents' attempts to speak English "unsettling." He would "grow nervous" hearing them, his "clutching trust in [his parents'] protection and power weakened" (15). His own problems with English were that he could not stretch words far enough to form complete thoughts, and that he didn't know the words he did speak well enough to make them into distinct sounds (14).

   Rodriguez's attitude toward the sounds of "los gringos" changed as he began to perceive the importance of having a public identity, an identity that called for the adoption and use of a public language—English. This change is complete, as he describes in paragraph 12, when he hears the sounds of English with pleasure because they are now the sounds of *his* society and a reminder of home, rather than a source of alienation.

5. The great lesson of school for Rodriguez was learning that he had a public identity.

6. The nuns wanted to know what language was spoken in Richard's home because they understood that he needed to speak a public language; yet he resisted their demands that he practice and use English at school and remained "dazed, diffident, [and] afraid" (27). The nuns also connected Richard's behavior with the slow progress his brother and sister were making in school.

   After the nuns' visit, Richard's parents gave up the language "that had revealed and accentuated [his] family's closeness" (38) and began to speak to him, at home, in broken English. The family members also began to practice their English after dinner each night, and the three children attended daily tutoring sessions at school.

7. Rodriguez believes his first-grade classmates could have become bilingual more easily than himself because they would have regarded a second language simply as another public language, whereas he did not believe he could speak even one public language.

Questions on Rhetoric

1. Rodriguez is suited to speak on bilingual education because, as he states in paragraph 6, he "was a bilingual child, a certain kind—socially disadvantaged—the son of working-class parents, both Mexican immigrants." In other words, he was just the type of child the advocates of bilingual education hope to aid with their program.

2. The personal narrative is effective in conveying the difference between public and private language and therefore strengthens Rodriguez's point about the need for children to develop a public identity—the main thrust of his argument against bilingual education.

3. The first four paragraphs highlight the difficulties and fears a child faces when he begins school without adequate knowledge of the language spoken there. They connect with the rest of the essay by establishing Rodriguez's childhood experiences with language as the basis for his argument against bilingual education, as Rodriguez himself suggests in paragraph 6: "Memory teaches me what I know of these matters; the boy reminds the adult."

4. The juxtapositioning of English and Spanish words emphasizes the differenec in *sounds* between the two languages and this is the basis for Rodriguez's identification of each language with a separate world, one public and one private.

As he describes growing older and changing his attitude about English, Rodriguez intersperses the Spanish and English words without the corresponding translations to indicate that the sounds have merged and are no longer as noticeable as when they represented two distinct worlds for him.

5. These words reveal that Rodriguez felt he had no "place" outside the world of his family, that he had no public identity because he could not communicate with that outside world.

Vocabulary

endorsed (5): supported; approved of.
intimidated (7): made timid; made to feel fear.
gaudy (8): obtrusively brilliant in color; flashy.
counterpoint (9): a contrasting but parallel element, item, or theme.
nasal (12): characterized by or resembling a resonant sound produced through the nose.
barrio (17): a chiefly Spanish-speaking community or neighborhood in a U.S. city.
canopy (21): a high, overarching covering.
diffident (27): hesitant to assert oneself from a lack of self-confidence; timid.

Writing Topics

1. As a prewriting discussion for this assignment ask your students to relate what role their families have played in the development of their language skills. Find out, for instance, how many of them were read aloud to as children and whether they feel it had any effect on their facility with language. Or discover what, if any, similarities exist in the experiences that have contributed greatly to students' learning language skills. Your discussion may lead students into areas of thought they can follow up on in their essays.

2. Though many of your students may not have experienced being placed in a schoolroom where the language was foreign to them, they may have encountered situations on vacations or during travels where they did not speak or understand the native language. For those who have, discuss in class whether they can identify with Rodriguez's description of how foreign sounds affected him, or with the alienation he felt at not being able to understand. This may provide a better understanding of what Rodriguez means by not having a public identity and can serve as a focus for this writing assignment.

3. Before students begin this assignment it may be helpful to conduct a brief class exercise in which they must classify various speaking and writing situations as either public or private. Using the distinctions Rodriguez establishes in his essay, have them consider situations such as speaking on the telephone, writing a letter to a friend, addressing an audience of strangers, etc.; then have them decide if each specific situation reflects a public or private use of language. Their analyses may lead students to discover differences between the two that Rodriguez does not address, and can aid in the development of their essays.

III. THE LANGUAGE OF POLITICS AND PROPAGANDA

POLITICS AND THE ENGLISH LANGUAGE, George Orwell   (p. 111)

Questions on Content

1. Students should base the summaries of Orwell's argument on the first two paragraphs of his essay. Basically, Orwell feels that "the English language is in a bad way" (1), but that it can be improved.
2. For Orwell, a mixed metaphor is "a sure sign that the writer is not interested in what he is saying" (5). If the writer's mind were engaged, he would avoid inconsistency. Orwell, then, is concerned about the ways that formulaic writing both reveals and encourages thoughtless writing.
3. Orwell notes that "an effect can become a cause, reinforcing the original cause and producing the same effect in an intensified form, and so on indefinitely" (2).
4. Formulaic writing is prefabricated writing. As such, it discourages both fresh ideas and imaginative composition. Unfortunately, the prefabricated phrase is easier and quicker, so there is a great temptation to use it. Good writing is often painstaking and slow if our words are to serve rather than control our thoughts.
5. Orwell is careful to avoid such errors. His first paragraph, however, contains "it is generally assumed," "so the argument runs," and "must inevitably share," which are all trite; his second paragraph contains "modern English," which is a vague term, at least at this point in his essay. By a careful analysis of other paragraphs, your students will be able to identify additional "errors."
6. Orwell's four prewriting questions from paragraph 12 are:
   a. What am I trying to say?
   b. What words will express it?
   c. What image or idiom will make it clearer?
   d. Is this image fresh enough to have an effect?
      Orwell says that scrupulous writers will probably ask themselves two more questions as well:
   e. Could I put it more shortly?
   f. Have I said anything that is avoidably ugly?
7. Not all dictionaries will contain the term "question-begging." It is a logical fallacy that occurs when the conclusion of an argument is a rephrasing of its beginning assumption. The argument is circular, goes nowhere, and thus is said to beg the original question. For example, "Alcohol is bad for children because it is illegal." "Why is it illegal?" "It is illegal because it is harmful." Most examples of this fallacy are not so easy to detect. Ask your students to find additional examples in their daily reading and to bring them to class.

27

Orwell believes that political language has deteriorated because politics has deteriorated. As he puts it in paragraph 14, "In our time, political speech and writing are largely the defence of the indefensible." He believes that politicians have become less sensitive to the needs of humanity and therefore try to be evasive—to hide behind vagueness in speech and writing.

Most linguists would agree with Orwell that the progress of any language is both uncontrollable and controllable. Its history over a long period may be inevitable, but its more meaningful short-term development can be consciously controlled by just the kinds of suggestions that Orwell offers.

Questions on Rhetoric

1. Orwell presents the five samples (3) as representative examples of how the "English language... is now habitually written" (2). He continues: "These five passages have not been picked out because they are especially bad ... but because they illustrate various of the mental vices from which we now suffer" (3).

   In paragraphs 11 and 12, Orwell returns to these five passages and makes critical remarks about them related to the various vices he discusses.

2. Each of Orwell's metaphors and similes turns an abstraction into a concrete image and thus makes it easier for the reader to understand his argument. Each is vivid, memorable, and striking in its novelty. You may wish to ask your class what figures of speech they would use to convey the same information.

3. Orwell classifies "the tricks by means of which the work of prose construction is habitually dodged" (4) into the following categories: "Dying Metaphors," "Operators or Verbal False Limbs," "Pretentious Diction," and "Meaningless Words." In this part of his essay, Orwell is attempting to explain and clarify various types of language abuse and finds classification (a type of exposition) useful for this purpose.

4. The terms or concepts that Orwell defines include: metaphor, dead metaphor, dying metaphor, false limbs, pretentious diction, meaningless words, and euphemisms. A clear understanding of these terms is crucial to the success of Orwell's argument since they help explain what is wrong with the language he criticizes.

   For each of these definitions Orwell first describes what the term or concept means and then provides a concrete, illustrative example to help clarify that meaning.

5. The transition from criticisms to proposals occurs in paragraph 18: "I said earlier that the decadence of language is probably curable.

   By organizing his essay this way Orwell establishes a clear and complete understanding of the problem before addressing how to attack it. He also aids this approach by notifying readers early in the essay (paragraph 2) that "the process [of the decline of language] is reversible" and that he will return to this aspect of his topic after analyzing the process of decline.

6. In that "habits" and "vices" are correctable or reversible, Orwell's use of these terms is consistent with his thesis that language corruption is also reversible.

7. The sentences rewritten in the active voice are as follows:
   a. John hit the line-drive single.
   b. You should add two eggs and one stick of butter to the other ingredients.
   c. Doctors cannot release information of a confidential nature.
   d. The administration released figures today showing that the cost of living rose sharply during the past twelve months.
   e. Someone decided that a meeting would be held on each Monday.

When the actor is unknown or when the writer prefers to deemphasize or not mention the actor, the passive voice is appropriate.

The active voice is more direct than the passive voice about who is doing something. The passive voice, because it permits concealment of the actor, can be used to deceive, as was frequently the case in some Watergate testimony and Pentagon releases during the Vietnam War.

Vocabulary

decadent (1): in a state or condition of decline or decay.
frivolous (2): unworthy of serious attention.
inadvertently (4): unintentionally.
implication (5): act of implying or suggesting; that which is implied.
impartiality (7): lack of prejudice; neutrality.
biased (7): prejudiced.
reconciled (8): made compatible.
pretentious (12): showy, affected.
scrupulous (12): principled; painstaking.
humanitarian (15): one devoted to the promotion of human welfare.
evolutionary (18): gradually changing or developmental.

Writing Topics

1. Orwell would probably find much to complain about in this ad, especially in regard to his ideas about the "defense of the indefensible." Students' analyses of the ad will probably focus on the following phrases and sentences:
   "smoking has always been an adult custom"
   "even among adults, smoking is controversial"
   "as if you were a child"
   "just because you're no longer a child doesn't mean you're already an adult"
   "you're kidding yourself"
   "That's about as straight as we can put it."
   As a prewriting activity you can look at a couple of these lines in class and ask students to identify which of Orwell's devices for deceptive language they are examples of.
2. Another way students can collect examples of "political English" is to watch TV news broadcasts for a few days and record suitable selections of this type of communication.
   Whatever means students use to collect examples, once they've gathered their five you may want to consider some of them in class to see if they reflect the "tricks" Orwell mentions or if there are, indeed, new tricks apparent in them. Your discussion can demonstrate to students how to analyze their own collections of examples as they develop ideas for their essays.
3. Before students write about their own experiences involving attempts to conceal meaning through the manipulation of language, it may help to discuss examples outside the realm of politics that also illustrate this idea. Here are a few examples you might consider:
   celebrity responses to scandal
   reactions of sports figures and officials to charges of drug abuse
   a business spokesperson's defense against charges of harmful or unethical practices
   public disputes between management and labor during negotiations to end or forestall a strike

SELECTION, SLANTING AND CHARGED LANGUAGE, Newman P. Birk and Genevieve B. Birk (p.125)

Questions on Content

1. The Birks define and explain the principle of selection in the first paragraph: "What we know or observe depends on what we notice; that is, what we select, consciously or unconsciously, as worthy of our notice or attention. As we observe, the principle of selection determines which facts we take in."

   They later add that the principle of selection "holds not only for the specific facts that people observe but also for the facts they remember," and is influenced by "our whole mental state of the moment" (3). The Birks then summarize their explanation: "The principle of selection serves as a kind of sieve or screen through which our knowledge passes before it becomes our knowledge" (4), and "it is important to remember that what is true of the way the principle of selection works for us is true also of the way it works for others" (5).

2. Slanting differs from the principle of selection in that it occurs as "we express our knowledge in words" rather than as "we take in knowledge" (note to paragraph 6). The three devices that a writer or speaker can use to slant knowledge are: (1) the selection of facts and feelings from our store of knowledge; (2) the use of charged words; and (3) the use of emphasis to communicate meaning.

3. The first example illustrates how, by changing the word that is stressed, the meaning of the phrase "wise old man" changes also. Then the authors demonstrate other ways of slanting through emphasis by changing the connectives and word order of this same phrase:

   old but wise (emphasis on *wise*)
   old and wise (balanced emphasis)
   wise but old (emphasis on *old*)

   In note 4 the Birks illustrate how punctuation marks can provide emphasis and slant meaning:

   He called the Senator an honest man?
   (The question mark places doubt on the statement's accuracy.)

   He called the Senator an honest man?
   (The stressed "He," along with the question mark, questions the credibility of the speaker who called the Senator an honest man.)

   He called the Senator an honest man!
   (The exclamation point expresses surprise or astonishment at the speaker's action.)

   He said one more "honest" senator would corrupt the state.
   (The quotation marks signify the ironic use of the word "honest.")

   And in the final series of examples the authors show, again, how connectives and word order can influence meaning:

   He is awkward and strong.
   He is strong and awkward.
   (In these two, word order determines emphasis.)

   He is awkward but strong.

30

He is strong but awkward.
(In these two, the connective "but" determines emphasis.)

Although he is somewhat awkward, he is very strong.
He may be strong, but he's very awkward.
(In these two, the combination of connectives and word order determines emphasis.)

4. As the Birks explain in paragraph 31, charged words are those that "convey any kind of inner knowledge—feelings, attitude, judgments, values... [It] is the natural and necessary medium for the communication of charged or attitudinal meaning."
Examples of charged language from the two descriptions of Corlyn include:

Slanted for	*Slanted against*
well-cut	plain black dress
draped subtly	hung
slender form	thin frame
chiseled features	stringy
Simple frame	bleached
engaging smile	harsh features
rare talent	inane smile
one man in the world	last man on Earth
descended	fast and ungainly
effortless grace	reached for some coffee
spoke with equal ease	flickering light...
Ethereal quality to her	revealed every flaw
beauty	loud talk
eyes danced with each	gulped down
leap of the flame	eyes grew red with each
	leap of the flame

5. Students' responses may vary, but they should address the issues of selection and slanting.
6. Without charged words we would not be able to express attitudinal meaning and would be left with a language that could only convey verifiable facts, as the Birks explain in paragraph 33:"[Charged language] shapes our attitudes and values even without our conscious knowledge; it gives purpose to, and guides our actions; through it we establish and maintain relations with other people and by means of it we exert our greatest influence on them."

Questions on Rhetoric

1. Students' reactions to these examples may vary, but it seems apparent that had they not been included the essay would lack the clear and concrete illustrations that help clarify the meaning and purpose of the Birks' essay.
2. Paragraph I presents a definition for "the principle of selection," and paragraph 2 illustrates the definition by providing a concrete example showing the principle in operation.
3. the Birks have used a logical order to present their information, beginning with the least difficult point to understand and ending with the most difficult. In doing so, they have arranged their material in a very structured, almost outlined, manner. The combination of these organizational schemes is appropriate and effective for the explanatory nature of their essay because it makes it easy for readers to follow the successive points and to comprehend the discussion that accompanies each.

4. The Birks' purpose is to *explain* some of the linguistic processes involved in human communication. Their essay serves more as a definition than an argument.

Vocabulary

exhaustive (2): comprehensive; thorough.
blushed (3): became red in the face, especially from modesty, embarrassment, or shame.
sieve (4): a utensil of wire mesh or closely perforated metal used for straining or sifting.
attitudinal (6): characterized by being a state of mind or feeling.
verifiable (11): able to be proved true by the presentation of evidence or testimony.
inconspicuous (26): not readily noticeable.
abstractions (29): general ideas or words, considered apart from concrete existence.
turbulencies (33): violently agitated, disturbed, or chaotic experiences or emotions.

Writing Topics

1. This exercise is designed to allow your students to attempt to create different realities through language. By maintaining essentially the same facts, adding material that is not totally objective, altering diction, and changing the point of view, the total impression of a passage can be changed. Of the following three paragraphs, only the first presents an objective statement of facts; the other two create different impressions:

> At a press conference, President Carter announced that he had sent Secretary of State Cyrus Vance to the Middle East to confer with both Menachem Begin and Anwar el-Sadat about the peace initiatives there.

> President Jimmy Carter, in a major effort toward world peace, has announced that he asked Secretary of State Cyrus Vance, who has just returned from Moscow, to go to the Middle East to attempt to improve the uneasy truce there.

> With the hope of drawing the attention of Americans away from his personal political problems, Carter has ordered Vance to the Middle East to confer with leaders concerning the tense situation there.

2. To evaluate the success of the students' attempts at slanting, you can ask some of them to read one of their three descriptions aloud and have the rest of the class identify which of the three it is. In most cases, the ones slanted for and against will be easily identified, but students may have some difficulty recognizing the balanced versions if the writers haven't been especially careful in the selection and arrangement of facts. In any case, after each version is identified discuss what, specifically, led to that identification.

3. The article entitled "Little League Bans Foreigners: No More Chinese HRs" appeared in the *New York Daily News*, a tabloid. The other version appeared in *The New York Times*. Both appeared on November 11, 1974. Students should base their decisions on the following types of evidence:
   1. headlines
   2. diction
   3. opinion versus fact
   4. tone
   5. attitude
   You may wish to have your students analyze the following version of the same story, which

appeared in the *Boston Globe*. Stylistically, this version shares some qualities with the articles in both the *Daily News* and the *Times*.

TAIWAN OUT: LITTLE LEAGUERS BAR "FOREIGNERS"

Associated Press

WILLIAMSPORT, Pa.—Little League will confine future World Series to teams from the continental United States.

The announcement made yesterday was an apparent aim to exclude Taiwan, which has won the series the past four years, and in 1957 and 1958, Monterrey, Mexico, took the baseball title for boys under 12 years old.

The League said all of its local leagues had been advised of the change made by the board of directors after a review of the competition.

Little League said regional championship series would be continued in Canada, the Far East, Europe and Latin America and its playoffs for senior or big league programs would not be affected.

A spokesman cited travel costs for foreign entries and the nationalistic approach taken abroad as the reason for the change. He described the U.S. Little League programs as regional in makeup.

Since the Little League broadened its scope in 1957 and 1958 to include teams outside the continent, 20 foreign teams competed in the program. There are 9,000 leagues in the U.S.

The Little League World Series will be played here Aug. 19-23.

Only four teams, the U.S. regional champions, will be entered. Whether it will be a sudden death or double elimination series has not been determined.

There were eight teams in the series when foreign teams competed.

The first Little League World Series was played in 1947.

The ruling eliminates children of American servicemen stationed in Europe because a spokesman said they were considered "foreign."

GOBBLEDYGOOK, Stuart Chase (p.138)

Questions on Content

1. Gobbledygook is verbosity—"using two, or three, or ten words in the place of one, or using a five-syllable word where a single syllable would suffice" (2). In short, gobbledygook tends to obscure instead of clarify.

   In thinking of examples of gobbledygook, students should try to remember the language typically found in legal documents, government guidelines and regulations, political speeches, insurance policies, product guarantees, and so forth.

   Chase objects to the use of gobbledygook because it makes communication difficult, if not impossible.

   In this statement from paragraph 33, Chase means that if we thought of ourselves as receivers as well as transmitters of messages we would be more careful and precise in the sending of our messages.

2. Professionals use gobbledygook, or "professional jargon," for a number of reasons—to deceive, to conceal, to impress, to dumbfound, to clarify, and so on.

   Professional jargon is justified when all parties involved are "in the know" (for instance, when a lawyer is talking to another lawyer or a doctor is addressing a medical convention). Students may wish to reread George Orwell's comments on meaningless words in "Politics and the English Language."

3. This is essentially an exercise in vocabulary choice. Students can also brush up on their paraphrasing skills. You might ask your students to collect interesting current examples of gobbledygook from magazines and newspapers and then have the class "ungobble" them.

   Students will probably find Chase's revisions a big improvement on the originals, but you may wish to find out whether they believe he eliminated too much.

4. Gobbledygook tends to reduce human beings to abstractions and thus to dehumanize communications. Orwell feels that the way to combat such abstraction is to use concrete terms.

Questions on Rhetoric

1. Chase's purpose is to define gobbledygook and to explain where and how it is used.
2. In the opening paragraph, Chase translates Roosevelt's pointed statement into "standard bureaucratic prose." It is from this example that he deduces his definition in paragraph 2.

   It is necessary for Chase to establish a definition of gobbledygook before he can proceed to a discussion of the areas in which it is chiefly manifested.

   According to Chase (end of paragraph 9), the difference between gobbledygook and double-talk is the intention of the speaker or writer; the intentions of the user of gobbledygook are usually honest, whereas the intentions of the user of double-talk are usually dishonest.

3. Chase uses many examples and quotations to illustrate his points, to document his contentions, and to indicate how widespread the use of gobbledygook is.

   The examples are important because they are themselves concrete and not abstract like the word *gobbledygook.*

4. Most students will probably find the ending effective, both for its illustrative quality and for its humor.

   Chase could have ended his essay at paragraph 36, since it ends on the notion of "ungobbling" bureaucratic prose. It does not, however, have the overall summary effect or the inherent humor of the plumber story.

Vocabulary

pretentious (2): showy; affected.

immortal (4): not subject to death.

squandering (9): wasting.

tautologies (11): needless repetitions of the same idea in different words.

advocates (13): speaks in favor of.

proposition (16): a plan or scheme suggested for acceptance.

murky (25): confused or muddled.

clients (25): those for whom professional services are rendered.

Writing Topics

1. Students react to this passage in different ways. Some are awed by the writer's diction ("I wish I could write like that"); others are confused by the passage and admit that they had to read it several times; and, finally, some recognize the passage for what it is—gobbledygook. Some have great difficulty in trying to condense the paragraph. Duplicate a dozen student responses in order to discuss the differences among them in class. Basically, one could translate the paragraph as follows: "We can't always have everything we want, so we must pick and choose."

   Students can enjoy creating their own technical jargon, or what Arthur Herzog aptly calls "Sci-speak." Ask students to think of a three-digit number. Then have them form a "technical term" by linking the corresponding words in the table below.

COLUMN 1	COLUMN 2	COLUMN 3
0. evaluative	0. coalition	0. equilibrium
1. functional	1. power	1. relation
2. hyperbolic	2. influence	2. attribution
3. intuitive	3. communication	3. contingency
4. interactive	4. sociometric	4. gradient
5. reciprocal	5. role	5. structure
6. negative	6. activity	6. decision
7. operational	7. task	7. network
8. centralized	8. status	8. matrix
9. interdependent	9. interpersonal	9. index

   The table is taken from p. 146 of Arthur Herzog, *The B.S. Factor: The Theory and Technique of Faking It in America* (New York: Simon & Schuster, 1973). According to the table, the number 514 produces a "reciprocal power gradient." After working with Herzog's table, ask your students to comment on jargon and the dangers inherent in its usage.

2. This exercise provides an opportunity for students to deal directly with an example of gobbledygook. The main problems with this example are that it merges the present, past, and future tenses; it eliminates the distinction between masculine and feminine pronouns; and it makes the singular mean either singular or plural and the plural mean either plural or singular. This is not the way English works, and students' reactions should range from confusion to laughter to outrage.

   Students should also recognize that the depersonalizing nature of bureaucratic agencies and the legal system makes them especially prone to impersonal, writer-oriented "gobbledygook."

3. This assignment offers a good means for evaluating students' comprehension of the essays they've read. After reading their essays, you may wish to select two or three to share with the class and use as a focus for discussion of the differences between these terms. The ones you select should contain effective, illustrative examples accompanied by clear and concise explanations for what those examples demonstrate in regard to "jargon," "technical language," and "gobbledygook."

PROPAGANDA: HOW NOT TO BE BAMBOOZLED,
Donna Woolfolk Cross   (p.149)

Questions on Content

1. Propaganda is "simply a means of persuasion" (1).
   Propaganda is used by all kinds of people, for good and bad causes.
   It is used for the purpose of influencing the behaviors and attitudes of people.
2. Cross feels that "propaganda pervades our daily lives, helping to shape our attitudes on a thousand subjects" (2). People should, therefore, be informed about propaganda so that they can distinguish between deceptive propaganda (that can be used to mislead,) and reasonable argument.
   Cross's advice for dealing with propaganda is to become informed about the various devices that propagandists use.
3. "Begging the question" occurs when "a person assumes as already established the very point that he is trying to prove" (37). This device is explained in paragraphs 37 and 38.
4. In paragraphs 47-50, Cross discusses what she believes is the most common propaganda device: the testimonial.
   Examples of testimonials abound in advertisements and political campaigns.
5. Cross believes that we should become informed about the methods and purposes of propaganda "so we can be the masters, not the slaves of our destiny" (52).

Questions on Rhetoric

1. Classification allows Cross to bring a sense of order to her discussion of the various types of propaganda used today. Cross organizes her discussion of each type of propaganda device as follows:
   a. identify and define device
   b. provide examples of device
   c. offer advice on how to combat device
3. Cross uses examples extensively in her essay. She provides one or more to illustrate and clarify each explanation for the types of propaganda devices. She also continually returns to the fictitious politician Senator Yakalot, since politics is an area where the devices are often employed.
   Students will probably find the examples very helpful in understanding the descriptions of propaganda devices.
4. People, like lemmings, are "often the unwitting victims of the bandwagon appeal" (23).
   Cross qualifies the analogy by pointing out that lemmings are driven by instinct whereas people choose to join the crowd.

Vocabulary

connotations (8): the associated or secondary meanings suggested by a word, as distinguished from its denotations.
elicits (10): draws or brings out.
colloquial (14): characteristic of ordinary or familiar conversation.
insidiously (15): deceitfully or deviously.
spectrum (40): a continuous sequence or range.

Writing Topics

1. Most students will probably agree that the ends do justify the means, but it is nonetheless useful to have them consider their acceptance of propaganda in these instances. Do we become inured to propaganda through such easy acceptance? Why do organizations whose intent is to help others use propaganda devices? Are there not other ways to generate support?
2. When students have completed this assignment ask a few of them to read their essays in class so others can evaluate how persuasive they are and can identify the types of propaganda devices they have employed. Then discuss which devices Cross mentions are most effective for the purpose and subject matter of each essay.

INAUGURAL ADDRESS, John F. Kennedy (p.161)

Questions on Content

1. Kennedy is referring to advances in agriculture and the advent of nuclear power, which did not exist when our country was young. The first can be used to bring prosperity to poorer countries; the second can annihilate all people.
2. Kennedy addresses his remarks to allies (6), post-communist nations (7), third-world countries (8), South American countries (9), the United Nations (10), and our political enemies (11–20). By not naming names, Kennedy allows the groups he is addressing to identify themselves silently, to slip the shoe on if they decide it fits. In the case of enemies, this tactic may seem less confrontational, yet Kennedy maintains his dignity without name-calling and still conveys the strength inherent in the suggestion that, "I don't have to call you by name, you know who you are."
3. "If a free society cannot help the many who are poor, it cannot save the few who are rich." (8) "Let us never negotiate out of fear, but let us never fear to negotiate." (14) "And so, my fellow Americans, ask not what your country can do for you; ask what you can do for your country." (25) These phrases are short and catchy and seem to sum up in a line several sentences worth of ideas. They are effective aspects of Kennedy's style because they are well-crafted and easy to remember. In fact, many of these phrases were well known.
4. Few presidents outline the "how to's" of the "must do's" in an inaugural speech. Such details, if stated at all, are usually reserved for campaign speeches, press conferences, and state of the union speeches. An inaugural address is generally more of an occasion of inspiration than of strategy, thus Kennedy's speech does not come across as lacking in an essential detail.

Questions on Rhetoric

1. Paragraphs 6 through 10 begin with the word "to." Paragraphs 15 through 18 begin with words "Let both." In paragraphs 25 and 26 Kennedy uses the phrases, "my fellow Americans" and "My fellow citizens of the world." Parallelism is a chief component of Kennedy's writing style. It strengthens his writing by stating key phrases over and over again, thus

37

ingraining them in the mind of the reader. It also lends a pounding rhythm that makes his speeches easier to listen to and to follow.

2. Throughout his speech Kennedy has addressed other nations, the United Nations, and political enemies using the "we" pronoun. Finally, he calls for the listener, his fellow Americans to join him in that "we." It has the effect of verbally tapping the listener on the shoulder and reminding him or her that the listener is also "we." It is also a powerful means of empowering the voters, of making them feel as responsible as the president for carrying out his agenda.

3. Kennedy's tone in addressing the first several groups outside the United States is one of friendship. It is intended to express good intentions. However, toward the "enemies" of the state, he takes on a more menacing tone. Although he is extending the olive branch, he has the other hand in his pocket ready to draw if necessary. His speech was made during the height of the Cold War, when relations with Russia were tenuous. When he speaks to the citizens of his own country, Kennedy's tone is no less forceful; however, instead of a threat he issues a challenge to join him in the fulfillment of his vision. Kennedy uses a different tone with each group for the simple reason that his message and his expectation for each group are different. Throughout his speech, however, his overall tone is marked by a forcefulness of purpose which lends unity to his style.

4. Kennedy addresses each group separately; he does not shift back and forth among them. He addresses first the allies of the United States, then the new friends, then the acquaintances, each time affording them one paragraph. Kennedy then devotes paragraphs 11–20 to the "adversaries" of the United States, warning them that he will not be weak, and calling for an effort toward peaceful cooperation. Paragraphs 21–27 address his fellow citizens.

5. Kennedy uses a metaphor to warn South American nations that if they align themselves with Communist countries, the short-term gains might end in long term misery.

Vocabulary

oath (1): a solemn appeal to God to witness the truth of a statement
asunder (6): in separate pieces.
tyranny (7): government in which rule is vested in a tyrant.
prey (9): victim.
subversion (9): the attempt to overthrow.
invective (10): abusive language.
invoke (17): to put into effect or operation.
shrink (24): to draw back or away; withdraw.

Writing Topics

1. Ask students to share in class what they know or have heard about the Kennedy administration. Experience suggests that, 25 years later, students are still excited by discussions of this period. Some will know fairly little; some will probably hold a rather romanticized image of the Kennedys (will, in effect, have been impressed by the "Camelot" myth); some may be knowledgeably critical. Be sure that students know what "Camelot" refers to (the site of King Arthur's round table, handily theatricalized during the Kennedy years by the Broadway musical of the same name). Those students who take an oppositional view of JFK may want to consider what Orwell would make of, e. g., (4) or (24).

2. Students will probably need some information on the global political climate of the 1950s,

including not only the relations between the superpowers but also the colonial uprisings in the developing countries.
3. To relate the assignment more closely to the Kennedy speech, ask students to compare the two speakers' situations, audiences, and motives. The essay might be easier, for some, as a comparison and contrast between the two speeches.

THE RONALD REAGAN BASIC 1984 CAMPAIGN SPEECH,
The New York Times (p. 167)

Questions on Content

1. Reagan's definition of partriotism as a recognition that one's country is a decent place to live and is a force for good in the world conforms closely to the dictionary definition of the word, i.e. a love of one's country. However, some students will argue that love of country does not imply, "my country right or wrong," as Reagan's definition does. They will argue further that a proud citizenry has the right to question the policies of its country without being labeled unpatriotic.
2. The question some students will raise is "freer than what?" In order to understand Reagan's use of the word "freer", we have to understand Reagan's concept of the word "free."
3. Reagan was referring to the Carter administration. The word "they" connotes a formless, faceless reality and in this case is slightly mocking in tone. It is similar in its effect to the "they" President John F. Kennedy used in his inaugural speech, earlier in the section. It permits the audience to nod assent, to agree with the speaker that the faults of the "they" are so well-known that "they" don't even have to be identified by name. It allows the speaker to imply, "I don't have to call you by name, we all know who you are."
4. Hopefully, most college students know that statistics can be used to "prove" almost anything. For example, in order to evaluate the relative accuracy of Reagan's statement that six million new jobs were "created" during the first four years of his administration, a student world also have to know how many jobs were "lost." Reagan alludes to reductions in federal spending, (11) however, he does not say how those reductions may have resulted in increased state spending. In the matter of interest rates, some economists maintain that these rates are slow to react to policies and that each administration bears the gift or the burden of the policies of the previous administration. So in order to answer the question of who can legitimately take credit for improvements, a student needs a sophisticated and broad-based understanding of the various factors that influence change and economics. For the most part, presidents are made or broken on the popular perception of the truth of their claims.
5. Reagan promised to improve education, simplify the tax system, lower taxes, and provide a job for every American who wants one. Obviously, not all these promises were kept. However, campaigning politicians often make promises they cannot possibly keep, because some of these promises are simply too grand in scope. Reagan promises jobs to every American who wanted one. However, the job market is influenced by factors (such as the world economy) which are outside a president's control.
6. By reminding his listeners that he was once, and still considers himself, a member of the

Democratic Party, Reagan is bridging the gap that many Democrats would normally feel exist between themselves and a Republican presidential candidate. In effect, Reagan is suggesting to the voters in his audience that he shares their ideology.

Questions on Rhetoric

1. "There's a feeling of patriotism in out land... And I don't know about you but I'm tired of hearing people run her down." (1)
    "For them to introduce that blueprint for bondage in Philadelphia,... was a betrayal of the American people." (12) "They see an American where every day is April 15th, tax day. We see an American where every day is the Fourth of July." (15)
    "I am telling you that what I felt was that the leadership of the Democrat Party had left me and millions of patriotic Democrats in this country who believed in freedom." (28)
2. "I will say, however, their policies were fair. They didn't discriminate—they made everybody miserable." (5) "You know, I have to tell you, I'm afraid that the age issue may be a factor in this election after all. My opponent's ideas are just too old." (14)
    Reagan's brand of humor is intended to be easy-going and good-natured. It adds to his image as a "nice guy."
3. Reagan uses simple phrasing and avoids a fancy vocabulary, which makes it easy to follow his speech. He also asks the members of his audience questions in an almost evangelical style that elicits an energetic response and draws them into his thinking. Another aspect of this style is his ability to fire up a crowd with frequent reference to America's best image of itself as a patriotic, decent place to live.

Vocabulary

patriotism (1): love of one's country.
legacy (2): inheritance; bequest.
malaise (4): a sense of physical ill-being.

Writing Topics

1. Reagan's use of the victorious Olympic athletes as a figure for the inevitable success of American perserverance works in several ways. It flatters his audience with the thought that they each personally partook in the athletes' victories. It also comforts them with the thought that the real challenges that America faces are really no more complex than shot-putting or broad-jumping. It implies that, in facing those real challenges, there will be clear-cut"winners" and "losers," which is not only a simplification but a preparatory move toward declaring the world's "losers" insignificant—one basic thrust of Reaganite ideology. Finally, it transfers to Reagan himself some of the glory of the athletes' victories by implying that they were due to the so-called rebirth of patriotism with which Reagan was so closely associated. To fully unpack the workings of this figure and others like it is to understand the complexity of that process summed up in the familiar cliche about Reagan: that he became enormously popular by "making Americans feel good about themselves."
2. Students who come to this assignment assuming a wide ideological disparity between JFK and Ronald Reagan may be surprised, in working out their comparisons, to find how similarly the two politicians employ these terms.

IV. ADVERTISING AND LANGUAGE

THE LANGUAGE OF ADVERTISING CLAIMS, Jeffery Schrank   (p. 179)

Questions on Content

1. Advertisers try to impress morals and standards on society by displaying beautiful, wealthy people as the American ideal. Immunity to advertising means not succumbing to the pressures exerted to have fresh breath, bouncy, healthy hair, and the ability to pick out the right processed cheese for your family. Although this is what most Americans speak of when they claim they are immune to advertising, Schrank suggests that there is more to being immune to adwriters' tactics. He claims Americans are not aware of unsubstantial claims being make. He makes a good case with examples such as Palmolive, which outsells many brands of dishwashing detergent based on the claim that it leaves dishes "virtually spotless."
2. Chromacolor is a copyrighted name that Zenith has invented for a quality common to most color television sets. However, because by copyright law no other manufacture can say it uses "Chromacolor," Zenith creates an impression of exclusivity and superiority by inventing a name for a common manufacturing process.
3. Schrank may be wrong when he suggests that parity products are so similar that such products cannot claim superiority over other products on the market. For example, some shampoos may be telling the truth when they claim they leave your hair healthy. Many shampoos on the market contain sodium chloride which dries hair leaving it damaged. Shampoos which do not contain sodium chloride are, in the opinion of many hairdressers and dermatologists, significantly "better" and "healthier" for your hair.
4. In open defiance of elementary school grammar lessons, legal minds have reinterpreted the words "better" and "best." "Better" has been interpreted as a comparative to mean "best," and "best" has been interpreted to mean "equal to."

Questions on Rhetoric

1. Schrank introduces the concepts of immunity to advertising and parity products in a lengthy introduction. Then in a weak, two-sentence transition discussing parity products he introduces his list of ten basic techniques. This may give the false impression that these techniques apply only to parity products. Also, many of his examples overlap without explanation which makes them unclear.
2. Schrank may have intended his list of ad claims to be the meat of his essay and felt that it spoke for itself leaving nothing to conclude. Also, Schrank is thorough enough in his discussion of ad claims that a conclusion or summary of those ideas might be redundant.
3. Schrank's analogies are clever and helpful for being graphically to the point. His best is the "wet is better," claim for an ad that says something that is already true for any product of its

41

kind on the market. Another apt analogy is the action of the weasel with an egg, which parallels the substance of the weasel claim.

4. Schrank could have been more explicit in his defining of ad claims. The "Vague claims" are not the only ones that overlap. Many of Schrank's examples could fit other categories. Good classifications have distinct categories. If this is not possible, the author should not only point out the overlaps, but explain why they occur.

Vocabulary

notorious (1): generally known and talked of, mostly in a negative sense.

psychosell (1): selling tactics especially directed toward the will or toward the mind specifically in its connotative function.

pseudoinformation (4): information that is apparently rather than actually useful.

parity (4): the quality or state of being equal.

gambit (11): a remark intended to start a conversation or make a telling point.

subjective (14): characteristic of or belonging to reality as perceived rather than as independent of mind.

Writing Topics

1. Since the first part of this assignment asks merely for paraphrases of Schrank, the real opportunity for creativity (and demonstrated comprehension) is in the second part, the student-written ads. Alert them to the possibility that ad *visuals* might make these claims no less effectively than ad copy, and allow free rein on the media they might want to work in: radio, print with or without illustration, telescript, or even full videotape production, given the available technology. The important challenge is to make one of Schrank's claims on behalf of the product with maximum creativity and impact.

2. This is fairly self-explanatory. It will be most effective with pairs or groups of ads that do explicitly compare their product to the competition or even—more interestingly—compare *themselves* to the competitors' *advertising*. Recently there seem to be a number of campaigns that have advertising, rather than products, as their subject (and which, of course, implicitly promote themselves as more honest than other ads since they share an ironic knowledge with the viewer about the artificiality of advertising).

3. As with #1, this opens up the question of visuals and their capacity to "make claims" about a product. This may be particularly interesting to students in as much as since Schrank's essay was written, there seems to have arisen an entire genre of advertisement, influenced by MTV and targeted toward a student aged market, in which the visuals call dramatic attention to themselves and the spoken word is barely a presence at all. Given this phenomenon, perhaps the question would do well to allow for video as well as magazine ads, and to raise, in addition, the question of music and how it works in ads. On the other hand, if you are doing an extensive unit on advertising, you may want to save this as an assignment to accompany Jay Rosen, "The Presence of the Word in TV Advertising."

THE HARD SELL, Ron Rosenbaum (p. 188)

Questions On Content

1. Rosenbaum describes the Hard Sell as the "no more Mr. Nice Guy" school of commercial strategy, or the "take-it-or-leave-it approach." These commercials contain hard, fast facts; aggression is taken out on products, and the idea is always present that life is tough. For example, Dodge trucks are "ram tough," and Ford trucks are "built tough." The Humiliation Sell reminds readers that they better use a deodorant that "works over-time" and a detergent that removes "ring around the collar." Rosenbaum is not opposed to "love" in advertising as long as it is cuddly and emotional. He is opposed to "murder [being] committed" in some commercials as materialism over-takes Christmas for the poor husband who did not buy his wife a Longines.
2. Adwriters exploit the idea that life is tough so that manufacturers become saviors when they produce products that make life easier. In this tough life we can turn to the makers or Excedrin to relieve our headaches, and the makers of heavy duty paper products to quicken dinner clean up. These producers become the heros by recognizing our needs and sympathizing with our daily stress and strain.
3. Ad writers portray love as either sentimental or selfish, according to Rosenbaum. The most outstanding example of selfish love in Rosenbaum's essay is the Longines watch ad. In this ad, a wife lets her husband know in no uncertain terms that in spite of his sacrifices, his Christmas gift is a disappointment because it is not a Longines. Sentimental love is presented in ideal scenes such as couples walking hand in hand along the beach or sharing quiet evening in front of the fire.
4. Rosenbaum does not like the Hard Sell ads. In paragraph six he calls them the "no nonsense ads." Nor does he like the "Aching '80s" or "Bull Apart" ads as evidenced in his sarcastic suggestion that the bull of yesterday's brokerage advertisement has suffered PBB poisoning or cattle mutations. It is, however, obvious that Rosenbaum does like "happy ads." In paragraph 25 he uses words such as "warmth," "spiritual," "camaraderie," "lyrical," and "beauty," which contrast with words such as "abruptly," "survival," "combative," "anger," "assault," "dank," and "lonely" used in the rest of the essay.

Questions On Rhetoric

1. Rosenbaum's vocabulary and tone indicate that his audience is mature and sophisticated, perhaps a group of young professionals rather than the students Schrank addresses. He uses words such as "sophistry," "concierge," "insidious," and "malleable," and discusses investments and Renoir's painting of Louis XVI. This contrasts with Schrank's simpler vocabulary and his discussion of television sets, dishwashing detergent, and gasoline. Schrank's reference is to Bing Crosby rather than to Renoir.
2. Rosenbaum uses words such as "us," "we," and "our," in an attempt to relate to the reader more personally. Thus Rosenbaum joins with the reader in being subjected to the tactics used by ad writers.
3. Brokerage firm ads display the two ends of the ad continuum, i.e. the "tough life," and the "loner" ad. Not only do these two ads show that the ideals ad writers want to portray are changing, they also emphasize the similarly "infamous" reputation shared by brokerage firms and the ad industry.

43

4. Rosenbaum does not use the superior voice of the teacher; as pointed out earlier, he includes himself with the reader by using the first person plural. And although his diction is witty, his purpose is not solely to entertain. While Rosenbaum introduces an idea he wants the reader to consider, his strong language indicates that his ultimate goal is to persuade the reader to his point of view.

Vocabulary

pugnaciously (6): belligerently.
cloistered (13): secluded from the world.
sophistries (19): subtly deceptive reasoning or argumentation.
intone (20): to utter in musical or prolonged tones.
harbinger (21): one that presages or foreshadows what is to come.
bode (28): to foretell.
gestalt (30): a structure of physical, biological, or psychological phenomena. So integrated
    as to constitute a functional unit with properties not derivable by summation of its parts.
malapropism (46): the use of a word sounding somewhat like the one intended, but ludi-
    crously wrong in its context.
ethos (47): the distinguishing character, sentiment, moral nature, or guiding beliefs of a
    person, group, or institution.
crestfallen (48): feeling shame or humiliation.
hoodwinked (53): deceived by false appearance,
malleable (56): flexible; having a capacity for change.
precipitous (58): deeply descending.

Writing Topics

1. The first part of this assignment—predicting a nickname for the coming decade—should make an interesting classroom discussion, with some students envisioning a resurgence of '60s-style nonconformism, others a deepening conservative trend, others a time of sober, moderate altruism, *etc.* The assignment challenges students to think about how ads (and by extension other forms of artful communication) *reflect social values* rather than merely engage in manipulative pragmatics.
2. This assignment resembles some of those for Schrank and Rosen, and is fairly self-explanatory. For a somewhat more sophisticated exercise, you might ask students to compare and contrast the schemata devised for classifying ads by, say, Rosenbaum and Schrank. How do their different concerns influence their analytical methods, and what does each writer's system of classification allow him to say that the other's doesn't?

THE PRESENCE OF THE WORD IN TV ADVERTISING,
Jay Rosen (p. 199)

Questions on Content

1. The idea of verbalness through visual effects means that adwriters express a certain word or abstract idea without using the spoken word. For example, the spoken word is hardly used in Levi's 501 jeans commercials, yet the feeling of "blue" is portrayed through scenery, actions, and tone.
2. The technique of visualization in ads is achieved by creating more images that arrive "at a faster clip, and [pack] more of a punch." The images are presented with one theme in mind, (for example "night" in Michelob commercials) which if successful, then become linked to the product. Rosen terms this the "deep structure" of the advertisement.
3. Rosen claims that Phil Collins' lyrics merely contribute to "the presence of the word" in the Michelob commercials. However, Rosen believes that it is not necessary to have this music play throughout the commercial to express "night." The fact that Phil Collins has written a song called "Tonight" was convenient for the adwriters. They could, of course, have written a song about "night." Instead, by using a popular song written by a popular rock star, they were able to associate Phil Collins and Michelob.
4. Adwriters use visual persuasion to develop verbal ideas, so the spoken word is less necessary. Visualization is also used to hide a deeper meaning in a commercial. It is for both of these reasons that watching television with the sound turned down can prove interesting. This may be the only way to catch the hidden meaning of a commercial.

Questions on Rhetoric

1. Rosen seems to be appealing to the college-aged person. This is apparent by studying his references to beer, MTV, rock stars, and jeans. These are products and interests common to the fun-loving spirit of the younger, more carefree population.
2. The irony in this essay is that in order to see the true meaning of an advertisement, one must turn the sound down on the television. Another irony is that the more visual advertisements become, the more they are about ideas that are verbal. Rosen believes this is so well depicted that not only are visual words such as "blue" and "night" portrayed, but even abstract phrases such as "what if."
3. Rosen's introductory sentences serve as good transitions between paragraphs. Theses sentences move the ideas along quickly. For example, note the transition between paragraphs three and four. Rosen begins discussing flipping channels and then discusses visualization in the next paragraph. The opening sentence connects these two seemingly unrelated ideas.

Vocabulary

provocation (2): something that arouses or stimulates; provokes.
visualization (4): the process of interpreting in visual form.
license (4): freedom of action.
obliterate (6): to remove from existence.

Writing Topics

1. Like many of the assignments in this section, this allows the student room for considerable creativity. The very abstractness of the concepts listed may meet resistance from some students, at least initially, and many may opt for the terms more conventionally associated with advertising, such as "inexpensive" and "improved." On the other hand, each week seems to bring a new post-MTV-styled ad (the Phil Collins/Michelob ad, incidentally, was one of the very first of these) that bears out Rosen's thesis, so students may be increasingly acclimated to ads that are altogether too "cool," too detached and ironic, to make a vulgarly explicit pitch.
2. If your class seems up to it, you might preface this assignment with some sort of classroom presentation of basic semiotics. Many students find some of the essays in, e.g., Barthes's *Mythologies* accessible enough; you might simply throw out a few examples of what it means to "read" all the visual elements of a filmed narrative, just to expand their conceptions of what to be looking for.

GETTIN' RICH BY DROPPIN' THE G, Edwin Newman (p. 204)

Questions on Content

1. Ad writers may misuse the English language in order to appeal to the average American consumer who is not a stickler for "proper" English, or as a means of getting the consumer's attention. Dropping the "g," misspelling words, and using a homonym for the intended word all serve as flags in the jingle to help the reader remember the product.
2. In some instances ("Me and my buddies," "Get major credit cards easy"), the effect of correction is minimal; in others ("Ain't nothing like the real thing," which Newman doesn't seem to realize is an allusion to a rock song, or "It looks as good as it performs"), the corrected version would be quite different in tone. Presumably, the writers of the more discordant misuses are consciously breaking rules, while others are less self-aware.

Questions on Rhetoric

1. The technique of naming the product and not the brand name catches the reader in a kind of "name that advertising claim" game and hence catches our attention. Or alternatively, perhaps it communicates some of Newman's contempt for these advertisers; to identify the brands would be to do them a favor, and Newman implies that they don't deserve the recognition.
2. Newman discounts the adwriter in his essay. He claims that products are not only speaking, but boasting their own qualities. He puts the products on the same level as the actors and actresses who endorse the products. Students will find many examples of the personification of products.
3. Newman does not thoroughly expand on his thoughts in another attempt to get the reader to think, as he does by not mentioning product names. Newman gives the reader enough information to lead the reader to his thought process, but does not complete the thought. So,

when Newman says in paragraph 8 "there are enough of the other kind," the reader knows that "the other kind" refers to unintentional mistakes.

Vocabulary

semiliteracy (1): the ability to read and write on an elementary level.
elitist (4): of the upper classes.
simper (5): to smile in a silly manner.

Writing Topics

1. Students may well be put off by Newman's judgmental tone regardless of how they feel about "ain't," so they may be fairly gleeful about putting him on a level with the advertisers he loathes. Either before or after the writing, however, you may want to ask them whether the "tricks" they've identified in Newman's work are really equivalent to the abuses he criticizes. Asking them to compare his situation, audience, and intentions to those of the adwriters might even lead into a discussion of whether a rhetorician's strategies really deserve to be thought of as "tricks" in the first place. Overall, this assignment is a good opportunity to think about where one draws the line between abuse and creativity in language.
2. Again, students put off by Newman's tone may jump to defend even adwriters at his expense. They should be dissuaded, however, from identifying all analysis of advertising with judgements on the sins of advertisers.

IT'S NATURAL! IT'S ORGANIC! OR IS IT?, *Consumers Union* (p. 207)

Questions on Content

1. Americans are eager to buy "natural" foods because they believe "that they're somehow better for [them]—safer or more nutritious" (6). Foods that carry the label "natural" can be a rip-off, though, if that label is used more as an agent for profits than as a genuine indication of safety or nutrition.
2. Manufacturers are getting into the natural food business because their market research tells them it's what consumers want to buy. These so-called natural foods can also carry higher prices since consumers are willing to pay more for what they believe are healthful foods, and this means higher profits for manufacturers.
3. The essay suggests that there is usually little, if any, relationship between natural and nutritious. "Natural" generally refers "to the character of the ingredients (no preservatives or artificial additives) and to the fact that the food has undergone minimal processing" (6). Although the essay does state that many processed foods are less nutritious than fresh foods (24), the main point seems to be that the label "natural" is often used as a selling device, with little regard to the accuracy of the claim. The authors use the example of "natural" potato chips, for instance, to demonstrate that such labels can have nothing to do with the nutritional value of a product (21).
4. Some benefits of processing are: (1) Freezing preserves nutrients that could be lost if fresh

foods are not consumed quickly; (2) Pasteurization kills potentially dangerous bacteria in milk; (3) Some additives are safe and useful.
5. In paragraph 27 Moskowitz explains that "our palates have become attuned to many unnatural tastes," so we often prefer artificial flavors to natural ones.
6. The tactics for convincing consumers that products are natural are presented in paragraphs 29-38:
   a. The indeterminate modifier: Use a string of modifiers but claim the "natural" modifies only the next adjective in line.
   b. Innocence by association: Imply that a product is natural by associating it with nature.
   c. Printer's error: Claim that a false "natural" label was the mistake of a printer.
   d. The best defense: Attack the competition's claims for natural products.
   e. The negative pitch: Point out that a product doesn't contain something it wouldn't contain anyway.
7. Consumers Union suggests that "the word 'natural' is so vague as to be inherently deceptive, and therefore should not be available for promotional use" (39). Recognizing the difficulty of getting such a proposal into law, however, the essay also presents a revised FTC proposal that says "the word 'natural' can be used if the product has undergone minimal processing and doesn't have artificial ingredients" (41).
8. Consumers Union would probably have complaints about the implication that these soups are natural products. Though the ad highlights their fiber content, it does not reveal what other ingredients the soups contain that might not be considered so healthful.

Questions on Rhetoric

1. Consumers Union's purpose is to *inform* its readers of the ways manufacturers use the label "natural" to sell products, so that they can make informed decisions about what to buy.
2. Since the article discusses how these two terms are often misused by food manufacturers, it is first necessary for readers to understand what the terms are supposed to mean when used correctly and honestly.
3. Students will probably find the examples essential to a clear understanding of the deceptive practices used by manufacturers to promote "natural" foods. Their responses on which examples work best may vary according to how familiar they are with the practice each example illustrates.
4. This essay is organized as an informational process analysis that explains how food manufacturers use the term "natural" to sell their products, and what can be done about such deceptive practices.

Vocabulary

trade (1): dealings or the market involving specified commodities.
foster (5): help to grow or develop; stimulate; promote.
implication (6): something indicated indirectly or by allusion; a hint or suggestion.
premise (6): statement or assertion that serves as the basis for an argument.
bandwagon (12): popular position or appeal.
ploy (13): an action intended to deceive or outwit.
touted (17): praised or recommended highly.
carcinogen (26): any substance that produces cancer.
palates (27): roofs of people's mouths, often referred to as a source for their senses of taste.
derision (33): ridicule.

Writing Topics

1. You may want to review writing definitions with your students before they begin this assignment since they will no doubt need to define these two terms in their arguments either for or against banning them from advertising.
2. As a prewriting activity you can analyze an ad in class, discussing what tactics of deception are employed in it and what benefits are implied through the use of the word "natural." After you've drawn conclusions about whether the ad is deceptive, discuss possible ways of organizing these conclusions into an essay. Students can then apply the same process to the development of their own essays.
3. To demonstrate how students might approach this assignment you can bring in (or have students bring in) copies of magazines that contain advertisements. Have students leaf through them looking for words or phrases that appear frequently in the ads. Once they've identified some often-used expressions, discuss whether the ads they appear in contain any of the tactics of deception described by Consumers Union.

ADVERTISING'S FIFTEEN BASIC APPEALS, Jib Fowles (p. 216)

Questions on content

1. We do not agree that buyers have become stoutly resistant to advertisements. Buyers are aware, to ascertain extent, of the morals being inflicted on them and some of the emotions being appealed to. However, there are some appeals and claims that buyers are not aware of. We find that Schrank and Rosenbaum are convincing enough in their arguments to make readers aware of how frequently they are fooled. Students will no doubt have many examples of their own gullibility.
2. Students will have various answers.
3. Fowles suggests that Florence Henderson is the main appeal in Wesson Oil commercials; however, the food plays an equally major role. The sight of fried chicken and french fries soaking in Wesson Oil appeals to a simple, basic need, the desire for good, hot, greasy food. We maintain that most food ads rely on the sight of mouth–watering food to make the sale. Fowle's assessment of ad writers' intentions may be correct; however we think it possible that consumers are not so easily influenced. More than any other product, food is subject to tests which have an immediate and definite influence over the consumer. They are less likely to be fooled just because it is endorsed by a perceived motherly image or has a history.
4. Mere opposition to an ad might not bring it to a halt. The bottom line would be sales. Adwriters can be satisfied with ads that get attention, positive or negative—that is the idea. Halting a campaign that is doing well would probably take an act of Congress, or legal action.

Questions on Rhetoric

1. Fowles's thesis is that the emotional appeal of every ad is a variation on one of a number of basic appeals; this is stated directly in paragraph 11.
2. Fowles draws on the ideas of several well-known psychologists, as well as introducing a large number of examples from which he draws his conclusions inductively.

3. Fowles's tone may seem somewhat overbearing to the student unfamiliar with psychological terms. His tone seems to us crisp, direct, and quite self-confident. His diction is aimed at an educated reader ("parsimonious," "obduracy"), as is Rosenbaum's.

Vocabulary

hawked (3): offered for sale by shouting in the street.
abhorrent (3): not agreeable.
circumvent (5): to get around or avoid, especially by ingenuity or stratagem.
importuned (7): requested or begged for urgently.
profane (13): not concerned with the spiritual or religious.
titillated (17): excited, stimulated, especially in a sexual way.
inveigle (18): to win over by wiles or flattery.
facsimile (33): an exact copy.
gibes (46): taunting words.
nimbus (64): a cloud or atmosphere about a person or thing.
aesthetic (73): related to the question of artistic quality.
avant-garde (85): an intelligentsia that develops new or experimental ideas in the arts.
avid (95): eager, intensely interested.
curried (96): attended to, flattered.

Writing Topics

1. Students are unlikely to find the *concept* of subliminal advertising controversial, and will probably have little difficulty taking a position on it. Researching it may turn up some interesting material, however, though students should simultaneously be evaluating the trustworthiness of some of the schlockier books they're likely to turn up on the subject.
2. Assuming the student brings to the assignment a basic sympathy with Fowles's position, this is an exercise in laying out as simply and clearly as possible an opposing position and closely examining its logic. Students should have little problem discerning the vulnerability of the first premise, and will probably have things to say about the others as well.

INTENSIFY/DOWNPLAY, Hugh Rank (p. 235)

Questions on Content

1. By "professional persuaders" Rank means advertisers, government officials, and any other people who make their livings by trying to persuade others.
2. Persuaders intensify by repetition, association, and composition. Through repetition, a slogan, product name, or logo is used again and again until it is familiar. Association connects a product or idea with something to which the audience already reacts. Composition intensifies through pattern or arrangement. Students will find examples in current advertisements, political materials, and so forth.
3. Persuaders downplay by omission, diversion, and confusion. Through omission, informa-

tion is concealed. Diversion downplays by distracting attention to side issues whereas confusion complicates until the issue is obscured. Students will find examples in current advertisements, political materials, and so forth.

4. It is possible for someone to intensify and downplay at the same time; the advantageous features of a product may be repeated many times in an advertisement, while the disadvantageous features (usually price) may be omitted.

Questions on Rhetoric

1. Rank developed this schema so that ordinary "individuals can better cope with organized persuasion" produced by "professional persuaders."
2. Rank has used classification to organize the common methods of intensifying or downplaying.

Vocabulary

logo: a distinctive company signature or trademark.
slogan: catch word or phrase or motto that is used to advertise a product.
certitude: feeling of absolute sureness or conviction.
assumptions: ideas that are taken for granted or naturally supposed to be true.
explicitly: in a clearly stated or distinctly expressed manner.
analogies: explanations that draw comparisons between the points of similarity that exist in things that are otherwise dissimilar.

Writing Topics

1. You may wish to have your students supplement the ads in the text with ones of their own choosing. Students should become more aware of just how contrived and purposeful most ads are; they should, as well, come to appreciate how advertising affects their buying habits and shapes their lives.
2. This activity has proven to be not only entertaining but also quite an eye-opener for students. In addition to comparing one realtor's offerings with those of another, students should compare a modest city home:

    CITY LIVING IS GREAT in this three-bedroom, two-story home. Features include game room, 12 baths, den, enclosed porch; close to services. $63,000.

    with a modest country home:

    A COUNTRY HOME—On one acre. L-shaped ranch, three bedrooms, dining area, fireplace, garage. $77,000.

    And a more expensive city home:

    LUXURIOUS COLONIAL—Four bedrooms, 2½ baths, fireplaced family room, center foyer. Huge private deck. Deluxe with many extras. In Pinewood Manor. Now $119,600.

    with a more luxurious country home:

    BRISTOL—Four-plus acres of pines and open, with a new two-story rustic Dutch Colonial, 16' x 26' living room, with fieldstone fireplace, knotty-pine kitchen, refrigerator, and built-ins, four bedrooms, two baths, large open porch, pretty country location. $126,000.

Other worthwhile comparisons can be made between new and older homes, between new and remodeled or renovated homes, and so on. Having analyzed the language of real estate advertisements, students are now well prepared for writing assignment 3.

As an alternative to analyzing real estate advertisements, have students work with the "employment opportunities" listings in the newspaper. For example, what can your students tell you about the following job listings?

REAL ESTATE—Career? We'll train. Two vacancies exist. Send resume. Box 115.

REAL ESTATE SALESMAN—Send resume to Box 231.

GALS—Please let me show you how I earn top pay and still am home when my family needs me. Car and phone. KL5-4435, 9-5.

BRAINS WANTED!—Looking for interesting work where you can use your intelligence and earn big money? International educational publisher has part-time and full-time positions open. No experience necessary. Flexible hours. Call 555-3056, 12-1 only, for interview.

BUSINESS EXECUTIVE—Person with executive ability, good education, or good business background. Write stating qualifications to Box 325 or call 555-2569 for interview. All replies confidential.

Can they identify the encyclopedia salesperson? The Tupperware salesperson?

An amusing lexicon of real estate terms appears in *Harper's* (November 1973), p. 112, and is abridged in the *Reader's Digest* (February 1974), p. 119.

V. PREJUDICE AND STEREOTYPES

THE LANGUAGE OF PREJUDICE, Gordon Allport (p. 247)

Questions on Content

1. James simply meant that without words we would not be able to group our experiences into manageable categories. Words allow us to group objects, experiences, or ideas on the basis of one or more particular features even though other groupings are possible.

   If we could not determine categories, we would have, as James said, a "sand-heap" of experiences. Life would be total confusion.

2. Nouns "cut slices" by presenting narrow views of reality such that they may even "prevent alternative classification" (4).

   Allport says in paragraph 3 that "a noun *abstracts* from a concrete reality some one feature and assembles different concrete realities only with respect to this one feature." Nouns are therefore always "unfair" in that they must include and exclude. Refer your students to Allport's anecdote about the blind man (3), and ask them to comment on it. Can they recall similar instances of nouns "cutting slices"?

3. Allport says, "The common use of the orphaned pronoun *they* teaches us that people often want and need to designate out-groups (usually for the purpose of venting hostility) even when they have no clear conception of the out-group in question" (19).

   It is used so often because it depersonalizes and is nonspecific, thus making it easier for the speaker to be critical.

4. Allport says in paragraph 4 that "Some labels, such as 'blind man,' are exceedingly salient and powerful. They tend to prevent alternative classification, or even cross-classification." These are "labels of primary potency."

   Their tremendous power to control our perceptions of reality makes them very important.

   We can and should be wary of such labels even when they are favorable; since they are so emotionally charged, they obscure the finer distinctions that should be made.

5. Changing a label of primary potency from a noun to an adjective may cause it to lose some of its force because it is associated with another word (the noun it modifies), and the presence of the noun "calls attention to the fact that some other group classifications are just as legitimate" (9) as the label of primary potency.

   For this reason—to have at least two attributes of the person to consider rather than only one—it is useful to "designate ethnic and religious membership where possible with *adjectives* rather than with *nouns*" (9).

6. Allport's essay seems an obvious reaction to the McCarthyism of the 1950s and its preoccupation with the "red menace." Many of the associations attached to the label "communist" were established at that time and remain in place even today.

7. Because Allport does not explicitly define these terms, students may wish to consult the dictionary.

reify (36): to regard or treat an abstraction or idea as if it had concrete or material existence.

verbal realism (35): the literal truth of words; words denoting the essences of things (usually used to refer to someone other than oneself).

symbol phobia (33): fear of words; often characterized by the confusion of words with actual things (we are usually inclined to symbol phobia when we ourselves are concerned).

word fetishism (36): the excessive attention to or reverence for particular words.

symbol realism (33): synonymous with *verbal realism*.

Allport believes any attempt to reduce prejudice must include semantic therapy because people cannot always say "whether it is the word or the thing that annoys them.... Hence to liberate a person from ethnic or political prejudice it is necessary at the same time to liberate him from 'word fetishism'" (36).

Questions on Rhetoric

1. Allport's thesis is the first sentence in paragraph 5.
2. Paragraph 1 discusses words in general and their relationship to thinking and to the forming of generalizations. Paragraph 2 discusses our need to use words to categorize human beings into various groups. Paragraph 3 discusses the nouns that we use to categorize people and how these nouns focus on only one aspect of an individual. Thus the topics of the paragraphs move from words in general to the use of words to categorize people to the nouns that label these categories.
3. All six quotations in Allport's article provide specific examples or illustrations of a general point that he is developing.

   The quotations are effective; they provide concrete details to support his generalizations.
4. The topic sentence of paragraph 17 is "Especially in a culture where uniformity is prized, the name of *any* deviant carries with it *ipso facto* a negative value-judgment."

   The paragraph is developed primarily through the use of examples. Three sentences dealing with the "fact that even the most proper and sedate labels for minority groups sometimes seem to exude a negative flavor" precede the topic sentence. The topic sentence is followed by further examples that illustrate and explain the generalization it sets forth.

Vocabulary

rudimentary (1): elementary; in the earliest stages of development.
ethnic (4): characteristic of a religious, racial, national, or cultural group.
inherent (12): existing as an essential part or characteristic.
ludicrous (12): laughable or hilarious through obvious absurdity or incongruity.
sinister (13): suggesting an evil force or motive; ominous.
morbid (13): pertaining to disease; gloomy.
sedate (17): serenely deliberate in character or manner; composed; collected.
array (29): an impressive display of numerous objects; an orderly arrangement.
cohesion (36): the process or condition of sticking or holding together.
intrinsic (36): pertaining to the essential nature of a thing.

1. This activity is intended to make students consider the extent to which words actually shape our opinions. Basically the article maintains that opinions are shaped by words and that if the words are changed, opinions will automatically change also. For example, in changing from *jungle* to *savanna*, the negative connotations of the former word supposedly disappear. In discussing the article, students usually divide into two grounds: those who accept the underlying assumption of the article (that is, that language controls perception) and those who reject it. In order to explain the differing positions taken by the two groups, you may want to review the Sapir-Whorf hypothesis.
2. You may wish to have students share their essays in class so they can discover what labels their classmates find offensive—a small measure of "semantic therapy."

WORDS WITH BULIT-IN JUDGMENTS, S. I. Hayakawa (p. 259)

Questions on Content

1. According to Hayakawa, informative connotations are essentially dictionary definitions; they describe what the word *denotes*. Affective connotations, on the other hand, are what we usually mean by "connotation" as opposed to "denotation": suggestive implications that may accompany the literal, explicit meaning of a word. Informative connotations refer to facts; affective connotations refer to judgments about the facts.
2. "Newspapers and polite people" in the American Southwest have stopped using the term "Mexican" because it has acquired so many negative affective connotations that it is an insulting term (2).
3. Many names or labels for groups of people or things both arouse very strong affective connotations and suggest misleading implications. By so doing, they actually "dictate traditional patterns of behavior," essentially knee-jerk responses unaccompanied by much, if any, thought. Hayakawa cites, among others, the terms "drunkards" (3), "leprosy" (3), "little hoodlums" (4), and "maladjusted" (4).
4. Hayakawa argues in paragraph 4 that "verbal stratagems" are often necessary in order to avoid eliciting the "traditional patterns of behavior" caused by the "strong affective connotations."
5. It is important to realize that the meanings of words may change "from speaker to speaker and from context to context" (5) for two reasons: first, to avoid insulting people unintentionally, as can happen when a term that you use neutrally is perceived as derogatory by the person to whom you are speaking; and second, to avoid feeling insulted by a term that has no negative connotations for the person who uses it. We must realize that, in a sense, words do not have meanings; rather, people have meanings for words—and different people may have different meanings for the same word.

    Had the black sociologist realized that his white benefactors intended no insult or feelings of contempt in their application of the term "nigger, " he could have felt more at ease and enjoyed their sincere hospitality without feeling he was being denigrated.

6. Both Hayakawa's "words with built-in judgments" and Allport's "labels of primary potency" function in the same way: they "act like shrieking sirens, deafening us to all finer discriminations that we might otherwise perceive" (Allport, paragraph 4).

Questions on Rhetoric

1. Most of Hayakawa's paragraphs begin with a topic sentence, with the rest of the paragraph expanding, explaining, or illustrating the topic sentence. This type of paragraph organization contributes to our sense that Hayakawa's article is clearly and logically organized and developed.
2. Hayakawa uses the meaning attached to the word "communism" to define *informative* and *affective* connotations. Students will probably agree that this concrete representation of what might otherwise be an abstract explanation of these terms makes it easier to understand the definitions.
3. Hayakawa uses a number of transitional devices. These include:
    paragraph 3: repeated key idea
    paragraph 4: pronoun reference and repeated key idea
    paragraph 5: transitional expression ("as we have observed")
    paragraph 6: transitional expression ("similar")
    paragraph 7: repeated key word
    paragraph 8: repeated key words
    paragraph 9: repeated key word
    paragraph 10: transitional expression ("such")
    paragraph 11: transitional expression ("one other")
    These transitions clarify how his ideas are connected and link each paragraph logically to the one before.
4. The "greased runway" metaphor is effective. It suggests a rapid and unstoppable descent along an already established course, not a bad description of the way in which the use of language with very strong affective connotations leads inevitably to a predictable result—"old and discredited patterns of evaluation and behavior."

Vocabulary

simultaneously (1): happening, existing, or done at the same time.
repellent (1): inspiring aversion or distaste; repulsive.
contemptuous (2): scornful; disdainful.
psychopathic (4): manifesting aggressive antisocial behavior; having a pathological mental condition.
rehabilitation (4): restoration to useful life through education and therapy.
innocuous (5): harmless; innocent; having no adverse effect.
benefactor (8): one who gives financial or other aid.
dissent (11): difference of opinion or feeling; disagreement.
candor (11): frankness of expression; sincerity; straightforwardness.

Writing Topics

1. This activity is intended to heighten students' awareness of the numerous and frequent terms that "arouse both informative and affective connotations simultaneously" (1). Students

should have no difficulty in suggesting such terms; a few that come quickly to mind are *chauvinist, fascist, homosexual, left wing, lice, addict, cancer,* and *welfare recipient.*

2. Before beginning this assignment students may find it helpful to discuss an instance when violating verbal taboos hindered clear thinking because of the prejudices conveyed or thought to have been conveyed.

   Your discussion can also incorporate students' reactions to people who "tell it like it is" as an excuse to tread on other people's feelings. By examining these aspects of prejudice in our use of language students may be better prepared to address the issue of how it can be better to talk in roundabout terms to avoid such prejudices.

THE ETYMOLOGY OF THE INTERNATIONAL INSULT,
Charles F. Berlitz (p. 264)

Questions on Content

1. All of these words, innocent enough in themselves, were originally nonpejorative and later evolved into racial slurs. The Spanish word "negro," which gave rise to the word "nigger" is another example of one of these words.
2. the word "Eskimo" is an Algonquin word, adopted by the white man, meaning "eaters-of-flesh." The Eskimos call themselves "Inuit." However, through use, and because of the white man's occasional insensitivity to native customs, the word has become a permanent fixture in the English language.
3. The socio-racial obstacles that blacks must overcome are no doubt familiar to most students. Blacks are working to overcome the bigotry that they say results in their obtaining inferior education, employment, housing, and an all around unfair slice of the American pie. Semantically, they must make the word "black" sound "beautiful" even though it connotes "evil," "illness," "danger," and a host of other negatives aspects that have nothing to do with racial bias.
4. The tendency among tribes and peoples to differentiate the "we" and "they" along lines of good and evil is the well-spring of racial bias. It allows a people to declare that facial features, skin color, and language in themselves possess the possibility for being good or bad. Once that judgement has been made, and no matter how superficial it may be, a people can justify their own sense of superiority and self-righteousness.

Questions on Rhetoric

1. Berlitz may not have intended to shock his readers; nevertheless it is unnerving to read so many of the words that we associate with feelings of hatred and bigotry. Berlitz reveals negative feelings toward racial slurs in several places. For example, "One of the epithets for Negroes has a curious and tragic historic origin, the memory of which is still haunting us." (6) "Jap, an insulting diminutive that figured in the ... (1968) national U.S., election (though its use in the expression "fat Jap" was apparently meant to have an endearing quality by our Vice President) is a simple contraction of "Japan." (11)

2. Berlitz identifies slurs that originate as nonpejorative words in the language of the people being insulted. A second group is made up of words associated with the history of the people. A third group is derived from the eating habits of a nationality. And a fourth derives from the geographic location of a people. Other groups are based on facial features or language, while the last and one of the largest groups describes the despised people simply in terms of "the other." Students may have experience with other forms of racial insults, either those they have heard used against others or those used against themselves.

3. Berlitz's thesis is that racial slurs have their roots in ancient inter-group antagonisms that are inappropriate and destructive to perpetrate in the modern world. Berlitz achieves what many writers achieve when they wait until the end of their essay to present their thesis. By then Berlitz expects he has made his point and has a better chance of convincing his reader of the obvious merit of his thesis.

Vocabulary

pejorative (2): disparaging.
appellation (3): name; designation.
vulgar (3): offensive to good taste or refined feelings.
opprobrious (3): outrageously shameful or disgraceful.
trenchantly (3): caustically; bitingly.
picturesque (4): graphic; vivid.
swarthy (5): dark-skinned.
epithets (6): a characterizing and often abusive word or phrase.
santified (15): holy; consecrated.

Writing Topics

1. For the student, researching these questions should be a fairly engaging exercise in etymology. The Berlitz essay will already have given some idea of what to expect.

2. Most students are unlikely to disagree—at least on paper—with the humanitarian sentiments here. The sticking point for them will probably be the words "even linguistically," by which we assume Berlitz means something like "not even in the symbolic realm of language—leaving actual behaviors to one side—can we afford to perpetuate the equation of Stranger with Enemy." If this is fairly accurate, then the assignment becomes an occasion for reflection on the relative importance of racial language, as when for instance someone excuses the use—in a heated argument, say—of "nigger" on the grounds that "it's only a word."

3. Essays on this question need not necessarily limit themselves to racially or ethnically-designated groups; following the example of African-Americans, women and minorities such as gays, lesbians, and the disabled have insisted on the importance of being called by the terms they choose.

WHAT IT MEANS TO BE BLACK, William Raspberry   (p. 269)

Questions on Content

1. In basketball doing it "black" means playing with speed, grace and accuracy. In singing it suggests an energetic, soulful delivery, and in dance it connotes an unselfconscious, sinewy ease of motion.
2. In wishing not to be labeled "white," black children form too narrow a definition of what it means to be black. (6)
3. Ethnic gifts are not innate; they are the result of a people's belief that they do something well. Raspberry's argument, with the added explanation of the importance of the role of tradition, could easily explain the phenonenon of "innate" talent.
4. "The real problem is not so much that the things defined as "black" are negative. The problem is that the definition is much too narrow." (14) Raspberry has a point that is valid for anyone. The more narrowly we define ourselves, the fewer choices we have. However, the fact that the word "black" has negative connotations for some people is not insignificant.

Questions on Rhetoric

1. What it means to be "white" or "black" is not easily defined, because the terms represent an accumulation of attitudes. Raspberry expects that his readers share an understanding of these attitudes. This assumption of our shared understanding is effective because it emphasizes how prevalent these attitudes are.
2. The examples from the two paragraphs contrast the ways we react to the word "black" in different situations. They serve to support Raspberry's thesis that the positive aspects of the word are expressed narrowly.
3. Raspberry's use of questions not only is an effective way to draw readers into the discussion; it also forces readers to examine their own views on the subject.

Vocabulary

racism (1): a belief that some races are by nature superior to others.
conducive (6): leading or contributing to a result.
quintessentially (9): typically representative of.
elocution (10): the art of effective public speaking.
inculcated (11): to teach and impress on the mind by frequent repititions.
concede (12): grant; yield.

Writing Topics

1. This question is difficult and abstract enough that it might best be used as the basis for a class discussion before the students are set loose on it. One lead-in to such a discussion might be the example of the very successful Bill Cosby TV show. The show has been widely praised for presenting a positive image of black success, both familial and professional; on the other hand it is often criticized for all but ignoring race as a theme, for presenting black success on a thoroughly "white" model. Is this an instance of a minority's "fostering a good opinion of itself," or remaining "at the mercy of the majority's opinion"? (Incidentally, one thing to emerge from Raspberry's essay, we would hope, would be an understanding that the success

of a few black figures in sports and the performing arts does not mean that the doors of opportunity are equally open to all, as a few pundits have opined regarding Cosby's popularity). In any case, we hope that students will be able to see that there are ways in which a minority *is* and ways in which it *isn't* "at the mercy of the majority's opinion." Some students may resist Raspberry's suggestion (despite Raspberry's being himself black—a point which should perhaps be established early on, though most students will have discerned it) that black children *don't* "understand that they are intelligent, competent people," or have a good opinion of themselves; this seems to us worthy of debate.

2. Students may come up with some rather wild surmises regarding the origins of black/white symbolism. Some may be inspired to go beyond their own dictionary to the OED or even such culturally-illuminating texts as the Bible or the works of Shakespeare, for both of which concordances are available.

VI. SEXISM AND LANGUAGE

SEXISM IN ENGLISH: A 1990S UPDATE, Alleen Pace Nilsen   (p. 277)

Questions on Content

1. Nilsen lived in Kabul, Afghanistan for a couple of years and observed the subservient role of women in that society and her own. When she returned to the States, she saw that many women were questioning "the expectations they grew up with." Nilsen chose the study of sexism in the English language as a quieter, nonviolent means of examining women's role in society. She discovered that language and society are so intertwined that she could not avoid facing social issues head on.
2. Nilsen makes the following points:
   a. English words derived from the name of a person: A very large number of everyday words have come into modern English from the names of men. A very much smaller number of words have entered the language from the names of women, and most of them come from Greek mythology (6).
   b. geographical names: Many American place names refer to women's sexual features, especially their breasts (7, 8, and 9).
   c. pairs of words, one masculine and the other feminine: Often "sexual connotations are given to feminine words while the masculine words retain a serious, businesslike aura" (10) as *callboy/call girl* (10), *sir/madam* (11), and other pairs illustrate. Furthermore, in masculine-feminine pairs of words, the masculine word "is the base with a feminine suffix being added for the alternate version" (12), and the masculine words appear in far more compounds than do the feminine words.
   d. the use of words referring to foods, plants, and animals in connection with women: Women in our society "are expected to play a passive role" (15); our language reveals this expectation by its large number of words describing women in terms of foods or something to eat (16), plants (17), and pets rather than aggressive animals (18).
   e. the first names given to male and female infants: "Girls are much more likely to be given names like *Ivy, Rose, Ruby, Jewel, Pearl, Flora, Joy*, etc., while boys are given names describing active roles such as *Martin* (warlike), *Leo* (lion), *William* (protector), *Ernest* (resolute fighter), and so on" (19).
   f. the use of Ms.: Women who ask to be identified as *Ms.* rather than as *Miss* or *Mrs.* are protesting against being defined in terms of their relationship to a man (20).
   g. dictionary entries concerning famous women: Even women who are famous in their own rights are almost always identified in dictionary entries in terms of their relationships to some male-husband, brother, father, even lover. Such listings are not given for men (21, 22, 23, and 24).

61

h. positive and negative connotations connected with the concepts "masculine" and "feminine": Nilsen argues that "there are many positive connotations connected with the concept of masculine, while there are either trivial or negative connotations connected with the corresponding feminine concept" (26). She discusses this idea at length in paragraphs 27 through 35.

3. If the purpose of a dictionary is, in fact, to lay out how the language is actually used and not to pass judgments on that usage, then dictionary makers cannot be faulted for including definitions that betray cultural biases. Students' opinions on this matter may vary, but they should be encouraged to explain the reasoning behind their attitudes.

4. In paragraph 14 Nilsen reveals that only in the areas of sex and marriage do women appear more important than men.

5. In paragraph 36 Nilsen lists several changes she has seen in the language over the last 20 years. One is the increased use of inclusive language, the use of she; he or they when the gender is unknown or unclear, publishers now use guidelines to help writers use language that is fair to both sexes, newspapers list women by their names instead of their husbands, business letters begin with "Dear Colleagues," and "Dear Reader," instead of "Dear Sir," nouns which add "ess" to render it feminine are being dropped from the language, and both men's and women's names are being used for hurricanes. These changes show Nilsen that "sexism is not something existing in English... it exists in people's minds." Instead of being the alternative to both *Mrs.* and *Miss* that it was intended to be, *Ms.* has replaced *Miss* to become a catch-all business title for women.

Questions on Rhetoric

1. Nilsen supports her conclusions primarily by amassing large numbers of examples based on a thorough examination of one particular standard desk dictionary.

   Her evidence is convincing.

   It is complete and presented objectively.

2. Nilsen has organized her essay using division and classification together with comparison and contrast. She first divides her essay into areas where sexism occurs in dictionary definitions and classifies her examples of male and female oriented entries accordingly. Then, as she discusses each area, she compares and contrasts what the male and female examples reveal about cultural biases.

3. The tone of this essay is reasonable, logical, and good-natured.

   Nilsen maintains this tone by carefully describing her procedures, by drawing conclusions only after she has presented a good deal of evidence, and by including humorous examples and inviting the reader to share her amusement at their ludicrous nature.

   The tone is appropriate; she is persuasive because her tone is detached and calm.

4. Short transitional paragraphs in Nilsen's essay are paragraphs 5, 15, and 26.

   They are effective; they present her principal conclusions and are followed by longer paragraphs that give the supporting evidence.

   Short transitional paragraphs should be used in essays of substantial length to move from one important idea or section to another.

   They should be avoided in short essays and in cases in which a smooth transition can be made in the first sentence of a new paragraph.

5. Nilsen compares language to an x-ray as it provides "visible evidence of invisible thoughts." Many students will appreciate the simile for summing up Nilsen's point simply and clearly.

Vocabulary

inherent (1): belonging to by nature.
eponyms (7): anything, real or imaginary, from whom something, as a tribe, nation, or place, takes or is said to take its name.
gender (13): sex.
semantic (14): of or related to meaning.
temperance (21): habitual moderation in the indulgence of the appetites or passions.
trivial (28): commonplace; of little importance.
ambivalent (30): simultaneous attraction toward and repulsion from a person, object or action.
quaint (36): pleasingly old-fashioned or unfamiliar.

Writing Topics

1. Students should be reminded that as they explain how improvements can be brought about they will need to provide specific examples to illustrate exactly how changes can occur. You may also wish to analyze how Nilsen has incorporated the discussion of examples into her essay before students approach their own.
2. The opposition to women's attempts to change language is in part a reaction to change itself; many people fear and distrust change. Other opponents feel that the suggested changes are silly and either are not needed or would have no effect.

    We do not think that the opposition is justified because many attitudes and prejudices are unconsciously transmitted and reinforced by our language.

    The most effective technique employed by an opposition is ridicule, as Jonathan Swift and other satirists have long known. Some changes in the language would be silly (for example, *hurricane* to *himicane*), and even though no serious feminists support them, opponents make fun of them and ignore the serious sexual biases of English.

REAL MEN DON'T: ANTI-MALE BIAS IN ENGLISH,
Eugene R. August (p. 289)

Questions on Content

1. According to August, language studies operate under the assumption "that men control language and that they use it to define women as inferior." August asserts that in reality both men and women shape language and hence both are complicit in the definition of gender roles and the distribution of power.
2. The three kinds of anti-male bias are: First, gender-exclusive language that "omits males from certain kinds of consideration." For example, "alma mater" is a gender exclusive term to describe a university. And "mammal" is a biological classification made according to the female's ability to suckle her young through her mammary glands. Second, gender restric-

tive language includes terms applied to males only and according to August is designed "to keep them within the confines of a socially prescribed gender role." The Real Men Don't syndrome is just one example of language that defines what is expected of a "real man." Third, negative stereotyping characterizes the male as inherently evil or dangerous. "Nearly all the words for law-breakers," such as murderer, swindler, mobster, hood, and terrorist, bring to mind the image of a male rather than a female, August says.

3. August agrees that such terms are implicitly insulting to women; however, he points out (rather tautologically) that since boys are the target of these insults, it is the boys who are most insulted by them. August appears to consider this claim a corrective to the "one-sidedness" of the commentary on these terms, but the single example he cites is not sufficient to establish that these usages are seen by "most commentators" as disparaging exclusively to women.

4. To be a man, boys and men have to conform to a socially prescribed gender role which isn't always clear because most boys are raised by women and because most demands on boys are given in the negative, such as "real men don't." Yet, if a boy or man behaves in a way which does not conform, he is ridiculed. Early in life a boy is expected to be "all boy" and when hurt, "a brave soldier." If he fails he is a "sissy" or a "mama's boy." In school, if he doesn't show an easy manner with the girls he is a "nerd," or a "drip." If he does not take dares, he is a "coward." If his masculinity is open to question he is a "queer" or a "pansy"; if he rejects the military he is a "draft dodger," a "peacenik" or a "traitor." If he behaves badly with women, he is a "louse," a "rat," or a "Don Juan." If he marries and fails as a breadwinner, he is a "loser" and a "deadbeat." Students may have a hard time coming up with terms that August has left out.

5. August suspects that the masculinization of evil has its roots in the western depiction of evil in male terms, such as the Biblical Evil One who is always referred to as "he." He claims that this perception of evil as male shows up in attitudes about crime, in which generic names for criminals such as, "mugger," "killer," "rapist," and "child abuser" tend to connote male rather than female perpetrators. News reports emphasize male participation in any given crime more heavily than female responsibility even if both sexes are involved—or so August claims on the basis of one example.

6. If the problem of anti-male bias in language is ignored, August believes that having been labeled as the enemy, men will act like the enemy.

Questions on Rhetoric

1. August quotes Mead and Dinnerstein because they are recognized intellectual figures, but also, clearly, because they are women. August hopes to lend their authority to his claim that women's sexism, as reflected in English, is as serious a problem as men's sexism. Somehow one doubts that either of these thinkers would accept this argument.

2. August divides gender-restrictive nouns into two groups: those that restrict females and those that restrict males. The female-gender-restrictive list is comprised of one word, while the words to imply that a boy is not all-boy includes 11 terms. This suggests that our society feels it is far less acceptable for a male to behave like a female than it is for a female to behave like a male. Whether this indicates a greater anti-female bias than anti-male is a question August does not, we believe, address adequately. Compare Nilsen (29).

3. August's title is effective because it allows readers to finish the phrase for themselves, thus engaging them in stereotyping even before they begin to read the article. Other similar, but not nearly as effective titles might be, "Take It Like a Man," and "Be A Man."

4. The opening sentences of August's essay state his position in a straightforward, scholarly

manner. They set the tone for an essay that purports to be written without anger or vindictiveness.

Vocabulary

symbiotic (2): together in intimate association or close union especially when mutually beneficial.
denigrates (4): casts aspersions on.
notorious (7): known as talked of, generally negatively.
virtual (9): being in essence or in effect though not formally recognized or admitted.
slurred (12): made a slighting remark.
enjoined (13): commanded; ordered.
castigated (14): punished, reproved or criticized severely.
homophobic (16): suspicious and afraid of homosexuals.
deferential (18): courteous; respectful of another's wishes.
obtuse (21): dull; slow-witted.
bane (32): a source of woe and harm.
yahooism (32): the cries of uncouth and rowdy persons.

Writing Topics

1. August's experiment and the conclusions he draws from it are extremely vulnerable, as we hope the students will discern. He presumably hoped his students would check "could be either" for most of the terms, but the wording of the other options—"primarily males/ females"—seems to have suggested to the students that they should calculate whether the *majority* of thieves, killers, mobsters, *etc.* were *likely* to be male—though of course, they literally *could* be either. That the students checked "primarily male" in most instances seems perfectly predictable, not because of some "anti-male bias in English" (would a classful of Spanish or Russian speakers yield very different results?) but because of the predominantly male make-up of most of these categories, as measured in easily-available statistics.

GENDER BENDERS, Jack Rosenthal   (p. 303)

Questions on Content

1. Rosenthal never defines the term explicitly, but Hidden Gender refers to the phenomenon whereby people, asked to name the genders of two paired objects, will generally be able to identify one as "masculine" and the other as "feminine" despite the absence of any biological criteria for doing so.
2. With any given pair, most people respond similarly, *i. e.* confronted with Ford and Chevrolet, a majority of those who see any gender at all will take Ford to be masculine and Chevrolet to be feminine. The game doesn't work with single items; Hidden Gender is relative—the same item may appear feminine in one pairing (the fork in fork / knife) and masculine in another (fork / spoon). Among other things, this suggests that Hidden Gender resides *in the*

observer; it (and perhaps, by extension, other kinds of gender?) is not an inherent quality of the object under observation.

3. Rosenthal suggests that, confronted with an object (again, a *paired* object) of no immediately apparent gender, we look for whatever among its qualities—size, color, strength, delicacy, gracefulness, *etc.*—can be aligned with those attributes our culture defines as feminine or masculine.

4. The other kind is "ceremonial" gender, as when a nation, ship, invention or engine is designated a "she."

5. Students will have no trouble naming successes. "Extreme" instances which are seriously proposed and have gained acceptance will be harder to cite. Of course, what a student considers "extreme" will depend on how discommoded she or he is by change. The use of the feminine in indefinite pronouns is probably still considered "extreme" by some, yet it has become fairly common and many would consider it a "success."

Questions on Rhetoric

1. The opening question immediately hooks us into the "game" upon which Rosenthal has based his essay, and is *off-beat* in a way that instantly attracts attention. The remainder of the opening paragraph again defies our expectations by indicating that the seemingly frivolous game we've just played points to a serious issue.

2. Each of these sentences directly addresses the reader, asking questions or giving instructions, calling on us to join in Rosenthal's inquiry as if the essay would be somehow incomplete without our participation.

3. (1) introduces the subject of Hidden Gender.

(2)-(3) differentiate Hidden Gender from other kinds of gender which societies have traditionally attributed to inanimate things. (4), despite its patronizing jibe, indicates a third kind of gendered language—usages that implicitly exclude women.

(5)-(8) introduce and describe the Hidden Gender game and its typical results.

(9)-(10) explore possible explanations for the game's predictability.

(11)-(14) explore the implications of the game's indication that Hidden Gender is relative.

(15) broadens the essay's implications. The phenomenon of Hidden Gender suggests how deeply sexism runs in our culture and how large the task of transcending it will be.

Paragraphs (2), (3), and (4) do interrupt the essay's flow by interceding between the introduction of the Hidden Gender concept and its elucidation. They are there to distinguish Hidden Gender from other, more familiar forms of gendered language. The lesson here for the student is that in introducing a new and unfamiliar concept, it may be useful to distinguish it from associated, more familiar ones. Ultimately, Rosenthal wants to argue that the concept he is introducing poses a more serious issue than these more familiar instances of gendered language.

Vocabulary

formal (1): following the established form, custom, or rule.
superficial (1): lying on, not penetrating below, or affecting only the surface.
callous (2): lacking sympathy with others.
inherently (14): involved in the constitution or essential character of something.
purging (15): making free of something unwanted.
cosmetic (15): affecting the appearance.

Writing Topics

1. This question should engage students in some hard thinking about whether any adjectives are truly value-neutral—a difficult question that is, in interesting ways, given an entire new difficult dimension by Rosenthal's essay. Would the word "frail," for instance, seems *other-than-neutral* if not for the deep-seated sexism which, Rosenthal claims, emerges in our terms for describing objects? You might suggest they look in the Thesaurus for a synonym for "frail" that seems truly neutral, and to think about why there are or are not such words.
2. When the students try this with their friends, we predict that lively discussions will ensue—in fact, those who are able may want to keep a tape recorder going for reference during their writing. In the ideal instance, the group would include some whose responses go against the grain. You might also suggest they follow up the game by telling the participants about Rosenthal's account of Hidden Gender and asking how they account for the phenomenon; they may wind up in a nature-vs.-nurture debate that will provide a lot of material for thought.

ONE SMALL STEP FOR GENDERKIND, Casey Miller and Kate Swift   (p. 307)

Questions on Content

1. The notion that "everyone is male" "operates to keep women invisible." In other words, according to Miller and Swift, women go "unsung" and they are "kept in their place."
2. In paragraph 10 the authors define sexist language as "that (which) expresses... stereotyped attitudes and expectations, or that assumes the inherent superiority of one sex over the other." Women are also guilty of expressing their attitudes toward men in sexist language, such as "just like a man."
3. Male and female are designations applied objectively to people and things. "They are graphic and culture free." Masculine and feminine cannot be used "without invoking cultural stereotypes." Certainly, to refer to anyone as "male" or "female" when referring to gender would fall into the first category. "Manly and" "virile" are two dictionary words describing "masculine" virtues. In contrast, "womanish," "feminine wiles," "womanish tears," and a "womanlike lack of promptness," describes "feminine" attributes in the same dictionary. The authors conclude that words associated with males are positive while words associated with females are negative.
4. The press defines women through "external of superficial concerns," such as their age, appearance and occupation. The Chicago chapter of N.O.W. drew up guidelines which include: leaving out descriptions of women that would be considered inappropriate if used on men, using language to convey that women and not only men are included in the ranks of the professions, and using the same discretion in printing generalizations that would be extended to minority groups.
5. Women are in the forefront of efforts to reexamine Judew-Chirstian traditions both in their efforts to gain ordination and their contribution to the scholarly work of theological reform. According to the authors, the press has treated these efforts with a sneering disrespect.

Questions on Rhetoric

1. The authors have reconstructed the original metaphor, "One small step for man, one giant step for mankind," spoken by astronaut Neil Armstrong in 1969 when he and two other astronauts were the first human beings to set foot on the moon. No doubt the authors saw this as a perfect example of the way in which language excludes women.

2. These two riddles prove the authors' point before the authors state what that point is. The riddles put the reader into the right "mood" for the argument that follows.

3. The riddles at the beginning of the essay and the various lists of derogatory nouns used for men and women support the authors' argument effectively. However, some students will argue that words such as "mankind," "man" and "he" when used to include both men and women are practical and not demeaning.

4. The authors use strong language, which can be read either as unflinching or as angry. In our opinion the authors have skillfully arranged and included descriptions of sexist attitudes toward women and some of the "names" they are called to communicate their anger about the issue.

   "The language makes her a 'lower caste',... it works to 'keep her in her place.'" (6) They ask why women have to keep explaining that it is demeaning to be depicted as "decorative objects, breeding machines and extensions of men, not real people?" (20) "The sexual overtones in the ancient and no doubt honorable custom of calling ships "she" have become more explicit and less honorable in the age of air travel: "I'm Karen. Fly Me." (25) The authors characterize attitudes of "ridicule, contempt and disgust toward female sexuality," and the attendant epithets and insults as related to "the savagery of rape." (25)

5. The authors waited until the end of their essay to present their solution because they hoped that by then the reader will have come to agree with them as to the severity of the problem, the difficulty of a solution, and the need for a solution. In other words, by the 45th paragraph, the reader is ready for the news.

Vocabulary

riddle (1): a puzzling question to be solved by guessing.
intrepid (8): characterized by resolute fearlessness, fortitude, and endurance.
skewings (9): meats held on a pin for roasting.
nomenclature (9): a system of names used in a science or art.
invoking (12): calling forth by incantation: conjuring.
incongruous (15): not consistent with or suitable to the surroundings of circumstances.
approbation (17): approval.
surreptitiously (17): clandestinely; underhandedly.
invidious (18): injurious.
lexicographer (18): editor or maker of a dictionary.
repudiate (23): refuse to have anything to do with; cast off.
euphemism (27): substitution of a pleasant expression for one that is unpleasant.
supersede (43): take the place of; replace.
progenitor (45): direct ancestor; forefather.
progeny (45): offspring; children.

Writing Topics

1. Although much has changed in the recent past, students may be surprised to learn how many

of Miller's and Swift's criticisms still apply. The definition of "womanish" they quote, for example, survives in *Webster's Ninth New Collegiate Dictionary* (1988). One of the synonyms offered for "tomboy" in that dictionary is "hoyden"—a rather *less*-than-subtle disparagement of females. "Masculine" has as one of its definitions "of or forming the formal, active, or generative principle of the cosmos," while the only equivalent for "feminine" is "the female principle." Also, compare "masculine: having qualities appropriate to a man" with "feminine: characteristic of or appropriate or peculiar to women." There is, of course, the possible objection that dictionaries should reflect the way people use words, sexist or not, rather than dictate usage, but even by that standard, the latter two examples seem unnecessarily androcentric.

2. Although the authors oppose *-ess* endings, they grant the usefulness, in some circumstances, of feminine endings that take the form of exchanging *-woman* for *-man*, where *-man* is an established part of the word. The difference is that in *poet/poetess*, the *-ess* acts as a qualifier, marking a deviation from the norm signified by p*oet*. In the Case of *Congressman/congresswoman*, symmetry is more nearly approached (though not perfectly, given the Adam's ribbed character of the latter).

3. Our suspicion is that at least the major metropolitan newspapers have become conscientious enough so that howlers like "Blonde Hijacks Airliner" will have become relatively rare, although egregious instances continue to crop up. The *San Francisco Chronicle* ran a story fairly recently about a man who shot his wife because of the dinner she'd served him, headlined "Wife Cooks Last Pork Chop." One valuable addendum to this assignment would be to have those students who do find offensively sexist language write letters of complaint to the editor.

IN DEFENSE OF GENDER, Cyra McFadden (p. 320)

Questions on Content

1. McFadden objects to the neutering of English because she finds it makes language appear "self-conscious," and it slows further a language "already fat, bland, and lethargic" (22).
   That she sees this neutering as a language fad is evident in her belief that we can do away with this "game" if we simply "decide not to play it" (22).

2. In McFadden's terms, "person" suffixes and "he/she's" in print " jump out from the page, as distracting as a cloud of gnats, demanding that the reader note the writer's virtue" (4). In speech, "they leave conversation fit only for the Coneheads on "Saturday Nite Live'" (5). Students' reactions to McFadden's opinions may vary, though most will probably admit that these suffixes and pronouns are a source of irritation and frustration in their own writing.

3. McFadden offers three objections to hyphenated names: (1) they are hard to remember; (2) they defeat answering machines; and (3) they retain overtones of false gentility (20). Students may or may not find these objections valuable. Some may feel the benefit of declaring the husband separate but equal outweighs such troublesome considerations.

4. McFadden suggests that the neutering of English accomplishes nothing in the area of sexual bias, and only serves to confuse and frustrate writers who try to work these unworkable suffixes and pronouns into some kind of fluent expression.

5. McFadden does *not* offer any solutions and, in fact, wishes that "person or persons unknown would come up with one" (3). It may be a good class exercise for students to share any solutions they are able to devise so classmates can respond to them and determine whether they are any less "ludicrous" or cumbersome than those McFadden objects to.

Questions on Rhetoric

1. McFadden states her thesis in paragraph 4: "Defend it on any grounds you choose; the neutering of spoken and written English, with its attendant self-consciousness, remains ludicrous." She then supports this idea with numerous illustrative examples.
2. McFadden's tone is lighthearted and humorous, yet serious enough to let readers know that her objections to the neutering of English are more than just a trivial concern. Since her purpose is to demonstrate what is wrong with this kind of language and not to offer solutions, her approach is appropriate and effective.
3. The claim in paragraph 2 establishes that McFadden understands the motivation behind the neutering of English, since she herself has had to suffer the sexist bias inherent in our normal use of language. Her point, therefore, is not to argue that there is no need for the elimination of such bias, but rather that there has to be a better way to accomplish it.
4. The metaphors and similes in McFadden's essay include:

Metaphors

"I nonetheless *take off my hat*..." (3)
McFadden conveys the sense of admiration or respect that is indicated when someone takes off his hat as a show of regard.

"Those 'person' suffixes and 'he/she's' *jump out from the page*..." (4)
McFadden indicates that the words make a very distinct impression when they are encountered, by suggesting they contain qualities of animation.

"So much for *sounding brass and tinkling cymbals*." (6)
The brass and cymbals refer to sensations that Bible verses are supposed to arouse when they are read, and McFadden uses the metaphor to show that the neutered language eliminates any chance for these sensations.

"but slashing is not the answer; *violence never is*" (9)
McFadden uses the images associated with the word "violence" to indicate the severity of the disruption caused in language when someone uses the he/she-type construction.

"feminists out here *wrestle the language, plant a foot on its neck and remove its masculine appendages*" (12)
McFadden gives concreteness to an abstract concept—language, and suggests that feminists' attempts to eliminate sexual bias from language is comparable to the struggle of a fierce wrestling match.

"So the *war of pronouns and suffixes rages, taking no prisoners except writers*" (19)
McFadden compares the battle to eliminate sexual bias from the language to a military battle.

"Neuter your prose with all those *clanking he/she's*" (19)
McFadden attributes qualities of substance, enough to create a "clanking" noise, to items that have no such substance—words—to indicate the awkwardness and disruptiveness caused in writing by "neutered" language.

"a language already *fat, bland, and lethargic*" (22)

McFadden again uses qualities of substance and animation to refer to an abstract concept, this time to indicate that English is a hard language through which to convey a sense of fluency and grace in writing.

"*I'll be dragged behind a saddle bronc*" (22)

McFadden's description of a scene in which serious physical harm could occur indicates the degree to which she opposes the use of neutered terms like "cowpersons."

Similes

"as distracting as a cloud of gnats" (4)

McFadden compares the distraction caused by "person" suffixes and "he/she" pronouns to the irritation created by a cloud of gnats.

" In a Steig cartoon, the words would have marched from her mouth in the form of a computer printout." (5)

Though she doesn't use the familiar "like" or "as" this is still a simile since it draws a comparison between the way the woman at the San Francisco restaurant spoke and the way a computer emits information.

"like a replay of the Manson killings" (8)

McFadden compares the repetition of the word "slash" to activity associated with the menacing use of a knife.

5. McFadden's continual references to the "person" suffixes and "he/she" pronouns, as well as her incorporation of the suffixes into her own explanations (e.g., "in the interest of retaining their own *personhood*"), provides evidence for how these devices can make language awkward and ridiculous.

6. Though the primary meaning of "neuter" within McFadden's context is "neutral, " to indicate the kind of language that is not biased toward either sex, the connotations attached to its other meanings (asexuality or the castration and spaying of animals) suggest the kind of treatment the language itself has undergone in the effort to eradicate its sexist bias. In this respect, it seems a remarkably apt choice of diction.

Vocabulary

fusing (1): joining.
scourging (2): eliminating by severe means; afflicting; punishing.
aspirant (3): one who longs for or desires.
liturgy (6): a collection of prescribed forms for public worship.
replete (8): full to the uttermost.
render (8): to state formally.
generic (9): general; representative of a group or class.
appendages (12): parts attached to the main body, as limbs, tails, leaves, etc.
suffuses (18): spreads over.
lethargic (22): slow moving; sluggish.

Writing Topics

1. As a prewriting activity you can lead a discussion of feminist issues such as the push for ERA and the notion of comparable worth. By analyzing aspects of these issues in class, students may be able to draw conclusions about the "serious intent" of the proposed changes.

2. It may be helpful to share the results of this assignment with the class to demonstrate both the variety of ways that sexism creeps into language and the variety of ways that people can try to eliminate it.

GIRL TALK-BOY TALK, John Pfeiffer   (p. 325)

Questions on Content

1. The newest branch of language study deals with the role of gender in speech, with an emphasis on discovering how, why, and under what conditions the sexes talk differently. The new studies began about ten years ago. When researchers, inspired by the women's movement, began to examine earlier language studies that belittled women's conversation.
2. The continued belittlement of women's conversation reveals that sexist attitudes are more than skin deep. These attitudes show up in places as diverse as medical journals, bra ads, campaign speeches, and government offices in modern Japan.
3. Women ask 70 percent of the questions, encourage others to speak in all-female groups, tend to narrate in the third person rather than tell stories about themselves, and speak in a higher pitch than men do. Men meeting a woman for the first time make 75 percent of the interruptions; with women they know better, men make 96 percent of the interruptions. In both cases, men usually choose the topic of conversation. Other, more subtle differences include a male habit of not listening to what women say and women's being "first-named" by men who address other males by their last names. All can be seen as indicative of sex-bias attitudes. However, interrupting and not listening are the most blatant means anyone can use to disallow the relevance of another person in a conversation.
4. When men and women who had never met before were mixed in conversation, the men " softened" while the women became more aggressive and adopted an "every woman for herself" attitude. It is interesting to suppose, as Pfeiffer does, that the male behavior was a "mating display" and that the male participants were likely to revert to their usual behavior upon closer acquaintance. We may reasonably assume that the women were likely to do the same.
5. Language research is now exploring conversational patterns used man to man, woman to woman, culture to culture, profession to profession, doctor to patient, and social group to social group.
6. Men and women are shifting in their relationship toward each other. Women ask fewer of the questions in a conversation as they become more intent on expressing their own point of view, and men are listening.

Questions on Rhetoric

1. This method is effective and appropriate because the comparison and contrast of male and female conversational patterns is the point of the work being done by the researchers. Pfeiffer's use of quotes is particularly effective because this is one of those times when

readers can easily match the findings of the experts to their own experience. The reports of the experts ring true and so serve to support Pfeiffer's argument.

2. These two paragraphs give historical background or the early forms taken by feminists' concern with language.

3. Students may not all agree that Pfeiffer's tone is sarcastic or angry.

4. The immediate explanation for the preponderance of women among researchers in language and gender would be that women have generally led the way in gender-related research, because they have more to gain than men from dispelling the ignorance that helps to perpetuate patriarchal abuse. (Note the first sentence of paragraph (12).) By saving this observation until the end, Pfeiffer closes on a note of challenge: there is still a long way to go before men are as interested as women in understanding gender and its relation to power.

Vocabulary

unobtrusively (1): inconspicuously.
rogues' gallery (3): a collection of portraits of criminals and suspects maintained by the police for purposes of identification.
culprits (5): ones accused or guilty of a crime.
intonation (7): rise and fall in pitch of the voice in speaking.
agenda (10): a list of things to be done.
affronts (12): insults.
constellation (23): a group of ideas, feelings, objects, or characteristics that are related.
coalitions (27): temporary unions for a common purpose.
phenomenon (28): an observable fact or event.

Writing Topics

1. Obviously, without recording equipment and an extremely detailed transcription system, students will not be able to catch all the nuances in which gender-relations reveal themselves. But for inspiration (and for more ideas about the kind of things to be looking for), they can be referred to Robin Lakoff's *Language and Women's Place*, itself rather impressionistic yet extremely interesting. (Lakoff doesn't pretend to statistical rigor, and her research method amounts to what the student will be required to do—careful listening.

2. Note that Pfeiffer never calls the tendency to ask questions a sign of weakness, any more than he calls the tendency to speak in declaratives a sign of strength. Obviously there is much to be said in favor of asking questions. It demonstrates interest in one's partner, curiosity about the world at large, and a polite willingness not to dominate the conversation. The statistic remains disturbing in some ways. For one thing, it means that men ask only 30% of the questions, which suggests at least a relative degree of incuriosity and impoliteness on their part (a suggestion that is further borne out by the statistics on interruption). Furthermore, the imbalance suggests that, nice as asking questions may be, there is at least some element of de *facto* self-censorship on women's part (socially determined, to be sure).

3. As with #1, finely detailed analysis is probably too much to hope for, but the multitude of speakers under observation here may result in richer findings. Again, students may want to look at Lakoff's book or some other examples of the literature, beyond just Pfeiffer's essay, for more ideas of what to be on the lookout for.

THE "F" WORD, Catharine R. Stimpson   (p. 334)

Questions on Content

1. The word "feminism" entered the English language in 1895.
2. On the "puny" side, women still have little clout in certain areas: podium, pulpit, TV studio, White House briefing room. However, feminism has three potent gifts to offer both men and women: "a moral vision of women,...; political and cultural organizations that translate the vision into action; and psychological processes that enable men and women to re-experience and re-form themselves." (4)
3. Type A is the neoconservative who wishes to maintain the status quo, the "barefoot and pregnant" ideal of womanhood. Type B blames women for society's problems. Type C includes women who separate themselves from the feminist movement claiming in effect that "we can do it on our own." Type D sees feminism as a crusade against motherhood. Type E accepts the benefits of the feminist movement while disavowing any allegiance to it. Type F is the feminist who has grown weary and frightened in the face of the enormity of their task.
4. Feminists fear feminism because it is demanding and difficult and because many of them are as confused as anyone else about what the new woman is supposed to look like. Her humble confession makes Stimpson more accessible and reasonable sounding to her readers. The "feminine mystique" is the popularly accepted image of woman as she is "supposed" to be, not as she is. In replacing this image, feminists sometimes experience fear and guilt about the new mystique they are building.
5. Stimpson suggests referring to feminism as the "F-word," because "It might deflect a little of that hostility back where it came from." She also suggests that feminists use more humor and more audacity, and declare "I am a feminist," more often. Her strategies may work for the reasons she offers in her final sentence, "The more we say it, the more reasonable it will become and then it will be G-rated."

Questions on Rhetoric

1. Stimpson encourages feminist thinkers to examine their own prejudices and the prejudice of others around the word "feminism" as a means of revitalizing their thinking and their efforts in the movement. The first words of Stimpson's essay are a shock to readers who are expecting an essay on a profanity. It alerts them to the kind of association some people have to the word "feminism."
2. Stimpson was justified in expecting her readers to be both sympathetic and informed on the subject of her essay because *Ms.* is a leading feminist magazine. The inclusion of other feminist experts would have detracted from the easy, personal style of her essay.
3. Stimpson uses a simile in paragraph 10 to emphasize the careless squandering of rights that were hard won. In paragraph 1 she uses the metaphor of the x-ray to compare the similar roles each "new word" had in our culture and to contrast the ease and disease with which each of them was assimilated into our language.
4. Stimpson practices what she preaches by using a forceful and sometimes humorous tone. The effect is one of good will rather than of hostility and may attract more "x-raters" and "feminaphobes" to her point of view. Students will find several easy examples of her diction throughout the essay.

74

Vocabulary

feminism (1): theory of the political, economic, and social equality of the sexes.
zany (3): crazy; foolish.
lurches (3): sways or tips.
ideologues (8): those who hold the assertions, theories, and aims that constitute a political, social, and economic program.
repress (9): restrain; suppress.
belligerence (10): truculence; pugnaciousness.
mystique (11): a set of beliefs and attitudes developing around an object or associated with a certain group.
compelling (12): driven or urged with force.
nuance (13): a shade of difference; a delicate variation.

Writing Topics

1. Students will have no trouble finding material on the history of the women's movement. The real interest in this assignment will lie in the students' efforts to reconstruct the geneses of the six forms of resistance, and their speculations on the ways in which each of these voices has gained a measure of social legitimization and power.
2. Alert students will have recognized most if not all of these "voices" from their own experiences in the family, on campus, and in front of the TV. However, Stimpson's treatment of each, while very incisive and suggestive, is brief (as befitting an essay for a popular magazine), and you may want to spend a fair amount of class time collectively elaborating on the attitudes and interests embodied in each "voice."
3. This assignment, of course, requires some extended thought on the definition of "individualism" as well as of "feminism." Students will probably arrive fairly quickly at the formulation that feminists are individualistic to the extent that they advance the individual interests of women, but that their individualism is qualified to the extent that they envision collective and legislative remedies for the social ills they identify. This can become an occasion for reflecting on the adequacy of "individualism" as a principle of social cohesion. The assignment may be somewhat misleading insofar as it suggests Stimpson virtually equates feminism with individualism; the dish-washing example can be viewed as rather tongue-in-cheek, and in the paragraph's first sentence, Stimpson describes the individualistic assumptions of Americans as "self-deceptive."

VII. EUPHEMISMS AND TABOOS

EUPHEMISM, Neil Postman   (p. 345)

Questions on Content

1. Euphemisms have gotten such a bad name because people have frequently used them to deceive others.
2. When people consider a thing and the name for that thing the same they confuse the thing with its abstract representation, as it is expressed through language. The name has meaning only in the mind, whereas the thing itself exists separate from anyone's ability to identify it. For further discussion of the principle that "the word is not the thing" see S. I. Hayakawa's *Language in Thought and Action*, 3rd ed. (New York: Harcourt Brace Jovanovich, 1972), pp. 21-30.
3. As Postman explains in paragraph 3, "if you change the name of things, you change how people will regard them, and that is as good as changing the nature of the thing itself." In paragraphs 5 through 7, Postman's examples include *senior citizens, chairperson, blacks*, and *sanitation engineers*. Students will mention other comparable examples of job titles, names for groups, and so forth.
4. Postman means that the term *blacks*, in place of *Negroes*, is more, rather than less, direct about racial color.
5. Postman believes that earthy language and euphemisms simply express different conceptions of what an event means. To put it another way, he believes that there is no single "real" term for a concept or action.

Questions on Rhetoric

1. Postman's point is that euphemizing, as a process, has "no moral content" (7).
2. Postman begins with a definition of *euphemism* because he wants to make sure his readers understand the meaning of the term. He also wants us to see beyond the word's connotations, to see its literal or denotative meaning.
3. Postman's examples serve two primary purposes: (1) they help clarify exactly what euphemisms are; and (2) they clearly demonstrate the distinction between euphemisms that are used to deceive and those that are used honestly and can help shift perceptions and attitudes. All of Postman's examples are functional and therefore enhance his essay.
4. Postman uses transitional expressions (*and, of course, for example, but, for*), repeated key words (*names, people, thing, illusion*) and pronoun references (*it, that*). Each of these transitions links two or more sentences in paragraph 2.
5. Postman's last two sentences are an appropriate conclusion because in them he returns to the two most prominent examples in his essay. The two examples remind us of the extremes to which the euphemizing process can be put.

Vocabulary

auspicious (1): favorable.
exalted (1): elevated or noble.
expunge (1): to strike out; obliterate.
hideous (1): repulsive, very ugly.
evokes (1): recreates or brings to mind.
amiss (1): improper.
semantics (2): the study of meanings.
illusions (2): things that deceive by producing false impressions.
contemptible (4): despicable.
categorically (7): absolutely; unconditionally.

Writing Topics

1. The euphemisms that students are likely to find contemptible are: *orderly withdrawal, resources control program, health alteration committee,* and *convenient terms.* To some degree students feel that the intent of these terms is to deceive.

   As they consider the basis for each of the euphemisms listed, students should be stimulated to generate examples of their own. They may then want to distinguish between those that are contemptible and those that aren't, and use this as one of the structuring principles of their essays on the uses to which euphemisms can be put.

2. As a prewriting activity for this assignment you may want to discuss situations where a person can benefit from the use of euphemisms. Consider, for instance, Postman's own example involving the terms "shithouse" and "restroom," or even just "bathroom" and "restroom," and ask students to explain why the euphemism might be the better term to employ in either case.

VERBAL TABOO, S. I. Hayakawa (p. 350)

Questions on Content

1. Hayakawa classifies taboo words into the following categories:

Categories	Examples
excretion and sex	rest room, powder room
money	sums, remittance
death	passed away, went west
anatomy and sex	white meat, retire
religious	"Gee," "gosh almighty"

2. Words that have strong *affective* connotations arouse strong feelings or stimulate an emotional response through the unspoken associations attached to them. *Informative* connotations convey more neutral associations, and while these associations may provide additional information about a word, they usually do not "affect" a person's feelings or emotions.

3. In paragraph 5 Hayakawa states that taboos "prevent frank discussion of sexual matters."
4. According to Hayakawa, "uttering these forbidden words provides us with a relatively harmless verbal substitute for going berserk and smashing furniture; that is, the words act as a kind of safety valve in our moments of crisis" (6).
5. Hayakawa discusses this relationship in paragraph 8. When people attempt to ban the use of a word (for instance, communism or any four-letter word), they are often confusing the word with the thing or action the word symbolizes.
6. The relationship between taboo words and euphemisms is, basically, that the latter are used to avoid the former. Euphemisms are words with agreeable connotations and are often substituted for words that carry more unacceptable connotations, such as taboo words. Hayakawa mentions the terms "toilet" and "rest room," for example. The more pleasant sounding "rest room" connotes a place where one goes to relax and rest, while the more taboo "toilet" carries more direct and often socially embarrassing associations.

Questions on Rhetoric

1. The controlling idea of the paragraph is presented in the first sentence.
   Hayakawa supports this topic sentence with numerous examples of euphemistic usage.
2. Hayakawa makes the transition between the fifth and sixth paragraphs by establishing a contrast between verbal taboos and even stronger verbal taboos. The word *however* signals this contrast.
   Hayakawa makes other transitions by using the transitional word *another*, the pronoun reference *these*, and the repeated key word *primitive*.
3. The intent of this question is to alert students to the decisions a writer must make concerning audience and degrees of explanation. Responses about the story of Rumpelstiltskin will vary.
4. Hayakawa's examples provide concrete illustrations for the general principles stated in his essay. In paragraph 3, for instance, he writes: "The fear of death carries over, quite understandably in view of the widespread confusion of symbols with things symbolized, into fear of the *words* having to do with death." The meaning of this abstract and general statement is more easily understood as Hayakawa goes on to present specific examples of symbols and explains how they are confused with what they symbolize.
   You may wish to discuss with students which of Hayakawa's examples they find most effective, and then determine what makes them so useful in understanding his essay.

Vocabulary

inhibited (2): restrained or held back.
symbols (3): things that represent something else by association, resemblance, or convention.
coincidence (3): accidental sequence of events that appear to have a causal relationship.
anatomical (4): of or pertaining to body structure.
ignorant (5): unaware or uninformed.

Writing Topics

1. An excellent discussion of the semantic principle that "the word is not the thing" appears in S. I. Hayakawa, *Language in Thought and Action*, 3rd ed. (New York: Harcourt Brace Jovanovich, 1972), pp. 21-30.

The child in the anecdote has confused the phenomenon of death with the word *death*; she mistakenly believes that reality will change if it is relabeled. Hayakawa gives many good examples of the prevalence of this confusion in everyday life.

2. Such objections to dictionaries are examples of a central point in Hayakawa's essay: the confusion of words with the things being symbolized. By eliminating dictionaries from schools and libraries, parents seek to protect their children from certain "objectionable" words. The children, while protected from the dictionaries themselves, would in all likelihood encounter these objectionable words in other situations.

FOUR-LETTER WORDS CAN HURT YOU, Barbara Lawrence (p. 354)

Questions on Content

1. In paragraph 3 Lawrence dismisses two popularly held explanations of the existence of taboos before giving her own explanation: "the sources and functions of the words themselves." The explanations she dismisses are that taboos exist because of sexual hang-ups, or as a result of class oppression.

2. In paragraph 10 Lawrence states why, as a woman, she objects to obscene language: obscene language tends "to deny women their biological identity, their individuality, their humanness."

   Men could object to obscene language on the same grounds; see paragraph 7.

3. In general, students will agree with Lawrence's argument. Get them to discuss their reasons for agreeing or disagreeing.

   The question of whether Lawrence's view is strictly feminist may generate more debate. You may wish to discover exactly what students believe a "strictly feminist" argument is.

4. In presenting the etymology of "the best known of the tabooed sexual verbs"; Lawrence demonstrates that from its origin the word has carried sadistic or denigrating connotations, which is the main reason she objects to obscene words in general.

   Most students will probably be surprised to discover how the word has developed etymologically.

Questions on Rhetoric

1. Lawrence's questions in the first two paragraphs serve three main functions: to capture the reader's attention, to involve the reader, and to establish the topic and suggest its development.

2. Lawrence's avoidance of four-letter words shows that they are not essential even in an essay such as this. Their absence lends seriousness and dignity to her essay.

3. Lawrence's use of *eloquently* and *piously* underscores the hypocrisy of those people who, while ignoring the plight of women, will jump to the defense of racial or ethnic minorities.

4. We feel that the two paragraphs, although related in subject, should not be combined because the emphasis that Lawrence wants to give her final question would be lost.

5. The effect of her final question is to persuade the reader. One is led to answer the question as she would with a resounding "No!"

Vocabulary

preferable (1): more desirable or worthy.
grimaces (1): sharp contortions of the face expressive of pain, contempt, or disgust.
oppression (3): subjugation or persecution.
analogy (5): correspondence in some respects, especially in function or position, between things otherwise dissimilar.
antecedent (5): going before; preceding.
implicitly (6): indirectly expressed.
contemptuous (8): scornful; disdainful.
pejoratives (12): words that disparage or downgrade.

Writing Topics

1. Discussion can focus on the problem of women who, in seeking equality through forceful language, defeat their purposes by using language that has long been used to denigrate other human beings, especially women.
2. As a prewriting activity for this assignment you may want to present students with writing samples from authors like Norman Mailer or Henry Miller, that exhibit their use of "obscenities." You can then discuss how students respond to such passages and whether this kind of language does, in fact, conjure up mental associations that are sadistic or denigrating. Your discussion may help students formulate their opinions on this matter as they prepare their essays.
3. In conjunction with this assignment you may want to review the "descriptive" purpose of dictionaries in relation to their inclusion or exclusion of obscenities. Ask students whether the fact that obscenities are commonly used in the language, even those that denigrate a class or group of people, justifies their inclusion in dictionaries that attempt to reflect how language is actually used.

   They might find it helpful to review S. I. Hayakawa's "How Dictionaries Are Made" in Chapter IV.

THE LANGUAGE OF NUCLEAR WAR STRATEGISTS, Stephen Hilgartner, Richard C. Bell, and Rory O'Connor (p. 358)

Questions on Content

1. The authors refer to "the world of nuclear warfare" as doublethink because of the paradoxes inherent in preserving peace through the threat of war, obtaining security through insecurity, and thinking the unthinkable. The image of the hall of mirrors accurately portrays these paradoxes since the concepts reflect back on themselves in inverted form.
2. Students' reactions to this language may vary, but most will probably agree that it lacks the emotional intensity that one associates with considerations of nuclear warfare. This "cool and clinical" language allows war strategists to discuss these issues in a "rational" manner

and masks the destructive implications of the decisions and policies they arrive at. This is exactly the kind of masking at work in the War Department's name change, disguising the central purpose for which that agency was created—to analyze, prepare for, and conduct war.

3. The authors present their explanation for "deterrence" in paragraph 3: "Nuclear deterrence is, in effect, a mutual suicide pact: if you attack me, it may kill me, but I will kill you before I die. The civilian population of each superpower is held hostage by the opposite power."

   Nuclear war planners fear a "preemptive first strike" because it would "cripple the enemy's ability to retaliate" (7), thus encouraging first use of nuclear weaponry. The threat of a preemptive first strike is therefore the catalyst for what we know as the "arms race," since "the perception of the possibility of an enemy attempting a splendid first strike" has caused the superpowers to reach "higher and higher levels of destructive power" (9).

4. The neutron bomb differs from a conventional nuclear bomb in that it produces "less explosive blast... releasing a greater fraction of [its] energy in a deadly burst of neutron radiation" (16). In other words, the aim of a neutron bomb is to kill troops while reducing the overall blast damage.

5. The technological developments in the 1970s that have destabilized the situation between the United States and the USSR are: (1) the deployment of "multiple independently targetable reentry vehicles" (MIRVs); and (2) improvements in missile accuracy.

   Additional threats to deterrence are the recognition that the C-3 systems (command, control, and communications) of both superpowers might be vulnerable to nuclear attack, and "the possibility of a system failure in either superpower's nuclear-war-fighting computers " (32).

6. The students' substitutions for italicized words should reveal a more direct and frightening presentation of nuclear war information.

Questions on Rhetoric

1. The authors' purpose is to *argue* against the use of such language by explaining its highly specialized vocabulary and the implications hidden behind it. Their stance on the issue is evident in the tone and diction of the following passages:

   "Cities are *bargaining chips*; they are not destroyed, they are *taken out* with *clean surgical strikes*—as if they were tumors" (1).

   "The driving force behind the arms race is a treacherous double-bind known as the *security-dilemma*" (10).

   "The superpowers' *hawks* watch each other closely, passing what they see through the gloomy filter of worst-case *scenarios*" (11).

   "Equipped with this array of armaments, nuclear warriors are ready to play the game of *escalation*, using threats and counterthreats to deter, influence, coerce, and block their opponents" (24).

   "A terrifying web of perceptions and misperceptions is possible. *Spiraling tensions* could start a thermonuclear war even if no one wanted it" (24).

2. The authors use the strategies of classification and cause and effect extensively in their essay. The paragraphs that contain elements of classification include: 5, 6, 13, 14, 15, 22, 27, and 28; while those that rely on some form of cause and effect analysis include: 4, 7, 8, 9, 10, 11, 20, 24, 27, 28, 31, and 34.

3. The analogy of the game of chicken reflects how the superpowers dare each other to carry

the nuclear escalation game further and further until one backs down from fear of self-destruction, granting the other victory. Most students will probably find this analogy a recognizable and effective means for explaining the notion of escalation strategy.

4. The example in paragraph 21 illustrates how it is possible to be rational by pretending to be irrational or acting irrationally. Nixon's strategy of appearing obsessed to the point of madness was intended to bring the war in Vietnam to a speedier conclusion.

In paragraph 30, the example demonstrates how the recognition that the superpowers' C-3 systems might be vulnerable to nuclear attack has destabilized the situation between the United States and the USSR, by providing a "strong incentive to strike first."

The two examples in paragraph 32 reveal how much of a destabilizing influence the possibility of computer failure may be, despite the Department of Defense's assurances that it is insignificant. The examples show how close we have already come to the "nuclear edge" as a result of computer malfunctions.

Vocabulary

esoteric (2): beyond the understanding or knowledge of most people.
carnage (4): bloody and extensive slaughter, especially in battle.
retaliate (4): to return like for like, injury for injury, wrong for wrong, etc.
construed (6): explained, deduced, or interpreted.
arsenal (9): a story or collection of weapons and other munitions.
conjunction (14): a joining together; union; combination.
purportedly (16): apparently intended to get or do.
array (17): an impressive display of assembled persons or things.
tacit (18): not declared openly, but implied or understood.
orgasmic (19): in a frenzied or greatly excited manner.
insensate (19): without sense or reason.
hypothetical (17): assumed or supposed.
vulnerable (28): open to attack by armed forces.

Writing Topics

1. Students should be reminded to include more accurate substitutions for the terms they believe present an inaccurate picture of the realities of nuclear warfare. They should also provide explanations for why it would be more beneficial to use such realistically descriptive language.

2. As a prewriting activity for this assignment you may wish to discuss whether the nuclear war strategists can be classified as a profession that Hudson would believe requires a technical language exclusively suited to its professional needs. In other words, find out if students believe that the planning for nuclear war is an activity that can legitimately exclude the lay person from its "professional" considerations. Your discussion may help students draw conclusions about which of the italicized words in this essay can be considered euphemisms, technical language, or jargon.

3. As students consider how Postman might react to the language of the nuclear war strategists, you might reemphasize his belief that euphemisms can positively enhance change in society's priorities or values. Students can then decide whether the changes that the nuclear war strategists' language might bring about would be beneficial or detrimental to society. This may provide an approach from which they can discuss whether it is acceptable to use euphemisms to deal with matters that pose psychological difficulties.

VIII. MEDIA AND LANGUAGE

"NOW... THIS", Neil Postman   (p. 373)

Questions of Content

1. The words "Now... this" are frightening to Postman because no matter how serious the information that comes after them, they are uttered "without knitted brow—indeed with a kind of idiot's delight." "Now... this" has become a new conjuction which separates everything from everything, according to Postman, and as such is a metaphor for the discontinuity of thoughts and ideas that are the content of "conversation" in present-day America. It confirms the media belief that thoughts that follow each other need not be related. In other words, the world has no meaning or order.
2. Television time is perfect for this "Now... this" world view because it is already broken into short segments both to allow for commercial breaks and to keep the viewer from dwelling too long on any single thought.
3. Hampered viewer acceptance means simply that "viewers do not like looking at the performer" either because he or she is unattractive or because he or she is not credible. In theatrical terms this means that the viewer is not persuaded that the performer is the character being portrayed.
4. Postman distinguishes a "reality truth" as one which can be judged to be true or not true based on empirical observation. The other "new" kind of truth evident on broadcast news is based on the performer's giving the "impression of sincerity, authenticity, vulnerability or attractiveness."
5. (1) New shows spend no more than forty-five seconds on any news story thus preventing the viewer from taking them seriously. (2) Film footage provides easy diversion. (3) News casters reveal little emotion or reaction to the stories they report so as not to alarm or otherwise upset the viewer. (4) Frequent commercial breaks discharge negative feelings a report may arouse in viewers. (5) All news shows have musical themes.
6. Contradiction is the uttering of two mutually exclusive statements in the same context so that one or both of them must be untrue. Because "Now... this" divides the world into endless segments, it does away with "context" and the possibility of contradiction disappears.

Questions on Rhetoric

1. Postman's example of the Burger King break after the nuclear war announcement will seem exaggerated only to students who never watch television news. Most readers will find it an effective example because it recalls the blunt interruption of hard facts they experience every time they tune in the nightly report.
2. In paragraphs 6 and 7 Postman asks a series of questions designed to get the reader thinking

about the meaning of "truth" as interpreted by television news producers. He expects the reader to answer "yes" to all his questions which will make them his allies in his concern over the nature of television "truth." In paragraph 10 Postman asks the reader to question the necessity for music on a news broadcast. This question and others like it in the essay force readers to question elements of a news show they take for granted. In paragraph 18 Postman "quizzes" readers to let them see for themselves how little they actually "learn" from the news.

3. The order in which Postman lists the various examples of anticommunication has everything to do with its startling effect on the reader. First he names Dadaism and nihilism, two schools of thought which may or may not be familiar to most readers and so may have less impact. Schizophrenia however is a term both familiar and alarming to most people, while his final example is a punch line in itself offered as the final insult to television news broadcasting. Postman has moved almost literally from the sublime to the ridiculous.

4. In his constant use of the words "you" and "we" Postman adopts the reader (and also the television viewer) as his ally and confidant. However, his description of the successful tactic television news uses suggest that television producers may be right about their audience. For example, "...as long as the music is there as a frame for the program, the viewer is comforted to believe that there is nothing to be greatly alarmed about." (10) Postman paints television news producers as deceivers who, rightly or wrongly, have a low opinion of an American viewing public which does not want to be troubled by reality. For example, "Viewers are rarely required to carry over any thought or feeling from one parcel of time to another." (3) "It is also of considerable help in maintaining a high level of unreality that the newscasters do not pause to grimace or shiver when they speak their prefaces or epilogues to the film clips." (12)

5. Postman subtly predicts the end of our civilization by stating his belief that without an understanding of the nature of truth and history a civilization cannot survive. Having already shown the degree to which our civilization has achieved ignorance, Postman's prediction becomes a statement of the inevitable and so is a fitting and frightening conclusion to his essay.

Vocabulary

tantalizing (2): teasing by presenting something desirable but keeping it out of reach.
perverse (3): turned away from what is right or good; corrupt.
discrete (3): individually distinct.
epistemologists (8): philosophers who investigate the origin, nature, methods and limits of human knowledge.
verisimilitude (9): the quality or state of appearing to be true.
leitmotif (10): a recurring theme.
juxtapositions (13): instances of two or more things being placed together.
nuances (15): subtle distinctions or qualities.
anachronism (15): a thing from a former age that is incongruous in the present.
abjures (16): to abstain from.
conceit (18): a fanciful notion.
perspicacity (25): acuteness of mental vision.
paradigm (26): model; pattern.
analogue (29): something similar to something else; analogous.
ubiquitous (29): widespread; everywhere.

Writing Topics

1. The immediate instance Postman cites is the Iranian hostage crisis; television played up the spectacle for months, yet left very little content in the minds of its viewers beyond an indeterminate sense that, in some irrational way, America was being picked on. In a broader sense, the entire essay is loaded with evidence for Postman's claim. Note his comments on magazines like *Us* and *People*, and TV shows such as *Entertainment Tonight* (which has recently begun promoting not only celebrities as news, but TV commercials as entertainment). Caution students against trying to attack or defend Postman's *superlatives*; the idea is not to argue over whether, say, the French are better entertained. They can, however, probably offer observations from their own experience on the relation between Americans' taste for diversion and their relative degree of public-spiritedness. For those who are stuck, suggest they think about television's post-Gary-Hart fascination with the sex lives of politicians, or the vast increase in prominence given in the last decade or so to opinion polls and weather, or the following oxymoron, the name of an actual TV show: "MTV News."

2. Radio call-in shows reflect, and participate in, the debasement of public dialogue. At best, they perpetuate the illusion that listening to a discontinuous series of fragmentary opinions, most of which are never examined or backed up, is a way of getting information about the world. At worst, they present aggression and hostility as the tone for public debate. Most major media markets will have some such shows; ask in class whether any of the students know of times and stations, so that all can locate the programs. Otherwise, TV shows that most students will have seen essentially replicate the effects described above: Oprah Winfrey and Phil Donahue at the "at best" end of the spectrum, Morton Downey in the nether regions.

3. In covering the hostage crisis, most television news devoted little attention to Iranian and Islamic history or culture. In the absence of such knowledge, it became difficult for Americans to see the hostages' captors as anything other than retrograde, irrational, or sadistic, if not demonic. You might encourage the students to think, not only about what information is neglected in coverage of a given event, but *why* such neglect occurs. For instance, in the Iran case, was it unconscious ethnocentrism on the broadcasters' part? A calculated decision that viewers would find the information boring? A cynical deference to viewers' xenophobia? A fear that presenting information about Islamic culture would look like sympathizing with the enemy?

THE MESSAGES BEHIND THE NEWS, Herbert J. Gans (p. 385)

Questions on Content

1. Topical values, like fads, are transient. For example, the idea that every patriotic American ought to invest in war bonds was universal yet fleeting. The notion that every American ought to be able to own his own home is taken for granted nowadays, but is really quite recent in our history. While Gans seems to make a reasonable distinction between these and enduring values such as the superiority of America over other countries, an altruistic

democracy, and the value of rural living, they are all subject to the proof of time. As we move into a more crowded, more complex world, some of Gans' "enduring" values may turn out to be "topical" after all.

2. Ethnocentrism expresses the belief that one's own culture is superior to all others. In newscasting this manifests itself as a valuing of the news of the newscaster's own nation over all others.

3. Domestic news holds forth the ideal of "altruistic democracy" which is characterized by a concern for the public interest. As a result politicians and public officials are expected to be efficient and above reproach.

4. Big cities are hotbeds of "racial conflict, crime and fiscal insolvency." The suburbs on the other hand breed "homogeneity," "boredom" and "adultery," and more recently have assumed some of the big city problems of crime and racial tension. Small town virtues come through most clearly in stories about the faults with "bigness," such as developers' despoiling of the land, the take-over of small family farms by farming conglomerates, and big business' polluting of the air are some examples of stories that imply the virtue of "smallness."

5. The "ideal" individual struggles against adversity and more powerful forces on his own terms, but with the public good in mind. However, the enduring ideal which discourages extremism controls the individual and casts doubt and suspicion on those who break the law and violate the public perception of morality. It also shuns atheists, religious fanatics, conspicuous consumers, hippies, highbrows, lowbrows, and users of slang, to name a few of Gans' examples.

6. Youth is almost entirely judged according to the adult rules it is breaking, says Gans. Most students will probably agree that his observation confirms their experience.

7. The several enduring ideals Gans lists describe a Progressive Reformist ideology extant in the early 1900s. Neither liberal nor conservative, it can be described in modern terms as an independent ideology having either liberal or conservative leanings depending on the issue.

Questions on Rhetoric

1. Gans' purpose is to inform his reader about the infrastructure of values he has discerned informing news reportage. There is little in his matter-of-fact, academic tone to suggest a polemical intention; his emphasis is on detached explanation and analysis.

2. Gans' exposition of the eight clusters of "enduring values" is analytical. He takes them up one by one, in no particularly purposeful order that we can perceive. His intention here is to build up, piece by piece, as thorough a picture as possible of the value-structure underlying the news. Since that structure is itself multifaceted and complex, he aims to simplify it and make it as accessible to inspection as possible. Summing up, he compares the structure to a historical analogue, the Progressive ideology of the early 20th century, in order to leave us with a sense of completion, integration, and historical resonance.

3. Since Gans' audience is largely made up of professional journalists and sociologists, he does not go out of his way to simplify his vocabulary.

4. Gans is trying to summarize the results of two decades' observations, and so his evidence does tend to come in generalized descriptions ("Although the news has little patience for losers, it insists that both winners and losers be scrupulously honest," etc.). Specific, attributed quotations (such as the *Time* example in paragraph 17) are more the exception than the rule. Students who tend to be querulous may feel that this damages his persuasiveness, which raises the question: Does Gans, or does he not, project an authority sufficient to suggest that, if pressed, he could furnish the specifics to substantiate his claims? And how does he do this (or fail to do this)?

5. Some students will offer examples of Gans' non-neutral diction. Others will argue that Gans uses these same non-neutral verbs and adjectives to describe the newscaster's attitude toward that story and not his own. For example, "the news celebrates old technology and mourns its passing." (27) "People who consume conspicuously are criticized, but so are people such as hippies, who turn their backs entirely on consumer goods." (29)

6. Gans' argument in this paragraph is circular and hard to follow as a result. First he argues that the news is not subservient to the elite; then Gans says the elite are subject to the standards expresses in the news; next he points out that the elite set these standards; and he finishes by insisting that when all is said and done, the news is autonomous. The paragraph bears the ring of contradiction.

Vocabulary

inferred (2): derived as a conclusion from facts or premises.

scrutiny (4): a careful going over; examination.

disparages (6): degrades; belittles.

scrupulously (9): minutely careful; abiding exactly by the rules.

habeas corpus (11): a writ requiring a person to be brought before a judge or court, especially for investigation of a restraint of the person's liberties.

countervailing (14): furnishing an equivalent of or a compensation for; offsetting.

pastoral (21): having the simplicity, charm, serenity or other characteristics generally attributed to rural areas.

rapacious (22): inordinately greedy; predatory.

anthropomorphically (25): ascribing human form or attributes to a being or thing not human.

proviso (35): a stipulation or condition.

promulgate (41): to set forth or teach publicly (a creed, doctrine, etc.).

antipathy (43): a natural, basic, habitual repugnance; aversion.

Writing Topics

1. With the advent of the crack "epidemic" and the so-called "war on drugs," students will probably find a good deal of talk about cities as "war zones," *etc.* Bernhard Goetz (who shot four teenagers he believed to be threatening him on a New York subway) probably became more of a national news figure than he would have if the incident had occurred on a small-town bus. Our perception is that the folksiness of Charles Kuralt's "On the Road" pieces survives as well, in the human-interest pieces that typically wind up a newscast loaded with stories of global tension and impending disaster; whether set in a small town or not, these generally concern "little people" whose spunkiness or eccentricity enable them to strike charming blows against the ever-threatening "bigness." On the other hand, small-town and rural settings seem to figure ever more prominently in stories on ecological crises.

2. Two cautionary notes should probably be sounded here: First, the student may need a videotape machine to record the news broadcast in order to assure accuracy and enable detailed study of its language (although since the assignment focusses on the spoken word, an audio recorder set close to the TV may be adequate). Second, it is important to stress that Gans' findings are based on extensive observation of a great number of different newscasts. Not every story will yield language as clearly value-laden as "turned up" is in this instance, and it would be somewhat misleading to draw large conclusions from studying the coverage of a single news story. Still, striking examples may emerge, particularly in stories concerning

members of one "outsider" group or another (minorities, dissidents, foreigners, the homeless). Mark Crispin Miller's recent book *Boxed In* contains an astonishing analysis of the derisive messages coded into CBS News's coverage of the 1984 Democratic Convention.

WHEN NICE PEOPLE BURN BOOKS, Nat Hentoff   (p. 398)

Questions on Content

1. One book burning took place at a liberal church while the other took place at a right wing school. At the first burning, books were destroyed for containing sexist language. At the second burning the book *Slaughterhouse Five* presumably was destroyed for graphic language and sex. Both burnings, as far as Hentoff is concerned, displayed a "lack of faith in the free exchange of ideas." In other words, people at both gatherings violated the spirit of the First Amendment.
2. Any book burning is intended both to destroy books and symbolically to destroy all similar books not present. Such burnings are not intended as a means of providing warmth. To declare that a book burning is "merely symbolic" is a dangerous ignorance of the both the power of symbolism and the literal destruction of the written word.
3. Hentoff uses the word "bad" as a sarcastic reference to right-wing conservatives most despised by liberals, who by contrast would characterize themselves as the "good" guys. Certainly people such as William F. Buckley, Jr. and Phyllis Schlafly (both mentioned in Hentoff's article) would be prominent among "bad" companions.
4. There are several candidates for such a sentence: "[T]he way to handle ideas [one doesn't] like is to set them on fire;" "If you don't like certain ideas, boycott them;" "[T]he first amendment isn't for just anybody." One of Hentoff's favorite rhetorical strategies is to fashion a blunt, utterly noneuphemistic paraphrase of what he takes his opponents' position to be; the implication is that, when all the cant is stripped away, *this* is what my opponent's position looks like. The device can be effective, but risks striking a bullying tone if the paraphrase seems unfairly reductive.
5. Symbolic speech is simply the silent expression of our views, through our behavior, our dress, or the company we keep. In suppressing symbolic speech we open the door to further suppressions, including those of verbal speech.

Questions of Rhetoric

1. Hentoff assumes his audience is educated and politically aware and in fact readers of *The Progressive* are knowledgeable about left-wing and right-wing ideology. Because Hentoff is a well-respected advocate for the left, readers are apt to pay attention to his views even though he is, in a sense, advocating for the right.
2. Hentoff's audience, being leftist, will be less inclined to dismiss Hentoff's argument if they can be convinced that offenses against the First Amendment by liberals don't amount to just an isolated incident or two.

3. Hentoff demonstrates a liberal distaste for leftists who violate the spirit of the First Amendment as evidenced in his sarcastic references to their behavior. For example, "As all right-thinking people know, however, the First Amendment isn't for just anybody." (45) "Aside from the ACLU's, how many amicus briefs do you think the Imperial Wizard is likely to get from liberal organizations devoted to academic freedom?" (46) Students will find many such examples.

Vocabulary

pernicious (1): very destructive or injurious.
expurgated (2): cleared (as a book) of objectionable passages.
homily (8): sermon.
salubrious (10): favorable to health.
apostasy (11): a renunciation or abandonment of a former loyalty (as to a religion).
secularist (15): one who is indifferent to or excludes consideration of religious values from political and social systems.
riven (29): split; rent.
promulgates (31): makes known or puts into force by open declarations.

Writing Topics

1. Hentoff's concluding remark implies that the well-intentioned people who had attempted to censor a symbol (the Klan robes) ended up letting themselves be manipulated by it. In effect, they affirmed the power of the Klan by demonstrating the lengths to which they would go to prevent its symbol from being seen. Meanwhile, by its clearly tongue-in-cheek understatement (most people would say that what's *really* "just like the Klan" is encouraging *in*decent people to do *worse*-than-dumb things), the remark establishes Hentoff as one who will not let the Klan make him lose *his* cool.

   For Hentoff, freedom of speech is an absolute. The targets of his criticism here are leftists who infringe on that freedom, not because he is not himself on the left—on most issues, he is—but because he wants to dissuade leftists from imitating the tactics of the authoritarian right.

2. Hentoff does not actually say that "offensive" expression prevents more serious consequences, as if uttering, say, racist sentiments were a safety valve to prevent one from committing racial attacks. He does say that when someone engages in racist expression, the best response is not to censor but to use it as an occasion for public dialogue. In any case, this assignment—asking the student to take a clearly-defined, well-argued position on one of the most controversial and discomfiting features of our democracy—is the sort of thing every college student should be asked to undergo at some point.

3. This is another important exercise, in that many students have given only scant thought to the question of the university's purpose as more than a place for job training. Ask them to discuss not only what Hentoff thinks (there should be little difficulty in discerning this), but how his conception compares to their own, past or present.

NOW YOU TAKE "BAMBI" OR "SNOW WHITE"—THAT'S SCARY!, Stephen King (p. 406)

Questions on Content

1. King thinks children should avoid plots involving children turning against other children, matricide, cannibalism, and murderous children because they are all plots that would "freak children out."

2. Literally the "high shelf" is where King puts videos he doesn't want his kids to reach. Later he uses the term metaphorically to mean parents' limiting of those things they consider unsuitable for their children and as the late hours of television programming reserved for older audiences.

3. Any censorship smacks of the "Big Brother" syndrome to King. He does not believe that people who do not know his children should have the power to determine what is right for them. In King's opinion, only parents have the right to decide what their children may or may not watch.

4. Parents can decide what plot elements they want their kids to avoid and can check television listings to see what plot elements a movie contains. If the plot elements are not clearly described in the listing, parents can call the television station and ask about the movie. Watch scary movies with children and discuss them afterwards.

Questions on Rhetoric

1. King's choice of a title is a good one because it foreshadows King's point that many of the fairy tales we think nothing of reading to our children are every bit as scary as the "horror" movies we do not want them watching on television. Students may suggest several titles using the names of other scarier fairy tales.

2. King wants to persuade his readers that children's television viewing should be monitored but that only parents have that right. He states this position directly in paragraph 13.

3. King refers to the possibility of "catharsis" as being the mitigating factor that makes some horror stories more suitable than others. This factor makes sense except that as King points out, what is a catharsis for one child might be scary to another.

Vocabulary

matricide (9): the murder of a mother by her child.
catharsis (12): elimination of a complex by bringing it to consciousnes and affording it expression.
arbitrarily (13): determined by will or caprice.
queried (17): questioned.

Writing Topics

1. Students will probably find that the dictionary definition of "fairy tale" emphasizes the essentially fantastic quality of the tale's characters ("fairies, wizards, goblins," *etc.*), while King's modernized version has all the signs of recognizably novelistic verisimilitude, and hence becomes unnervingly credible. Of course, students who assume that fairy tales are normally as sweet and unthreatening as the version of "Hansel and Gretel" they probably

heard as children will be interested to read some fairy tales in their *real* "original" versions, pre-Grimm Brothers. Inasmuch as these older versions generally have longer and more involved plots than the Grimm versions, they may provide the bases for true gore-extravaganzas at the students' hands. Students should, of course, consider not only what they have lost with their modernized versions, but also what they have gained (like, for instance, a saleable movie treatment?).

2. "Catharsis" is a concept many students find interesting. Since catharsis can be attributed to almost any piece of violent trash, it may be helpful to try in class to identify some well-known books or films that *lack* catharsis. Note that King does not say that if a film offers catharsis it necessarily *is* OK for a child; *Carrie* might be a good example of one that does and isn't.

ADVERTISING IN DISGUISE, *Consumer Reports*   (p. 412)

Questions on Content

1. A news story carries the weight of truth to the average viewer and so is more valuable than advertising to a corporation. However, it is the function of the news media to present unbiased reporting of business stories and that function is imperiled when the distinction between news and ads is blurred.
2. The Report describes four ways that P.R. firms have honed their canning techniques.
   (1) P.R. firms offer "canned" stories to the networks or local reporters can "voice over" silent, canned material.
   (2) Agencies provide the names of local retailers of their product which can be added to the packaged report to give it local appeal.
   (3) "The vanishing interviewer" trick allows a local station to dub the face or voice of one of its own reporters over the footage of an interview that has been conducted by a P.R. person. "In effect, the reporter serves as an actor in a commercial."
   (4) Footage is packaged in videocassette form or can be beamed in via satellite.
3. Canned news appears in the special sections of newspapers, such as those covering real estate, automobiles, travel and food. The commercial plug usually is "buried" so readers will mistake the "ad" for a feature article.
4. Most articles of this kind run in papers with a circulation under 80,000. Larger papers sometimes run canned news for big advertisers. The more ads a paper sells, the more news stories it can afford to run. If a paper lacks genuine news stories, it sometimes fills extra space with "canned" news.
5. Some students may answer that "business is business." Others may answer that they were struck by the "shameless" tone of the responses of the P.R. people.

Questions on Rhetoric

1. The thesis is stated in paragraph 6: "by blurring the distinction between news and advertising, such activities imperil an important function of the media: providing consumers with accurate, unbiased information about the marketplace."
2. The lengthy illustrations are necessary to describe the methods, motives and effects of these ad campaigns.

3. Consumer Reports is written for the average consumer as is evidenced by the use of a reasonable vocabulary, clear, interesting illustrations, and to-the-point quotes from both sides of the issue. For example, the first six paragraphs ask nothing of readers but that they hear the story of one ad campaign that was used as a news story. This illustration is also effective for being familiar to most readers who watch television.

Vocabulary

imperil (6): endanger.
guise (7): external appearance; semblance.
insinuating (8): winning favor and confidence by imperceptible degrees.
savvy (8): grasp practical or pragmatic matters.
formatted (13): produced in a particular form.
blurb (27): a short publicity notice.
vigor (44): intensity; force.

Writing Topics

1. "Entertainment news" programs like *Entertainment Tonight* now often present reports *on advertisements*, as if a new commercial were as hot an item for insider gossip as a new movie or concert tour. When Michael Jackson or Madonna signs a multimillion dollar contract to make Pepsi commercials, the story makes the regular newscasts and the commercials become as avidly-awaited as these stars' new videos. Morning shows like *Today* sometimes feature interview segments with entrepreneurs, passed off as reportage on new trends (for instance, having the owner of Sharper Image on to talk about the popularity of catalog shopping). Although these "news" reports are not created by the companies, they seem intriguing borderline cases: "real news" stories or thinly disguised plugs?
2. This assignment might be combined with #1; that is, students working on this should not be confined for their examples to the two cases recounted in the essay. We hope that students will understand that the issue cuts at least two ways, that "ads-as-news" not only flirt with deceiving the consumer, but also affect journalistic standards and public expectations of the news media.

PIGSKIN ENGLISH, Robert MacNeil   (p. 420)

Questions on Content

1. MacNeil expected to find "mangled grammar" and other signs of the decline of the English language in sportscasters' English. He feared this misuse of English sets a poor example for the millions of viewers around the world whose only means of learning about our language and culture is by watching television.
2. Sportscasters provide the verbal "razzle-dazzle" that masks the dullness or the game. More

than any other sportscaster, John Madden is master of "reach-for-it metaphors," which by their sheer audacity and glibness, distracted the viewer. Madden also speaks the everyday speech of the average American.

3. Broadcasters speak Network Standard, a Midwest accent characterized by "clarity, intelligibility and neutrality." Sportscasters speak a "very regular, colloquial American, filled with "lotsa," "gotta," "musta," "woulda."

4. MacNeil explains that Madden's English is "something to relax with, like the act of watching football itself. It is a way of crossing economic class and finding fellow feeling." Some students will defend the purist position and maintain that good English is always desirable. Others will agree with MacNeil that it is possible to assume different language patterns to suit the occasion without doing lasting harm to the language.

Questions on Rhetoric

1. MacNeil refers to the "Gothic Hordes" and "The Visigoths" in his opening paragraph as metaphors for the brutality sportscasting wages against the English language. These are particularly appropriate images because they conjure the football "hordes" which are wreaking a similar havoc on each other.

2. Without sacrificing good grammar MacNeil uses humor and words and phrases to create a relaxed, easy style. Clearly he is having fun with his essay. For example, "I thought it world be a snap... I assumed all I had to do was turn on the television, watch a little football and fill a notebook with mangled grammar." (1) "...Often in the two-shots so comically close together that you wonder about bad breath...." (7) "Leaving anxious language students in Singapore aside for the moment,..." (15)

3. Edwin Newman is a respected journalist and television commentator who has written several books criticizing the incorrect use of the English language. For an example of his work, see p. 59.

4. MacNeil organizes his material so that the reader follows him step by step through his inquiry into sports English. First he states his own misgivings about sportscasters' English, (misgivings which are probably shared by many of his readers.) Then MacNeil reveals the facts which led to his own shift in opinion. This parallel journey is an effective means of persuading readers because it offers them the same evidence, in the same order, that led MacNeil to his new conclusion.

Vocabulary

epic (1): a long poem in elevated style describing the deeds of a hero.
pandemonium (4): a wild uproar; tumult.
compelling (6): driving or urging with force.
paradox (9): a seeming contradiction.
glaring (12): very conspicuous or obvious; flagrant.
colloquial (13): characteristic of informal conversation.
deplorable (15): lamentable.
finicky (16): excessively particular in taste or standards.
ingratiating (17): winning favor; pleasing.
consummate (18): complete; perfect.
penchant (18): a strong inclination; liking.

Writing Topics

1. To evaluate the use of language in sportscasting, students will need to consider, as MacNeil does, the purposes commentary is intended to serve. They will probably find MacNeil an attractive alternative to Newman, and not only because they tend to dislike judgmental types. The virtue of MacNeil's position isn't so much its *laissez-faire* attitude as its recognition that linguistic proprieties are flexible and situation-specific.

2. Students might compare not only the types of language used in commentary on different sports (some may justly point out that Howard Cosell is pretty much Howard Cosell, whether he's reporting on boxing or football), but the types used by different individual sportscasters. They might try to arrive at "profiles" of two or three sportscasters, compare and contrast them, and speculate on what sorts of viewers find each most congenial.

3. Discussion of this question might hark back to Postman's essay. While some might say that the fact MacNeil cites proves that TV doesn't do so much harm after all, others might say it suggests that despite the hours people spend consuming TV broadcasts, their *content* is difficult to retain in any very determinate way.

IX. WRITING WELL: USING LANGUAGE RESPONSIBLY

HOW TO SAY NOTHING IN 500 WORDS, Paul Roberts (p. 429)

Questions for Study and Discussion

1. The writer's essential task is to make dull subjects interesting. This task is especially difficult for college students, according to Roberts, because often they are asked to write about topics that have been discussed to death. Many students will agree that their college experience jives with Robert's assessment.

2. Roberts advises students (1) to avoid the obvious content, (2) take the less usual side in an argument, (3) slip out of abstraction, (4) get rid of obvious padding, (5) call a "fool a fool," (5) beware of the pat expression, and (6) and use colorful words. All of these are sound, effective tricks, and each student will have his or her favorites. We find his advice to "take the less usual side," and to "avoid the obvious content" are the most unusual and most likely to lend students a new perspective on their writing.

3. Although Roberts advises against unnecessary padding of a subject, he says a student can reach a goal of 500 words by simply coming up with more content. In other words, instead of saying too much about too little, say less about more.

4. According to Roberts, modern science, particularly psychology, has come up with too many big words intended to convey what should be simple thoughts. Thus "schoolboys are maladjusted or unoriented or misunderstood or in need of guidance or lacking in continued success toward satisfactory integration of the personality as a social unit, but they student received a portable typewriter for graduation. More currently the gift world have been an electric typewriter or even more probably a computer. His list of "popular topics" might also give him away for including, College Football, Fraternities, Is Chivalry Dead. Today college campuses buzz with talk about Aids, Sexist Language in College Texts, and the Pros and Cons of Women's Rugby. Roberts's proposed sentence on sororities (18) speaks for itself.

5. Roberts presents his material in the same steps he advises students to take as they take on a writing assignment. In his case, Roberts uses the worn-out topic of the pros and cons of college football and grapples with it from beginning to end moving from the blank page, to the possible ways to handle a topic, to a finished product. He makes a clear and effective use of the method of "show" don't "tell."

6. Robert's casual and friendly style is appropriate for his young audience. Throughout his essay, he uses an unexpected, colorful choice of words to illustrate his points. For example, "When I hear Gerber Spinklittle play "Mississippi Man" on the trombone, my socks creep up my ankles." (18); or "Picture poor old Alfy coming home from football practice every evening, bruised and aching, agonizingly tired, scarcely able to shovel the mashed potatoes

into his mouth." (15) In many cases, the unexpectedness of his words is also what makes them humorous. He also manages to convey graphically, and without resorting to cliche, the sense of fatigue and frustration that many students feel when confronted with this task. For example, "It comes to you that you do your best thinking in the morning, so you put away your typewriter and go to the movies." (3)

7. Roberts's title seems to promise a method for stretching minimal content into a college essay, and his first section more or less delivers just that. The major part of his essay, though, is taken up with the opposite: a method for finding something to say in 500 words. Presumably he chose his title to entice the student reader; imagine how much more alienating "How to Say Something" would be.

WRITING HONESTLY, Donald Hall (p. 441)

Questions for Study and Discussion

1. Hall presents his thesis in the first sentence of the essay: "Writing well is the art of clear thinking and honest feeling."
2. Hall believes that we "fool ourselves" with the passive voice and personification which help us "avoid blame" (2), cliches which "become meaningless substitutes for feeling and thought" (2), and jargon which lacks content and feeling.
3. Hall believes that declarations of sincerity could easily be used to justify or mask just the opposite impression. Just because a writer claims to be sincere does not mean that the message that he or she is conveying is a sincere one. Hall's example in paragraph 4 illustrates this point well.

    For Peter Elbow sincerity is an unwillingness to mask or hide one's intended message especially when one professes to be totally honest.
4. In paragraph 8 Hall uses the analogy of the computer to explain how people's brains send out programmed messages and "printouts of ready-made pseudo-thoughts and pseudo-feelings." The analogy is effective because the brain is in many ways a computer and people are increasingly familiar with computers and their components.
5. Although spontaneity is useful in learning how to write and in uncovering things that we did not know we knew, it is limited in that it cannot by itself constitute good writing. It is helpful in discussing this question to review paragraphs 10 and 11 with students.
6. Hall's conclusion is appropriate because it not only summarizes the major points in his essay but also emphasizes the importance of those points. Furthermore, this last paragraph is effective because it causes the reader to reflect on what he has just said and on the importance of writing well.
7. We feel that Hall very much practices what he believes in this essay. Students also find Hall's voice to be authentic and clear.

WRITING FOR AN AUDIENCE, Linda Flower (p. 447)

Questions for Study and Discussion

1. In her opening sentence Flower states that "the goal of the writer is to create a momentary common ground between the reader and the writer" (1).
2. When Flower refers to the "distance" between writer and reader, she means the differences in age, background, attitude, etc., that can stand in the way of successful communication.

   The first step in closing this gap is for writers to "gauge the distance" between themselves and their readers by analyzing the audience they are writing for.
3. According to Flower, the three critical differences between writers and readers are knowledge, attitude, and needs. She devotes most of her essay to the latter two since *knowledge* is the "easiest to handle" and does not require the explanation that *attitude* and *needs* do (3).
4. Flower defines *knowledge* as "conscious awareness of explicit facts and clearly defined concepts" that "can be easily written down or told to someone else." *Attitude*, on the other hand, is more like an "image" or "a loose cluster of associations" (4).

   This distinction is important because "a reader's image of a subject is often the source of attitudes and feelings that are unexpected and, at times, impervious to facts" (5). Writers, therefore, need to be conscious of this distinction to bridge the "distance" between themselves and their readers.
5. In Flower's view, "the ability to adapt your knowledge to the needs of the reader is often crucial to your success as a writer" (8). To determine just what these needs are, writers must ask themselves what readers need to know in order to make a decision about their subject matter.
6. Flower says "a good college paper doesn't just rehash facts; it demonstrates what your reader, as a teacher, needs to know—that you are learning the thinking skills his or her course is trying to teach" (9).

   Writers *use* knowledge rather than just expressing what they know when they "meet the demands of an assignment or the needs of their reader" by reorganizing or rethinking their ideas.
7. Students' responses to this question may vary, though it seems apparent that Flower has made some conscious attempts to suit her essay to her college audience. In her discussion of needs, for instance, she focuses on writing done on a job and in college courses—both examples of the kinds of writing college students are concerned about.

SIMPLICITY, William Zinsser (p. 451)

Questions for Study and Discussion

1. In paragraph 7 Zinsser states that "it is impossible for a muddy thinker to write good English." He also states that "clear thinking becomes clear writing; one can't exist without the other" (7).

2. Clutter consists of "unnecessary words, circular constructions, pompous frills and meaning-less jargon" (1).

   Zinsser feels that we can free ourselves of clutter by stripping every sentence to its cleanest components. We should also clear our heads of clutter by asking ourselves, "What am I trying to say?" and "Have I said it?" (12).

3. Zinsser assumes that the reader is a person who has a short attention span and who "is assailed on every side by forces competing for his time" (8) including newspapers, the media, his family, his household responsibilities, and sleep.

   Therefore, writers have the responsibility to hold a reader's attention by being clear, concise, purposeful, and interesting.

4. In paragraph 12, Zinsser points to the questions that writers should constantly ask themselves.

   These questions are important because honest answers to them will help the writer eliminate clutter.

5. "Simplicity" for Zinsser means uncluttered. Uncluttered writing is writing that says precisely what the author wants to say.

   Students' opinions on whether our "national tendency is to inflate" may vary. You might discuss with them whether they have noticed such a tendency within their college or university environment.

6. Zinsser uses short sentences in paragraphs 1, 6, 8, 9, 17, and 18. These short sentences lend emphasis and interest as well as variety to Zinsser's prose.

7. Students find the pages of Zinsser's manuscript to be a fascinating example of a writer's work in progress. After studying the passage, they should be able to point to the following types of changes:

   1. elimination of whole sentences
   2. elimination of words or phrases
   3. substitution of one or two words for a longer passage

   Of course, there is no substitute for examining each change that Zinsser has made. Our students find it useful to determine the advantage that Zinsser gains by eliminating specific words, phrases, and sentences and particularly by making certain substitutions. It has been our experience, as well, that several students always like one or more portions of the original better than the revision and the reasons they give for their preferences have provoked lively classroom discussions.

THE MAKER'S EYE: REVISING YOUR OWN MANUSCRIPTS,
Donald M. Murray (p. 457)

Questions for Study and Discussion

1. Murray states that most writers view revision as the opportunity "to discover what they have to say and how best to say it" (2). Revision, therefore, is an important element in the process of writing because it produces "a progression of drafts, each of which says more and says it more clearly" (3).

2. Murray's purpose is to *explain* the importance of revision, and how one can develop good reading skills for revision.
3. According to Murray, a writer must be conscious of the following in the process of revision: (1) information; (2) meaning; (3) audience; (4) form; (5) structure; (6) development; (7) dimension; and (8) voice.

    Most students' processes of revision will not be as complete or deliberate as Murray's. You may wish to focus, particularly, on the order of Murray's steps as you compare them to the students' revision practices.
4. When Murray states that "Writers must be their own best enemies," he means that they must not rely on the criticisms or praises of others for evaluation of their work, but must instead "detach themselves from their own pages so that they can apply both their caring and their craft to their own work" (4).
5. Murray's quotations add credibility and authority to his comments on revision, since professional writers are most qualified to speak on what constitutes successful writing. The message from these professionals seems to be that good revision skills are essential to a successful writer.
6. Murray reveals that professionals view first drafts as the very beginning of the writing process, the point from which "real" writing can begin. Peter F. Drucker goes so far as to refer to the first draft as the "zero draft" since he doesn't feel he can "start counting" until after the initial draft is complete.

    Students should recognize that this kind of attitude can aid in their development as writers, since it will help foster effective revision practices.
7. Murray states that "Most readers underestimate the amount of rewriting it usually takes to produce spontaneous writing" (9), because "in school we are taught to decode what appears on the page as finished writing" (3). He recommends a special kind of reading ability, therefore, that focuses on one's own writing, "critically and constructively," to see how words "can be changed and rearranged, can set off a chain reaction of confusion or clarified meaning" (3).
8. In Murray's view, the revision process never really ends, it is just stopped for one reason or another. He ends his own essay in mid-sentence to dramatize this notion, implying that had he not been forced to send a draft off for publication he would still be busy revising it.

THE QUALITIES OF GOOD WRITING, Jacqueline Berke   (p. 462)

Questions for Study and Discussion

1. Berke considers the following six elements to be essential to good writing: economy, simplicity, clarity, readability, information, engagement. At its best, good writing is also "poetic."
2. "By the time we are old enough to write, most of us have grown so self-conscious that we stiffen, sometimes to the point of rigidity." (5) Most writers will confess that writing as naturally as they talk is as difficult as it is to "act natural" on a stage in front of a roomful of people.
3. Most students will agree with Malrois' assessment of Presidents Abraham Lincoln and John

F. Kennedy. E. B. White, Mark Twain, Tillie Olsen, and Alice Walker are just a few other writers known for their clean, clear writing.

4. Obscure writing is the dead giveaway of unclear thinking.

5. Berke intends the word "human" in paragraph 10 to describe writing that does not forget that, no matter how technical the subject matter, the audience is still made up of human beings.

6. In her first paragraph, Berke compares a famous sentence by Patrick Henry with a "high-flown" paraphrase. Later in the essay she repeatedly compares examples of concise, pungent writing with sloppy, circumlocutory expressions of the same idea.

7. Berke states her central idea then uses examples and illustration to support it. Because she is an interesting and to-the-point-writer her paragraphs tend to read quickly, thus the reader would have lost more than she would have gained in the use of shorter paragraphs that included less information.

8. The author draws an effective and poetic parallel. One could also compare good prose to a well-dressed woman, one who conveys her style and grace without the use of too much make-up or jewelry.

9. Berke compares a writer who uses unnecessary words to a dentist who inflicts pain and a lawyer who incurs risk. These imply a sort of responsibility owed the reader by the writer.

St. Martin's

0-312-02080-5